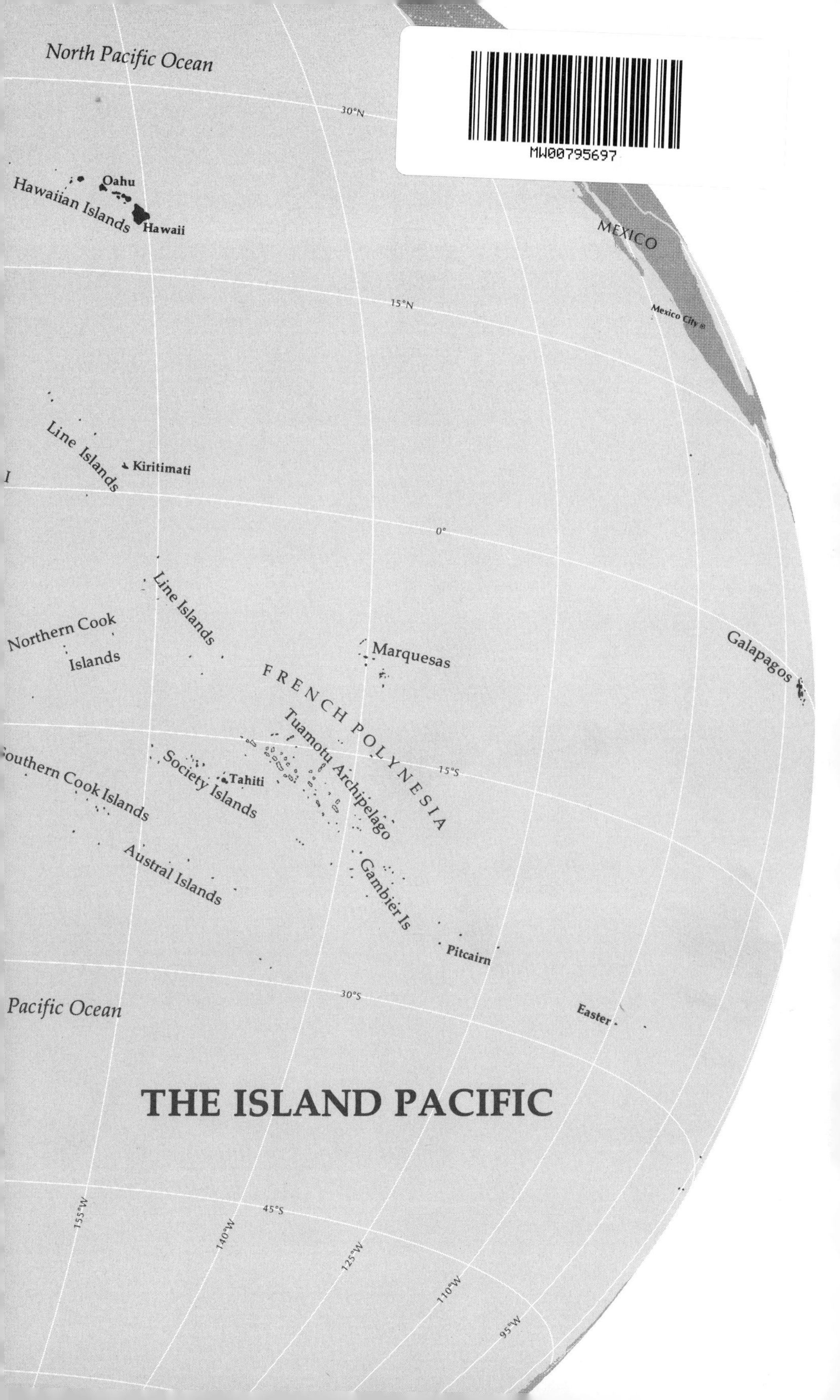

North Pacific Ocean

30°N

Oahu

Hawaiian Islands Hawaii

MEXICO

15°N

Mexico City

Line Islands ▲ Kiritimati

I

0°

Line Islands

Northern Cook

Islands

Marquesas

Galapagos

F R E N C H   P O L Y N E S I A

Tuamotu Archipelago

Southern Cook Islands

Society Islands Tahiti

15°S

Austral Islands

Gambier Is

Pitcairn

30°S

Pacific Ocean

Easter

THE ISLAND PACIFIC

155°W

45°S

140°W

125°W

110°W

95°W

Wealth
of the
Solomons

OTHER VOLUMES IN THE
PACIFIC ISLANDS MONOGRAPH SERIES

Pacific Islands Monograph Series, No. 3

Wealth of the Solomons

A history of a Pacific archipelago, 1800–1978

JUDITH A. BENNETT

Pacific Islands Studies Program
Center for Asian and Pacific Studies
University of Hawaii
UNIVERSITY OF HAWAII PRESS • Honolulu

© 1987 University of Hawaii Press
Manufactured in the United States of America

93 92 91 90 89 88 6 5 4 3 2

Library of Congress Cataloging-in-Publication Data

Bennett, Judith A., 1944–
  Wealth of the Solomons.

  (Pacific islands monograph series; no. 3)
  Bibliography: p.
  Includes index.
  1. Solomon Islands—History. I. Title.
II. Series.
DU850.B46   1986   993'.5   86–16080
ISBN 0–8248–1078–3

To four of my teachers—
my Dad, the late David Thomas Bennett,
Val White Heitfeld,
Murray Chapman,
and Dorothy Shineberg—
with gratitude and aroha.

EDITOR'S NOTE

IT IS A PLEASURE to write an introductory note to this third volume of the Pacific Islands Monograph Series. The history of the Solomon Islands is in itself an intriguing story, and Dr. Bennett tells it more than well. The depth and breadth of the work is impressive in at least two respects. First, it covers events in the Solomons from initial European contact in the middle-1500s to the country's emergence as an independent and sovereign state in 1978. Second, all facets of colonial history are covered; to name only a few: the early contact period, the whaling trade, the development of plantations, the nature of British colonial rule, and missionization. Considering the scope of this volume, it represents a definitive history of the Solomon Islands, and it will remain so for many years to come.

The above is self-evident to even the most casual of readers. Not explicit is that Dr. Bennett's research combined the research strategies of both the ethnologist and the historian. Extensive and standard historical research was conducted in archives and libraries in Australia, New Zealand, and Hawaii. Like an ethnologist, Bennett conducted field research on the weather (south) coast of Guadalcanal for five months in 1972 in conjunction with the Guadalcanal weather coast project. She returned to the Solomons in 1975 for a year's travel and residence in villages on Guadalcanal, Malaita, New Georgia, San Cristobal, and the Shortland Islands. This research focused on oral histories with Solomon Islanders who had experienced life under colonial rule prior to World War II.

The publication of the Pacific Islands Monograph Series is subsidized by private funds raised by the University of Hawaii Foundation. From the outset, Mr. Donald Mair, executive vice-president of the Foundation, has shown great interest and support for the series, and his assistance and that of the Foundation is greatly appreciated.

ROBERT C. KISTE

CONTENTS

FIGURES

PHOTOS

TABLES

PREFACE

THIS BOOK IS A HISTORY of socioeconomic changes occurring among Solomon Islanders since contact with outsiders from about 1800. In it I have attempted to trace the resilience of Melanesian values in the face of expanding Western commercial influence and eventual political control, addressing both change and continuity.

My definition of the Solomon Islands is that area so described at independence in 1978 and that name will be applied to the same archipelago both before and during the British protectorate. Solomon Islanders are, in the main, Melanesians as defined by anthropologists and by modern Melanesians themselves. In this book, the name Melanesians is sometimes used to mean Solomon Islanders, just as the term Europeans may be applied to Australians when the cultural aspect rather than geographical origin is stressed. However, because at first European contact the peoples of the Solomon Islands typically lived in small separate societies, I have concentrated on three major themes as bases for organization and generalization: Solomon Islanders and their relationship with their environment; their relationships with each other; and their relationships with the outside world.

Solomon Islanders have had a long and intimate knowledge of their particular island environments and identify closely with them, both materially and spiritually. At the beginning of the historic era it was evident that although Solomon Islanders could win a living from their own lands, disparities of resource availability existed. The majority of the people lived in the inland "bush," yet their life was harder than that of most coast dwellers. The "saltwater" people could exploit the bounty of both land and sea and were more accessible to traders from other islands. When European whalers and traders came, the coastal folk were placed to reap the benefits from the new goods and opportunities. This relative deprivation was not confined simply to bush dwellers vis à vis coastal people. In general, the eastern islands, particularly Malaita, had very few products to offer the trader. There, Islanders could obtain few trade goods until they were able to go to sell their labor on the cane-fields of Fiji and Queensland. So began a tradition of migrant labor that extended into the plantation era. After World War II the pattern contin-ued, though the destination more often than not was Honiara, the capi-tal. Alongside this pattern existed its obverse—those who had access to trade produce or, later, the land on which to grow cash crops, stayed at home to work and, compared to the eastern Islanders, sacrificed little in satisfying their wants. Inherent in these fundamental differences, inten-sified by the cash economy, was the genesis of the notion of island-based deprivation.

Not only has involvement in capitalism changed Solomon Islanders' perceptions of the resources of their own particular region in compari-son to others, but it has also altered their perceptions of the utilization and ownership of these resources. Prior to contact, land and reef resources were available to anyone within the local land-holding group who had the energy to cultivate the soil or fish the waters. Once cash crops and commercial exploitation of the reefs became more common, from about 1910–1920 onward, disputes arose as to who owned and inherited the land and reefs and/or who had the right to the wealth obtained from the sale of their products. Inland people migrating to land on the coast injected a further element of contention, as had early land sales to Europeans. Resources that had once been a major part of the entire group's wealth were increasingly becoming the saleable com-modities of individuals.

A primary aspect of Solomon Islanders' relationship with the environ-ment was their dependency on it, as all cultivated gardens and/or fished to survive. Growing involvement in barter trade with Europeans and then the cash economy did not bring an end to this. Subsistence activity expanded or contracted in response to the fall or rise of produce prices or the rare swings in the labor market. This pattern of keeping all options viable has persisted in the post–World War II period, despite a certain amount of pressure from the government.

My second theme focuses on the relationships among Solomon Island-ers. During the years between 1800 and 1978 Solomon Islanders came to be just that—Solomon Islanders. Certainly, their identity as "Solomon Islanders" is but one among the multilayered texture of various place loyalties, but it is uppermost in the people's minds when they think of their place in today's world. In the main, that identity was developed by Solomon Islanders themselves in the face of introduced economic and political forces. The parade of whalers, European and Chinese traders, labor recruiters, government officers, missionaries, planters, and the Japanese and Allied armies created challenges and opportuni-ties that brought groups of Islanders into new relationships with one another. First, the peoples of small islands, then big islands, and then regions began to see themselves as having more in common. This process was fostered by the depth and breadth of communication arising from the spread of Pijin via plantations as well as mission languages, and by the mobility of thousands of plantation laborers and native mission personnel with their gospel of Christian love. The government's pacification policies at the turn of the century provided the milieu in which these changes could flourish. Ironically, increasing regional consciousness in the thirties and forties made Solomon Islanders a force to reckon with in their dealings with that same government.

In their interaction with one another, leadership has always been important to Solomon Islanders. The relationship of leaders to supporters has changed little over the years (barring recent national politics), though the means to leadership were transmuted as warfare and certain other practices became outlawed. Many old-style leaders lost authority, and were soon replaced by younger men who exploited new, government-sanctioned ways to power.

The final theme concerns Solomon Islanders' relationships with the outside world, a world predominantly of Westerners, at least until World War II. Almost from initial contact a dependency was created because Solomon Islanders wanted and soon needed Western goods. In the trading period this dependency did not imply any real loss of autonomy. However, when the continuing search for Western goods meant that some Islanders became a significant component of the Pacific labor pool, their incorporation into some colonial framework was virtually inevitable. Once the islands officially became a British possession, there was also a kind of inevitability about how the administration would finance itself, given the apparent abundance of land and labor. These developments were largely beyond the control of the fragmented peoples of the Solomons, but soon involved them more deeply in the world economy. On such a wide stage they could play only the most insignificant role. Control by the government, the merchant and planting companies, market trends, the advance of foreign armies, and major features of the impetus toward decolonization itself originated far beyond the islands. Only through consideration of these institutions and forces in their own right will their power be understood.

Ultimately, their relationships with the outside world gave birth to most of the changes in the relationships between Solomon Islanders and their environment and with one another, because of the impact of new goods and accompanying ideas and value systems. While some ideas and values were rejected, others were not and many were transformed to become more the intellectual artefacts of Solomon Islanders than of Europeans. Pagan, bush Malaitans clung tenaciously to their traditional cultural beliefs to justify their behavior on plantations, just as

Nggela Christians used gospel teachings to attempt to prick the conscience of their bishop and the colonial government in the late thirties. A decade later, the ideologues of Maasina Rule cleverly constructed a philosophy to unite both pagans and Christians in forging a new identity for their people in the eastern islands. Elements of the European world interested and intrigued Solomon Islanders, but never to such an extent that they became mere tabulae rasae on which that culture's entire value system could be imprinted.

Only recently have historians begun to look at the involvement of Pacific Islanders in trade and commerce. Given the fragmentary nature of the evidence, that is understandable, especially for the whaling and trading era which usually provides far more qualitative than quantitative data. The records I consulted for this early period are varied, including whaling and labor recruiters' logs and journals, memoirs, newspapers, the records of the Royal Navy (Australia Station), Colonial Office records, entries in the Customs House records in Sydney, and family histories along with, at the close of the period, the writings of C. M. Woodford and the records of the Western Pacific High Commission established by the British government in Fiji in 1877. From 1896 on, the correspondence between Tulagi, Fiji, and London forms the bulk of the administrative records consulted, but others include plantation company registry records in Queensland and New South Wales as well as a range of records from the Australian National Archives. The records of the Land Titles Office, Department of Forestry and Lands (Honiara), were a very valuable source not only for land transactions, but also for tracing both individuals and their fortunes. Books written by participant traders, recruiters, government officers, planters, anthropologists, doctors, missionaries, and visitors have been useful for the twenties and thirties, as has the *Pacific Islands Monthly* for the decade before the war. Particularly valuable and previously unused sources were the records of Burns, Philp & Company and, to a lesser degree, the surviving letters of W. R. Carpenter & Company, Tulagi. The records of Lever's and the Pacific Islands Company located in England were useful for the period c. 1896–1920 as were those of Fairley Rigby and Company for c. 1910–1920. Regrettably, I was twice refused access to records of Lever's Solomon Islands plantations. Since Lever's (Lever's Pacific Plantations Limited) are still very active in the Solomons and are exploiting their claim to timber on the former "waste lands" of Kolombangara, one can only assume that this was company policy. Mission records have been used selectively. The *Southern Cross Log* (Melanesian Mission) and some of the papers and diaries of the Melanesian and Methodist missions have been helpful, particularly the Goldie papers for the postwar period. Besides the lack of access to the records of the Seventh Day Adventists and the South Sea Evangelical Mission, the main reason for my consulting only a selection of mission records has been the research already done on the history of Christian missions. David Hilliard's work on the Protestant missions, in particular, is a comprehensive study of the impact of those missions on Solomon Islanders. Hugh Laracy's book, *Marists and Melanesians*, is a useful account of the Roman Catholic mission, and A. R. Tippett's missiological study, *Solomon Islands Christianity*, offers insights into the wider effects of Christianity.

As I was not granted access to government records from about 1950 on, I have used a range of other sources for the period up to 1978. Official publications, the writings of former civil servants and the coast-watchers, a corpus of specialized doctoral research by anthropologists and geographers, and Hugh Laracy's collection of Maasina Rule documents were consulted.

One of the major sources of information is oral evidence, which has provided both new data and, frequently, a different perspective from the predominately European-written records. To gather this material from Solomon Islanders, in 1976 I spent ten months based at Vatumanivo (Guadalcanal) where I had lived for three months in 1972 doing research; Heuru (San Cristobal); Maoa (Malaita); and Nuhu (Shortland Islands); as well as a few weeks between Gizo, Vella Lavella, Munda, and Tulagi. People who were adult before World War II were interviewed in villages near the bases either by me directly in Pijin or with the help of an interpreter who worked consistently with me in any one research site. Once the informants were familiar with the aim of the research—which was announced over Honiara radio and the "coconut wireless"—the procedure was to elicit the employment history of each informant, with specific questions regarding motivation, village reactions, recruiting, relations with government and employer, and type of work, wages, and conditions. Another area of study was villager involvement in trading and copra production along with, in some cases, wartime experiences. As most of some one hundred sixty informants had good memories for names of employers, ships, and government officers, it was not difficult to date the various events using a historical calendar drawn up from government documents and specific to each area. The interviews were tape-recorded and later transcribed. Transcripts of the material collected from informants, once completely typed and analyzed for other research, will be lodged eventually at the Solomon Islands National Archives and the National Library of Australia. Because this material amounts to some four hundred foolscap pages of handwriting, it is impossible to include it in an appendix to this book.

A final word. There are as many histories of any one country or people as there are historians. I hope that other histories of the Solomon Islands will follow and that Solomon Islanders will be among the historians. To you especially, I offer this book as a gift and as a challenge. Take it as you will.

ACKNOWLEDGMENTS

IN EXAMINING THE GENESIS of this book I have realized how extensive my debt is to others. The book is based on my doctoral thesis for the Australian National University, Canberra, but was revised and its scope extended during 1983 when Massey University in Palmerston North provided me with a postdoctoral fellowship. I am grateful to these institutions, as I am to the East-West Center in Honolulu for its support in introducing me to field work in the Solomons back in 1972.

For assistance in the tasks of documentary research I am indebted to the staff of the Mitchell Library, Sydney, the National Library of Australia, Canberra, and the Hocken Library in Dunedin. Bruce Burne and Paddy Macdonald (then based in Suva) were especially helpful at the Western Pacific Archives in 1975–1977 along with the staff of the Australian National Archives in Canberra, Sydney, and Melbourne, the Queensland State Archives in Brisbane, the University of Melbourne Archives, the Turnbull Library in Wellington, and all contributing agencies to the records now on the microfilms of the Pacific Manuscripts Bureau. Sally Edridge, formerly attached to the National Library of the Solomons and now of the National Library of New Zealand, in both capacities has been very helpful, especially in allowing me to consult her excellent bibliography of the Solomon Islands, now published.

I owe special thanks to C. T. A. Black and the management of Burns Philp for allowing me to use their archives in Sydney. My thanks go to the staff of the Land Titles Office in Honiara who assisted my study of all land records except those still in the process of registration.

I wish it was as easy to summarize and thank those who assisted in the task of research into the oral record. All informants are listed following the bibliography and have my gratitude. I wish particularly to thank Luvusia Willy of Guadalcanal, Jonathan Kuka of Malaita, and Hari Drew Ramo of San Cristobal for their help in leading me to those informants and acting as interpreters when Pijin would not suffice. Other people in the Solomons who made my journey and my work easier include Remesio Eresi, John Bana, Luka, Bernard Pilowa and Kweni, Silverio Otuana, and the priests and sisters at Nila in the Shortlands; Andrew Kukuti, Bruce and Phillip Palmer, Eileen Shick, Rolf Novak, Billy Binskin, the late Bill Gina, Willy Paia, Kitchener and Annie Wheatley, John and Joyce Kevisi, and Alice Kera in New Georgia; Francis Chuku, Seti, Kekekae'a, Rosa, Didon, and the DMI sisters at Avuavu, Guadalcanal; Jonathan Fifi'i, Salimauri, Seti, Justus, Joseph Jephlet, Jo Gonai'ilae, Anna and Brian Havill, the staff at SSEC High School, Su'u, and the Catholic sisters Patrick Mary and Placida at Buma, Malaita; Basile, Father Frederick, Joanna, Briton, Nestor, Mrs. and Dr. John Kinnon, Jack Campbell, Leslie Fugui, John Derrick, the priests and sisters at Wanione Bay, Geoffrey and Linda Kuper, and Joseph Tooruomae on San Cristobal.

My thanks go too to the late Tommy Elkington and his wife, Naysa, for their many kindnesses to me during my stay at Tulagi and for their trust in giving me certain documents. I thank the following for their support while I was in Honiara: Francis Bugotu, Anna Craven, Lawrence Foanaota, Peter Larmour, Ann Springfield, Andrew Gough, Jennifer Jones, Margo and Ian St. Ives, Ralph and Jane Wingfield, Eva Lamda and family, and John Gina. I am especially thankful to Lyn Haywood for her continued assistance during much of my stay in the Solomons and in Canberra.

For their helpful criticisms on parts of this book that formed the Ph.D. dissertation, I am grateful to the staff of the Department of Pacific and South East Asian history, ANU, Canberra, especially Gavan Daws, the late Norma McArthur, and Oskar Spate. Anyone who studies the colonial era in the Southwest Pacific cannot but thank Deryck Scarr for his pioneering study of the Western Pacific High Commission. To the ever-generous Bob Langdon whose work in the Pacific Manuscripts Bureau over the years continues to make the historian's research simpler go my thanks. I also thank Dorothy Shineberg of the Department of History, ANU, for her useful critiques, constant encouragement, and friendship. Thanks, too, to John Langmore for his suggestions, to the late Keith Willey for his sense of humor, and to Winifred Mumford for her help with the original graphs and figures.

More recently the staff of the History Department at Massey University (then under the leadership of Bill Oliver), provided a congenial environment in which to both teach and write. I thank Barrie Macdonald and Kerry Howe for needling me to get the book finished. Ralph Ngatata Love of Massey also gave support and kindness—Kia ora, Ralph. Thanks, too, to the University of Otago, Dunedin for financial assistance with the indexing of the book. To Joan Herlihy and Colin Allan I offer my sincere thanks for their perceptive comments on the postwar period of the book; both gave generously of their time and knowledge. And at the last, as he was at the beginning of my interest in the Solomons, Murray Chapman of the University of Hawaii came forward with wise recommendations for rounding off the manuscript. Many, many thanks to Linley Chapman for her editorial guidance and endless patience, and to Robert Kiste and the Pacific Islands Studies Program for their support for the publication of this book.

I owe a special debt of gratitude to Stewart Firth who most generously gave me helpful suggestions on the Ph.D. and the encouragement which spurred me to tackle the book. I wish, too, to thank Hugh Laracy, who has always assisted with information and hospitality, and to Margaret Cronin go many thanks for her help and letters of encouragement over almost twenty years.

I also would like to acknowledge three gentlemen who at various stages of my research did their best to discourage me. Regarding the possibility of a history of trade and plantations one stated, "No records exist." This gave me the real challenge. Thank you.

Kia Pōwhiri Rika-Heke, tōku hoa, he tino mihi aroha ki a koe mō tāu atawhai.

To a veritable regiment of typists I owe thanks for their patience in deciphering my scrawl and making such a professional job of it—Robyn Savory, Vicki Baas-Becking, Judy Poulos, Gloria Chechuti, Anvida Lamberts, Heather Read, Glenis Foster, and most recently, Isabel Campbell. Marta Langridge at ANU translated the German works for me. Many thanks to you all.

Without the help of all these people this book would not exist. However, for the use made of all sources and suggestions and for the book's conclusions, I am responsible.

Dunedin, Otago,
Aotearoa (New Zealand)

MEASUREMENTS
AND SPELLING

Measurements

UNITS OF WEIGHT, DISTANCE, AREA, AND MONEY are given in the forms used in the sources. In the Solomon Islands, the imperial system was used and the currencies in circulation during the twentieth century prior to World War II were the pound sterling and the Australian pound, which retained parity until the onset of the Depression. To facilitate rough comparisons, in 1932, sterling was equal to A£1.25, or US$4.00. In 1966, the Solomon Islands followed Australia into the decimal system, when A£1 converted to A$2.00 (= 16s.sterling = US$2.25). At independence in 1978, the Solomons introduced their own decimal currency. Measures of weight, distance, and area were converted to the metric system in 1975.

Spelling

Spelling of Solomon Islands Pijin words follows *Pijin Blong Yumi: A Guide to Solomon Islands Pijin*, by Linda Simons and Hugh Young. The more usual spelling of 'Pijin' is retained only in compound terms such as 'Pidgin English'.

Wherever possible, place names are spelled as in Hackman's *Guide to Spelling and Pronunciation* . . . (1968). However, that document is not exhaustive, and spellings not covered in it follow the sources, where they are consistent. Where they are not, the spelling most frequently used or the spelling in current use has been adopted.

CHAPTER 1

The Solomon Islands in 1800

> . . . the Melanesian Way was a lifestyle which was com-
> munalistic and egalitarian, making its decisions by consensus
> and achieving its aims by co-operation. It emerged in small
> communities, in a moneyless, subsistence economy, which
> lacked crops which could be stored for any but quite short
> periods. Affluence by hoarding was impossible—the best that
> could be aimed at was prestige by giving away. The Melane-
> sian Way was egalitarian because it had to be, not because of
> some inward urge to egalitarianism deeply planted in the
> Melanesian soul.
>
> Sir Percy Chatterton

Land, sea, and people

THE FIRST EXPLORERS of the archipelago to leave a permanent written
record were the Spanish, led by Alvaro de Mendaña. So potent was
their account that four hundred years later the Solomon Islands—an
independent nation of 235,000 people—still carries the name given by
Spanish cartographers to islands all but barren of the fabulous gold of
King Solomon's mines.

When the Spaniards sighted their first island in the group they
believed it to be part of a continent because of the high mountains and
the extent of the coastline. Like its near neighbors, the Bismarck Archipelago and Vanuatu, the Solomon Islands group is part of a chain of
islands known today as Melanesia. The islands of Melanesia extend
across the southwest Pacific Ocean from the large island of New Guinea
in the west to New Caledonia in the south and to Fiji in the east, on the
threshold of Polynesia.

The Spanish explorers and their European successors were eventually
to learn that the Solomons consisted of six major islands—Choiseul,
New Georgia, Santa Isabel, Guadalcanal, Malaita, and San Cristobal,
ranging in length from 80 to 200 kilometers and in width from 15 to 50
kilometers. The climate of the islands is generally hot and wet, producing a perennial and luxuriant green canopy over most of their surface.
These large high islands are volcanic in origin, as are most of the smaller

1

islands such as the Santa Cruz group. All of them are subject to earth-quakes, which are virtually a monthly occurrence for the Solomons as a whole, often causing major ecological destruction. Dotted in the ocean at the remote edges of the modern Solomons are tiny atolls, sparse in vegetation and human settlement—Ontong Java, Sikaiana, Anuta, Tikopia, Rennell, and Bellona (Figure 1).

As the Spaniards observed, central mountain ranges dominate the main islands. Except for north Guadalcanal, and particularly in the eastern Solomons, there is little coastal plain, as the land rises abruptly into a system of rugged razorback ridges, reaching 1000–2000 meters high.[1]

Variable factors such as location, topography, rainfall, soil type, and vegetative cover provide a great range of microsystems for subsistence agriculture. In historic times, these have changed little, although the availability of introduced food plants, especially the sweet potato *(Ipomoea batatas)* has expanded the potential of coastal lands. How-ever, various blights have affected taro *(Colocasia esculenta)* in the last forty years, reducing both the cultivation of this vegetable and its status as a dietary staple.[2]

Some notion of the variability of environmental factors can be gained from a comparison of four areas within the modern Solomons—Langa-langa (the artificial islands of north Malaita and the adjacent 'Aoke coast and hinterland), Tikopia, Roviana Lagoon (New Georgia), and Tadhimboko (northeast Guadalcanal) (Figure 1). The artificial islands of Langalanga contain no land for cultivation, but the nearby low-lying coastal area with its alluvial and saline soils offers some land suitable for growing taro, sweet potato, and tree crops such as the coconut *(Cocos nucifera)* and the canarium almond. In this area of quite heavy rainfall (3000 to 3500 mm a year), the vegetation consists of mangrove and plants typical of floodplain forests and swamps, including wild sago *(Metroxylon* spp.). The leaves of the sago provide thatch for houses and the pith is used as food for pigs on occasion. The fruit of the *Bruguiera* mangrove is collected for food. The "saltwater" people of Langalanga rely heavily on the sea and reef for food, for the raw materials for manufacturing shell valuables, and for porpoise teeth, all of which pro-vide the means to barter with the inland people for greater supplies of vegetables and pigs. The inland "bush" people live as high as 900 meters above sea level, but have most of their gardens between 200 and 350 meters. Unlike those of their coastal neighbors, their gardens are on slopes, mainly because there is little well-drained flatland in the moun-tains. Their main crops are taro, sweet potato, and bananas *(Musa* spp.), with trees like the *ngali (Canarium harveyi nova-hebridiense)* and breadfruit *(Artocarpus incisus)* typically growing in former garden sites among upland forest. Here, as elsewhere, certain soil types are pre-

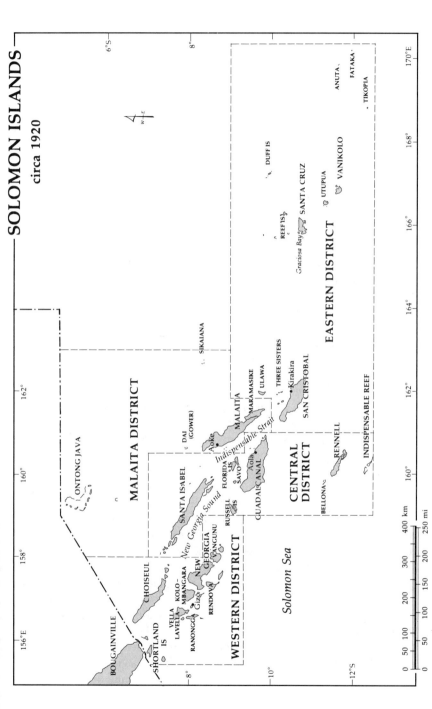

SOLOMON ISLANDS

circa 1920

Figure 1

ferred for cultivation, but with the bush-fallow method (described later) maximum use is made of the organically rich topsoil.

On far-flung Tikopia, a low-lying Polynesian outlier of volcanic origin and Andosol soils, the rainfall is heavy throughout the year (around 4000 mm). Most of Tikopia's lowland and montane forests and savanna woodlands are used for gardening under a brief wild-grass fallow. Here, unlike most other outliers, mulching is not used for fertilizing the soil. Tikopia's flat, open areas of high water table grow taro, but in sloping areas mixed gardens of taro, yams *(Dioscorea alata)*, and bananas are usual. Like Langalanga, there is some wild sago, and fishing in the lagoons and sea provides a substantial proportion of the food supply.

Cultivators in Roviana Lagoon and Tadhimboko exploit different coastal environments yet grow similar crops—taro, yams, sweet potatoes, and bananas. *Pana (Dioscorea esculenta,* a type of potato) grows well in north Guadalcanal and was, with yams, the staple in former times. The terrain in both areas is similar in elevation, but Tadhimboko is drier (about 2000 mm a year, seasonally) and in a distinct rain-shadow typical of the grasslands and savanna woodlands of north Guadalcanal, compared to the lowland forest of Roviana, which receives about 4000 mm a year. In both areas the sea and reefs supply some food, but the further inland settlements are, the less their people rely on these. Tadhimboko people hunt wild pigs, birds, opossums, and the odd bat and collect wild yams.[3]

Despite the difficulties of steep slopes and a range of soil types and vegetative cover, each of the major islands provides similar resources for the subsistence cultivator, although in varying proportions.[4] How a cultivator held rights to such resources varied from place to place and, since many of the present land tenure systems appear to elude classification by anthropologists, generalizations about the past may not be reliable. Almost all systems were based on the principle that the primary cultivators, their heirs and assigns had first claim to the land. Of course, family groups and clans accumulated these rights. An individual might acquire the right to use some of a group's land, but the group's approval, mediated sometimes by a chief or big-man or sometimes simply by consensus among the elders, would be essential. Moreover, land that was not used for cultivation, but was in some way associated with a particular family or clan—perhaps their ancestors were buried there or they went there periodically to gather certain products—remained group property. Rights to land, rather than being held by a village (which could contain a number of unrelated individuals), were generally vested in descent groups, people who shared a common ancestor or ancestor-figure. Often, especially in hamlets or small settlements, the nearby land that the people used for subsistence belonged to all of them.

This was less frequently the case in larger settlements where land-use rights might be granted to other clans and incomers or where land owners by descent might be far away because of marriage or extended residence in another village. The latter case required greater flexibility in land allocation, to permit those with the greatest need to use the land. However, contention could arise when land became a scarce resource or distant relatives returned to reassert their claims.[5]

Where the land ends, significant differences start. The modern Solomons state occupies an area of over 777,000 square kilometers, of which 96 percent is sea. Everywhere the sea offers food and valuables, but its bounty is profuse and most easily won in the areas of reefs and lagoons. The open sea offers abundant fish, especially tuna (bonito), tunny, and mackerel. Porpoises are common and highly valued for their teeth, especially in the eastern and central Solomons. A range of fish abounds in the reef areas and lagoons, as well as crayfish, crabs, shellfish, and bêche-de-mer.[6] Hawksbill turtles were probably more plentiful in the precontact period, as was the crocodile, which is now virtually extinct. While a few places in the east, and north Malaita, have such resources, reefs and lagoons are most frequently found near the western islands, and, to a lesser extent, the Florida Islands.

The sea is a major influence on the climate of the Solomon Islands. Because of the sea's great mass relative to land in the equatorial zone, mean values of temperature and humidity vary little throughout the year at any particular altitude. Average day-time temperatures range from 20 °C to 33 °C.[7] Moisture-laden winds from across the sea mark the year's passage here as elsewhere in the southwest Pacific. From about March until November the trade winds blow from the southeast and are strong and steady, creating constant choppy conditions on unprotected seas. By December the winds have reversed and come from the northwest until April; at this season, the winds are much more variable and sudden squalls can make seas turbulent in unsheltered areas. The northwesterly season is slightly drier than the southeasterly, with the annual rainfall ranging from 2500 to 5000 millimeters.[8]

The western islands are also influenced by westerlies, which contribute to the heavier rainfall received on the southern side of the major islands during the southeasterly season. However, from about 160 °E the westerlies peter out and the trade winds from both hemispheres meet in a single convergence zone. Between this longitude and 175 °W (Wallis Islands), cyclonic depressions usually occur from December to April, and sometimes develop into tropical cyclones following erratic southerly paths that may include the Solomons. Detailed, long-term meteorological records for the Solomons are scarce, making it difficult to say just how often and where cyclones strike. One or two occur each year, with the eastern Solomons apparently more often affected. The damage cyclones do varies with their intensity and the geographical features of the land over which they pass. Heavy rainfall causes flooding and landslips that destroy gardens, and sometimes villages, as do the severe winds reaching up to 100 knots. High winds can uproot trees and strip the leaf cover from 20-kilometer-wide swaths of vegetation, so reducing the supply of food and building materials. In more exposed areas, the winds carry salt spray from the sea up to 5 kilometers inland, burning all the vegetation.[9]

The sea is a dominant factor in the perception of the Islanders, no less than in their environment. The people who live on the coast are called "saltwater" people; those inland are "bush" people. On the bigger islands, such as Guadalcanal, the "bush" might begin one-half to two kilometers from the coast. Even on some of the smaller islands like Simbo precontact tradition tells of the same conceptual division even when the islands concerned might be only two to three kilometers wide. Although not universal, this dichotomy of people was common in Solomon societies and is today not dissimilar in connotation to the Western world's "city slicker" and "country cousin." The saltwater people see themselves as being more articulate, cleverer, and wiser to the ways of the outside world than the bush people. With few exceptions, such as the Lau and Langalanga lagoon communities, the coastal people have extensive gardens, yet their reputation lies in their abilities at fishing and swimming. The bush people also see them as morally inferior and somewhat corrupted by foreign influences. In contrast to the saltwater people, the bush people see themselves as being simpler, stronger, more honest, and truer to the real values of their society. They are excellent horticulturalists, know the bush environment intimately, and are tireless walkers. However, the saltwater people often consider them stupid, slow, and backward in their customs.[10]

The saltwater–bush division rarely corresponds with linguistic boundaries. On Malaita, the most densely populated island of the postcontact period, there are four to eight languages, with many dialects. Most of these languages extend from the east to the west coast across a segment of the island. Here, as on other islands, saltwater and bush communities lack political cohesion and are usually at odds with one another, but share a common language.[11]

In the Solomons there are over eighty indigenous languages, the majority of which belong to the Austronesian group. This language family extends from southeast Asia as far as Easter Island, New Zealand, and Hawaii. The ancestral speakers of these languages first entered the Pacific from the west about 4000 B.C. and probably reached the Solomons about 2000 B.C. But they may well have found parts of the islands already occupied by peoples related to the first settlers of New Guinea, who moved slowly from the southeast Asia region more than thirty thousand years ago. These people probably spoke languages described as Papuan or Non-Austronesian. One subgroup of this very old language family is the East Papua phylum to which belong some of the present languages of Vella Lavella, Rendova, New Georgia, Savo, and the Santa Cruz Islands.[12] It would be a nice correlation for the linguist and the prehistorian if these ancient Non-Austronesian languages were all spoken by isolated communities living in the interior whence they were driven by later coastal Austronesian-speaking settlers. But as in so many aspects of human culture in the Solomons the picture is far more complex. In some areas today, two peoples of similar culture, one speaking a Non-Austronesian language and the other an Austronesian language, live side by side along the coast. Elsewhere, the coastal people speak a Non-Austronesian language and their bush neighbors an Austronesian language. It would also be a nice correlation for the physical anthropologist and the lay observer if the coal-black people of the western islands all spoke languages of the one family and the brown people of the central and eastern Solomons spoke another. Again the reality is less simple. All the Shortland Islands people speak an Austronesian language, while many of the New Georgians do not.[13]

Among the Austronesian-speaking newcomers were the Lapita people, so called because one of the earliest finds of their distinctive incised pottery was made at that place in New Caledonia. Radiocarbon dating suggests that around 2000–1300 B.C. they rapidly colonized parts of island New Guinea, the Solomons, Vanuatu, New Caledonia, and Fiji. From Fiji they voyaged to Tonga and Samoa to become the first settlers and the ancestors of the present-day Polynesians. Excavations of other artefacts along with Lapita pottery provide evidence that these people were very mobile seafarers who exploited coastal resources in Melanesia and Polynesia. Among such artefacts was obsidian from New Britain, which has been found at sites as far away as the Reef Islands (Santa Cruz) and New Caledonia, indicating that the Lapita people either traveled up to 2600 kilometers on their voyages or maintained links, at least for a while, with related communities throughout the Melanesian chain. In time, the Lapita people were either replaced or absorbed by other communities, but they may well have left a contribution to the subsequent technology.[14]

Although the present inhabitants of the Solomons have long forgotten those ancient migrations, their oral traditions record more recent movements of people across considerable distances. It is unlikely that these will ever explain the totality of cultural and linguistic diversity existing even on one island, but they do provide a model of the type of movement and resultant complexities that were common in precontact times. Traditions of the Bougainville Strait communities tell how refugees from warfare left Alu (Shortland) Island and fled to the southeast coast of Bougainville, possibly in the second half of the eighteenth century.[15] The 'Are'are speakers of eastern Guadalcanal settled hundreds of years ago on the offshore islands of Marau after leaving their homes in west Malaita.[16] Perhaps, like the Alu, they activitated old trade and marriage ties to win entrée. Not long before European contact, some Lau people from the artificial islands of north Malaita migrated south to Port Adam, probably because of population growth.[17]

Population pressure, often resulting in land disputes and warfare, was the likely motive behind most major migrations. Areas obviously unfit for human settlement, such as the Three Sisters group which presently lacks fresh water, or the mosquito-ridden Lauvi Lagoon of south Guadalcanal, were either abandoned or avoided. Where the basic needs for food, water, and shelter could be satisfied, security and defense were the main criteria for selecting a site for settlement. Inland, the bush people invariably built their houses on ridge tops even though this entailed arduous climbing to bring home water and garden produce. Most of the saltwater people similarly positioned their homes atop coastal peaks or spurs. These coastal and inland settlements were hamlets rather than villages. A bush hamlet might consist of one or two households (about ten people), although coastal settlements tended to be larger. In some coastal areas, where the foreshore was wide and large numbers of related people had access to plentiful food supplies, "villages" were really a series of strung-out hamlets, each consisting of about five houses clustered together. Paths connecting adjacent hamlets passed through undergrowth, betel, *ngali* (canarium almond), and coconut groves. Depending on terrain, hamlets were about 185–275 meters apart, a distance that would allow shouts and conch-shell blasts to be heard above the noise of the surf. As enemy attacks were always a possibility, the strung-out arrangement of the coastal settlements was strategically advantageous because once the alarm was given the inhabitants of neighboring hamlets had time to organize defense or to flee. These extended settlements usually had from 100 to 250 inhabitants. In particularly favorable positions, such as Sa'a in south Malaita, the number could be higher, but these were exceptional.[18]

The general pattern of small, dispersed settlements benefited the health of Solomon Islanders. Diseases such as leprosy, respiratory complaints including tuberculosis, and dysentery may well have been endemic but introduced varieties of these have masked the original disease base. Certainly both before and during the early contact period some protection from disease was afforded by the isolation of settlements. Moreover, most people tended to keep away from neighboring hamlets where illness was rife. Sometimes the very sick, including lepers, were driven off—drastic but effective preventive medicine. People perceived hamlets where unnatural deaths had occurred as being under the pall of spiritual disfavor, and consequently deserted them.

Sites might be abandoned because of natural catastrophe—a flood or earthquake—but more commonly people moved their homes to remain no farther than an hour's walk from their gardens, providing, of course, they could find a secure location. Some settlements, especially inland ones, might be moved every three to ten years, depending on the land's fertility and the density of the population. Frequently, maybe every twenty-five to fifty years, an abandoned site, always remembered by the former occupants and their offspring, would be reoccupied, with the new buildings following the ground plan of the old.[19] In some areas such as Guadalcanal and Choiseul there was a system of dual residence. The strategically placed main village was where all residents had houses, was the center of ceremonial activity, and was sometimes fortified. During the yam planting and growing season, the members of each family or subclan lived in a hamlet adjacent to their gardens. After harvest or in times of enemy attack the people would leave these hamlets to return to the central village.[20] Such sporadic but continual occupancy played havoc with the archaeological record, just as so many abandoned sites confused early foreign observers who equated them with massive population decline.

Village isolation was no protection from some afflictions. Malaria, yaws, and hookworm were certainly endemic. On the high islands every ecological zone inhabited by human beings was also shared by one or other variety of anopheles mosquito, the malaria vector, although it was probably less common in the high bush areas where most of the pre-contact population seems to have been located. Yaws, less common at altitudes above 500 meters, is usually contracted by children from adult carriers. It was hardly a minor complaint even in the early twentieth century, as one long-time resident noted:

> To the casual observer the native appeared . . . a strong and healthy race. More closer inspection would find, hidden away in the houses and living apart in little huts, human beings covered with frightful sores and suffering the ravages of secondary and the last stages of the disease. Nearly every small child exhibited the sores of the first stage. Women eager to bear and rear children aborted time after time, no doubt the effect of yaws on their constitution.[21]

The combination of yaws and malaria probably did have an adverse effect on the fertility of the women. Those who gave birth saw 40 percent of their babies die from malaria. The survivors of this and yaws by adulthood developed some resistance to both diseases. Hookworm, spread by pigs, caused anemia, as did malaria. Like malaria and yaws, it was debilitating and, in combination with those other diseases, was sometimes fatal. Some people survived into old age, but the majority could expect to live no more than about thirty years.[22]

Life for the people in the Solomon Islands was never a round of incessant toil for bare survival; but sickness and death hovered very close, despite the fecundity of land and sea.

Production, exchange, and social organization

Almost all Solomon Islanders made gardens by the swidden or bush-fallow method. The cultivator cleared a patch of primary or preferably secondary forest, and planted root and tree crops in the first year, sometimes with further plantings of root crops in the second and occasionally the third year. Following the harvest, the garden was left to regenerate to jungle, except for the exploitation of tree crops. During the second or third year, the gardener, having found one or more suitable sites, began new plantings and the cycle commenced again. The first plot lay fallow for anything from three to twenty-five years, depending on the fertility of the soil, the stability of the site, and the density of the population, but a ten-to-twenty-year fallow was probably most common.[23] In a few areas on New Georgia and Kolombangara, taro was grown on irrigated terraces, a far more labor-intensive form of cultivation that produced high yields.[24]

Until contact with outsiders, taro was the main root crop in the Solomons, followed by yams. In a few places, such as Simbo, bananas were a staple too.[25] Elsewhere they, along with breadfruit, sugarcane, papaya, and different kinds of green vegetables, contributed variety and balance to the diet. The canarium almond was an important tree crop, as was the coastal-growing coconut. Although widespread, sago was a regular part of the diet only in the Shortlands and, in a few areas, an emergency food in time of shortage.[26]

The swidden method of horticulture is one of the most efficient in the world in terms of return on labor input. However, it requires quite a large area of land: approximately 1250 square meters for each person (and each dependent adult pig) each year. This means about 3.75 hectares per person for a lifetime of thirty years. These figures are ideal. In reality, the villagers had to allow for the unexpected in order to reduce the risks inherent in an often volatile social, political, and climatic environment. The ambition of a big-man to gain prestige by feast-giving might mean hundreds more pigs needing to be fed and necessitate more land being cultivated. The wise villager, knowing the local area's vulnerability to raids by enemies, would make an extra garden or two in hidden corners of the bush, just in case. The land itself might dictate more extensive garden making. For example, in areas of steep slopes, where erosion and landslips were common, the gardener had to make more or larger plots in the same way as where the soil was poor. For all this, there was probably little land shortage on the big islands.[27]

Widespread famine was rare, but during the "hungry" months when taro and yam supplies were running low and new gardens being planted, Solomon Islanders turned to the forest for foods such as wild yams and small game. This period of scarcity varied from place to place, depending on microclimate and dominant food crops, but fell roughly between December and May.[28] The valued pig was a source of protein, but was normally consumed only on festive or ritual occasions. For coast dwellers, fish and shellfish were a more regular supplement to a primarily vegetable diet.[29]

Some areas were famous for a particular crop and some notorious for their lack of it. The Saʻa people of south Malaita and their neighbors on Ulawa Island apostrophized Uki Island accordingly:

> Uki with its oily yam mash
> Its flying sands
> Uki of the sandy shore
> Disappear in the coconuts
> Net fish with yells
> Uki where yam sets die.[30]

Apart from regional differences in the foods produced, some places were known for their particular natural resources: stone for adze-making, iron pyrites to blacken teeth. Other areas achieved prominence because of craft specialization. Pondokona, New Georgia, was known for fine wickerwork shields, southeast Santa Isabel for lime spatulas. Valuables made of shell, feathers, and opossum or porpoise teeth were also made or assembled in some place. The most prominent centers of production of this kind of currency included Langalanga, Malaita, and Hounihu, San Cristobal, where small red or white circular shell beads were made and threaded on strings; and Roviana and Marovo, where various sizes of arm rings were manufactured from fossilized clam shells.[31] These valuables, or currency, were used in transactions creating social relationships (like marriage), and preventing or repairing a break in existing relationships (such as mortuary payments and blood money). They were the means of reciprocal and redistributive payments, but were not used for commercial exchange.[32] Apart from these relatively durable valuables, little if any wealth could be accumulated for transmission from generation to generation. It was rare for any concentration of wealth, including these valuables, to remain in the hands of one person or family for long, as there were social mechanisms that kept valuables in circulation, providing the basis of the egalitarianism typical of Melanesian societies.

Specialized crops, resources, and manufactures all led to the growth of trading networks throughout the Solomons. Coastal communities formed the nodes of such systems. To their bush neighbors they regularly offered fish, coconuts, and sometimes goods from far away; they received in return vegetables, pigs, and often specialized products like string bags. Barter between strange groups occurred on neutral ground, with the women doing the haggling and the armed men hovering in the background. When business was over each party returned to its own territory.[33] Some coast dwellers, however, had to make long and often dangerous journeys across the sea to get what they needed for themselves and to exchange later with trading associates. The length of the journey and the vagaries of the weather meant that time was needed for recuperation at the voyagers' destination.[34] Over the ages, individuals from distant settlements became protected trading partners, even to the extent of exchanging names. These relationships were cemented by presentations, usually before barter began. Men of Ulawa and Santa Ana would welcome their brother trader with an exchange of red shell money and the greeting, "Your house is ready for you at our village, may no harm come to you. May you and your party find happiness during your visit and may you all have a safe journey home."[35]

Another commodity exchanged was human beings. In order to ensure its own continuance every community needed marriageable women, and for many societies this meant finding women outside their own immediate group. Throughout the islands, individuals identified with a particular descent group either unilineally (*either* mother's *or* father's side consistently) or ambilineally (through mother or father). In San Cristobal, Santa Isabel, Guadalcanal, and Nggela, most traced their descent through the clan of their mother back to an ancestor with a special totemic association with some nonhuman living being like a bird or snake: thus, a "hawk" clan mother would have "hawk" children. Such clans were exogamous and had to establish relationships with other clan groups to obtain wives: that is, "hawks" married "doves," "eagles," "snakes," or "flying foxes," but never "hawks." In general these groups lived in adjacent areas and spoke the same language or similar dialects. However, on Malaita and most of the western islands descent was traced generally from a particular ancestor through males and females. In these ambilineal descent societies individuals could marry anyone except those within the first-cousin (and sometimes second-cousin) range. Most seemed to prefer to marry members of their own residential group because it was safer to marry relatives than strangers and because it lessened claims of outsiders to land use-rights. But since the small size of the group frequently precluded this, "trading" in women was an important consideration for almost all groups at some time. It was never a one-way transaction. Bride-wealth was handed over by the groom's male relatives to those of the bride to compensate them for the loss to the clan and family.[36]

This was one of the rare public acknowledgments of the economic worth of women in the society. As well as being childbearers, women held a significant role in production. Men cut down trees and cleared the undergrowth to make gardens, but the women did the daily weeding and tending of plants. In addition they carried home huge loads of produce and firewood, and cooked and cleaned for the household. As elsewhere, men did the sporadic and interesting tasks of fishing, hunting, and fighting, while women regularly collected shellfish, drinking water, salt water for cooking, tended pigs, made tapa or grass fiber clothing, and in some areas pottery, and carried out the most tedious stages of shell valuable manufacture. Although a woman's economic worth was recognized in the marriage transaction, her social status relative to a man's was low. The Polynesian concepts of *noa* ('common, secular, ritually unclean'—the negative female element) and *tapu* ('special, sacred, ritually holy'—the positive male element) also prevailed in varying degrees in the thinking of Solomon Islanders. Women's paths led into and around the hub of home and hearth; men's radiated outward and upward, beyond the commonplace to the frontiers of the known world. Women's lives were circumscribed by men, but such unequal relationships were sanctioned by every element of culture, intangible and tangible, be it language or bodily deportment, myths or eating practices, time concepts or the siting of village buildings. To men and women alike the social order, constantly reinforced and reinforcing, seemed normal, inevitable, and unchanging.[37]

Through women the old men indirectly controlled the young men. Young men needed wealth to present to their future bride's family and to get it they did what the elders wanted: adventurous work like joining war parties and trading expeditions, but more often the mundane tasks of working the garden and building houses. Because a single man past the age of marriage was considered by all to be a person of no account, the young strove to obey, even when the old men exploited them.[38]

There was yet another source of labor and wealth—slaves. These were either captives in war or offenders against the society's norms who were sold to neighboring peoples. Slaves were more commonly found among the more powerful coastal societies, which had exceptionally strong leaders. They provided extra labor and were sometimes kept in reserve for the occasion that called for a human sacrifice. As an institution slavery was limited. Slaves lived very much as did their masters. They were not numerous and in no way constituted a class. Often, especially with those who had esoteric knowledge of such things as sorcery or the weather, slaves became accepted as members of their new society. Young slave women were frequently made to act as prostitutes for the district but in time they were usually married off by their managers for a reduced bride-price and their past forgotten.[39]

Through migration, trade, marriage, and slavery, new ideas and practices percolated through Solomons societies, especially in coastal areas. Just how these affected precontact communities can only be guessed, because the work of the archaeologist in exploring even the material culture has only just begun. It seems that considerable changes have occurred even in relatively recent times. In the three to four centuries between the visit of Mendaña in 1568 and the arrival of subsequent European visitors, the people of Ulawa and Arosi (northwest San Cristobal) stopped using bows and arrows in warfare, retaining only spears.[40] Oral tradition told of the manufacture of shell money at a "mint" near Talise on the south coast of Guadalcanal that ceased production before European contact. The tradition of the Oau people of Malaita relates the successive cultural innovations they made over several generations before the white man came.[41] Undoubtedly tradition and conservation were strong in the Solomon Islands, but the people were pragmatists, incorporating from the new what appeared to serve their ends while discarding the superfluous.

Political organization

Political groupings in the Solomons were generally small and localized. The level of operation determined the nature and size of the grouping involved. In, say, a region containing a dozen hamlets of related kin, each hamlet would consist of one or more households containing a nuclear family. The senior male in each household, usually the father of the nuclear family, would exert authority over and speak for the household. On matters concerning all the hamlets the most senior males, usually in the grandfather's generation, would be deferred to. It might happen that from within one of these hamlets or from an adjacent, more distantly related group, a man might arise who was ambitious and desired power above the ordinary, an individual who aspired to be a big-man.

Quite simply, a big-man was a man who could win followers, certainly within his own clan group, but also beyond. Although the usual size of an established big-man's following in precontact times is not known, most anthropologists would reckon it at a maximum of around two hundred. The big-man's influence could also be great outside his own group. Other big-men had to take his power into consideration because he could be a potential ally or enemy in a dispute with a third group.

To gain and sustain a wide following a big-man had to bring renown to himself and his supporters by conspicuous demonstration of his wealth and, above all, his generosity. This involved extensive and intelligent manipulation of his own resources and those of his clan to create surpluses, particularly of pigs and vegetables. Feast giving, dance entertainments, and assistance with the financing of young men's bride payments and of funeral offerings, were all essential acts of a big-man. But, as in all aspects of economic activity, such actions were embedded in and subservient to the social context. A big-man was considered wealthy insofar as he redistributed the wealth among his supporters and gave them a feeling of significance. In precontact society his ability to organize and mobilize professional assassins or war parties, particularly to revenge any injury to his followers, was also an essential component of his leadership, although not all big-men actually led such parties, preferring to leave this to others who were specialists. A big-man, while infrequently an expert in religious and magical knowledge and practice, had to be able to finance sorcerers to protect himself and his followers, as well as be able to honor the ancestral and other spirits by appropriate rededication of shrines, the opening of men's houses, and, in coastal areas, the launching of canoes. Often the big-man possessed a thorough knowledge of local history, especially regarding the inheritance and distribution of land. In precontact society, just as a big-man grew in importance so too did the spirits of his ancestors or other tutelar spirits who consequently became greatly revered among the big-man's followers. An exceptionally powerful big-man was frequently attributed to have a special supernatural power or quality, resembling mana, which derived in part from his connection with such powerful spirits. This gave such a rare individual great authority over others and an ability, while at the apex of his powers, to command obedience from his followers.[42]

In a few societies, such as on Kolombangara, the major roles of the big-man might be shared among several persons. One big-man of the society was the expert on genealogical knowledge and the manager of the group's land, another was a religious leader, and another the leader in warfare.[43]

Although the major attributes of the big-man were to be found in all leaders in the Solomons, in some areas a more chiefly system based on inheritance of status prevailed. But, as in Polynesia and its tiny outliers in the Solomons, ability and performance had to set the seal on hereditary preference. If a young man lacked these qualities, elders of the family would support a more able uncle, brother, or cousin. Even in these societies, a commoner with outstanding qualities could by his achievements become chief. Such chiefly societies existed in the Shortlands, New Georgia, Florida Islands (Nggela), Lau Lagoon, and at Sa'a on south Malaita.[44] These people were all coast dwellers, in areas where travel by sea or along the coast was relatively easy, and an aid to efficient communication. Moreover, these communities were particularly rich in natural or manufactured resources.

Relative affluence and ease of communication did not automatically produce a chiefly political organization, but in areas lacking these, societies were invariably very small scale with either big-man leadership or, at times, simply government by the gerontocracy. Such groupings were typical of bush areas. All groups, whether large or small, could ally temporarily with neighbors for warfare. But alliances were constantly shifting—an ascendant big-man might need to make a name by avenging some insult to one of his supporters. Usually the insult originated from a quarrel about the major sources of wealth and security in the Solomons—land, pigs, and women. Warfare was sporadic and, for coast dwellers at least, more common in the growing season, when the northwesterlies blew. The demands of the subsistence economy and the inability to store food over long periods meant that the men simply did not have the time to indulge in months and years of unremitting warfare. The occasional early morning raid bringing death to four or five people, or the ambush of one or two bushmen foolish enough to wander down to the coast to fish were the norm; the pitched battle on open ground was unusual, if for no other reason than the adverse terrain. Solomon Islanders had long memories for unrevenged killings. In time, they or a hired third party would even the score unless compensation was offered by the erstwhile enemy. Like other Melanesians, Solomon Islanders were adept at making war but no less talented at making peace.[45]

Peace meant trade could resume and marriages could be arranged. But periodic warfare coupled with the small political units kept people suspicious of strangers. A stranger was automatically an enemy.[46] Why would a man leave his land, relatives, and the protection of his ancestral spirits, to come to a foreign territory, unless it was to cause trouble?

Religion

No one knows what religious concepts Solomon Islanders had before European contact. What emerges from early postcontact sources no less than from contemporary culture is that Solomon Islanders believed in spirit-beings and occult forces, which their rituals concentrated on communicating with and manipulating. The spirit-beings fell into three general categories: first, the autonomous deities and culture heroes usually associated with creation or the regulation of the conditions conducive to human existence; second, autonomous spirit-beings—demons and tricksters who wantonly harmed and annoyed; third, the spirits of the dead. Another class of beings was associated with totems, such as the eagle, hawk, or snake. Some societies have totems that are the supposed founders of a unilineal descent group or were adopted as a kind of emblem because of some ancient association. No rituals of worship or placation are associated with totems. Prohibitions exist: One does not marry into one's own totem; nor does one kill or eat either the actual totemic animal or, in many areas, members of the same totem.[47]

In general, the autonomous deities and culture heroes associated with creation finished their work long ago. Such beings were never truly human. One such spirit figure was a female snake who, for some, was the mother of a woman who was their primary ancestor. She also brought death into the world and the multitude of languages into parts of the Solomons. On Guadalcanal she was called Koevasi; on San Cristobal, Kahausibware. Most societies had no supreme creator being at all and if they did that being was no longer concerned about its creatures and their behavior. These gods lived in permanent retirement.[48]

Other deities or heroes were active in ensuring fertility, and success for the group and its concerns. These spirits were specific to clans or localities, although a particularly potent spirit might attract followers beyond these limits. Sometimes such spirits had originally been human, but to other groups similar figures might not have had any corporeal presence at all.[49]

The ancestral spirit-beings were of universal importance. With death a person passed into another dimension. One aspect of a person's being, the "shadow," remained around the village; the other aspect, the "soul," passed to one or other of the abodes of the dead, such as Marapa off east Guadalcanal or Laulau off Isabel. Although generally invisible, the ancestral spirits maintained an interest in their living relatives. All people could call upon a recently dead near relative for help in time of stress, but those ancestors who had been powerful in their own lifetimes, those with mana, were worshipped. Over time, some ancestors supposedly continued to demonstrate their mana by positive intervention in the fortunes of their living descendants. Such ancestral spirits continued to be venerated while the less active ones were slowly but politely forgotten and allowed to slip into complete oblivion.[50]

Creator spirits were not worshipped, but deities or heroes with an ongoing role in human existence were, as well as the ancestral spirits. Trickster or demon spirits were feared, placated, and occasionally invoked through sorcery to do evil, but rarely worshipped.[51] Active culture heroes and deities as well as the ancestral spirits would initiate communication with their followers through a dream or by certain signs —a firefly in the house, or a butterfly hovering over the head. The recipient of such signs would then attempt to find out which spirit was calling and what it wanted. Sometimes the spirit then manifested itself in the form of a shark, snake, lizard, bird, crocodile, or fish, or in more vivid dreams. Worship of these spirits usually consisted of prayers with sacrifices (pigs, fish, human beings) or offerings (food, shell valuables) at a shrine, which often might contain some relic of the deity or ancestor. Many Melanesian societies had priests, but this role was usually in addition to all those of other men, as there was no priestly class.[52]

For most Solomon Islanders the relationship between them and both the regulative deities and the ancestral spirits was one of reciprocity, a reflection of their own socioeconomic relationships in the empirical world. If the spirits were treated with reverence, the living expected them to provide assistance in their endeavors. It seems that regulative deities in particular were viewed not so much with fear and awe as with respect and affection. In many places people held regular religious festivals celebrating the role a deity played in the fertility of the land. These first fruits or harvest festivals were usually held for about three days in February and were joyous occasions that reconfirmed the unity of the community and its devotion to its deity.[53]

Such spirits, if antagonized by their followers' failure to offer sacrifices, could cause misfortune. However, Solomon Islanders attributed major troubles to the actions of sorcerers. In the Melanesian's view nothing happened by chance; people attempted to channel spiritual forces to their own ends. Consequently whatever happened—be it illness, a famine, the death of a pig, the falling of a branch onto a child, the achievement of leadership, or victory in battle—all occurred because someone had access to power from the spirits. One major way of gaining access was through sorcery, with the sorcerer using magical ritual to invoke a deity, an ancestral spirit, or, less commonly, a demon spirit. Sorcery was universal and, in its negative aspects, greatly feared. A form of social control, it usually restrained the more ruthless and exploitive members of the community and ensured conformity to socially accepted moral values.[54]

Particular spirits were invoked for this purpose by individual sorcerers, but in many societies this oblique involvement was the sum total of the spirits' interest in the moral behavior of the living. The prime religious duty of the Kaoka people of Guadalcanal, for example, was to carry out ritual observances to the spirits. For them to imagine that the spirits would be offended by immoral behavior was ludicrous. Other societies had different ideas. On Malaita, many believed that if a man killed his relative, the spirit of an ancestor common to both would be so offended as to cause the death of the killer.[55]

Such might be the fate of a few of the living, but beyond the grave there was little expectation of particular reward or punishment for deeds in life. Some groups believed that exiles or the unborn child of a dead mother, being members of no human society, were in death destined to wander alone forever through the forests. These were unusual cases, for the afterlife itself was a vague state. What happened in the various abodes of the dead was not of interest.[56]

Little was known about the afterlife simply because Solomon Islanders were preoccupied by life in this world. Right behavior in the ritual attendance to the spirits' demands was rewarded by observable success in this world, not the hereafter. Religious systems based on the attainment and manipulation of spiritual power for earthly success had no place for the weak. They offered little solace for the maimed, the sick, the failures, the deviants, and the dispossessed. Unrewarded and unredeemed in life, these people suffered and waited for an empty death.

Other worlds

For most Solomon Islanders, the world they knew well was bounded by a range of mountains, rivers, and the sea.[57] Many had some understanding of near neighbors, including those on adjacent islands. What really lay beyond those islands or the high mountains became increasingly speculative as the distance lengthened.

From their own hemisphere the Europeans too had speculated as to what was beyond Asia and then the Americas, the boundaries of their world. Geographers from early times had propounded a great southern continent—Terra Australis Incognita—a land mass necessary, they believed, to keep the earth balanced on its axis. This southern land was all the more fertile a soil for the imagination because it was unknown. Here the hopes and fantasies of the European could flourish unabated, creating a land of riches, the fabled Ophir. From the sixteenth century on, with the way opened by Magellan, explorers began to criss-cross the Pacific in search of this great continent.[58]

Europeans discovered the Solomons relatively early in the era of Pacific exploration. In 1568 the Spaniard Mendaña came ashore on Santa Isabel. On this first visit Mendaña and his ships stayed six months and visited half the major islands in search of gold. Despite the intruders' terrifying strangeness, the Islanders soon learned how to manage the one hundred fifty men who tramped over their lands demanding food and water.[59] Rudimentary though they were, the European firearms were intimidating; but, as Dorothy Shineberg has so well shown, the various groups of Solomon Islanders quickly adapted their defensive and offensive strategies to contain the alien technology.[60] Although disappointed with the lack of gold, Mendaña on his return to Peru and later Spain tried ceaselessly to convince his superiors of the Solomons' potential as a place of settlement, the mirage of the land's apparent fertility having gripped him. Finally, in 1595 he once again was in command of four ships from Peru. The expedition sailed west in search of the islands that would form a way station for Spanish ships plying between Manila and South America. Except for a remnant of survivors who reached Manila, this enterprise ended in the disappearance of the vessel *Almiranta*, and death for Mendaña and the rest on Santa Cruz. About this time castaways from a lost Spanish ship founded a settlement near Pamua on San Cristobal. But its people and all memory of both Spanish expeditions were soon swallowed up by the dark jungle.[61]

As far as Europeans were concerned, the sea had likewise swallowed up the Solomons because sixteenth-century navigators had not discovered a method to fix longitude. Finding the Solomons again would almost be a matter of chance.

With the awakening in Europe of scientific interest in the Pacific in the late eighteenth century and the contest for mastery of the sea lanes, a second wave of explorers resumed the search for the southern land. Major discoveries were made in the Society and Hawaiian islands, Australia, and New Zealand. Because of their wealth and mild climates these lands soon dominated the concerns of trading and colonizing Europeans. Once again Europeans sighted the Solomons: Bougainville in 1768, Carteret and Surville in 1769, then the naval captains, merchantmen, and whalers who gradually pinned these elusive islands in the mesh of longitude and latitude.[62]

While the "ship men" stayed on board their vessels, scribbling on bits of paper, the world of the Solomon Islanders remained intact. Despite the Solomons' difficult climate and multiple political units, the Europeans slowly learned more and more as the maps made access easier and the ships' journals told of their products and peoples. For Solomon Islanders, the great ships were portents of new experiences and a superior technology. By the close of the eighteenth century both Europeans and Islanders were increasingly crossing the beach for commerce. Those first simple transactions were to link the destinies of both peoples forever.

CHAPTER 2

The ship men
(c. 1800–1860)

One day, long long ago, a man was fishing on the reef, and he
saw something out in the sea. It appeared to be an island, but
it moved. He ran to the beach shouting, "An island is coming
here," and quickly the people gathered on the beach to watch
a sailing ship approach and anchor off the reef. The inhabitants of the island came ashore, and our island world ceased
to be.

Casper Luana, "Buka! A Retrospect"

[The Solomon Islands are] of little importance, . . . for in
the course of these discoveries they found no specimens of
spices, nor of gold and silver, nor of merchandise, nor of any
other source of profit, and all the people were naked savages.

Juan de Orosco, 20 March 1569

DURING THE FIRST HALF of the nineteenth century regular visits by whaling ships to parts of the Solomons gradually replaced occasional contacts by European explorers or passing merchant ships. The Melanesians
saw these first Europeans in terms of what they already knew—the visitors had to be spirits. Distinctly unspiritual behavior soon convinced
them otherwise and more human intercourse began. The whalers were
interested in food, water, wood, and women and bartered accordingly.
At this stage, trading by whalers for items to sell in the metropolitan
centers was simply a sideline to the main commercial enterprise of
whaling. The whalers' stays were short and their demands few, yet the
iron, infection, and ideas they left behind set in motion changes not
only in the basic technology but also in the economy and wider society
of the Solomons. Some islands, because of their lack of resources or inac-
cessibility, remained on the periphery of this new iron age, just as did
the people high in the bush areas. Yet because the technological demands of communities near the whaling ports were changing, the trade
linkages of those communities with the more isolated areas were
affected also. Those who had iron did all they could to maintain their

supply because for many it became more and more essential to their altered life-style.

First contact

The initial meeting of Solomon Islanders with Europeans was a fearful experience for both. The Solomon Islanders tried to fit the ships and their company into their own cosmology. Because many societies disposed of their dead in the sea, it was the home of ghosts. Great vessels with white flapping sails and white-skinned crew could only be ghosts' ships.[1] Where these dead ancestors bringing rewards or retribution?

The Europeans, unaware of their temporary spiritualization, perceived only the difficulties of their situation. Despite their traveled sophistication and arms they were outnumbered in an unknown land and poorly charted seas. Away from their ships, as they would have to be on occasion to collect fresh supplies, they were extremely vulnerable to attack. The appearance of the Solomon Islanders in their swift, graceful canoes could hardly have reassured them. The Islanders' naked blackness, dyed hair, distorted ears and noses, conjured up visions of savagery and cannibalism that overwhelmed almost all thoughts of a common humanity.[2]

Imprisoned in the limitations of their respective cultures, both sides hoped for the best at meeting, but anticipated the worst. With communication limited to signs and actions, first contacts frequently resulted in conflict. Almost by accident both parties stumbled on gestures that had sufficient shared meaning to facilitate basic exchanges. Once this occurred the way was open. When the first ship called at Simbo, a man named Paragusara marshaled enough courage to go on board, offering the "ghosts" a green coconut as a gesture of friendship. So great was his apprehension that he blurted out, "I am afraid." Although these words were, of course, incomprehensible to the visitors, he was not harmed. When he returned to his village he persuaded his companions to take food to the ship. In return they received tobacco, ship biscuits, and hoop iron.[3]

Knowledge of the existence of iron and metal tools was probably widespread in some coastal parts of the Solomons by as early as 1790. The few early explorers had had an impact, but the wreck of La Pérouse's two ships in 1788 at Vanikolo provided such a bonanza that news of the marvelous iron spread rapidly over the eastern Solomons and perhaps beyond, following existing trade linkages. Possibly, the survivors of La Pérouse's expedition, after leaving Vanikolo in their newly built craft, were wrecked elsewhere in the Solomons, so further spreading the knowledge of iron. Certainly, before this could have occurred, the inhabitants of Simbo in 1788 demonstrated to Shortland "a manifest preference to whatever was made of iron."[4] This suggests either an extremely quick perception of the potential of the metal or prior knowledge from drift wreckage or from the islands' communication network reporting on explorers.[5]

Iron, in the form of hoop iron, axes, tomahawks, plane blades, fish-hooks, and nails, was, to a stone-age society, almost magical. Its great strength and durability were readily appreciated. It outperformed the local products in its ability to maintain a keen edge after many hours of work. The first iron tools were seen as having an inherent value, a special quality or mana. They were treated as valuables or luxury goods, not simply as tools, and were revered as such. As late as the 1860s, John Renton, a castaway who came ashore at Sulufou, testified that the people regarded tomahawks as sacred:

> They possess indeed some tomahawks of European make obtained by trading with the natives of Isabelle, the island . . . frequented by ships. These tomahawks however they prize too highly to put them to common use and generally keep as articles of special virtue, hung up in the part of the hut specially devoted to their gods.[6]

Initial contacts with Europeans created a natural association between them and their powerful tools and weapons. The Solomon Islanders' first perception of white men as ghosts with mana would soon change as contact increased, particularly when the people could observe a white man apart from the material props of his culture—as was the case with castaways, deserters, and fugitive convicts. The north Malaitans had two examples before them—of the unfortunate Renton and of an earlier castaway of the 1820s, "Doorey." They saw the white men as

> a nomadic race eternally roving about over the sea in big canoes. If the white man had any islands at all . . . it must have been little . . . otherwise they would not require to leave it and come trading for yams and coconuts. They [the Sulufou] themselves traded for such things because they could not live without them, and they could come to no other conclusion except the white man was governed by the same necessities.[7]

Even by the early 1800s, some groups of Solomon Islanders in coastal areas had a fairly accurate picture of the capabilities of the ship men. The strangers were undoubtedly men, albeit with peculiar ways. In spite of their odd behavior the white men did possess iron and metal goods of great utility, far superior to any island-made items. For these goods, the Islanders would tolerate many of the strangers' idiosyncrasies.[8] Increased knowledge of the Islanders by Europeans offered no comparable consolation. When the early Europeans behaved badly they soon found that the Solomon Islanders retaliated with force and drove them away. Their initial image of the Islanders was etched deeper into their consciousness. Moreover, their reconnaissances in the islands provided nothing in the way of commercially exploitable products that might have compensated for the risks involved.[9]

Whaling: The beginning of long-distance trade

To the French and British explorers of the 1760s and succeeding decades it was apparent that little was to be gained in the Solomons. The islands and their people seemed destined to maintain their independence, and also their isolation, cut off from the Westerners and their metal. The colonization of Australia and New Zealand, coupled with the exhaustion of the Atlantic whaling grounds, brought white men back to the Solomons in the 1790s. Neither the islands nor the people were the attraction. The seas were the roads of ships and whales. For the East India Company and American merchant ships, the Solomons happened to be islands along a short route to the East from Port Jackson; for the whalers, the islands delineated the paths of the great sperm whale.

The East India Company ships brought cargoes of convicts to New South Wales while the American traders brought the means to sustain them. In Europe the wars had so curtailed English shipping that until 1813 the Navigation Acts were temporarily unenforced, allowing the Americans to sail across the Pacific to New South Wales, where they exchanged speculative cargoes for specie to buy tea at Canton.[10] Both the East India Company and American ships used (and in two cases had "discovered") passages through the Solomons to the north: the strait of Bougainville, between Choiseul and the Shortland Islands; the sea between San Cristobal and Santa Cruz; the infrequently used Manning Strait between Choiseul and Santa Isabel; and the Indispensable Strait between Malaita in the east and Nggela and Guadalcanal to the west (Figure 1).[11] These passages were but a way through, not a way to, the islands. For the period 1790–1820, actual landings from ships in the Solomons were exceptionally rare, although contact was sometimes made with canoes at sea and sightings were numerous (Figure 2).

Whalers, as opposed to merchant ships, had more opportunity and inclination for both contact and landing because they were constantly plying the waters around the Solomons. The first few ships came as early as the 1800s, increasing in numbers in the 1820s as colonial whaling, for a decade or so, helped to make the South Seas the primary commercial frontier of the infant Australian settlement. As the Atlantic whaling grounds became less profitable, American and British whaling ships increased their activity in the Pacific. The sailing ships went with the prevailing winds—north from South Pacific ports to the Solomons from May until about November, or south from Micronesia to the islands during the remaining months. The peak of the industry and the

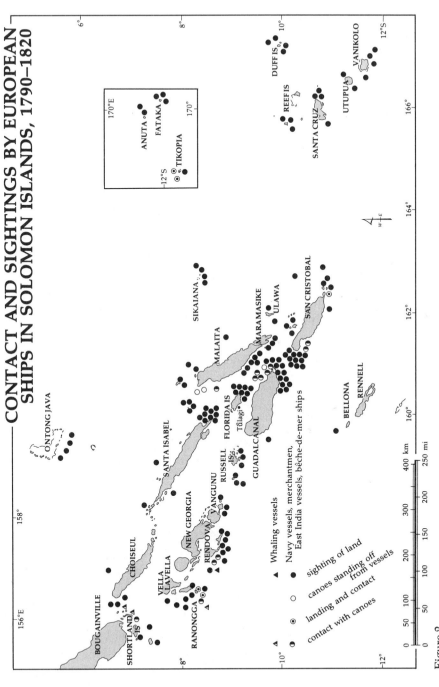

CONTACT AND SIGHTINGS BY EUROPEAN
SHIPS IN SOLOMON ISLANDS, 1790–1820

ONTONG JAVA

BOUGAINVILLE

SHORTLAND IS

CHOISEUL

VELLA
LAVELLA

RANONGGA

NEW GEORGIA

RENDOVA

VANGUNU

RUSSELL

SANTA ISABEL

MALAITA

SIKAIANA

FLORIDA IS

Tulagi

GUADALCANAL

MARAMASIKE

ULAWA

SAN CRISTOBAL

BELLONA

RENNELL

ANUTA

FATAKA

TIKOPIA

REEF IS

DUFF IS

SANTA CRUZ

UTUPUA

VANIKOLO

▲ Whaling vessels

● Navy vessels, merchantmen,
   East India vessels, bêche-de-mer ships

▲ sighting of land

○ canoes standing off
   from vessels

◉ landing and contact

● contact with canoes

| 0 | 50 | 100 | 150 | 200 | 300 | 400 km |

| 0 | 50 | 100 | 150 | 200 | 250 mi |

Figure 2

contact it engendered in the Solomons was reached in the 1840s and 1850s. It declined dramatically in the two succeeding decades, with the last recorded whaling ship in Solomons waters in 1887 (Appendix 1).

During the first few decades of the whaling era certain places in the Solomons became known and valued for their sheltered anchorages, their victualing capacity, their supplies of wood and water, and their women. Simbo (or Eddystone, Figure 9) was one such place and probably the earliest to achieve a reputation among the whalers as a safe place for white men. By 1803, the Simbo, whose contact with whites went back fifteen years, had long since lost their early fears.[12] They were more than confident about meeting the *tie vaka* 'ship men'—a confidence not initially shared by the captain of the *Patterson*, which reached Simbo on 15 December 1803:

> At 7 A.M. upwards of 30 canoes full of men (nearly 200) came along the side from . . . Simboo. They were entirely unarmed—one spear being the only weapon we saw. After preparing ourselves in some measure in case of an attack proceeded to trade with them giving them bottles, knives, nails, iron hoop etc. in exchange for coconuts, trinkets, plantains, etc. They are a very handsome set of men, few of them (the boys excepted) falling below the middling size of . . . Europeans—they had no clothes on except a small strip of something like a cloth about their middle. . . . They are a very Thieving set, one attempted to get into the quarter rail, but by shaking a cutlass at him he went off with great confusion. While we were trading with them one had the impudence to take one of our hats off and jumped instantly into the water, got into his canoe and then began to laugh at us. We did not suffer any of them to come farther than the outside of the quarter rail. They are quite sharp in trading, not suffering anything (for a considerable time at first) to go out of their hands until you handed something in payment for it. They appear to know the use of hatchets, gimlets, knives, etc. and signified a preference for these articles. One of them cut off a block from the chains swam off with it and then set up a loud laugh—they are a shrewd cunning lot of fellows. They expressed a wish that we would go ashore among them and told us they had women on shore . . . .

> [The next day] . . . we traded with them as yesterday but did not allow any of them to get on the side. They behaved much better than yesterday —indeed I could not but consider them quite a hospitable ingenious people. . . . They are expert swimmers. We amused ourselves by throwing nails, etc. into the water for them to dive after—they will go to a great depth and stay under a long while. They showed a great eagerness after iron of all kinds but more particularly for cutting instruments . . . .[13]

Despite the mutual uncertainties, trading between Islanders and whalers at Simbo had become a regular thing. Like Simbo, Mono (Treasury), Santa Ana, Santa Catalina, and Sikaiana became places of resort to the whalers (Figures 1, 3, 8). Being small islands, they were relatively secure from attack by neighboring groups, and their products suited the whalers' needs. From the late 1840s, as whalers became more familiar with the inhabitants of San Cristobal, Makira Harbour with its natural advantage of a sheltered harbor also became popular. Simbo, Mono, Santa Ana, and to some extent, Makira Harbour, had been entrepôts for local trade prior to the coming of Westerners, because of their locations, particular products, and their people's expertise.[14] The coming of the whalers marked the beginning of a golden age for indigenous traders at these places.

At Simbo, for instance, trade goods were exchanged for tortoiseshell and other articles of native manufacture from the people of New Georgia. The astute Simbo chief Lobi in 1844 had much to say about the treachery of the neighboring New Georgians to the bêche-de-mer collector, Andrew Cheyne. Lobi told of massacres of crews of whalers on New Georgia. These may have happened, but independent evidence indicates that the New Georgians were no more aggressive than any other people.[15] With the help of Cheyne's influential writings, Lobi's warning did serve to frighten whalers away from New Georgia for some years—with considerable profit to the Simbo people.[16]

Each of these major ports had its own speciality. Despite a scarcity of wood and water, the atoll of Sikaiana was favorably located in the passage between the Santa Cruz Islands and the main islands of Malaita and San Cristobal. Its first recorded visit by a whaler took place in 1828, when the *John Bull* brought a Sikaiana castaway home from Ontong Java, a gesture that generated much goodwill.[17] By the 1840s pigs, fowls, and coconuts were the principal items bartered to whalers. Santa Ana and Santa Catalina offered coconuts, personal ornaments, fresh water, and some wood. Mono, away to the west, was a source of vegetables and tortoiseshell as well as wood and water. With a safe anchorage it was ideal for the general refit of a ship. Makira Harbour excelled all the other ports of refreshment. The people there, like the Simbo, soon gained a good reputation among the whalers, one of whom remarked, "They are cannibals, they are thieves but with us they will keep faith."[18] While whalers were anchored, peace prevailed even between rival groups at the harbor and inland, permitting maximum trade and encouraging future visits.

Makira Harbour had pigs, and an abundance of fruit and vegetables (Figure 3). The harbor was secure, wood and water plentiful. "Curios" —clubs, wooden bowls, weapons, and carvings from the men's house— were removed from normal use and traded, the demand probably producing the first artefacts manufactured in the Solomons for export. All these, as well as shells and tortoiseshell, were offered for iron goods and glass bottles, the latter being broken up to make sharp cutting edges for removing arrow- and spear-heads from wounds, as well as for razors.

SAN CRISTOBAL (MAKIRA)

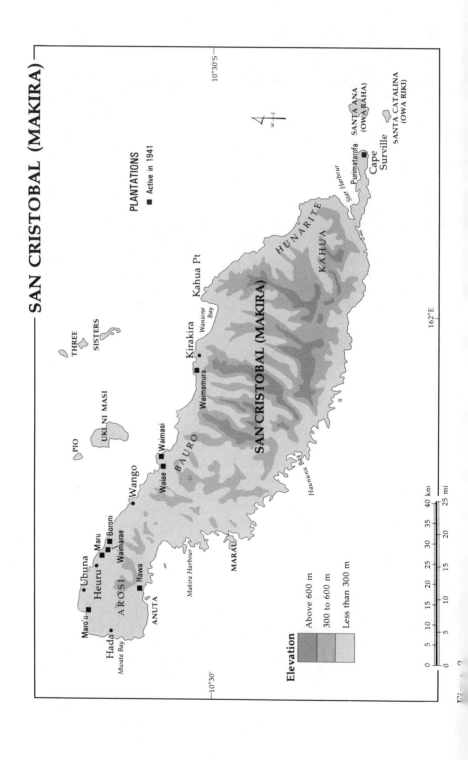

PLANTATIONS

■ Active in 1941

THREE
SISTERS

PIO

UKI.NI MASI

Maro'u

Ubuna

Heuru Maru

Hada Waimarae Boroni

Hawa

AROSI

ANUTA

Mtvata Bay

Makira Harbour

MARAU

Wango

Waiae Waimasi

Waimasi

BAURO

Waimamura

Kirakira

Wanione
Bay

Kahua Pt

Haununu Bay

SAN CRISTOBAL (MAKIRA)

HUNARITE

KAHUA

Star Harbour

Purimatarofa

Cape
Surville

SANTA ANA
(OWA RAHA)

SANTA CATALINA
(OWA RIKI)

10°30'S

162°E

10°30'

10°30'

Elevation

Above 600 m

300 to 600 m

Less than 300 m

0   5   10   15   20   25   30   35   40 km

0   5   10   15   20   25 mi

Fi...

The whalers particularly wanted tortoiseshell as a sideline to their main concern because it was durable, portable, and brought good prices, varying in London from 28 to 45 shillings per pound in 1832.[19] To Europeans it was a luxury item used mainly in making ornaments, combs, hair pieces, and buttons.

Another requirement of the whalers was women. In a place like Makira Harbour the supply of these was guaranteed by the prevailing mores, which allowed young women (and men) great sexual freedom until marriage. When a young woman was unwilling a gift paid to the parents usually brought compliance.[20]

During the period 1850 to 1870 an average of only three whaling ships a year would have visited Makira Harbour, allowing but brief opportunity for the people to obtain trade goods. With approximately twenty-five to thirty men aboard, business was doubtless brisk during a ship's stay.[21] When the demand for women exceeded the supply in the immediate coastal villages, the bush people sent their women to the ships, capitalizing on what must have been virtually the only saleable items they had to offer. While the whalers were at the harbor, women from the bush passed in safety through the coastal villages and went to the ships where they "were on board each night, and a good portion of every day, the bush people were . . . well satisfied with what they received from the ship."[22]

Both parties were almost frantic to use what little time they had to their mutual satisfaction. Whereas the sailors faced long months of forced celibacy or homosexuality at sea, the Solomon Islanders had only a brief few days to extricate as many trade goods as possible before the ships departed. It did not seem to matter if the women concerned were professional prostitutes *(urao)* or not, since almost all the unmarried women flaunted themselves and searched for clients.

The naturalist MacGillivray, following aboard the HMS *Herald* in the wake of the whalers, caught the mood of intense and successful soliciting by the Makira Harbour people as he observed from the upper deck the doings of the lower:

> The women of Makira are of diminutive stature. Some of the young girls are well made and often have pleasing and occasionally even pretty features. . . . I do not think that in any part of the world less regard is paid to female chastity—in fact such may be said to have no existence at Makira. Prostitution is carried on in the most shameless manner. Little boys and girls may be seen pimping for their sisters and the female who is said to have enjoyed the greatest amount of patronage from the ship during our stay was not old enough to have attained the outward signs of puberty.[23]

Because most San Cristobal societies forbid mention of sexual matters between brothers and sisters (and first cousins), MacGillivray may have been incorrect in classifying brothers and sisters as pimps for older sisters. More probably, however, he was observing the temporary suspension of the normal social code for the purpose of maximizing the return of trade goods from the ship's crew, as a variation on the practice of offering women in marriage to cement an alliance with a wealthy group.[24]

More exploitative was the situation where slaves—whether captured in war or purchased from neighbors—were involved. They had little control over their destinies and were the obvious choice for the white man who was "mad" for women.[25] Particularly in areas where trading opportunities were exceedingly few or sheer greed obtained, women were sometimes forced into submission and offered to the whalers.[26] At Veuru, on the weather coast of Guadalcanal (Figure 12), the following scene was witnessed by the officers of HMS *Herald* in 1852:

> A young girl was . . . dragged down to the canoe which afterwards in her struggles she capsized and attempted to escape, but she was brought back by a man who threatened her with an axe. On reaching the ship she was offered for a kila kila [axe].[27]

At Santa Isabel, the whaler Cattlin saw women brought out on the beach to tempt the crew into landing. The very fact that they were held by the men, an obscene public act in all but violent exchanges, indicated unwillingness on the part of the women.[28]

No matter how Solomon Islands men obtained women for the sexual purposes of the whalers, they had found a consumer commodity par excellence. During the whalers' stay their recurring need could be satisfied only by purchase. For the first fifty years of contact from about 1800, no other commodity was found to match this one. As a result, the whalers were by no means the economic winners in the trading relationship and welcomed continued "exploitation."

Although the whalers sometimes called at other islands besides these more frequented ports, they rarely visited the two large islands of Malaita and Guadalcanal. The inner coastlines of the double chain of Solomon Islands were avoided because there was little chance of finding whales and much danger from reefs and shoals. Moreover, the inaccurate nature of the navigational charts as late as the 1860s and 1870s also made whalers reluctant to ply between poorly mapped islands.[29] South Guadalcanal, facing the open ocean, had no safe all-year anchorages, except at Marau Sound where mariners needed to be familiar with the passages to get safely through the reefs. The large island of Malaita, despite some forbidding coastline in the east, did have good harbors (Figure 10). Yet it was generally avoided, though not because of any suggestion of the excessive ferocity of the inhabitants. The killing of a ship's captain and the kidnapping of his second officer in north Malaita

in 1827 were not enough to scare the *John Bull* away and certainly were
not of major concern to whalers sailing near other parts of the island.[30]
Malaita simply had little to offer. Cattlin, on first meeting canoes off
north Malaita, remarked of their occupants that "they had no notion of
trading" and suspected that the cooked piece of taro they offered was
poisoned.[31] Coconuts, a few yams, and taro were about all the whalers
ever got.[32] Their contact was restricted to the northern tip of the island
where all communication, except for the 1827 incident, was with
canoes. As soon as the more productive and more hospitable Makira
Harbour became known among the whalers in the late 1840s, they
ceased contact with the people of Malaita.

Malaita, because of its poverty and perhaps its strict sexual code,
remained on the periphery of the new trade. The few goods that
reached the Malaitans were traded by groups from adjacent islands.
Other areas that were in a similar position because of their geography or
limited productivity (at least until the 1850s when suppliers other than
whalers would begin to come) included Guadalcanal, the Floridas,
Savo, Rennell, Bellona, and the bush districts of Choiseul, Isabel, and
the Bauro region of San Cristobal.

In the areas of frequent contact, a working relationship was built
up. Both sides perceived contact to be mutually beneficial, yet, despite
the increased familiarity, their understanding of each other remained
superficial. Neither side had much idea of how the other functioned as a
complete society, or of its underlying values and attitudes. Because each
group quite naturally tended to interpret the behavior of the other in
terms of its own reality, there was ample potential for conflict between
Solomon Islanders and visitors, as two incidents on Mono illustrate.
Early in 1842 the English whaling ship *Offley*, captained by Lazenby,
was at Mono when three men deserted. The captain demanded their
return by the chief. When no action resulted, he shot the chief. This "so
insenced [*sic*] the savages, that they rushed upon and killed them without let or hindrance with their clubs and spears."[33] Eighteen of the
whaler's crew of twenty-eight were killed.[34] It was highly improbable
that the Mono chief shared the officers' appreciation of either the precarious state of discipline aboard whaling ships or the need to maintain
numbers so that the ship functioned efficiently. Keeping a crew together
was such a major preoccupation of ship captains that they sometimes
held Islanders hostage until runaways were returned. On occasion
rewards were offered and paid for bringing in deserters.[35] In the
Offley's case the chief's lack of understanding and the captain's flash of
anger brought fatal results. The incident shook the confidence of both
sides, but whalers still called, albeit cautiously, and the Mono people
continued to gain much from the connection.[36]

Eighteen years later, in May 1860, the American whaler *Superior*

visited, bringing back a Mono man from Simbo.[37] At Mono the crew
painted the ship and traded normally. Although the log-keeper makes
no reference to the *Offley* disaster, the captain "kept the king on board
nights as a hostage," just as a precaution. The *Superior* left after five
days and sailed north, returning in September. The log ends with the
entry for the fourteenth: "Weather fine, to work cutting wood. Took in
100 lbs of water. Traded for some vegetables."[38]

A day or two later the Mono people attacked the crew, then stripped
and burned the ship. This time, the misunderstanding arose from the
captain's ignorance of the culture. In Mono (and Alu), certain matters,
most of which concerned sexual activities or organs, were considered
insulting if mentioned in conversation or alluded to by other actions. At
the time of the *Superior*'s visit to Mono the people wore very little cov-
ering. Captain Woods happened to see the genitals of chief Bagara and
burst out laughing. In what would have been a situation for bawdy buf-
foonery in his own society, Woods' action brought about his death in
Bagara's. The chief had no quarrel with the rest of the *Superior*'s party,
but some of the crew retaliated and all but six were killed.[39] Thereafter
whalers avoided Mono.

The greatest check on violent abuse of one party by the other was self-
interest. As the Mono examples show, the cultural reflex or immediate
needs occasionally displaced considerations of long-term possible benefits.

The most obvious area of conflict was between Solomon Islanders
and Europeans. Although it is convenient to so label these two groups
they were by no means homogeneous or harmonious. Long-standing
conflicts between different political units of Islanders, just as between
individuals or cliques confined aboard the whaling vessels, existed independently of contact between the two groups. But when contact
occurred a third party could be drawn in by one or other of the major
protagonists, as happened at Makira in 1860 when a group of bush people carried out the only recorded killing of a whaler there. At the time
there was a strong suggestion that the Tahitian second mate of the *Onyx*
had a grudge against the first, and bribed the bush men to kill him. As it
happened, another man, the carpenter, who was popular among the
coastal Makira Harbour people, was killed by mistake. The Makira
Harbour big-man, anxious to maintain friendship with the whalers,
volunteered his people's services to combine with the crew of the *Onyx*
in an assault against the bush village, using the vessel's arms. This
would afford the big-man double advantage since, in the opinion of one
of the crew, he did "not only revenge the wounded man but [did] a little
private revenge with the Bark's arms for himself."[40]

Such occurrences were uncommon, with violence being a feature of
less than 10 percent of the contacts between whalers and Solomon

Islanders[41] (see Appendix 1). On this frontier the working relationship functioned with but few incidents because the whalers generally did not interfere in an overt, purposeful way with the activities of Solomon Islanders unless there was a danger of crew being lost. The whalers' needs were relatively few, the beach being the real limit to their temporary territorial incursions. When they hunted whales, there was no encroachment on the indigenous fishery because the Solomon Islanders did not hunt whales. Nor was there any attempt by the whalers to incorporate the Solomon Islanders into their world economy.[42] When the two groups first traded they offered merely their surpluses in exchange for nonessentials; their respective economic systems were independent of each other.

To the whalers, the goods offered to the Solomon Islanders were of relatively little value. Hoop iron was cheap and abundant on whaling ships, where casks to store the whale oil were made aboard as it was produced. Nails and glass bottles were similarly inexpensive and axes only a little less so. Beyond the beach, the Melanesians must have viewed the products they offered to the traders in much the same way. They had to grow taro, yams, and other vegetables, but there was often a surplus. Many cultivated gardens and bred pigs on a scale greater than was necessary for subsistence because of the round of feasts where a superabundance of food was an indicator of a big-man's power to manipulate the means of production. Tortoiseshell, especially from the western Solomons, was used and traded within the islands for fishhooks and personal ornaments, but the amounts required were small.[43] Both groups offered to sell goods of low value to themselves and wished to buy ones of high value. When trading between whalers and Solomon Islanders first began, the durables they exchanged were luxury items and therefore dispensable; neither group depended for its existence on obtaining the products of the other.

Technological innovation and consequences

The significance of the whalers lies in their introduction of iron on a fairly large scale. The Solomon Islanders could not escape far-reaching consequences once they accepted the whalers' trade. Changes were generated from within Solomons societies as they sought a new equilibrium to accommodate the technological innovations that iron made possible.

Iron goods were the greatest prize to the Solomon Islanders and soon replaced indigenous counterparts, but during the first decade or so of European contact in any one area, the people retained the knowledge necessary to produce their own stone and shell tools should the external supply of iron be cut off. For example, in 1851 the people in the vicinity of Makira Harbour still used stone adzes, although they greatly desired iron goods. They were not yet dependent on the introduced substitutes, which were still fairly scarce.[44] Doubtless the supply was occasionally cut off in some places, but the number of visits of whalers and traders would gradually increase over the years, ensuring a fairly constant supply of iron. Effectively, the old technological expertise became redundant and subsequently atrophied. For increasing numbers of Solomon Islanders what had been a luxury was becoming a necessity.

Iron was sought avidly because it had distinct economic advantages over stone and shell. The many hours necessary to produce a stone adze moved from the debit to the credit side of the time ledger. Aside from its durability, the use of iron could reduce the Melanesian males' working day for subsistence, shelter, and ceremonial by 30 to 40 percent.[45] Clearing the jungle and felling trees to make gardens were done more quickly with metal axes than by tediously burning a green tree and picking away at it with stone tools. In coastal areas the time and effort saved must have been at least 30 percent, because along with the usual Melanesian horticulture, canoes had to be constructed so that fish could be caught. Felling a tree, trimming it for carrying, hollowing out the base, cutting and fitting the planks, carving the decorations, all proceeded much more quickly with metal axes and iron adzes (made from either hoop iron or planes). Housebuilding, too, could be finished in less time. In some areas, metal fishhooks replaced the older bone or shell ones, but this was not universal as some hooks made from mother-of-pearl acted as lures. Nonetheless, the lures were produced in less time because they could be more easily shaped with a metal file or rasp. Even lopping off heads became easier as metal axe heads mounted on long handles made superior weapons.

Iron tools saved a third of the men's time, but except in a few cases of specific expertise, women gained little extra leisure from the new technology.[46] Men did the work of felling trees, clearing thick undergrowth, and fencing. As the digging stick was (and still is) the principal tool of the women, their labor on subsistence must have remained about the same.[47] The options open to the men were to do the same work in less time or to do more work in the same time. If they did more work the burden on the women would be increased proportionately. Salisbury has shown that for the Siane people of New Guinea, garden production remained fairly stable despite the introduction of metal tools, as the men used their extra time in other things and there was a limit to the number and capacity of women in that particular society.[48] This may also have occurred in the New Georgia area, but since there was a tradition of slavery, raiding may have increased to provide extra labor units to do the planting and weeding that was women's work. Certainly any increased ceremonial feasting would have required additional garden produce and pig raising, both of which demanded the time of women.

Iron also revolutionized one of the bases of the Solomon Islands economy: the production of shell currency and valuables. Instead of fiber from a bush creeper the Roviana people used a taut metal wire to cut *poata* 'arm rings' from clam shells. Drills, made from rat-tail files and similar tools, were substituted for stone chips for boring the fine holes in threaded shell valuables.[49] With greater efficiency the supply could have remained constant, with less time spent on production. More probably, it increased, introducing an inflationary trend and concentrating more power, through the accumulation and conspicuous consumption of other forms of wealth, in the hands of groups who manufactured shell valuables.

The introduction of iron made clearing and other subsistence activities easier and, in some districts, contributed to a better standard of living.[50] Iron saved time and effort, but how was this new-found leisure used? Salisbury concluded that in the New Guinea situation it "was used for politicking, ceremonials, legal disputes and fighting."[51]

By the 1850s there were signs that this was happening in parts of the Solomons. Jackson, taking up a theme suggested by Tippett, had argued that head-hunting, a concomitant of increased ceremonial activity, though practised on a limited scale in precontact New Georgia, increased and spread dramatically over the western and central Solomons by the 1880s and 1890s.[52] This process was well under way within the New Georgia Islands by the 1840s, stimulated in part by the search for supplies of tortoiseshell and slaves.[53] By the 1850s the practice, not a traditional Santa Isabel one, had reached Gao and Mbughotu. Retaliation was necessary for self-preservation. Ivens' description of a Gao raid in the 1850s on Basakana Island (north Malaita) and the "payback" attack that followed has almost all the elements of the raid, retaliation, and imitation formula.[54] Jackson stated that head-hunting was only a next step after revenge killing since it was an act that was meaningful to the original aggressors. The head was the seat of mana, the power to manipulate the natural world. This specific location of mana was recognized by the practice in many Solomon Islands societies of preserving and venerating the skulls of the ancestors. The taking of an enemy's head therefore did not conflict with general religious values.

The increase of head-hunting where it was indigenous, and its imitation by borrowing where it was not, may have been an intensification of ritual to counter a deeper malaise. From the New Georgians' traditional standpoint raids were made for heads when a new canoe or canoehouse was to be inaugurated, a shrine rededicated, or when a chief died. They also believed that disharmony in the natural order was a result of someone bringing the influence of malevolent spirits or forces to bear. With the introduction of iron, much about the natural order was changing, not simply the economics of the society. The power structure altered as wider and wider alliances were made for mutual protection and combined assault. Some clan leaders declined in influence vis-à-vis the more vigorous warrior leaders having the organizational ability to mobilize larger groups and provide the feasts and ceremonials so dear to the people. Young men could build reputations overnight through skillful raiding and reap rewards in the form of shell and introduced valuables from the new leaders. New enemies were made in the competition for tortoiseshell and slaves. Old allies and trading partners were discarded when their stone and shell products lost their exchange value in the iron-dominated economy. Some groups momentarily lost their place and worth in the world. Disorientation may also have come in the wake of introduced diseases from whaling ships, arousing suspicions of sorcery by other groups. Such disorder may have fed on itself, with the taking of heads in an attempt to control the evil spiritual forces in turn creating more confusion and the need for more heads.

Excessive head-hunting was an attempt to control the new forces unleashed in the western Solomons by the advent of iron. Similarly, the shell valuables of Roviana and Marovo (Figure 7), rather than remaining simply items that acknowledged socially significant events such as marriage and death, became more and more like money with a set value range. In New Georgia arm rings came to be used to bind relationships arising almost invariably from conflict, the value offered being determined by the relative importance of the particular situation.[55] In order to increase the production of shell rings and control local conflicts and alliances, more slaves were needed, a situation that in turn created the impetus for raiding farther and farther afield.

The heightened warfare and raiding was eventually to depopulate vast tracts of land in the western and central Solomons. In precontact times, raiding resulted in a few deaths only, with perhaps some slaves taken. Even where a state of continual warfare existed between two groups, as, say, between the Wango and Fagani peoples on San Cristobal, casualties were rarely of an order to depopulate an entire district. The number of casualties was limited by the comparability of the combatants' weapons as well as the conventions for peacemaking and trading.[56] When iron was channelled through only certain groups, comparable weaponry and attrition declined as factors in the control of warfare. In about 1840 the people on the island of Gizo were no longer able to defend themselves and fled to join allies at Mbilua on Vella Lavella (Figure 9). About a decade later a party of a thousand canoes organized by a big-man from Vaela on Vella Lavella raided the island of Mbava (Baga) killing and driving off its inhabitants.[57] The merciless attack on the people on Basakana Island by the Gao demonstrated the heightening ferocity of raiding and the resultant decimation of some populations.

While most Solomon Islands societies on the coast (and probably those beyond) were affected by an increase in the level of warfare, not all followed the New Georgia model of expanded ritualistic killing. In the Shortland Islands, for example, the old custom of taking a life to cap the launching of a canoe or as a redemptive act to avoid adverse spiritual repercussions following a chief's death, continued unchanged throughout much of the precolonial period. A raid across to Telei, Buin (Bougainville), with two new canoes resulted in four Buin deaths. On another occasion of launching new canoes "Big" Gorai led a party of seven canoes to Tiarama, Choiseul and killed two chiefs.[58] Although this kind of ceremonial killing remained as before, the level of homicide and fratricidal warfare within the Shortland Islands themselves was escalating by the mid-nineteenth century. A series of wars by the Mono with the Alu scattered or killed most of the "old" Alu people.[59] Ambition was well served by the new weaponry. The chief Bagara, who was "Big" Gorai's uncle, wanted supremacy over the other chiefly clans on Mono: "There shall be no other chief. I am the only one."[60] His power and the fear it engendered among the common people enabled him to control any trade contact, and he was aided by the Europeans' need to deal with a fixed leader.[61] Iron was used in warfare at this period, as the killing with tomahawks of the *Superior*'s crew (in which Bagara was involved) demonstrated.[62] Beyond Mono, Bagara almost wiped out entire villages on Alu because he "lust[ed] for the wealth of the land and its waters."[63] Part of this wealth was the shell used in the manufacture of traditional valuables and, the whalers' choice, tortoiseshell.

Some coastal communities found that the advent of iron lessened their dependence on other groups. Before regular contact with Europeans the people of Santa Ana, Santa Catalina, and the Surville Peninsula of San Cristobal (Figure 3) had obtained their large plank-and-rib canoes from other areas. Because the large canoes were expensive to purchase, smaller outriggers were made for everyday use. Since the Santa Ana and Santa Catalina people obtained considerable quantities of vegetables from the gardens of the more fertile San Cristobal mainland, they experienced difficulties getting this bulky cargo across the often turbulent waters of the strait in such flimsy craft. In just "a short generation" with the aid of iron tools, the people of the Santa Ana–Santa Catalina region appear to have learned the art of making the larger six-to-ten-meter plank canoes so well that they themselves became exporters to San Cristobal.[64]

Some communities that had been closely linked and interdependent maintained their relationship after the coming of the Westerners. This was a function of the nature of the linkages. Where each contributing group manufactured specialized items, none of which were stone or shell tools, the introduction of iron was less disruptive. In the Santa Cruz group, the fortuitous holing of La Pérouse's ships in 1788 had opened a cornucopia of iron goods that gave Vanikolo a favorable trade balance for many years vis-à-vis its traditional trading superiors in the complex economic system, Nendö (Santa Cruz) and the Reef Islands (Figure 1). This advantage was eventually offset by those islands' greater productivity and by visits of ships including whalers throughout most of the group. There is no tradition of heightened warfare as a result of the introduction of iron. The main impact was to increase production and interisland trade, and to raise the standard of living.[65]

Introduced diseases and ideas

Although the economic system of the Santa Cruz Islands was not dislocated by the advent of iron, the diseases that the whalers and other Europeans brought introduced some disequilibrium into the societies in this group and elsewhere. When the whaler *Lady Rowena* visited Tikopia in 1832, the chief told the captain of an illness that had been among the crew of the French ships that had come seeking traces of La Pérouse (d'Urville in the *Astrolabe* and de Tromelin in the *Baionaisse* in 1828). This illness—vomiting and pains in the bowels—spread among the Tikopians, carrying off many, including three "kings" in succession.[66] D'Urville's ship appears to have been responsible as de Tromelin reported the deaths of 115 Tikopians following the *Astrolabe*'s departure.[67]

Other diseases seem to have been introduced at this time. Venereal disease was present in contemporary European populations and, since sailors in port were not always the most discerning in choosing their sleeping partners, such diseases were not uncommon aboard whaling vessels. In the Solomons, endemic yaws and resultant immunity to other *treponema* bacilli eliminated syphilis, but gonorrhea and other venereal diseases may have affected fertility among women on such places as San Cristobal where sexual contact with whalers was constant.[68] These diseases made fewer inroads where death was the remedy for women found to have them, as in the New Georgia group.[69] The introduction of both venereal diseases and "consumption" in southern Bougainville and the adjacent Shortland Islands has been attributed to whaling ships.[70] "Consumption" was common among the crews of the whaling ships and had the potential to spread quickly among the islands. The whaler *Ontario* was at Sikaiana in 1863 and, at their own request, discharged two consumptive sailors, George Williams and Hiram Morse, the latter dying within two months.[71] In 1858 an earlier visitor to this island had seen signs of smallpox and attributed assumed population decline to this and other diseases.[72] In a later and better documented era, from about the 1870s onward, the very lack of deaths from such diseases as measles, mumps, and chickenpox suggests that earlier outbreaks may have conferred some immunity on survivors.[73] These diseases with shorter incubation periods were probably introduced by ships coming north from Australian and New Zealand ports.

Increased mobility by Solomon Islanders themselves provided another means for diseases to be transmitted from the outside world. Every year from the late 1820s, about half a dozen Solomon Islanders, particularly Polynesians from Tikopia and Sikaiana, shipped aboard as whalers' crew and passengers, sometimes for the period the ship was in Solomons waters and sometimes for extended voyages to foreign ports.[74] In 1828 Captain Lewis of the *Alfred* employed as crew four Tikopians, one of whom at least went to Sydney; later, as captain of the *Wolf*, Lewis returned him to Tikopia.[75] The *Lord Rodney* in 1835 took aboard three men from San Cristobal who traveled with the ship around to other islands and then to Sydney where they stayed for two years with the Blaxland family of Newington. They were returned after further voyaging, having learned to speak good English.[76]

By the 1860s such voyaging was commonplace. The *Eugenia* in 1862 took on three men for Sydney from Makira Harbour, with the usual Europeanized names of "Lewis," "Dick," and "Jack" Markela (Makira) respectively. They traveled with other similarly anonymous Pacific Islanders—"Peter," "Jack," and "James" Kanaka, "Charles" Tahiti, "Jack," "John," "Long Jack," and "Henry," who were Maori, as well as "Bill" and "Jack" Mangea (Mangaia).[77] Some crewmen never returned home. The *Stephania* took on Ontong Javanese who journeyed north to the Carolines, Japan, the Bering Strait, and on to the Arctic where the crew hunted polar bears. Here, "at one P.M. Duffee, a native of Lord Howes Islands died. At 4 P.M. hove to and buried the dead." The ship sailed south again to Honolulu, the Gilberts (Kiribati), to Pohnpei, back to the Solomons, and on to Sydney.[78]

One of the most remarkable instances of islander mobility facilitated by whaling ships was not the voyaging of Solomon Islanders beyong their lands, but of other islanders moving into the Solomons. The *Two Brothers*, while "on the Line" between the Solomons and the Gilberts during September 1861, found two lost canoes from Woodles Island (Kuria) filled with men, women, and children, numbering forty-three in all. They were taken aboard and soon after put ashore at Sikaiana by Captain Joshua Davis.[79] The next known whaling ship to visit that

island was the *Ontario*, in December 1863, leaving behind the two consumptive sailors. It returned in February 1864 and took off from the
island, "a lot of passengers that we are going to carry to Pleasant Island
[Nauru], 2 white men and 7 native women and 2 natives besides George
Williams the Boatsteer. We left him here some 67 weeks ago."[80] The passengers disembarked at Nauru, perhaps the original destination of the
people in the canoes. Whatever the case, the infusion of forty-three (or
that less nine) would have had a substantial demographic and cultural
impact on the Sikaiana population, which was estimated in 1851 to be
only 180.[81]

Along with iron and infection, the whalers brought ideas. At first
these were transmitted only through signs and demonstrations because
of the language barrier. By the 1830s people on Santa Isabel could
repeat to d'Urville and his men English words learned from whalers.[82]
Of Sikaiana in 1847, Cheyne reported that "nearly all speak more or less
broken English."[83] Elsewhere, at places like Makira Harbour, English,
broken or otherwise, was not, with the exception of a few individuals,
in frequent use until the 1850s.[84]

In the oral tradition of Sikaiana it is said that whalers used the atoll of
Matuavi as a depot to render down the blubber, the only account of any
shore-based processing. From these men the Sikaiana learned how to
distill spirit from the toddy they made from the coconut-palm blossom,
and then sold it to visiting ships. These people, like those on other Polynesian outliers, had a long tradition of adopting new techniques from
visitors and castaways. People who drifted in from the Gilbert Islands
taught them the process of making the actual toddy *(karevi)* and molas-
ses, just as women from Nauru and Niu introduced the manufacture of
certain mats and fans.[85]

Not all the ideas and languages introduced to the Solomon Islands by
the whalers were of Western origin. As the *Eugenia*'s crew illustrates,
many of the sailors came from other Pacific islands as well as Europe,
Asia, and the Americas. Crew lists abound with "John" Kanaka,
kanaka being originally a generic term for Hawaiian males. In this way
the whalers spread the word to the western Pacific. Certainly, at San
Cristobal in the 1860s an old man trying to pimp among the officers of
HMS *Curaçoa* was speaking "coarse Hawaiian gibberish," along with
others who spoke English.[86] The very word used to describe the whaling
ships, *vaka* and variants *(faka, haka)*, for at least some Solomon Islands
societies was an introduction from either neighboring Austronesian language groups within the Solomons or from Polynesian whaling crews.[87]
Certain Polynesians, for example, Maoris, Rarotongans, Tongans, and
Samoans, would have had the advantage of being able to communicate
with people of the Polynesian outliers of the Solomons.

Polynesian fashions also spread. The crescent-moon neck ornament of gold-lip pearlshell was not worn until the mid-nineteenth century and after in most of the eastern Solomons. Tahitians are said to have been responsible for this, with supplies of gold lip later coming from the Floridas (Nggela) and the western Solomons.[88] The whale's tooth was valued in the Simbo area and on Ontong Java, its supply guaranteed by whalers and its veneration perhaps learned from Fijians or Tongans.[89]

Besides whalers and the occasional trader, the only other "ship men" who tried to have extended contact with Solomon Islanders were a group of French Roman Catholic Marist missionaries. In 1846 the first encounter between Bishop Epalle and the people of Astrolabe Harbour, Santa Isabel, ended in the bishop's death from wounds inflicted with an axe he gave as a gift. It appears that the killers saw Epalle as having first allied himself and his party with a rival group and therefore classed him as an enemy.[90] The surviving Marists resided for twenty months among the people around Makira Harbour, San Cristobal, but their stay did nothing to convince the Islanders of the validity of the white man's religious ideas. The Marist priests and brothers were welcomed at first for their trade goods. Later, they failed to share their possessions and food during a famine, refused to join the coast people in their forays against inland tribes, and were seen as responsible for the introduction of an epidemic illness. After one brother died of fever and dysentery and two priests were killed by the bush people, the Catholic missionaries abandoned the Solomons and did not return for fifty years.[91]

Deserters and castaways from whaling ships were less scrupulous than the missionaries about becoming involved in intertribal conflicts, as such activity guaranteed them a place in the society. At Makira Harbour alone, from the 1850s to the early 1870s, about thirty deserters or signed-off men from the whaling ships lived at different times with the people, who welcomed the white men for good reasons:

> The Makira people many of them know the use of fire arms and appreciate their value, they also value any pure white man, they do not seem to care much about negroes, or natives, and will readily give them up [to their ship's captain] for a small gratuity such as powder, lead, beads, or pipes and tobacco, but a white man they will not so readily part with, they want him to go to war with them, even if he does not fight, his presence appears to inspire them with a confidence they did not possess in his absence, and the opposite party vice versa.[92]

Such men, along with a few escaped convicts from Australia, may have had an input not simply into warfare, but also into the gene pool of the population, as was the case on Tikopia (see Appendix 2). With a couple of exceptions, such as the runaway convict "Dani" (Dennis Griffiths) from the HMS *Herald*, which came to Wanderer Bay in 1854 searching for William Boyd's killers, these men did not become perma-

nent residents. Their cultural impact, beyond their goods and mechanical skills—if they had any—was minimal.[93]

Necessities and luxuries

The long-term contact that resulted from temporary European residence and from Solomon Islanders joining whaling ships had two outcomes. It gave Solomon Islanders the opportunity to learn more items of
the foreign culture as well as to form a more realistic perception of the
Westerners. In 1858 the captain of the Austrian naval vessel *Novara*
found the Sikaiana to be excellent draughts (checkers) players and anxious to trade for playing cards so that they could play "odd fourth."[94]
Through contact with whalers and Cheyne's bêche-de-mer gatherers,
the Sikaiana people became probably the first group in the Solomons to
learn the habit of smoking tobacco. According to Cheyne they would
trade a 100-pound pig for 5 pounds of tobacco in 1847.[95] By the 1850s
tobacco and pipes were in demand on Simbo and were beginning to be
used in parts of San Cristobal and the adjacent islands.[96] Elsewhere in
the Solomons the practice is not recorded until at least the 1860s.[97]
Whalers and traders now had an eminently consumable item, almost as
quickly spent as the sexual favors of the Makira women.

The whalers frequently mentioned the type of trade goods they
offered, but gave little indication of the prevailing exchange rates (see
Appendix 3). At Makira Harbour in the late fifties an empty bottle
brought five yams; a tomahawk brought twenty to thirty yams, depending on their size.[98] The captain of the *Novara* provides a record of
exchange rates at Sikaiana, with no inflation in the tobacco prices in the
ten years since Cheyne's visit:

For 5 lbs tobacco	one pig
For 20 steel fish hooks	one pig
For 5 strings red corals	one pig
For 5 strings green and red glass beads	one pig
For 5 packets of needles and thread	one pig
For 10 ells of calico	one pig
For 5 fish hooks	ten eggs
For 5 fish hooks	two hens
For 10 fish hooks	30 pieces taro
For 2 packets needles and thread	30 pieces taro
For 1 packet old playing cards	4 hens[99]

On Sikaiana in the fifties a new feature of trade emerged in the form
of a demand for goods with little utilitarian value. When the whalers
first came to this island and the rest of the Solomons the desire of the

Islanders was overwhelmingly for iron tools and, a lower second, glass.
After cruising around the western Solomons, the log-keeper aboard the
Gipsy had quickly perceived this:

> I remarked that handkerchiefs or anything however gaudy, or that they
> did not perceive the necessity of they invariably rejected after the first
> burst of wonder, and craved after those things only of obvious utility, a
> trait not always observed among savages. It is plain that they are utilitar-
> ians: knives, fish-hooks gimlets were in greatest request. An axe or adze
> was prized as a handsome or rare acquisition, so it was [?] and saved them
> a world of labour.[100]

The gap in levels of affluence between groups within the Solomons
was widening. In mid-century large numbers, if not the majority of the
population, lived in the bush on the big islands. These people looked
with helpless and envious eyes at the largesse visited upon some of the
saltwater people who, as ever, exploited their geographical advantage
to the full. At this time, in a few places such as some atolls, Makira Harbour, and Simbo, the market for iron, by now almost an essential to
these people, was becoming sufficiently saturated to allow them to
trade for new luxury items—caps, calico, playing cards, tobacco, and
pipes—while communities in the bush owned not even a single axe.[101]
Because of their continued contact with Europeans, the Tikopia in 1838
were using muskets to defend themselves and the Sikaiana in the 1850s
were using firearms for hunting, in stark contrast to the bush people of,
say, Malaita or Guadalcanal.[102] The latter communities had rarely been
as materially well off as those on the coast and the advent of iron elsewhere made them even more disadvantaged, as many of their own
products became redundant. Where a state of war was constant, the
coast people made certain that the supply of iron tools to the bush was
kept to a minimum, so as to retain the military advantage. When iron
tools were traded to different groups (usually those with other strategic
disadvantages), such as from the Shortlands to isolated Siwai or Buin,
one can imagine that profits were high in terms of goods or human
beings.

Away from the whaler ports, some groups had the human and natural resources necessary to maintain the expanded economic activities
stimulated by the whalers. Groups in more direct contact competed for
these resources once their own supplies were exhausted. As long as some
had access to the new trade and others had the wherewithal to sustain
it, warfare increased both in extent and ferocity. The price of iron was
proving more expensive each year to the "have nots" within the Solomon Islands. To the "haves," almost without their realizing it, another
price was being exacted along with the disturbing social and political
consequences. A slow but growing dependence on the wider European

world economy developed because iron, once a luxury, was for some coast dwellers becoming increasingly essential to sustain their changed way of life.

THE "SHIP MEN" had brought these technological, economic, and social changes to Solomon Islanders almost incidentally. With the exception of the Catholic missionaries, it is doubtful that any European before the mid-nineteenth century was consciously trying to change Solomon Islanders beyond the rather superficial level of substituting aspects of technology. Certainly sailors, whether brown or white, told their wondrous tales, but the mundane concerns of ordinary life soon recalled the attention of the audience from this fantastic world beyond the great ocean. Knowledge and ideas without practical application were only of amusement value to Solomon Islanders.

Likewise, although the whalers and other European visitors had no intention of bringing pestilence upon the people they visited, this was far less controllable than trade goods or knowledge. Unless there would be no human contact, they could not help but bring in new diseases, which must have had deleterious effects on the population, especially in places where it was concentrated and confined, such as Tikopia. All this occurred before any European remained in one place long enough to record the impact of introduced sickness on isolated, vulnerable peoples. When entire communities perished, there was no one left to remember.

Yet even after experience taught that the Europeans could bring troubles, no Solomon Island society, once the purpose of the whalers was understood, ever refused to receive more ships. The Islanders held the advantage, in terms of both strategy and resources. The whalers' lives depended on the hospitality of the people. Although the Solomon Islanders dearly wanted the iron of the Europeans, their deepening dependence on it was never such that they abdicated their autonomy to the strangers. From the ships' array of goods, fashions, technological processes, language, and even the strangers themselves, the Islanders selected only what was of use or pleasure to them. They were in control.

CHAPTER 3

The traders and their masters
(c. 1860–1900)

The treasure islands were his desired landfall:
past the grey discipline of streets and past
the minatory towers with their clocks
the sails rose bannering on the saltwhite mast,
The islands ran like emeralds through his fingers
(Oparo, Manahiki, Tubuai)
till he turned truant, cleared the heads at dawn
and half-forgot the seasons, under that sky . . . .

Judith Wright, "The Idler"

. . . traders put into Melanesian ports, taking what they
wanted by force.

Harold M. Ross, Baegu

TRADERS LEARNED of the commercial possibilities of the Solomon Islands
from the whalers. At first, like the whalers, the traders sought tortoiseshell, but in response to the changing demands of the world economy
they soon began to purchase other tropical products. To obtain these the
traders had to expand the limited demands that had been induced
among the people around the whaler "ports" and extend the geographical scope of foreign trading to areas untouched by the whaling ships.
They established bases and visited adjacent islands to gather sufficient
cargo to fill their vessels. Their visible presence on a fairly permanent
basis was a major factor in increasing the demand for their goods. Not
only did the traders provide a constant supply of a wide variety of
manufactured goods, but they also used many of them in their daily
round and in the households they established with Solomon Islands
women, thus providing, unlike the whalers on their brief visits, a continuous demonstration of the uses of the new goods for their customers.

From about 1870 the traders' business was assisted considerably by
the intercolonial labor trade, which introduced thousands of Solomon
Islanders to many of the products of Western technology. Where they
had something to offer the traders, the returners from Queensland, Fiji,

45

and Samoa were able to satisfy the new wants they had developed overseas. In some areas the missionaries of the Melanesian Mission (Anglican), like the white traders and the labor trade, were the means of
introducing new artefacts and tastes to many Islanders.

For the trader, living in the Solomons was not easy. Because survival
in this alien environment depended on support from metropolitan-
based backers, the trader was, to a great degree, susceptible to their dic-
tates. Solomon Islands political units were small and their leaders' influence usually extended no farther than a few adjacent villages. A trader
had to seek out and ally himself to the strongest of the leaders. As well as
having to contend with the difficulties of a strange culture, the trader
faced competition from other Europeans. Virtually unfettered by the
legal restraints of their homelands, the traders often resorted to desperate measures against one another to win the custom of the Islanders.
Their activities were circumscribed by their backers, their customers,
and their competitors, to say nothing of the occasional intervention of
ships of the Royal Navy on their annual round of the western Pacific.
Few traders made great profits, yet most seem to have found some measure of relief from the constraints of European society which, for many
of them, had proved even more restrictive.

The growth of long-distance trade

The first European trader to visit the Solomons on a regular basis,
Lewis Truscott, had learned of the abundance of tortoiseshell while cap-
taining whaling ships there in the late 1840s. From New Georgia in
1851 he brought back to Sydney more than a thousand pounds of tortoiseshell as well as sperm oil. Two years later, in the trading vessel
Oberon, he collected tortoiseshell and occasionally took on barrels of
sperm oil, off-loaded from whaling ships.[1] Like Truscott, colonial whaling captains were apprehensive of crew running off to the Californian
and Australian gold-rushes and preferred such transshipment as a
means of keeping their ships at sea as long as possible.[2]

By the early 1870s all this had changed. The traders had the tortoiseshell to themselves because fewer whalers came to the Solomons. Whaling in the Pacific had declined with the rapid progress of the petroleum
industry and the destruction of the American fleet during the Civil War.[3]

By this time tortoiseshell was only one of several articles the traders
wanted. In the late 1850s they were collecting pearlshell in the western
Solomons.[4] Like tortoiseshell, it was used for ornaments and in button
manufacture. Although this luxury trade continued, alongside it grew a
demand for goods that were becoming essential to Europeans. In the
mid-sixties traders were gathering increasing tonnages of bêche-de-mer

because, like the Vanuatu sandalwood by then almost exhausted, it was a commodity acceptable to the Chinese, the main suppliers of tea to Australia and New Zealand.[5]

The advance of the industrial revolution in Europe and the United States and the concomitant population boom created a need for coconut oil for use in making soap and chemicals, especially explosives.[6] By the late 1860s traders were systematically collecting the oil made by some Solomon Island societies, but this form of trade was merely a brief episode because buyers found it more profitable to have the value added to the product in the factories of Europe than on the beaches of Pacific islands. The Godeffroy process of copra manufacture, which was perfected and rationalized by Weber in Samoa in 1869, had already been used in the Carolines in 1865. By processing the dried kernel of the coconut in Europe, the manufacturer reduced transportation costs, obtained a purer product, and could sell the copra meal residue as cattle feed. The new process spread rapidly throughout the Pacific.[7] By 1876 the export of processed coconut oil from the Solomons had ceased, with an accompanying upsurge in copra production from fewer than 10 tons a year in 1874–1875 to 379 tons in 1879 (see Appendix 4 and Figure 4).

High prices for copra and a steady demand for other Solomons products in European and Asian markets meant that there was incentive for traders to increase their activity in the islands.[8] The potential trader acquired useful information not only from the whalers but also from labor recruiters coming from Fiji and Queensland after 1869. The intercolonial labor trade was responsible for educating a generation of seamen who brought knowledge of Solomon Islands products back to Australia, Fiji, and even New Zealand. Furthermore, the labor trade vessels were regular visitors to many of the islands, especially the central and eastern groups.[9] Although many a trader was later to resent their presence because in some areas they offered an alternative source of trade goods and took away some of the village labor force, the labor recruiters provided regular contact with metropolitan centers—a new communication link for both itinerant and resident traders.[10]

Indentured Melanesian labor played an important role in the development of agriculture in central and northern Queensland in the last thirty years of the century. Agriculture, along with a mining boom, drew more and more coastal ships north of Brisbane. It was only a few extra days' sailing for them to cross the Coral Sea to the Bismarck Archipelago or the Solomon Islands for a cargo of valuable island produce. From early experimental voyages emerged fairly regular shipping direct from Sydney to the Solomons.[11] Throughout the 1870s the volume of Solomons shipping arriving in Sydney gradually increased, peaking at the close of the decade (see Appendix 4). Concomitantly, imports increased, with bêche-de-mer, pearlshell, ivory nuts, and copra reach-

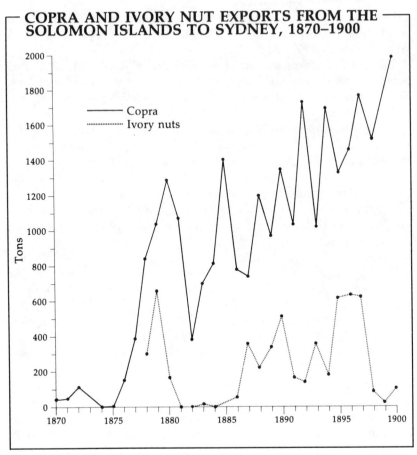

COPRA AND IVORY NUT EXPORTS FROM THE SOLOMON ISLANDS TO SYDNEY, 1870–1900

Figure 4 (*Note:* Real exports were greater because some ships' cargoes were unquantified. Data from Appendix 4.)

ing their highest level in 1878–1880 (Figures 4, 5). After this boom came a decline that lasted until about 1884 and appears to have been caused by a combination of factors: a price fall for some products, such as copra and bêche-de-mer; less profitability because of intense competition; the loss of six vessels in 1880 and another in 1882; and the withdrawal of the business firm of Cowlishaw and Ferguson.[12] The years from 1884 to 1900 saw a decline for most products from the 1878–1880 level, except that copra steadily increased in volume reaching almost 1900 tons in 1900, thus becoming the staple export of the Solomon Islands (see Figures 4, 5, 6).

Like their Australian colonial neighbors, a few New Zealand shipping companies with Pacific connections extended operations to trading in the Solomons. They met with little success.[13] Although in the 1870s

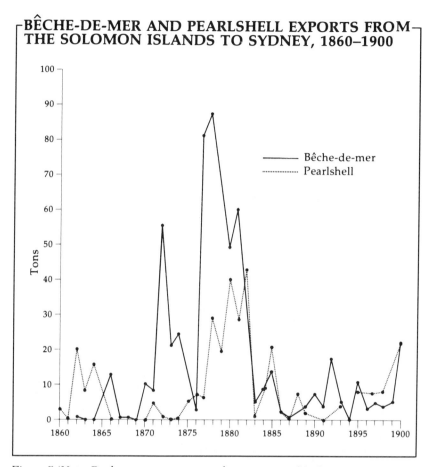

BÊCHE-DE-MER AND PEARLSHELL EXPORTS FROM THE SOLOMON ISLANDS TO SYDNEY, 1860–1900

Figure 5 (*Note:* Real exports were greater because some ships' cargoes were unquantified. Data from Appendix 4.)

and 1880s their traders became involved in serious disputes with Solomon Islanders, the main reason for their failure was the dominance of Sydney as a port of entry for trade throughout the southwest Pacific. Produce shipped first to Fiji or Auckland from the Solomons was not as profitable as that taken to Sydney direct. With few exceptions, trade remained Sydney based and financed.[14]

Traders and backers

Neil Brodie and Alexander MacKenzie Ferguson were the leading competitors for the Solomons trade in the 1870s. Brodie employed resident traders at Gizo as early as 1869 and in the following decade installed European agents at Savo and Marovo Lagoon (see Appendix 5). Fergu-

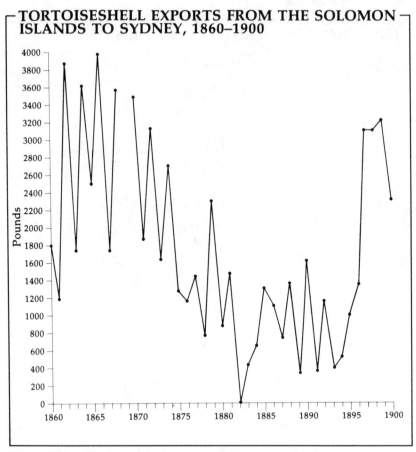

TORTOISESHELL EXPORTS FROM THE SOLOMON ISLANDS TO SYDNEY, 1860–1900

Figure 6 (*Note:* Real exports were greater because some ships' cargoes were unquantified. Data from Appendix 4.)

son used local traders in the western Solomons and beyond in the Bismarck Archipelago, as well as European agents at Uki ni Masi and at Makira Harbour. Well established by the mid-seventies, Ferguson's business expanded after he entered a partnership with the Sydney merchants and shippers Cowlishaw Brothers in 1877. By 1880 the partners had white traders at Marau and Tadhimboko on Guadalcanal, and at Savo and Roviana as well as Uki.[15]

To facilitate the collection of produce from around the islands, Ferguson introduced the first steam-powered vessels: in 1875 the *Ripple*, an auxiliary schooner to tender the barque, *Sydney*. With the Cowlishaws he purchased another steamer, *Emu*. These were used in conjunction with a variety of schooners, cutters, and launches that were controlled by the men at the company's stations. When a full cargo had accumulated at these stations the company's larger sailing vessels, *Avoca* and *Gazelle*, would take it to Sydney two or three times a year. This organization was continued by Cowlishaws' buyers, Kelly, Williams and Woodhouse, and an allied company of J. Williams. G. T. Waterhouse, also of Sydney, was a competitor from the mid-1880s, introducing one of the first chartered overseas steamers in 1894 (see Appendix 4). Brodie, and his 1880s partner Clark, continued to rely on sailing vessels, as did all the other smaller companies and independent traders.[16]

The financial arrangements between the Sydney backers and the trader on a ship varied. Some firms gave a prospective trader credit to buy a schooner of twenty to thirty tons and a cargo of trade goods. The debt was reduced as the trader sold produce to them. Other metropolitan companies might, as in Ferguson's early career, hire the trader, usually giving him a proportion of the profit from the sale of cargo. By this means, some traders were able to purchase their own vessels and use the Sydney connections as agents only. Other traders received a share of the profits in return for services and investment of capital; for example, Cowlishaws reached an agreement with Stephens of Uki whereby he paid half of the cost of the schooner *Atlantic*, half the crew's wages, and half the cost of trade. Stephens was paid no wage, but got half the net proceeds of trade, after the purchase price of goods and the freight from the Solomons to Sydney at a rate of £4 sterling a ton. Cowlishaws were to be his only buyer and could post him at any of their stations.[17]

Such agreements could limit the traders' real income. Substantial profits were to be made from trading in tropical produce, as Table 1 shows. But these prices represent the Sydney market values. Freight charges from Sydney to London for the period were about £3 a ton for copra. A cargo of 100 tons in 1880 could fetch £1850 in London, but the Sydney agent immediately deducted £300 for freight. With the cost of transportation from the Solomons to Sydney at £2 to £2 10s. a ton, a further £250 was deducted from the payment to the trader. The gross price paid to the trader, or beach price—disregarding all other expenses— was then £1850 less £550, or £1300, about £13 a ton. But the other expenses, including the costs of the Western trade goods, of paying Solomon Islander agents, and of paying local workers to prepare the copra for shipment, and so on, were accountable. In 1880, when a hypothetical £13 a ton beach price was a possibility, Stephens at Uki was being paid a mere £2 10s. by Cowlishaws, this being, according to his agreement with them, half of the clear profits they made together. During that period the real profit to Cowlishaws was more like £11 a ton for copra, rather than £5, but since they were charging Stephens £4 a ton freight Solomons to Sydney instead of the usual £2 to £2 10s., as well as charging him for half the cost of the trade supplies, they may have been weighting other costs more in their own favor as well.[18]

TABLE 1
Market prices of various tropical products, 1860–1900

	Coconut oil/copra (£/ton)	Tortoise-shell (s./lb.)	Bêche-de-mer (£/ton, S[a])	Pearlshell (£/ton, S)
1860	37 (L[b]), coconut oil			
1865	45 (L), coconut oil			
1868		14–21 (S)		70–90 (best quality mother-of-pearl) 35–45 (small) 45–50 (black-lip, S)
1872	31–35 (S), coconut oil	21–28 (L)		180–240 (best quality) 130–150 (small)
	10–18 (L), copra			32–38 (black-lip)
1873	16–32 (L), copra	12–32 (L)		
1879			100	
1880	20 (L)			
1882	10–12 (S)	10–13 (S)		
1883	14 (S)	12 (S)		
1885			25–70	
1886	10 (S)		35–75	
1893	10 (S)			
1898–99	10 (S)	12 (S)		25 (black-lip)

SOURCES: *SMH*, 16, 24 Nov., 1, 8, 28 Dec. 1860, 2 Jan. 1880; *Fiji Weekly News and Planters Journal*, 29 Aug. 1868; *Fiji Gazette*, 10 Oct., 7 Dec. 1872, 18 Jan. 1873; *Fiji Times*, 23 June, 3 Nov. 1875, 27 Feb., 5 Sept., 26 Dec. 1877, 4, 29 May, 26 June 1878, 7 Aug. 1880, 15 July 1882, 10 June, 12, 19 Dec. 1885, 22 May, 9 June, 21 July 1886, 13 July 1887, 1 Sept. 1888; *New South Wales Customs' House Statistics 1882, 1883* (Sydney 1883, 1884); Biskup 1974, 27, 63n.; Maude 1968, 274; Ribbe 1894, 134; Woodford Papers: Diary 23 Oct. 1886; AR German New Guinea 1898–1899, MS in English in possession of Dr. Peter Sack, ANU.

NOTES: [a] S, Sydney; [b] L, London

Of all those involved in the network of trade, transport, and distribution, the resident trader was easily the most vulnerable. When the market price declined, the Sydney company that bought the produce and usually shipped it from the Solomons absorbed very little of the loss, instead passing it on to the resident trader by cutting his beach price. An independent trader theoretically had some room to maneuver because he could sell to another ship, but this was uncommon because a trader needed to put in orders for trade and supplies well ahead of time. When his shipper brought the goods he was not only under a moral obligation to sell him his copra, but probably was forced to because he had so often to pay for the incoming goods with money or credit earned on the sale of produce. If a resident trader owned an interisland vessel, the original outlay and upkeep had to be considered in calculating his profit. A trader who agreed to trade solely with a particular firm, as Stephens did, was obliged to accept the firm's prices since he was financially dependent on it.[19]

Profits and losses

In the boom period of the late 1870s the profit margin among resident traders was high—about 60 percent, disregarding any limiting agreements they may have had with their backers. Gradually, intense competition coupled with the bargaining of the Solomon Islander producers reduced the traders' ability to do this. A ton of copra should have cost, at 1870s prices and at the stated prices of the following decade, about £3 in trade goods. In 1887 tobacco in Sydney cost the trader about 1s. 9d. to 2s. 0d. a pound (with 26 sticks to a pound), plus freight charges of 1d. to 2d. The number of coconuts (smoke-dried) needed to produce a ton of copra varied, depending on the size and quality of the nut. In some areas 10,000 were needed, in others 6000. To buy, say, 7000 nuts, the trader in the 1880s, at the ideal rate of 1 stick of tobacco for 10 nuts, would have to give 700 sticks or almost 27 pounds of tobacco. This would cost him about 2s. per pound, or a total outlay of between £2 10s. and £3. When a resident trader could sell his copra to the shipper at a beach price of £7 to £8 (while Sydney prices were about £10 to £11 a ton), he could get a gross profit of about £4 a ton. But, by 1886, with the increasing number of traders and, in some places, alternative sources of trade in the labor recruiting for overseas, the trader was in fact paying more for his copra. He was forced to accept from Solomon Islanders 70–80 coconuts instead of 100 for 10 sticks of tobacco (approximately 1s. in value of general trade goods); his outlay to buy 1 ton of copra became £4 17s. 6d., leaving him a reduced £2 10s. to £3, or between 35 and 40 percent profit, a drop of about a third from the profit of the late 1870s.[20]

Although cost factors fluctuated, profits remained at this level or slightly below until 1900. By 1896 the Sydney price of the preferred American tobacco was down to about 1s. a pound. The freight to the Solomons amounted to 16.6 percent of the Sydney invoice price, which meant that the trader paid ½d. for each pound of tobacco landed. At the exchange rate of 1 stick of tobacco for a string of 10 coconuts, with the reduced price, the trader was now apparently able to buy 7000 nuts for the sum of £1 10s. But underfilling of strings was now habitual. In 1896 a trader was offered, and actually accepted, a string of *seven* half-nuts (3½ nuts) for the price he once would have paid for twenty! Such a small string as this was probably uncommon, but dealing in strings of 14, 15, 16, 17, and 18 half-nuts was not. Such a practice kept the traders' outlay to buy a ton of copra to just about what it had been in the 1880s with tobacco at 2s. a pound.[21]

Some counterbalancing effect was provided by the slight decline in freight charges after about 1895, as the merchant shippers Burns, Philp & Company, in their steamship *Titus*, competed for cargo from the Solomons against Waterhouse's steamer *Kurrara* and his 217-ton sailing ship *Chittoor*. Freight charges ex Solomons for Sydney were then £1 15s. a ton, 5s. to 10s. less than in 1880.[22]

By 1900, the trader's gross profit margin increased very slightly when the price of tobacco in Sydney dropped to 10d. a pound. The trader could now buy a ton of copra for about £1 6s. As copra was selling to Burns Philp at about £7 10s., the trader's gross profit was £6 4s. However, at this time, "the cost of trading" including the license fees paid to the government, was easily £3 for each ton. On top of this, the trader had to pay someone to cut up the copra for shipment. The net profit would then not have been more than £2 10s. to £3, or about 33 percent.[23]

The commodities the trader offered the Islanders varied in cost. A trader who dealt in pipes and matches could make more profit than one dealing in tobacco. On the other hand, profit on cutlery was much less.[24] Where traders supplied traditional Solomon Islands valuables, profits could be considerable. In the 1890s traders bought and sold dog and porpoise teeth among themselves at 25s. and 12s. 6d. a hundred respectively. These were then traded to Solomon Islanders at the rate of £2 10s. and £1, giving substantial profits of 100 and 62.5 percent respectively, apart from the additional return earned from the sale of the goods exchanged, such as copra.[25] Even when some Solomon Islanders began to demand cash for their goods and labor at the turn of the century, much of what the trader lost on the profits inherent in barter exchange was regained by the use of coins of no lower denomination than a shilling because where, say, a pipe was worth 9d. a Solomon Islander would have to pay 1s. and get no change. (Threepenny coins were unpopular because their small size meant they often were lost by people without pockets, wallets, or coin purses.)[26]

A resident trader's profits could be affected by fluctuations in metropolitan prices, his own industry, and his location. Ivory nuts in 1890 fetched about £3 a ton in Sydney. Three years later the price jumped to £12 because they were found suitable for the manufacture of wheels for roller skates in Vienna. The high prices produced a glut and the price dropped to £5 a ton in 1896.[27] In the same year, copra, which in 1880 had been up to £16 a ton in Sydney, was down to about £8 or £9.[28] Charles Olsen, shipping his goods through Waterhouse, was getting £2 a ton beach price at Santa Ana. As he collected about 25 tons yearly from the adjacent islands, his annual income was about £50. In more productive areas, such as the western and central Solomons, a more industrious trader, say Nielsen at Nggela, was able in the same year to ship 50 tons of copra, 1 ton of bêche-de-mer, 15 hundredweight of pearlshell, and 30 pounds of tortoiseshell, to earn a total of £200.[29]

Despite the vagaries of the marketplace, a few traders made a lot of money, simply by supplying highly prized but scarce commodities. Peter Pratt was earning almost £1000 a year in the early 1890s, when Acting Resident Commissioner C. M. Woodford was on a salary of £200. Much of Pratt's earnings came from trading in arms and ammunition, since, as a Frenchman, he was outside British jurisdiction and the law of 1884, which prohibited British subjects from selling those items in the islands.[30] Likewise, Oscar Svensen, a Norwegian, did well out of the firearms traffic until 1896 when the establishment of the protectorate government checked such trading.[31]

In financial terms it is exceedingly difficult to calculate the overall profit or loss in the life of the resident trader. Yet their deaths illuminate their lives. Probate of the will of Joseph Emmanuel ("Portuguese Joe") in 1902 revealed an estate of £1 4s. 11d., after almost twenty years trading at Nggela and Savo.[32] Charles Atkinson's executors reckoned his assets at £36 14s. 0d. and his debts at £523 6s. 3d. Among the debts was a sum owed to T. G. Kelly, who was one of the partners in the company of Kelly, Williams and Woodhouse, which had bought out Cowlishaws in 1880. After sixteen years of trading, Kelly was bankrupt and Thomas Woodhouse a crippled old man living in fear of his life at Uki.[33] The last days of the "Old Commodore" (Woodhouse) at Gizo were made easier by the charity of Wheatley and Wickham to whom he owed over £200. After his death they waived their claims, to allow an inheritance to pass to Woodhouse's daughter in Sydney. Without encumbrances, the estate amounted to £12.[34]

Uncertain profits meant intense and frequently bitter competition among traders. Deception and even theft were sometimes used in the war to win a cargo. Brodie's business suffered in 1885, when his local agent on Santa Isabel was put in irons by the sometime trader Peter Niels Sorenson until he had extorted "4000 bêches-de-mer, 24 turtle shells, 3 hogs and a pig." Hawkins of the *Fairlie*, concerned by the Royal Navy's campaign against gun trafficking, sold his stocks to the Frenchman Pratt. With this, the most attractive of all trade goods, Pratt had little difficulty in persuading Wickham's Solomon Islander trader at Karuhare to part with the tortoiseshell collected in readiness for Wickham's next visit.[35]

Traders occasionally went further in their attempts to undermine their competitors. Following the killing of the trader Tom Dabelle at Anuta, southwest San Cristobal, Samuel Keating made an unsuccessful appeal to the navy to hang Sono (Johnson) of Hada, stating it would be "conferring a favour on the white traders of the Solomon Islands."[36] That Keating worked for Captain Woodhouse of Kelly, Williams and Woodhouse, and Sono traded for their arch-rival, Waterhouse, hardly made his testimony impartial.[37] Rivalry and antagonism was so rife between traders in the 1880s that the visitor Woodford was only slightly exaggerating when he said the traders "rejoice to hear of the murder of one of their number immediately flocking to the spot on the chance of picking up some of his leavings or buying them from the natives."[38]

In such a competitive business, any new contenders, particularly if they were non-British, faced a wall of opposition from the established traders. In 1880 Eduard Hernsheim sailed from Jaluit on a commercial reconnaissance of the Solomons and New Ireland. His main informant on trading conditions in the Solomons was Captain Davis, a former employee of Cowlishaw and Ferguson, then just starting to trade on his own. To scare the German off, Davis told him that 30 sticks of tobacco was the going price for 100 coconuts. This would be the highest nineteenth-century price ever recorded in the Solomons, amounting to an incredible £7–£8 paid to Islanders for 1 ton of copra, or three times what the resident trader Stephens got from his backers. Confronted with this apparent unprofitability, Hernsheim turned his attention from the Solomons and concentrated on his stations in the Bismarck Archipelago.[39]

In human terms the risks were great. Combined with the non-human vagaries of the Solomons environment, the risks made trading an extremely hazardous livelihood, as the career of the best known of the early traders, Alexander Ferguson, demonstrates. Leaving his clerical position at O'Dowd's of Sydney for a time, he came to the Solomons in the late 1860s as a steward to Delaney of the *Marion Rennie*, on which Brodie sometimes served as chief officer. In 1867, the *Marion Rennie* deposited Ferguson at Makira Harbour to collect produce, sailing on to Rendova where the entire company was massacred. When in 1868 HMS *Blanche* investigated, three Solomon Islanders were "punished" and a fine of three tons of tortoiseshell imposed, to be ready for collection by the end of the year. Delaney's son wanted the shell on behalf of the estate, but extracting such an amount was impossible, as his agent, Brodie, found in 1870.

Ferguson, now with his master's certificate, returned to the Solomons in 1871 in the *Captain Cook* as trader and agent for O'Dowd's, the backers of Delaney. There, in the following year, he acted as a go-between for the navy and the chiefs of Rendova. The captain of the man-of-war, quite exceeding his powers, authorized the "tribe" to execute the man Sondo, said to have instigated the crime. The navy's intervention was most unsatisfactory: the Delaney family's move for compensation was lost, Sondo was supposedly executed by the chiefs in 1872, and, when Ferguson brought the *Kate Kearney* past Sydney Heads in 1874, it carried a rich cargo of 1700 pounds of tortoiseshell. Among island hands it was said that Ferguson himself had purchased most of the shell from the Rendova chiefs who had been accumulating it to give to the man-of-war.[40]

Although Ferguson obviously had an eye to the main chance, over the years he earned a reputation for fair dealing among both Europeans and some Solomons communities. He often took Islanders to Sydney to show them the sights, thus winning friends. He had two children, Margaret and a son, by Mariki of Fead Island (Nuguria) off Bougainville. A close friend of the Gorai of the Shortlands, Ferguson was respected by the chief, who named a nephew after him. Following an attack by certain Nggela people on the *Dancing Wave* in 1875, Ferguson's friends from that island warned him to keep away as those involved wanted more blood.[41]

Europeans, including missionaries and labor recruiters, respected him because of his generosity and honesty. With the Methodist missionaries, he helped survivors from the ill-fated de Rays settlement on New Ireland. This was not an isolated incident. He had saved crew from the shipwrecked *Delhi* and *Latonia* in 1879. A year later he assisted people off the wrecks of the *Meteor* and *Trevelin Family.*[42] In doing this he lost almost £1000 for himself and his partners, Cowlishaws. The partnership had suffered a series of major reverses since August 1877, when their vessel, *Witch of the Wave*, went on a reef off Choiseul. Although the crew survived, the vessel and cargo were lost. In July 1878, the company's ship *Sydney* sank off the Shortlands, a loss of £2000. Late the following year the *Esperanza* was plundered at Kolombangara. Excluding the death of her crew, losses amounted to £2000. During those years attacks on the firm's shore stations at Guadalcanal cost them £700. In one attack in 1879, their Marau agent, Halgate, and a Savo man were killed by the 'Are'are *ramo* 'fighting chief' Vaisare and his followers because Ferguson in 1878 had reported a theft by the *ramo* to the Royal Navy. The captain of HMS *Sandfly*, meeting with the unsuspecting Vaisare, had fined him ten fathoms of shell valuables. He eventually retaliated by killing Halgate.[43]

In August 1884, Ferguson, aboard the *Ripple*, called for the first time to trade at Numa Numa, Bougainville, on the recommendation of another trader. While trading on the ship, the people attacked the crew and killed the thirty-four-year-old Ferguson with an axe blow. Their motivation is not clear. Ferguson had told them his vessel was "ship belong Gorai" which may well have antagonized them as Gorai's people in the past had attacked the Numa Numa.[44]

Ferguson's career is representative of that of the white Solomon Island trader. Even this résumé of his life demonstrates that the trader had to proceed with care in visiting Solomon Island coasts because greed, dissatisfaction with some trading deal, the desire for revenge, or a village's need for a head to fulfill a ritual demand could all mean open conflict and death.[45]

Of motives and men

With profits so variable and futures so uncertain, why did the traders choose to make their living in the Solomon Islands? For a few—perhaps the young Wheatley dreaming over the books of Robert Louis Stevenson in cramped Liverpool, or Ferguson, clerking in O'Dowd's stuffy offices in Sydney—there was a dash of romance and a strong measure of dissatisfaction with "the grey discipline of streets."[46] Some traders seem to have found themselves in the islands as residue of a failed enterprise and simply stayed on until something better came along. Others, with less innocent motives, sought an island where their own race could no longer sit in judgment on their behavior.

John Champion Macdonald came to San Cristobal to find such an island. A Canadian, known in the Solomons as an American, he was a former sea captain working out of Fiji on labor vessels.[47] In about 1877 he opened a trading station near Star Harbour for Houng Lee of Levuka, general merchant and owner of the recruiting ship *Dauntless*. By 1880 Macdonald, said to have absconded with Lee's ship, *Star of Fiji*, had established himself as an independent trader on the small island of Santa Ana with his brother William, who had deserted a wife in Fiji.[48] In 1877 also, Fred Howard came first to San Cristobal on the *Mary Anderson*, as an agent of the New Zealand firm, McArthur and Co. After he upset the Ubuna people he was forced to leave, but was working three years later on Uki for the trader Stephens. As a young man, Frank Wickham ran away from his home in Somerset, England. Shipwrecked in the Bougainville Strait, he was rescued by Ferguson, who brought him to his trading station at Kolo Hite. Lars Nielsen seems to have been on the same vessel. Both men settled in the Solomons, worked as agents for other traders and, by the 1890s, had established themselves as traders, with Nielsen at Savo and Wickham at Hombu-hombu, Roviana Lagoon.[49]

Unlike Frank Wickham, several traders were running away from far more than the restraints of the parental home. A few of the assistants employed at traders' stations were escaped convicts "on a trip round the world via New Caledonia."[50] In 1878, Henry Townsend, tried on homosexual charges in Samoa and Fiji, hoped to find refuge at Uki as a trader with a young male Melanesian companion, only to be killed a few days after his arrival.[51] After stealing a ship and cargo from Fiji in 1887 and trying their luck as traders, Queen and Marsden met a similar fate on Rendova.[52]

Norman Wheatley likewise fled to the islands with his past snapping at his heels. Family tradition tells how the young Wheatley was working in a factory in Liverpool and, in an argument with the foreman, hit the man over the head with an iron bar. Thinking he had killed him, Wheatley stowed away on a ship to the East only to have to flee from a cholera epidemic to Australia. From there, inspired by somewhat romantic visions of the Pacific, he made his way to New Georgia in 1892.[53]

Despite dark and dubious pasts many of these "copra peddlers" were men of some education.[54] "Jack" Cooper, who lived at Marau in the 1880s, was a graduate of the Whitgift School in England.[55] Aubrey Griffiths, "an old Harrovian" and trader at Roviana, impressed visitors with his intelligence and manner.[56] Commander Rason of HMS *Royalist* found Peter Pratt to be "the best educated" of the traders he had met.[57] Nicholas Tindal, who came to the Shortlands in the early 1890s, had doubtless been to the best of schools since his father was a British vice-admiral.[58] Fred Howard, a German, was a "thoughtful and well educated man," but a visiting naval officer found him "very reticent as to his reason for having left the Fatherland."[59] Almost all of Ferguson's white traders were "college bred," but like the homosexuals and convicts had "come to grief in other spheres."[60]

In number, the resident traders were few. In 1870 there were about seven, in 1875 perhaps four, in 1880 six, 1885 ten, 1890 fourteen (see Appendix 5). Yet, in any one year the number of whites engaging in trade in the Solomon Islands was much higher. Temporary residents played a significant role in trading. Ferguson had "a dozen centrally situated stations" in 1877 and Ribbe knew of "about twenty stations and as many traders" in 1893.[61] Many of these stations were manned for only part of the year. A ship placed an agent at a station for a few weeks or months to organize produce and later collected him plus goods on the return trip through the islands, or from Sydney.[62] Numerically, the itinerant traders in ships were more significant. In 1870, for example, at least three Sydney-based vessels, *Captain Cook*, *Aurora*, and *Rose and Thistle* (the last made two trips) were in Solomon Islands waters (see Appendix 4). Each had a European captain and a crew of about five or six, besides Islanders taken on in the Solomons. Ten years later, in the boom period, the arrivals in Sydney increased to twenty-one. That meant about 100 to 130 European itinerants, including men who might have sailed on more than one voyage a year.[63] Although there was some variation in subsequent years, some 70 or more Europeans annually would have been on trading ships alone around the islands until 1894, when Burns Philp and other companies commenced steamer runs from Sydney and began to change the pattern of Solomon Islands shipping (see Appendix 4).

The price of survival

With such small numbers and little effective political backing, the Europeans had to develop a range of survival strategies. Sharing a similar cultural background, the traders could communicate with the other agents of Western influence appearing in the islands—the Royal Navy, the labor recruiters, and Christian missionaries. Except for two or three white resident missionaries of the Melanesian Mission, the resident traders had a greater knowledge of Solomon Islanders than any other Europeans,[64] and could exploit their position as mediators. The traders were generally prepared to use their influence with other Europeans to assist the local community adjacent to where they lived, since they depended on those people for their existence. Olsen, a trader on Santa Ana, had little to lose and much to gain in goodwill in helping the Ghupuna people to regain one of their women, who tried to run away with a Malaitan on the labor recruiting ship, *Sybil*, in 1895. Olsen did his utmost because, as he later told the commander of HMS *Ringdove*, not to do so would "make things unpleasant here for me as a trader."[65]

To secure their own positions, the traders played off one power against another. In the Shortlands, the death of Gorai was followed by a struggle for succession. To add to the uncertainty, John A. Macdonald, son of J. C. Macdonald, had married Tanutanu Galaga, Gorai's daughter, who subsequently died in childbirth, being weak from "consumption." This turned the people against John for a time because they believed he had poisoned her. Afraid of being attacked, in 1893 he appealed for help to the German New Guinea authorities, since all the Shortland Islands except Mono were then German territory. When the cruiser *Sperber* appeared, Macdonald, having demonstrated the apparent might of his support, took the role of mediator and protector, ostentatiously begging the commander not to punish the people.[66]

Although they might have threatened to call in a roving man-of-war, few traders did so because, like Macdonald, they were aware that, unlike the navy, they had to live with their neighbors on a permanent basis. When Peter Pratt appealed for naval assistance in a letter to the *Sydney Morning Herald* in 1889 it was an act of sheer desperation. Two of his Malaitan workers had been killed and his station plundered while he was away from Nuza Zonga. Suspicion fell on the Simbo people, but when Captain Hand in HMS *Royalist* came to investigate, Pratt had reconsidered and refused to go with him to identify the men, knowing "it would injure his trade."[67]

Like Pratt with the Simbo, Wickham withheld information to protect
his trading relationship with two big-men of Mbaniata, Rendova, who,
in 1885, had become involved in the taking of the head of a trader,
James Howie.[68] Wheatley similarly resisted pressure by Resident Commissioner Woodford to reveal evidence against the people of Kolokongo,
in Roviana Lagoon, incriminating them in the murder of two white
traders, Kerr and Smith, in 1895.[69] His reticence was understandable
since he had just purchased an island adjacent to Kolokongo. Had
Wheatley assisted the enquiry it would have spoilt "his business there or
render[ed] the island altogether untenable."[70] Woodford found that
Wheatley's involvement in local affairs did not stop at mere refusal to
divulge information. Despite Woodford's pacification campaign in the
late 1890s, Wheatley, in order to steal a march on his rival Wickham,
secretly helped Hingava and neighboring chiefs with their head-hunting expeditions, by supplying them with illegal firearms.[71]

Traders maintained generally amicable relations with the other permanent agents of European influence in the islands—the missionaries—
although the traders' style of life sometimes earned clerical reproach.
Ferguson's civility to the Reverend Alfred Penny clearly paid dividends.[72] Penny noted in his diary that he intended to go aboard Ferguson's ship, *Emu*, "to show the people I cordially approve of trading
fairly."[73] Some traders, like Swartz, Svensen, and Nielsen, actively
courted the missionaries' favor through gifts of supplies and money as
well as free passage and accommodation.[74]

After they returned to the Solomons in 1898, the Roman Catholics
depended on traders for transportation until they purchased a vessel in
1903. Svensen and Keating assisted the establishment of the mission at
Rua Sura, off Guadalcanal. When in 1899 the Marists tried to win over
the Makira Harbour people by large payments of tobacco and pipes in
return for land and fresh vegetables, the traders' attitude changed. Mission generosity meant undercutting the traders' prices and endangering
their livelihood. Tension subsided when the Catholics opted for cash
transactions on San Cristobal and shifted their attention to the treacherous south coast of Guadalcanal—a region unfrequented by traders.[75]

Trading rivalries in large part determined the course of Christian
evangelization of New Georgia (Figure 7). Wickham and Wheatley
encouraged the Methodists to come to Roviana in 1902, believing that
the mission might assist the sickening and decreasing population and so
bolster production. With the great chief Hingava's decline as he neared
death, perhaps they feared that a switch of allegiances would undermine their position. The mission, too, might make the people more
amenable to the new order of the protectorate government.[76] Wickham, a Methodist who had sent his son to Newington College, Sydney,
presumably had some sympathy for their aims. Because Wheatley fan-

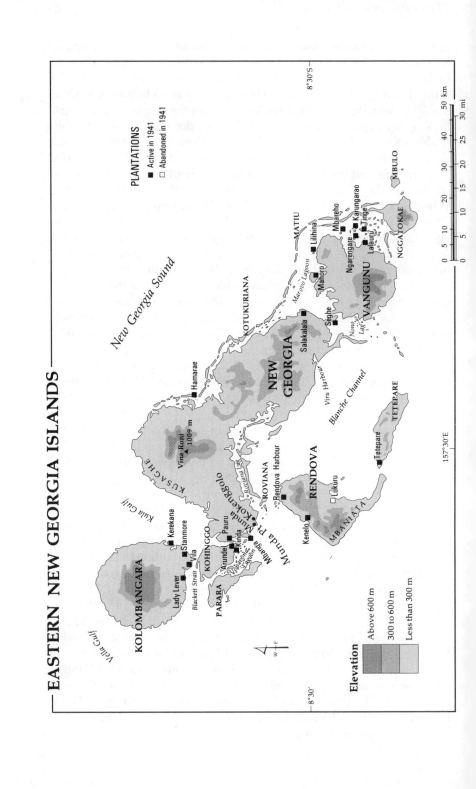

EASTERN NEW GEORGIA ISLANDS

PLANTATIONS
- ■ Active in 1941
- □ Abandoned in 1941

Elevation
- Above 600 m
- 300 to 600 m
- Less than 300 m

cied himself as a patron of the whites in the western Solomons, this action would not have been out of character, but subsequent developments alienated him from the Methodists. Wickham's friendship with the mission aroused the antagonism of Wheatley, his long-time social and commercial rival. Of greater importance was the steady growth of the personal power of the Reverend John Goldie, the mission chairman. Goldie's authority in the eyes of the people eventually excelled that of the government. Wheatley, for years a big-man in the Melanesian sense, resented Goldie's increasing influence so much that he tried to undermine the mission by inviting other Christian sects to the district. Over the years he unsuccessfully canvassed both the Salvation Army and the Roman Catholics. Eventually Wheatley's third choice was to prove attractive to the Melanesians. In 1914, eager for mission work, the Seventh Day Adventists settled at Viru to become a thorn in the side of Goldie for the rest of his long life.[77]

In the Solomons, such one-upmanship had been an established ploy in the traders' survival strategy. With no central regulating authority until the establishment of protectorate government in 1896 and a lack of efficient communication, the numerically weak traders acted as individuals rather than as an organized group in attempting to manipulate their relationships with Islanders. The only external authority, the Royal Navy, could do little damage to persons and property except in areas susceptible to sea-based attack, such as Roviana where the destruction of villages and canoes by Davis in 1891 did have a chastening influence.[78] On land, the Solomon Islanders were masters of guerilla warfare and had the advantage of the navy's ignorance of their alliances as well as its short memory for their faces, to say nothing of the ambivalence of the traders toward such intervention.[79]

A more effective method of control would have been, as Bishop Selwyn of the Melanesian Mission advocated, the withdrawal of trading facilities from the district.[80] This tactic had been successful on Kolombangara and, briefly, on Guadalcanal in 1876–1879 following the killing of white traders. But the early eighties saw an influx of new traders hungry for business and the boycott broke down.[81] Under preprotectorate political conditions, such concerted action was rarely possible because traders were locked in competition and would suffer if trading ceased in a particular area.

Having to rely on their own ingenuity for survival, the traders usually established their stations on small islands—the position was more defensible than a mainland site, and the population easier to negotiate with, being more contained. The island had to have a sheltered anchorage and be central to areas where people could obtain sufficient produce to sell to the trader. In the east, Santa Ana and Uki filled these criteria. On Guadalcanal the traders chose a little island off Aola called Gera

Figure 8

(Mbara), as well as Tavanipupu and "Ferguson" Island in Marau
Sound. Savo, and Ghavutu and Mbangai in Nggela were also sites. In
the western Solomons, the Roviana Lagoon provided islets like Kolo
Hite, Hombuhombu, Hombupecka, and nearby Nuza Zonga. In the
Marovo lagoon, resident traders lived on Lilihina throughout most of
the 1880s and 1890s. On Simbo, Narovo was Jean Pascal Pratt's station
in the 1890s (see Appendix 5). Further west, the Macdonalds, after leaving Santa Ana via Aola, settled at Siniasoro, Fauro, in 1885, with William living later at Munia. Although Fauro is a large island, its small
population of no more than 300 in the eighties and nineties enabled the
Macdonalds to choose a secure site in a strategic position. In the early
1890s the Tindal family settled nearby on the small island of Faisi (Figure 8).[82] On mainland stations traders could survive only by living
under the protection of a particularly powerful big-man, such as Sono
of Hada, San Cristobal, or by living in a Christian district, as Nggela
was by 1890.[83]

Although most of the trading stations were occupied on a fairly continuous basis, the small European trading population was fluid. In the 1870s, for instance, Ferguson, on his return trips to Sydney, used to take two or three of his agents to recuperate. When McArthur and Company of New Zealand made their brief foray into Solomons trading they relieved their agents by sending replacements within a year.[84] Many of these one-year visitors never returned to the Solomons and have left very little record. The resident traders Halgate, Provis, Townsend, the Dabelles, and Guy were killed within a year of their arrival. Between 1860 and 1896 the total number of whites involved in trading who were killed was about eighty. If a period of two years is taken to qualify a trader for permanency, then Morrow, Nyberg, Cooper, Howard, Atkinson, J. P. Pratt, and Hamilton Wright were the only long-term residents killed by Islanders. Even after the culling out of the inept, the failure rate was almost 10 percent. Replacing them meant a fairly regular stream of new faces coming to the Solomons (see Appendix 6).

The permanent resident traders, by definition, had learned how to survive in the social and physical environment of the islands. Most of them were former seafarers who were not unused to difficult conditions with a minimum of comforts. Many a trader lived in a house like the one at Faisi (Photo 1)—little different from his Solomon Islands neighbors'—with sago palm walls and roof and dirt floor, or perhaps a raised one of split palm or even dressed timber, such as Olsen's house at Santa Ana (Photo 2). When the trader could afford it he might have his agent in Sydney send up Australian hardwood and corrugated iron to build a more substantial, but far hotter house. The trader was considerably safer in the latter since the walls could stop a bullet or an axe blow—"during the day the natives spy out where the white man has his sleeping place and mark it on the wall outside."[85] At particularly dangerous stations the trader would adopt the practice of the Melanesian who did not trust his neighbors, and change his sleeping place every night or surround his bed with bulletproof materials, such as tobacco cases. The corrugated iron roof not only caught fresh water, but was also fireproof. Most houses fronted the beach, limiting the exposure to attack as well as providing for a quick escape to the boats in case of trouble.[86]

Because of their accumulated day-to-day experience with Solomon Islanders, the resident traders learned much about local custom. Wickham, for example, knew the significance of the sacredness of the head to New Georgians when he agreed to call at the Russells to collect the head of a Roviana warrior who had died on a raiding party's voyage to Guadalcanal. On another occasion he intervened to save the life of a man whose wife had been killed on suspicion of having cast the "evil eye" on Ngetu, chief of Mbili, causing death to him and others.[87]

There were limits to this kind of intervention. When the traders were confronted with aspects of Solomon Island culture they found person-

Photo 1. Tindal's station at Faisi, c. 1895. *(Ribbe 1903)*

Photo 2. Charles Olsen and Santa Ana children at the trader's house, c. 1895. *(Festetics von Tolna 1903)*

ally distasteful, the wise, chameleon-like, adopted a tolerant attitude. Woodford relates John C. Macdonald's eyewitness account of an incident that occurred in 1883, describing the sacrifice of a boy captured from Santa Isabel and a sow during the launching of a war canoe at Nono, New Georgia. After the child had been exhausted by repeated dunkings in the sea he was carried on the back of the "chief devil-man" around the canoe house three times, then

> the chief took up a 12-inch trade knife and with a gash across the child's throat and then a chop the head was off and the blood streaming from the neck. The man still carrying the child on his back then ran round and round the house as before scattering the blood on the house and ground till the body ceased to bleed. It was then thrown down in front of the house. The pig . . . which had been tied up close by was brought and killed by being thumped and jumped on and stifled in the usual way and the two were then cooked together. They were afterwards eaten with the other [human] bodies and the child's head was stuck up in the clubhouse.[88]

Macdonald could but remain silent among so many and carried this gruesome memory back to his home on Santa Ana. There, two years later, his knowledge of the people's customs enabled him to save the life of another little boy, his own son John. The boy had accidentally shot a chief's son with an arrow. Macdonald senior quickly got his boy into the men's house, which was as much a sanctuary to the people as the Christian churches were to fugitives in medieval Europe. While the boy was safe, Macdonald arranged compensation by buying a slave from the mainland for the dead man's clan. Nonetheless, the incident and increasing competition for trade in the area led him to move his family to Aola and later Fauro.[89] Over the years Macdonald had learned much of Santa Ana culture and had been able to earn a position of respect among the people. He knew the language and used Western medicine to help the sick. He protected the people from the more exploitative element among the labor trade recruiters, since he and his white employees frequently worked on a temporary basis as interpreters and crew for Fijian vessels when they called at Santa Ana. Macdonald's partner, Sproul, had helped the people by shooting a crocodile that had been troublesome. Macdonald was also a friend to big-men on San Cristobal, including Taki of Wango.[90]

Resident traders like Macdonald took pains to cultivate good relations with the nearby people, having more at stake than traders aboard ships. In 1880, for example, the mate of the *Venture*, while in a whaleboat with resident trader Bateman off Ubuna, accidentally shot a big-man, Aurua, who was with him when his gun misfired. The captain, Wolsch, set sail for Sydney but Bateman, at considerable personal risk, chose to return to the village to explain events and conciliate the people.[91]

Photo 3. Peter Edmund Pratt trading for coconuts at New Georgia, c. 1895.
(Ribbe 1903)

The traders' consideration for the cultural sensibilities of their neighbors won them allies, just as their ability to defend themselves and their property drew grudging respect from potential foes. Peter Pratt's survival was due in part to his skill with the revolver that he carried while trading (see Photo 3).[92] Likewise, Howard's successor on Uki in 1895 was "a dead shot with the rifle: he is consequently much feared."[93] On the other hand, if a trader simply allowed himself to appear vulnerable and powerless then he was doubly so. Traders attributed the stealing of Woodhouse's boat from Roviana by the men of Gisu, Fauro, to an earlier incident involving a German schooner. The ship *Hapai* was wrecked near Gisu, but the master and crew had managed to get ashore, saving some cargo and pigs. When the people came, the captain, who like his crew was well armed, "went down on his knees to the natives and begged for his life, while they killed his pigs and stole his stores before his eyes."[94] Such weakness nearly always invited exploitation.[95]

Although the trader who survived was the trader who could protect himself, most were wary of extending this protection to Solomon Islander associates outside their immediate employ, especially if it involved armed participation. Certainly Wheatley assisted Hingava by supplying him with arms for distant head-hunting raids to Choiseul and Santa Isabel, and Peter Pratt got into a dispute with Maghratulo, a Vella Lavella big-man, in 1890 when he tried to take back the big-man's Ontong Java captive to the lad's father for a reward. However, in the main, the traders avoided involvement in serious altercations between groups of Solomon Islanders in the vicinity of their stations.[96] During the years Macdonald was on Santa Ana, the Ghupuna people were at war with the Nataghera on the opposite side of the island. Macdonald personally deplored this and the depradations of the Santa Ana big-man, Mai, who terrorized the Hunarite people on San Cristobal, yet in both cases he remained aloof.[97]

The one foe that the whites could not protect themselves from was malaria, which carried off a high percentage of the indigenous population in infancy, perhaps as many as 40 percent. But those who survived had greater resistance to it than the Europeans.[98] Every year or so at least one trader died from malaria.[99] Although quinine was in use as a quasi-prophylactic and a palliative, opinion varied on what was a safe dosage and on just when it should be taken. An overdose could induce blackwater fever, a very dangerous, often fatal, illness.[100] It was no wonder traders came and went so often in this period, since the best treatment for malaria was to leave the tropics, although the sufferer still remained prone to bouts of fever. Nor is it surprising that the traders, with malaria only "80% men,"[101] became sometimes lethargic, "their brains dried out by the tropical sun," and vulnerable to attacks by Solomon Islanders and the more subtle depradations of the bottle.[102]

Alcohol assuaged the loneliness and stresses of the traders' lives. When traders met it helped to create a feeling of fellowship, of warmth that most missed in their relationships with both Solomon Islands men and, when sober, rival traders. For some who could afford it, alcohol helped to pass the leaden days that dragged as they waited for the wind to turn or for the sight of the Sydney ship. But it could be a treacherous comforter. The captain of one of the ships lost in 1880 had run aground at Marau Sound. The cause of the wreck was explained by a Solomon Islander: "Man stop ship he plenty kai kai grog. Man he no look out. By and by big fellow wind he come, ship he go ashore. By and by he finish."[103] The long-time trader at Santa Ana, Frankie Nyberg, got himself killed in retaliation for deeds done while he was drunk.[104] Like Nyberg, William Macdonald at Fauro indulged in periodic drinking binges, but seems to have survived because he had a Solomon Islands wife to protect him from his temporary derangement.[105]

For many traders, including Macdonald, P. E. Pratt, Wheatley, Woodhouse, Nielsen, Wickham, Olsen, and Griffiths, the key to their longevity in the islands was often to be found in the relationships created by marriage to Solomon Islanders. With their shady pasts and less than attractive futures these men had little to offer white women but a difficult life away from their kin. In the preprotectorate era only one white woman came to live permanently with her trader-husband. Melinda Macdonald, a New Zealander, followed John to Santa Ana after he had prepared a house there in the late 1870s, and twice Solomon Islanders threatened her and her children.[106] A number of sea captains brought their wives with them, but only for the round trip to Sydney. A few other women came to live with their trader-husbands, but could not cope with the harshness of life and soon returned to Australia.[107] To find a wife, the white trader had to seek elsewhere.

Although some traders, like so many of the official builders of the British Empire, may have had a distinct psychological preference for women of color, expediency was the primary determinant of their coupling.[108] Throughout the islands were women whom Europeans considered good-looking. The fine-featured, coal-black New Georgia women, many of them descendants of Choiseul and Santa Isabel slaves and adoptees, were particularly pleasing to the whites. Their counterparts in San Cristobal and Santa Ana in the 1880s, still were, as in the whaling days, "singularly and fatally pretty."[109]

On a more practical level, the Solomon Islands woman, inured to hard physical work and to the climate, kept the trader's household running well, providing him with fresh food from her own garden and with pigs she had reared. Were she from a different island, her contacts with other women still gave her access to information the trader could not himself always obtain. She was more alert to the little signs of a change of mood or activity among village people. Such sensitivity often provided timely warnings of potential trouble for the unsuspecting trader.[110]

Both Europeans and Solomon Islanders realized that such a marriage was the strongest possible link they could have with each other. In some cases, of course, Solomon Islanders offered their women on a temporary basis for immediate but limited rewards to less reputable traders, just as they had to the whalers. These women were, as before, either slaves with little control over their own destinies or, in some societies, the young unmarried girls who were allowed sexual freedom.[111]

The traders who seemed successful, stable, and more likely to funnel back substantial benefits on a continuous basis were usually given free women, the daughters of respectable families. Solomon Islanders realized that this would encourage a trader to reside among them. This was Gorai's motive behind the marriage of his daughter, Tanutanu Galaga, to Macdonald.[112] Where the trader had a secure relationship with the local big-man, as in the cases of Wheatley and Wickham, marriages were made with women from neighboring areas. Frank Wickham's first wife, Ameriga, was from Bougainville and his second from New Georgia.[113] This arrangement had social advantages, but also drawbacks. A husband was expected to contribute to his wife's clan on various occasions, such as feasts for funerals. To limit such obligations, a trader might marry a woman from a distant place. For example, William Macdonald first married Alice Male, and second, Marota, both from Santa Isabel where he traded sometimes in the *Sea Ghost*.[114]

Occasionally clan interests clashed with the trader's, but usually the trader lost. Peter Pratt, after some resistance from his future in-laws, was permitted to marry Simaema. Some years later and shortly after the murder of his assistant at Nuza Zonga, Pratt wished to leave the island. His wife's relatives persuaded him to use their land at Sosolo, at Munda Point on New Georgia, as a trading base. Meanwhile another trader and fierce rival, Kelly, who also had a Roviana wife, Lelenduri, was trying to establish his own station nearby. As Kelly's mother-in-law was a Munda woman, he had an excellent means of spreading the opinion that Pratt was trying to alienate the land to himself. The owners did not want this because it could mean strangers moving in who would be less receptive to their demands and because the land was to remain with the clan of the Pratts' children. The local people, led by Kelly's great friend Hingava, won the land back by using the Europeans' law and court against Pratt.[115]

A few traders, such as "Jack" Cooper at Marau in the mid-eighties, formed polygamous unions with two or three women.[116] To the white visitor, appearances were preserved by calling the women "laundress, cook, gardener or house-maid" and these roles were certainly part of the duties involved.[117] Even with two or three women and attendent obligations, the trader benefited substantially from such relationships. The costs of supporting a Solomon Islands woman were small—few clothes, no necessity for trips south, and little real need to have children educated overseas since in most societies they inherited rights to land use through the mother and formal education was by no means universal in Western countries. If the trader tired of the woman, there seemed to be little difficulty in most cases in obtaining a divorce—the trader simply sent the woman back to her home, probably with gifts for her family by way of compensation for her labor. In a domestic crisis, when an argument developed "the black wife does not mind if the trader takes a stick to her."[118] "Minding," and being able to do something about it, was a dilemma the Melanesian wife of the trader shared with her sisters in the islands and in the traders' homelands of the time. Nonetheless, there were some limits to gross maltreatment. With a free woman and even with a slave, when her economic value created a vested interest, her generative or proprietorial clan might retaliate. William Fraser, a trader at Aola in the late 1890s, went berserk while suffering from *delirium tremens*, and assaulted his woman with an axe, severely wounding her. So great was the public outrage, that he was forced to leave the islands.[119]

Many traders grew genuinely attached to their families. When Charles Olsen died in 1897, his fellow traders testified to the truth of his unwitnessed will, which left all his possessions at Santa Ana to his wife, Kapunakai, and her three children by a previous marriage.[120] The fierce

attachment of one old trader, Aubrey Griffiths, to his wife surprised a
visitor, Count Rudolf Festetics von Tolna, who thought the woman
ugly, diseased, and unfaithful. The trader's concern for the welfare of
his family was no ephemeral emotion. After his wife, Margaret, bore
him a son, Griffiths applied to the High Commission in Fiji to have the
birth registered. Before his death Margaret's father, Alexander Ferguson, had arranged for a missionary, George Brown of New Ireland, to
care for her young brother.[121] Even Woodhouse, old and ailing in 1896,
thought more of his ten-year-old part–Ontong Java daughter's future
than his own comfort when he sent her south for schooling.[122]

The trader's domestic arrangement had a wider significance than
simply the relationship it embodied with the local community. Most
traders induced their wives to wear more clothing than the average
Solomon Islander, just as they did their children, as the photographs of
the Atkinson, Wheatley, and Pratt families illustrate (Photos 4–7).
Although in Wheatley's and Pratt's cases the families may well have
dressed for the occasion, it was apparent by this very emphasis that
clothes were a status marker for Europeans. Employees on a trader's
station, in places untouched by missionaries, soon adopted the type of
clothing the trader wore. The photograph of Peter Pratt trading in the
early 1890s well illustrates the progression. Pratt's offsiders are wearing
clothes like his, while one of the villagers has a shirt on and his friends
are in traditional garb (Photo 3). Clothing appears to be one of the
items the trader is trying to barter for copra. Trader's households would
have employed most of the hard and soft wares that Europeans were
used to at home. Occupants of the trader's station who moved in and
out of local villages could provide a continuing demonstration of how
various articles of Western manufacture could be used, steadily increasing the range of goods desired by Islanders.

Traders' marriages were a corporeal demonstration of the preprotectorate relationship between Europeans and Solomon Islanders. The
marriages, particularly when children were born, established a special
alliance between the races that was of mutual advantage.

Men in the middle

Despite their attempts to meld the two worlds they knew, the traders
found that the necessary compromises created their own stresses and
inconsistencies. For them, ambivalence was the most characteristic attitude. Because many of them had left their homelands to escape real or
imagined public or personal disgrace, the islands were both places of
refuge and of banishment. The traders openly defied European conventions when they married or lived with one or more local women, yet
wished, not always realistically, to maintain their identity with European culture as they understood it. Visiting Europeans tended to

Photo 4. Pierre Pratt (wearing hat) among villagers at New Georgia, c. 1895. *(Ribbe 1903)*

Photo 5. Mrs. Charles Atkinson, in dress, New Georgia, c. 1895. *(Ribbe 1903)*

Photo 6. Norman Wheatley, wife, and family, c. 1908. *(Burnett 1911)*

Photo 7. Wheatley's children, c. 1908. *(Burnett 1911)*

deplore their way of life. Ribbe condemned the traders' tendency to "go native," observing that they lived like this

> because the concept of better things that civilization offers has been lost to them. In their language they use many island expressions, even among people who do not understand them; "white man's potatoes" for European potatoes and "white man's grog" for gin are expressions used by the traders everywhere.[123]

William Macdonald used to send to Sydney for the latest in women's fashions, including undergarments and high-heeled shoes, for his Isabel wife on Munia, despite the fact that she sensibly discarded them for a *kaliko* and bare feet after a day or two.[124]

The way the traders behaved when confronted with their own society reveals the same contradictions. After years of frugal existence with a Solomon Islander wife the trader who had saved a few hundred pounds would go on a spree of lavish living in Sydney or even Europe for a few months.[125] At such times the traders could enjoy a brief period of relative importance, of bought power among their own people which their often precarious position in the Solomons rarely, if ever, offered. Yet such excursions brought home to them unpalatable truths. In time, and almost unwillingly, the traders gradually became more and more attached to the piece of land where they lived, their Solomon Islander families, and the people they knew there. Each trip "home" highlighted the growth of this bond and their deepening feelings of alienation from all that they had once known well. Some, when confronted with their former way of life, must have experienced reverse culture shock—like Mouton, a trader from the Bismarck Archipelago, when he reached Sydney:

> I will never forget that day, when I went on shore the noise and the traffic affected me very much, and I was quite useless in the street, this lasted only a few days then I got my nerves quietened and in time I was o.k. the only thing I could not get out of my imagination is that I had the impression that everybody was looking at me, I know it was only imagination but there it was and it made me very miserable.[126]

Life in the islands increased the traders' feelings of ambivalence toward their own society, but the contradictions did not stop there. Most seem to have had a love-hate relationship with Solomon Islanders and their culture, verging at times on a kind of moral schizophrenia. Wheatley had been sufficiently close to the people to be able to hire assassins to murder a rival trader. He understood the New Georgia people to such a degree that their chiefs came to him for advice. He contracted at least two marriages to New Georgia women and virtually established a dynasty in the western Solomons. Yet in his will the only Islanders he considered were his Roviana wife, Sambe Vindu, and his children.[127] The residue was to go to his own race since the will stipulated that the money, called the Norman Wheatley Fund, be set aside for a hospital, the Norman Wheatley Sanatorium, "for white men and white women."[128]

His neighbor, Pratt, married by custom and a Roman Catholic priest to Simaema of Vonavona, fathered two sons and four daughters. In his best years he gave his wife a "European education," taught her to speak good English, and to run the house well.[129] He took her to Sydney, where their young children received some schooling. But later Pratt was to divorce her, leave his children in the Solomons, sell up his station and vessel, and go to Australia by himself. His young daughters came to the notice of the resident commissioner, who put them under the care of the Reverend John Goldie.[130] Some years later when Pratt tried to see them in Sydney, Goldie, alert for moral inconsistencies, condemned his "conduct in leaving three helpless girls to be dragged up in dirt, disease and sin in the filthy native village of Rubiana [Roviana]."[131]

THE TRADER'S LOT was a far remove from both romantic and anthropological fantasy, being neither a life of adventure, ease, and unbridled sexuality nor one of rapacious looting of the products of the unfortunate "natives." At all times before the establishment of a permanent government presence, and often beyond, a situation of inequality existed between traders and Solomon Islanders, skewed strongly in the latter's favor, defining their wider social and economic relationships.

Besides being in the control of the Melanesians for both life and livelihood, the traders were vulnerable on other points. The incessant competition among them was all the more fierce for its trickery and sporadic violence. A drop in prices for tropical products in the metropolitan center always meant they bore most of the loss. They were at the mercy of the Sydney merchants who expected high returns on the capital they provided to start them off in business. Few traders made much money and when they did accumulate a substantial sum they usually frittered it away on a spending spree in Sydney. In part, this was a form of compensation for their psychological vulnerability. The resident traders bestrode two cultures, neither of which they could truly claim as their own. White they might be and many of them educated too, but they had fled their own society because of some real or fancied failure. Coming to the islands as adult men, they could not shake off all the values of their own people. They could never live completely like Solomon Islanders or adopt the culture; they remained apart, though familiar. The familiarity attained through several years of living among and with Solomon Islanders gave the traders a deep understanding of the customs and social organization of particular communities. Because it was integral to their livelihood, the traders extended and created the markets for

Western goods among Solomon Islanders, becoming specialists in the needs and greeds of their customers. The traders had a wide knowledge of both Solomon Islanders and their islands, rivalled among their white contemporaries only by a couple of missionaries of the Melanesian Mission.

The traders were always mediators between the goods of the West and Solomon Islanders, and they were sometimes called upon to mediate between the forces of the two societies. When they did, their special knowledge momentarily gave them a very powerful role because visiting Europeans, like the naval captains, were ignorant of Solomon Islanders and their ways. As such visitors were extremely rare and transient until the turn of the century, the trader remained virtually powerless—the thrall of many masters.

CHAPTER 4

The attractions of trade
(c. 1860–1900)

Great is the greed of our eyes for the valuables from abroad
which came with disaster.

Raymond Firth, *We, the Tikopia*

I had made up my mind at the beginning to go with the
bishop [to New Zealand] for this reason: I wanted to go
myself to the real source of things, and get for myself an axe
and a knife, and fish hooks and calico, and plenty of other
such things . . . . I did not go for any other reason but only
because I had seen lots of these things on the ship, and
wanted to go and get plenty for myself.

George Sarawia, *They Came to My Island*

To the Solomon Islanders the trader's ship carried much more than
simply material goods: it was a floating island of opportunities. On
board were the means by which the people could reduce the labor spent
on subsistence and become stronger opponents of their enemies. For
those who could manipulate the supply of the new goods there was the
promise of power greater perhaps than any Melanesian had held in precontact society. To many, the price they paid seemed insignificant—a
few weeks a year cutting copra or catching turtles. But some, especially
in the eastern Solomons, were disadvantaged because their natural
resources were scant or because they were remote from direct contact
with traders. So anxious were many of these for the new goods that they
traded years of their labor, the only commodity they had that the white
man wanted.

Although the "valuables from abroad" were accepted because they
were perceived as beneficial, they also inevitably created a dependence
among Solomon Islanders on the outside world and its economy. Developments and readjustments within the society and polity were necessary
to accommodate and to exploit the new economic forces. Solomon
Islanders not only used previously untapped natural resources to obtain

the trade, but they also attempted to produce substitutes for some of the imported goods as their need for them increased.

The trading relationship: The Melanesians

With the advent of the resident trader, the Solomon Islander's role in overseas trade was not simply as producer. If a trader could not draw enough produce from around his station to fill a ship, he was obliged to travel to more distant settlements. Here and there were to be found men who had some prior experience of Europeans—as ship's crew, on overseas plantations, or, occasionally, through mission activity—as well as a knowledge of the jargon "pidgin-English." Some of those who became agents were big-men in their own right, but others were go-betweens for big-men unfamiliar with Europeans. The trader gave such men an advance of trade valued at 10 shillings, or more with reliable agents, and expected them to have the copra and other produce ready to load on his next visit.[1] These local traders received part of the goods as their share of the profits. From the 1870s they were heavily involved in operations, and by 1881 were organizing virtually all the trade at the production, collection, and exchange stages.[2]

Although both the foreign and the local traders were always trying to maximize their own profits, the relationship between them was one of interdependence. A fairly high standard of reciprocal trust seems to have prevailed, rather like that between partners in the traditional Melanesian trading networks. As Woodford observed,

> Taking everything into consideration the natives are fairly honourable in keeping their engagements. Traders have told me that natives have faithfully handed over the amount of produce owing sometimes months and months after the trade advanced was gone and perhaps after they had accepted trade from another white trader. I consider that it speaks well for the natives that the system has been able to exist at all.[3]

Doubtless, traders could get the best end of the bargain on occasion—when, say, the indigenous trader demanded articles that were a new fad and relatively cheap, such as the small bells that the Marau women favored at one time.[4] But a trader who consistently bartered inferior articles would soon be eclipsed by rivals. The Solomon Islander traders were in a strong position since they were always working on the white trader's capital. Even when they got into debt the Europeans were usually prepared to advance more credit in the hope of recovering their original outlay as well as maintaining access to produce.[5] "Billy" Pope, a Guadalcanal-based trader, extended credit to his agent Tarohoasi at Heuru, San Cristobal, of nearly a ton of copra, worth about £10 in Sydney. In the Russells, "Cookie" owed Swartz 20,000 coconuts or £30 market value.[6] But this was modest in comparison to Gorai's operations in the Shortlands. Gorai found it easy to play off one trader against another because of the number visiting his area, particularly after 1884 when the Germans were extending their New Guinea protectorate to include Bougainville, Choiseul, Santa Isabel, the Shortland Islands, and Ontong Java. He could choose between the traders from German New Guinea, the resident traders on Fauro, the Macdonalds, and later Tindal on Faisi (Figure 8) or the colonial traders from the non-German areas of the Solomons. In 1886 his financial position was made up of advances in trade goods to the extent of 30,000 coconuts from Sam Craig, 30,000 from Woodhouse, and 60,000 from Macdonald. This amounted to about 20 tons of copra or £200 at Syndey prices.[7] Gorai could operate like this because he dominated the traders' access to produce. He could see to it that copra was imported from south Bougainville to the Shortlands, could organize Bougainville labor to cut copra on Magusaiai and adjacent islands, and could make a trader's trip to southern Bougainville a success by sending one of his sons or nephews to assist in the negotiations.[8]

As in Gorai's case, the Solomon Islander factor could usually get very favorable trading conditions because several independent traders were clamoring for produce. Increased competition in the 1880s and 1890s also meant that consumers were paying less for their goods, by mean of the simple mechanism of underfilling a "standard" string of coconuts, described earlier.[9]

The amount of labor required to produce a sample year's set of goods (see Table 2) was about 80 days out of 365, which meant that although a quarter of any one year was devoted to fulfilling the new economic demands, a great deal of time was still left for traditional activities. At this period commercial production was, for the Solomon Islanders, just a sideline done by the family, a profitable investment of time to get goods that made the pursuit of traditional activities by the men easier and less demanding of heavy labor.[10] In cases where producers were concerned with satisfying their own individual or family wants, rather than wider, politically dictated urgencies, Solomon Islander traders could maintain a large measure of control in their relationships with Europeans.

Many aspects of the relationship between foreign and indigenous traders were similar to those existing between partners in traditional Melanesian societies. The mutual interdependence was one, although the Solomon Islanders had a distinct advantage since in most places they could choose from a number of traders. This meant "their" trader had to give them a good business deal. Just as Wickham, Pratt, and Wheatley protected and assisted their contacts, so too did the local traders sometimes warn their foreign partners of plots against their lives.[11]

TABLE 2
Cost of trade goods, 1878–1893

	Value £ s. d.			Coconuts	Man days[a]
1878[b]					
1 Snider	3	0	0	6,000	50.00
1 musket	1	0	0	2,000	16.60
25 sticks of tobacco (1 lb.)		6	0	600	5.00
15 pipes (quality unspecified)		1	0	100	0.80
1 flask of gunpowder		2	0	200	1.60
1 box caps		1	0	100	0.80
1 ring (from Roviana)		1	6	150	1.25
1 half-axe		4	0	400	1.25
Total	4	15	6	9,550	77.30
1885[b]					
1 Snider	3	0	0	6,000	50.00
50 cartridges		10	0	1,000	8.30
1 bolt calico		10	0	1,000	8.30
1 shingling hatchet		4	0	400	1.25
1 lb. beads		2	0	200	1.60
1 lb. tobacco		2	0	300	1.60
1 fantail hatchet		1	0	100	0.80
1 fathom calico		1	0	100	0.80
1 sheath knife		1	0	100	0.80
1 half-axe		4	0	400	1.25
Total	4	15	0	9,500	74.70
1893[c]					
1 rifle (Winchester?) and ammunition	5	0	0	10,000	83.300
15 clay pipes		3	0	150	1.250
2 pieces of tobacco			1/2	10	0.083
1 long knife			6	50	0.400
1 large knife		1	0	100	0.800
1 box wax matches			5	10	0.083
1 Jew's harp			1 1/2	30	0.250
1 hatchet		1	0	100	0.800
1 fathom calico			7	100	0.800
Total	5	6	8	10,550	87.766

SOURCES: BSI-LTR: Conveyance of 8 July 1878, file 205–002–1, pt. 3 application 156/70, LR 41 Bara Island, and Conveyance of 13 Feb. 1885, Ozama, LS, LR 117, Red Book 112, f.6; Ribbe 1903, 95; Frazer 1973, 76–77.

NOTES: Ribbe is the only one of these sources that lists goods, value, and price in coconuts. His rate of 100 coconuts to 1 shilling was used to calculate the number of coconuts equivalent to the value of the trade goods in 1878 and 1885. However, in real terms, goods were probably more expensive for the Solomon Islanders in 1878.
[a] The man-day is defined by Frazer as an 8-hour working day for male labor processing coconuts into copra.
[b] The lists of trade goods and their value for 1878 and 1885 are given as goods paid for land in the Land Titles Records.
[c] The data for 1893, in prices and coconuts, are taken from Ribbe.

When the trader came to a village he received hospitality from his business associate, a courtesy that was reciprocated.[12] In some cases the relationships were cemented, as in traditional society, by the exchange of women on a casual basis or in marriage—except, of course, that it was one-way. As marriages produced offspring the relationships developed further, and often children, living on their mother's land, became involved in the indigenous culture.[13]

The Solomon Islanders, familiar as they were with trading before European contact, had not far to seek in their repertoire of cultural responses to find ways of manipulating the traders to their own benefit. There was always a place for the "foreign" trader in their society. The Europeans were simply a new "tribe" who offered an array of trade goods technically superior to most of the indigenous counterparts. For the purposes of trading, both parties were well matched, with any advantage usually to the Melanesian.

The penetration of Western goods

Throughout the 1860s and 1870s many areas that had no contact with whalers were being visited by traders. A typical run by a vessel was from Santa Ana to Uki, Aola (Guadalcanal), Roviana, and back (Figures 1, 3, and 7). Another circuit might take in Santa Isabel, Vella Lavella, Choiseul, and Nggela (Florida Islands).[14] Before, what little trade was received by areas outside the whaler ports had been filtered through the hands of intermediaries. During these decades, in such previously uncontacted areas, there was still a great demand for the basic metal commodities—axes and tomahawks. For example, in 1877, at Nggela, which had been well off the whalers' run, copra, coconuts, and vegetables were traded to *Witch of the Wave* for axes, tomahawks, and sticks of twist tobacco.[15]

This pattern might have been expected to continue, but to come much later, if at all, in commercially unproductive areas that were not frequented by traders, such as Malaita, southern Guadalcanal, Santa Cruz, Rennell and Bellona, southeastern San Cristobal, and much of Choiseul and Santa Isabel. However, in the 1870s the colonial labor trade brought an abundance of metal tools and utensils, guns, tobacco, and other trade items. Now those beyond the traders' ambit had the chance to possess the products of Western technology and to lessen their own labors. Equally important for some groups, such as the people of Choiseul and Isabel, was the opportunity they now had to redress the balance of power held by their more affluent and better-armed neighbors. The "beach payments" to the passage masters, who acted as intermediaries in the dealings between the recruiter and the recruit, and to the relatives of recruits anticipated the goods that they eventually brought home.[16]

Had it not been for the hunger for such goods among the islands too poor to attract the traders, the number of recruits to the colonies would have been substantially lower. Where alternative means to the possession of trade goods were available, the recruiter had a difficult task filling his ship. This was the case in the New Georgia Islands, Nggela, northwestern San Cristobal, parts of northern Guadalcanal, and, excluding imported labor from southern Bougainville, the Shortland Islands. Other areas like Savo and Uki, which had provided recruits in the early 1870s, were unresponsive to the appeals of the recruiter a decade later as regular contact with traders became established.[17]

By the 1880s most of the coastal people of the Solomon Islands had discarded stone and shell implements in favor of metal ones that were more effective. In 1887 Woodford found in the northeast of Guadalcanal that stone adze heads were regarded as antiques. He did manage to get a few excavated from the dirt floors of village houses, but had met the same problem in the Shortlands as Guppy had earlier there and on San Cristobal.[18] In the early 1890s it was virtually impossible to get any stone tools in the New Georgia Islands.[19] Stone adzes were still used in the mountains of Bougainville, the San Cristobal bush, and presumably the more isolated mountain areas of Malaita.[20]

Western trade and Solomon Islands economies

In trading, the coastal people still wanted metal tools, but the metal's very durability eventually modified and diminished the demand. In many places indigenous preference forced the trader to become a supplier of traditional valuables in order to survive commercially. Depending on an area's productivity, this change took anywhere from about ten up to twenty years.[21] Traders probably became involved after seeing their Solomon Islander crews trading in valuables at various islands where they could "make a good deal more . . . by private barter . . . than in wages."[22] To obtain the valuables the trader had often to become an intermediary in the traditional trade network. At Nggela in 1887 the people wanted dog teeth from the trader "Jack" Cooper of Marau, in return for their copra. They would give 50 coconuts for 1 eye tooth of a dog. The Uki people and the bush dwellers of San Cristobal had supplies of dog teeth, but were reluctant to part with them unless they could obtain the valuables they most prized, porpoise teeth. For 2 porpoise teeth they would give 1 dog tooth. The trader having told him that at Hada, Mwata, and Makira Harbour porpoise teeth were available in large numbers after the yearly porpoise hunts, Cooper went to Makira

Harbour, now well past its prosperous whaling days, where the people craved tobacco. For 1 stick of twist tobacco he exchanged 4 porpoise teeth that at Uki brought him 2 dog teeth and were then traded to the Nggela people for 100 coconuts.[23] Although more effort was involved, most traders dealt in traditional valuables as part of their operations because it was extremely profitable. In Cooper's case, he would have paid out about 70 sticks of tobacco worth 5s. 4d., to buy 1 ton of coconuts that would earn him £7 to £8, exclusive of overhead.

The increasing involvement of traders in the exchange of valuables may have lessened the profit to their own crew, who traded as a sideline, but in some cases the competition lowered the price to the consumer. The demand for valuables for distant markets meant that the bush people, in a few places at least, had a chance to get some of the traders' goods directly and not through profiteering coastal intermediaries. The bush people of the Bauro area near Wanione Bay, for example, brought down dog teeth to trade with Hamilton Wright in 1896.[24] Sometimes, too, the traders expanded the circulation of the indigenous product beyond precontact limits. Tortoiseshell was much desired by the Tanna people of Vanuatu. Robert Towns' traders, who needed pigs from the Tannese to trade with the Santo people in return for sandalwood, called at the Solomons to obtain tortoiseshell as early as 1859.[25] Later, in the 1890s, traders found that the red shell valuables manufactured at Langalanga were identical to those used at Sudest (Tagula) in New Guinea. The Melanesian there, saturated with the trade goods offered by the gold-miners, showed a preference for traditional forms of wealth; Nielsen and others bought the Langalanga valuables from the Nggela people for the miners, who used them to barter for gold. This increased demand led to a rise in the price by 1896.[26] The southeastern Solomon Islanders continued their demand for gold-lipped pearlshell introduced by the whalers. Stephens at Uki bought copra from Ulawa with these pearlshells, which had to be imported or purchased from the few deep-sea divers at work at Nggela and the Manning Strait.[27]

In Roviana, the mint of shell valuables for much of New Georgia, the people profited from the traders even though the immediate Roviana Lagoon area itself did not produce an abundance of copra and tortoiseshell (Figure 7).[28] Until the end of the nineteenth century they continued and, with the help of iron tools, expanded the manufacture of the clamshell rings that were treasured as far away as Santa Isabel, Choiseul, the Shortland Islands, and south Bougainville.[29] To obtain their copra and tortoiseshell, the traders often had to provide these rings along with articles of Western manufacture, thus guaranteeing an abundance of goods for the Roviana people. It was no wonder that Roviana chiefs had so many axes, rifles, and whaleboats or that they had to maintain a regular supply of slaves to keep the wheels of Roviana's commerce turning. The demand for the Roviana rings was constant because they were frequently used to adorn the skull houses of the ancestors as well as to consolidate the alliances of the living.[30] The traders, in order to be less dependent on those who made the valuables, introduced substitutes—white porcelain armlets—but the New Georgians spurned the ersatz product, although some of their island neighbors accepted it, perhaps because its price was lower than that of the genuine article.[31]

Substitutes such as these could induce inflation within Solomon Islands societies, just as added demand could raise prices, but this was sometimes offset by increased supply. For example, in exchanges between Europeans and Solomon Islanders, valuables such as dog and porpoise teeth kept a stable value from the 1880s to the 1920s at around 2 dog teeth or 5 porpoise teeth for 1 shilling, although there was some variation with area, say between Nggela and San Cristobal.[32] This stability seems to have been an outcome of two counterbalancing factors. First, traders (and later labor recruiters for the Solomons plantations) expanded both the geographical and social circulation of these products. The valuables became available in some areas where before contact they had been a rarity. Moreover, an ordinary villager, not just a big-man who earned part of his prestige from alliances and warfare, could trade copra or other products and obtain valuables that had been virtually unavailable through exchanges before the white traders appeared. Secondly, by importing them from outside the Solomons, traders provided greater quantities of these items than the Islanders produced. In the 1890s, for example, as well as bringing in live dogs from Sydney as did other traders, Svensen seems to have been importing vast quantities of their teeth. By the 1900s, dog teeth were coming from London and Sydney fishermen were supplying porpoise teeth for the Solomon Island trade.[33]

Inflation could not be controlled when demand alone increased. The white traders could find no acceptable substitute for, or additional supply of, the type of shell valuables made at Langalanga.[34] Already inflated by the Papua gold-miners' demand in the 1890s, shell valuables (fine, red) went steadily from between 1s. and 1s. 6d. a fathom in 1896 to £1 a fathom in the 1920s, where it remained until World War II.[35]

The overall effect of such inflation in the last decades of the nineteenth century and the early twentieth century may have been to further increase the wealth and power of those big-men who could still achieve eminence from traditional activities, especially in coastal areas.[36] Coast people with access to the new essentials and the increasingly available valuables such as dog teeth were able to use their wealth to obtain women for marriage as well as pigs from inland groups. Using a portion of the traded goods, these groups in turn drew on more distant communities for women and pigs, not being able to pay the coast group's inflated prices. In this manner, inflation radiated out from the coast through intermediate groups right into the central bush communities.

On Guadalcanal, for example, the bush people near Tatuve in the 1890s would have obtained their metal tomahawks only through trading their pigs and women with the coast people, as none of their young men had yet been overseas.[37] Even when commodities such as vegetables were able to be produced more quickly than pigs or women, the pattern was similar. The people of Santa Ana and Santa Catalina, as well as their San Cristobal coastal neighbors at Star Harbour and Hunarite, controlled the inflow of iron goods and tobacco from traders and labor vessels (Figure 3). Not only were these people able to obtain vast quantities of vegetables and pigs from the people of inland Kahua and eastern Bauro to supply the labor vessels and their own increased ceremonial feasting, but also they were able to draw on the bush people's reserves of precious shell valuables.[38]

Similarly, Uki (Uki ni Masi) from the late 1860s came to be a trading and victualling center for Europeans. This gave the Uki people an added advantage in trading in human beings with the relatively poor Bauro hinterland of San Cristobal. Many of the Uki women, like their counterparts in the Shortlands, were unwilling to reproduce, since bringing up a child from birth entailed heavy physical labor. When pregnant they often procured abortions, preferring to import an older child from the people of the San Cristobal bush.[39]

Had this continued, those farthest from the coast would have ended up with depleted human, animal, and accumulated productive resources. They would have been prey to communities stronger in numbers, arms, and wealth, as occurred among groups inland from the prosperous coastal communities around Aola and Rere in northwest Guadalcanal in the 1880s. In such areas, where direct trade with Europeans was common, there was a pull toward the coast. Although tribal fighting in this period made any large-scale migration difficult, refugees from weakened communities often fled their bush villages and joined stronger coastal communities where they had some relatives.[40]

Coastal areas supplied the first of some 30,000 Solomon Islanders who went to Queensland, Fiji, Samoa, and New Caledonia between about 1870 and 1910 as laborers. Often chiefs or big-men profited extensively from this trade. In the Shortlands Mule Kopa obtained recruits from Bougainville and even distant Buka through the relationships he had with their big-men. In 1882, from the captain of the *Sea Breeze*, he received for one man 1 musket, 1 big axe, 4 half-axes, 1 tomahawk, 1 long knife, 2 handfuls of beads, 4 pieces of cloth, 4 tins of caps (for muskets), 40 sticks of twist tobacco (3 lb.), 3 fishing lines, and 100 fish hooks. From his store of goods Mule Kopa paid the Bougainville source 1 big axe, 1 tomahawk, 4 necklaces, 10 iron hoops, and 3 strings of beads, which left him quite considerable profit.[41] The Bougainville people living a few miles inland on the great coastal plain worked on entirely the same business principle in dealing with the bush people of the interior. They bartered to their inland neighbors 1 metal axe for 300–400 coconuts and then on the beach would give 100 coconuts for 1 identical axe.[42]

This process was the same for other forms of precontact wealth. Once a coastal population had a reserve of trade goods and was able to draw on more inaccessible groups for additional women, pigs, and other valuables, the imbalance so caused encouraged the inland groups to offer their young men for labor recruiting. Since it was difficult for these men to get wives because of the inflated bride-price, the group could well afford the let some go overseas. Access to labor vessels was allowed by coast dwellers who, like Mule Kopa or Kwaisulia of Ada-gege, Malaita, by consent or coercion, took a toll of goods from the recruits.[43] Their profits were even greater, since the passage master reaped rewards and a reputation from being the go-between for the naive bush recruit and the labor recruiter. Although some recruits still came from coastal areas in the 1890s, the majority were from inland districts. The coast people were now peripheral to the Western world economy while the bush people produced the labor it needed at no opportunity cost to that economy or to its coastal intermediaries.[44]

But the cost to the laborers for access to Western goods was high. Aside from all the social and personal cost—upheaval from home, the risks of ill treatment, and perhaps illness or death overseas—the recruits of the eastern Solomons were getting far less for their labor than their western and central Solomons neighbors who sold produce to the traders. For three years of labor new recruits to Queensland earned £18 while those to Fiji got £9. To earn an equivalent amount through trade, the maximum time the producer would have to work would be one year in the former case or six months in the latter. In other words, the laborer worked three to six times as hard for trade goods as did his producer neighbor.[45] Western goods were now accessible to all, but half the Solomons was now "rich" and the other half "poor" by comparison, and the poorest of these were the bush people of the eastern islands and Choiseul.

Western trade and Solomon Islands polities

The general impact of foreign trade was to generate centripetal forces within Solomon Islands societies that pivoted on prosperous coastal trading settlements.[46] This process was further intensified by the nature of the trade goods offered by the Europeans. Iron axes had made a tre-

mendous difference to the New Georgians' performance as headhunters
even in whaling days. When guns were added to their arsenal such
groups became more formidable, especially as Snider breech loaders,
Martini-Henry rifles, and the occasional Winchester rifle began by the
1880s to supersede the inferior single-shot muskets.[47] Naturally, men
used these new weapons in pursuit of traditional goals, but they were to
find that the socioeconomic relationships necessary to obtain firearms
and other trade goods would alter, in part, the scope of those goals.

Maghratulo of Vella Lavella (Figure 9) had gradually gained power
in the eighties by giving feasts and organizing expeditions for head-
hunting and to get tortoiseshell to sell to the traders. He won the support of the leaders of major clans in the Mbilua district where his own
clan, the Lingi Lingi, had no land and obtained from the Sikuni clan
usufructory privileges over the unoccupied islets of Ozama and Liapari.
At Liapari his followers and slaves planted coconuts; Ozama (adjacent
to the present village—Figure 9) he permitted traders to use as an
anchorage. In turn, by acting as middleman to the traders, he assisted
the clan leaders who had helped him.

As well as trading, Maghratulo sold the islet of Ozama to John Macdonald and Jesse Davis. The real owners of the land complied because
they knew this would keep the traders near at hand and they had
obtained guns and trade goods in the initial transaction. Maghratulo
built up the people's arms supply through his trading contacts, but was
opposed to fighting among groups on Vella Lavella itself and directed
raiding outside his island, a policy that allowed copra growing and
trading to proceed relatively undisturbed there. In and beyond the Mbilua area, Maghratulo gained a reputation as a leader of his people
because of his prominence in trading. Traders preferred to deal with
him because he was used to the ways of the whites and a good speaker of
Pijin.[48]

Maghratulo died in 1894, before the colonial government was established.[49] In his lifetime he was able to use the new means offered by the
relationship he had with traders to gain old and enlarged ends, for he
"not only maintained a trading monopoly but he used the profits from it
to finance parties to raid areas such as Santa Isabel and Choiseul to
obtain heads."[50]

Across the Gizo Strait at Roviana (Figure 7), Hingava, chief of Sisieta
(Munda), was also extending his political power (Photo 8). He had
grown to manhood at a time when traders wanted to establish stations
at Roviana. Agents of Kelly, Williams and Woodhouse, as well as Peter
Pratt, Wickham, and Wheatley all operated under the protection of
Hingava or his friends the neighboring chiefs.[51] He had good reasons for
encouraging the traders. As chief he was responsible for organizing
head-hunting expeditions and the associated rituals.[52] Heads for the

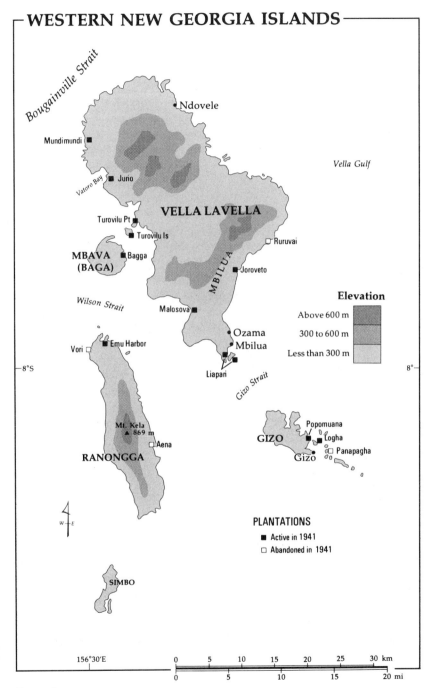

Figure 9

Photo 8. Hingava of Sisieta, New Georgia. Note
mbakia, the large pendant around his neck. *(Edge-
Partington 1907)*

ancestors, slaves for the village, and tortoiseshell for the traders were
the dividends from this investment of time and resources. The better
armed and prepared the expedition, the greater the chance of success.
With the traders at hand, Hingava and his chiefly allies had access to
iron axe-heads which, on long handles, were the perfect weapon for
head-hunting.[53] Firearms were also of great value in surprise attacks on
sleeping villagers. The traders around Roviana had little compunction
about selling guns and ammunition because, by the late 1880s, these
goods were virtually the only foreign items that could get them payable
quantities of copra, tortoiseshell, bêche-de-mer, and other products.[54]

When Peter Pratt's employee, William Dabelle, was murdered at
Nuza Zonga in 1889, Hingava and his adviser-priest Wangi may well
have been implicated, at least in harboring the killers.[55] However, since
over the years Hingava had presented himself to naval captains as the
cooperative chief of the whole Roviana area, his home and canoe house
were spared when Captain Davis of the *Royalist* shelled all the Munda
and Roviana villages in 1891.[56] Throughout the nineties Hingava con-

tinued to give the appearance of assisting the navy, going with them and
C. M. Woodford, the first acting resident commissioner, to Rendova in
1896 to find the killers of Gibbons, a trader. The following year, with
Wangi and Gemu, his own nephew and later successor, Hingava again
aided the colonial government in the same investigation, as did Gemu
when he accompanied Woodford to Ranongga and Vella Lavella in
search of the killers of Pratt's Melanesian crewman. Hingava's association with Europeans in authority brought him kudos in the eyes of his
own people, particularly when he won the first ever land court hearing
between a Solomon Islander and a European, in this case Peter Pratt.
Hingava so cleverly acted the role of assistant to Her Majesty's government that the navy, Woodford,[57] and even some visiting missionaries
regarded him as "paramount chief."[58] Perhaps traders like Wickham
and Wheatley who lived near Hingava knew otherwise, but as he was
their protector it was to their advantage to have Hingava's importance
magnified. A disgruntled Peter Pratt certainly knew otherwise, even if
he did somewhat overstate the fact when he said, "Hingava has no
power whatever except individually in among his own small tribe."[59] In
truth the chiefs of Simbo and New Georgia were a fellowship of equals;
among themselves they gave mutual aid and respected one another's
wishes.[60] Hingava could ask chiefs in other districts for men and canoes
to accompany his own on head-hunting raids to Choiseul and Santa Isabel. On one raid to Mbambatana (Choiseul), in about 1894, Hingava
mustered 500 men and twenty-two war canoes from his own and
another chief's resources. With the help of traders, he was able also to
find two English-built boats, 300–400 rifles, and 5000 rounds of ammunition for the expedition.[61]

By the time the protectorate government had suppressed head-hunting in the late nineties, Hingava was in his declining years and lost little
of his great personal prestige because of peace.[62] He had spurned the
missionaries partly because he had been warned against them by some
of the early traders who feared a check to their own activities. More
important, in Hingava's heyday no advantage was to be gained by association with the missions.[63]

Until 1880 the only missionary body active in the Solomons, the
Anglican Melanesian Mission, could record little success although it had
contacted some Islanders as early as the 1850s. The strategy of taking
Melanesian youths as "scholars" to New Zealand for short periods, and
later to Norfolk Island for longer stays, had not been a success. Most
came because they wanted trade goods or simply for adventure. Once
home, isolated from any mission support other than occasional brief
visits by itinerating clergy after the 1860s, these young people quickly
returned to the usages of their own culture and forgot most of the little
they had learned of Christianity. The various Solomons societies, confi-

dent in their own ways, could see little use for the new teaching. But these conditions would change by the end of the century, just as the missionaries' stays became more frequent and extended.

On Santa Isabel, Soga was a leader who used the missionaries and, to a lesser extent, the traders to consolidate his own power base. His father, Bera, with axes and guns obtained from traders and labor recruiters, was able to offer some protection to a scattered and demoralized people whose society had been in upheaval for years because of attacks by the New Georgians as well as internal warfare. In the 1880s, Soga chose to identify himself and his own considerable abilities with the pioneering efforts of the Melanesian Mission and became, through alliances and subsequent shows of force, a peacemaker and a man of great mana. On the one hand he was admired, deferred to, and assisted by the missionaries and other Europeans; on the other, in exploiting the new "way" he was respected by the Isabel people as the first and perhaps the greatest paramount chief of Isabel, who had saved them from virtual extinction.

In Nggela (Florida Islands), the Melanesian Mission worked alongside the trader. Here, too, the leaders realized the value of internal stability as a key to unlocking the traders' chests. Nggela was, in fact, the first embryonic proto-state of the Melanesian Solomons. There the *vaukolu*, an annual council of chiefs, elders, and church leaders was held and, in 1888, drew up laws for the Florida group years before the protectorate was established (see Photo 9). Both traditional and introduced trade expanded on Nggela, with its resident traders and its centrality to Savo, Guadalcanal, Malaita, and Isabel.[64]

The pattern was similar elsewhere, although less common in areas supplying primarily labor. Kwaisulia of Adagege, using goods and firearms obtained from labor recruiters, achieved power over a large area of north Malaita. In the eyes of his followers, this influence brought the recognition of the Royal Navy and later the protectorate government, thereby in turn further validating his authority at home.[65] On San Cristobal too, chiefs like Taki of Wango and Bo'o of Heuru were able to profit from the nexus of diverse Western influence.[66] These San Cristobal men were chiefs of clans in their own right and used customary avenues to power, but they also exploited the opportunities provided by the trident of European penetration—the traders, the missions, and the Royal Navy (and later the protectorate government)—to increase their mana and status in the eyes of their people. As this occurred and they became more and more important, one or other representative of the European trident approached them repeatedly when communication was necessary. In this spiral of reinforcement their influence grew beyond the limits of traditional, precontact polity. A contemporary observer distilled the essence of Taki's power: "He has obtained the dou-

Photo 9. Gathering on Nggela for the *vaukolu* attended by Christian chiefs, clergy, and teachers, and one-tenth of the "respectable" males of each Christian village. The first *vaukolu* was held in 1887. The meeting pictured here was held in the 1890s. *(National Library of Australia)*

ble reputation of being a friend to the white man and of being the most accomplished head-hunter of San Cristobal."[67]

Satisfying new needs, modifying old skills

During much of the pre-protectorate contact era, the demands and ways of the Islanders came to dominate the Solomons trade. This dominance was neither continuous nor unidirectional because initially the Islanders had desperately wanted metal tools. In time, with the greater availability and wider distribution of goods, the people in any one area demonstrated increasing selectivity and were able to pressure the traders into supplying their specific needs in traditional valuables and Western goods. This buyers' advantage of the Islanders was offset as the use of the introduced tobacco spread. Initially, acceptance was fairly slow, but Islanders taught their fellows how to smoke and by the early 1870s the knowledge had followed both ships' and traditional trade routes.[68] From this time until the turn of the century and often beyond, tobacco increasingly became the small change of the Solomons.[69] A trader, labor recruiter, or missionary who needed yams for food could buy ten for a stick of twist tobacco.[70] Tobacco had brought the trader porpoise teeth valuables at Makira Harbour. In the early 1880s 10 coconuts could be obtained for 1 string of white shell valuables or 1 stick of tobacco, since by then equivalence of the introduced and the traditional currency had been established in many areas.[71] For the Solomon Islander, the difficulty with tobacco was that although it was often a medium of exchange and a rough unit of account, after being used for its intended purpose it was gone.

As the liking for tobacco, begun in the sixties, became an addiction in the seventies and eighties the Solomon Islander came to depend more and more on the traders for supplies. This dependence did not long remain total. After labor recruits in Fiji and Queensland saw tobacco growing and learned the rudiments of drying it, they smuggled the seeds home.[72] Some measure of self-sufficiency was reestablished by the development of indigenous tobacco growing in the eighties, although the imported product was (and is) usually preferred because the people remained ignorant of how to cure it properly.[73] Among most Solomon Islanders, tobacco ranked behind only metal axes and firearms in order of popularity. For many, like the bushmen photographed in 1895 at Deep Bay, Malaita, the only foreign items among their entire personal accoutrements were tobacco and pipe (Photo 10).[74] The Solomon Islanders had been quick to find local substitutes for the imported clay pipes that were brittle and easily broken. Some used cone-shaped sea shells with a hollow reed stem attached; others whittled their own pipe bowls from soft local stone. In the eighties the southern Bougainville people actually manufactured their own clay pipes and exported them to the Shortland Islands.[75] Tobacco was a new crop and preparing it a new process quickly adopted by the people who first learned how by observation overseas. The manufacture of pipes was an adaptation of existing technology and materials to a new end, once again done independently.

Just as copra manufacture was learned from resident traders, many Islanders familiar with drying and smoking fish learned the difficult processing of bêche-de-mer. As early as 1845, the Sikaiana people were curing tons of it to offer to the trader Andrew Cheyne. In the Melanesian Solomons what little processing occurred was done by other Pacific Islanders until the 1870s, when a price rise motivated traders to involve the local people.[76]

Turtle hunting to get shell was likewise an extension of an existing practice. Whether or not the turtle "farms" of New Georgia and Ontong Java were indications of a new technique employed to increase production is not known, but there is no record of their existence pre-1890, when turtles were relatively plentiful in the wild.[77] By the 1890s they were very scarce in the New Georgia area, necessitating turtle-

Photo 10. Bushmen at Takataka Bay (Deep Bay), east Malaita, c. 1895. *(Festetics von Tolna 1903)*

hunting (and often head-hunting) raids as far as the Russells, as well as continuing raids to Choiseul and Santa Isabel.

Solomon Islanders skillfully modified other processes in order to obtain the trade goods they desired. Traders found there was a market overseas for the island "curios."[78] Soon the Solomon Islanders realized that most Europeans knew very little of the finer points of the shape, size, and quality of particular artefacts and, using metal drills and adzes, they fell to work to mass produce the most popular articles. The people of the cyclone-susceptible Santa Cruz Islands, who had very little copra to sell, got some trade goods by bartering curios, including models of the graceful *taumako* outrigger canoe. These and bêche-de-mer remained the principal exports of Santa Cruz from the 1880s until the close of the century.[79] At Roviana, craftsmen produced model war canoes and carvings of warriors. As demand increased in some areas so, too, did the price. Naval officers visiting Mono in 1886 found that the clamor for artefacts, particularly imported Bougainville spears, had sent the prices sky-rocketing.[80] Not even the new resident commissioner could winkle a superb Guadalcanal club from its Savo owner for less than £1 sterling.[81]

The Solomon Islanders could adapt existing skills and processes, but because they had no knowledge of metal technology there could be no indigenous substitution for firearms. Demand for these was constant

from the 1870s to the 1890s. Guns were far more sensitive to tropical
conditions than axe or tomahawk, and even when there was a regular
supply, wear and tear along with the frequent ignorance of maintenance procedures kept the demand fairly high.[82] Obviously guns, like
axes, were of great practical value—as weapons or for hunting. When
the Solomon Islanders sought other trade items, they seem to have continued in this preference for utility. An example is their desire for whaleboats, which were ordered by the leaders of wealthier communities,
such as Gorai of the Shortlands, Tomimasi of Fauro, Hingava of
Munda, and Sono of Hada.[83] Under the protectorate, for some it
became ideologically convenient to use whaleboats because (in the New
Georgia Islands, for example) no heads or rituals were required to
launch a foreign boat. Labor could be diverted from canoe making to
copra making, which, being an introduced process, likewise had no
associated ceremonial.[84]

Metal fishhooks were often the first modification in fishing technology, followed by the boats. In the richer copra-producing areas, canvas
was used on these boats and by the 1880s substituted increasingly for
woven leaf sails on the indigenous canoes.[85] Other elements of Western
material culture were used to improve returns from the sea. The Solomon Islanders soon adopted dynamite as used by captains of labor
recruiting ships for in-shore fishing. Because dynamite had to be ignited
and tobacco smoked, matches and even the burning-glass came to
replace the carrying of fire or the slower method of fire making by rub-
bing sticks.[86]

Where the entrepreneurial big-men and chiefs were able to control
most of the trading, they acquired many Western goods not normally
possessed by other members of their communities. The Marau Company at Tavanipupu Island imported a large bell for one big-man who
used it to signal assembly for his people. A neighboring big-man, perhaps recalling sights he had seen in Australia, wanted a lighthouse, but
the traders were not able to oblige.[87] In the Shortland Islands, Gorai
obtained thirty pairs of sash windows for his house, in which he used
kerosene lamps and Western furniture.[88] A room set apart for entertain-
ing foreign visitors contained "a small ship's cannon, a dozen rifles of all
types, a picture of the Queen of England, a variety of wall clocks, some
large mirrors . . . ."[89] Gorai's nephew Ferguson, deeply involved in
trading himself, lived for a time at Sanae (an islet off the north coast of
Alu) in a huge house of local materials, full of Western goods. Hingava
chose to build his dwelling in the European fashion with separate
rooms, perhaps inspired by the houses of Wheatley and Wickham. Taki
of Wango, like Gorai, had a fondness for glass windows and European
clothing.[90]

In the eighties and nineties, Solomon Islanders began to demand European garments and cloth. Practically, in the tropical climate there was very little need. Nor did this trend reflect missionary influence because, except for a few cases, the missions were not entrenched at this time, and those that were rarely equated clothing with Christianity.[91] Even the unconverted, the "custom" people, showed a liking for clothing. Although they wore very little by way of normal attire, they nonetheless attached meaning to bodily decorations. A particular *mbakia* worn by a chief such as Hingava (Photo 8), had a long history. Who owned it, the occasions on which it had been worn, its age, even the circumstances of its manufacture added a special value to it beyond the ordinary. To a Malaitan, a flower worn in the hair in a particular position meant that the wearer was looking for a kill.[92] The *araha* 'master of peace' of the 'Are'are people of south Malaita wore a net-like garment edged with teeth to show he wished to draw people together, to catch them in his net of peace (Photo 26).[93] Adornments and garments usually had a symbolic meaning and carried an intrinsic worth. Although all Solomon Islanders may not have known it, the average European in the Solomons rarely wore clothes for any reason other than habit or protection from the elements. To the Islanders the very fact that the Europeans felt obliged to wear clothes had some significance. Clothes were part of them, of their way of life. The stories about cannibals trying to eat the shoes of white victims and of Melanesians becoming terrified when a white visitor removed his shirt for the first time illustrate the validity of the aphorism, clothes maketh the man. On San Cristobal, the name the Arosi people first gave to Europeans was not the usual *tie vaka* 'ship men' or *mane sere* 'white men' but *waabemarasini* 'the people with bodies like a parrot'—because these men, like most whalers, wore red shirts.[94] Obviously, the Melanesians quickly perceived that shirts and other garments could be taken off and put on without anything untoward occurring. They probably began wearing them out of curiosity. In time, long after the initial fascination had worn off, the realization grew that perhaps the whites laughed privately at their nakedness, just as the whalers from the *Superior* had at Mono. The clothing they chose to wear then became a tunic of their humanity, a statement to the European that they too could partake of the world beyond their shores and possess its products if they so desired. Since Solomon Islanders did not have to prove this to their fellow villagers, clothes were rarely worn continually except, perhaps, for hats or the occasional shirt on a chilly evening. Clothing, like heirlooms and shell valuables, was stored away in their houses, to be there as something of value, of status. It was put on when a ship appeared.[95] Gorai was an impressive sight in the full dress uniform of an admiral of the British

Navy "even to the belt and sword."[96] In his declining years he was still a distinguished figure in European eyes in his "hat, trousers and a 'stars and stripes' blouse."[97]

Of course, some Solomon Islanders, not having the cultural experience of Europeans or even of Gorai, appeared very incongruous in their trading clothing. When a visiting man-of-war came to Uki, the chief, Rora, would dress himself in a cast-off naval officer's coat, with all sorts of spurious military decorations pinned to his chest (Photo 11). To the visitors, Rora's dressed upper half contrasted rather oddly with the undressed lower half of his body. The wearing of clothes, no matter what strange juxtapositions they took in the eyes of Europeans, signified to Solomon Islanders an equality between black and white. They were not so much trying to ape the whites' manners as attempting to show through the symbols of clothing that equality was possible and existed. This was something that both societies knew and the traders accepted. And it explains why British Resident Commissioner Woodford later took the officer's coat and decorations from the recalcitrant Rora. The colonial ruler could not tolerate, albeit in virtually burlesque form, the wearing of symbols that suggested equality with, or authority beyond, that of the British government and its representative.[98]

The symbolic meaning inherent in the wearing of clothing served a useful psychological purpose to the Solomon Islanders in alleviating some of the stresses of the cross-cultural situation. On a more tangible level they found a few items among the white man's medicines that were of benefit in relieving some of the illnesses that resulted from other cross-cultural meetings. The traders kept Western medicines on hand for their own use and occasionally dosed their employees. Early missionaries used medicines together with nursing care among the Solomon Islanders.[99] Returners from the colonial canefields had learned of the efficacy of some Western remedies, although in the pre-antibiotic era this was limited to certain diseases. One disease that was unresponsive to customary remedies was *bakua*, which is believed to have been introduced from other Pacific Island areas. A scaly fungus skin infection, it is unsightly and frequently results in an itchy irritation.[100] The population of Savo was "clean" by the late nineties because the people there were buying and applying a mixture of chrysophane and kerosene they obtained from the traders.[101] Although endemic yaws prevented syphilis epidemics, gonorrhea and other venereal diseases were introduced through the sexual intercourse of whalers, traders, and sailors with local women and of Melanesian men with prostitutes on overseas plantations. By the 1890s the repercussions from these diseases, particularly gonorrhea and ulcerating granuloma of the genitals, were noticeable in the islands, especially the Shortlands and New Georgia. Sterility in women and congenital blindness were not uncommon. By that time too the peo-

Photo 11. Rora standing in front of canoe house, Uki, c. 1895. *(Festetics von Tolna 1903)*

ple had started purchasing copper vitriol crystals from the traders in an attempt to treat veneral diseases.[102]

Alcohol was another remedy for some of the ills of the white man's flesh and spirit. It was imported in large quantities by the traders yet very little seems to have found its way to Solomon Islanders.[103] A few traders offered "square gin" in exchange for produce and it features now and again as an item of purchase in early land sales.[104] Some observers attributed its low consumption to a matter of taste on the part of the Solomon Islanders.[105] Although the traders chose not to curtail

their own consumption, the majority were wary of the seeming unpre-
dictability of their customers at the soberest of times and appear to have
refrained from trading in alcohol for fear of the consequences. Alcohol
may have been difficult to get from the trader, but the Solomon Islanders were sampling a range of other imported edible goods. At this time
bulumakau 'tinned meat' was a good seller in Roviana stores.[106] Nielsen's Nggela trader wrote to him in 1896 asking for goods to restock his
store, including requests for 20 tins of beef, 3 tins of biscuits, 1 bag of
rice, 20 pounds of sugar, 4 tins of curry powder, and 4 tins of pepper.[107]
On Sikaiana, where feast giving bestowed great prestige, the consumption of rice, tinned biscuits, and meat managed to outstrip that of
tobacco.[108] Rice, which had once been totally unacceptable to Solomon
Islanders as food, was now increasingly sought.[109] At the turn of the
century the astounding amount of 1000 bags of rice was landed on
Ontong Java by a trader. Ordered by Chief Uila, this represented about
£400 in value, or at beach price, 80 tons of copra, Ontong Java's main
export commodity.

Uila was able to produce this and more because as a Polynesian chief
he brought new areas under cultivation, as well as drew on the supply
from existing coconut groves. Uninhabited atolls were planted in coconuts, one of the few crops that do well on their sparse soils.[110] The big-
man trader and headhunter, Maghratulo of Mbilua, had done the same
at Liapari, extending the exploitation of the land's potential. On New
Georgia, coconut groves that had been planted to provide sustenance to
headhunters on their journey north were, by the turn of the century,
given over to surplus production, being more systematically exploited
by the bush people who could now frequent the coast in safety. Among
some Solomon Islanders there was a growing awareness of the value of
coconut trees and the relatively easy profit to be made from establishing
new coconut groves on unplanted land, an extension from crops for food
to crops for cash or trade goods.[111]

WITHIN THE SOLOMONS, the trading era brought fundamental and inter-
connected changes. At the core of this matrix lay the Solomon Islanders'
demand for the products of Western technology. Such a demand set into
motion a train of processes that transformed substantial elements of the
indigenous technology, the economy, and ultimately the polity and
social organization. The cries of battle and the report of the gun did not
drown the crack of the bush knife splitting open the coconut for drying.
Although warfare seems at first to have become more intensive and
bloody in many areas, the alliances necessary to the waging of it drew
people into larger and larger groupings. Simultaneously, because trade
needs peace in order to prosper, leaders in the western and central Solomons tried to eliminate warfare, at least within their own regions.

Political blocs of new and larger magnitude were coalescing by the 1890s, and there was very little fighting within the individual islands of the New Georgia group and the Shortlands. For those who were sufficiently accessible to it, the Christian message provided a new ideology that permitted them to abandon warfare readily. Areas that had been harassed by headhunters and whose society was in disarray produced leaders who grasped the hope of a new unity and peace in the gospel of the Melanesian Mission. Santa Isabel and Nggela prospered under Christianity and drew traders there more than ever because of the increased security and productivity.

In the western and central Solomons the political changes demonstrated a consistent trend: The disequilibrium introduced by Western technology and trading itself was being counterbalanced by a new internal, integrating relationship among peoples, primarily through extensions of traditional methods. In a similar way a new relationship also developed between the people and the land. Old crops and products such as coconuts and tortoiseshell were directed to commercial ends, while others that had been totally unutilized, such as bêche-de-mer and ivory nuts, were gathered and sold to the traders. The locally grown tobacco resulted from an experimental introduction from overseas and a desire for self-sufficiency by Solomon Islanders. They quickly learned new processes such as copra making and bêche-de-mer curing and adapted old processes such as carving and pottery making for good financial returns.

In the last three decades of the nineteenth century, because it was relatively simple for Solomon Islanders to use untapped resources and processes for commercial purposes, production remained very much an individually determined matter and, to the outsider, small scale. For those with the natural resources, access to Western goods was comparatively easy. With metal implements, little or no extra labor was required for additional commercial production beyond the time spent on subsistence in the precontact period. Resident Commissioner Woodford, with his experience of neighboring Pacific countries, summed up the advantages of the Solomon Islanders in 1896:

> I consider of all the natives of the Western Pacific with whom I have come in contact the Solomon Islanders of the British Protectorate are able to supply their demand for articles of foreign trade with the least exertion.[112]

In the eastern Solomons and Choiseul, in areas that had nothing for the trader, things were different. Warfare increased, as elsewhere, until most communities had their share of metal goods and firearms. But, because the people got trade goods by offering their labor rather than their produce, there was no general tendency for leaders to emerge with power greater than in traditional times, with the minor exception of a few coastal passage-masters. Moreover, the fragmentary sociopolitical organization most common in these regions hardly provided the infrastructure or the ideology for such leadership. There was little economic need to enforce peace as long as men could continue their usual activities and not deprive themselves of their supply of Western goods. Passage-masters and elders might persuade the young men to "volunteer" for overseas plantations, and get their percentage, but there was little to be gained in offering captives. The recruiters could not accept captives without legal consequences in the colonies and there was no guarantee that what they earned overseas would get back to their captors three or more years later. There was another difference too: Laborers from the eastern Solomons and Choiseul were paid far less than their contemporaries in most of the western islands. Capitalism was creating rich and poor Solomon Islanders.

CHAPTER 5

The colonial government and pacification

(c. 1896–1920)

Whether a district has been taken in hand by the trader first or by the missionary first, or by both simultaneously, the efforts of both classes of pioneer have sooner or later led to the recognition of British rule. The form of that rule has been what best suited the occasion and the moment.

Australian Parliamentary Papers 1919

There has never been any conquest or cession of the British Solomon Islands and the rights of the natives whether chiefs, communities or private individuals remain precisely the same as before the Declaration of the Protectorate.

C. M. Woodford, 8 June 1899

WESTERN POLITICAL CONCERN with the Solomons soon followed in the wake of Western economic interest. Within the world economy the Solomon Islands contributed only a mite to the factories of Britain, but they did provide the bulk of Melanesian labor to the plantations of Britain's colonies in Queensland and Fiji from the 1870s on. It was no coincidence that the British established a loose control over the Solomons a few years later. Rivalry among European powers for territory and labor in the Pacific, along with alarms from the vulnerable Australian colonies, drew Britain into declaring a protectorate over the Solomons. Later, a real presence was established there unwillingly, not because of any particular aversion to assuming sovereignty, but because the British Treasury did not wish to finance a new dependency. Not only did Britain want to have its cake and eat it, but also to enjoy the privilege free of charge. The British government took the Solomons on the proviso that they would pay for their own administration. Consequently, Woodford, the first resident commissioner, had to find ways to raise revenue. Taxes on traders would help, but Woodford saw the development of plantations as the only viable solution. Capital would be attracted if he could

103

provide land and labor. An abundance of labor was assumed on the basis that the Solomons had provided thousands of recruits for the overseas labor trade. Land had to be alienated—an easy task in Woodford's opinion—and once alienated, it had to be held in security. For that, it was necessary to pacify the Solomon Islanders.

Pacification was both slow and piecemeal: slow, because of the nature of Solomon Island societies and the limited resources of the government; piecemeal, because the government aimed to make the Europeans and their property secure rather than the Islanders and their land. In most places pacification only barely preceded European commercial plantation development and often limped behind it. The government adopted tactics appropriate to such frontier conditions, recruiting other Solomon Islanders, traders, and planters to assist its own scant regular forces. Although the government was loath to admit it, the Christian missionaries were its greatest allies and not infrequently its precursors in pacification. Through the missionaries' intercession and ideology thousands of Solomon Islanders came to accept more peaceable ways of conducting their affairs, thus avoiding conflict with the government.

Peace had its price for Solomon Islanders. It shook the foundations of much of their social, political, and economic activity. During this time of change and reassessment, new spokesmen and old leaders could vie for power only in ways that would not attract government repression. One major way to acquire wealth was by selling their own and others' birthright—the land.

The protectorate established

From 1877 until 1893 the Solomon Islands were within the loose jurisdiction of the British high commissioner in Fiji. Under the Western Pacific Order in Council of 1877 the high commissioner was given extraterritorial authority over British subjects in the Solomons, but lacked control over other European nationals and the native people. The only way the High Commission could settle major disputes between Islanders and British subjects was to regard an attack on the latter as an "act of war" and retaliate accordingly. Shelling of accessible villages and even the occasional execution by naval commanders on their annual tour of the islands were neither effective nor, from the point of view of international law, justified.

Despite the administrative and humanitarian discomfort this odd situation sometimes engendered, it suited the level of British influence in the Solomons. Except for the yearly visit of the man-of-war, the British were saved the expense of direct political control yet were able to obtain a small amount of raw materials for their industries and, more important, cheap labor for their colonies in Queensland and Fiji.

Events in the 1890s provided the impetus for a change in this policy. Britain was faced with a contracting market for its manufactured goods because Germany and France, as well as the United States, were producing similar articles at competitive prices. In order to safeguard their markets Germany and France attempted to keep Britain out by seeking new colonies. The "scramble for Africa" was reenacted in the Pacific, with some variations. German annexation of New Guinea and Samoa, together with French hegemony over the Society Islands, New Caledonia, and Vanuatu (formerly the New Hebrides), aroused the concern of the British government because Britain's southern Pacific colonies perceived their strategic and economic interests to be threatened. Australia, in particular, was one of the more valuable colonies whose interests Britain could not afford to disregard.[1]

When in 1892 the Griffiths ministry in Queensland reversed its 1885 decision to eventually abandon the much-criticized Pacific labor trade, Britain was provided with a "plausible excuse for 'protecting' the Solomons" and so protecting their labor reserves for Queensland and Fiji recruiters.[2] By declaring a protectorate, the British were able to justify keeping out other colonial powers, particularly France and Germany.

The secretary of state for colonies, far removed from the political realities of the Solomons, believed that treaties could be made with local rulers and a revenue provided by them in return for loose British "protection." The High Commission soon showed the Colonial Office that this was not feasible with so many small political units and pressed for a minimal establishment of a resident deputy commissioner in the Solomons. The Colonial Office vacillated because it did not want to spend any money on the Solomons and hoped that Australia would eventually govern the group. By shuffling funds from one vote to another, the high commissioner, wary of possible Australian control, managed to send Charles Morris Woodford to the Solomons as acting resident commissioner in 1896. Woodford soon produced a detailed report on the islands, based on direct observation plus his experience there as a naturalist in the 1880s, demonstrating how he could raise more than £700 a year in revenue. So impressed was the Colonial Office with the potential financial viability of the group that it urged the Treasury to give a grant-in-aid of £1200 to inaugurate the new government.[3]

This sum was barely enough to fund the skeleton staff of one British administrator, a few Fijian police, and a residency at Tulagi, let alone allow for any extension of government superstructure. The only internal source of revenue in the Solomons in 1896 was the traders. For Woodford to raise any more, economic activity in the islands would have to

expand. If he were to rely on increased indigenous production, Woodford realized, the process of creating new wants would be too slow to
raise the revenue he sought. His answer was to encourage overseas
developers to invest in plantations.[4] This meant that the government
would have to assist them in obtaining land, but peace needed to be
enforced before land alienation could be carried out with any hope of
successful occupation and planting.

Methods of pacification

At first glance, pacification appeared to be a formidable task, but the
nature of the Melanesian societies precluded any large-scale resistance,
as was demonstrated when Gibson of HMS *Curaçoa* sailed around the
group to declare the protectorate in 1893. The only Melanesian opposition to what must have been a mystifying procedure was at Langalanga
Lagoon, Malaita. Since in nineteenth-century international law nominal compliance by the inhabitants was necessary for a foreign power to
"protect" another, Gibson inquired why Britain's flag was not wanted.
The Laulasi villagers were afraid that their acceptance of it would signify to the bush people that by aligning themselves with Britain the
lagoon dwellers were preparing for war. This would lead the bush people to discontinue the trade on which the Langalanga people, who had
no gardens, were dependent for food.[5] Although this reasoning was
quite consistent with the traditional polity, it exemplified the weakness
of such fragmented political units—a weakness that on the one hand
made Britain's pacification of many thousands of Solomon Islanders a
fairly easy task involving comparatively few European officers, but on
the other meant that each unit had individually to be convinced of Britain's power. While Britain needed only minimal resources on any one
front, under such limitations the process of pacification of the entire
group was bound to be prolonged.

Woodford labored under considerable logistical disadvantages. He
had eight Fijian policemen, and in the first few years of the protectorate
could move from island to island only on visiting warships or mission or
trading vessels. Wherever possible he used naval company to carry out
punitive expeditions, giving at least the impression of a legitimate government presence. However, as only two or three ships visited each year,
Woodford had to find other means of pacification.[6] He adopted the
standard colonial strategy of using "friendly tribes" against other island
groups and he also recruited white traders as armed militia.

In general, pacification was enforced where European interests were
threatened, either directly or indirectly. If peace between warring
groups was usually the consequence, this was not the primary focus of
government policy. As with other forms of outside influence, the people

who lived on the coast or adjacent hill country were the first to feel the effects of the government's pacification policy because they were accessible to Europeans and because they resided on or near suitable plantation land. In the early years of the protectorate, most of the land readily available for plantations appeared to be in the New Georgia Islands and northern Guadalcanal, and it was to these areas that the government's efforts were first directed.

In New Georgia in 1898, Woodford used his new assistant Mahaffy and warships to soften up resistance by the Roviana and Simbo headhunters, appointing Mahaffy as resident at Gizo the following year. Mahaffy and his canoe-borne "police" force from Santa Isabel were quickly on the scene of any trouble in the southern New Georgia group. So effective was this mobile force that by 1900 they had stopped headhunting from Roviana, Simbo, and Mbilua and enforced peace among adjacent peoples.[7]

There were dangers in employing nongovernment personnel. Both Solomon Islander and European militia could use opportunities to plunder, to even old scores, or simply to ingratiate themselves with the government. Even under the ideal circumstance of direct supervision, the civilians' lack of training and discipline could lead to disaster when fighting broke out, as Woodford early discovered on Guadalcanal in 1897. Following the killing of Svensen's employee Jean Porret at Kaoka (the Marau Company's new plantation, Figure 12), Woodford led a group of ten white traders and his Solomon Islander sergeant to capture the killers. In the confusion the traders wounded two suspects and almost shot the policeman.[8]

This unsatisfactory outcome was more by accident than design, but frequently white traders who had been powerless prior to the protectorate's establishment could not resist the chance to humiliate any Solomon Islander who offended them. In the Marovo area in 1908 Ngatu and some companions killed Oliver Burns, an agent of Wheatley.[9] A punitive expedition consisting of traders and Sykes, a temporary government officer, set out with the intention of "killing anyone they came across in the locality."[10] Fortunately, the presence of the Methodist missionary Shackell moderated their actions. Soon after, HMS *Cambrian*, with Woodford aboard, came to Marovo where the crew burned the homes and canoes of suspects. Following the plundering of plantation stores by the same people, Woodford returned a few months later aboard the *Belama* with Heffernan, the district magistrate of the Shortlands, and a militia of Shortlands men, leaving in their wake raided gardens, burned houses, and wounded villagers.[11] "The lesson inflicted . . . has been a severe one," wrote Woodford in 1909. Marovo had been made safe for the white man.[12]

Missionary intervention prevented the first Marovo expedition from becoming a massacre. The Methodist missionary Nicholson played a similar role at Mbilua on Vella Lavella in the same year. Edge-Partington, magistrate at Gizo, learned that the professional warrior Sito Latavaki was somewhere on the Mbilua coast (Figure 9). The magistrate was anxious to capture Sito because he had been responsible for an attack on Jean Pratt in 1897, in revenge for Peter Pratt's failure to fulfill an arms contract. While trying to capture Sito, the government party shot Sito's wife and children. In retaliation, from his bush hideout Sito sent his men to Mbava to kill the Malaitan wife and children of the trader Binskin, who had participated in an earlier raid on Sito's people in 1901. The murder of Binskin's family resulted in a punitive expedition consisting of government officers, revenge-crazed traders, and an undisciplined Malaitan militia who swept over Vella Lavella in a random wave of killing and destruction. Nicholson intervened, sheltering hundreds of refugees at the mission station while persuading the government officer to allow the local people to catch Sito.[13] They soon accomplished what a "fortnight of bloodshed and plunder" by the government had failed to do, capturing Sito and his companions alive.[14]

These incidents set the tone of the future relationship between the peoples of the New Georgia Islands and the government. The Methodist mission sheltered, protected, and assisted them, even when most were still pagans. The New Georgians were not the only ones to fear the government's punitive actions. On San Cristobal in 1915, when a recruiter, Laycock, was killed, the pagan bush people inland from Wanione fled to the Roman Catholic mission there to hide from the government. Although the government resented such competition for the people's loyalty, the missions, particularly the long-established Melanesian Mission, were undoubtedly its auxiliaries in pacification—as events on Santa Isabel and Nggela had shown—and the alliance had to be maintained.[15]

Consequently, wherever the missionaries encountered violent opposition the government came to their aid. On northwest Guadalcanal both Melanesian and Roman Catholic missionaries and converts were continuously harassed in the late 1890s by Sulukavo who, like Sito, was a warrior cum bounty hunter or *malaghai*. Throughout the 1880s and 1890s he was paid by big-men and others to conduct raids or kill people who had offended against the social mores. The missions had to contend not only with the violence caused by the vengeance of the *malaghai*, but also with the raids of the Savo people and New Georgia headhunters. Such warfare hindered the mission, but kept Sulukavo employed and wealthy. As he saw the spreading effects of the Christian emphasis on peace, he realized that his way of life was threatened and determined to drive out the missionaries. By 1900 his attacks were becoming so bold that the missionaries appealed to Woodford, who led a militia of fifteen

Savo men into Sulukavo's deserted village, Tasule, about five miles inland from Maravovo, and burned down several of the houses. Since the government had stopped the New Georgian and Savo raiding and the missions had brought peace to the area, Sulukavo's function had become redundant; he could do little but obey Woodford's order that attacks on the missions were to end.[16]

Missionaries and traders were not the only Europeans who, either by co-option or cooperation, became agents of the government's pacification policies. The pioneer planter was drawn, usually unwillingly, into "taming the frontier." In the government's view, one way to pacify an area was to encourage European settlement there. Contradictions were inherent in such a policy. Was the government urging settlement so that if Europeans were attacked it could justify to the high commissioner additional spending for punitive expeditions and a call for British warships? Or did it expect the white settlers to be front-line troops in pacifying the population? In 1909 Acting Resident Commissioner Barnett urged the high commissioner to approve a land transfer to a European on Vella Lavella because "it is a distinct advantage to encourage settlement on the coastlands of Vella la vella as by this means the more troublesome bush tribes can be better brought under control."[17] From similar actions in the 1910s on San Cristobal and Malaita the government clearly was not only encouraging the establishment of European plantations in uncontrolled areas, but also expecting the settlers to pacify any troublesome neighboring tribes with little, if any, government aid. Frontier conditions bred frontier attitudes among the Europeans, who often became a law unto themselves.[18]

Under such circumstances, when a European life was taken, the government compensated for what it lacked in consistent and balanced administration by massive overkill. Even Malaita, left virtually to itself for many years, began to receive some attention from the government when white men were killed. In 1908 an inexperienced labor recruiter, C. C. Mackenzie, was killed near Bina (Figure 10). Before HMS *Cambrian* was used in the Marovo punitive operation, Woodford and the entire ship's company landed at Bina, going inland to destroy the villages of those implicated. Although the guilty parties avoided capture on that occasion, a punitive expedition following the murder of the missionary Daniels had more effect. In 1911, Daniels, of the South Sea Evangelical Mission (SSEM), aided a local man who had seduced the daughter of a big-man of Busu village and then sent the pair to safety at the mission headquarters at Onepusu. Such a crime against the rigid Malaitan sexual code could not go unpunished and Daniels was killed. The SSEM clamored for government intervention to such an extent that HMS *Torch*, with High Commissioner Sir Francis May on board, was eventually sent to east Malaita. A surprise attack on Farisi left five vil-

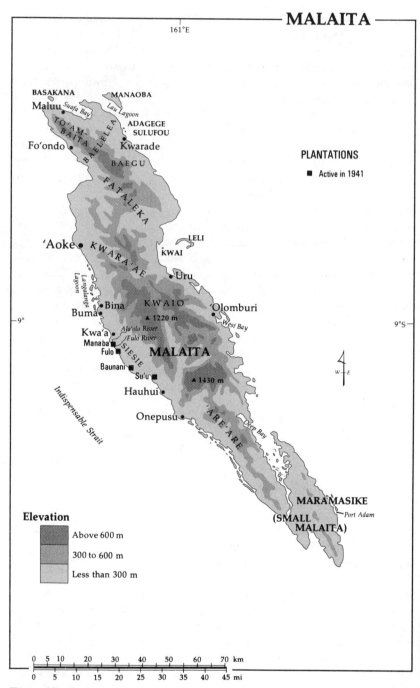

Figure 10

lagers dead. Then the *Torch*'s company destroyed the village of Uru, whose big-man had been involved in the killing. The shots fired at Farisi reverberated throughout Malaita. Not only was Farisi a hilltop village, difficult of access, but, like Uru, it was in the heartland of the Kwaio people, who had acquired a fearsome reputation dating back to their daring attacks on overseas labor recruiting vessels. If such a people could be humbled by the government then surely this was a force to be reckoned with.[19]

Less dramatic, but still effective, punitive action by the government did not always merit a mention by Woodford in his dispatches to the high commissioner, but were probably fairly common. In 1904, for example, the coastal people hired bushmen to kill the Catholic missionaries at Avuavu, Guadalcanal. Warned of the plan, the missionaries notified Woodford, who arrested the culprits and took them away to work for a year on the government gardens at Tulagi. A few years later the Catholic station at Moli, Guadalcanal, was attacked and plundered. Again, government intervention followed.[20]

Not all Solomon Islanders opposed the will of the government. The demonstration effect of punitive action was not lost on neighboring groups. Moreover, many eastern Solomon Islanders had acquired first-hand knowledge of the power of the white man from experiences on overseas plantations. Many of the government's earliest supporters came from among such men, as did the missions' first followers. These contacts or unofficial "headmen" were helpful to the government in parts of Malaita, Guadalcanal, and San Cristobal long before the formal system of district headmen was created in the early 1920s. Within a few years of the establishment of a government station on Malaita in 1909, District Officer Edge-Partington was receiving reports from "government headmen" at Fo'ondo and Maluu in the north of the island. As early as 1902, Woodford's former police sergeant, William Buruku, after twenty-three years in Fiji, returned to his home at Wanderer Bay, Guadalcanal, where he became the means by which the new law was introduced to the area. Further east at Talise another man, David Sango, returned in 1907 from twenty years in Queensland. As a Christian he worked with the SSEM to evangelize the district, doing so successfully and also reinforcing the government's pacification policy. In 1911, through his influence, people along the central south coast came together and destroyed their valued firearms as a gesture to signify the end of fighting.[21]

Although Sango's memory is respected in the Talise region to the present day, not all who assisted the government were so benevolent to their neighbors. Around Aola, Guadalcanal, for example, the big-men of Nggela ancestry, most of whom had returned from Queensland, supplied information about the culture of the Mbirao bush people to the government, which was attempting to understand native law. Much of the information was misleading and resulted in a series of informal and later formal government regulations that contributed to the decline of the bush population. For example, regulations against cremation meant that disease spread and regulations for the consolidation and establishment of permanent villages meant that the people came to have difficulty feeding themselves properly because their gardens gradually were made farther and farther away from the permanent villages.[22]

The government had opened the Aola station under C. C. Francis in 1914.[23] On neighboring San Cristobal, the former first chief of the Native Constabulary, F. M. Campbell, acting very much on his own initiative, brought the island's eight thousand people under government control within two years, his task made easier by mission activity and the weakness of a population emerging from a series of severe epidemics. Opening the Kirakira station in January 1918, Campbell soon divided the island (with Uki ni Masi and Ulawa) into eight districts, each under a "district chief" who was held responsible for carrying out Campbell's ideas regarding sanitation, the fencing of pigs, and the consolidation of hamlets into "substantial villages," as well as bringing criminals before his court.[24] On Santa Isabel the first district officer, Heffernan, appointed in 1918, inherited the structure of Melanesian Mission government, but except for some passive resistance from church leaders, had no one to "pacify."

With stations at Kirakira, Aola, and Tanabulli, as well as at Shortland Harbour (1907), Gizo, 'Aoke, and the residency at Tulagi, by 1918 the government had established a basic administrative framework of about ten officers and a hundred local police for control of the most productive and most populous islands (Appendix 7). During the first thirty years of the protectorate, official government forces assisted by other Europeans had punished attackers of whites and their interests, while preventing the people of the smaller islands and the coastal inhabitants of the larger islands from engaging in warfare and following customs repugnant to Europeans.[25] By the twenties, much of the area where commercial activity was centered had been pacified and made secure for Europeans.

The effects of pacification

Pacification meant the loss of power by traditional leaders. In the western Solomons, the government enforced laws against the acquisition of firearms, suppressed head-hunting by massive destruction of canoes and canoe houses, and moved against the slave raid and slave trade between New Georgia and Isabel and Choiseul. In doing this the government rapidly destroyed the link between the chiefs' organization of productive activities (slaves for labor, tortoiseshell in exchange for trade goods, head-hunting as productive of spiritual welfare) and ceremonial activities (canoe launching, the reconsecration of skull houses, the killing of slaves to placate the ancestors) and so undermined much of the basis of their power.

There were also inescapable internal factors that spelled the end of the old ways. The population of the New Georgia Islands was declining. Years of head-hunting and retaliatory raids within the islands themselves and beyond to Santa Isabel, Choiseul, and even the Russell Islands and Guadalcanal, had taken their toll.[26] Diseases such as influenza and dysentery frequently swept through the islands, their introduction assisted by the regular and rapid steamer service that commenced in 1895 from Australia. The migration of people from the bush areas of the New Georgia Islands to the coast, where they could more easily tend their coconuts and make copra, was facilitated by both the *pax Britannica* and the missions and continued, in more isolated areas, until the 1920s. The bush people saw the advantage of dealing directly with the traders instead of through the saltwater dwellers, such as the Roviana people.[27] Although this may have proved of benefit commercially, the gradual fusion of scattered bush hamlets into larger coastal settlements also aided the spread of droplet-borne infections as well as increasing the incidence of malaria among the former bush people.

With so much sickness, the rudimentary medical aid provided by the Methodist mission from its inception in 1902 proved an attraction to some of the New Georgia people.[28] The decline in numbers meant less pressure on available food resources. Consequently, there was a large surplus of such long-term food crops as coconuts, which the people readily sold to the traders. Following pacification, there was little occasion for an aspiring big-man or chief to organize any new productive enterprise because the surplus satisfied any increased wants among the depleted population. Since the population was smaller there was no land shortage, and this in turn removed the opportunity for a clan leader or chief to manipulate the availability of land for cash crops for his own aggrandizement. Furthermore, after fifty to a hundred years of contact with Europeans, many ordinary villagers were able to deal with the outsiders without the mediation of a chief. Copra growing and production could be done by family groups and, by the turn of the century, needed no one to mobilize large numbers, unlike head-hunting. Both politically and economically, the chiefs' position was weakened. Among themselves, the traders were very competitive and, since the 1880s and 1890s, had been calling regularly at the villages along the coasts of the New Georgia Islands where a great deal of copra was being made.[29] An individual could sell copra, ivory nuts, bêche-de-mer, and tortoiseshell and get trade goods directly from the trader.

Although many New Georgians for years stayed aloof from the Methodist mission, the chiefs, persuaded in part by Wickham and in part by their own observations, sent their sons and chiefly heirs to the mission school to obtain the apparent key to the white man's power—reading and writing. Other young people, along with "slaves" and adoptees who may have perceived the changing political and economic conditions, attached themselves to the mission in the hope of finding the means to exploit new opportunities. Each year the mission's following grew, especially after the Mbilua and Marovo punitive expeditions. Hingava's death in 1906 epitomized the sunset of the old gods, for even his funerary rituals were abbreviated.[30] Discussing the status of the older chiefs in 1908, informants told Hocart: "no one is mighty now; they are all alike; they have no money, they cannot go head-hunting, they all 'stop nothing'."[31]

Elsewhere the pattern was similar. Pacification destroyed many traditional sources of wealth for big-men. On Guadalcanal, children had regularly been sold at Sahalu near Visale. These *cheka* were bought by big-men of Guadalcanal, Nggela, and Savo. Some of the females so purchased eventually became professional prostitutes or *rembi*. Their favors were paid for in dog teeth, most of which went to their manager, the big-man. Many of the male *cheka* became warriors and followers of the particular big-man who had purchased them. By buying *cheka*, a big-man could increase his wealth, his support, and therefore his power.[32] The government's opposition to killing dried up one of the sources of such children, and the Christian missions' condemnation of "slavery" and prostitution meant that the institution virtually disappeared and, with it, a source of wealth and power to big-men. Elsewhere, warriors like Sulukavo of Nggai, Guadalcanal, who gained their living and influence solely from killing, saw the whole rationale of their existence condemned by peace.

In the Shortlands the end of the overseas labor trade plus the policing of the border by German colonial officials in the early 1900s cut off Bougainville as a major source of exchange goods and human beings for the chiefs. Their wealth had encouraged extended polygamy: Gorai alone had one hundred wives. Coupled with introduced disease, the decline of chiefly authority appears to have brought about a rapid decline in population, an outcome deplored by the Roman Catholic Marists who opened a mission in the Shortlands in 1898. Their preaching, plus the support of the government officer resident there from 1907, reinforced the trend toward abandoning polygamy, an outcome of shrinking wealth and inability to provide multiple bride payments. With less trade and fewer wives, the chiefs no longer had as many labor units at their disposal and their relative power declined.[33]

Big-men who had made their names by being able to deal with the traders successfully found that the old mutually beneficial relationship was beginning to change as the government enforced pacification. The white trader understood the Western concept of a state-wide government based on a written law. Moreover, he had language and something of a shared culture on his side and was able to use these to his own advantage with government officials in confrontations with the Solomon Islanders.[34] Within the framework of the new polity, the relationship was no longer skewed in favor of the Melanesians, but entirely vertical, with the Europeans as superiors and the Solomon Islander big-men as subordinates. This weakening of the prestige of Solomon Islander trading partners did not go unnoticed by their own communities. For others the erosion of authority was more subtle.

When the white men came in numbers to the Solomon Islands, they little understood the religious values of the Melanesians and so flouted them, through either ignorance or, more often, disregard. Europeans touched or even carried away sacred objects such as offerings at ancestral shrines, bathed in spirit-haunted streams, walked alone at night, and, again and again, broke taboos that Solomon Islanders believed would bring sickness and death in their wake. Sorcerers could vent their magical fury on the white man and see scant result.[35] Not only were the white men able to survive sorcery, but they also seemed able to marshall stronger supernatural power, since they were able to defeat great warriors who had called on the support of their own ancestors. Consequently, Solomon Islanders began to doubt the wisdom of generations. The young lost respect for elders and big-men who could give no answers to the new questions of the time. In some places, such as Roviana, the old answers were lost irrevocably as priests and elders died in epidemics, taking their esoteric knowledge with them.[36] Part of the apparent apathy and lack of interest in life observed in some groups was probably a kind of passive resistance to Europeans by people who had not yet found other legitimate ways of expressing their feelings within the constraints of the imposed law. But such behavior was so pervasive that contemporary travelers and ethnographers, bemoaning the passing of the formerly vigorous and perhaps somewhat idealized culture, predicted the extinction of the Melanesian race.[37] Although many of the younger generation found new answers and hope in Christianity, most of the older people and holders of traditional authority adhered to the old way. This was what they understood, even though it seemed to be failing them.

Selling a birthright

Since virtually all the old means of acquiring and, more important, maintaining power were closed, many of the elders attempted to prop up the ruins of their authority by obtaining and redistributing wealth from other sources. In areas where peace had been established men could get money and Western goods by selling something other people—usually the whites—wanted. Only three classes of items could be offered in return for money and goods: labor, products (such as copra), and land. Those who wished could risk going to a plantation on another island to earn £6 a year. In the early years of the twentieth century, when pacification was gradually being enforced, this was a much more dangerous and less familiar proposition than going to Queensland or Fiji. To earn the equivalent by making copra a person would need to grow, cut, and dry from 12,000 to 14,000 coconuts (or 2 tons of copra), which entailed 40 to 100 work-days. The only remaining way to obtain money and goods was to sell land.[38] Often the land that was sold was only used intermittently and was undeveloped, and so the price offered by the trader seemed attractive.

Such prices were infinitely more attractive to those who had no alternative means of earning money. Old men were too weak to go to work on distant plantations or, if they were fortunate enough to have large groves at their disposal, to cut substantial amounts of copra. Younger big-men had the strength, but, to many of them, such servile, time-consuming labor did not befit their position in society.[39] These men, clan elders and fading big-men, sold or authorized the sale of most of the land to Europeans.

When the young chief Ngatu took part in the killing of Burns, he was acting in a valid and approved way in the terms of his own society. A tribesman of his wife had been taken to Tulagi by the government on suspicion of being involved in a double killing at Marovo, and had hanged himself. Burns' life was taken to atone for the death. Ngatu, a chiefly hero in his own society, was a criminal in the alien one, and was imprisoned. Owing partly to the intervention of the Reverend John Goldie, Ngatu was ultimately freed and then became a Christian. This meant he was no longer able to take heads. With cash becoming important for the new religious activities as well as secular concerns, Ngatu had good reason to sell 800 acres at Seghe to the government in 1913.[40]

Ngatu, by attaching himself to the new order, had found an alternative route to prestige and power, as did many of the young chiefs and chiefly heirs of the New Georgia group. The Methodist mission was remarkably successful with the younger generation in New Georgia, but one of the chiefs of Roviana, Gemu, clung to his old beliefs. Gemu was Hingava's successor and, unlike his cousin Gemi, he refused baptism. Gemu, not in conscience able to attempt to gain status through being a Christian leader, was nonetheless able to sell land. In 1905 Gemu sold Hombupecka, an island that Wickham held under permissive residency, and later, in 1912, he sold his share of Kolo Hite (a small island near Munda), receiving from both sales a total of £25 or the equivalent of four years of plantation wages.[41]

Photo 12. Laborers using the plough to break up turfs of lang-lang grass on Guadalcanal plains, c. 1910. *(Burns Philp Archives)*

On Guadalcanal, Sulukavo's decline as a *malaghai* left him only one way to retain some of his tarnished glory. In 1907, in one of the earliest land sales in the district, he sold Lavuro to a planter for a combination of both new money and valuables and traditional valuables: £20, 2000 porpoise teeth, 200 dog teeth, 1 case of tobacco, 1 case of pipes, 2 gross of matches, 1 piece of calico, 2 knives, and 2 axes.[42]

European planters were attracted to the northern coastal plain of Guadalcanal because the land was relatively flat and covered mainly by savanna, which appeared easier to clear than virgin bush (Photo 12). Very few Melanesians lived on the northwest coast and even fewer on the exposed north coast, mainly because of the effects of raids from New Georgia, the Russell Islands, Savo, and Nggela from the late 1870s through to the 1890s.[43] Trading was concentrated on the east coast because both people and produce were there.[44]

In other parts of the island the main sources of trade goods were returners from the labor trade, many of whom were bush people. The few who did trade with the whites were mainly coastal ex-laborers who, as elsewhere, were better able to understand what the traders wanted. Not only did these people trade with the whites, but they also at times acted as passage-masters to overseas labor recruiters.[45] Because they were usually attached to a big-man (either of their own clan or, by adoption, another), they had some control over the clan's land.[46] These sophisticates were the channels by which most of the Western trade goods came into the society. By the time repatriation from Queensland was under way (1904–1908) the demand for trade goods was increasing and it was met for a time by the four thousand returners to the Solomons.[47] At the same time the bush population was starting to move to the coast because warfare had virtually ceased and because many newly converted Christians, encouraged by missionaries, wanted to found Christian communities there.[48] Before this, the bush people had received some trade goods, but only from returners of their own or through coastal intermediaries.

On the coast, as a result of the demonstration effect of returners as well as local and foreign missionaries, the relocated bush population was anxious to obtain more trade goods. For a few years following repatriation from Queensland the returners' wealth filled the demand. Trade goods were distributed and cash was used to buy more from traders as well as to pay church contributions. So much coin flowed to traders and the church that the government listed accumulated gold coin to the value of £2500 as one of the Solomons' principal exports in 1908–1909.[49]

By this time the people of northwest Guadalcanal were beginning to feel the pinch. Although labor recruiting within the Solomons was soon to involve Guadalcanal men, in the early years of the century the few that went on two- or three-year contracts from the north coast to plantations could not immediately fill the demand for goods.

The former passage-masters cum traders realized that the easiest and quickest way to get trade goods and money was to sell land. People in the Nggai area claim it was these men with only vague rights to the land who sold it. This certainly could have happened in relation to land formerly held by women. Land-buying Europeans, carrying their own cultural bias with them, always dealt with male representatives of a group. Women, who would have been most anxious to preserve their land for their own children as members of their clans (not the fathers'), were at a great disadvantage, which was further exacerbated by their inability to speak or understand the plantation pidgin spoken by the men.[50] Murray Bathgate, who has done extensive field work in the area, considered that former Queensland laborers alone duped their own people, but it is more likely that many big-men and clan leaders acquiesced in land transactions because they received a share of the trade goods and money. In this way they were able to maintain the economic base of their status in the face of changes that were undermining other foundations to their authority. Nonetheless, the eventual effect on the ordinary villagers was probably the same. As Bathgate stated, in the Nggai area, land was sold by

> ex-Queenslanders and seldom did they share out any of the proceeds. In fact many villagers did not know that the land which they had an interest in had been sold until planters arrived with labourers to clear away the forest and regrowth. Even those who did know that the land had been sold, and who may have received a few sticks of tobacco or a clay pipe,

were never to know whether or not the amount they received from the settlers was commensurate with their particular interests.[51]

Just as knowing individuals were in a position to exploit their own
people through the emerging weaknesses in traditional sociopolitical
organization, so were others able to use loopholes in the customary land
tenure system to attain their own ends. Such legal loopholes had little
significance until land became a marketable commodity. The Reverend
Charles Fox, speaking against "unjust" native land laws in 1916,
described how on San Cristobal the sole survivor of a group of land-
owners sold land to Europeans even though another group had been in
permissive occupancy for generations.[52] The owner received the full
purchase price, but the occupiers had to leave the land. In both cultures
—Solomon Island and European—the letter of the law prevailed, but
the spirit was often ignored, creating subsequent resentment.[53]

Despite such cases the San Cristobal people appear to have escaped
the worst of opportunism in land dealing. With a few exceptions,
mainly of land puchased by Svensen, the sales on San Cristobal were
made after 1912, when a law was introduced making the government
the sole purchaser of land. Almost all of the transactions involved the
mediation of respected clan leaders who understood what was involved.[54] Moreover, most were witnessed by either Fox or the Reverend
Mr. Drew, ministers of the Melanesian Mission who, at the time, had
extensive knowledge of the coastal peoples' wishes in regard to land and
were in a position to explain the ramifications of selling to outsiders. In
Guadalcanal, on the other hand, more than half of the land in the
Nggai area and half of that along the rest of the north coast was sold
before 1912, at a time when the witnesses involved had less concern
with protecting the interests of the sellers.[55]

Some big-men, trying to maintain their status as generous givers,
became deeply indebted to traders. Ferguson, chief of Alu (Figure 8),
had been advanced trade by Sam Atkinson until he owed the trader
12,000 coconuts or about two tons of copra. Ferguson agreed to give the
islet of Bakiava, south of Fauro, to redeem the debt in 1901. Although
the government appears to have disallowed this transaction, there were
probably other cases where land was sold for a nominal sum because of
pressure of debts.[56]

Other motives were behind land sales. In the optimistic early years of
plantation development, several crops besides the known coconuts and
bananas were planted experimentally. Cotton, rubber, and coffee were
crops unfamiliar to most Islanders. Perhaps some sold portions of their
land in the hope of learning how to cultivate them from the white man's
demonstration.[57] Some sellers might well have expected to enter into a
relationship with the newcomers similar to the one they had had with

the resident traders and thereby gain greater access to trade goods. Others, beyond the orbit of government control, felt the presence of a white man offered some protection from their enemies.[58] When they sold land to the powerful government they also may have believed, as so often was the case in customary land transactions, that they were creating a special bond whereby the government would protect their future interests. In the wake of introduced diseases, some of the old men may well have believed that their people were dying out and therefore selling the land and using the proceeds would be a sensible move.

Realizing the immensity of arbitrary force the government could marshall to carry out its will in pacification, many Solomon Islanders felt not simply a loss of confidence, but an absence of power. Land transactions carried out in such an atmosphere of fear were hardly legitimate. The traveler Frank Burnett related a case that occurred in about 1909, involving a group of Kolombangara people whose land was to be granted to two white men. Burnett went with his friend Wheatley to the area.

> Upon landing, and after Norman had transacted his business with the native trader, a deputation, headed by the Chief, waited upon him, and, through an interpreter of their own, stated they were led to understand that the Government proposed to take from them their best property, upon which they planted their coconuts that practically constituted their livelihood. That as they were not powerful enough to dispute the action of the authorities, in respect to this contemplated spoilage, and as it appeared inevitable that the lands in question would pass to the white man, they preferred that Mr Wheatley, whom they had known and traded with for years, should have them. They, therefore, proposed that he should accept a deed of the property in question, containing, however, a stipulation that they should be allowed to collect the cocoanuts from all the existing trees. The Chief also signified his willingness to obtain the signatures of the owners to such a conveyance of the property to Mr Wheatley, so that, in this way, outsiders should be prevented from settling in their midst.[59]

The last frontier: Conquered yet entire

Since the government's policy of pacification was not extended throughout the Solomons simultaneously, there remained some places where the overall patterns did not prevail in the early decades of the twentieth century. In general these areas were not proven producers of coconuts, possessed fairly large bush populations, had few, if any, resident Europeans, and were on islands more distant from Australia. In these places, the elders and big-men had the chance to keep their traditional authority much longer than, say, in New Georgia.

On Malaita, for example, except for the lagoon villages and some small Christian settlements, very few large permanent villages were on the coast, the people preferring the more defensible hilltop sites. The advent of the protectorate had caused hardly a ripple in the bush country. By 1911, only a coastal strip in the north of the island had been "pacified." In the resident magistrate's words there were "thousands of natives in the bush who did not care a fig for the government."[60] The substantial bush population, despite decades of exposure of their men to the outside world through the overseas labor trade, clung proudly to their traditional ways. A clannish and fractious people, they had used the iron and guns obtained overseas to intensify their feuding and to further their personal vendettas.[61] The fighting made it exceptionally difficult for any would-be planter of coconut palms on Malaita to move from the hills to the narrow, exposed coastal strip to grow them. The products might have drawn the trader, but he too would have had to avoid involvement in the local fighting.

The labor trade had meant that the young men became the suppliers of Western goods, a new economic role that potentially threatened elders' authority. But the former laborers, the majority of whom were bushmen, went back to a closed society when they returned to their small, isolated hamlets atop mountain spurs in the Malaitan hinterland.[62] In his whole lifetime, the average returner would have little if any further outside contact unless mediated by neighboring and frequently warring groups. Until other outside influences were to be felt (and for a few communities this came as late as World War II), the elders were able to continue to exploit their ritual role in a religious system centering on ancestor worship as well as their politico-economic position. As the traditional holders of shell valuables, needed for a myriad of social transactions including marriage, they could manipulate the flow and the economic output of the women. In the absence of many of the young men, the women, as gardeners, were the main producers within the society. Not only did the elders sustain their authority, but also it is likely that they increased their power relative to such young men. Where traditional beliefs remained intact, as for virtually all Malaita during the overseas labor trade, a returner had to "purchase" his readmittance to membership in his clan. In doing so he gave out to clan elders a major portion of his new wealth. As most returners had no gardens and pigs they soon became indebted to kin. In time, much of what remained of their wealth was whittled away by use or as presents to friends and relatives. In the eyes of the returner this was a small price to pay for the prestige of having traveled so far and for the assistance his elders would provide in the form of shell valuables for "payment" for his future bride.

Had a young man and his family struck out on their own and made a plantation on the coast, the authority of the elders would have been weakened because the man would have had not just the results of three years of overseas employment at his disposal, but also the prospect of a lifetime of earnings from selling coconuts to white traders. There were ideological as well as institutional economic barriers to such a course. Within the traditional beliefs, it would have been spiritually dangerous for a family to set itself up far from the priests and ancestral shrines. There was little support from within these societies to encourage the prerequisites for foreign trade. Among existing coastal and lagoon settlements, the entrepreneurs who had arisen as traders-in-men during the labor trade had had to enter into social and economic relationships with the elders of the young recruits. They did not so much alter the established order of the bush communities, as strengthen the power of the elders and big-men.

Malaita, the major supplier of Solomon Islands laborers to the overseas labor trade, was also a source of local plantation workers. To obtain them, the recruiters had only to anchor their vessels off-shore (as they had done for decades), keeping European contact with Malaita to a minimum. Although the government did attempt to punish the killing of whites on Malaita, it paid scant attention to the establishment of internal peace in early years of the century. Undoubtedly the personnel and resources of the government were scarce, yet its inertia on Malaita was reinforced by the general belief among the white community that pacification would mean a decline in the labor supply so vital to the new plantations. Most significant, as the visitor Hubert Murray of Papua remarked in 1916, the Europeans were convinced that the Malaitans would no longer sign on because the elders, with the expected loss of authority after pacification, would not be able to pressure them to go.[63]

Not until the late twenties and early thirties would the government, with more staff, begin to make its presence felt throughout Malaita—at a time when the demand for laborers was far less acute.[64] Along with the influence of the Christian missions, the government's pacification policy started to erode the elders' authority by forbidding and punishing killing. Such killing was usually the outcome of offences against the inflexible sexual code, sorcery, or a personal insult. Because these offences threatened the good name and continued assistance of the ancestors *(akalo)*, atonement was necessary to reestablish a harmonious relationship between the living (the visibly present) and the dead (the invisibly present). Frequently, a *ramo* 'warrior-leader' was hired to do the necessary killing. At best *ramo* were justice men, but often they were more like bounty hunters, extorting shell valuables and pigs by fear. Nonetheless, killing was central to the maintenance of the existing order.[65]

When the government stopped it, the *ramo*, like warrior leaders elsewhere, lost their customary power and income, the ancestors could never be fully placated, and the young people began to doubt the legitimacy of the elders. Associated with Christianity, which devalued certain cultural beliefs such as female pollution, pacification effectively weakened the power of the traditional elders on Malaita, just as it had on other islands.[66]

On less populous Choiseul, the pattern was similar except that the Methodist and Roman Catholic missions, despite their animosity toward one another, were the prime movers for peace rather than the government, which exerted no real administrative control over the island until the late 1930s. By 1925, intergroup fighting had ceased as a direct result of mediation by New Georgian and European Methodists, along with the people's growing interest in trading. Since the mediator role was characteristic of big-man behavior on Choiseul, it was not long before the mission teachers took on other aspects of peaceful leadership, weakening the authority of local big-men. Prior to 1920, very little land was alienated on Choiseul and most of that was unoccupied land resumed under the Waste Land Acts.[67] By the 1930s, when both Choiseul and Malaita were pacified and under the kind of government control conducive to extensive plantation development, the Europeans' interest in obtaining land had evaporated and the government alienated very little. Clan leaders and elders in coastal areas had little chance of selling land to get wealth to prop up their status.

THE ESTABLISHMENT OF THE PROTECTORATE had been an act arising from concerns outside the Solomon Islands and their people. Uninvited, the British ran up their flag before small communities of Islanders under the watchful eyes of the *Curaçoa*'s gunners. Yet when a government had to be financed the Colonial Office expected the islands and the people to facilitate the process. It was expected that they would provide the land and labor so vital to the overseas capitalist planter. For the three elements of land, labor, and capital to work in harmony, peace was necessary in the islands. At first, pacification was aimed at offenders against white men and their interests, but gradually it was extended to all. The government marshaled an array of forces, the bulk in fact being unofficial—Solomon Islanders, traders, missionaries, and even planters. The use of irregulars with vested interests ensured cooperation, but opened the way to many injustices against innocent Islanders and encouraged a frontier mentality among European settlers. Undoubtedly, pacification benefited the colonizer and eventually the colonized in terms of personal security. But at the time, those "pacified" must have seen things very differently because their world had been drastically reordered. The Europeans were now in control, whereas before 1896 they had been subservient to the Islanders. The government introduced new methods of settling quarrels, punishing wrongs, winning wealth, and, in condemning certain local practices as repugnant to humanity, it created new crimes. Island societies had to adjust to all this or suffer what was often violent punishment.

The adjustment was considerable. It was not simply a case of the new replacing the traditional, but the new replacing ways already greatly changed by the coming of Western technology. This technology had created some extremely powerful big-men and chiefs and had made some societies wealthy in relation to others. Similarly, in areas rich in produce, its mediators, the transient whalers followed by the resident traders, had given the impression that Europeans were people who would be easily controlled. Groups deeply involved in the trading and use of Western goods as well as the new relationships they entailed, felt the installation of the protectorate government as a particularly heavy blow to their self-confidence.

Many found both solace and a rationale for the introduced order in the new religion, Christianity, and hoped to discover in it the key to the white man's knowledge and power. Peace and British law severely curtailed existing avenues to power and leadership for Solomon Islanders. Some, especially the young, found new opportunities in missionary organizations. Many, particularly returners to the eastern Solomons after many years overseas, used their knowledge of white men to win support among their people by acting as go-betweens for the European government and the missions. Where they possessed suitable land, many leaders, both old and aspiring, saw the sale of it as a novel, but government-sanctioned, way to obtain wealth and authority.

Land as a marketable commodity was an entirely new concept for Solomon Islanders and only a minority understood the ramifications of tenure transfer. The Europeans understood it well, but except for a few missionaries, most of them kept that knowledge to themselves.

CHAPTER 6

The colonial government and land alienation

(c. 1900–1920)

I said to him [Wanu of Santa Ana] what I did to all others I
interviewed during the cruise that "I came as a friend, and to
redress all grievances—those made by the black man as well
as those made by the white man." After a while he asked me,
"If white man come and take my land will you stop him?" I
replied, "Certainly": but I failed to find out what was on his
mind when he asked that question.

Captain G. H. Hand, HMS *Royalist*, 1890

There are millions of acres of waste land in tropical countries
waiting to be developed, and all that is wanted is a little help
from the authorities to convert waste tropical possessions into
veritable gold mines, producing wealth beyond the dreams of
avarice.

Sir William Lever, May 1912

WITH PACIFICATION underway Woodford set out to attract investors in
the Solomons just as world prices for tropical products like copra and
rubber were starting to rise. Such plantation development required
extensive tracts of land and Woodford facilitated its acquisition by
European planters. Lands were obtained by resumption under the
Waste Lands regulations, by freehold purchase, and later by government purchase for leasing. Capital flowed into the Solomons as new
companies were established and older merchant companies extended
their operations.

Apart from the aim of making the Solomons self-supporting there was
no overall plan in the Colonial Office or even the High Commission for
the islands' eventual future. A general belief among Europeans that the
Melanesians were destined to die out provided a comforting rationale
for administrators as they permitted the alienation of thousands of acres

of Solomons land. Neither concept was particularly conducive to the protection of indigenous interests by those in power and both frequently led to practices that were reprehensible and legally questionable.

Commercial infrastructure

When Woodford came to the Solomons in 1896 in search of ways to finance the new protectorate he was encouraged to find that the trader Lars Nielsen, living peacefully among the Nggela Christians, had a small plantation at the stage where the coconut palms were bearing. At Marau too, the traders Theodore and Oscar Svensen, with their partners the Nerdrum brothers, had begun planting coconuts on small offshore islands and planned to establish a cacao plantation on the Guadalcanal mainland near Kaoka. Before this the only other attempts by Europeans to grow coconut palms commercially had been Brodie's planting of an acre or so at southeast Gizo and Stephens' purchase of the right to collect coconuts at Uki in the 1880s.[1] Traders had been unwilling to venture on a large scale into planting or buying coconut-bearing land because they lacked security of property and person.

With the establishment of the protectorate there was a strong possibility that extensive plantation development by Europeans could be safeguarded. Equally encouraging in the isolated Solomons was the advent of the first steamer service from Sydney. In 1894 G. J. Waterhouse extended his existing trading interests by sending to the Solomons on charter first the SS *Aldinga* and then the SS *Kurrara*.[2]

The *Aldinga* called at Papuan ports, cutting in on the trading and shipping interests of Burns, Philp & Company, a thriving north Queensland firm. To compete with this threat Burns Philp chartered the SS *Hesketh* to race the *Kurrara* to the Solomons.[3] With such service offered by Waterhouse and Burns Philp to traders in the Solomons, the *Sydney Morning Herald*'s shipping writer predicted:

> Let it be only known by the copra-getting white traders who live among the Solomon Islanders that two steamers a month will call on them and the stimulus for production will be so great as to lead to results scarcely yet conceivable.[4]

The potential business in the Solomons coupled with that in east New Guinea induced Burns Philp to buy its own vessels and start a regular steamer service to those islands. The steamer service did not produce any immediate boom in production—copra exports to Sydney in 1892 were 1650 tons and in 1900 they were almost the same.[5] But it did provide a regular means of transporting people and produce between the metropolitan center and the islands. To a world largely ignorant of island conditions the semimonthly steamer was a continued source of information. It became the protectorate's unofficial publicity agent in Australia.

The "waste lands"

Despite the encouragement of the steamer service, the static nature of export income worried Woodford because the Treasury was becoming more insistent on cutting all financial aid and having the Australian colonies administer the Solomons. In response, Woodford settled on a course he had recommended in 1896 to High Commissioner o'Brien, "Your Excellency should assume ownership of all unoccupied lands in the absence of native ownership. A system of long leaseholds or conditional purchases might then be inaugurated which would be a source of revenue . . . ."[6] Woodford, like many Europeans elsewhere in the tropics, was fascinated by the seeming potential of the "numberless uninhabited and most fertile islands" and their suitability for coconut growing.[7] It was but a small step, with a compliant Colonial Office seeking solutions to the Treasury's difficulties, to marry Woodford's political ambitions with the economic aims of the Pacific Islands Company, which in 1898 sought from the Colonial Office a concession for "all the unoccupied islands" of the British protectorate.[8]

The Pacific Islands Company, based in England, had grandiose schemes for economic and political penetration of the Pacific, an outcome of the background and character of its principals. One of the directors, John Thomas Arundel, brought into the company most of his assets, including those he had acquired from the New Zealand company of Henderson & MacFarlane—specifically, licenses to remove guano from, and plant coconuts on, a number of small mid-Pacific islands. Other directors were Sir John Bramston, former assistant under-secretary of state, Sir Robert Herbert, recently retired permanent under-secretary of state at the Colonial Office, and Lord Stanmore who, as Sir Arthur Gordon, had been the first high commissioner to the Western Pacific and governor of Fiji.

These directors applied for a land concession in the Solomon Islands to operate and govern as a chartered company, after the style of the British North Borneo Company or the New Guinea Kompagnie in the German territory. That the company should have a concession was supported unanimously by the Colonial Office, the high commissioner, and Charles Woodford. However, the Colonial Office rejected the concept of chartered companies because, as the Congo Free State was demonstrating, they were inefficient or often inhumane. The application was refused.[9]

After protracted negotiations the company was granted 200,000 acres for selection, but final agreement was further delayed, first by a counterclaim of the Deutsche Handels- und Plantagen-Gesellschaft (DHPG) to lands supposedly purchased in 1886, and second by consideration of the questionable legality of the Crown's assuming waste lands in a protectorate where there had been no existing state structure. The outcome was the British government's offer in 1903 of a "Certificate of Occupation." This rather tenuous instrument was hardly the kind of proprietary right the Pacific Islands Company wanted, since it forbade subletting and was of itself insufficient security for borrowing.[10]

The English company of Lever Brothers, manufacturers of soap, had meanwhile become interested in the Pacific Islands Company. William Lever was anxious that his company should gain direct access to raw materials and so control input prices for metropolitan processing. In order to avoid Australian tariffs on imported soap, Levers opened their Balmain factory in Sydney in 1900.[11] A year later, a chance meeting of William Lever with Arundel brought Levers a step closer to gaining control over the copra supplies so vital for soap manufacture. The original Pacific Islands Company was to be liquidated and a new one formed, along with the Pacific Phosphate Company (later well served by Lever on its board of directors).[12] By buying shares in the new Pacific Islands Company (1902), Lever obtained the rights to collect copra on small islands in the Cook, Line, and Phoenix groups, thus gaining a "foot-hold in the Pacific."[13] Levers now controlled a source of raw materials as well as a factory in the South Pacific area, but difficulties with shipping between the scattered islands and Sydney brought the enterprise to a halt.[14]

This apparent failure made William Lever cautious for a time. Meanwhile, the discovery of phosphate deposits on Nauru and Ocean (Banaba) islands drew his and other shareholders' concern to the more lucrative allied company, the Pacific Phosphate Company. The greater importance of the phosphate, the Pacific Islands Company's decreasing capital reserves, and the delays in negotiations meant that by 1903 the company's interest in getting the huge Solomon Islands concession had waned. Levers finally bought the concession from the company in 1906 for a mere £5000, but only after earlier arranging to purchase almost 80,000 acres of freehold land in the Solomons. This freehold buying had been urged on Lever by the firm's Sydney manager, Joseph Meek, who in 1905 anticipated commercial benefits from owning consolidated holdings in one area that combined a suitable climate and cheap labor with closeness to Australia.[15] With the rapid rise in the price of oils in 1906 (a result of competition from a new source, margarine manufacturers), Lever was even more determined to have his own source of raw materials for soap making. Moreover, he now believed that the best way to reduce the cost of vegetable oils and fats to his manufacturing company was to increase the world supply. The economic contradictions inherent in this dual role as producer and consumer were not to become apparent for another ten years.[16]

Levers had managed to obtain the concession for 999 years, instead of the 99 years originally offered by the Colonial Office. Woodford, thoroughly disgusted with the postponements and procrastinations of the Pacific Islands Company, had strongly supported the extension of the concession period[17] because he was anxious to have Lever as a "millionaire tenant" in the protectorate.[18] Despite this further concession, William Lever did not feel that the length of occupation could compensate for the insecurity of title by Certificate of Occupation.[19]

At first glance Burns, Philp & Company, as wholesale traders and shippers in the Solomon Islands, had little to lose by the appearance of Levers. The Sydney-based company conducted its business in the islands from the trade-room of its ship while anchored at such central places as Faisi, Gizo, or Tulagi, where all the traders' vessels assembled on "steamer day." In 1901, Burns Philp had shown no interest in establishing plantations or trading depots and declined to purchase Nielsen's station at Ghavutu (Figure 14), which Svensen subsequently bought. Two years later Svensen offered this land to Burns Philp again, along with 22,000 acres on Guadalcanal and in the eastern Solomons. Once again they declined.[20]

In 1904 Burns Philp acquired more than 800 acres of plantation land in the western Solomons. This apparent reversal of their former stance was forced on the company, not by any particular ambition to extend into plantation development, but by the threat of a competitor for the cargo that filled their ships. The competitor was the German firm of Eduard Hernsheim. Since the Shortlands were German territory prior to the incorporation of the northern Solomons into the British protectorate in 1900, German traders had had free access to the islands.[21] Not surprisingly, Hernsheim, whose Sydney agent was Justus Scharff, got a great deal of the business of the three related families of European traders there, the Macdonalds, Tindals, and Atkinsons. To win custom, Burns Philp obligingly took over mortgages held by Hernsheim on the properties of these families, and financed other undertakings. By 1904 the Tindals were both dead, as was John Champion Macdonald. In buying up the residue of the Tindal estates and foreclosing on the mortgages of Macdonald and Atkinson, Burns Philp at one swoop relieved itself of debts of £1200, and gained control of commercial plantations. They also gained control of Faisi which they believed to be "the finest harbour in the Shortlands and may possibly become a government coaling station." In view of Hernsheim's interest, their decision was motivated by the belief that "The Shortlands would be a stronghold for the company from which to extend operations in the event of trouble with anyone who might threaten our Solomon Islands trade in the future."[22]

When it came, the threat was not from Hernsheim, but from Lever Brothers. This company, aware of earlier difficulties arising from Burns Philp's grip on southwest Pacific shipping, purchased the first of their own vessels in 1903 to carry supplies from Australia and seed nuts from Samoa to their plantations in the Solomons.[23] Except for small tracts on the freehold lands that they had purchased, Levers' holdings by 1907 were either just being cleared or still in virgin bush; there could be no significant production until about 1913 or later as coconut palms take six years to start bearing. To get a paying return cargo for their SS *Upolu*, Levers began buying copra from the resident traders. In most areas where Levers held land, they installed their own agents to buy copra directly from the local people at more than double the going rate.[24]

By 1907 Burns Philp found they were losing more than half of their freight to Levers' ships—only two years after they had been forced out of German New Guinea by the government-subsidized Norddeutscher Lloyd Line. The company's position was precarious. In 1902 they had signed an agreement with the Commonwealth of Australia to provide a steamer service to carry mail to Papua, the Solomons, and the New Hebrides (Vanuatu) in return for an annual subsidy of £6000. The contract still had over four years to run. In an attempt to regain their commercial supremacy and fill their ships, the company contemplated extending forward, from being predominantly shippers and traders into fully fledged plantation operators, producing their own cargo.[25]

To do this Burns Philp, like Levers, had to get land. Like Levers too, they acquired some from the government as "waste land." The concept of waste land was well established in British law, but it was foreign to Solomon Islanders. All Solomon Islands societies believed that there were degrees of individual or clan interest in a particular piece of land, depending on the use to which it was put. A man had a strong claim over garden land, provided it belonged to his clan whose ancestors were the first to make gardens and build ancestral shrines there. Continual, if sporadic, use of an area implied some rights of ownership. Around New Georgia and the Manning Strait, particular groups of people had claims to certain small uninhabited islands because they went there at the full moon to catch turtles as they came ashore to lay eggs in the sand. Although they might not actually use it, land on and near certain mountains, such as Tatuve on Guadalcanal, was important to some of the Islanders because of its religious significance. Certain other inland areas, particularly the moss forest zone, were rarely used by any groups —but no European ever wanted this land for plantations and only a handful had ever visited such regions by the turn of the century. Very little arable land was "waste"; it was there to be used for various purposes. Most Europeans had little if any understanding of this, or of the amount of apparently "bush" land needed to sustain a population by swidden agriculture.[26]

Woodford, from his earlier Solomon Islands experience and conversations with traders in the 1880s, was convinced that depopulation had left whole islands virtually uninhabited. That depopulation had occurred from head-hunting, introduced diseases, and migrations in the western Solomons may have been true, but the way the resident commissioner investigated the current status of the ownership of the islands prior to alienation for "development" was cursory indeed. He sailed around the islands in the *Rob Roy* in 1899 with representatives of the Pacific Islands Company, but spent most of his time viewing the land from the foredeck. Woodford's description to the high commissioner of the large areas of land the Pacific Islands Company wanted indicates that, except for Kolombangara and Vaghena, very little ground surveying or exploration was done of the lands of Vonavona, the north coast of New Georgia, islands in the Manning Strait, and the south coasts of Santa Isabel and Choiseul. After the resident commissioner's tour, the north coast of New Georgia remained "quite unexplored" by Woodford's own admission, and the south coast, then claimed by the company, was "not visited." Woodford went on to say "I have never visited this place but I believe it to be quite uninhabited." In his report there is no evidence to show that any landing was made on the smaller islands in the Manning Strait. On the south coast of Santa Isabel, Woodford relied on the testimony of *one* "native of Bugotu" (a district on the southeast coast of the island), as to the entire area's being uninhabited. Woodford's view of south Choiseul from the sea (a view the Choiseulese knew a raiding party from, say, Vella Lavella, would have seen too) revealed that the coast was "entirely uninhabited" and so "no possible objection could ever be made to the alienation."[27] The high commissioner obviously shared Woodford's enthusiasm for the concession because, despite the incredible vagueness of the boundaries, the lack of any survey, and the sheer perfunctoriness or, more truly, neglect of the inquiry into who had interests in the land, he acquiesced in the transaction, never questioning Woodford's opinion.

Yet Woodford's opinion was not totally uninformed. His writings in 1886 and 1898 show that he well understood the process whereby an indigenous group of people might temporarily relocate or disperse in the face of enemy attack or natural calamity. He also knew that the survivors of such groups always kept on hoping to return to their ancestral lands when the threat receded.[28] Despite this knowledge, he seems not to have applied it to the lands he alienated under the Waste Lands Regulations of 1900, 1901, and 1904. The 1904 regulation defined waste land as "land which is not owned, cultivated or occupied by any native or non-native."[29] Most of the land in the western Solomons that Woodford inspected from the *Rob Roy* was not apparently "cultivated or occupied" but he never really tried to find out if it was "owned" and, in doing so, left a legacy of land troubles for future generations.

The original Waste Lands Regulation of 1900 was not a creation solely for the benefit of the Pacific Islands Company or its purchaser, Levers. Woodford had lobbied to have the claims of the Hamilton Pearling Company recognized by the high commissioner. Captain William ("Squeaker") Hamilton who owned almost half the shares in the small company had first visited the Solomons as a Queensland labor recruiter in 1883.[30] In 1899 Hamilton had learned from the trader Aubrey Griffiths that the pearlshell beds of the Manning Strait and Port Praslin, Santa Isabel, had been worked successfully by Svensen and a partner, Charles Wilson. Hamilton obtained a license from the German authorities in New Guinea because the area in which he wished to work was still German territory. Recognizing that the transfer of these lands to the British was a fact and wanting only the ceremony of lowering one flag and raising another, Hamilton asked Woodford for a license when the resident commissioner was aboard the *Rob Roy* with the representatives of the Pacific Islands Company in 1899. As Hamilton gathered shell and entered into general trading with the resident traders in Roviana, he found he needed a base for his eight small vessels, three boats, and supplies. His application for a further concession, including the rights to turtle fishing,[31] received Woodford's unconditional support because the resident commissioner gained £85 a year from this one concern in revenue from licenses and taxes—"the largest single contributor to the revenue of the Protectorate" in 1901.[32]

In allowing the grant of unoccupied lands to Hamilton, Woodford admitted no contradiction when he warned that any survey of them would be "certainly fatal to the surveyor."[33] If such islands were uninhabited, as he claimed, then how could a surveyor be killed? Woodford knew very well that groups of Solomon Islanders visited the area every year. Parties from New Georgia stayed on the islands of Manning Strait on their way to Choiseul and Santa Isabel. As they had been doing for generations, they caught turtles for their own use and to trade for the white man's goods. Likewise, the Kia folk of Santa Isabel also hunted turtles regularly on the islands.[34] By dismissing these people, who clearly had some rights to the islands and an undeniable claim to the turtles, with the pejorative word "head-hunters," Woodford clouded any indigenous claims to legitimacy. His logic became increasingly circuitous in trying to deal with such rationalizations. He told High Commissioner o'Brien that the natives of New Georgia "fully expect a veto will be put [by the government] on their visit to Ysabel and Choiseul on account of their past misdeeds." He went on to say that if they tried to visit these areas he would arrest them "on suspicion." Thus, he reasoned, "No hardship would therefore be entailed upon the natives of the group by the granting of a concession of the nature asked for by Captain Hamilton."[35] In 1904 Hamilton officially got his concession of a ninety-nine-year lease to the Manning Strait islands, including half of Vaghena (Figure 11).[36]

Throughout that year Hamilton and his agent Julius Oien started planting these islands (including Vaghena, Salakana, and Carpenter islands) with coconuts. The company, used to fairly immediate returns, found plantation establishment to be more capital intensive than they had expected. By 1907, when the pearlshell beds were becoming depleted and the price of pearlshell had dropped, the company was looking for quick profits from selling its land.[37]

One of the companies that was notified of this offer was Burns Philp, not surprisingly, since Hamilton's brother was the Melbourne manager of the Australian United Steam Ship Company, whose board of directors was virtually identical to Burns Philp's.[38] In almost every particular, Hamilton's lands seemed what the company wanted. Their plan for plantation development centered on getting an immediate return so that their steamers could be filled. They aimed first to buy up plantations that were established and near bearing and, second, when opening new land, to plant bananas interspersed with rubber or coconut seedlings since there was a good market for the fruit in Australia. Hamilton's offer included a pearling plant aboard a schooner, a lugger, the fishing rights to the islands, and about 400 acres planted with coconuts. The fact that the land was held under a Certificate of Occupation, which meant that within the first ten years the new owner had to spend 2 shillings per acre on improvements or forfeit the land, was considered by Burns Philp's man on the spot, Gerald Gordon, to be one of the few drawbacks to the purchase.[39] Following additional favorable reports by company representatives Robertson and Walter Henry Lucas, Burns Philp in 1908 agreed to the purchase for £8000 and unsuccessfully petitioned Woodford to extend the Certificate of Occupation for another nine hundred years, in line with Levers' concession.[40]

Burns Philp also obtained land directly from the government under the Waste Land Regulation of 1904. Not only did Woodford wish to see further investment in plantations, but he also wanted as many companies as possible involved in the islands because he was fearful that such a massive enterprise as Levers could become a monopoly and therefore a potential threat to the government's autonomy.[41] In 1908, on the understanding from the resident commissioner that a substantial grant would be made, Burns Philp formed a new subsidiary company, the Solomon Islands Development Company with a capital of £100,000 to develop plantations. The previous year the traders Svensen, "Billy" Pope, and T. Wilden, as well as the resident commissioner, had tried to find an

CHOISEUL (LAURU)

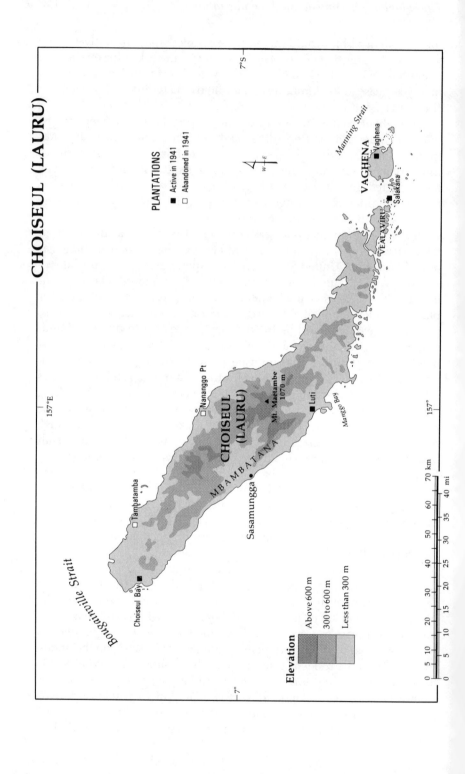

PLANTATIONS

■ Active in 1941
□ Abandoned in 1941

Elevation

■ Above 600 m
■ 300 to 600 m
□ Less than 300 m

unoccupied stretch of 10,000 acres for the company on Guadalcanal, an island preferred because it was closer to Australia. If successful, the traders were to have been paid a commission by Burns Philp. Presumably, for Woodford the company's investment in the development of the Solomon Islands would have been sufficient reward.[42]

A suitable area, Muvia, was found inland from Tetere on the Guadalcanal plains; it was bisected by the Ngalimbiu River (Figure 12). Because the sea frontage and areas to either side of the river were clearly occupied or planted with gardens, Woodford felt that the company should eventually get these reserved lands by direct freehold purchase from the native owners. Burns Philp, desirous of consolidating their "waste lands" concession and obtaining a sea frontage, was amenable to this suggestion since freehold conferred stronger title. Woodford's rationale for maintaining the reserves on the concession implies that he knew that the people did indeed hold rights to this so-called waste land and that he was consciously circumventing them. In creating the reserves he reasoned that the people "would accept the alienation of the large blocks."[43]

In 1908, W. H. Lucas made three attempts, with and without traders' assistance, to persuade the local owners to sell their land, displaying before them coveted gold sovereigns. This proved futile as the Melanesian Mission had strongly discouraged its followers from selling land in the area to Europeans. The people were also apprehensive of an influx of Malaitan plantation laborers.[44] Woodford was contemplating further compulsory resumptions to assist Burns Philp, but, because of conflict with Levers over labor-management relations, feared that Levers would expose any favoritism he showed Burns Philp. The plan that evolved to deal with this situation speaks eloquently for the kind of action Woodford was prepared to take to "develop" the Solomons. Lucas wrote in November 1908:

> At [Woodford's] suggestion I went over to Guadalcanal yesterday in a small open launch and have at last fixed up an arrangement with a native for a piece of foreshore. He has sold to a trader for a trading station only and I am giving the trader ten pounds to transfer to me. Mr Woodford will refuse to recognize the sale to the trader and will resume it for us.
>
> This roundabout method will stop any complaint that land was resumed forcibly which the natives required for themselves, as the rejected sale agreement will be on record.[45]

In the midst of these machinations, the secretary of state in England in 1912 finally approved amendments to the land laws, forbidding direct purchase of land from the native owners by non-natives. Any purchases were henceforth to be made by the resident commissioner

GUADALCANAL

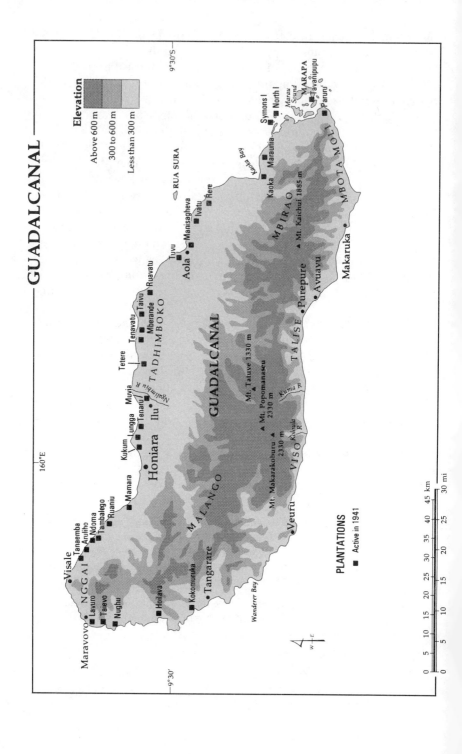

160°E

9°30'S

Elevation

Above 600 m

300 to 600 m

Less than 300 m

Visale
Maravovo
Tanaemba
Aruliho
Lavuro
Ndoma
Taievo
Tambalego
NGGAI
Nughu
Ruaniu
Hoilava
Mamara
Kokomuruka
Tangarare
MALANGO
Honiara
Kukum
Lungga
Muvia
Tenaru
Ilu
Tetere
Tenavatu
Mberande
Taivu
Ruavatu
TADHIMBOKO
Ngalimbiu R
GUADALCANAL
Mt. Tatuve 1330 m
Mt. Popomanaseu 2330 m
Mt. Makarakohuru 2330 m
VISO
Kohraja
Veuru
Kuma R
TALISE
Purepure
Avuavu
Makaruka
MBIRAO
▲ Mt. Kaichui 1885 m
Kaoka
Maraunia
Kaoka Bay
Symons I
North I
Marau Sound
MARAPA
Tavanipupu
Paruru
MBOTA MOLI
Wanderer Bay
Tuvu
Aola
Manisagheva
Ivatu
Rere
RUA SURA

PLANTATIONS

■ Active in 1941

W—E

0   5   10   15   20   25   30   35   40   45 km
0   5   10   15   20   25   30 mi

who could then lease them to suitable applicants. Burns Philp objected
to this in regard to the Guadalcanal lands because it debarred them
from obtaining under freehold the lands adjacent to their Muvia property. So began a protracted wrangle between Woodford, the high commissioner, the Colonial Office, and Burns Philp. Burns Philp argued
that Woodford had led them to believe they would get the coastal land,
in time, under freehold title. They quoted private letters from Woodford of 16 July and 6 October 1907 respectively:

> I think I can get you a block of ten thousand acres of the grass land upon
> Guadalcanar upon Occupation License as waste land. . . . The grass land
> is absolutely useless to the natives, so I see no reason why it should not be
> put to good account. . . . There would be no frontage, but I propose to
> arrange for you to have access to the coast where you require it, and before
> many years there is no doubt you would get the frontage too.

> I propose to recommend that the coastal frontage be reserved for you if it
> should come into the market, as it will eventually do in a few years time.[46]

Woodford was thus in a very embarrassing position when the Act
came into force on 1 January 1912. He was obliged, because of his
arrangement with Burns Philp, to recommend to the high commissioner
that the Colonial Office should be advised to grant special permission to
the company to purchase 5000 acres of freehold in the area, including
1210 acres the government had already purchased in 1912–1913. After
his retirement in 1914 Woodford personally approached the Colonial
Office on Burns Philp's behalf.[47]

When Colonial Office representative R. Vernon had visited the Solomons in 1912 to report to the secretary of state on political and economic affairs, he had also recommended that Burns Philp be allowed
the option of purchasing the land as freehold. Despite this pressure and
Burns Philp's London lobbying of Sir H. W. Just, under-secretary of
state for colonies, the Colonial Office remained adamant.[48]

Undeterred, Burns Philp launched a publicity campaign complaining
of their treatment and that of another Australian concern, the Vella
Lavella Plantation and Trading Company, by the Colonial Office. They
published their views in a series of articles written by the *Times* former
Australian correspondent, Arthur W. Jose, and edited by W. H. Lucas,
which appeared in the *Sydney Morning Herald* during May and June of
1915 and were subsequently assembled in a booklet, *British Mismanagement in the Pacific, No. 2*, distributed in Australia and Britain.[49] The
company highlighted its land problems, advocated the establishment of
an advisory council to consult with the high commissioner on matters of
local concern, and recommended that the high commissioner have
greater autonomy from the Colonial Office, that the administration of

Fiji be separate from the small protectorates' administration, and that the high commissioner reside "within easy reach of the islands." Australia was considered a suitable site for the high commissioner's headquarters.[50] The last proposal had been entirely supported by Woodford who frequently clashed with im Thurn, the high commissioner.[51] The assumption was that in Australia the high commissioner would be more responsive to local concerns and, by implication, more susceptible to pressure by Australian commercial and political interests.

The campaign did not achieve many of its wider aims, but Burns Philp received considerable satisfaction regarding their land grievance. Although they did not get freehold title, they were granted the land they wanted—Ngalimbiu, the river reserve, and Gavaga, the seafront reserve, under Certificates of Occupation for 999 years, along with a revised certificate on the adjoining block, Muvia, giving them the same period of occupancy on it—extending the original certificate by 900 years. This was done under special legislation in 1918 (King's Regulation No. 10 of 1918), four years after the Waste Land Regulation of 1904 had been repealed.[52] As Vernon of the Colonial Office had noted during his visit, "Most things are legally practicable in a Protectorate."[53]

The promise of the Solomons

The years from 1905 to 1913 were peak years for plantation development in the Solomon Islands. During this period the attention of investors all over the world was drawn to profits to be made from tropical products. In Malaya (now part of Malaysia), rubber was the most spectacular money-spinner. With the development of the pneumatic tire and the increased production of the motorcar, rubber was at a premium. The first boom came in 1905 when cultivated para rubber *(Hevea brasiliensis)* brought 6s. 10d. per pound. By 1909 the price had risen to 9s. 8d. per pound, with production cost in Malaya only 1s. 0d. to 1s. 3d. a pound.[54] While copra remained more steady, the European market prices were also gradually increasing: £15–£19 per ton in 1908, £18–£23 in 1909, £21–£28 in 1910 and 1911, £24–£28 in 1912, £22–£33 in 1913. Copra's importance appeared to be guaranteed following the discovery of a method to deodorize coconut oil that made it suitable for use in the manufacture of margarine.[55] In the Solomons, although other crops were possibilities, experts advised investors to concentrate on the coconut as a reliable and proven commercial crop.[56]

Plantations in the tropics became an attractive proposition in the eyes of the financial pundits.[57] In Australia, on 6 August 1910 the Sydney *Sun* published a full-page spread, amply illustrated, entitled "The Wealth of the Solomons." The article spoke of progress and prospects in the islands, emphasizing the dual theme of their potential and Australia's role as the "natural protector" of the area. On 12 August, Macmillan Brown hammered home his impressions in the *Sydney Mail:*

> The number of estates is growing every year. . . . For land is cheap . . . and there are vast areas that might be acquired from the native. . . . Rubber has not yet begun to be tapped. But if the price of rubber keeps up the Solomons will become a great field of its production. And some planters have assured me that 9d a pound on the plantation would pay.

> There are other tropical products that will always hold a good place in the Solomons though they will never approach to copra and rubber in importance. . . . Cocoa and coffee . . . vegetable ivory . . . .

A year later hopes were just as bright. The Melbourne *Age* of 23 March 1912 spoke glowingly of "the prospects of the copra industry."

The most significant book on the coconut industry was *Coconuts, the Consols of the East* by H. H. Smith and F. A. S. Pape, published in mid-1912. Full of practical advice to future growers, it placed high expectations on the potential of coconut planting. Its foreword was by W. H. Lever who supported the book with an almost evangelical fervor and was not altogether disinterested since his factories would be fed by the coconuts and increased primary production would most assuredly lead to a drop in the price of raw materials.[58] This kind of publicity, plus the fact that by 1908 both Levers and Burns Philp had pioneered investment in the Solomons, encouraged Australian capitalists.

By 1912 a number of companies with the aim of establishing plantations in the Solomons had been registered. Levers had started with a capital of £300,000, double that of Burns Philp's subsidiaries, Shortland Island Plantations and the Solomon Islands Development Company, combined. About twenty smaller companies were registered in Australia, ranging from minor concerns like the Fatura Island Development Company with a nominal capital of £8,000 to the widely advertised and subscribed Mamara Plantations with £130,000 (Table 3). The majority of the shareholders in these companies were Australians from the eastern states, most of whom lived in Brisbane or Sydney. Several owned shares in more than one company. Some had also lived and worked in the Solomons. Oscar Svensen, for example, invested extensively in Solomon Islands Rubber Plantations, Mamara Plantations, and Domma Plantations.[59]

Freehold land and the traders

All the plantation companies preferred freehold land because it gave both security of tenure and greater leeway regarding future use of the land. Rubber trees take six to seven years to mature and have a life of twenty-five to thirty-five years. Coconuts do not achieve full bearing

TABLE 3

Smaller plantation companies in the Solomon Islands, 1912–1913

Company	Nominal capital	Type of land title	Location	Specific sources
Bugotu Plantations Ltd.	?	?		
Domma Plantations Ltd.	?	Freehold	Ndoma	LTR: 191–149–1, no. 102/67 LR 40, Doma
Fairley Rigby & Co. Ltd.	10,000	Public lease	Boroni, Waimasi	QSA: COR, 30/1912; LTR: 252–809–1, LTO Pt. 3; LTR: 237–001–1, no. 15/68 and 18/69 LR 218 Boroni
Fatura Island Development Co.	8,000	Public lease	Papatura Island, Suavanu	LTR: 071–002–1 and 071–003–1, no. 88/71 and 89/71, LR 23, Papatura and Suavanau
Gibson Island Ltd.	20,000	Public lease		
Gizo Solomons Plantation Pty. Ltd. (F. Snowball)	?	Public lease	Nusaburuku	LTR: 097–013–3, Appl. for 1st regn., no. 42/67, LR 386, Nusaburuku, Gizo
		Freehold	Rendova Harbour	
		Freehold	Agana and Vangoro Islands	
		Freehold	Mbukimbuki	
		Freehold	Kenelo and Banyatta	LTR: 120–005–1, no. 81/67, LR 629, Kenelo
		Freehold	Buka Buki	LTR: 123–003–1, no. 55/71, LR, Buka Buki
		Freehold	Veuru	LTR: 123–003–2, no. 56/71, LR 25, Veuru
Hamilton Plantation Choiseul Bay Co. Ltd.	20,000	Freehold		NSWSA: COR 3/5838, no. 4388
Hivo Plantations Ltd.	10,000	Public lease	Haevo	QSA: COR, 139/1912; LTR: I08–004–1, no. 101/71 LR Kwarkiulo, Haevo
Kindar Ltd.	15,000	Freehold	Kinda	BPA: Kindar file; LTR: 098–006–2, LTO Pt. 3; 120–006–1, no. 37/1/73, LR

...ter description, LR 64, Barakai

Company	Area	Tenure	Location	References
Lavoro Plantations Pty. Ltd.	50,000	Public lease	Samarae and Repi	QSA: COR, 40/1910; LTR: 190–004–1, no. 92/68 and 123/68, LR 244 Taievo
		Public lease	Taievo	LTR: 190–004–2, Pt. 3, LTO nos. 93/68, 124/68, LR 220 Nugu
		Public lease	Nughu	LTR: 190–005–1, 96/98, LR, Lavoro, no. 2; 190–005–2, 97/68, LR 19 Lavoro no. 1
		Freehold	Lavuro	LTR: 190–006–1, 95/68, LR no. 17, Hoilava
		Freehold	Hoilava	
Mamara Plantations Ltd.	130,000	Freehold	Mamara	QSA: COR, 106/1911 See Chapter 6, note 81
Malayta Company Ltd.	50,000	Freehold	West Malaita	
		Freehold	Mbanika	LTR: 193–003–4, no. 29/1/72, LR 105, LR 106, LR 113, Ruavatu
		Freehold	Ruavatu	LTR: 205–002–1, Pt. 3, LTO, no. 156/70, LR 41 Bara Is.
		Freehold	Mbara Island	
Molie Plantation Ltd.	?			
Mundi Mundi Co. Ltd.	?	Freehold	Mundi Mundi	LTR: 063–003–1, no. 3/1/72, LR 1; LTR: 063–001–1, no. 83/66, LR 1, Mundi Mundi
Phil. Dickenson & Co. Ltd.	?	Public lease	Waimarae	LTR: 237–002–1, no. 19/68 and 29/69 LR 215, Waimarai
Gatere Plantations Ltd.	20,000	Freehold	Ghatere	
Solomon Islands Rubber Plantation Ltd.	15,000	Freehold	Chojoruru	QSA: COR, 28/1919; LTR: 107–002–1 to 107–002–3, no. 353/71, LR 174, LR 176, LR 177, Santa Isabel
Union Plantation & Trading Co. Ltd.	15,000	Freehold	Liapari	QSA: COR, 3/5789, no. 3148, Ullberg's Plantation Ltd.; LTR: 079–004–0, no. 28/69, LR 61 Liapari
Vella Lavella Plantation & Trading Co. Ltd.	?	?		?

SOURCE: WPHC 1734/13: BSIP-AR 1912–13.

(an average of fifty nuts per tree per year) until the eighth year, and have an assured life of fifty to eighty years depending on planting conditions.[60] Both crops, being long term, tied a planter's investment to one place for several years. The safer the title to the land, the more secure that investment.

Before 1912 a planter could obtain freehold land from either a non-native or a native owner. Buying from a European had its advantages since both the buyer and the seller worked within the same cultural and legal framework regarding tenure transfer. Because initial planting had already been started on some properties offered for sale by Europeans, plantation companies could be assured, first, of a title confirmed by use and occupancy and, second, of an earlier return than on virgin land. Therefore, with the boom conditions and particularly after the 1912 Regulation, European owners were in a position to demand high prices for their freehold land.

Almost all of the European owners had started business in the Solomons as traders. But by the early 1900s the whites were finding trading an increasingly unrewarding occupation. From 1896 they saw their profit margin whittled away almost yearly as the government imposed taxes on their heads, their ships, and their stations. Perhaps the worst blow was the introduction of an import duty on tobacco in 1906. At one shilling a pound the duty effectively doubled the price of the traders' principal trade staple.[61] In return for their taxes, traders in the "pacified" areas now had more security. Some, mainly newcomers, used their common race with the government's officers as a means to cheat the Solomon Islanders, who no longer had might on their side and who, as yet, had little understanding of the rules of the new power game, let alone how to manipulate them. More security also meant an influx of traders, more competition, and falling profits, especially as the government clamped down on gun trading.[62]

Yet the established resident traders held a trump card: they were men in the middle. For the first time in their careers as traders they could use this mediator's role to make themselves a fortune. They now had the chance to buy the respect they craved—the respect superior European visitors and even Solomon Islanders had long denied them. Because of their long association with the Islanders they could purchase land cheaply.[63] With one or two exceptions none had bothered to buy extensive tracts of land before 1900, but as some realized the possibilities of plantations, they purchased land from local owners. They could either start planting it themselves or hold it as a speculative investment, providing they could sell before the five-year development clause became effective.[64]

Although the European sellers sold at high prices, their indigenous neighbors, who were not privy to the negotiations of traders with big business, were less fortunate. The traders had no desire to tell of their huge profits for fear of causing resentment among the original owners and preventing further purchases. Big business was equally unlikely to advertise its payments to Europeans because prices would have risen, even on inferior or undeveloped plots, as the native sellers came to realize the value the whites placed on their lands.[65] Even the missionaries, where they had vested land interest, did little to enlighten the people. In the western Solomons, the Methodist chairman Goldie, later to complain stridently of other Europeans' land dealings, remained silent in 1907 while he bought up 7000 acres, 6000 for his own plantation company and the rest for mission use, at fourpence an acre.[66]

A brief overview of some of the major transfers of freehold land during the early years of the twentieth century illustrates the relative gains the landholding traders made. Between 1890 and 1907 as a trader, pearler, and later planter, Svensen managed to buy land from native owners as far apart as Guadalcanal and Santa Cruz. He also purchased lands from other Europeans who either had overextended themselves financially or wished to retire from the islands. By 1907, Svensen owned about 40 acres at Ghavutu, Tanambagho, and Ghaomi (Nggela); 17,500 acres at Lungga, several acres at Tadhimboko, 160 acres at Aola, 25,000 acres at Kaoka, islands near Marau amounting to about 110 acres (Guadalcanal); 2000 acres at Uki, 1200 acres on the Three Sisters, about 30 acres at Santa Ana, 1000 acres at Maro'u Bay, the island of Monagai near Anuta (San Cristobal); 1000 acres at Graciosa Bay (Santa Cruz); 2500 acres at West Bay (Russell Islands); and a trading station on Savo. In all, Svensen held 51,000 acres, of which about 200 acres were planted and 2000–3000 acres were cleared. For the purchase of this land he paid about £4000 (of which £3000 was paid to Lars Nielsen for the Nggela lands alone). In 1907, Svensen received £40,000 for the 51,000 acres, or about 15 shillings per acre, from Levers.[67]

As well as buying from Svensen, Levers acquired lands in the western Solomons from Norman Wheatley, who owned land at Logha, near Gizo, which he had purchased for £30–£50 worth of trade in 1899 and had improved by planting coconuts. He sold it to Levers in 1911 for £12,000.[68] Wheatley also sold the island of Mbarikihi, for which he had paid £24 in 1910, along with his leasehold on Samarae and Repi, to Kindar Limited for £7300.[69]

In 1909 Burns Philp bought Mberande on Guadalcanal from Justus Scharff, who had financed the bankrupt partners, Derbishire and Harding. Derbishire had bought the estate from Svensen paying £400 for the land—for which Svensen had originally paid £76. Under Derbishire and Harding, 424 acres of the approximately 2000-acre block had been cleared and planted with coconuts. They had asked for £10,000 but Scharff, who wanted the debt settled, accepted £5000 for the estate

and some boats. To Burns Philp the actual cost for the plantation land
was £3500 or about £8 10s. for each planted acre, which the company
considered a bargain since W. H. Lucas had estimated the cost of clearing virgin bush to be $5 per acre.[70]

Another substantial company began buying land in 1910. Its leading
shareholders were the Young family of Bundaberg, Queensland, who,
with their relatives the Decks, had become involved in evangelizing
Melanesians on their Queensland sugar plantations in the 1890s. From
the Bundaberg Queensland Kanaka Mission came the South Sea Evangelical Mission, which followed Solomon Islands Christians back home
after the cessation of the Queensland labor recruiting. The planting
concern, later known as the Malayta Company, purchased the major
holdings of the trader "Billy" Pope on Guadalcanal and in the Russell
Islands for £35,000. These lands had cost Pope no more than £300.[71]

In 1907 Pope had purchased a large block of land on northern
Guadalcanal, called Domma (Ndoma), paying the native sellers £30.
Three years later he sold it to the partners Oscar Svensen and d'Oliveyra
for £5142 17s. 1d.[72]

The Gizo Solomons Plantation Proprietary Limited was anxious to
buy land in the west for planting cotton and other tropical crops. Their
main shareholder, F. Snowball, paid £6400 for Mbukimbuki and Veeru
(Araro Island) at Rendova, to Harry Wickham in 1908. Between 1885
and 1905 Wickham had paid a total of £66 for the land.[73]

Since such high prices were being asked and obtained by European
sellers the companies might have been wiser to purchase directly from
the local people. That the traders had already selected much of the best
land and had portions of it cleared and planted were major considerations for the buying companies. Even more important, company representatives realized just how difficult it was for them to arrange direct
purchase. Burns Philp, with over ten years' experience in the islands,
advised their agent Gerald Gordon when he was sent to obtain lands on
Guadalcanal in 1907: "If . . . Mr Woodford decides that he cannot
actively help you, then it would be better not to attempt to do anything
by yourself, as a stranger would have no hope whatever of negotiating
any deal with the natives."[74]

The difficulty the companies faced was that they lacked any social
bond with the Islanders and did not know who were the rightful owners
of the land. In almost every case of freehold purchase pre-1905, Solomon Islanders sold land to men whom they knew well and whom they
believed would live among them on a permanent basis. The traders,
because of their long experience, could usually distinguish the true from
the spurious claimants to a piece of land.

The companies therefore turned to the traders to act as go-betweens
in arranging to buy native lands. From the company's viewpoint there
were risks attached to this too since a trader might decide to keep the

land for himself and sell out later at a high profit. In 1907, when Burns Philp commissioned Wheatley to buy lands for them, they were wary of his "usual keen sense of self-interest."[75] That Wheatley had been in debt to Burns Philp as early as 1901 and had mortgaged his Logha property to them for £1000 two months earlier, doubtless stimulated his "generous offer" to help the company obtain land.[76] Commissioned for £50 by Burns Philp, Wheatley purchased almost the entire island of Tetepare from the owners, Condor and Hindi. Burns Philp gave Wheatley £100 with which to pay the owners for over 30,000 acres. Although much of the land was to prove unsuitable for plantations, at three farthings (³/₄d.) an acre Wheatley had certainly made a bargain for the company.[77] Woodford recommended the sale, which was allowed despite some mild scolding by the high commissioner, who wondered what the acreage of Tetepare was and whether the consideration was adequate.[78]

One major company that did purchase lands directly from the local people was the Malayta Company. By the time it started looking for land in the Solomons much of the best, most accessible, and more extensive tracts of land had already been taken up. The attention of its directors was drawn to Malaita because some of them were relatives of the founders of the South Sea Evangelical Mission (SSEM). Here the company could not use traders as go-betweens because there had been no trade to draw such men to Malaita. The only Europeans who knew anything about that island had been the ship-bound labor recruiters, but their acquaintance with land matters was, of course, negligible.[79] The company tried to employ the missionaries, Dr. Norman Deck and Miss Florence Young, as intermediaries in purchasing lands near Bina on western Malaita in 1910. Since at this time there were no significant Protestant Christian settlements in the area, the SSEM missionaries' rapport with the people was little greater than the company's.[80]

Moreover, the Roman Catholics, using Catholic-converted returners from Fiji as go-betweens, had already bought land for a mission station at Bina from the rightful owners. Thereafter the Malayta Company's representative showed little understanding of either indigenous land tenure or indigenous opportunism. The company's huge purchases from just south of Kwaʻa to Suʻu (except for the land between the Fulo and Alaʻolo rivers and the Baunani block) remained uninspected by the district officer of Malaita, Edge-Partington, who nonetheless recommended them to Woodford. As the company took up occupation, the conflicts that arose made it abundantly clear that the west Malaitan purchases were riddled with misunderstandings on both sides. In some cases, plots of land had been sold by people with no rights to the land in question. On other occasions younger brothers or cousins sold land while their elder brother and clan spokesman was away working on a plantation on another island. Yet other quarrels arose when one or more of the owners was not given a share of the purchase price paid to the sellers. In some of the transactions no one bothered to pace out the back boundary of the coastal strip, leaving ample opening for further arguments. The company's managers, despite "tabu" reserves marked on maps, neglected to preserve shrines of clan ancestors, cutting down the sacred groves and angering the inhabitants.

Although it sometimes profited spurious claimants to ownership, the Malaitans' sharp dealing in land was well matched to that of the Europeans. It is bitter irony that these transactions, so hotly disputed from the time of the Malayta Company's occupation even to the present day, involved the highest prices ever paid for land by private purchasers to local owners for a virtually unoccupied and totally undeveloped area of poorly drained, shallow soils. For example, the land between the Fulo and Ala'olo rivers, about 2000 acres, was bought from Alick Guifoina and Lamouri for £140, 1500 porpoise teeth (value about £8–£10) and 4 cases of tobacco (value £40)—a rate of about 2 shillings per acre.[81] The Malayta Company was forced to offer such high prices for land because Malaitans, with their extensive overseas experience, had by this time a greater understanding of land values elsewhere than their less-traveled kindred in the copra-producing west.[82]

Although the Malayta Company's purchases were poorly supervised, Woodford was not always so careless. He usually refused to recommend the sale of lands where there was a substantial population in occupation or where existing groves of coconuts had been planted by nearby villagers.[83] However, Woodford generally supported sales where it seemed clear that the people would soon die out. He did this with the Mberande land Svensen wanted, but his rationale hardly said much for the "protection" the government afforded Solomon Islanders:

> I find that the native owners are not only willing but anxious to sell. The only natives at present living on the land are the two old men, Orri and Mallegai. They are anxious for the advent of a white man to protect them from the incursions of bushmen from the interior. Their rights are reserved during their life time.[84]

The landlord government and the leasehold system

By the end of the first decade of the twentieth century, Woodford, looking back over the twenty-three years since he first visited the Solomons, was convinced that the people of the islands, like the remnant that Orri and Mallegai represented, were doomed to extinction. He explained this view in a letter to Sir Everard im Thurn, the high commissioner, in 1909:

> The whole population of the British Solomons . . . will disappear. . . . My opinion is that nothing in the way of the most paternal legislation or fostering care, carried out at any expense whatever can prevent the even-

tual extinction of the Melanesian race in the Pacific. This I look upon as a fundamental fact and as certain as the rising and setting of the sun.[85]

Believing this, the resident commissioner reasoned that since all the islands would one day be totally depopulated it would be in the best interests of the government and the future of the Solomons to buy up the land. That the Melanesians were destined to disappear was not a view held solely by Woodford. It was true for most administrators in the dependencies of the Western Pacific High Commission at the time. For once, im Thurn agreed with Woodford.[86]

Despite this, he had refused to support Woodford's first scheme to amend the existing land laws. As early as 1906 Woodford had suggested that the government should buy land "from the native owners at the price they ask and that it should then be transferred from the government to the would-be purchaser at a price of not less than two shillings an acre." Woodford resented the "absurdly inadequate" prices being paid for land by private buyers, including Levers.[87] The basis of his resentment was not that the Solomon Islanders were losing or that their remnant population was in need of protection, but that government revenue gained nothing. Had such a scheme been adopted at the time, the government, instead of the land-dealing traders, would have made a profit on Solomon Islands land.

High Commissioner im Thurn rightly pointed out that Woodford himself had recommended the purchases at the "absurdly inadequate" prices and, since Woodford obviously planned to offer native owners the same low payment, refused to submit the proposal to the secretary of state because he believed it would be rejected.[88] Im Thurn and Woodford were frequently at variance, much of the conflict stemming from the fact that im Thurn was not only high commissioner of the Western Pacific territories but also governor of Fiji. He saw Woodford's success in attracting investment to the Solomons as a loss of potential capital for Fiji. Woodford, sometimes with justification, tended to read into all of im Thurn's policies a desire to subordinate the interests of the Solomons to those of Fiji.[89]

Woodford doggedly pursued his ideas on leasehold, finally putting them directly to the Colonial Office without im Thurn's knowledge. A modified scheme was approved by the Colonial Office, subject to im Thurn's support, which was eventually given. The government was to buy the land and lease it, rather than sell it, to prospective settlers.[90]

Such a system of leaseholds with an appropriate forfeiture clause would also give the government a large measure of control over the land, a control Woodford sought because he was critical of the lack of development on lands already purchased as freehold or held under Certificates of Occupation. Levers' concentration of expenditure on their freehold lands, to the neglect of the "waste lands," was particularly galling since Woodford saw such occupation without development simply as a ploy to keep out potential competitors.[91]

Woodford's recommendation for the introduction of a system of lease-holds was accepted by the secretary of state for colonies and became law on 1 January 1912. Under the regulation, the government became the sole purchaser from local people of land that was then leased to Euro-peans for ten to ninety-nine years, depending on how it was to be used. For a 10 percent commission the government was also empowered to arrange "Native Leases" between native owners and Europeans for terms ranging from five to ninety-nine years. In 1913 most of the Native Leases were for small areas, usually station sites of traders or mission-aries. The lands leased out by the government ranged from plots of 2 to more than 1000 acres, the latter being mainly for agricultural use, pre-dominantly on San Cristobal, Santa Isabel, and the New Georgia Islands.[92]

There is little evidence to show that Woodford saw the government's role as one of honest broker, even in 1911. It was not the emerging prob-lems over earlier transactions that brought him to opt for leasehold instead of freehold and "Certificates of Occupation," but rather the pecuniary benefit that was likely to accrue to the government. The stan-dard price paid by the government for native lands was 2s. 0d. an acre, a good price in comparison with some paid earlier to local owners for freehold land, but one that would earn for the government an average of 3s. 2d. per acre per year for the first thirty years of the lease, or a gross profit of 4620 percent.[93] Other than extending government control and policing labor recruitment, what all this extra revenue was to be used for was anyone's guess because neither Woodford nor the Colonial Office had any plans for medical or educational services in the Solomon Islands.[94] The main effect of the 1912 land regulation was, besides increasing potential revenue, to give the government greater control over lands and to stifle the emergence of market forces. There is clear evidence from the rising prices asked by some native owners that they had begun to become aware of market forces as the history of the Malayta Company's transactions demonstrated.

By the eve of World War I, of the estimated 9,500,000 acres of land in the protectorate, over 463,425 acres or about 5 percent had been alien-ated, over half under the Waste Land Regulations.[95] In absolute terms this is not great, but it is significant in terms of the accessible coastal land available for coconut planting.[96] Woodford had met all the land needs of potential investors, attracting over £1 million in capital from plantation companies. In his last annual report before his retirement, the resident commissioner could justifiably boast of the progress of development in the protectorate that "during the last six years a larger area of land has been brought under coconuts in the Solomons than in any other group of islands in the Western Pacific" and the applications for land for coconut planting were continuing to pour in.[97] His land policies, it appeared, had been a success.

BETWEEN ABOUT 1890 AND 1920, official Colonial Office policy toward tropical colonies where there was a substantial native population ranged between, at best, protection and paternalism and, at worst, exploitation carried out as efficiently and painlessly as possible. In the Western Pacific and elsewhere, local commissioners were largely the real policymakers, with London rubber-stamping decisions, except on matters likely to draw discussion in the British Parliament. There was little, if any, concept of the "development" of native peoples or of major resources for these people.[98] The Solomons was one of the most insignificant areas of the British Empire, with policies determined mainly by leisurely correspondence between the resident commissioner in Tulagi and the high commissioner in Fiji, with occasional glances over their shoulders to possible Australian attitudes.

In the Solomons the dominant motivation behind all government policy decisions was the need for the islands to be self-supporting. The colony was run like a business and the revenue column had at least to balance with the expenditure column, if not to exceed it. With such constraints it was not surprising that Woodford set out to alienate lands for expatriate investors, particularly since he, like most Europeans, assumed that the Solomon Islanders were a dying race. Woodford used contrivances like the Waste Lands Regulations to make legal fiat out of legal fiction. The resident traders generally assisted the process of alienation by selling out the lands of their erstwhile customers to the planting companies at huge profits. Woodford had the power to disallow further speculative freehold transactions, but allowed them to proceed until 1912. Even then, when he gained total control of new land dealing by a system of leasehold, he was motivated by a desire to gain profits for the government, not to protect the people from their own ignorance and individual cupidity or to raise money for measures to halt their extinction.

Recognizing all this—the ad hoc nature of Colonial Office policy, the demands for revenue, and the prevailing beliefs of administrators—Woodford still emerges as blameworthy in his role as the architect of Solomons land alienation. Not only did he fail to investigate the state of occupancy and ownership of thousands of acres of so-called waste lands, as well as many freehold parcels, but he also resorted to secret and illegal maneuvers to assist Burns Philp to acquire land. The capitalists had received far more than "a little help from the authorities" and the Islanders far less in this new colonial world.

CHAPTER 7

The colonial government and labor

(c. 1900–1930)

Having given the matter our closest attention and having
regarded it from every aspect, we are compelled to come to
the conclusion that, in our considered opinion, no change of
administrative policy or no voluntary action on the part of
employers in offering more attractive conditions of service
can possibly provide a local solution of the vital problem of
labour shortage with which the Protectorate is at present
faced.

Report of Labour Commission, 1929

THE PROTECTORATE GOVERNMENT met the land demands of the commercial planter with comparative ease. Providing a supply of labor to
develop that land was far less simple. Logically, the European belief
that the Melanesians were dying out meant that sooner or later the
demand for labor would outstrip the supply. Even when recruiting for
the overseas labor trade ended, the planters were still short of the numbers of men they needed. The obvious solution was to import indentured labor as had been done in the 1870s when Indians were brought to
Fiji. But the Colonial Office opposed this policy, and its position hard-
ened with the passage of time. After World War I the Colonial Office
showed an increasing interest in the labor conditions of the British territories, although its power as policymaker was circumscribed.

From the start the protectorate government had opposed the blatant
abuse of human rights as understood in British law. But enforcement
was another matter since, in the first decade or so of the protectorate,
frontier justice was the order of the day for the Solomon Island laborers.
By the 1920s the government had greatly improved conditions of indenture, following its recognition that the protectorate's laborers were
essential to the economy and had to be preserved. The dominant concern of the government was always to develop the plantation economy;

as its control on the Solomons tightened, legislative measures were formulated with this goal in mind. Laws were introduced to fix wages in the employers' favor at the same time as a head tax was imposed, compelling men in poor areas to seek work on plantations for a time.

The Colonial Office and labor policy

The white planters of the Solomons had been supplied with an abundance of land by a cooperative government and they expected similar assistance with labor. Both the government and the planting companies neglected to consider the extent of the potential supply. Without a census there was no way of counting the population, although estimates ranged from 100,000 to 150,000.[1] Nonetheless, Woodford believed that numbers were declining and that eventually the labor supply must also dwindle. Even the heaviest investor, Levers, had been careless in assessing the labor supply, expecting that with the cessation of the overseas labor trade, enough workers would be obtained from the larger islands.[2] As late as 1910, the normally perspicacious W. H. Lucas thought that the labor crisis "would not be reached for several years."[3]

His was a singular opinion. By 1909 Woodford and most of the planters found that as more and more acres were cleared and planted, the demand for labor exceeded the supply. With the model of Fiji's development using Indian labor in mind, Woodford requested that such labor be introduced to the Solomons, arguing as he had on the land question that the Solomon Islanders were a dying people. The high commissioner favored the request, as did the secretary of state for colonies, but he sought the reaction of newly federated Australia, which it was thought might soon be responsible for the Solomons. The response was not encouraging: the Australians could see no logic in importing "coolies" while Solomon Island labor was still being recruited for Fiji and urged the protectorate to ascertain the strength of its uncounted, partly unpacified population.[4] Nevertheless Woodford raised the issue with the high commissioner again in 1910 and 1911, pointing out that experiments in growing rubber and cotton, which required specialized, intensive labor, were being abandoned because of the labor shortage.[5]

For their part, Levers developed a plan similar to Fiji's for the introduction of indentured labor, but the secretary of state for India, harking to the stirrings of Indian nationalism in 1911, would not consider it unless only free laborers were involved.[6] At the end of 1912, when it was apparent that the closing of the labor trade to Fiji had not solved the difficulty, Vernon of the Colonial Office visited the protectorate and recommended the importation of laborers. Encouraged, Levers and Burns Philp, the largest employers, increased their lobby in Britain and in the Solomons.[7] But they had reached a stalemate. Any company willing to spend money on recruitment and transportation of overseas labor required some kind of contract or indenture of the laborer to guarantee a minimal return. The Colonial Office would not permit the introduction of labor to the protectorate under these conditions and the companies refused to risk capital to import free labor.

The first World War (1914–1918) and its local effects caused a lull in the planters' complaints. The invasion of German New Guinea by Australian forces led many to believe that it too would soon become a British territory giving them free access to Bougainville labor. However, the peace settlement saw Australia as administrator of the new mandated territory and all labor reserved for New Guinea's own needs. Since on the eve of the war Burns Philp had deployed some investment funds intended for the Solomons to Bougainville because of the availability of freehold land there, its success as a plantation concern was not completely tied to the fortunes of the protectorate.[8] Levers, heavily committed to the Solomons, had to make the best of its operations where they were. By 1923 the company had cultivated only 20,000 of its 400,000 acres, being unable to expand further without additional labor. Once again Levers proposed elaborate schemes for importing either Indians or Chinese. Despite the protectorate government's support, the Australian government, in line with its "White Australia" policy, was firmly against the migration of large numbers of Asians to islands so close to its own thinly populated shores.[9]

By this time, too, other influences on the Colonial Office were taking effect. The war stimulated British public interest in colonial peoples, just as the creation of the International Labour Organization (ILO) in 1919 drew world attention to labor conditions in colonies. The passing of the India Emigration Act in 1922 brought the Colonial Office under pressure from the India Office to regulate the employment of contract labor within dependencies.[10] The possibility of introducing any new scheme for large-scale recruiting of plantation labor from one dependent territory for indenture in another was now out of the question. By the end of the twenties British officials in the Solomons had to concede that without outside labor there would be "no hope or prospect of further development."[11] But the framers of wider policies in the Colonial Office could suggest no solution other than making the best use of the Solomons' own labor.[12]

After the war, Colonial Office opinion was slowly becoming important on other general policy matters. Lacking the power of the purse, the Colonial Office was not often able to force the financially independent Solomons to legislative positive advancements, but it was more successful in preventing what might internationally be considered as regressive legislation, especially in labor matters. For example, the

Solomon Islands Planters Association, formed in 1914 to represent the smaller planting companies, constantly tried during the 1920s to have the two-year contract period extended to three; but the secretary of state for colonies remained adamant. Similarly the planters found the Colonial Office consistently against the recruiting of married men without their wives "because the statistics in many parts of the Empire show that it adversely affects the birth rate."[13]

The protectorate government and labor

Despite these constraints, the protectorate government assisted the planters to maximize the existing labor supply and minimize its cost. Broadly, the evolution of policy and practice of labor regulation and supervision falls into three periods: 1897 to 1913, 1914 to 1920, and from 1920 until the outbreak of the Pacific War. During the first period, the abuses of labor by employers were at their worst because of poor government supervision and a concomitant frontier mentality among many of the overseers and managers. From about 1914 to 1920 employment conditions gradually improved, partly because of stricter government regulation and inspection and partly because employers and employees realized that labor was a scarce resource. By the early 1920s, the entire system of indenture and its regulation was stable, with channels of communication and action established and generally known to both employer and employee.

In 1897 Woodford introduced the first labor regulation in the Solomons, but at this time concern was more with establishing the government's interest in labor matters in the face of competition from Queensland and Fiji than with setting out detailed conditions for the employment of indentured labor. Contracts were limited to two years, planters were to send in reports of their labor every three months, and laborers were to be repatriated free of cost. Control of labor employment within the Solomons was vested in the resident commissioner, who was empowered to issue licenses to employ and had the right to inspect plantations.[14] In practice Woodford tended to ignore the abuse of labor, more often noticing the positive side of the laborers' plantation experience. In 1908, he maintained that laborers were "extremely well treated," that the "condition of the natives employed on coasting vessels and upon plantations in the Protectorate is infinitely better than the sordid conditions under which most exist in their own homes," and that after their indenture they returned to the villages with better physiques.[15]

But conditions on some plantations were sordid in the extreme. In 1908, for example, Fulton, the assistant general manager of Levers'

Rendova plantation, wanted a photograph of a young Solomon Island woman called Likin. Hermes, an overseer, asked Likin to undress in a nearby store in front of a group of Malaitan laborers, telling her to put on fresh clothes for the occasion. This angered one of the men, Aho, who tried to shove Hermes out of the store. In the fight that followed Hermes shot Aho three times, killing him.[16]

Such incidents were not uncommon. Guadalcanal and Malaita men who worked on plantations at the time recall many conflicts, which rarely got into court. About 1912, a Mr. "Jack" at Yandina, Russell Islands (Figure 13), used to wield a stockwhip to encourage the men to work; he eventually kicked a Makira man to death, and left the country. At Levers' plantation at Mbanika, in the same group, an overseer shot Sunde, a Malaitan, in the head and killed him because he had broken the standard company rule of not eating the flesh of the coconuts. Said to have killed another Malaitan called Arimauri, the overseer was whisked out of the islands by Levers. Another Levers man, Thompson, attacked an 'Are'are laborer at Ilu, Guadalcanal, killing him with a mattock; he, too, found sanctuary in Australia.[17]

Physical violence was the order of the day on most plantations. Levers' European employees were notorious for it, but others acted similarly. At Baunani (Malayta Company) Allen, when provoked, would belt men with a *loia* cane, just as McAlpine and McIntyre did at Tetepare (Solomon Islands Development Company). At Salakana, another plantation held by the same Burns Philp subsidiary, the French-Tahitian James Gibson ("Jimmy the Gib") hit the men as a matter of course when they refused to obey (Photo 13). Malaitans who worked at Levers' Pipisala plantation (Russell Islands), remember an overseer, E. H. Glasson, who would hit them if they stood up from their work to straighten their backs.[18]

Government documents paint a similar brutal picture. Glasson was involved in a court case in 1915 against disobedient laborers, and two years later killed Bluie, a laborer at Levers' Faiami estate and a former Queensland migrant. Glasson fled the protectorate and enlisted in the army in Sydney. Leaving the country voluntarily or at the urging of their employer or the government was the standard way of avoiding a possible murder charge.[19] In 1915, V. J. Francis of Kau Kau (Levers' Kaoka plantation) departed on a steamer after killing a Santa Cruz man, proclaiming, "what does it matter if I did kill a nigger?"[20] Despite this and the widely held public opinion that he was guilty, the government allowed him to leave. Before 1914 the Solomons had no judicial commissioner to try major cases. Because officials knew that legal action involving court cases in Fiji could cost the government hundreds of pounds, they preferred deportation. With Islanders being tried and hanged for murder of their own people and the occasional white man, it

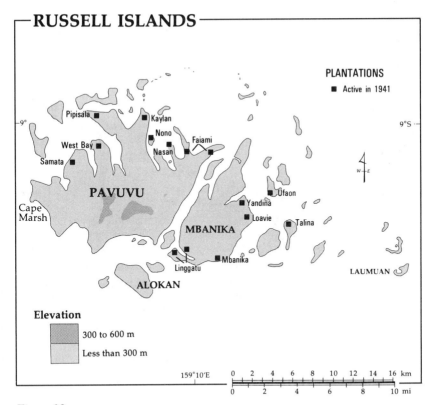

Figure 13

did not take long for them to realize that "the government hanged a native for killing white people, but if a white man killed a native it was nothing; the European just went away."[21]

Lack of government personnel, judicial and otherwise, was the underlying cause of maltreatment of laborers on plantations. Although Woodford could not spare staff to check conditions on plantations near to government centers, he allowed planters to settle in areas still uncontrolled. As well as being unable to police the labor practices of these planters, the government could not protect them from the local community. At Uki in 1908, Levers' manager Munster, fearing an attack by visiting Malaitans, armed his laborers with Sniders. Evidence in this particular case proved Munster to be an extremely unsavory character, yet Levers made the point to Woodford that some of Munster's actions were understandable because Uki was a dangerous place and the government offered no police protection for the planter.[22] Likewise on Malaita from 1911 to 1917, despite the presence of a district officer at 'Aoke, the Malayta Company had to station its own armed guards around its plantations at Su'u and Baunani to protect employees and

Photo 13. Typical early plantation house of Solomon Islands Development Company at Salakana, c. 1910. Front seated: James Gibson and his Tahitian wife, Turai Miriami A. Tehei. Back, seated on left, Walter Henry Lucas. *(Burns Philp Archives)*

property from marauding bushmen.[23] Planters on San Cristobal also had to rely on their own resources to cope with trouble. In 1914 Mumford wrote to his company in Australia:

> The Bushmen here at Boroni are still very liberal with their threats, and native reports are to the effect that we are to be honoured with a repetition of the raid last Xmas, but I don't know when, and it is probably only bluff, although it would not be quite so easy to drive them off now I have only 7 boys here with me as they can muster 2[00] to 300 all well armed. They are the same crowd that killed and ate those Malayta boys some months ago and they often visit me here 20 to 30 strong. However, I do not lose any sleep and my home is always open and my Winchester always ready.[24]

Such conditions meant that the Solomons had a limited appeal as a place of employment for Europeans. As the bigger companies tried to hire personnel to run their plantations they had to accept the best they could get. The best frequently proved to be the worst when it came to labor management. Young men from the Australian cities, abundant in hopes but deficient in experience, often became unbalanced because of loneliness and took their frustrations out on their laborers.[25] Experienced men came too, men who were used to maintaining their authority by force and could each say of themselves, "I can handle niggers and am salted to malaria. . . . I have guts . . . and am . . . used to uncivilized life in tropical countries."[26] Men of this ilk, often both unchecked and unsupported by government, rationalized their fear of the odds they faced by assuming their own superiority. An old hand instructed the newcomer Jack McLaren in 1910 in methods of controlling native labor: "Treat them as muck. Remember that a white man's the only human being and that there isn't any other kind. That's the only way to get anything out of them."[27]

Such frontier attitudes shocked Mahaffy when he visited the protectorate in 1908 to report on developments. He warned the high commissioner that the mainly Australian managers of Levers were

> for the most part unable to deal with native labour, and this is not surprising when it is remembered that they have every opportunity of manifesting their dislike for "niggers" upon the somewhat isolated plantations of the firm. Desertions are not infrequent among the native labour, and . . . in some cases they may be accounted for by a lack of consideration, and in some cases by actual cruelty. It is not denied that floggings take place upon the estates, and to put such a power into the hands of ignorant and prejudiced persons constitutes a real danger.[28]

To avoid the abuses Mahaffy recommended a more stringent labor regulation that would be rigorously enforced. Besides his humanitarian concern for the laborers, Mahaffy realized more clearly than Woodford that harsh treatment, although it might produce short-term gains, would soon lead to a decline in the numbers offering for contract work with certain planting companies.

In 1910, as a consequence of Mahaffy's report, Woodford introduced new labor regulations, which detailed conditions of employment and repatriation, fixing the minimum age of recruitment at fourteen (soon after changed to sixteen) and setting out how the maximum fifty hours of work a week was to be allocated, with Sunday as a day of rest.[29]

Not long before Mahaffy's report Woodford had appointed Sykes as inspector of labor, but his duties were mainly to supervise the final repatriation of Queensland returners and to act as government agent on the *Samoa*, a German vessel recruiting in Solomons waters.[30] In 1911 an Australian and former government agent on Fiji labor vessels, William Bell, took over the position. Bell found himself in a ludicrous situation: With no ship, he could not inspect plantations or ratify contracts beyond the confines of Tulagi. Since Woodford had failed to have more than a few copies of the 1910 regulations printed, planters did not know the new laws. It was common knowledge that recruiters often neglected to sign on recruits in front of a government officer and that planters kept poor records of the names and length of contracts of their laborers. Bell, not cut to the strict mold of the British colonial servant, volubly criticized these faults to all his superiors, including the secretary of state.[31]

In 1914 the years of neglect of labor conditions took tragic toll. Dysentery broke out among plantation laborers and spread rapidly, exacerbated by lack of medical care and filthy, crowded conditions on recruiting vessels, plantations, and at Levers' and Burns Philp's transit depots near Tulagi—Ghavutu and Makambo (Figure 14). Bell's first official inspection of plantations revealed how inadequate facilities were to deal with any of the medical problems of laborers, let alone a dysentery epidemic. Of approximately 150 plantations, there were

> not three plantation hospitals which by the greatest stretch of imagination would be considered sufficient. . . . Almost all the so-called plantation hospitals are miserable structures of rough native material even worse than the ordinary labour house with a floor of ordinary earth on which the building is erected, and no attempt at cleanliness and sanitation. . . . The treatment of dysentery patients during the epidemic was in many cases inhuman and dangerous to the community. I have seen a labourer in the last stage of dysentery lying unattended on the ground with a covering of only a sheet of roofing iron leaning against a packing case.[32]

So alarming was the epidemic that F. J. Barnett, who had replaced Woodford, ordered all recruiting suspended from August until December. Even so, the overall death rate among laborers was almost 5 percent, reaching a terrifying 10 percent on Levers' plantations. The Colonial Office demanded to know why.[33]

Barnett and his successor were more supportive of Bell's approach than Woodford and, with the impetus of Colonial Office scrutiny, began to implement the regulations and improve supervision. By 1915, the inspector of labor had got a vessel, the *Mala*, and was able to inspect 54 of the 147 plantations. In the following year all were inspected.[34] Levers' overseers, left to their own devices for so long by their employers and government, did not want anyone "buggering about [their] labour" as Bell was told, but the court proceedings that followed in the wake of his early inspections proved they could no longer act with impunity toward labor.[35] Reports of the most notorious cases involving Francis, Glasson, and Levers' local manager, Norman Ross, flowed from Tulagi to Suva and thence to Whitehall and the Colonial Office. In turn, the Colonial Office queried Sir William Lever, who for years had been trying to convince it just how well his company would care for coolie labor should it be allowed into the protectorate. A few months later Ross and his associates were replaced.[36]

During this time more rigorous regulations were introduced: Recruits had to sign on and off in front of the inspector of labor or other government officers at either Tulagi or district headquarters to ensure that laborers understood the nature of their contract, were in good health, and, at the end of their term, to check that they received the balance of

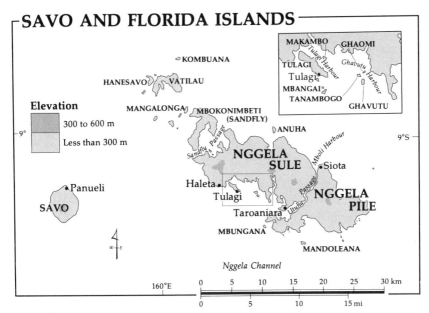

Figure 14

the wages due to them. As new stations were opened at Aola and Kira-kira and district officers were equipped with vessels, the work of the labor inspector was supplemented, allowing for closer government attention to labor-management relations.[37]

The rights of the laborer were increasingly protected by 1915, but the government also guaranteed the employers' rights under indenture. The Solomons (Labour Amendment) Regulations of 1912 strengthened the legal sanctions so that every hour of work lost to an employer because of the laborer's disobedience or "want of reasonable diligence" would be compensated for by the deduction of two hours' pay. Bell pointed out that this was a trivial deterrent in terms of the court procedures neces-sary and urged that the penalty be increased with a clause allowing for the imprisonment of recidivists and the extension of contracts to cover the time lost by imprisonment.[38] In the planters' view there were good reasons for this. Levers, for example, calculated that they had lost the equivalent of "7½ years of one unit's time" as a result of eleven men being imprisoned following an assault case.[39] Losses like this meant that there was less likelihood of planters taking a laborer to court for offenses against the regulations because the planter would suffer no matter what the outcome. Further abuses were likely as overseers tried to solve their problems out of court.[40] The penal provision became law in 1921, but to the annoyance of the planters, only the resident commissioner could

grant the extension of contracts. In cases where further and possibly
dangerous conflict seemed inescapable, he ususally denied such requests
by planters.[41]

Although in the early twenties blatant abuse of labor was rare, there
were still opportunities for exploitation. As the concept of a daily task
was just beginning to replace that of working for a number of hours
each day, the management of the Malayta Company ordered its overseers at isolated Baunani to extract 510 pounds of copra from each
worker instead of the conventially accepted but legally unstipulated 450
pounds. Despite such occasional avoidance of the spirit of the law, by
1922 the system of labor administration was well established and its
procedures routine.[42] K. J. Allardyce, a special commissioner sent from
Fiji to investigate the wage scale and other labor matters, was able to
declare that the system was responsible for "satisfactory" employment
conditions for indentured labor.[43]

Wage policy

In the early years planting companies had found that they were not
dealing with an entirely unsophisticated labor force. Certainly many
young men, some no more than adolescent boys who had been rejected
by the vessels recruiting for Queensland and Fiji, were willing to go to
work on Solomon Islands plantations for from 5 to 10 shillings a month.
Attracted by the shorter contract of two years and the recruiters'
embroidered tales of far distant places, away beyond the sunset in "Roviana," these rejects of the overseas labor trade signed on to do the
pioneering work of clearing plantation land.[44] Older men with Queensland or Fiji experience were not as easily beguiled. At Bina, Malaita,
Leslie Gill tried in 1912 to recruit labor for "Roviana," but found that
the disgruntled passage-master's only response was to rail against the
injustice of the various "govamun" involved in closing the colonies to
Solomon Islanders.[45]

Aside from the loss of seeing new places and sampling life overseas,
the source of the Islanders' discontent was economic. They knew that,
although the Queensland wage for the "new chum" was 10 shillings a
month and the Fijian half that, a man who had "finished time" with
three or more years' experience could get much higher wages. Corris
estimated that about 25 percent of the Melanesian labor force in
Queensland and Fiji from at least the mid-1880s were "old hands" and
received more than the minimum wage.[46] By the 1890s, Queensland
employers were discovering, much to their regret, that "the Kanaka is
finding his real market value and refuses to re-engage on the original
terms."[47] While the labor trade was flourishing, experienced returners
in the Solomons had no difficulty bargaining with Queensland recruit-

ers for above-minimum wages during the early 1890s.[48] By 1906, following the cessation of recruiting, the demand for experienced Melanesians in Queensland increased and men remaining could get over £1 a
week.[49]

Islanders saw themselves being excluded from these relatively good
employment opportunities, perhaps not realizing that the diminishing
supply was forcing up the demand for seasoned workers. Among those
deported from Queensland were men whose income had for many years
been above £50 a year; a few of them had operated small businesses,
such as wood carting or boarding houses.[50] Consequently, many returners and deported laborers had raised expectations when employment opportunities offered in their homelands. Certainly in 1896 pioneer planters such as Svensen and Nerdrum had accepted that they had
to compete with the colonies in hiring "finished time" men if they
wanted really experienced workers: They were willing to pay them double the Queensland minimum wage. Levers and later planters did not
have to do so because the closure of Queensland in 1906 and Fiji in 1911
took away the real competitors for labor. Levers followed the recommendations of the Pacific Islands Company agent, Grant, who said that
a minimum monthly wage of 10 shillings had to be general if profits
were to be made.[51] As a result, in the years following the cessation of
overseas labor recruiting, less than 1 percent of the labor force was
employed at 10 to 15 shillings a week and the majority received only 2s.
6d., or 10 shillings a month.[52] Although some returners worked at the
going Solomons rate, they found that their money could purchase less
than in Queensland. Even before 1906, when Woodford imposed a duty
on tobacco,[53] the cost of duty-free tobacco and other goods was offset by
the extra freight plus the fact that traders marked up commodities and
sold them at "native prices."[54]

Solomon Islanders began to understand that they had lost much with
the end of the labor trade. Shortly after his return to Malaita in 1908, a
dissatisfied Peter Ambuover (or Ambuofa) petitioned the king of England for a Solomon Islands basic wage of £1 a week and complained of
his deportation from Queensland. In 1912, discontented with their
increasingly apparent loss of options, Ambuover, Benjamin Bowra
Footaboory, Jackson Kefeety and his brothers (sons of Kwaisulia of Ada-
gege), Jack Gwoefoon, Harry Rumsalla, and Harry Umfirra of north
Malaita, petitioned Woodford for an improved local wage, for "European" food, and for more humane treatment on plantations. They
asked that young boys from twelve to fourteen years of age receive £1
per week, men of fifteen years and over who were new to the work
receive £1 5s., and "old hands" £1 15s.[55] Footaboory and his friends,
using their new-found Christianity as a weapon to argue their case,
pointed out to Woodford: ". . . we are now under the British flag so we

should get wages and treatment equal to the whites. We are all one in the law and in the eyes of Jesus, our Lord."[56] (See Appendix 8.)

Although Woodford ignored the petition and kept the minimum adult wage at 10 shillings a month, the increasing demand for labor from about 1913 on began to affect the cost to the planter of obtaining workers. The recruiters, receiving orders from the planters, were confronted with the growing difficulty of finding recruits. To attract them, the competing recruiters were compelled year by year to increase the customary "beach pay," which was usually trade goods. Naturally, they passed their increased costs on to the planters. Recruiting fees rose steadily: £6–£8 in 1911, £10–£12 in 1915, £14 in 1916, and £20 in 1920.[57] Although the legal wage remained stable, the market was forcing up real costs.

Labor concerns dominated the first meetings of the Advisory Council in 1921 and 1922. The council consisted of two official government members, two representing commerce, and one, Bishop John Steward, representing the missions. Of course, no Melanesians were on the nominated council, their interests presumably being represented by the missionary and government members.[58] The planters called on the government to control the rising beach pay by banning it, or at least setting a limit to its value. They were willing to agree to a 100 percent increase in the wage. After discussion with High Commission advisers and consideration of world trends regarding native indentured labor, the government in 1923 agreed to set the beach pay at £6 cash advance on the total wage, providing the overall wage doubled and recruiting vessels carried no trade store.[59]

The planters were to regret this decision. From 1921 to 1923 the government introduced a head tax of £1 a year on all able-bodied native males between sixteen and sixty years of age. Although the government adamantly denied the connection, both Bishop Steward and many Solomon Islanders perceived the tax as simply a means for guaranteeing the maximum labor supply by forcing men from poor areas like Malaita to find employment. Certainly the planters expected that the tax would stimulate the number of men signing on for work. The tax was instrumental in maintaining the supply, but did not appreciably alter the numbers offering to work. In some years between 1910 and 1920, the supply had reached 6000. By the early twenties it was apparent that the ceiling was 6000 to 6500 under contract in any one year and no ordinary incentives could increase it (see Figure 15).[60] By 1923, Levers in particular had realized that the combination of a limited labor supply and the tax incentive would reduce the need for them to pay the additional wages; they belatedly opposed the cash increase. Like the other planters, they could console themselves with the knowledge that the beach pay could not legally be raised by recruiters. Moreover, they knew they

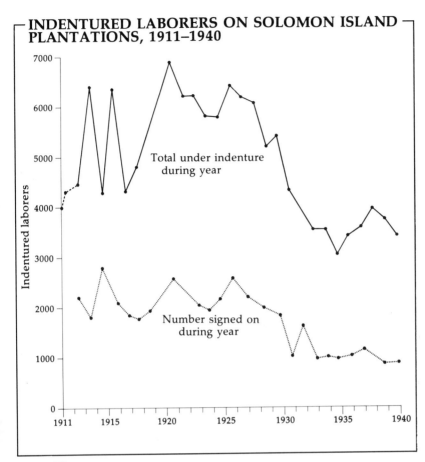

INDENTURED LABORERS ON SOLOMON ISLAND PLANTATIONS, 1911–1940

Figure 15

would get back a large portion of the wage by continuing to charge 100 percent and more on the landed costs of goods at their plantation stores, where laborers were largely captive customers.[61]

The effects of this change in wage policy were considerable, especially on Malaita. Along the coasts of this large island (only partly pacified until the late 1920s) at anchorages such as Kwari'ekwa and Maoa were men like Funiloge and Jonah Alisifiona, who earned cash and goods by acting as go-betweens for recruiters and recruits, just as many had done in the labor trade days.[62] The European commercial community, with uncharacteristic concern for the welfare of the individual recruit, described these passage-masters as "touts," "pimps," "loafers,"[63] and "bullies" who extorted money from the "unprotected native" from the bush.[64] While there were undoubtedly many cases of extortion and misappropriation of beach payments by passage-masters, the real basis for the ire of the Europeans was that the experienced passage-master, usually a clan elder and returner from the colonies, operated for the recruits' benefit (and his own) to the disadvantage of the recruiter and the planter. Not only did the bush people often reward the passage-master for his services with presents from the recruits' beach pay, but also the recruiter gave him trade goods or, by the twenties, from 10 shillings to £1 for each recruit.[65] The new regulations of 1923 reduced the importance of the passage-master, who could no longer bargain to increase the recruits' beach pay. Nonetheless, such men still received some reward, often because they convinced the recruiters, rightly or wrongly, that they remained influential in obtaining recruits. By the early 1930s, however, with pacification, the spread of Pijin as a lingua franca, and the increasing use of well-known north coast saltwater Malaitans such as Sali (Charlie) Kamai and Jo Velakona as full-time assistants on recruiting vessels, the old passage-masters' remnant of authority had all but vanished.[66]

The 1923 regulations had other, more immediate, effects. Malaitan and south Guadalcanal recruits and their families were pleased at first with the higher wage scale, but had difficulty in finding anywhere to buy the tobacco and calico they wanted, as recruiters could neither give out trade goods nor operate stores on their vessels.[67] Before 1925–1926 many recruits assumed that the advance payment of £6 was the equivalent of the old beach payment and expected to get the full two years' wages at the end of their contract. Recruiters had done little to enlighten them as to the new arrangments. Not until those who had been recruited in 1923–1924 signed off did the terms become more widely known.[68] With the monetization of the beach payment, new recruits would increasingly take some of their cash advance with them to spend at Tulagi or at the plantation; the individual, rather than his family or clan, was the main beneficiary of the change.[69]

With the imposition of the head tax in 1921–1923, some of the new earnings were lost immediately. On Malaita in 1923, £3000, about one-tenth of the wages bill, went in head tax, excluding tax paid by employers for their laborers.[70] As a result of the tax, real earnings for most Islanders dropped. Moreover, men who were eligible to pay tax, who did not go off to work, and who had no produce to sell had to rely on kin for the cash. The tax was thus a new external pressure compelling men to work where formerly the choice had been their own and their community's.[71]

The continuing labor crisis—the search for solutions

Desperate as the planters were to obtain labor, they tried to find reasons why the combined push of the tax and pull of higher wages could not induce more men to sign on. A few recognized that Solomon Islanders who had land could subsist, and needed only target work to buy a few manufactured goods or pay their tax.[72] But the majority of the planters continued to tinker with the secondary causes of the inadequate labor supply. In 1927 they were telling the government that the shortage was now the result of advancing cash instead of goods to recruits. The bulk of the cash went to the bush people of Malaita but, as the planters pointed out, "the money is of little use to them without the opportunity to spend it and they do not encourage the young men of the village to earn more."[73] Through the Planters' Association and the Advisory Council, the planters then argued that recruiting vessels ought to have trading facilities aboard. They called for a public inquiry into this and other aspects of the labor question, including the length of time of indenture and the control of the resident commissioner over extension of contracts following imprisonment. The inquiry was carried out in 1929 by a commission whose substantial report made it clear that planters wanted not only continuance of the indenture system but even greater control of labor by the government on their behalf.[74]

Not until 1934 did the resident commisioner draw up the proposed consolidated labor regulation, based in part on the findings of the Labour Commission. Meanwhile, the first census of the protectorate had been carried out in 1931. Malaita, the source of 68 percent of the labor, had a population of 40,000.[75] With about 4000 of its adult males working on plantations, 10 percent of the island's population was absent in any one year. In neighboring Papua and New Guinea, government policy during the thirties was that no more than 7 percent of the adult males should be absent lest village life and health suffer. Even during the emergency of World War II, anthropologist Ian Hogbin was to warn of the dangers of exceeding this percentage.[76] Malaitan societies in the 1920s were supplying more. It is doubtful that they could have provided even more men to the plantations and still have survived.

By the time the census results were known, the protectorate was beginning to suffer the effects of the Great Depression. This economic slump allowed the government to successfully resist Colonial Office reaction to the consolidated labor regulation. The government argued that the indenture system protected the worker. This it might have done, but it also meant that the employer could control almost all aspects of the laborers' existence. Moreover, once the contract was signed the laborer was compelled to stay. All weapons of labor protest—resignation, strikes, work-to-regulations, go-slow strikes—were legally forbidden and would have resulted in a court case and a fine or imprisonment for the worker. Without indenture, costs to the planter would have risen as, for example, the seasoned hand would have been better able to bargain for higher wages than would the raw recruit. Under the existing system the experienced worker usually obtained a better wage only if he signed a second contract while he was still on the plantation, thus saving his employer a recruiting fee.[77] The Colonial Office disapproved of the continuing penal clause, along with the system of indenture itself. In practice, in a time of economic stringency, it could do little more than periodically remind the protectorate that the system ought to be improved.[78]

BOTH COLONIAL OFFICE policy and protectorate government practice were largely determined by economic and political realities in the Solomons. Wider policy considerations of the British Empire did impose some limits, the most important being the ban on coolie labor. Similarly, the awakening of greater international interest in dependent peoples following World War I meant that although the protectorate could hang on to the indenture system, the laborers' rights had to be protected. Within these parameters, however, the government had above all to consider the needs of the commercial planters because they and their associated merchants and shippers represented the source of the protectorate's revenue.

The planters wanted two things that were to some extent in conflict: first, more laborers and, second, a maximum of work from the laborers for the least expenditure. During the first twenty years of the century the planters' real costs of obtaining the scarce resource of labor climbed. The planters demanded government intervention to control the cost of labor and to stimulate the flow of men offering for work. They received it, through wage fixing and the head tax. But though the tax meant that men would always seek some paid employment, the labor supply was limited and the incentives the planters were prepared to offer could not induce more men to leave their villages for plantation work. Besides the limitation of population numbers, what most planters and the government did not fully grasp until the late 1920s was that even the poorest of Solomon Islanders, the laborers from the eastern Solomons, "have plenty of land. They are on a different footing to labourers elsewhere in that they are not forced by economic pressure to work."[79]

The government's policies failed to increase the supply of labor. But failure of an exploitive policy no more excuses it than does success. The government had institutionalized the exploitation of labor—by fixing wages in the employers' favor, so choking market forces, and by introducing a head tax that made it imperative for men to take up some employment or break the white man's law.

CHAPTER 8

The plantation
(c. 1900–1930)

[Solomon Islanders] combine for fishing, trading, or looting
expeditions, and share in the results, but no man is called to
work and paid for it either by the day or piece. And when
men are invited to help in housebuilding, for instance, which
at certain points requires many hands for a single day, they
receive their food only, and the debt is paid by similar help
when occasion requires. Hence they have no traditional
knowledge of the relations of master and servant to one
another; and by not understanding this many white men are
offended at the free and easy bearing of the brown man;
which is considered as impertinence but which is not.

Reverend Dr. W. H. Welchman, 1906

It will be many years before the average native can work for
himself and his family with any degree of continuity of
method, this achievement will be helped by the knowledge
and discipline he may acquire while in the employ of a white
man.

Major F. F. Hewitt, 1931

THE PLANTATION pervaded a substantial part of the lives of most Solomon Islanders. Generally, men recruited for plantation work out of
necessity because they had no other option for earning cash. In every
way the plantation was an alien institution and when men went there
they renounced their old lives and adopted a style of living geared to the
one aim of production for commercial exchange. Although the rules of
this institution were formulated in an arena outside the direct control of
the laborers, it would be misleading to see them as having no role in the
evolution of those rules. Many of the major revisions of the labor regulations were in part an outcome of resistance by labor to inhuman treatment by employers. The resistance was often crude and sporadic, but it
was maintained as long as the evil continued.

Even when regulated by law, plantation life was unappealing, especially to those who could only be field hands. Once the initial novelty of

a new place had worn off, it had little to offer other than cash that was soon spent on imported manufactured goods, and, from the early 1920s, on the tax of kinsmen.

For most men the plantation was their initiation into the commerce of the European and it gave them a common experience. That experience taught them that their role, though essential to the plantation economy, was considered a servile one by the European. It also taught them about one another.

Motives for recruiting for plantations

Before the tax there had been internal pressures within society for a young man to go away and work on a plantation, pressures that sprang from the individual's own desires as well as from the needs of the particular community. On Malaita, Guadalcanal, and San Cristobal, which provided on average 68, 16, and 6 percent of plantation labor respectively from 1913 to 1940, the main incentives for recruits were trade goods and cash. These were brought home to be distributed to parents, uncles, older brothers, and other clan elders whom the returner could ask to contribute shell valuables for his bride payment when he wished to marry. Without such valuables, a man, particularly a pagan, simply could not marry.[1]

The pattern began with the overseas labor trade. The goods brought home were a substitute for the "credit" that in precontact times a young man would have built up with his elders by working in their gardens, building their houses, caring for their pigs, fighting in their battles, and being respectful to them. As iron tools made gardening and house-building easier, and as warfare gradually lessened under the protectorate, the temporary loss of the young men to the community was more than compensated for by the continuing supply of Western goods they brought home.[2]

Moreover, there were few alternative attractions to keep the young unmarried men in the village. Virtually no societies had prolonged initiation ceremonies demanding the presence of men of a certain age. Until marriage, young men were free from any onerous social demands.[3] Marriage was the most significant action in a man's life, a move which set him apart from the immature, socially irresponsible world of youth and brought him into the serious, responsible world of adulthood. Before marriage, young men from about fifteen to twenty-five enjoyed a period of freedom, although as they became older they were increasingly drawn into accepting more responsibilities if they wished to gain the clan's support for their future bride payment. Until this happened they were probably something of a danger around the village because their intrigues with women and quarrels with other hotheads could draw their entire clan into a dispute. In Christian settlements in the eastern Solomons this may well explain the weakness of missionary opposition to young men going to Solomon Islands plantations.[4] The overseas labor trade had established a tradition of employment away from home, but it was one that blended easily into the life cycle of Solomon Islands men.

The coming of the protectorate government and, in some places, Christianity allowed the tradition not only to continue but also to expand as the role of the young man as warrior virtually vanished. Contrary to the beliefs of the planters, pacification seems to have released more young men from "military service" at home because the numbers that had offered for the overseas labor trade, assuming a relatively fixed population, had been fewer than half of the steadily increasing numbers signing on for local plantations in the 1910s and early 1920s.[5]

Besides the direct material returns, there were other motives for signing on. Many of the young recruits of the first two decades of the century had heard accounts of the white man's world in Australia and Fiji from older male relatives. Their curiosity aroused, they set out to sample what they could of it on the plantation.[6] For some, curiosity was reinforced by the knowledge that many young women considered a man with plantation experience to be more attractive.[7] Others went away so that their involvement in village conflicts might be forgotten, and yet others fled broken socioreligious taboos.[8]

A few had special duties laid upon them by their clan. In the early thirties the recruiter Tommy Elkington was surprised to find his boat full at Folotona Taeloa in northwest Malaita with twenty strong men all wishing to go to Kinda in New Georgia. Hardy fellows, they easily passed the scrutiny of the medical officer and labor inspector at Tulagi and then were taken west to Kinda on Burns Philp's steamer. At the first morning's "line," when the men assembled to receive their day's orders, they attacked the European overseer, breaking several of his ribs. Earlier, this man had abused a young man of their clan; they had signed on in order to mete out some rough justice.[9]

Laborers' input into labor policy and practice

As the Kinda incident shows, laborers had ways of resisting maltreatment by planters. The most common, as with the enforcement of discipline by the planter, was physical violence, even after the 1910s. Planters regularly gave laborers a blow over the ear or a kick in the backside to make them do what they were told. Violence was so much a part of the expected disciplinary methods of the planters that a white man had to prove himself competent in it to be a success. It was common practice for companies to ask prospective overseers and managers if they could fight. The "new chum" overseer was always "tried out" by plantation laborers. Men would openly defy the overseer and expect him to hit them or lose face. Sometimes they would try to get him down to the labor lines at night when he would be an easy target. Everyone involved in plantations, including the government, knew that fisticuffs, or a brawl, were a standard and acceptable way of enforcing discipline —provided the laborer was in the wrong, knew it, and was not caused serious physical harm.[10]

If, however, the laborers felt they had been wronged they would frequently gang up on an overseer and beat him. This was particularly true of the Malaitans. Many such cases never reached the courts, although the Europeans were often severely injured. In cases where injuring the overseer without cause would mean a jail sentence for the laborers, they would provoke him into assaulting them by, say, working excessively slowly or acting stupidly. The resulting court case usually meant that the overseer was fined or even fired by the company.[11]

Of course, not all laborers felt that they could resort to violence, either physical or moral. By the thirties, many men who signed on for plantations were Christians and faced the moral question of the form their resistance should take. At Tetepare (Solomon Islands Development Company) a laborer wrote a desperate letter to a friend complaining of frequent beatings, shortage of food, and being required to work on Sunday, a day of rest on plantations. The laborer, Batini Bosuri, explained his predicament:

> We sign long government—we do not come here to be beaten. We want to beat him [the overseer]—but our teacher Napthali says we don't beat because we belong God now. Tell Turner [Officer in command of Constabulary]. We report to Government in labour office and I said I want to beat if master beats us—he said no—we must tell government.[12]

From the early twenties laborers had exploited the opportunities offered by regular government inspection to take their problems to the district officer's court. Some men, usually *bos-boe* 'boss-boy' of long experience, became adept "bush lawyers." Jack Mainagwa, formerly a boss-boy for Levers, claimed that he was involved in ten court actions, all of which were judged in his favor. Of course, if the boss-boy became too partisan, he would find he could not renew his contract.[13]

Another way of resisting the white *masta* was to despoil his property. Planters found that copra driers often caught fire and that they were unable to ascertain whether the cause was accidental or not.[14] Stealing of anything but tobacco and food made little sense to laborers because of the difficulties of hiding things around the plantation and getting them onto the boat to go home. Nonetheless, because they made the *masta* angry, thefts could give a kind of satisfaction to laborers.[15]

As anywhere, men on institutional food were alert to opportunities for varying their diet. Because of the shortage of labor, the larger plantation companies began importing cattle from about 1912 to keep down secondary growth among the coconut palms.[16] At Pipisala a boss-boy and his friends used to drive a beast to an isolated part of the plantation, take it into the bush, and then kill and eat it. In time, they consumed fourteen cattle. Unfortunately, their feasting was stopped as a result of a complaint to the *masta* by another laborer who had been hit by the boss-boy.[17]

In the twenties and thirties the least successful form of resistance was running away, because the district officer usually caught up with deserters. In earlier years, planters who maltreated their labor found that some would try to run away. In 1913 on Boroni, where Rigby had taken on local labor under indenture, they simply disappeared into the bush. Mainly for this reason, planters always tried to get recruits from a distant island. Even then, men were known to desert from as far afield as the Gizo district or Guadalcanal to get back home to Malaita.[18]

Life on the plantation

To most Europeans the laborers' lot seemed to be "one drab round of working, eating and sleeping."[19] It was a wise planter who took care of the most important of these in the laborers' eyes—eating. By 1910, an exact ration scale had been laid down by regulation. Few planters consistently underfed their labor, but some, particularly paid employees of the larger companies, were negligent. In 1920, for example, the labor inspector F. L. Pinching heavily criticized conditions on the estates of the Shortland Islands Plantation Company. At Harapa he found the laborers in such a distressed state that he issued food from the *Mala*'s ration store.[20] Two years later, the same company was issuing the weekly meat or fish ration at a pound a man, instead of a pound and a half. The labor inspector fined the company, observing that "now Mr Lucas has no control over the properties their status might improve."[21] As in that instance, overseers were sometimes merely carrying out company policy. The Malayta Company in the early twenties instructed its staff to issue only one pound three ounces of rice daily instead of the regulation one pound eight ounces.[22] Laborers, by this time well aware of their legal ration, were quick to report any abuse to the government officer. Of all the complaints heard by the government, this one was invariably remedied.[23]

The men also expected as their due the weekly issue of tobacco that had been supplied by employers from the earliest days of plantation development (Photo 14). Workers on general tasks—maintaining copra drier fires, collecting coconuts, catching beetles, clearing underbrush,

Photo 14. Tobacco issue, c. 1910, probably at Tetepare. Notice coconut seed-lings planted in background and the youth of the laborers. *(Burns Philp Archives)*

cutting firewood—got three sticks whereas the copra-cutters usually received six.[24] Because of the likely consequences it was rare for the tobacco to be withheld. If a worker acknowledged a breach of some regulation such as eating plantation coconuts, planters could get away with deducting tobacco from rations as a punishment; but without the worker's acquiescence this was difficult. At Levers' Pipisala plantation in the mid-twenties, the overseer refused to issue tobacco as a way of punishing some slow-working copra-cutters. This caused so much ill-feeling that the boss-boy who was in charge of the store defied the overseer and gave out the tobacco himself. There was a quarrel and a fight. The overseer informed the inspector, but was found guilty of illegally withholding the tobacco and was fined.[25]

As long as it was rainproof, the standard of their accommodation rarely worried laborers. Most of the larger plantations had a *haos kapa* —a building with galvanized iron roof, either iron or timber walls, and a timber floor raised off the ground. These were easier to clean and maintain than the leaf houses, although far hotter. Moreover, in places distant from a fresh water source, their roofs formed a catchment for rainwater, which was stored in tanks.[26]

The recruit was more concerned about who shared the house with him than about the quality of it. To avoid quarrels, both planters and men generally preferred to house laborers from the same area in one building, separate from other groups. Despite this there were often arguments between laborers, sometimes resulting in physical attack, but rarely in serious injury or death.[27]

At the center of almost every dispute was a Malaitan. Since Malaitans constituted over two-thirds of the labor force this is not surprising. With the power of numbers they frequently tried to impose their values on laborers from other islands. When the Malaitans' beliefs and sensibilities were offended there was usually an argument. Being called a "bloody shit" and "fucking bastard" was mild in terms of what Malaitans called each other when they made a "big swear," but it was enough to provoke anger and a demand for compensation in cash. When only Malaitans were involved the fine was usually paid, but with Guadalcanal men the demand for £1 to £5 was usually answered by a fight.[28]

Sometimes married men from Guadalcanal and San Cristobal took their wives with them to plantations on north Guadalcanal and in the western Solomons. The Malaitans, few of whom were married, only very occasionally did this. Trouble resulted when the women had to go to a common tank for water because pagan Malaitans considered that this act polluted all the water still in the tank, making it unfit for them to drink.[29] This near obsessional fear of the power of women to pollute touched other matters. At Bagga plantation on Mbava the Malaitan boss-boy forced the wife of a Guadalcanal man to go into the bush to give birth, to avoid possible contamination. With no preparations for giving birth under such circumstances, the woman lost the child. To defy the Malaitans and protect the woman during her next confinement the planter, Joseph Binskin, allowed her to use his house and refused to permit the 'Are'are boss-boy to "sign back" when his contract finished.[30] Laborers, mainly from Guadalcanal, who had wives had to guard them carefully since men outside their group would try to "steal" them. This stealing was the cause of many fights and occasionally brought government intervention.[31] For this reason, along with the cost of married accommodation and transport, few planters wanted married women on plantations, although Darlington of Solomon Islands Rubber Plantation (which, in spite of its name, produced copra) always told labor recruiters to try to get him a few married couples with female children verging on puberty. The women worked well at weeding and at clearing the drains on the plantation. Moreover, these couples, mainly from south Guadalcanal and San Cristobal, found that their daughters could earn quite a deal of money from the male labor. Darlington was also satisfied because he had a contented labor force, many of whom signed new contracts in order to stay on at "Mbugotu" (Santa Isabel).[32]

Like Darlington, most Europeans regarded the virtually all-male world of the plantation as unnatural. One visiting Colonial Office representative in 1928 went as far as suggesting to planters unofficially that single women be recruited for plantations on a large scale.[33] Such a course was impossible because of the socioeconomic value Solomon Islands societies placed on their women and because of inevitable missionary condemnation, to say nothing of the international conventions on the status of women as promulgated by the League of Nations.[34] Although plantations were often located near villages, indentured labor had limited contact with the people except for markets, which were generally held at the plantation rather than in the village. Casual laborers would often bring indentured men home at weekends, but the visitors usually stayed with the friend's family. Cases of village women being prostituted to, or sexually assaulted by, laborers on adjacent plantations were rare. When it came to heterosexual involvements, laborers either ran the risks entailed in "stealing" someone else's wife or consoled themselves with fantasy in labor line songs of sexual adventure.[35]

Consequently, homosexual relations "were practically universal" on large company-owned plantations.[36] Planters and inspectors ignored evidence, such as single beds pushed together in the labor lines, because sexual acts were difficult to prove and really mattered little to the Europeans as long as the plantations functioned efficiently. The government rarely took the matter seriously. In 1924 Heffernan, the Santa Isabel district officer, came across to Yandina to investigate a case of sodomy among the laborers, but the visit developed into a drinking party with the manager and the case was forgotten.[37]

It was not uncommon for "old hands" to assess the "new chums" as they came off the ship. The older men would pair off with the young newcomers, passing over a substantial gift of tobacco or calico to the older men of the young man's clan, *olketa wantok*. Malaitans, by culture and circumstance on plantations aggressive, were invariably the senior partners, although men from Guadalcanal and San Cristobal also acted this role. Such attachments, which also thrived among workers in the womanless world of the Solomon Islander in Tulagi, were often very strong. The older man showed his affection by giving the younger gifts and being in his company as much as possible. When a third party became more favored, jealousy was extreme and the younger man was often beaten. This kind of relationship was usually temporary and peculiar to all-male establishments. Although sodomy and other homosexual acts were not unknown on Malaita and elsewhere they were certainly not the norm and the prevailing ideology was against such activity. Sodomy occured on plantations, but mutual masturbation seems to have been much more common.[38]

Arguments and brawls sometimes originated in homosexual jealousies, but there were many other and more common reasons for fights among the laborers. As employers had found, food was the cause of many quarrels. If the cooks appeared to dish out more food to their friends than to those from other places there was sure to be strife. Some-times it was not the cooks' fault as men strolling in from distant parts of the plantation frequently found that the first comers had taken more than their share.[39]

Gambling often led to fights. Men bet on dice and cards, sometimes losing considerable sums of money. This in turn made stealing more likely. Although men who lost all their money were likely to "sign back," being too ashamed to go home empty-handed, the planters discouraged gambling because of possible fights and because a man who had been up all night playing was not able to work well the following day. Accordingly, the government banned the practice in 1927, but it merely went underground.[40]

Discontent that was expressed in complaints about rations or even in assault on an employer sometimes arose from sorcery. Malaitans had a reputation for sorcery even among the Guadalcanal people, who had their own effective and feared forms, *piro* and *vele*. On Levers' Three Sisters estate, for example, Malaitans threatened to assault the manager and his wife, ostensibly because of an insufficient food ration. As it transpired, the day after his arrival as a recruit, a notable sorcerer announced to his fellow Malaitans that he had dreamed that one of their number had poisoned two others who were ill at the time. When the laborers assaulted the poisoner, the manager's intervention diverted their anger toward him and his wife.[41]

In order to protect themselves from such danger, pagan Malaitans often brought some relic or item, such as a small section of a shell valu-able that had been associated with the shrine of their *akalo* 'ancestor spirit,' and hid it in the roof of the laborers' house or in the bush adja-cent to the plantation. They naturally prayed to this spirit in time of trouble.[42] After the cattle-killing incident at Pipisala, the masters of Jack Mainagwa determined to teach him a lesson by thoroughly fright-ening him. Apparently, they made him take an empty tin some distance to place on a fence so that they could take pot-shots at it. When his back was turned they fired six shots at him. They probably would have said they used blanks or had aimed wide of his body; however, Jack attributes his surviving the hail of bullets to his *akalo*'s powerful inter-vention.

A few laborers found that their *akalo* had deserted them. When Jo Totaka at Faiami died of what the Europeans called beriberi, his Malaitan friends attributed his death to a failure to make a propitiatory offering for an offense to his *akalo* before leaving for the plantation.[43]

Perhaps as a result of this kind of reasoning, laborers were not overly concerned by the high death rates on plantations in the early years. Mortality reached almost 5 percent in 1914 following the dysentery epi-demic, and remained between 2 and 3 percent until 1928 (see Table 4).

TABLE 4

Estimates of labor mortality in the Solomon Islands, 1915–1940

Year	Labor employed at beginning of year	Recruits for year	Total labor employed	Labor mortality	Mortality rate per 1,000 plantation years worked
1915	1,403	2,855	4,255	119	48.0[a]
1916[b]	—	—	—	—	—
1917	2,303	1,967	4,270	74	28.5
1918	2,898	1,888	4,786	76	23.9
1919	3,462	2,028	5,490	104	28.7[a]
1920[b]	—	—	—	—	—
1921	4,182	2,668	6,796	140	35.3
1922	3,743	2,400	6,143	115	29.8
1923	3,964	2,188	6,152	90	23.5
1924	3,704	2,062	5,766	68	18.9
1925	3,509	2,232	5,741	71	19.4
1926	3,703	2,665	6,368	103	27.6
1927	3,755	2,360	6,115	83	21.9
1928	3,840	2,176	6,016	83	23.7
1929	3,166	2,005	5,171	58	17.5
1930	3,454	1,909	5,363	50	15.1
1931	3,189	1,112	4,301	26	9.7
1932	2,187	1,726	3,913	17	7.5
1933	2,430	1,103	3,583	28	11.5
1934	3,410	1,163	3,578	23	10.5
1935	1,871	1,122	3,096	17	8.5
1936	2,109	1,146	3,457	44	21.1
1937	2,059	1,264	3,607	40	17.3
1938	2,560	1,129	3,993	22	8.7
1939	2,478	1,015	3,796	33	14.0
1940	2,278	1,023	3,459	18	7.9

SOURCE: Chapman and Pirie 1974, Table 2.3, p. 2–50.

NOTES: [a] Assumed that half of labor employed at beginning of year left by the end of the year and that recruits and departures were spaced evenly throughout the year.
[b] Not available

Besides dysentery, the main diseases were influenza and pulmonary complaints, as well as low-level malaria.

By the early twenties, with regular inspection, the government was able not only to pressure planters to provide regulation medical facilities, but also to assist them by publishing a handbook on common diseases and their treatment.[44] Levers, chastened after their several admonitions by the Colonial Office during 1914–1916 and still hopeful of importing coolie labor, became sticklers for the labor regulations. Although they employed trained medical personnel from 1917 onward, their strict adherence to the regulation ration of mainly polished rice and the labor-preferred tinned meat meant that some laborers died of beriberi, due to a lack of vitamin B_1 (thiamine). Before the late twenties some of the deaths from this disease seem to have been attributed to heart-failure or paralysis because of the similarities of some of the symptoms.[45] In 1933, there were six deaths from beriberi at Levers' Faiami plantation (Russell Islands) in four months. There probably would have been many more, had not most laborers supplemented their ration in their spare time—by fishing, by trading for fresh food with local villagers, or by the illegal consumption of the company's prized coconuts. However, a period of exceptionally rainy weather had cut off two of these sources and many men were affected. Moreover, some estates in the Russells were too far distant for villagers to come to barter their produce. The government doctor remedied the situation by altering the ration to include mealies, dried peas or beans (which the laborers disliked), and Marmite (a yeast extract used as a spread), and by ordering that coconut milk or cream be added to the rice before serving.[46]

Although its medical care of the general population was almost negligible, the government acted quickly in 1914, 1919, and 1929 to suspend recruiting and repatriation in the hope of preventing the spread of epidemics of dysentery, influenza (Spanish flu pandemic), and poliomyelitis into the villages.[47] Heeding the pleas of the Marist missionaries in the Shortlands regarding the steadily declining population, the government forbade recruiting in these islands in 1912, much to the annoyance of western planters who used the traditional links of the Shortland Islands with south Bougainville to siphon off labor illegally from the German territory. By 1923, Ontong Java, Tikopia, and Sikaiana, whose Polynesian populations were apparently dying out, were also included with the Shortlands as prohibited districts.[48]

The health of the plantation laborer by the late twenties and early thirties was probably better than his village counterpart's. He was medically inspected at recruitment, often treated for *bakua (tinea imbricata)* and hookworm, and was readily accessible for yaws treatment. By this time too, "sore leg" or tropical ulcers were not such a problem on plantations because little new land was being opened up and there was less likelihood of men injuring their legs on cut branches or fallen trees (Photo 15). Nonetheless, in an age before sulfa drugs and antibiotics, there were limits to what Western medicine could do. Many planters relied on traditional European remedies that were of marginal value. Up until the war, a dose of Epsom salts each Saturday morning was the unpleasant lot of every laborer. As late as 1931 planters were using this as well as castor oil to treat cases of dysentery.[49] It was more the improved sanitation, diet, housing, and care of the sick, rather than such basic medicine which reduced the death rate in the thirties in between 0.75 and 2 percent (see Table 4).

Photo 15. Laborers clearing land for a Burns Philp plantation in the western Solomons, probably Manning Strait, c. 1910. *(Burns Philp Archives)*

The planters

Health care, like all of the physical conditions of the laborers' employment, varied according to the size and location of the plantation. In general, planters on small holdings, though they might not have always issued regulation mosquito nets or the three monthly *kaliko* 'cloth', tended to be more concerned with their laborers as individuals. Because they were often pressed for money, small planters allowed their labor time to make gardens, so providing fresh and more nutritious food than the rice ration. In the early thirties as the Great Depression worsened, planters like F. M. Campbell at Waimamura, San Cristobal (Figure 3), entrusted the management of outlying plantations such as Hawa to a reliable boss-boy who treated the laborers well. Because small planters tended to have more casual labor from the neighborhood, they had to treat their workers fairly in order to remain on good terms with the local community. In the twenties and thirties almost all of the men in Arosi and many from the Bauro district worked for Campbell or on other local plantations on a casual basis, preferring this to indentured labor on other islands.[50] Compared with men on the large plantations such as Cape Marsh or Tetepare (Figures 7, 13), such laborers suffered little deprivation of normal village life. Struggling planters perforce had to rely on Islanders for assistance on tasks that the bigger companies gave to white overseers or Chinese carpenters. Some taught their boss-boy or offsider such skills as boat building, engine maintenance, and how to keep an inventory of stores. In this process affection and a mutual respect sometimes grew up, as Leslie Gill found with Johnny Kevisi of New Georgia, whom he came to regard as "the most courageous and most honest man" he ever knew. Paternalism was a strong element of these bonds, but occasionally a genuine friendship developed, particularly with Europeans who were born and grew up among Solomon Islanders.[51] Eventually, by either design or circumstance, small planters who had put all their resources into their plantations made the islands their life. They were more likely to marry locally than the white contract employees on the larger plantations, as, say, at Mberande. Although such marriages obviously did not guarantee mutual understanding between the races, they certainly made most of the Europeans involved more receptive to the Solomon Islanders' points of view. Some details of men who took local wives to live with them on their small plantations are given in Table 5. These and a few others were probably the 10 percent J. C. Barley spoke of in 1933:

> Speaking with over 21 years' experience of conditions in the British Solomon Islands, I regret to state that my considered opinion that—with the notable exception of the Missionaries—scarcely 10% of the European settlers in the Protectorate regard the native otherwise than a "necessary evil" in the economic life of the community or as being entitled to any sort of sympathetic attention or interest outside his sphere of utility as a customer or labourer. He is almost universally looked down upon as belonging to a somewhat unclean and definitely inferior order of creation, as one who does not know the meaning of gratitude, loyalty or affection, and who will invariably mistake kindness for weakness and immediately take advantage of any person rash enough to trust him and treat him as a fellow human being. My personal experience of the native of the Solomon Islands has always been diametrically opposite to this.[52]

Larger plantations, particularly those of Levers and Burns Philp, were controlled at the local level by salaried managers and overseers employed under contract. Such men frequently occupied a large plantation house and rarely had the time or inclination to get to know Solomon Islanders. Unlike the small planters, they did not engage in itinerant trading as a sideline to their operations, and contact with Solomon Islanders in their natural setting was uncommon. Moreover, most managers and overseers were not allowed to leave the plantation where they were stationed except to go occasionally to Tulagi. Some of the larger estates, including those of Levers and the Malayta Company in the Russell Islands, Burns Philp at Tetepare, Levers at Kolombangara, and Three Sisters plantations, were sufficiently isolated from villages that all their overseers knew of Solomon Islanders was the mass of men on the plantation.[53] By the early twenties, "the time of the brutal 'Nigger-driver' and the ideas he thought necessary for the proper working of natives" had passed, mainly because of frequent government inspections and a realistic approach by larger companies to the management of labor.[54] None-

TABLE 5

Small-plantation owners who took local wives

Name	Location and map reference	Remarks	Sources
Fred Green	Liapari and adjacent mainland (Figure 9)	Purchased the plantation at Liapari and land on the adjacent mainland in 1933 for £11,000 from Ross and Clark, formerly shareholders in Union Plantation and Trading Company	LTR: 079–004–0, no. 28/69, LR 61 Liapari; Leslie Gill
Henry Kuper	Makira (Figure 3)	Married Augusta Kavakamurirongo, chiefly woman of Santa Ana	G. Kuper; WPHC BSIP F66/13 vol. 1
F. M. Campbell	Makira	Married Kapinihari of Makira	Jack Campbell; WPHC BSIP F66/13 vol. 1
Albert M. ("Andy") Andressen	Ulawa (Figure 1)		Tommy Elkington
Arthur ("Masher") Thelfall	Tenavatu, Guadalcanal (Figure 10)	Married Isobel Sura, da. of Jimmy Sura (Guadalcanal) and Agnes Brown (Scottish-born)	Tommy Elkington; WPHC BSIP 48/29
Victor Paulsen	Sasamungga, Choiseul	Mainly involved in trading	Tommy Elkington; WPHC 2249/37
W. H. ("Mad") Bennett	Kia, Santa Isabel (Figure 0)	Lease cancelled in 1926	WPHC 3598/28
J. Binskin	Bagga, New Georgia (Figure 9)	First wife a Malaitan, killed by Sito Latavaki's men from Vella Lavella in 1901. Second wife was Florence Wheatley, da. of Norman Wheatley and Nautale.	Billy Binskin; Tommy Elkington; WPHC 41/02; WPHC BSIP 78/7/19; WPHC 2327/30

P. S. Palmer	San Jorge Is., Santa Isabel	Second wife was Annie Wheatley, da. of Norman Wheatley and Sambe Vindu	WPHC BSIP 78/7/14; WPHC 3600/28
H. Markham	Seghe, Nono Lagoon, New Georgia (Figure 7)	Married Lily from Ontong Java	Johnson 1940, 122–126; WPHC BSIP F48/4
C. Gorringe	Huhurangi, Santa Isabel		WPHC 2892/31
H. Beck	Aena, Ranongga (Figure 9)		WPHC BSIP F49/26/3
L. C. McMahon	Bolu Is., Ranongga	Small plantation and trading station. Lease cancelled 1932.	WPHC 3496/30; WPHC BSIP F30/6
A. Cant	Batubasi, Malavane, New Georgia Tinuvalu in Nono Lagoon, New Georgia	Married Sesu Sube	WPHC BSIP F48/4; F52/1/5 vol. 1
T. B. Mason-Robinson	Paru—a little island east of Fauro (Figure 8)	Bankrupt 1929	WPHC BSIP F30/5; WPHC 1030/29
J. K. Buchanan	Pidgeon Island (Mbiki), Sandfly Passage, Nggela (Figure 13) Vatiluna, Russell Islands (Figure 12)	De facto wife from Sikaiana	WPHC BSIP 30/1

NOTE: These planters were active in the late 1920s and early 1930s. Because some of them were out of the business by 1941, their plantations do not appear on the maps, which are listed here merely as a guide to the locations; nor do they appear in Table 8.

theless, the planters ran the larger plantations on authoritarian lines in order to control the one hundred fifty to two hundred men living in one location away from the normality of village life. They did this by imposing a strict discipline and, through social-distancing mechanisms, maintaining a hierarchy. Every working morning the men lined up shoulder to shoulder in front of the planter and received their instructions. These were relayed through one or more boss-boys who, although Islanders, were always paid more and given better rations and accommodation than the ordinary laborers. At the *laen aot* 'line up,' the sick would stand aside to be inspected by the planter and sent either to work or to the plantation hospital where they were treated, usually by the planter. Throughout the day the planter moved around the plantation inspecting progress and issuing further instructions. The laborers' day, if not their life, was divided by bells—*"belo," "belo-baek"*—which the planter or the boss-boy rang at set times. Things were done *antaem*— the white man's time. Meals were cooked regularly and if men were absent from the serving they usually did not get any food. There were no seasons, and no holidays; the only days that were different were the half-day on Saturday and the rest day on Sunday.

Planters on the larger estates rarely interacted socially with laborers, except perhaps to preside, patron-like, over an all-male dance and feast at Christmas. Occasionally, a few reliable men might be selected to go hunting or fishing with the planter, but they went as servants rather than companions. The planter never joined such expeditions when they were organized by groups of laborers in their spare time. It would have been unthinkable for a planter to join in the men's gambling sessions, although at Levers' Russell Island plantations the Chinese carpenters and drivers often took part in the betting.[55]

The need for the planters to maintain a social distance and group solidarity was apparent in matters pertaining to sex between the races. Although they turned a blind eye to homosexuality in the labor lines, whenever one of their own number was involved with a Solomon Island male, legal and social condemnation by the government and the rest of the white community was immediate—and stronger, perhaps, than their reaction to one of their group committing homicide.[56] Similarly, the merest suggestion that an Islander might be sexually interested in a white woman provoked a strong response among white males, although their own interest in local women was taken for granted. In the Shortlands during the thirties, a European gave an old magazine to a Malaitan laborer who worked for another European. When the laborer took a pinup from the magazine and nailed it on the wall of the labor house, his master tore it down, telling him that such things were all right for white men, but not for natives.[57]

Despite the double standard, few European men appear to have used coercion on the Solomon Island women with whom they cohabited; the few who did were assaulted or even killed by the women's kinsmen among the laborers. The government also maintained a check on the recruiting of unmarried and unaccompanied adult women for plantations, lest they be forced to act as prostitutes to either planters or laborers. The wives of laborers sometimes became concubines to unmarried planters, who paid them for their services, with the payment usually making its way back to the husband. Most European men, especially managers or overseers, tried to hide such liaisons from their fellows, out of shame or the fear that their company superiors—or more often their superiors' wives—would deem them unsuitable for promotion. In the small world of the plantation, the laborers always knew of any sexual contact between white men and brown women, no matter how elaborate the attempts at secrecy, finding in it an enormous fund for salacious speculation and humor. Women from neighboring villages, particularly on San Cristobal, sometimes lived with planters. Their families were content with the arrangement because it benefited them materially. Even when the local mores were defied, as in the case of the district officer on San Cristobal who committed adultery with a woman while her husband was in the government jail, if the offender compensated the injured party adequately—in this instance with a £5 bullock— the matter was forgotten. One well-known eastern Solomons planter and trader, who was married to an Island woman of good family and had enormous influence among her people, boasted to his white friends in the thirties that his score of local virgins was greater than Don Bradman's record number of cricket runs—335.[58] In all these liaisons the Europeans as a group had the economic and political advantage. Perceiving this, most Solomon Islanders acted accordingly. As in traditional practice, most societies traded their women for the general good. Such easy and generally mutually acceptable arrangements provoked little active resentment among Solomon Islanders.

When the situation was forcibly reversed, no such tolerance prevailed among the whites, since a threat to "their" women was a threat to their property and prestige. During the twenties and thirties a few relatively harmless and rather pathetic peeping Tom incidents, minor assaults on, and propositioning of white and usually unmarried women by Islander men occurred, culminating in the trial of the *haos boe* 'house boy' Punuhuru of Rendova for attempted rape of Pearl Downs at her husband's plantation house in 1933. The European planters demanded that Punuhuru be flogged, but, because of a deficiency in the magistrate's understanding of the law, he was charged under the wrong section and sentenced to five years' imprisonment. Although the supreme court judge in Suva reduced the sentence to two years because of this and other legal defects, he did point out that attempted rape could be punished by flog-

Photo 16. The big house on Mberande plantation, Guadalcanal—a rare occasion when Solomon Islanders were allowed on the verandah. Seated on steps, in a dark shirt, is W. H. Lucas at the center of laborers and villagers, c. 1918. *(Burns Philp Archives)*

ging, but only if an attempt to choke or suffocate the victim was made. Accordingly, in 1934 the law was altered so that flogging could be administered in cases such as the Downs incident. The European community was appeased.[59]

Although many European males were willing to engage in sexual intercourse with Solomon Island women, no planter would think of publicly shaking hands with an Islander, as the missionaries did. The planters, of course, were not isolated in their attitudes.[60] In the twenties and thirties, District Officer Miller in the Shortlands demanded that the people wash their tax money before presenting it to him. If he touched the "dirty money" or shook hands with Shortland chiefs, he would wash his hands where all could see.[61] Even the respected Dr. Crichlow, passed over by the government for promotion because of his part-Chinese parentage, dismissed a San Cristobal crewman of the *Hygeia* for speaking to him with a pipe in his mouth.[62]

On the plantation, except for domestic help, laborers were rarely allowed near the planter's house. The line of final demarcation was at the steps or the verandah, and few were permitted to cross it (Photo 16). The social distance between master and laborer was also reflected in the terms of reference the planters used to speak of their employees. "Boy" was universal, "coon" and "nigger" common. Levers counted laborers as mere "units," not as men.[63] Under such conditions the plantation was a "total institution," remaking its inmates temporarily into creatures geared to obey and produce by controlling every aspect of their lives.[64] For those whose lot it was to be nothing more than a laborer, life on the plantation was stifling and often brutish.

The plantation economy—opportunities and limitations

At least two-thirds of the people of the Solomons had to rely on the plantation and associated activities for getting the money they wanted to buy trade goods and, after 1921–1923, to pay their tax.[65] Within this general constraint imposed by the nature of the resource base and the location of their islands, some groups were even further limited in the choice of what kind of wage labor they sought. Prewar employment histories indicate that men from the central south coast of Guadalcanal and the north coast of San Cristobal worked on ships more than three times as often as men from the Siesie and west Kwaio area of Malaita (see Figure 16). This was an outcome of their origin. On the south coast of Guadalcanal, just as in the northwest of San Cristobal, there were, at the early contact period, extensive, long-established coastal and semi-coastal settlements.[66] Men from these villages were familiar with the sea and seacraft. Most who worked on ships seemed to have a pride in their vessels, in themselves, and in their abilities. They worked closely with Europeans and often a rough kind of camaraderie developed.[67] In Siesie, except for small hamlets at Kwa'a, Maoa, Fulo, Mbona, Baunani, Igua, and Kwari'ekwa, there were no substantial settlements on or near the coast. These villages may well have been bigger, but there is evidence that dysentery epidemics at the turn of the century, probably introduced by labor-trade returners, killed most of the original inhabitants.[68] Almost every Malaitan interviewed in this area had been born in a bush village and had migrated to the coast because of conversion to Christianity. Without knowledge of the sea and the ability to swim, few such men wanted to work on ships. Most of the Malaitans, being bushmen, had also been *wiked* 'pagan' at the time they signed on for plantations, whereas most of the Guadalcanal and San Cristobal men were Christians. Christianity meant that the Malaitan covered his nakedness. Even in the late 1930s recruits from the 'Are'are bush came along to the recruiters' ship naked. Just before the Second World War half of the population of Malaita was still pagan.[69]

Whether because of Christianity alone, or perhaps because of new hygiene and dress habits picked up with the message of the gospel, the Guadalcanal men were more often selected to be workers in the planter's own household and, for the most part, received gentler treatment than the ordinary laborer. The San Cristobal men had fewer opportunities for domestic work because they went less frequently than Malaitan or Guadalcanal men to plantations on other islands (see Figure 16). Indentured laborers from the Arosi district of San Cristobal showed a consistent reluctance to reengage after their original two-year contract, preferring local casual labor. Elders and big-men were against reengagement and often appointed a senior man among new recruits to

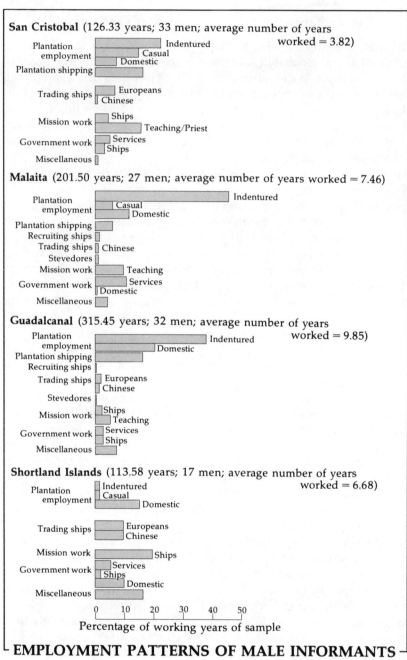

San Cristobal (126.33 years; 33 men; average number of years worked = 3.82)

Plantation employment — Indentured / Casual / Domestic
Plantation shipping

Trading ships — Europeans / Chinese

Mission work — Ships / Teaching/Priest

Government work — Services / Ships

Miscellaneous

Malaita (201.50 years; 27 men; average number of years worked = 7.46)

Plantation employment — Indentured / Casual / Domestic
Plantation shipping
Recruiting ships
Trading ships — Chinese
Stevedores
Mission work — Teaching
Government work — Services / Domestic
Miscellaneous

Guadalcanal (315.45 years; 32 men; average number of years worked = 9.85)

Plantation employment — Indentured / Domestic
Plantation shipping
Recruiting ships
Trading ships — Europeans / Chinese
Stevedores
Mission work — Ships / Teaching
Government work — Services / Ships
Miscellaneous

Shortland Islands (113.58 years; 17 men; average number of years worked = 6.68)

Plantation employment — Indentured / Casual / Domestic

Trading ships — Europeans / Chinese

Mission work — Ships

Government work — Services / Ships / Domestic

Miscellaneous

0   10   20   30   40   50
Percentage of working years of sample

EMPLOYMENT PATTERNS OF MALE INFORMANTS

Figure 16 (*Note:* From selected islands)

see that this wish was carried out on the plantation. Since, quite often, domestic employment was offered to a promising field hand, the San Cristobal men were rarely available to "sign back" into this kind of work. Positions at, say, Hawa or Maro'u were filled by women from the neighborhood. Although some pagan Malaitans conveniently shelved the taboos associated with female pollution while on the plantation, most normally would not touch a woman's clothes and were unwilling to work in proximity to a woman who might be menstruating. Consequently, both master and labor tended to avoid the issue of household work. Most Malaitans who worked as domestics were either Christians or employed by bachelor Europeans.[70]

The pagan bush Malaitan was therefore very restricted in his employment choices. Besides being a policeman or a warder—and the prerequisite for this was Pijin, which generally had to be learned during plantation employment—there was virtually nothing but plantation labor. The Christian missions offered some work, but obviously a man had to be a Christian to work as a teacher or catechist.[71]

The most remunerative employment for Islanders in the plantation economy was working on the six-weekly steamer, which involved traveling around the group loading copra at the main plantations as well as at Tulagi, Gizo, and Faisi.[72] Each member of the "steamer gang" received 3 shillings a day plus rations.[73] From the 1910s this job had been almost monopolized by organized groups of men from the Langalanga (including 'Aoke) and Lau lagoons—north Malaitan saltwater men used to dealing with the wider world since the early days of the overseas labor trade.[74] These men were a kind of elite, and far more efficient stevedores than their white contemporaries in Australia.[75] Tough, hard-working, their opinion of themselves somewhat inflated because of both their natural prosperity in the lagoons and their well-paying jobs, they brawled with the common laborers including other Malaitans on pratically every plantation in the group visited by the steamers.[76]

Of all the labor supply, it was the pagan bush Malaitans who made up the bulk of those employed on the hardest, least-stimulating work associated with the plantation economy. Although almost universally admired by Europeans for their working ability and their "service to their employer," their status was the lowest among the laboring group.[77] Similarly, other Solomon Islanders, while they knew Malaitans were the best workers, perceived them as unpredictable, rough "bushmen." To retain some of their own dignity many Malaitans made a virtue of necessity, glorying in their reputation and acting far more aggressively than they would have at home. But they knew they bore the brunt of the hardest and worst aspects of plantation life.

Former indentured laborers today pass lightly over the deaths through illness, the occasional short rations, and brawls with other Islanders, but still vividly remember with some bitterness the big plantations where the unsmiling masters always yelled and sometimes beat them. These laborers, with little, if any, tradition of servility and a natural dislike of embarrassment, have not forgotten occasions when they were forced to accept public and frequently undeserved humiliation from a master who not only often had a gun or whip in his hand, but also always had the penal sanction of the courts on his side.[78] Even men of the Langalanga steamer gang found the harshness of the masters hard to accept, as a visitor working on the recruiting ship *Kokorana* in the early thirties found:

> One day I sat with a Salt Water man at the door of his hut and chatted. He was a middle-aged man who had done occasional stevedoring work for many years, but his manner was shy. I asked him questions; we discussed the weather, this and that. Then there was a lull. And when I next looked at him his brown, kind eyes had filled with tears. Pacific Islanders weep readily when emotion touches them, but there had been no occasion that I know.
>
> When I inquired he shook his head, "You first white man, master, ever talk soft along boy."[79]

The price the Solomon Island laborer paid for the white man's goods and to get his tax money was a high one. This episodic semi-slavery eroded self-confidence and self-esteem. If many Solomon Islanders, particularly the Malaitans, had a chip on their shoulders, the plantation economy had nailed it there. Nor were there many spin-offs from this economy that might have made some compensation for the humiliation the plantation imposed. The buying power of their relatively poor wage was lessened by exorbitant prices at plantation stores and, at least until the 1920s, at the capital. Men learned few new skills on the larger plantations because there were few to learn. Some saw how to make copra for the first time, while others learned a more efficient way of removing copra from the coconut shell. A handful then tried to make it at home, but, like their neighbors in the west who made copra before plantation days, they could soon have learned this simple operation outside the plantation.[80] A couple might have learned to drive the few trucks on Levers' plantations, but most rode on the dashboard, jumping off to load coconuts, while a Chinese drove. The Chinese also built the "permanent" buildings, just as they did much of the boat building. A few men brought back orange seeds or "European" vegetables to grow in the villages, and one or two slightly modified the style of the houses they built. Of course, domestics and boat crews learned a lot more, as did the planter's factotum on some of the smaller plantations, and turned it to good use later in their lives. But the majority of laborers brought home from the plantation little that was useful, except for their trade-store goods. All had new food tastes as a result of plantation rations, the array of foodstuffs available at the plantation store, and the few meals they had at Chinatown in Tulagi while they were in transit. For the majority, the only way they could feed these and other new tastes, and achieve some variety, was to sign on again for the plantation.

The plantation sector drew surplus labor away from the villages, as the fact that about 10 percent of the entire population of Malaita and about 7 percent of that of Guadalcanal were working away from home during the period from about 1914 to 1939 attests. For the "weather coast" of south Guadalcanal, the percentage was probably higher, since the people of the north and east coasts could produce and sell copra. On south Guadalcanal the 32 old men interviewed in 1976 worked an average of almost 10 years away from home, a third of them spending 12 or more years on plantations or associated shipping. Except for 1 man who worked for the Catholic mission at Avuavu, every man interviewed, to say nothing of absent uncles, brothers, and brothers-in-law, had spent time away from home on plantations. One man had been away working for 28 years and another for more than 30. Likewise, in the Malaita sample, except for catechists and pastors, all the men old enough to have had prewar employment had worked on plantation-related activities. Almost a third had been away for 8 or more years, a quarter for 4 to 7 years, and another quarter for 2 to 3 years. And all of this took place in the most productive period of their lives. Few men did not return home at the end of each contract, and most stayed at least a few months before going away again. Those who were married left behind wives who felt the absence no particular hardship as they could call on kin and fellow villagers for assistance. In some cases on Guadalcanal, an absence followed the birth of a child, a substitute for the old postpartum taboo on sexual intercourse and the man's residence in the canoe house in pre-Christian times. Nonetheless, when husbands returned they were obliged to help those who had assisted their family, and for some months had little time to spend developing coconut groves or trying out other forms of economic enterprise. It is impossible to say with certainty how areas such as Malatia and south Guadalcanal might have changed without the plantation economy, but had the government been as helpful to the Solomon Islanders as it was to planters, perhaps these places would have become more like their neighbors in the western Solomons, at least as regards local copra production.[81]

The plantation system contributed very little to the overall economic development of Solomon Islanders, but it did have other, unexpected consequences that were to be of lasting social and political significance.

It would be fanciful to say that all men who went through the institution of the plantation developed a strong sense of Solomon Islands nationalism. But many certainly gained the prerequisites.

Although a man could make enemies on a plantation, he could also make new friends. Men who traditionally called only their kinsmen "friend," began to apply the same term to former strangers they had learned to trust.[82] Laborers sometimes went to visit their new friends in their home villages, stayed on, and with the friend's support, found a wife and married.[83]

Most important, they learned to talk with each other, directly instead of through interpreters. The overseas labor trade had fostered the development of a fairly unstable Pidgin English and Pidgin Fijian. The former was superimposed upon, and mixed with, the jargon of the whaler ports as trading ships and their crews sailed around the Solomons in the 1860s and 1870s. Through traders and the recruitment of some "old hands" on the new plantations, Pidgin English spread, reinforced by English-speaking planters, while Pidgin Fijian atrophied. Gradually, as thousands of men came in and out of plantations, the language Pijin both stabilized and spread, aided in the eastern Solomons by its use as the lingua franca by SSEM teachers and by some members of the Catholic mission. By the 1930s it had achieved a fairly standard form and was so widely known that recruiting vessels were no longer required by law to carry interpreters. "New chums" had to learn the language quickly as both the boss-boy and the master used it. As a result, men from the bush of Fataleka (Malaita) could soon talk to men from the south coast of Guadalcanal. Villagers near plantations picked up the language as they visited plantations to sell produce. Thus, men—few women could speak Pijin because few went to plantations—came to exchange ideas on their customs, their homes, their beliefs, and what they thought of Europeans. The insularity, particularly of the bushmen, was gradually broken down. Men began to realize that their own village was not the center of the world, and that they and people on islands hundreds of miles away shared certain values and problems. Taking an island view, Malaitan men learned that they as a people had many religious and cultural concepts in common.[84]

THE PLANTATION EXPERIENCE was common to most eastern Solomon Islanders, and all shared its culture, a culture that was unique—authoritarian, hierarchical, dominated by the clock, geared to producing a surplus for the Europeans' profit, virtually all male, and controlled by violent sanctions and often-harsh Europeans. The plantation was an institution that placed Solomon Islanders in a subservient, almost childlike role relative to the dominant European, a role that was the antithesis of the old nineteenth-century trading relationship. For most, the plantation was their introduction to Western commerce and, although they participated in only a minor way, it served to familiarize them with the ways of capitalism. What prevented the plantation culture from becoming the permanent culture of the men was the simple fact that as a society the plantation community did not reproduce itself and they were not bound to it forever. It was a temporary expedient that the subsistence villagers needed only occasionally.

Although not unbearable, the plantation experience created a general resentment among most laborers, especially the bush Malaitans, toward the European planters, particularly on the big company plantations. Such Europeans exercised a wide control over the laborers' existence. Aside from their wages, the material returns for years away on the plantation were negligible.

For all its strength at the time, this feeling of resentment remained unharnessed, dispersed, and largely unarticulated. The nature of the plantation system in the Solomons, superimposed on endemic small sociopolitical units, precluded any significant growth of a class ideology. Much unrest was funneled into legitimate expression by the institution of the labor inspectorate. There was also a high turnover of employees every two years. Many who "signed back" did so after a visit home and were members of an entirely new intake. Those who tended to stay on longer as boss-boys were co-opted by their slightly exalted position into identifying more with the management than with the workers. If they did not, they were not boss-boys for long. On the plantation, men of different groups, especially of different islands, were housed separately and tended to mix with their own. They had little in common with neighboring villagers, being perceived more often than not as potential trouble-makers. Moreover, even if some group awareness emerged on any one plantation, distances plus legal constraints prevented any consistent communication between groups on different plantations. Without some organization providing linkages, common grievances could not be readily aired, considered, or acted upon.

The plantation certainly gave thousands of Solomon Islanders a shared experience, a chance to learn about one another, and the means to speak together in a common language. These were important preconditions to any development of a group, regional, or even national consciousness, but the plantation system itself did not give birth to such an identity.

CHAPTER 9

Producers and consumers
(c. 1900–1930)

If you pay too much wages to the natives they would have so
much more money, and would then remain idle. The native
would only work for that particular time, so that if you
doubled his wages he really would only work half the time.
If you doubled the price for his copra, he would let the other
half lie on the ground and rot.

Joseph Meek, 1916

We do not share the widely-held assumption that equates
colonialism with exploitation. In our view economic exploitation occurs only when the exploited have to pay more for
their purchases than the price at which other sellers would
be willing to supply the required merchandise. Exploitation
likewise takes place when the people have to supply goods
or services for less than they would be able to receive on the
open market. Exploitation, in our opinion, must imply a con-
trived denial by coercive means of alternatives that would
otherwise have been available and preferred.

L. H. Gann and Peter Duignan, *Colonialism in Africa*
1870–1960

PACIFICATION IN ITSELF provided conditions under which local production could flourish. More Solomon Islanders gained access to imported
consumer goods as they moved from the bush to the coast, gradually
bringing more land into copra production. Missionary activity, especially in the western Solomons, also stimulated cash cropping. With
peace in the eastern islands, more men could go to plantations in the
1910s and 1920s. Solomon Islanders could play familiar roles, ones they
had learned in the trading and labor trade days. But they were limited
to those roles by the policies and practices of the government and the
commercial sector. Even as consumers, Solomon Islanders' interests
were subsumed to those of European business.

Although the head tax of the 1920s was an encouragement to greater
production of local goods and services, it afforded merely an extension

192

of Solomon Islanders' involvement, at the same level of the economy. In return for their money, taxpayers received little except closer control of their daily life by the government. Government policies in the areas of taxation and local administration, as well as with wages and the institution of the plantation, accustomed Solomon Islanders to participating in a cash economy, albeit on the bottom rung. As cash became important, land became a commercial asset to potential local producers. Consequently, aspects of the economic activity of Solomon Islanders gradually began to lose their old social framework. Where leaders no longer had an economic base, their authority crumbled.

Incentives to local producers

The government and the European commercial sector saw only two roles for Solomon Islanders in the new economy: as producers of labor and raw materials like copra, trochus, and pearlshell; and as consumers of imported goods. To the Europeans the significance of Solomon Islanders as local producers had varied over time. Between about 1896 and 1910, local production loomed large in government thinking because it employed white traders who paid license fees to the government, thus providing revenue. By the 1910s, once plantation development was under way, the planters and the government would have been content to see local production atrophy, so releasing more labor for the new plantations.

In spite of the dearth of encouragement from government and business, there were factors conducive to the expansion of local production, especially in the western and central Solomons. Among them, changes in settlement and demographic patterns were of paramount importance. Pacification meant that people could now live in exposed areas without fear of attack (Photo 17). Both missionaries and government officers constantly urged people to move downslope, from the hills to the valleys, from the bush to the coast, because more accessible settlements made for greater pastoral and administrative convenience. Following this migration in the late 1910s and 1920s, more people were on the coasts, where coconuts could be grown.

By the 1920s too there is evidence that the population decline in many areas had halted as a result of the cessation of warfare, medical aid given regularly by missionaries and sporadically by district officers, and the introduction by both missions and government of sanitation rules that better suited larger settlements than had traditional hygiene measures. Larger downslope settlements, especially along the coast, were also facilitated by the cultivation of a new crop, the sweet potato (*Ipomoea batatas*) which had been introduced by Solomon Islanders returning from Melanesian Mission headquarters at Norfolk Island and

Photo 17. Foate, a new Christian settlement on northwest Malaita, c. 1900.
Notice the lone coconut tree. The stone wall is to give protection against
marauding pagan bushmen. *(Beattie collection)*

from the Queensland and Fiji plantations.[1] The sweet potato grew well
in coastal soils, which were often unsuitable for other root crops. With
such supports the bush people of Choiseul, the New Georgia Islands,
Santa Isabel, parts of Guadalcanal, San Cristobal, and even pockets of
Malaita migrated increasingly to the coasts and more accessible river
valleys in search of better social and economic opportunities.[2]

But during the 1910s some found that large tracts of the coastal land
that they considered theirs by traditional use were claimed by Europeans, as companies, particularly Levers in the western Solomons,
gradually extended their plantations. Besides plantation development,
missionary advice and the activities of the government surveyor had
raised Islanders' awareness about the importance of land. Since the days
of effective armed resistance were past, the people sought other means.
A number realized that they could now consolidate claims to marginal
lands between formerly warring neighbors.[3] Some quickly grasped the
basics of the new game they had to play if they wanted to prove their
rights to so-called waste lands. With Methodist encouragement, the
Kusaghe people of New Georgia, for example, moved down to the coast
to reactivate their traditional claims there, as soon as they thought
Levers were likely to commence operations in the district.[4] Others
appealed to the government and the missionaries to redress their grievances.[5]

The government, although loath to admit injustice, could nonetheless afford to be sympathetic, because by the early twenties it was obvious that thousands of the acres claimed under the Waste Land Regulations could never be developed with the existing labor supply. So many quarrels arose that the government eventually established a commission of inquiry into several disputed land transactions, including those obtained under the Waste Land Regulations.

Judge F. B. Phillips began most of the investigations in 1921.[6] In the New Georgia group, native claimants were advised with a large degree of success by the Reverend John Goldie, on both "waste lands" and land claimed by the Seventh Day Adventist Mission.[7] As a consequence of the commission, about 45,000 of the 200,000 acres of Levers' "waste lands" were eventually restored to the people, providing some acknowledgment of what so many western Solomon Islanders had long known—that the government had never investigated the nature of ownership in the first place.[8]

Where land could be obtained or reclaimed, some of the settlers on the coast followed the example of their saltwater fellows and planted groves of coconuts. A few laborers returned from Queensland with new ideas of plantation agriculture and established sizeable holdings of coconuts for cash cropping, not simply the haphazardly planted village groves. With the pacification of north Malaita, several returners from Queensland left their inland homes with their families and were establishing settlements on the coastal plains, clearing new ground for gardens and coconuts on land owned and lent by others. Here, the pioneers of such "development work" were soon involved in quarrels with the saltwater owners because no longer was the land being used simply for subsistence, but for cash cropping on a long-term basis.[9] The commercialization of indigenously owned land—and the inevitable conflicts— had begun.

At Talise on the isolated weather coast of Guadalcanal, where little copra had been produced for traders in the nineteenth century, David Sango, a returner from Queensland, was the first to have ten acres of coconuts "planted in the European fashion" in the 1910s. His example encouraged one or two others to follow, but operations remained small because of the lack of suitable land in the area.[10] On San Jorge Island, Santa Isabel (Figure 17), another returner, Francis Kouselo, planted coconuts and, like Sango, came to be respected in his own community. Peter Waitasu, a business associate and friend of the trader-planter J. H. C. Dickenson, established an extensive plantation at Uki in addition to running a trade store and trading vessels.[11] Jimmy Sura, after returning from Queensland where he had married a Scottish woman, Agnes Brown, was the first Solomon Islander to formally register land to establish his right to use it to make money and to guarantee in British law the inheritance of the land by his children.[12]

These returners were exceptional, but the example of their efforts, plus the more significant activities of some four hundred Europeans engaged in the plantation economy, helped to stimulate indigenous production. Moreover, the majority of the Christian missions encouraged coconut planting in order that the infant church might become self-sufficient. Many missionaries believed it necessary for the "civilization" of Solomon Islanders that they should become involved in commerce.[13]

By chance, those missions that were exponents of the Protestant ethic happened to start their work on islands in the western Solomons where there was a long history of local production, so reinforcing an existing tendency. The first, the Methodist Mission, once it had established a following in the New Georgia Islands, Choiseul, Fauro, and Mono, took up annual collections of produce and some cash. The sense of competition between Methodist villages—partly a functional substitute for older rivalries—was strong, each trying to outdo the other in generosity.[14] As well as wanting funds for the church, the Methodist Mission viewed work as a necessity to maintain the changed material aspects of the civilized Christian's new way of life.[15]

> The man who earnestly follows the Lotu [church] leaves his weapons and looks after his coconuts, he comes for medicine and has his filthy sores healed, he bathes and has a beautiful glossy skin, he wears clean clothes and looks after his wife and children, he combs his fuzzy hair, he comes to school and learns the rudiments of knowledge, he tries to settle his disputes peacefully, he builds a house the pigs cannot get into, and makes good paths and plants crotons.[16]

The Seventh Day Adventists entered the Solomons mission field in 1914 and emphasized similar values to the Methodists. By the early 1920s their followers in the Marovo Lagoon area, at Ndovele (Vella Lavella), and at Ranongga were contributing tithes to the mission, in cash and in kind.[17]

In the central and southeastern Solomons in the 1910s and 1920s, the Melanesian Mission encouraged its adherents to set aside land to grow coconuts to sell for church collections as well as for their own use (Photo 18).[18] By 1920 the Roman Catholics were active on Shortland Island, Choiseul, Guadalcanal, San Cristobal, and Malaita. They called for some financial support from their followers, either by direct contributions or by working on the mission's small plantations, but generally were far less concerned than most of their rivals with having their people strive for the things of this world, especially those that cost money.[19]

The other Christian sect, the South Sea Evangelical Mission (SSEM), encouraged local production for a very short time only. Initially, male adherents were urged to work on the Malayta Company's plantations, since the major shareholders—the Young and Deck families, always

Photo 18. A Christianized village at Honggo, Nggela Pile, with coconut groves along the coast, typical of central and western Solomons, c. 1900. *(Beattie collection)*

favoring the plantation system—wished to provide a more Christian environment for laborers than that on other plantations. For a couple of years in the early 1910s the mission instructed its village followers to sell their copra to the Malayta Company and not to other traders, but came to grief as, in the words of a rival, "They are both sky-pilots and traders —absolutely rotten show—they are trying to cut everyone else out and have lost lots of money—they deserve to."[20] Thereafter, since the Solomon Islander missionaries received no stipend from the mission and the foreign missionaries were paid their emoluments from overseas contributors, the SSEM had little further to say about increasing local cultivation.[21]

On Malaita, where the SSEM's progress surpassed that of its nearest competitor, the Catholics, the major missions paid little, if any, attention to providing an ideological reinforcement of the virtues of capitalism, including the production of crops for cash. As ever, Malaita lagged behind economically.

Although the government had made no effort to stimulate local production throughout the 1910s, it did indirectly encourage it in 1921–1923 with the introduction of the head tax,[22] which was imposed to pay for "the general expenses of administration"[23] as personnel increased, and to encourage "the recruitment of labourers and also to induce cultivating native products for sale."[24] In the Solomons, unlike the other Pacific territories of Fiji, the Gilbert and Ellice Islands Colony, and

Papua, none of this tax was earmarked for welfare work such as education.[25]

Solomon Islanders had little prior warning that a tax was to be imposed. In areas where local planting was in its infancy or impossible, the tax—even when reduced from the basic £1 to 10 shillings or 5 shillings because of such hardship—meant that men had to seek employment on plantations, both to pay their own tax and to help the unemployed taxable men who were needed in the village.[26] The alternatives were few and harsh. The bush people of central inland Guadalcanal, as the district officer found in 1923,

> have no produce to dispose of except yams, and these they carry to the coast, two days hard march, where they are exchanged for "red money" and a little cash. The "red money" has then to be "hawked" about until a buyer is found for it. As they cannot possibly carry ten shillings worth of yams at one time, this journey has to be made on several occasions.[27]

Further east, in the Mbirao bush inland from Kaoka, the people gradually lost all their shell valuables because they were forced to sell them for tax money.[28] On Malaita, when taxes were being collected, some of the Solomon Islander police had their own "business" going by which they bought up cheaply precious shell valuables, often heirlooms, for the cash that would shortly after be taken by the district officer for tax payment.[29]

People who in the past had obtained trade goods and money by selling produce, extended their plantings of coconut palms as the old disinclination to work for wages away from home persisted.[30] By 1928, where villagers had the land, they were often planting a few acres with coconuts "after the European style."[31] In some places, such as Vella Lavella, they were merely exploiting existing groves more thoroughly. The cumulative effect of these new plantings and greater production from established groves was to increase the export of copra made by Solomon Islanders from 1350 tons in 1898, to 3000 tons in 1928, about 14 percent of the total exported for that year (see Table 6).[32]

For most Solomon Islanders, the head tax was a burden. But almost simultaneously another tax began to affect them as producers. In 1920, an export duty on copra of 10 shillings per ton was introduced and was inevitably passed on by the traders to the local producers.[33]

The effects of World War I on Solomon Islander producers and consumers

The introduction of the head native tax explains the gradual increase in local production despite the disincentives of the overall fall in the price of copra during the period 1922–1925 and the loss of income to pro-

TABLE 6
Value of exports of copra, 1910–1940

Year	Volume tons	Value, c.i.f. Sydney £	Value per ton £	Estimated price paid to white traders and planters in Solomons[a] £
1910	4,165	70,664	16.96	14.87
1911	3,745	58,331	15.57	13.50
1912	4,365	74,997	17.18	15.08
1913	5,831	116,662	20.00	17.85
1914	5,418	74,990	13.84	11.81[b]
1915	6,031	78,990	13.09	11.07
1916	6,030	91,663	15.20	13.14
1917	6,664	133,328	20.00	17.85
1918	10,000	155,000	15.50	13.44
1919	9,891	153,395	15.50	13.44
1920	8,160	194,046	23.78	21.55[c]
1921	11,127	300,206	26.97	24.68
1922	12,109	173,916	14.36	12.32
1923	16,711	209,387	12.53	10.52
1924	18,278	273,563	14.96	12.91
1925	16,508	287,702	17.42	15.32
1926	19,206	369,283	19.22	17.12
1927	22,316	411,597	18.44	16.32
1928	21,959	348,793	15.88	13.81
1929	23,525	387,079	16.45	14.37
1930	21,300	304,088	14.27	12.23
1931	23,681	271,828	11.47	9.49
1932	21,209	137,843	6.49	4.61
1933	22,256	153,426	6.89	5.00
1934	21,119	70,878	3.35	1.53
1935	18,093	54,013	2.98	1.17
1936	20,699	156,532	7.56	5.65
1937	25,073	293,054	11.68	9.69
1938	22,937	259,366	11.30	9.32
1939	21,666	150,000	6.92	5.03
1940	12,299	100,000	8.13	6.21

SOURCES: BSIP-AR 1918–1940; BPA.

NOTES: [a] Solomons price calculated on following basis: Solomons price = (Sydney price less 2% of Sydney price) less £1.75 (freight). The deduction of 2% of the Sydney price for insurance and handling charges is based on Burns Philp's price accounting 1922–1940, in notebooks of supercargo (BPA).
[b] Additional freight because of war (1914–1918) not subtracted.
[c] Exclusive of copra tax.

199

ducers because of the copra duty. Previously, when a dramatic price drop occurred indigenous producers reacted by tapering off copra making.

During World War I (1914–1918) copra prices in London were high, but the lack of shipping caused copra to be stockpiled either in the Solomons or in Sydney.[34] Although by 1916 Burns Philp was able to export most of this to the United States, the shipping shortage and war-risk insurance caused freight costs to increase, with Burns Philp's rates rising from about £1 15s. per ton prewar, to £2 5s. by 1918. The prices of the goods that merchants sold to traders rose 60–100 percent in the same period. Whereas the Solomons' staple currency, tobacco, had been priced between 1 and 2 shillings per pound in the 1900s, in February 1917 it was up to 3s. 9d.; in January 1918, 3s. 10d. to 4s. 0d.; and in January 1919, Levers were selling it to traders at Ghavutu for 6s. 1d. Initially the traders were able to absorb some of the increase by cutting their profit margin, but once the price got to 4s. 6d. per pound, in May 1918, they had to pass on the extra to the producers. On San Cristobal the manager of Boroni, George Mumford, doubled the price of copra to 20 full nuts for 1 stick of tobacco, a cut from £6 to £3 per ton to the local producer. Soon after, he ceased to trade because the people were making so little copra and because the price for the copra he could sell to Levers was too low.

Both Mumford and the Solomon Islanders were reacting in a similar way to the same economic forces.[35] Although they were responsive to increases in the price paid for their produce, they both had a critical lower limit or reserve price. From Shortland to San Cristobal, once prices fell below that limit, the Solomon Islanders made only the minimum needed to pay tax and perhaps buy tobacco, and then ceased to produce. Since cash crops were simply a useful sideline to the subsistence economy, they concentrated on the latter. The nature of the coconut palm was such that little damage was done by leaving it untended for a few years, and even then all that was needed was to cut down the undergrowth. In places where the sale of other produce, such as trochus shell, was profitable Solomon Islanders turned to that to earn the little they needed.[36] There were, of course, variations within the islands, depending on how close producers were to a steamer port of call. For example, during the war the New Georgia people near Gizo received higher prices than the San Cristobal people, because freight from Tulagi, the usual terminus for the steamers, to San Cristobal was £1–£2 both ways by early 1919, when copra was only £11–£12 a ton.[37]

In the immediate postwar years, following the dislocation of agriculture in Europe, the demand for copra remained high, with the Sydney c.i.f. price reaching almost £27 per ton in 1921 (see Table 6). But, as normality returned to Europe, prices fell dramatically, just when many commercial growers in the Solomons were facing financial difficulties. During and after the war, production costs such as the price of rice, like that of tobacco, rose; overseas capital, from Australia in particular, was difficult to raise; and many planters were facing an increase in the rentals on land held under Crown (public) and Native leases.[38]

The Solomon Islands Planters Association sought political intervention from Resident Commissioner Kane in 1922. The government had already given related concessions to Levers and Burns Philp by allowing them a three-year extension on the period stipulated for improvements on government leasehold land on the grounds that the inadequate labor supply had hindered progress. Kane recommended to Suva that the government lower rentals on Public leases and bring up all the 14,000 acres of Native leases for conversion to Public leases, thereby assisting planters and lessening administrative costs.[39]

Although the government permitted the initial low rental rate of Public leases to continue for an additional four years, it was reluctant to do the same on Native leases because of Colonial Office disapproval.[40] Yet pressure from planters for a decrease in the rental gained momentum because each year the rise on the Native leases came to affect more planters.[41] The government eventually lowered the rate on Public leases and on Native leases made after 1926, but the secretary of state for colonies denied all pleas for reducing payments on Native leases effective before that date. The secretary refused to permit "compulsory purchase of native lands," but allowed the protectorate's "surplus funds" to be used to pay the difference to the Solomon Islander lessors, on the planters' behalf, between the old and the new rates of rental.[42] On the face of it, the lessors involved were guaranteed their legal rights.

In reality, this compromise was at the expense of the Solomon Islanders. The lessors, along with the rest of the people, were subsidizing the relief provided by the government to the white planters. The "surplus funds" originated in part from the copra duty, the head tax, and the import duty (particularly on tobacco). Almost 40 percent of these funds came directly or indirectly from the contributions of Solomon Islanders.[43]

Barriers to greater Solomon Islander participation in the cash economy

The Solomon Islanders were disadvantaged in other ways. During the 1920s the revenue of the protectorate increased steadily as plantations came into maximum production (see Tables 6 and 7). In 1921 at least £3000 of this was lodged in a fixed deposit in the Bank of New Zealand in Sydney; by 1929 it had grown to £30,310. This fund was earning the protectorate interest at about 5 percent annually (for the times, a good

return), but, more significantly, it was available to finance development within Australia and New Zealand. If the Solomon Islanders had
been legally able to borrow they could not have done so because there
was no bank in the islands. Between them, the merchant companies of
Burns Philp and W. R. Carpenter provided most of the services a bank
offered—but only to the white community.[44]

Not only were surplus funds lodged overseas, but also much of the
cash income generated within the Solomons was expatriated. Government officers and the business community sent home some of their
wages to support their families and frequently purchased goods made
overseas. From 1920 to 1930, 80 percent and more of the annual export
earnings of the protectorate were spent on imports of rice, tobacco,
clothing, biscuits, meat, benzene, copra bags, timber, machinery, hardware, kerosene, beer, spirits, wine, sugar, and fish (in order of importance). Likewise, much of the money Solomon Islanders earned went on
these expensive imported goods, leaving little to accumulate as capital
to finance any indigenous enterprise.[45]

Some of the imports certainly could not have been produced in the
Solomons, but others replaced local products. Although the Solomon
Islands could produce sufficient crops to feed all of their people, the
major import during the period was rice—used to feed laborers on plantations. In the old labor-trade days, the recruiting ships coasting along
Guadalcanal, San Cristobal, Savo, and Nggela usually obtained fresh
food for their company from the saltwater people. When the destina-
tions were no longer Fiji or Queensland, but other islands within the
group, the shorter passage, together with the acceptance of rice by Solomon Islanders, meant that far less use was made of local food for plantation laborers. Consequently less trade and cash went to the people.
The government made no attempt to create a system of regional marketing whereby local food could have been used on plantations instead
of the expensive import. F. M. Campbell, planter and sometime acting
district officer on San Cristobal, suggested in 1926 that the government
permit the collection of the head tax in kind for some of the poorer areas
of the island, a practice quite common in Fiji and the Gilbert and Ellice
Islands Colony, both British territories. His plan was to purchase the
food so collected from the government account and use it to feed his
plantation labor. The resident commissioner forbade this because of a
conflict of interests, but the principle might have been applied in other
districts where the government had independent officers.[46]

Government inaction allowed the proven horticultural capacity of
the Solomon Islander producer to go unused. To step outside the pro-
ducer-consumer roles, Solomon Islanders had to face not simply government inaction, but also positive discouragement. Like the Europeans,
Solomon Islanders who wanted to open a store on shore or on a vessel
had to pay £10 a year for a license. In theory this applied to the home-

based Melanesian agents of the white traders, but was difficult to police.[47] The few who might have been able to raise £10 then had the task of setting themselves up as retailers without the benefit of credit facilities from the commercial firms. Under the Native Contracts' Regulation (no. 2 of 1896) no civil action to recover debts could be taken against a Solomon Islander. This was in line with British policy in Fiji, where it had been motivated by a desire to protect the Islanders from being stripped of their possessions, notably their lands. But the regulation was a two-edged sword.

It undoubtedly protected the Solomon Islanders, but it also meant that the amount of credit likely to be given to them by a European would remain insignificant. Only the small-time white traders could risk the loss of their trade advances against the promise of future produce. Even at this level, the government had done all within its legal power in 1897 and 1908 to encourage the competitive traders to operate on a cash basis, which would put them in a stronger position when buying, so that prices and therefore production would be higher.[48]

Although the government passed no legislation to cut off this one credit facility open to Solomon Islanders, it tried to give the impression that such a practice was in fact forbidden.[49] In 1916 Barnett told the chiefs and people of Alu:

> I will now speak about your land and coconuts. . . . You are at liberty to sell your copra where and how you like and get the best price possible, in order to do this you must do away with the old style of trading and learn to buy and sell like the white man for cash only. Credit and giving out trade is bad for the white man and worse for the native, therefore I hope you will now understand that there is to be no more credit.[50]

With and without credit many Europeans had been anxious to buy locally produced copra from 1905 to 1913. During those years the numbers of Europeans employed in trading and planting rose from 61 to 425.[51] The many small planting concerns, as well as Burns Philp and Levers, had to wait at least six years before the first of their coconut palms came into bearing. Having limited capital, managers or owners almost without exception took to trading. In larger centers like Roviana, produce might be brought to the trader's station, but in most cases the trader-planter went about the islands in a ship seeking trade. Fairley, Rigby and Company was typical of the small concerns. They kept one or two small vessels constantly on the move picking up copra and trochus shell along the western end of San Cristobal, going across with a full cargo to sell at Tulagi, and taking on returned laborers there to return to San Cristobal for a fee from Burns Philp or Levers while bringing back supplies for their own plantation at Boroni.[52]

Exclusive of the initial capital and calls on shareholders, these companies were partly self-financing during the growing period of the coco-

TABLE 7
Revenue and expenditure of
British Solomon Islands Protectorate, 1897–1941

Year	Revenue £	Expenditure £
1897–98	957	1,933
1898–99	1,257	1,030
1899–1900	1,454	3,120
1900–01	1,903	1,926
1901–02	1,907	2,179
1902–03	1,758	2,180
1903–04	1,632	2,253
1904–05	1,993	2,307
1905–06	2,378	2,341
1906–07	4,618	3,295
1907–08	7,430	6,483
1908–09	10,603	13,257
1909–10	11,356	8,456
1910–11	14,130	9,493
1911–12	16,040	22,639
1912–13	15,432	15,571
1913–14	24,520	16,500
1914–15	22,646	18,566
1915–16	22,006	26,425
1916–17	27,834	23,358
1917–18	30,563	26,120
1918–19	29,476	30,205
1919–20	34,544	37,639
1920–21	52,315	41,662
1921–22	56,432	45,450
1922–23	56,741	52,472
1923–24	64,329	52,655
1924–25	64,091	65,409
1925–26	71,430	60,330
1926–27	77,444	63,740
1927–28	75,664	73,993
1928–29	79,935	91,632
1929–30	76,678	68,807
1930–31	62,728	67,816
1931–32	56,744	55,323
1932–33	58,541	53,432
1933–34	53,039	56,822
1934–35	52,927	54,207
1935–36	58,465	49,224
1936–37	68,136	63,027
1937–38	82,809	69,002
1938–39	69,231	66,663
1939–40	58,983	74,084
1940–41	51,320	65,847

Sources: BSIP-AR 1897–1938; WPHC 397/38: Meeting of
Advisory Council, Apr. 1938, encl.; WPHC 3215/38: Meeting
. . . Nov. 1938, encl.; WPHC 1881/40: Meeting . . . July
1940, encl.; WPHC 2090/41: Meeting . . . June 1941, encl.;
WPHC F1/1: Meeting . . . Nov. 1941, encl.

nut palms, with the development capital so generated coming from the production of Solomon Islanders. But the Solomon Islanders were totally unable to tap the sources of overseas capital that were to some extent accessible to even the smallest of the European enterprises. The Islanders' language, lack of formal education, and ignorance of financial procedures, coupled with a lack of trust on the Europeans' side, precluded this.[53]

Within the islands, the larger business firms had been appalled by the casual arrangements between the resident traders and the people. When Burns Philp took over the Tindal interests at Faisi in 1906, W. H. Lucas learned to his horror that the people only recognized debts to the person who conducted the transaction, so that if that person were replaced the debt vanished. Such a system had worked well enough in the days of individual traders.[54] But, together with the impossibility of litigation to recover debts, it meant that the business companies, responsible to their shareholders, simply refused all credit to Solomon Islanders and set limits on the amount allowed to half-castes like Pierre Pratt of Ranongga. It was left to the small-time traders to run the risk of giving credit. Because of the risk, traders marked up by 50 percent the goods they left with their Melanesian agents, calculating a 16 percent loss as inevitable, and bringing real profit back to the usual 34 percent.[55] In this way even as producers the Solomon Islanders were debarred from receiving the best price because the merchant firms thought it safer to deal through the white traders.

This policy created a dilemma for Burns Philp when they extended operations from the trade room of the steamer to a shore-based store at Gizo in 1907, in an attempt to forestall Levers, whose Kolombangara operations were expected to result in the opening of their own store. In the view of Burns Philp, a store would also obviate the chaotic scramble of "steamer day" when the traders' haste to sell their produce and collect their cargo from Sydney, was exceeded only by their impatience to get to the bar.[56] On the other hand, with the opening of a permanent store the company would be setting up in competition with its customers, the white traders, for the trade of the Solomon Islanders. The traders not only provided cargo for the six-weekly steamer, but those of them involved in plantations were also customers for the more expensive items and bulk purchases.[57] The company therefore opened the store, "dealing with the traders, the government and white planters, all on an equal basis and with them only."[58]

However, Burns Philp always held that "the paramount factor in business is to make money" and when money could be made, business had no permanent loyalties, racial or otherwise.[59] Following the enforcement of regulations requiring labor to sign on and off before a government officer in 1914, Tulagi became the most important labor depot because it was centrally located for the passage of labor between the

Photo 19. Burns Philp's depot at Makambo Island, c. 1910. *(Burns Philp Archives)*

eastern Solomons and the western plantations. With so many paid-up laborers passing through Tulagi, Burns Philp modified its policy, at least on a retail sales for cash basis, and expanded its depot, opened at nearby Makambo in 1909 (Figure 14, Photo 19), into a full branch where Solomon Islanders could purchase goods—but in a section partitioned off from the "European" store.[60]

Enter the Chinese

Burns Philp's change of attitude was in part induced by competition, not only from Levers' depot at Ghavutu, an island near Makambo, but also from Chinese traders who started to open stores over the swamp at Tulagi in 1913–1914.[61] These Chinese had come to the Solomons in twos and threes, as builders and cooks for Burns Philp, Levers, and others, in earlier years. Using their connections with the Hong Kong, Rabaul, and Sydney Chinese communities, as well as their own savings, they soon left their trades, leased land, and became storekeepers. Based initially at Tulagi, they began to go about in ships seeking trade, paying higher prices for native produce, and charging less for trade goods than did the Europeans (Photo 20). By 1920, the Chinese numbered fifty-five and were becoming a serious threat to the white traders, who consequently attempted to convince the government that these "aliens" encouraged "social evils" among the Solomon Islanders.[62] Although it could find no evidence of malevolence among the Chinese community, the government refused to issue any more trading licenses to them for twelve months.[63]

Photo 20. Main street of Chinatown, Tulagi, in 1930s. *(Western Pacific Archives)*

Levers too resented the Chinese storekeepers at Tulagi. Most of the company's laborers passed through the capital, being housed at Ghavutu during their wait for shipping. As Chinese stores increased in number and became popular among the laborers, Levers' management realized that more and more wages were being spent at Chinatown than at the plantation stores or at Ghavutu, where previously they had had captive customers and sold well above Chinese prices. Levers accordingly pressed the government to witness the paying-off of their laborers at Ghavutu, thus preventing them from getting off the island to Tulagi. By 1916 Burns Philp demanded that they too be allowed to pay-off laborers at their depot.

Barnett demurred, not so much because Solomon Islanders were complaining of being unable to shop at Chinatown and the other stores, but because it was often inconvenient for officers to cross to Ghavutu and Makambo. Attempts by the companies to have the movement controlled continued until the early 1920s, when they gave up in the face of the opening of W. R. Carpenter's store on Tulagi and the Solomon Islanders' persistence. The local Nggela people, plying between the islets in their canoes to sell vegetables, provided the transportation as did the Chinese or their "boys," who sometimes broke the curfew on Solomon Islanders at Tulagi to ferry customers to Chinatown by night. Since the only weapon left to the merchant firms was competition, they enlarged their range of goods and periodically dropped prices to attract the "pay-off" business.

The one thing they failed to develop was rapport with Solomon Islanders. The Chinese, unlike the salaried white storekeepers, never hurried the laborers' interminable deliberations over purchases, and made an effort to allow for their customers' foibles. One Chinese store-keeper, "Sweetie" (Suete) was very popular because he would let the buyers fill up their boxes to what appeared was the set limit (say, £1 or £3, depending on how much the customer wanted to spend) and then, as a "present," add extra articles for nothing. The customers always believed they had a bargain, though in fact the extra cost of the seeming bonus had already been added to the original purchases.

In Chinatown, itinerant Solomon Islanders could find a place to sit down and eat well and cheaply, which no "native" would have been allowed to do at Elkington's Hotel or at the European Club. Laborers who, as boat crew or domestics, had acquired a taste for alcohol were sometimes able to buy it from certain Chinese, although this was illegal. Most laborers considered that the Chinese gave them better value for money. When it came to merchandise, their European business rivals thought the same.[64]

The merchant firms also opposed the Chinese because they presented a threat to some of the firms' indebted white trader clients. If Solomon Islanders bought from and sold to the Chinese, the traders' book debts with Burns Philp and Carpenters would not be reduced. However, the potential losses were limited to this one area as long as those firms remained wholesale suppliers and shippers to the Chinese.[65]

The government was sensitive to the antagonism of the merchants toward the Chinese but, as in the early days with Levers, did not want monopoly conditions in commerce. In 1918 a Chinese was allowed to open a store at Aola, next to the government station, because the Malayta Company store at Mbara had been the only one where paid-off laborers could buy goods.[66] Between 1921 and 1932 only four new ship licenses and six new store licenses were issued to Chinese. However, in 1926, after consultation with the Colonial Office, the government gave Alois Akun permission to open stores outside Tulagi, at Gizo and the Shortlands, in order to create competition for Burns Philp's stores, which the planters complained were selling goods at 70 to 100 percent mark-up.[67]

Similar extension of Chinese stores to other centers would have improved the position of Solomon Islanders as producers and con-sumers, but the government's concern was predominantly with the interests of the Europeans. On Malaita, District Officer Bell urged Kane in 1927 to issue store licenses to Chinese, since the regulation of 1923 had forbidden recruiting boats to supply trade as beach payment and substituted £6 in cash. Following the introduction of the regula-tion, Europeans had taken out five additional store licenses, making a total of nine in operation on Malaita by 1925—hardly sufficient to meet the needs of about 40,000 people living mostly in bush areas. To protect those ventures and to contain the anti-Chinese feeling among the Europeans, the government refused to issue any more store permits to the Chinese, even though the consumer would have benefited.[68] Chinese trading remained a ship-based operation except at Tulagi, Aola, and Gizo.[69]

Although the government used the law to control Chinese trading so as not to let them swamp "British" enterprise, it did nothing to encourage the development of a group of indigenous entrepreneurs, despite indications of this potentiality. The big-men who rose as middlemen to the whalers and traders and the passage-masters of the old labor-trade days were models from an earlier era when the odds were in favor of the Solomon Islanders. Even in the plantation period Peter Waitasu had gathered sufficient resources to buy and run trading vessels out of Uki. Sango at Talise not only had his own coconut groves, but also ran a few head of cattle for sale locally. Enterprising north Malaitans who owned cutters earned themselves 5 shillings per head when they took across to Tulagi the gang of stevedores from Langalanga who worked the island run on Burns Philp's steamers.[70]

From 1925 on, many Europeans abandoned trading away from their plantations, which were coming into profitable production and demanded most of their time.[71] Some white traders were forced out because of decreased profits resulting from both the slump in the copra price of the early 1920s and the imposition of the copra duty. The Chinese were under the same constraints but, because of their frugality, were both able and willing to work harder for less than the average white man and paid better prices to Solomon Islanders for their produce.[72] By filling the shipping and distribution hiatus, the Chinese effectively prevented indigenous participation at this level of the economy.

The merchant firms quickly sensed the new direction.[73] Burns Philp's management in 1926 were certain that

> it will only be a matter of time when there will be no white traders left. It is therefore good policy to look after and foster our trade with the Chinese so that when the time comes and these people control the bulk of native produce, we will have their confidence and good will.[74]

Through keener competition, the advent of the Chinese assuredly benefited the Solomon Islander producer and consumer. But from the point of view of the companies, and later the government, the Chinese were simply a more efficient and less troublesome replacement for the most minor of the entrepreneurs, the white traders. The actors on the middle level of the pyramid of capitalism were changing, but the Solomon Islanders were still at its base.

The blessing of settled government

The government let the Solomon Islanders remain as mere producers and consumers in the economy, but to expect more is perhaps to impose values of a later age on the government of a colonial backwater. Yet once the Solomon Islanders became direct taxpayers, in the 1920s, they had the right, in terms of the values of their "masters," to get some return from the government, just as their neighbors in the British territories of Fiji and the Gilbert and Ellice Islands Colony had in the form of medical aid and education. They had now become paying consumers of government services.

Some progress was evident in medical service to the Solomons by 1930, but, for an estimated population of 150,000, the service remained rudimentary.[75] By 1915 a government hospital had been built at Tulagi to serve the white community and the laborers who passed through the Department of Labour.[76] A government doctor visited some of the plantations perhaps once a year to check on the health of laborers.[77]

At Gizo, Shortland Island, and San Cristobal, Dr. Crichlow worked intermittently as both medical and district officer from 1916 until 1927, when he became the traveling medical officer on the *Hygeia*. By 1930, three government doctors were employed plus Dr. Lucy Holt-Macrimmon who cared for her husband's plantation labor at Su'u, Malaita, as well as the surrounding villagers, in return for a grant of £150 per year.[78] There were as many doctors again, receiving no government support, working for the Methodist and Melanesian missions, as well as one employed by the Vanikolo Kauri Timber Company. District officers also provided basic medical aid for the villagers near their stations from 1923 onward. In the mid-twenties a handful of illiterate Melanesian men were trained at Tulagi hospital as dressers. This was the only form of education the government provided, all else being left to the missions. By 1930 there were only seven dressers in government employment through the entire protectorate.[79] In the late 1920s, in the Solomons and the rest of the southwest Pacific islands, the Rockefeller Foundation's medical team commenced its beneficial campaign against the debilitating diseases of yaws and hookworm, but the 50 percent contribution of the Solomons government was mainly logistical.[80]

The government spent money on establishing a "Native Administration" in 1922. District and village headmen and village constables were selected and supervised by the district officers.[81] Formerly, the official line of communication and command had been from the district officer to the people. Considering the limited number of costly European personnel, this innovation was an inexpensive way of extending government control.[82] District headmen were paid £12 per year (the same as a plantation laborer, 1923–1934), village headmen £3, and constables £1

10s. For an outlay of less than a thousand pounds per year, or 1.6 percent of the protectorate's annual expenditure for the years 1922–1927, the demands of the government could be brought right into the villages.[83]

That this institution was introduced at almost the same time as the "Native Tax" is not accidental. Included in the duties of the headmen were census-taking and reporting to the district officer any movements of people into and out of the region. In this way the taxable population could be noted as well as the disappearance of defaulters from the tax or runaways from plantations. Under the new regulation, villagers were required to work on communal services—road making, house building, and clearing village compounds. Sanitation rules were to be enforced, including the building of separate cooking houses, latrines, and pig fences. While traveling, the district officer could demand that villagers supply such assistance as carriers and canoes as needed. In addition, laws relating to slander, adultery, abusive language, disorderly conduct, and the making of gardens were to be enforced by the headmen. A system of courts to try and, if necessary, fine offenders was also set up, with the district officer hearing the case and the district headmen acting as assessors.[84]

Although the regulation was gradually enforced in most districts, many problems arose from the choice of headmen. Often such men appeared influential to the district officer, but were not important in their own society. District Officer Hill on Guadalcanal believed "even the best natives" to be "so unreliable as to render them of no use in assisting in tax collecting."[85] Many of them called on the constable or the police patrols to enforce their will or the will of the government as they understood it, resulting in abuses of authority.

In 1927, as an outcome of resentment toward poorly supervised police and the often harsh enforcement of the tax collector, some Mbirao bushmen of Guadalcanal murdered a police patrol. A few months later, a group of Kwaio on Malaita, led by Basiana, killed District Officer Bell, the cadet Lillies, and their police. The Bell killings particularly disturbed the European population, the more nervous element anticipating a full-scale uprising. Most Solomon Islanders, including many Malaitans, were equally concerned, since they had respected Bell; despite his rough manner, he had helped many of them during his years as labor inspector and district officer. An official inquiry followed this unprecedented resistance to the government, and on Malaita reprisals among the Kwaio were to have tragic and long-lasting effects. Many aspects of administrative policy came under the close examination of the Colonial Office after the "Bell killings" attracted both Australian warships and British parliamentary attention.[86]

The government then adopted a more gradual approach to the

enforcement of regulations, allowing some latitude for local conditions, and admitting to the Colonial Office that in the past "recognition appears not to have been given to the fact that the native polity was not uniform throughout the Protectorate." Although Guadalcanal, San Cristobal, and Malaita clan leaders received some allegiance and respect from their own clans, placing them in authority over other clans imposed "an entirely foreign element."[87] However, by 1928 the government, having embarked on this course, felt it too late to revise the system. Despite its deficiencies, it was preserved, but under the closer control of the district officers. In the west the new system was not a major problem, since in New Georgia and the Shortlands almost all the district headmen were traditional chiefs who were owed some respect from other chiefs and their followers.[88]

Except for minor medical welfare and tightening control over its subjects, the government had done little for the people in return for their taxes of £10,000 a year.[89] Even at the close of the decade, when a real opportunity arose to set aside funds for Solomon Islander development, the government's concern was for the expatriate. Although the gesture was potentially a sop to unemployment in Great Britain, in 1929 the British Government underwrote some of its well-intentioned post-war pronouncements on its colonial peoples with monetary grants under the Colonial Development Act. The secretary of state for colonies was empowered to "make advances to the government of . . . any territory . . . for the purpose of aiding and developing agriculture and industry in the . . . territory . . . thereby promoting commerce with the United Kingdom."[90] Since copra was important to British industry, in 1931 the protectorate applied for and received a grant from the Colonial Development Welfare Fund for £5000. This was matched pound for pound by the protectorate government for research into coconut pests and diseases troubling plantations, especially those of Levers, which produced a third of the export crop. The thought that local producers might be variously assisted by the £10,000 never occurred to the committee concerned.[91]

Producers and consumers and capitalism

By 1930 cash was the basis for most relationships the Solomon Islanders had with Europeans. Interactions took place in order to give or get money. Even the missions participated in the process, since all but the SSEM paid their local clergy and assistants cash stipends.[92] The missions' concern for the people went beyond mere fund raising, but to some, particularly the Methodists, finance was an issue that often took center stage. In 1928 for example, Goldie and forty "Christian chiefs" of the Roviana circuit met to discuss methods to further the work of God, "the main topic [being] the best way to lift and maintain the income of the District" for mission use.[93]

For producers of goods grown or collected at home in the western and central Solomons, the process of monetization of the old barter system proceeded fairly slowly until the 1920s. Land sales and then lease rentals in earlier years had alerted many to the value of cash, but without simultaneous competition for their goods and money there seemed little real use for it. This situation began to change in the 1920s as a consequence of both business and government policies. Established traders like Fred Green at Simbo and later Gizo, and Leslie Gill at Roviana always dealt on a strictly cash basis. With the opening of stores at Gizo by Burns Philp, and Alois Akun operating on the same principle, Solomon Islanders could shop around and get better bargains; local producers increasingly asked for cash from the trader buying their copra or trochus. But the desire for cash was confined to places such as Gizo or Faisi, where people could shop at Burns Philp or nearby trader-planters like Atkinson and Scott. The majority of the people, living away from the centers, had only traders such as Evans at Mono, or the itinerating Chinese vessels like the *Nanui* in the Gizo district.[94] For them trade was still mainly on a barter basis.

The plantation was more efficient at educating in the ways of money than was barter trade. Many returners from overseas plantations had acquired an understanding of wages for services and buying with cash. A new generation learned similar things on Solomon Island plantations: their labor was exchanged for cash; cash exchanged for overpriced store goods; they were constantly reminded that their laziness, stupidity, and sickness cost the owner money; that rations, mosquito nets, and *kaliko* cost money; that time itself was money. People now had a value, not in social terms, but as units of production. This was a European definition of the worth of the Solomon Islander. In the institution of the plantation the metaphor began to influence the basis of the laborers' relationships with one another, cut off as they were from natural society. Money was the means of their greatest entertainment—gambling. When one group felt offended by another, compensation was demanded in cash, not in traditional wealth objects as at home.

With the opening in the 1910s of the "native" stores at Tulagi and elsewhere on a strictly cash basis for laborers, the old barter-credit system of the trader and labor recruiter found a competitor. But unlike the local producers of goods, the laborers almost always had access to the stores at the end of their contracts, as well as on the plantation itself, and could more quickly learn about cash buying.

The period 1921 to 1930 marks an acceleration of the monetization process, a direct consequence of government legislation. Cash consciousness increased dramatically with the introduction of the head tax because people in communities producing both goods and services had to have money to hand over to the tax collector or face imprisonment. Men now became indebted in a new way, by paying one another's tax. Elders often owed money to younger men. Social obligations, at least in this context, had a strict cash equivalent. The substitution of a cash advance for trade goods as beach payment in 1923 meant that laborers and their families in the eastern Solomons had to get used to dealing with cash if they were to obtain the trade goods they wanted.

In the east too, traditional valuables were assigned an equivalent in the introduced currency. This had begun in the trading days with so many porpoise teeth for a shilling, but the cash equivalent was a device for the trader to keep the accounts; Solomon Islanders were rarely given or asked for cash, unless they were returned laborers who were aware that cash gave greater buying power than barter on a competitive market. Such competition was rare in places like Malaita, south Guadalcanal, and Santa Cruz until well into the twentieth century; people in isolated places had insufficient resources to spare labor for plantations. With the tax, they sold off their traditional valuables in return for currency to give to the collector, and these valuables began to be perceived in cash terms. For the wealthier north Malaitans who did not have to sell their valuables to pay the tax, cash was nonetheless received for the shell money of Langalanga, which the steamer gang sold as far west as the Shortland Islands.[95] The establishment of the Native Administration and the payment of functionaries like headmen caused people to see their relationships with the government in cash terms where previously those who had assisted the government or any authority had seen it more as reciprocity.

During this period too there was a shift in the people's attitude toward the land that appeared first in closely settled areas, rich in cash-crop potential. On northern Malaita in the 1910s and in less populous New Georgia in the 1920s, quarrels over land, as well as the valuable tree crops of coconuts and ivory nuts, became more common because people wanted to claim ownership to earn money, not simply to establish use rights. In New Georgia, the disputes took the form of Methodists versus Adventists, a convenient ideological conflict to mask the divisions among families and clans as to who should have the land to use for copra growing.[96]

In all these areas—land, labor, obligations between men and between the individual and the community—the economic element was beginning to be separated from its social context. This had long been true of most dealings between Europeans and Solomon Islanders and now applied increasingly to those between Solomon Islanders themselves.

Political correlates of socioeconomic change

Pacification and mission activity had weakened the power of traditional leaders and many lost it completely, but this did not mean that their role disappeared. It certainly changed, but in many areas established leaders and those who were hereditary heirs to the leadership ranks successfully abandoned outlawed activities while taking on legitimate and legitimizing substitutes. After the initial conflicts and process of conversion, missionaries rarely denounced local leaders. Goldie worked side by side with a new generation of young, literate Methodist chiefs, giving constant and public recognition of their authority and probably freezing existing chiefly families in permanent positions of power. Although he became the greatest *ngati bangara* 'chief' of all the New Georgia group, it was a position he could only have won because he reinforced the system that sustained such chiefs.[97] With Goldie's support of the chiefs, the mission teachers, although respected, were not in a position to vie for political power because they were never based in their home villages and were dependent on chiefly patronage. The Catholics in the Shortlands, following the conversion of Gorai's son in 1909, showed similar deference to the chiefs, as did adherents of the Melanesian Mission to the leaders on Isabel, Nggela, and north San Cristobal.[98] In these areas, mainly in the western and central Solomons, the leaders could take part in production and the growing cash economy. Especially in the New Georgia group, these leaders were central in the annual fund-raising activities of the missions. They thus had both an economic base and a role to support their claims to political power. Moreover, in the western Solomons the government acknowledged their useful political role by appointing them as headmen.

Farther east, particularly on Malaita and most of Guadalcanal, there were great differences. Missions and government tried to work through existing leaders, but with the exception of a few coastal chiefly societies such as Lau and Sa'a (Small Malaita, Figure 10), these leaders came and went as big-men rose and fell. In such a fluid situation many of the missions' local teachers and catechists became contenders for political power as well.[99] The leaders of extended families and clans saw the ascribed status they expected from age and seniority gradually being devalued because the young men's plantation labor became the primary if not the exclusive source of cash—cash that men needed for the tax. The elders had been able to contain youthful challenges while trade goods or even cash flowed to them and thence to the community in return for their support and valuables for the young men's bride wealth. But once there was an external demand for cash in the form of the tax and no compensating return channeled through them, their power was in jeopardy. Moreover, government and missions were offering alternative ideologies with relatively weak sanctions on aspects of morality condemned by the old system. As the tax and other foreign influences gradually ate into the heartland of the bush pagans, the elders' authority waned.

THE EARLY 1900s had been a period of great optimism in the protectorate, not only for the white planter, but also for some Solomon Islanders. After large numbers of laborers returned from overseas in the first decade of the twentieth century, many Solomon Islanders realized that life in their islands could be improved "for we are waiting and looking for something better"[100] and their spokesmen wanted "to bring up our nation into the civilization states."[101]

But the means toward a better life were circumscribed. Where local production was underway the government did little to encourage further development beyond pacification, which had been necessary anyway for the establishment of commercial plantations. Where there was no local production the government simply let the people offer their labor to obtain the consumer goods they needed. Avenues to alternative economic development for Solomon Islanders were not only left unexplored, but also blocked off by legislation and by business practices that saw the European always as the only possible entrepreneur, even at the fundamental level of trader or storekeeper. When the Europeans were leaving trading and an opportunity offered for the Solomon Islanders, it was the Chinese who were permitted to take it. Considerable capital generated directly and indirectly by Solomon Islanders was never made available to them, but expatriated for development in the metropolitan centers or absorbed by the planters. A significant amount of government revenue came from the Islanders and part of it was used in the 1920s to tide the planters over their difficulties with lease rentals. But neither government nor business gave similar aid to Solomon Islanders, even when the Colonial Office supplied additional funds.

The tax was an impetus to greater production of both copra and labor, but it was an excessive burden on the people in poor areas, like inland Guadalcanal and most of Malaita. There too, the existing local political system came under threat through elders being beholden to youths. As well as demanding tax, the government simultaneously required new ways of doing a range of things in the villages—from where to cook to where to defecate. Often little explanation was given that might have justified these changes, except the threats of policemen and, on occasion, district officers. From the villagers' point of view, the changes brought few apparent benefits, except for some improvement in medical facilities—but those were only available regularly at district centers or plantations. The education so many Solomon Islanders had wanted at the turn of the century and beyond remained a mission preserve, so excluding active pagans. Most villagers would have agreed with Kane's 1922 assessment of the tax: "In return for this [tax] the natives enjoy the blessing of settled government. Practically nothing else is done for them by the government."[102]

For a people whose whole cultural ethos was reciprocity, the Solomon Islanders were not satisfied, but they lacked any but the most direct and unsophisticated means of expressing this feeling, since the government had not encouraged dialogue. The killing of government personnel on Guadalcanal and Malaita in 1927 was a result of long-term government insensitivity and often oppression. Just as they had on the plantations in the early days, Solomon Islanders resorted to violence when there appeared no other alternative. And just as it had with plantation conditions, the government took notice and improved local administration, but not without first punishing the vehicles of the discontent. It was in many ways an unequal struggle, but it sprang from a perception of the colonizers' injustice by the colonized.

From earliest contact, the Solomon Islanders had been producers and consumers, but as Western control tightened, not only were they confined to those roles by law and European practice, but also they were increasingly restricted within them and their interests made subservient to those of the colonizing power. Solomon Islanders were being educated in the ways of capitalism through the agency of the plantation, the government's administrative policies, business practices, and the missions, but none of their masters thought that education sufficient to give them entry to any but the lowest levels of capitalism.

CHAPTER 10

Weathering the storm
(c. 1930–1942)

. . . copra is the beginning and the end and the basis of
calculations in all matters . . . .

Australian Parliamentary Papers, 1919

There is unfortunately little likelihood of the price of copra
returning to the boom years pre-1929 again for some years.
We must weather the storm by holding on so that we may
be in a position to reap the benefit of any rise in the price of
copra which must in time recover.

Resident Commissioner Ashley, 11 November 1931

THE ECONOMY OF THE SOLOMONS depended on a single product—copra.
Never a great profit maker after World War I, copra was badly affected
by the Depression of the 1930s and there were repercussions on the Solomons right through to World War II. Among the expatriate commercial
community, the small planters and white traders were easily the most
vulnerable because they lacked reserves of capital to see them through
hard times. Their indebtness to the merchant companies increased,
leading eventually to foreclosure and bankruptcy. The larger commercial planters with cash reserves were able to survive by means of cost
cutting and the use of improved technology. The merchant and shipping
companies, carrying a large proportion of indebted clients and facing
competition from a new shipping line, commenced to trade directly
with the Solomon Islanders, buying their produce for cash. Through
sheer commercial necessity the merchants were forced to see an expanded role for Solomon Islanders, just as that role was being recognized by
the Colonial Office and even the protectorate government. Although
the administrative policies could be seen as becoming increasingly
benevolent, they sprang, like the principles of the merchants, from the
exigency of social and economic realities.

"King Copra"

In the Pacific, the Solomons were late in establishing commercial copra plantations. Neighbors to the east, Samoa and Fiji, had been exporting plantation copra for several decades by the time Levers and Burns Philp began to plant in the Solomons. To the west, the late nineteenth-century enterprise of the Germans in the Bismarck Archipelago had laid the foundation for New Guinea's twentieth-century supremacy as a producer of "South Seas" copra.[1]

The shortage of labor meant that by the 1920s copra was the major product of the Solomons, as it was for all southwest Pacific territories except Fiji with its sugar exports. From the 1910s to the early 1930s South Seas copra made up 13 to 15 percent of the total world production, the bulk of which originated in Ceylon (Sri Lanka) and the islands of Southeast Asia. The Solomons component of South Seas copra during this time was a little over 5 percent, or a mere 0.7 to 0.8 percent of the world's annual commercial output. Copra might have been "King" in the Solomons, but its kingdom was a tiny one.[2]

The quality of much of Solomons copra did nothing to offset its insignificant volume. Like most South Seas copra, it was smoke-dried and fit only for soap manufacture, with hot-air and sun-dried copra being reserved for margarine production. By the 1920s South Seas copra had the reputation of being the worst quality produced in the world.[3]

The lack of labor in the Solomons had not only prevented diversification of plantation crops, but had also slowed the development of copra plantations during the 1910s. Many planters were still pioneering when the copra market faltered during World War I. For some, like Fairley Rigby and Company and the Union Plantation and Trading Company, this early setback was sufficient to cause their winding-up.[4]

Thirteen years of plenty, when world trade favored agricultural products, were succeeded in 1914 by years when the supply of edible oils frequently exceeded the demand, causing fluctuations in the prices to producers. World population growth, which had called forth increased agricultural production to meet new demands following the great expansion of the industrial revolution and the vast migration of Europeans to the Americas and Australasia, was now stabilized. In the 1920s increasing supplies of edible oils from Africa and Asia competed strongly with copra for a share of the world market.[5]

To Solomons planters, the slumps experienced during the war and 1922–1924 were sobering, but improved prices in subsequent years provided sufficient encouragement for most to continue. But the prewar optimism was replaced in the 1920s by a realistic caution. Very little expansion of planting in new areas occurred and the European population remained stable at between four and five hundred persons. Consol-

idation and steady maintenance characterized the industry.[6] In 1929–
1930, when copra fell to its 1924 price, planters were concerned, but
expected an eventual upward trend. A year later the market worsened
and continued low until in 1935 copra at major Solomons ports was
earning less than £1 4s. a ton, or £13 below the 1929 price (see Table 6).

The Depression and the plantation system

At the onset of the Depression it cost planters between £4 and £9 to
produce a ton of copra, depending on the size, location, age, and fertility of their plantations.[7] With prices down to £9 10s. a ton for copra, the
planters naturally sought ways to reduce their production costs. Their
major fixed outlay was for recruiting labor. Each laborer on a two-year
contract cost the planter a total of between £70 and £80.[8] When copra
prices were low it made sense to reduce the labor force or to deploy it
more profitably elsewhere. But the indenture system and the plantation
monoculture were insufficiently flexible to respond immediately to
changed economic circumstances.

Indenture bound the laborer firmly to the plantation owner, but it
also tied the owner to the laborer. At the beginning of 1930, planters
employed almost thirty-five hundred laborers and signed on another
two thousand during the year. Thus, when prices declined further in
1931, they had these two thousand with almost two years to run on contract, plus a quarter to a half of the thirty-five hundred with one year
still to work (see Table 6 and Figure 15). The planters were not only
saddled with these men, but they could ill afford to cease recruiting
because the copra price, as had happened before, might suddenly
recover and then they would want to revert to maximum production.

There was little the planters could do to deploy their labor elsewhere.
They might concentrate it for a few months on brushing, weeding, or
repairing drains and local-material housing, but this was only a temporary expedient because under the plantation system laborers were
trained only in the limited operations associated with copra making.
Some planters directed labor to the growing of local food to replace the
expensive imported supplies of rice and tinned meat and fish. But this
was only a partial solution for a limited number because years of reliance on "European food" had created new tastes which recruits expected to be satisfied as part of the legal requirements for employment.[9]

As the Depression continued and copra prices fell still further, the
planters were unable to continue to indenture laborers at the pre-1930
level. They so pruned their indentured labor force that for the decade of
the 1930s it was on average almost 50 percent smaller than that of the
1920s (see Figure 15 and Table 6). All planters were forced to econo-
mize, but the smaller companies and concerns lacking capital reserves,

such as Phil Dickenson and Company, Clift and Clift, and Associated Plantations had to make the greatest retrenchment.[10] To maintain their holdings, they hired local casual laborers thus saving on recruiting and two years of maintenance costs. The disadvantage was that there was always the likelihood that copra prices would increase and casual laborers would abandon the plantations to make copra in the villages. Moreover, in the Gizo district, West New Georgia, the local people were so unused to plantation work that planters considered them to be only half as efficient as men from the eastern Solomons.[11]

Planters experimented with other systems of organizing labor.[12] In the Gizo and Santa Isabel districts they adopted the "partnership" or "profit-sharing" system in the early 1930s. Under this system a planter encouraged reliable time-expired laborers to stay on, gave them land to grow their own food, and paid them an agreed amount for each bag of copra made. This was a qualified success, since much depended on the relationship between the planter and the laborers. No sanctions, such as existed under the indenture system, could be brought to bear against a laborer, and a planter had to exercise both tolerance and tact to retain workers. The major drawback for the planter was the tendency of the laborers to work to target—once they had enough money for a specific want, they saw no reason to continue working and departed. Since they could earn up to four times as much under this system as they could under indenture, they generally worked for only a few months at a time.[13]

On San Cristobal in 1933, F. M. Campbell introduced a variant of the system on his plantations. Local people were to cut the copra, use his driers, and then sell the copra to him. Planters in the Gizo district also adopted such a system. In the west it was fairly successful, but in the east, with the additional freight on copra, the earnings were so minimal that the people refused to do the work.[14]

Production was maintained in most areas under these schemes until late 1933–1934, despite the reduction of indentured labor. Copra prices plummeted yet again to £1 10s. a ton in 1934 and then, on average, to £1 3s. in 1935 (see Table 6). At this time even the most financially viable concerns, like Levers and the Burns Philp subsidiaries, Shortland Island Plantations and Solomon Islands Development Company, showed signs of strain. In 1934 Levers closed down their Logha plantation and planned to do the same at Pauru and Noro, concentrating on their more consolidated and productive areas, such as the Russell Islands. Likewise, the Solomon Islands Development Company closed Luti and Manning Strait (Vaghena), leaving only a caretaker at Salakana (Figure 11).[15] On Malaita the Malayta Company almost ceased operating except for a few casual laborers.[16] By late 1933, in the Gizo district practically all the smaller companies had ceased production. There, a

222 Wealth of the Solomons

year later, Levers, the Solomon Islands Development Company (at
Tetepare), the Gizo Solomons Plantations (at Kenelo), and W. R.
Carpenter (at Lilihina and adjacent islands in the Marovo Lagoon)
were the only plantations making copra.[17] In the Shortlands a few of the
smaller plantations kept going with a handful of casual laborers. On
San Cristobal virtually all the plantation closed except those controlled
by Levers or Carpenters.[18]

The early bankruptcy of a few planters underscored the difficulties of
the majority. In 1930 T. B. Mason-Robinson at Fauro (Figure 8) and
Dickenson at San Cristobal were in such reduced circumstances that
they could no longer pay their labor. Harry Wickham in New Georgia
was in the same position a year later. In such cases the government, having ratified all labor contracts, was morally obliged to pay the due
wages or find itself with the whole indenture system under threat and
indigent "foreign" and unemployed laborers harassing villagers or
loitering in the main centers.[19]

As early as 1930 some of the planters unsuccessfully approached the
government for a reduction in the minimum plantation wage.[20] Similarly, when they applied for a change in the labor regulations so that the
tobacco issue could be eliminated, Ashley refused simply because it produced almost half the £30,000 excise duties.[21] As the Depression worsened, Resident Commissioner Ashley had to face the inevitable fact that
the government and the planters shared the same destiny. By 1933 the
demand for a wage reduction was universal. The planters presented a
petition to the high commissioner, Sir A. C. Murchison Fletcher, in
February 1934. In March, the secretary of state for colonies appointed a
committee of three Europeans to advise the high commissioner on the
proposed reduction "first from the point of view of the employer and
secondly from the point of view of the employed."[22] The employed, having no voice, were hardly considered. The committee was unanimous.
Laborers' wages or "what in effect is their pocket-money" were to be
reduced from 10 shillings a month to 5 shillings for light work, and from
£1 to 10 shillings for normal adult work, so cutting the planters' total
labor costs (wages, maintenance, recruiting fees) by one-sixth and the
laborers' take-home wage by half.[23]

The government considered other forms of relief to the planters. In
1930 Ashley suggested a bonus system whereby the government would
pay 10 shillings a ton to planters who had no more than 500 acres and
who produced no more than 240 tons, but the larger companies
objected to the inequity of the scheme. They wanted a total remission
for a year of the copra export duty (which was 12s. 6d. a ton) as this
affected all producers equally. The government found this less attractive
because it would mean a loss of revenue, but, in view of the planters'
predicament and substantial government reserves, granted a remission

from November 1930 to April 1931, when the duty was reintroduced on a sliding scale of 5 percent on the price of copra.[24] Another concession of the government was its acceptance of the depreciated Australian currency (worth 25 percent less than sterling), so that the planters could obtain the benefit of the exchange.[25]

In 1934 the economic situation had so deteriorated that the government remitted several Crown rents. This relief was too late for some. Between 1929 and the beginning of 1932, twenty-two Crown leases representing 8050 acres were canceled because rents were unpaid. In addition, fifteen Native leases for 2910 acres were surrendered. Although some of these were lots with no improvements, over a third had been substantially developed.[26]

The government maintained its subsidy of Native leases because, as both the Colonial Office and Resident Commissioner Ashley realized, if the contracts were interfered with by the government on the grounds of equity, "it might be considered on the same grounds of equity that we should reduce the native tax for the landlords."[27] The Colonial Office, as in the twenties, did not favor enforced reduction and since only two or three leases were involved by 1934—the others having been cancelled —the government did not press the matter.[28]

The merchant companies foreclose

Many small planters had overextended themselves in the 1920s and, when the Depression hit, got further into debt to Burns Philp or Carpenters. The merchants had given credit for supplies. In 1930 the government ruled that planters must have guaranteed funds to pay laborers before they could recruit them. As the merchants had to maintain their "investment" they usually acted as guarantors. Similarly they extended further credit in the hope that once copra prices rose they would be repaid. Because indebted customers were obliged to sell and ship through their creditors, Burns Philp in particular was able to safeguard a considerable proportion of its merchant and shipping business from competitors.[29]

W. R. Carpenter's had come to the Solomons as wholesalers and retailers in 1922, too late to have been caught up in the enthusiastic plantation investment of 1905–1913.[30] Nonetheless, as merchants and "bankers" Carpenters, like its rival Burns Philp, acquired both land and plantations in the 1930s as a result of foreclosing on mortgages held as security on advances or as part payment for debts of a company at liquidation. In general, when Burns Philp and Carpenters obtained property that was both leasehold and unimproved, they allowed the lease to lapse. However, if the land had been developed or was freehold, the companies usually retained it. In the late 1920s and 1930s Burns Philp extended mortgages or extensive credit to a number of small planters and companies including Pierre Pratt, Harry Wickham, Norman Wheatley, E. de Courcey Browne, F. M. Campbell, T. B. Walton, A. Olsen, Kindar, Fatura Island Development Company, Lavoro Plantations, and Clift and Clift. Carpenters held mortgages on many of Wheatley's freehold properties, on leases held by H. R. Sim and Gatere Plantations, as well as taking over from the liquidator the leases held by San Cristobal Estates.[31]

All of these properties eventually ended up in the hands of one or other of the two companies, much to the disgust of the original owners. To the majority of Europeans, BP were "Bloody Pirates" and WRC "Would Rob Christ."[32] Such feelings were not confined to the planters, for labor recruiters and traders also became indebted to the merchants. Ernie Palmer and Tommy Elkington, for instance, were partners in the mid-thirties in a labor recruiting business. Not called "Sugar" for nothing, Palmer got the business into debt with Burns Philp, which consequently obtained a mortgage of £120 over the partners' vessels, the *Mendaña* and the *Atawa*. Elkington, determined to clear the debt, earned the £120 in two years by recruiting mainly for Burns Philp, which stood as financial guarantor to the government for the various planters wanting recruits shipped. When Elkington went to make the final payment to Burns Philp's manager, J. C. M. Scott at Makambo, one of the office staff, Ray Shay, confidentially warned him not to pay in full, but to continue to work with the company on credit. Elkington persisted and never got another order for recruits from Burns Philp. The company gave the labor-recruiting contracts to its debtor-clients—such as Dick Harper of Mandoleana, who owed them £4000—because some reduction of the debt would be made with the earnings from recruiting.[33]

Burns Philp did not endear itself to traders having outstanding liabilities when in 1931 it cut off credit to those without assets.[34] Nonetheless, this policy encouraged the small planters to enter into trading and, once again, many of them adopted this old pattern of adjustment to straitened times. The solution was feasible only in the west and central Solomons because, at least for the white traders, profits were minimal in the east.[35] The white trader-planters found that trading was extremely competitive since the Chinese, and a few unencumbered European traders such as Fred Green and Leslie Gill, had an established custom among the Solomon Islanders.[36] Predictably, the old resentment toward the Chinese revived, with Europeans declaiming against their "merciless trading competition"[37] to the government and to a wider public through the *Pacific Islands Monthly*.[38]

Unfortunately for the white traders and the trader-planters the government's attitude was different from what it had been in 1921. The resident commissioner's main criteria as to whether or not a Chinese trader's license should be renewed were Solomon Islander public opinion and a more fundamental concern with the health of the general economy. As a consequence of the difficult times and the merchant companies' credit squeeze, many full-time white traders had already gone out of business. Between 1930 and 1932 the number of store licenses issued to Europeans fell from 117 to 59.[39] Since surplus indigenous earnings had to be spent to maintain both the production of Solomon Islander copra and the supply of labor, commercial outlets needed to be encouraged; the government refused to act against the Chinese.

For many small planters, turning to trading in the early thirties was merely putting off the evil day. At the end of 1933, with the fall in the price of copra, villagers virtually ceased to make it. As village production went down from about 3000 tons in 1931 to 300 tons in 1933, trader-planters were almost back to where they had started. In the western Solomons, trochus shell, fetching around £80 a ton, provided a little relief for some, but for many trading was not worth the cost of the benzine to run their vessels. It seemed as if the day of the small planter was all but past.[40]

The Depression and the big plantation companies

The major plantation companies were in a better position to cope with the Depression, which continued to affect the Solomons throughout the 1930s. Because these companies were parts of greater firms, their directors could transfer funds from the less profitable enterprises to the more profitable. Companies could also reduce costs by internal economies, such as the reduction by Burns Philp of the agency fee it charged for managing Solomon Islands Development Company. Although the profits of Levers Pacific Plantations through the Depression are not known, the parent company, Unilever, annually declared a dividend of 13 to 15 percent. Carpenters' entire Fiji, New Guinea, and Solomon Islands operations gave an annual dividend of 8 to 10 percent (exclusive of undisclosed earnings until 1932). The Solomons business alone paid between 4 and 8 percent. Burns Philp's (South Seas) operations in the same areas plus the New Hebrides and the Gilberts (now Vanuatu and Kiribati, respectively) earned an annual dividend of 5 to 6.5 percent.[41]

The bigger companies had additional means of offsetting some of the effects of the Depression. The Solomon Islands Development Company managed by Burns Philp, engaged in some boardroom manipulation to improve the appearance of its finances to both shareholders and taxation officials. By revaluing its assets in the Solomons using the 1934 price of copra as a basis, it was able to show a depreciation of £50,000. Early in 1935 the capital of the company was reduced from £100,000 to

£50,000. Since all of its one thousand £100 shares had been bought up to £95, the directors deemed that a £50 share would be considered paid up to £45, thus keeping the shareholders liable for the £5 reserve. However, whatever profits were made would appear to be quite substantial because they would be calculated on the basis of a reduced capital. Throughout the 1930s the Solomon Islands Development Company was able to engage in modest expansion without calling in the reserve capital, to maintain a credit balance, and even to declare dividends in 1930, 1932, 1937, and 1938.[42]

Besides such overall flexibility, these companies with large capital reserves were also able to adjust their organization within the Solomons. Levers developed an ingenious scheme to maximize production on the basis of the old "task" or "contract" system for its indentured labor. Under that system, once a copra cutter had cut a certain daily amount of green copra, usually 450 lb. (but on some plantations, 500 lb.), he could cease working and rest or, in some cases, allow his earned free time to accumulate so that he got all of Saturday off. In 1929, on its Russell Islands plantations, Levers experimented with paying cutters 3 pence for every 28 lb. in excess of 450 lb. a day—a rate of £1 for each ton of copra produced.[43] Since a laborer's take-home wage was only 5 shillings a week (before 1934) this system was a great incentive: Most laborers cut an average of 600 lb. a day and some earned from 15 to 25 shillings a week in bonuses.

Levers was not out of its corporate mind. For an expenditure of about £37 10s. a year for each indentured laborer, (including wages, board, recruiting fees, etc.) the company was paying out, in copra-cutting terms, 13 shillings a ton *if* a laborer actually produced 450 lb. a day, 5.5 days a week, 52 weeks of the year. But only under ideal circumstances did a cutter maintain the desired 450 lb. a day. Under the bonus system, which was extended in the thirties, Levers benefited enormously because it now had a sure way of guaranteeing output and eliminating malingering. For their part, the laborers found the proposition so attractive that Levers had waiting lists of men wishing to transfer from other tasks to work at copra cutting.[44]

Unlike the owner-operated small concerns, the larger companies were run by salaried managers. At this level, too, economies were made. The companies realized that it was possible for managers to channel plantation funds into their own pockets. Mild abuses, such as appropriating part of the laborers' rice stocks for the manager's household, were not uncommon.[45] On occasion, managers had been known to divert bags of plantation copra from the company steamer to the Chinese trader and keep the proceeds.[46] Burns Philp culled out such dishonest or inefficient managers in the early years of the Depression, expanded the duties of retained staff, and monitored plantation efficiency by means of an annual inspection by Allen Turnbull, head of their island agencies division.[47] The company also cut the monthly salary of white overseers from £20 to £16 and then to £12.[48]

Levers likewise pruned at the management level. Early in 1936 it amalgamated adjoining plantations to form single management units on Guadalcanal, in the Russells, and in the New Georgia group.[49] Levers had already eliminated some of its less profitable enterprises in the 1920s. Because their overseas vessel, *Kulumbangara*, had been losing about £5000 a year (it had no subsidy like Burns Philp), Levers took it off the run in 1916 and reached an agreement with Burns Philp to ship its copra. Trading had supplied much of the copra Levers had needed in the pioneering phase of plantation development, but by 1923 it was no longer necessary. The company sold its trading stations in such places as Ontong Java and Santa Cruz.[50]

During the Depression, Levers' Balmain (Sydney) factory absorbed the company's plantation copra easily, permitting savings on intermediary costs as well as the overhead of freighting to Europe.[51] Moreover, a cooperative buying policy by its sister company in Australia enabled the planting company to obtain higher prices than it could have on the open market. Some of the loss by Levers (Australia) was compensated for by a reduction in the taxes it had to pay. Levers (Solomons) did not by law have to pay a tax on its profits.[52] But these relationships worked both ways. The parent company, Unilever, based in Britain, was in fact responsible for some of the difficulties of other Solomon Islands planters. With improvements in edible oil technology, the company could substitute different types of oils and fats to favor those of lowest price on the world market, so keeping down its own costs, but also limiting the demand for copra.[53]

Having a guaranteed Australian market, Levers, except during the 1933 crisis, was able to maintain most of its consolidated holdings at maximum production and keep its estates in excellent condition (Photo 21). Ironically, the company's good husbandry was the indirect cause of one of its greatest problems. In the 1920s a number of plantations had been attacked by a condition known as "premature nutfall"—the nuts would fall off the palms before they were mature. And a beetle, *Brontispa froggati*, was attacking the immature unopened leaves and the palms. On some of Levers' plantations yields dropped from about 15 to 3 hundredweight an acre. From 1929, Levers had worked along the lines suggested by visiting entomologists, but made little progress. A full-time entomologist commenced work in 1931 and rightly concluded that the insect *Amplypelta cocophaga China* was involved in premature nutfall. What he and others did not discover before World War II was that an ant, *Oecaphylla*, normally preyed on the *Amplypelta*. But monocultures are not normal and, with the initial clearing and brush-

Photo 21. Levers' Vila plantation, Kolombangara, in the 1930s. These trees are about twenty years old. Various methods of spacing trees were tried to allow the palm the maximum exposure to sunlight. A space of ten or eleven meters between each tree was usual on plantations. In the center of the picture is a road with drains on each side. *(Terrain Study No. 54, 1943)*

ing of all secondary growth around mature palms, *Oecaphylla* was driven out or destroyed by other smaller ants and was unable to get from tree to tree via hanging creepers and vines as in its natural habitat. Thus *Amplypelta*'s biological control was removed and premature nutfall the consequence.

In the 1930s, plantations infested with the insect were mainly Levers' and, to a lesser extent, Burns Philp's. Because the smaller planters were forced to let their plantations run down and become overgrown, premature nutfall was rarely a problem to them. However, *Brontispa froggati* remained a perennial pest in the 1930s, and was combatted either by catching the beetles manually or spraying the palms with chemicals —both increasingly labor-intensive practices as young palms grew taller.[54]

Levers, planning for the long term, had always been willing to invest capital if eventual profitability was likely to be the outcome. The company was the first to introduce improved technology to produce a superior product. From the beginning of operations it had experimented with various hot-air driers so that in the 1930s it was the only company producing high-grade copra. By that time hot-air dried copra realized £1 to £2 10s. a ton more than smoke-dried.[55]

Levers' production in 1933–1934 of 8159 tons of hot-air dried copra accounted for 75 percent of the total hot-air copra produced. Almost all of the remainder came from the Malayta Company (later Fairymead Company) and Burns Philp's subsidiaries.[56] Most of the hot-air driers of these firms had been installed in the early 1930s to compensate for the decline in copra prices. Other planters were less able to respond with technological improvements; hot-air driers could cost up to £2000 each.[57] Even when a scheme was put forward to convert smoke driers to hot-air driers for as little as £90, few of the planters could find such a sum. The government had proposed a loan to assist conversion, but as most of the small planters were in debt to either Burns Philp or Carpenters the government could not get a first mortgage. Naturally the large companies, who considered half their debtors to be "bad," were not going to let them get further into the red.[58]

Competition and new directions

The losses the merchant companies experienced with their trader and planter clients were very real. Burns Philp's book debts at its Gizo store in 1933 amounted to £37,256 and well over 60 percent of them were "bad." The companies tried to compensate elsewhere for such losses. In order to attract some of Carpenters' customers, Burns Philp opened a store at Tulagi itself. Carpenters sold goods at prices 50 percent higher to Solomon Islanders than to Europeans. Burns Philp followed a similar policy.[59] Moreover, Burns Philp, which could have offered lower freight fees because of its subsidy, continued to charge the same rate as the chartered vessels of its rival, Carpenters.

In 1932 a new shipping company entered the Solomons. A German concern, Norddeutscher Lloyd (NDL) provided a superior service, calling at plantations such as Aruliho (Guadalcanal), where Burns Philp's captains had claimed the sea frontage was too dangerous for ships. NDL's trade room sold goods more cheaply than Burns Philp, but, more significant, it freighted copra to Europe via Hong Kong for £3 10s. to £4 a ton, compared to Burns Philp's £5 to £5 10s.

Burns Philp lodged its objections with the high commissioner, claiming that NDL ships would introduce smallpox, would provide a means for opium smuggling to the Chinese, and, most heinous offence of all, were subsidized by the German government to undercut British enterprise in the western Pacific. What Burns Philp omitted to mention was that it, too, like the German company, received a subsidy, then amounting to £12,000 a year, from the Australian government and the high commission to carry the mails. The protectorate's share of this subsidy was £3000. The resident commissioner understood, just as Burns Philp did, that if there were serious competition by NDL, planting companies such as the Malayta Company would soon transfer their freights and contracts from Burns Philp, so undermining the basis for the subsidies.

Needless to say, Burns Philp lowered its freight charges in 1933, just as it increased the copra price it paid at Solomons ports when Carpenters ran charters from Australia.[60]

The advent of NDL's six-weekly shipping service had immediate effects. In order to compete, the shipping side of Burns Philp's diverse enterprise had to accept any shipments available, including direct consignments from Sydney business houses. By this means even traders and planters indebted to the trading wing of Burns Philp could get goods, as long as they could pay the Sydney suppliers. Moreover, the NDL ships were also bringing in cargo from Europe and Hong Kong for the traders, especially the Chinese, as well as shipping their produce. Carpenters, of course, faced the same problem as Burns Philp. The trading business of both merchant firms fell off rapidly from 1932–1933 on. The usual strategies of price-cutting and paying higher prices to producers were tried, but resulted in reduced profits. There was only one alternative: direct trading with Solomon Island growers for the same cash prices as the white traders and planters received.[61]

Carpenters started this practice in the Marovo Lagoon in 1935.[62] Following that company's extension of direct buying into the Roviana district a year later, Burns Philp announced that they too would buy copra "at the same price for everyone." Not only would they give parity, but if Solomon Islanders had a minimum of 10 tons of copra ready at a village, Burns Philp would also provide transport to the shipping center at the ruling freight rate. At Gizo, where this first applied, the reaction throughout the entire community was "general consternation and perplexity and also an unprecedented rush on business."[63] So successful was the new policy that it was extended to Faisi and Tulagi, with plans in 1938 by Burns Philp to open two stores on Santa Isabel.[64]

Adjusting to the impossible

Early in 1934 Ashley summed up the state of expatriate planters:

> Outside the big companies . . . the plight of the private planters and small companies is desperate. They are almost all in debt to one or other of the large trading companies at Tulagi, and I understand that their credit is stopped except for food. They have no means of paying labourers as the cost of production is much more than the value of copra. The plantations they say must be abandoned and in many cases they have already paid off their labour and closed. The planters as a rule have a few head of cattle and some fowls, but they have no means of paying for tea, sugar, flour or tobacco.[65]

The government had considered various ways to tide the small planters over their difficulties. It had floated the proposed bonus scheme, the loans for hot-air driers, the temporary suspension of the copra tax, and the temporary remission of Crown rents—all of which foundered on the rocks of either the government's concern with safeguarding its solvency or the self-interest of the major planters and commercial firms. Likewise, the high commissioner's suggestion in 1934 that the protectorate could pay the freight for shipping the small planters' copra to the main ports was to come to nothing. Because neither the government nor Carpenters had storage space at either Faisi or Gizo, the government would have to pay for its construction or rely on Burns Philp. Burns Philp was not likely to cooperate as long as its companies were not to get assistance. Ashley concluded that even with this £3600-odd subsidy provided by the government the small planters still would not be able to make copra without a loss.[66]

The small planters as well as the surviving white traders received a brief reprieve toward the end of 1934. The price of copra improved following a severe hurricane in the Philippines and a drought in many parts of the world that resulted in a shortage of cattle feed. Moderately buoyant prices were sustained until July and recovered again in October 1935. The first nine months of 1936 saw fair prices, with a rise from £10 a ton to £17 15s. (ports price) in the last three months of the year. Encouraged, the small planters began to restore their deteriorated plantations, while Burns Philp and Levers reopened their more far-flung estates.[67]

A good price of £19 10s. a ton started off the year of 1937, but thereafter prices gradually declined. In that year too, the benefits of the period of improved prices were offset when Burns Philp increased its through freight to Europe from £4 to £5 a ton, despite the Colonial Office's claim that the true cost was closer to £3. By 1937 the only planters not in debt to either Burns Philp or Carpenters and still solvent were Campbell and Hug on San Cristobal; Corry on Guadalcanal; Younger on the Russell Islands; Bignell, Laycock, and Fulakora Plantation on Santa Isabel; and MacKinnon, Cant, Ruruvai Plantation, and the Methodist Mission in the New Georgia Islands. Only this handful were in a position to ship by NDL, which was finding running costs increasingly high as its customers became fewer. With so little real competition it was no wonder that even as prices for copra worsened in 1939 Burns Philp was still able to make 19s. 3d. a ton profit (7.5 percent) when the London price was £12 16s. 3d.[68]

At the close of 1937 the recovery was over.[69] Copra prices fell again and remained low until the outbreak of war in 1939 (see Table 6). World prices increased slightly in 1940, but, with the shortage of allied shipping and the resultant freight increase, copra production in the Solomons dropped to its lowest since 1922, with only 12,299 tons exported. For many producers in 1940, copra simply had not been worth making.[70]

At all levels, from the small planters to the planting companies, the

Solomons government, and the Colonial Office, there was a flurry of activity to try to adjust to what were almost impossible conditions. Trading was no solution for the small planters as the Japanese invasion of China had cut off the market for trochus. Once again the wages and rations of laborers came under scrutiny, with Carpenters arguing that the indentured wage scale should be halved again because employers in the Solomons were paying a minimum wage of 10 shillings a month compared to only 6 shillings in the Mandate of New Guinea.[71] The planters tried yet again to have tobacco deleted from the rations. But the government, with all its sources of revenue being inexorably closed off, was not about to give up the excise duty earned from tobacco imports.[72]

The government continued its policy of rental remission for those impoverished planters who resided in the Solomons and depended on their plantations for a living. By 1941 there were about thirty planters in this category.[73] Too poor or too stubborn to leave the Solomons, they were a remnant of a much larger group who, between 1929 and 1941, had held 40 percent of the Crown lease lands and who in those years had either had their leases canceled or the rentals remitted by the government.[74]

Carpenters appealed to the government for the remission policy to be extended to the lands it held under lease. Since the company had come by the lands through foreclosure on bad debtors in the 1930s and was without long plantation experience in the Solomons, it had ventured little on making improvements in bad times. Carpenters brought no new land under cultivation and continued to smoke-dry most of its copra. Since much of its land gave fairly low yields, by 1941 the company was feeling the pinch[75] (Table 8).

Likewise, the well-capitalized independent companies of Mamara Plantation, Solomon Islands Rubber Plantations, and Domma Plantations were in difficulties. Although these plantations had had sufficient reserve capital to tide them over the earlier crisis and to buy hot-air driers in 1938, the shortage of shipping in 1939 turned their very modest profits into losses. Without the means to move their copra their losses were bound to increase. Consequently, the group's chairman of directors, Oscar Svensen, the elder, asked the government for an advance against the copra the companies had in storage in 1940, but without success.[76]

The government made belated attempts to urge planters to use existing food resources since imports were increasingly expensive. In 1936 it had paved the way for greater use of local produce by revising the ration regulation to permit a higher proportion of local vegetables.[77] Although Burns Philp and other plantations followed government advice, by the close of the decade there were few laborers to be fed.[78]

Plantations of Principal Owners			Others	
Burns Philp	Levers	W. R. Carpenter	Plantation	Owner
Choiseul (Lauru) (Figure 11)				
Luti			Choiseul Bay	Associated Plantations Ltd.
Salakana			Nananggo[1]	
Vaghena			Tambatamba[1]	
Eastern New Georgia Islands (Figure 7)				
Tetepare	Arundel	Hamarae[2]	Kenelo	Associated Plantations Ltd.
Kinda	Kerekana	Karungarao[2]		
	Lady Lever	Lalauru[2]	Lukuru[1]	Methodist Mission
	Pauru	Lilihina[2]	Mbanga	H. Markham
	Rendova Harbour	Mahoro[2]	Seghe	
	Stanmore	Mbareho[2]		
	Vila	Ngarengare[2]		
		Salakalala[2]		
		Tinge[2]		
Guadalcanal (Figure 12)				
Hoilava[2]	Kukum		Aruliho	J. Clift
Lavuro[2]	Lungga		Gavaga (Tetere)	Solomon Islands Development Co. (SIDC)
Nughu[2]	North I.		Ivatu	H. C. Corry
Rere[2]	Ruavatu		Kaukau	C. E. Hart[3]
Ruaniu[2]	Symons I.		Kokomuruka	J. Svensen
Taievo[2]	Taivu (?)		Mamara	Mamara Plantation Ltd.
	Tavanipupu		Manisagheva	A. E. Palmer[3]
	Tenaru		Maraunia	C. E. Hart[3]
			Mberande	SIDC
			Muvia	SIDC
			Ndoma	Domma Plantation Ltd.
			Paruru	C. V. Hodgess
			Tambalego	M. Olsen
			Tanaemba	A. & M. Olsen
			Tenavatu	R. C. Symes[4]
			Tuvu	J. C. Williamson[5]

(continued)

TABLE 8
Commercial plantations and their owners, by island group, c. 1941 (continued)

Plantations of Principal Owners	Others	
Malaita (Figure 10)		
	Baunani	Fairymead Sugar Co.[6]
	Fulo	
	Manaba	
	Su'u	
Russell Islands (Figure 13)		
Faiami	Nasan	C. Younger
Kaylan	Nono	C. Younger
Linggatu	Talina	Fairymead Sugar Co.
Loavie	Yandina	Fairymead Sugar Co.
Mbanika		
Pepesala		
Samata		
Ufaon		
West Bay		
San Cristobal (Figure 3)		
Boroni	Cape Surville	H. Kuper
	(Purimatarofa)	
Maru	Hawa	F. M. Campbell
Waimarae (?)	Maro'u	S. M. Hug
Three Sisters	Waiae	F. M. Campbell
	Waimamura	F. M. Campbell
	Waimasi	F. M. Campbell
Santa Isabel (Figure 17)		
Estrella Bay[2]	Floakora	Fulakora Plantations Ltd.
Fera[2]	Chojoruru	Solomon Islands Rubber Plan-
Ghatere[2]		tations Ltd.
	Haevo	Effey & Kaufmann
Cuguha[2]	Hubugangi	F. H. R. Gorringe

Shortland Islands (Figure 8)

Alu (Tapokai)	Mrs Clara Scott
Balalai	Shortland Islands Plantations Ltd. (SIPL)
Bambagiai	SIPL
Faisi	SIPL
Harapa	SIPL
Kamaleai	SIPL
Kepiai	SIPL
Kokonai	A. Monckton
Lagugu	SIPL
Laomona	SIPL
Lofang	SIPL
Nusave	Cruickshank
Orlofi	Mrs Clara Scott
Parolang	Cruickshank
Piru	T. B. Mason-Robinson
Saeghangmono	SIPL
Taukuna	SIPL

Western New Georgia Islands (Figure 9)

Emu Harbour	Logha
Malosova	Popomuana
Aena[1]	H. Beck
Bagga	J. Binskin
Joroveto	L. F. Gill
Jurio	D. MacKinnon
Liapari	F. Green
Mundi Mundi	Associated Plantations Ltd.
Panapagha[1]	S. Marks & J. E. Davis
Ruruvai[1,7]	Formerly Ruruvai Plantation Syndicate
Turovilu Island	Martin
Turovilu Point	Klaucke
Vori[1]	

SOURCES: Files of Land Titles Office, Honiara; Allied Forces 1942–1943.

NOTES: 1 Abandoned; 2 Ownership transferred to mortgagee because of foreclosure; 3 Lessee of Levers; 4 Lessee of Isobel Thelfall; 5 Lessee of SIDC; 6 Malayta Company sold out to Fairymead in 1936; 7 Lease canceled.

In 1940 virtually all the smaller plantations cut or ceased production, and laborers' contracts were canceled by mutual consent. Burns Philp refused everyone credit except for copra against book debts and ceased buying smoke-dried copra from Solomon Islanders. The company's store at Faisi, which had a turnover of £14,000 in 1937, was scheduled for closure in late 1940. By August, Burns Philp along with Carpenters and Fairymead Company (formerly the Malayta Company) were beginning to shut down their estates. Burns Philp reduced its labor force on the plantations of the Solomon Islands Development Company by 36.5 percent in 1940, keeping on only the best workers, and, a year later, again closed Luti and Salakana. The firm also dismissed three of its four European overseers in the Shortlands and replaced them with Solomon Islander *bos-boe* under the direction of Carden Seton.[79] By 1940 the small planters in the Shortlands were so desperate for cash to buy food and pay a few wages that, like the Solomon Islanders, they sold their copra to a Chinese trader, Yee Poy, who was not long expected to be able to pay as he too was a debtor of Burns Philp. In lifestyle these struggling planters were now truly "a poor white class" reduced to living off the land like the Islanders.[80]

The Colonial Office and the future of the Solomons

When the economic situation worsened in the mid-1930s the government reached an impasse. Its measures to cope with the slump either had been impossible to implement or were ineffectual. Copra was still the basis of the economy, but that economy was failing. There was, among some colonial officials, a dawning realization that in extended times of low prices the overheads of a plantation system conducted by expatriates were too great for most to sustain. Even before this became apparent during the Depression, copra and other plantation crops like rubber never achieved their full potential because of the shortage of labor. As late as 1940, 85 percent of all alienated land still remained uncultivated.[81]

There were three kinds of producers—the big companies, the small planters, and the Solomon Islander growers. The Colonial Office predicted that the big companies could and would survive because they produced high-grade copra and were minimizing costs. The Islanders could produce and survive because "they had no costs." For the small white planter who could not make better copra and had no reserve capital there was "little or no future."[82] Since the economic well-being of Britain was uppermost in Colonial Office thinking, as revealed in the Colonial Development Act of 1929, there was no way the government could maintain this mendicant small-planter class. The white traders were in the same category. Their grave had been dug in the 1920s by the extensive credit-giving of the merchant firms and by Chinese efficiency. If trading had a future, the Chinese would dominate it.[83]

Harking back to the old Levers' theme, Levers' manager, Hewitt, took this a step further. In 1931 he had advocated the large-scale introduction of free Chinese immigrants, "greater than the numbers actually guaranteed employment." Such an abundance of labor would allow for some to sublease land from Europeans and a few others to go into "other industries." Since the Solomon Islanders were neither dispossessed of their remaining lands nor near starvation, a new class of landless proletarians was to be imported to develop alienated land cheaply, either as laborers or as *metayage* farmers (see n. 12), and to work as artisans and technicians in order to assure a "trade revival" in the Solomons. Islanders were to be left as they were on their land (or some might say, until it was needed) to make an occasional ton of copra while development raced ahead for other sections of the new society. Hewitt predicted

> . . . if the Chinese come here in numbers it would be almost certain that the last bit of outside native trade will fall into their hands and that the white trader other than the merchants and those in the more important places will become extinct.[84]

The British Colonial Office was not deaf to such a proposal, but it was cautious. Within the overall framework of assisting Britain and keeping the Solomons solvent, Colonial Office thought oscillated between the notion of eliminating the lower rung of white economic enterprise and replacing it with the indigenous grower, and a serious consideration of the sort of scheme Hewitt had proposed. In 1935 the Colonial Office instructed Ashley to do all he could to encourage indigenous production, even at the expense of the noncorporate white planter.[85] However, Britain provided no funds for this radical departure and was reluctant even to consider using the reserve funds of the protectorate. The middle of a depression hardly seemed an appropriate time to introduce major structural changes requiring extensive government spending.[86] Although Ashley had realized as early as 1930 that such changes were desirable, he was at a total loss to know where to begin.[87] Not surprisingly, two years later he was espousing the Hewitt plan. In some form of delayed revelation after years in the protectorate, Ashley suddenly decided that the indenture system, including the "strange food" of the plantation, was damaging to Solomon Islanders. Although he added this rationalization as a rider, there was no disguising his real motives:

> My grounds for advocating the introduction of exotic labour are that the country cannot develop without it. The planter must command settled labour, content to do monotonous work for a moderate wage, but such a force is not available in the Islands to-day. The indenture system may have

something to do with the rapid decline of the indigenous population. Increased production necessitates increased imports, and both mean increased revenue. Without funds it is not possible to administer the Protectorate thoroughly and satisfactorily.[88]

The only government-perceived brake on the implementation of this policy in 1937 was British concern with Australia's attitude. It is one of the supreme ironies of the protectorate's history that the commonwealth's "White Australia" policy threatened to keep the Solomons "black." Britain feared that spacious Australia with only about 6 million people would view the importation of coolie labor as an encroachment on the *cordon sanitaire* of islands the two countries had built to protect it from the Asian hordes. Ashley had an answer for this when he told the high commissioner in Suva that the orderly importation of a coolie population would fill the tempting empty spaces of the Solomons, so protecting the indigenous inhabitants and also Australia from the protectorate's invasion "by the land-hungry Asiatic nations to the north."[89] High Commissioner Richards was sympathetic to the Levers-inspired scheme and warned the Colonial Office that unless coolie labor was introduced the Solomons would remain a group of "semi-derelict islands which might be a decreasing instead of an increasing asset."[90]

Secretary of State for Colonies Ormsby-Gore was willing to entertain the proposal, provided a scheme could be spelt out by the Western Pacific High Commission and the Solomons government that would be acceptable to prospective employers and "at the same time would give no ground for justifiable criticism on the liberty of the labourers"—with the added proviso that the secretary of state for dominion affairs, which included Australia, was also to be satisfied.[91]

The scheme did not reach the stage of close examination by either the humanitarians or the secretary of state for dominion affairs. The movers of the proposal, Levers, could no longer guarantee their cooperation. By 1938 their difficulties in controlling the coconut pest *Amplypelta cocophaga* had increased and needed to be resolved before it would be worth their while to invest capital in a large labor migration scheme.[92] In the Solomons the new resident commissioner, Marchant, pointed the way to the only options left: Let the big companies continue as best they could; for the rest, the small planters, "the natives might well take over and run plantations by splitting them up into small holdings."[93] The pendulum now swung toward native development of resources, less because of policy than because of lack of an alternative, and a realization that by 1940 Solomon Islander producers with no government assistance were making 25 percent of the copra.[94]

The outbreak of war in Europe dominated British government thinking in 1939, but a year later a major change in colonial policy that had been prefigured in the 1929 Colonial Development Act was introduced. In general, because colonial development was seen as vital to Britain's own future, it was necessary to spend money to further the process. Moreover, in British colonies of far greater importance than the Solomons there was increasing, organized discontent with colonial rulers. The strikes and disturbances in Northern Rhodesia, the Caribbean territories, and Mauritius, for example, drew wide Parliamentary attention in Britain in the mid-thirties.[95] Without the power of the purse, Colonial Office policy, well-intentioned as it might have been, in most colonies remained just that—policy not practice. Consequently the British Parliament passed the Colonial Development and Welfare Act, which provided that a maximum of £1 million a year was to be set aside by Treasury to aid the colonies, not

> only for schemes involving capital expenditure necessary for Colonial development in the widest sense, but also for helping to meet recurrent expenditure in the Colonies on certain services such as agriculture, education, health and housing.[96]

From the Solomons, the resident commissioner submitted a proposal encompassing agricultural, educational, and medical services development and the initiation of an extensive road-building program. The plans for education were an outcome of the Groves inquiry carried out in 1939, with the support of Ashley, who had some hopes of opening government schools, but lacked funds and the commitment necessary to face strong opposition from the planting community, who feared a drain on their labor resources. The proposals were under consideration by the secretary of state in 1940–1941, when they had to be set aside while the British concentrated on the war effort.[97]

Despite the intervention of the war, a precedent had been set. The protectorate was no longer expected to be entirely self-supporting. Broader issues of social development could now be considered alongside the economy. With Britain supplying funds, it could force greater attention by the local administration to the wishes of the Colonial Office, wishes on such matters as a decent living wage, trade unionism, and the elimination of indenture, which for a decade had been ignored in the light of the parochial concerns of the protectorate.

FOR THE SMALL PLANTERS, no less than the traders, the 1930s were truly years of gall and wormwood. The bigger companies, for their part, had weathered the storm and, although by the end of the decade they were certainly not expanding, they were still capable of surviving. Had the war not intervened, and prices still remained low, even these highly capitalized operations were likely to have suffered eventually without radical change.

The Solomon Islands' bright prospects for multicrop plantation development in 1907–1913 had been limited primarily by three factors: land, labor, and the integration of production with the wider world economy. Although they failed to monopolize the land, the planters had, with government cooperation, obtained plenty of it, but this bore an inverse relationship to the labor supply. Labor was scarce and the existing alternatives to plantation employment provided subsistence for Solomon Islanders. Wider political and economic considerations on Britain's part, including the relationship with more valuable colonies such as Australia and India, had undermined schemes to obtain a supply of cheap coolie labor. Planters were hindered in their attempts to minimize production costs and maximize profits. Apart from this fundamental weakness of the plantation economy, many small planters lacked sufficient capital, so that when prices fell on the world market in the 1930s they became indebted to the merchant firms and, finally, were forced to sell to cover their debts. Lacking capital, they had not expended money on the technologically superior hot-air driers that would have earned them more cash in the 1930s and perhaps given them enough margin to continue.

Before World War I there had been a good market for the Solomon Islands staple, copra, but in the interwar years this market, over which the Solomons had no control, faltered and eventually collapsed in the 1930s. The only condition in the Solomons that really favored plantation development was the existence of legal and political sanctions, in the form of the indenture system with its penal clause, and the head tax, but even these were weakened by the alternative means of subsistence open to Solomon Islanders.

The Solomons possessed only some of the preconditions for a successful plantation economy, as became clear to its government and commercial firms at the onset of the Depression. This realization meant that new strategies had to be tried in order to guarantee the survival of the protectorate. The government and the Colonial Office eventually saw the possibility of a substantial part in the economy for the local producer. The merchants supported this development because it would assist them in cornering the trading market, by eliminating the intermediaries who had access to other suppliers and shippers. Yet with so much investment of capital and effort in the plantation economy, the alternative of development using imported labor was another possible solution, but one that never got beyond the discussion phase because of Levers' difficulties. As so often in the history of these islands, events outside the control of the government and people of the Solomons prevented such a scheme from being seriously considered, let alone implemented.

CHAPTER 11

A rumor of utopia:
The western and central Solomons
(c. 1930–1942)

In 1921 the Governor said that we shall pay taxes to help the
King's nation of England here in the Solomon Islands, and
we have paid taxes for 18 years. We have only been taught
the gospel, but nothing yet about trade and commerce. We
have been Christianized for 78 years now, the Church people
are anxious for collections and the Government for taxes, but
where is the money? Here in the Islands wages and prices are
very small, not enough for taxes and Church collections.

John Palmer Pidoke, A chief of Nggela, June 1939

PARADOXICALLY, THE DEPRESSION brought new opportunities and expectations as well as frustration and disillusionment to Solomon Islanders. As the lower rung of the alien commercial ladder collapsed, some Solomon Islanders took the opportunity to fill the gap with their own business ventures. But many of these ventures were new. The process of experimentation in conducting them took its toll of capital and time—and few among the European community attempted to assist the learning process. For many of these Solomon Islanders money became increasingly scarce and propitious time ran short at the end of the decade, leaving in place of hope a legacy of disappointment and often bitterness.

Along with the dimension of changing times there were variations among places. Generally, in the western and central Solomons the storm of economic and social troubles blew worst in 1933–1934 and again from 1937. In the eastern Solomons, despite occasional shafts of sunlight, the passing of the decade saw an intensifying storm of difficulties for the people.

In the west the majority of people involved in the cash economy were self-employed and grew or fished for their produce in their own home districts. In this region the worst of the trauma of conduct-induced

241

social change was over by the 1930s. Except for those of Choiseul, the people were under the *pax Britannica* and most, including the Choiseul-ese, under the *pax evangelica*. Under Christianity a new social coherence filled much of the gap created by the passing of many elements of the old culture. Although paternalistic, the Christian missionaires, like Goldie in New Georgia, were champions not only of their respective faiths, but also of the secular interests of their followers. In these areas those young people who received some formal schooling, particularly with the Methodists and the Seventh Day Adventists, were educated to a higher standard than their counterparts in the eastern Solomons. Coupled with their long experience with Europeans, this education gave them an air of confidence and bearing. Although equality in the colonial context was elusive, the westerners won a measure of respect from many whites that was not accorded their eastern neighbors.

The people of the central Solomons—Santa Isabel, Nggela, the Russells, Savo, and the northern coasts of Guadalcanal—did not feel the worst effects of the Depression until the late 1930s, just when they were beginning to articulate their needs in education, commerce, and cultural identity. They used the structure of the Melanesian Mission and the advice of one of its priests to express those needs to the government. In the main their petitions were reasonable and reasoned, yet the government refused to participate in dialogue, leaving the people further disillusioned.

The missions' support of the people in both the western and central Solomons brought to the fore the rivalry between church and state, a rivalry that had been present from the first years of the protectorate, but had increased from the late 1910s in proportion to the extension of direct government control.

The Depression and local producers

When the price of copra fell in the early 1930s the reaction of Solomon Islander producers was much the same everywhere—they stopped making it. Whereas once they had been able to get a shilling for 30 nuts, in 1931 they got half that for 100. Like the planters, the Islander producers looked forward to the day when the price would improve and conserved their resources to that end. In districts where Islanders had formerly produced significant quantities of copra, such as the Shortlands, the New Georgia Islands, Savo, and parts of the east and west coasts of Guadalcanal, the people set about expanding their food gardens, ceased buying "luxury" foods, extended the manufacture of local tobacco,[1] and in some cases reverted to the "old customs of dress."[2] The apparent ease of the transition amazed the white traders.

We find to our astonishment that the native can and is doing without our wares and to a much larger extent, and in a much shorter time than we thought possible, in view of the years it took to educate him up to buying what he did.[3]

But as the months and then years passed with no improvement in the price of copra, enough of the "education" of five or more decades of contact with the Western world remained to reassert itself among Solomon Islanders. The people were still capable of living quite well as subsistence villagers but over the years, particularly in the western and central Solomons, had developed new wants and expectations that depended for their satisfaction on cash. Undoubtedly, people in New Georgia could exist without the "gramophone and mandolins played in the village at all hours of the day," but many simply would not have chosen to, given the option.[4] Moreover, the Solomon Islanders still needed cash for their tax and their church.

Copra producers who wanted money had three alternatives in these times: they could try to sell what copra they made more profitably than before, they could find another product that gave them a greater return, or they could reduce their expenditure on what they considered nonproductive items. In the western and central Solomons all three strategies were tried with varying success.

From the start of the slump in 1929 until about 1934 some producers believed that by ceasing to produce they could revive demand. The people of the Shortlands, for example, restricted their copra making on this basis. Though such a policy might well have been effective if the Solomons had been a major producer of edible oils, on a world scale its contribution was insignificant. In some districts, such as Nggela, Savo, and Guadalcanal, the people attributed the slump to the machinations of the traders and the government. Since those groups had played an almost omnipotent role in the economic life of the Solomon Islanders from the establishment of the protectorate, it is not surprising that the fall in prices was seen as a conspiracy.[5]

The Gizo district—resistance and reorganization

Taking a more decisive stand, the people of the New Georgia Islands conducted a boycott of traders. The leaders of the movement were Boaz Sunga and Belshazzar ("Bill") Gina, members of the Methodist Mission and close associates of the Reverend John Goldie. Sunga, son of the *bangara* 'chief' Gemi and Goldie's clerk, was a chief in his own right who, with other chiefs and Goldie, had been received by the royal house of Tupou in Tonga in 1921.[6] Gina, grandson of an Isabel slave, was a candidate for the ministry and had spent some years in New Zealand. Both had received a solid formal education from the mission and were not afraid to question the activities of the Europeans. In 1932 they had "discovered the beneficial rate of [currency] exchange that exists between Australia and England and assumed that the European trader was hiding this for his own benefit."[7] The boycott spread through most of the Gizo district taking District Officer Middenway by surprise. He was concerned that the people, without their trading, would have cause to default on their tax. As ever, the traders blamed the government. Leslie Gill, long-time trader and planter at Munda, saw the boycott as a result of a discussion between a former district officer and Gina. With Goldie's long record of supporting the western Solomons people, many Europeans believed he was behind the boycott. It certainly enabled him and the traders and planters to pressure Burns Philp for a fairer price, with some success. Eventually, Goldie and Gill, both of whom obviously wanted to see copra production maintained, talked Sunga and Gina out of the boycott, but it was several months before copra making returned to normal.[8]

By 1933–1934, as reserves of cash and imported goods became depleted, some producers not only resumed copra making, but also experimented with new ways of processing and marketing. The lower price had meant fewer visits by fuel-conscious traders, particularly in outlying areas such as Ranongga (Figure 9). Many villagers who had made copra in preparation for the coming of an itinerant trader saw it rot before a vessel called. Consequently, people throughout the district started to cure their copra more effectively so that it could be stored for longer periods.[9]

Since money was harder to earn, the people in the Gizo district, as well as those of Santa Isabel, the Shortlands, Nggela, Savo, and parts of Guadalcanal, demanded and received cash for their produce, thus maximizing their income. As the traders' livelihood depended on the volume of their business they were forced to pay cash. Both people and traders alike realized that with cash the Solomon Islanders could buy where they wished. The fierce competition that resulted among European and Chinese traders benefited the Solomon Islanders, particularly in the west.[10]

The most significant innovation in copra making and marketing was the establishment of cooperative ventures by villagers. Because they had for many years worked together to make offerings of produce, including "gift copra," for the Methodist and Adventist missions, the people of the New Georgia Islands did not have far to look for a model. The first attempt was at Marovo Lagoon, led by the district headman and chief, Ngatu, in 1933. The people invested sufficient cash to purchase a vessel, but the scheme foundered and the ship became a derelict on the beach.

District Officer Middenway believed it would be years before "the natives develop sufficient concentration and perseverance to control successfully any business proposition."[11] Yet a year later, in July 1934, another group of people led by Headman Bambu of Ndovele, Vella Lavella, embarked on a similar venture. At the end of the year their cooperative had produced 375 bags of copra and 24 bags of ivory nuts. By shipping on consignment on the *Bremerhaven* (NDL), thus bypassing Burns Philp, they were able to get 3s. 6d. for a bag of copra when the local trade price was only 2s. 0d. In itself, the use of bags, enabling copra to be measured easily by weight rather than by numbers on strings, meant that the people received a better price. When prices were, for example, at £4 13s. 4d. a ton for copra purchased by weight, Solomon Islanders got only £3 10s. 0d. a ton for copra counted on strings. The Ndovele cooperative received some assistance from a sympathetic but bankrupt trader, Sydney Marks, who sold them the bags and twine to pack the copra. Although Middenway was surprised at the Ndovele people's success, he believed that following Marks' departure other traders, who wanted to purchase the copra themselves, would refuse to sell the necessary bags and twine. The bag problem did not eventuate in 1935 because the *Bremerhaven* bypassed Gizo that year. Nonetheless, the cooperative sold two lots of 400 bags of copra, the first at 7s. 6d. a bag and the second at £8 8s. a ton—a good price from the trader, who got only £9 10s. a ton landed at Gizo.[12] To rid themselves of their dependence on the trader, the cooperative proposed buying a five-ton motorized vessel to take their copra directly to Gizo. In spite of discouragement by Middenway and their Adventist pastor, Anderson, who both preferred a more easily maintained sailing vessel, the Ndovele people had accumulated the necessary £300 for the vessel by the end of 1936, after having sold 778 bags of copra at £9 a ton.[13]

Success inspired imitation. As the price of copra improved in 1935–1936, other villagers on Vella Lavella, particularly at Mandezavanga and Sirumbai, became interested in following the Ndovele example, as did J. Pitu of Nusa Roviana and Boaz Sunga of Roviana.[14]

Other ventures were tried. When the copra price was down in 1933–1934, the district officer found that the Gizo people were willing to try growing a new crop, rice. The Adventists had introduced the crop on an experimental basis at Ndovele. Middenway obtained seeds from the mission and distributed them despite the opposition of planters who feared that, just as Islanders were growing more of their own tobacco, they might also come to supply their own rice, further reducing the traders' business.[15] Needless to say, for a government which could state confidently that "with the exception of the copra industry there is no agriculture in the Protectorate" there had been no feasibility study. The experiment failed because birds ate most of the crop.[16]

The tax "revolt"

Fortunately, most people in the Gizo district did not have to rely exclusively on copra for cash and, with the exception of the Ndovele cooperative, few made it when the price fell to 5 shillings a bag. Along with the people of the Shortlands, Choiseul, Santa Isabel, the Russells, and to a lesser extent, Nggela, they had reefs around most of their coasts that were rich in trochus shell; in the early and mid-thirties, this sold for between £60 and £80 a ton, ports price. For collecting a four-gallon kerosene tin of shell (40–45 shells to a tin) Solomon Islanders got around 10 to 12 shillings from the traders. By 1933, all the available reefs in the Gizo district were being worked. That year, the 6000 people of the district earned £2000 from trochus shell alone and £300 from ivory nuts. About £440 was paid out by the government as wages to Solomon Islander staff as well as to headmen. Including salaries to mission teachers, the overall income of the district was around £3000 or 10 shillings a head.[17]

Although in absolute terms this was not a large sum, to the district officer the Gizo district appeared relatively well off and its 1500 taxable men able to pay the £1 tax. Most of these people perceived their first financial duty to lie with their missions, which for years had served their spiritual, medical, and educational needs. The extent of their commitment can be measured by contributions to the Methodist Mission in the Gizo district alone, amounting to £1724 in cash and £1915 in returns from produce in 1929. In the people's view, their "taxes" paid to the mission gave a return, whereas those paid to the government produced nothing.[18] Many felt at this time that the tax was excessive because not every island in the group had a reef and only a few men in each villager were able to dive for shell. The people posed the same question of the government as Goldie did: "Surely the Government does not claim that the natives have no other responsibility, and should be taxed to the amount of their total income or even more?"[19]

It was just this sort of attitude that the government resented. By 1930 the nature of the relationship between the missions, including the Methodists, and the government was very different from what it had been during the frontier era that was all but finished in the late 1910s, with some regional exceptions. The government, now strong, no longer had to compromise with the missions in return for the ideological and often logistical support in "taming" the Solomon Islanders. It still wanted their cooperation, but not their competition or criticism in secular matters. However, Goldie was not the sort of person to be intimidated by the government. He had been in the Solomons for thirty years, far longer than any itinerating colonial servant, and his power base among the western Solomons people was as unshakable as his personal influence in Australian and New Zealand church circles.[20] Publicly, the government could not fault him, for this Australian was always preaching loyalty to the Union Jack despite his ferocity in attacking any "injustice done to the native people."[21]

The tax question rekindled old animosities toward the government. The Kolombangara people remembered the "waste land" disputes. As a sign of their disgust the Methodist villagers on the island declined to pay the tax until the government again went through the ritual of explaining its purpose. They eventually complied, but had made their point to a government which did little, in their eyes, to earn the tax it extracted each year. As the price of copra fell still further in 1931, people in the Gizo district petitioned the government to take the tax in copra. Although the high commissioner was empowered to accept copra instead of cash, he refused because the government had no storage facilities and little shipping. Moreover, although district officers had discretionary powers to set a reduced rate, Middenway allowed a reduction in two cases only, from £1 to 15s.[22] In September 1933 most of the leading men in the district met with Goldie at Roviana to express their dissatisfaction. Their main concern was the tax, along with their objections to a foolish and fortunately short-lived regulation introduced by Ashley requiring Solomon Islanders to obtain a permit costing 1 shilling to move from one district to another. In his letter to the resident commissioner telling of the meeting, Goldie made the point that the tax had been set at £1 when the people were earning 15 shillings to £1 a bag for copra, and that now all they could get was 3 shillings.[23] The government was unsympathetic. During the following year, 38 tax defaulters were imprisoned by Middenway and some, allegedly, were beaten by Solomon Islander policemen. The Methodist synod registered a protest with the government early in November 1934.[24] In the same month the district officer found Boaz Sunga, who had been at the synod, again opposing him. The immediate issue was the dog tax of 2s. 6d. that had been introduced in the 1920s as a hygiene measure and revenue raiser, but the dominant concern was the head tax. Sunga declared that the tax was unfair and that he, too, would rather be jailed than pay. Using the mission-based lingua franca Roviana, Sunga had been sending letters to other chiefs, urging them to meet again at Gizo to petition for a reduction of the tax to 5 shillings. Early in November Middenway started collecting tax at Kolombangara and faced mass noncooperation. By this time the Adventists had joined the Methodists in what both Middenway and Pastor Anderson considered "a conspiracy."[25] Since 26 of the 38 people imprisoned for tax default were Adventists, the government could no longer attribute the resistance solely to the instigation of Goldie. The antipathy toward the tax had been sufficient to overcome sectarian differences and create political solidarity.[26] On 29 November, 600 people led by Gina and Sunga gathered at Gizo from all over the New Georgia Islands to present their protests to the district officer, with Goldie acting as their adviser and interpreter. Along with complaints about the rate of taxation, the people wished to know how their taxes were spent.[27]

Although the size of the gathering surprised and disturbed many Europeans, Middenway's only reply to the people was to point out that £2000 and more had been earned in the district in the year and that the people should start to make more copra or to seek work as laborers on plantations to get the tax money. Sporadic passive resistance, inspired in party by Gina and Jiriviri, headman of Simbo, continued until the end of the year. Goldie threatened to take the matter of the imprisonment of defaulters to the Colonial Office, but the situtation cooled as the copra price improved, making the tax less onerous.[28]

Prices of copra continued at an improved rate throughout most of 1936. This, along with the merchant companies' policy of equal prices, meant that most local producers left off shelling and returned to the now profitable task of copra making. As their incomes revived, the Gizo district's people once again began to spend more time on their cash crop and to buy more imported foodstuffs, particularly rice, and even such luxuries as bicycles—despite the lack of roads. In 1936, it seemed old times had returned:

> No longer are they content with only one decent hot meal a day consisting of vegetables and perhaps a little fresh fish, but are having three regular meals a day. Rice, biscuits, canned meat and fish, flour, sugar, tea and numerous other imported foods are being used extensively. Of course, the gardens are suffering as very little time is now devoted to gardening.[29]

But in 1937 copra prices fell again. As the trochus shell market had also collapsed, the people once again concentrated on gardening. Some extended their coconut groves in the hope of a future market recovery, but only made copra occasionally when they needed money for "the purchase of necessities such as clothing, kerosene and tobacco."[30] Although the government maintained the tax at £1, as a consequence of the "revolt" it was now willing to demonstrate more compassion in granting exemptions, allowing 500 to 600 a year, as opposed to only 2 in 1933, until the war broke over the islands. With their copra, their savings, and the help of their paternalistic missions, the people of New Georgia, having made their stand against the government in 1933–1934, were weathering the economic storm of the close of the decade with more grace than most of their compatriots.[31] No wonder then that in 1939 the visiting educationalist Groves said that in their district there was "a general air of satisfaction with life—a certain smugness, and a successful adjustment to European contact and culture-change."[32]

Beyond the Gizo district

Elsewhere in the western and central Solomons the pattern was similar. In the Shortlands, Choiseul, and Santa Isabel, the people compensated for their loss in income from copra during the early years of the Depression by expanding their fishing for trochus and other shell. The Shortland Islanders exploited the trochus shell resources of Alu and Fauro (Figure 8), although the Mono people were less well off, depending mainly on copra. They were served by European trader-planters in the area, two resident Japanese, Sasata and Kawakame, and itinerant Chinese from Gizo and Tulagi. Along with them, the resident Chinese trader, Yee Poy, also made frequent voyages around Choiseul to buy shell and some copra. Burns Philp's equal-price buying policy, the traders' supplying of bags at 1 shilling each, and the public posting of current prices by District Officer Keegan in 1936 encouraged renewed copra making among the people, who produced a quarter of the total exported.

The Shortland Islands also had at hand a range of employment opportunities that boosted the income of its small population of 1000, of whom about a third had to pay the tax of £1. The Roman Catholic Mission at Nila needed carpenters and crew as did the Methodist missionaries from New Georgia, who called regularly at Mono and Fauro. The staff at Burns Philp's Faisi store, along with the district officer at Korovou, required an array of personal servants—chicken-boy, wash-boy, house-boy, and garden-boy. The owners of small plantations, such as Mrs. Clara Scott, Mrs. Cruickshank, and the Atkinsons, preferred the Shortland Islanders as household help, sometimes counting their employees as part of their own families. Monckton's logging business on Alu provided work for local people (see Figure 15). Those at Maleai and Nuhu, who did not want to leave their homes even for casual labor, could sell shells and curios to parties of travelers from the Burns Philp steamer while it was anchored at Faisi. Plantation laborers were another source of cash, tobacco, rice, and soap for the people who traded betel nut and fresh food. A fillip to the local economy at the close of the decade was provided by the government market at Korovou and the regular purchase by the Shortland Island Plantation Company of fish caught by villagers.

The resident Catholic priest and former French cavalry officer, Maurice Boch, although not as involved in protectorate politics as his contemporary, Goldie, operated effectively behind the scenes to protect his flock's interests as he saw them. Few Catholic Shortland Islanders left the district on a long-term basis to work and certainly not as plantation labor, because of the combination of the ban on recruiting, ample employment opportunities at home, and the vigilant eye of Boch. With so much cash in the district, Boch had little occasion to confront the government.[33] However, in 1930, when the chiefs disputed Burns Philp's claims to certain lands, Boch stated their case to the company's representative, Alan Campbell. Military strategist still, he added that he did so only out of fear of his staunchly Catholic parishioners going "over to Goldie."[34] Shortland Islanders who witnessed the declining fortunes of the white planters and traders in the thirties do not remember the decade as a time of great hardship to village society. Choiseul was more peripheral to all these sources of cash income and consequently less dependent on it when copra prices fell. Its men, like the Shortland Islanders, found some work on Catholic and Methodist mission ships and on the mission stations at home and elsewhere in the west.

For most Santa Isabel people too, the period was generally prosperous. Having been favored by a long history of internal peace and virtual self-government through structures established by the Melanesian Mission in the late nineteenth century, they were in a position to exploit the natural advantages of an abundance of land and rich reefs to develop both internal and external trade (Figure 17). The mission assisted the people when it could by transporting their copra to Tulagi on the *Southern Cross*, but this was not done on a regular basis. The island's population in the early thirties was a mere 4100 on an area of about 388,500 hectares. Some of Santa Isabel's copra production was a result of the hated tax of 1922, which nonetheless had encouraged the systematic planting of coconuts for cash.[35] Despite the fall of copra prices in 1929–1930, trochus shell provided the means to sustain an altered style of living, as the Reverend Richard Fallowes noted at Kia in 1932:

> In some ways the Kia people are more intelligent and progressive than the others. Living close to a reef with shell they have been able to buy from the traders such things as they want and their homes are full of western comforts such as chairs, cushions and curtains. They possess two launches and a whaleboat.[36]

Along with selling their produce to traders, the Santa Isabel people made and traded among themselves canoes, paddles, baskets, and local tobacco.[37]

By 1931, they were anxious to have more commercial outlets and to widen their participation in external trade. After long discussions, the two district headmen, Walter Notare and Edmund Bako, petitioned the visiting high commissioner, Sir Murchison Fletcher, for a Chinese store on Isabel. More significantly, the people wished to take out store licenses themselves, despite the fee. The European traders and trader-planters on Isabel naturally opposed both proposals because they feared a loss of business. The Bishop of Melanesia, Baddeley, supported his church's followers regarding the Chinese store because he believed the people could

SANTA ISABEL

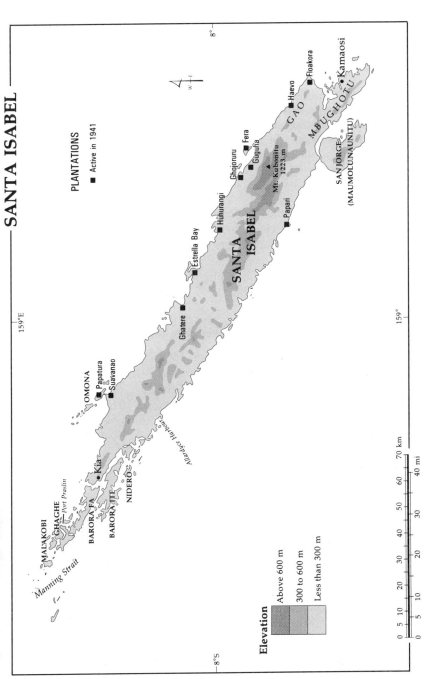

PLANTATIONS

■ Active in 1941

Elevation

Above 600 m

300 to 600 m

Less than 300 m

Figure 17

deal with the Chinese more easily than with the Europeans.[38] On the other hand, District Officer Fowler believed that the people's desire for a resident Chinese trader was an expression of their own feelings of inadequacy in dealing with Europeans, and urged a positive policy by the government.

> The Ysabel District is admirable ground for the introduction of a native trading policy; such a policy is necessary here and is far more to be desired than any innovations making more easy the way of non-natives. With encouragement and watchfulness by local Government authority natives may profitably advance in a direction towards which they now appear to be moving and the appeal for the possibly doubtful blessing of indiscriminate licensing of Asiatics for trading in this District removed.[39]

Influenced by this and the decreasing number of licenses being taken out by Europeans, Ashley ignored the pleas of the European traders and in 1932 introduced a reduced store license fee of £2 for natives as against £10 for non-natives.[40] However, he was less enthusiastic about restricting Chinese traders; by 1936, along with five European-owned stores, there was one Chinese on Isabel.[41]

Local traders, storekeepers, and capitalism

The effect of the lowered fee was soon apparent. By the end of 1933, 4 villagers on Santa Isabel had taken out store licenses in addition to increased numbers of hawkers who paid the government an annual fee of £1. The numbers of store licenses multiplied to 10 in 1934, 17 in 1935, and 52 by 1937, remaining about the same until the war.[42] The number of hawkers' licenses showed a similar growth.[43] By 1935, the coastal people were so well off from selling trochus shell and internal trading that they were said to be living "in a state of comparative luxury far above that of the majority of Solomon Islanders."[44]

Like the Santa Isabel people, other groups in the western Solomons earned cash from various combinations of internal trade and the sale of produce for export. In this way an individual who did not have access to trochus, for example, might still be able to trade pigs or vegetables with other Islanders in return for cash or other goods. In the western islands the cash flow continued throughout the first three-quarters of the decade. In the Russell Islands, the two hundred villagers not only sold trochus and copra, but also traded vegetables, other foods, and betel nut with some of the six hundred laborers on Levers' estates. Such was the level of their income that these "sophisticated natives" were said to have been even more prosperous than those of Santa Isabel.[45]

Lacking trochus, the neighboring island of Savo (population 700, Figure 14) had only copra to sell to the traders. However, its people maintained their cash income from the export of pigs to Nggela and Malaita. Just as in the Shortlands, when copra prices fell the pig population increased because more coconuts could be fed to them. The Nggela people profited as both intermediaries and breeders in the pig trade across to Langalanga on Malaita. It was far more economical for the people to use their coconuts to feed pigs, which they would sell at an average of £5 a head, than to make copra at a rate that required one or two weeks' labor to earn £1. Certain villagers continued to collect their share of shell valuables from visiting Langalanga divers. Cash was readily available at nearby Tulagi, where the people sold firewood, fish, poultry, and vegetables; but their biggest money-spinner was working as stevedores on Carpenters' or Burns Philp's steamers when they called at the capital.[46]

In the Shortlands, Choiseul, and the New Georgia Islands, indigenous participation in trade also expanded. By 1937, the Shortlands had 19 licensed local storekeepers and 18 hawkers. Neighboring Choiseul, rich in trochus and untaxed by the government, had 22 storekeepers.[47]

In the New Georgia Islands, although the people were effective producers in richly endowed islands, they were slow to become involved in ventures such as storekeeping, mainly because of the influence of the Methodist mission. The people were well served by the mission's stores at its head-stations, other stores at Gizo, and Gill's at Roviana, as well as by itinerating Chinese. Although the Methodist mission made an enormous contribution to the welfare of its followers in the west, the very scale of its operations, particularly in the field of village schools, absorbed most of the enterprising men. After completing their education, mission teachers were sent to villages other than their own, thus cutting off the economic base that could have supplied the labor and money needed for their undertakings. Because these men were engaged in teaching, the amount of time they could devote to economic activity was limited. Moreover, missionaries like Nicholson and Goldie, since the days of the Sito affair on Vella Lavella, had taken on the problems of the people as their own; in doing so, they gradually curtailed chiefly enterprise. The younger generation of New Georgians, remembering Goldie's stand on the Lands Commission and his advice in the tax crisis, looked to him and the mission for initiative and guidance, which he, in his own words a "benevolent despot," was only too willing to offer on most secular as well as religious matters.[48]

Goldie was a canny businessman—in 1923 he had obtained the first privately owned wireless in the Solomons so that he could monitor the copra market and not have to rely on Burns Philp's quotes (Photo 22). He was also a director of Mundimundi plantation, on land that he had bought cheaply in 1907. Despite his interest in the industrial side of the mission, Goldie had no policy of encouraging local enterprise beyond

Photo 22. John Francis Goldie, 1926.
(Metcalfe collection)

the level of producers, being for the people their manager in most things.[49] He approved of the white traders, providing they were honest, because they rendered "a real service to the people."[50] In fact, Goldie discouraged the development of the people's keen trading sense by virtually eliminating the need for intermediate traders, long before the merchant companies thought of doing so. To maximize the mission's bargaining capacity with the merchants, he had the people donate "gift copra" to the mission rather than the cash they would have earned by selling to the traders themselves (Photo 23).

Consequently, interest in the cheaper licenses developed slowly. The first store license holders obtained their finance mainly from relatives and friends in paid government employment. Their success in these early years was limited—in 1933, only 3 of the 7 licenses issued the year before were renewed. Thereafter, they increased gradually to 33 just before the war.[51]

Indigenous storekeepers and hawkers faced many organizational difficulties, not the least of which was their reliance on the Chinese or European traders for stock. The non-native traders still added all or part of their retail markup when they supplied the Solomon Islander traders; the margin of the latter's profit was slim. Often stores ran out of stock because of poor ordering or because a vessel called irregularly. For many local traders and entrepreneurs, the price fluctuations of the Depression compounded the difficulties that arose from inexperience and lack of formal education. On Choiseul, the missionary Metcalfe was horrified to find a new storekeeper promising gullible people £19 a ton for copra when the best price Goldie could get from Burns Philp was

Photo 23. Men ramming "gift copra" for Methodist Mission at Mono, 1939.
(Metcalfe collection)

255

only £9. Storekeepers were sometimes pressured into giving goods to kin on credit and then could not extract payment without causing family friction. Some did little or no business; others made a profit of up to about £4 10s. on a monthly turnover of £12, having added to their own substantial mark-up. Such a low level of individual trade militated in most instances against any large-scale arrangement with one of the merchant companies, with the result that many hawkers and even storekeepers were little better than agents for the non-native traders.[52] Yet without a vessel the villager-trader was locked into dependence on an intermediary, who in most cases was a Chinese trader who was more amenable to dealing in the small turnover of the local trader than the Europeans. The European traders resented this, particularly in the case of hawkers. They claimed that the Chinese traders paid the £1 hawker's license fee for the Solomon Islanders and set them up in business, taking custom away from the European traders who had to pay a much higher license fee.[53]

Following the direct buying policy of the merchants in 1935–1937, the intermediate trader's role weakened, and with it the means to ship local produce. To overcome this problem, one of the Chinese at Gizo, a trader and boat builder named Chan Cheong, and then Burns Philp, permitted groups of Solomon Islanders to buy cutters and auxiliary vessels on credit against incoming produce. Villagers in Roviana, Kolombangara, and Simbo opened accounts. For the first time ever, the merchants gave substantial credit to Solomon Islanders, if only because they were forced to do so by commercial necessity.[54]

With vessels bought either for cash or later on credit, individuals sometimes banded together to send across to a center to buy direct from Burns Philp or perhaps Carpenters, thus avoiding the intermediate trader. The Santa Isabel people at Kia, a highly unified community led by Bako, had sent boats over to Tulagi as early as 1932. Santa Isabel was such a center of trade that in 1937–1938 Burns Philp planned to open two stores there to buy direct on the same lines as those at Tulagi or Faisi, but the fall in prices of both copra and trochus precluded this. Even so, until the late 1930s, various groups of people on Isabel frequently combined their resources to go across to Tulagi to sell their produce and buy store goods.[55]

Local traders did better when they mixed their storekeeping with other cash-earning enterprises. Some who owned launches and cutters traded in canoes and local tobacco as well as imported goods. Others funded diving parties to collect trochus. Usually, the owner of the launch chose a group of divers, fed them, and paid them a percentage of the profits. Santa Isabel traders often employed Malaitans as divers on their boats, and, like their New Georgia neighbors, as copra cutters when prices were good. Ancient trading contracts of Santa Isabel with

Malaita were extended, with Kia people selling cutters there. Earnings from such ventures could be high—one Kia man earned £270 from shell in three months.

Cash earnings were not always evenly distributed throughout the population. There were signs that wealth was accumulating in the hands of a trader "class," the owners of trading and fishing vessels. With a money economy, capital formation was now possible. Certainly, there was a growing preoccupation among some of the people with the legalities of marriage and the inheritance of of property. By 1938, men of status and wealth, such as village headmen and priests, were asking £5 cash for their daughters' bride payment, while ordinary villagers got only 10 shillings to £2.[56] Such was the monetization of the economy in the New Georgia Islands that traditional valuables had all but disappeared even in ceremonial exchanges. Although the Adventists considered traditional valuables to be "of the Devil,"[57] the Methodists had no quarrel with their use in settling disputes and sealing friendly relationships; yet in the 1930s cash was almost always demanded as bride payment. Since the 1910s the availability of coin, as well as increasing rarity, the cessation of manufacture due to the competing demands of cash cropping, the ending of the traffic in slaves, and the disappearance of the old religious and warfare ceremonials had all combined to lessen the supply of traditional valuables. Cash was used increasingly instead of barter, even in ordinary exchanges of goods between villagers. Like customary valuables, coin could be stored and was in fact more durable. The government, anxious to keep the money flowing, decried the tendency for Solomon Islanders, including those in New Georgia and Choiseul, to hoard money, but praised the people's use of the newly opened Commonwealth (Australia) Savings Bank depots at Gizo and Faisi in 1931. Yet to Solomon Islanders these two methods of accumulating cash were functionally equal, even if the bank did pay a little interest.[58]

Cash was changing other relationships and further extending the potential for some individuals to accumulate wealth. In the New Georgia Islands, where traditionally the people did not recognize exclusive clan or individual ownership of the reefs, immature trochus was being moved from the outer reefs to the inner. Although the people who moved the shell did not claim ownership of the particular area of reef they had "planted," but only of the shell, it would have been virtually impossible for anyone else to look for trochus shell there. This process was further advanced on Santa Isabel. Just as in some areas there had earlier been disagreements about ownership of land when the cash crop copra was involved, rights to the use of the trochus-bearing reefs now became a lively issue, which the district officer could not settle without appropriate legislation.[59]

Hopes postponed

As the people became more involved in the cash economy they became increasingly aware of their educational limitations. Demands for education were not new: In 1896 on Malaita, Woodford had found that there was "a growing desire among the natives . . . to learn reading and writing."[60] Many had adopted Christianity in the hope that they could acquire the knowledge of the white man. By the 1930s that desire was still strong, but the people of various districts were increasingly disillusioned with the educational efforts of all but the Methodist and Adventist missions.[61] The Methodists in the 1900s had extended schools throughout their circuits and opened a Training Institution at Kokenggolo (New Georgia) in 1913. There, and at Mbilua (Vella Lavella) and Sasamungga (Choiseul) students received an education in a wide range of religious and practical subjects. Kokenggolo even boasted a kindergarten. The Methodists' neighbors and rivals, the Adventists, provided some education in English, a factor that won them converts both in the New Georgia Islands and later on south Guadalcanal. In the 1930s these two missions, particularly the Methodists, had educated the handful of native clerks employed by the government, many of the police sergeants, the first few students for the Suva Medical College to train as Native Medical Practitioners (NMP), the first western Solomons candidates for ordination, the first students for training as agricultural officers in New Guinea, and the first trainees for a wireless operators' course in Suva, to say nothing of scores of village teachers who brought literacy in the Roviana language to all the youthful population of New Georgia and beyond.[62] These schools were exceptional. Most mission education was rudimentary and involved little more than learning to read or recite parts of the Scriptures in one of the vernaculars, Pijin, or Bible "English."[63]

The initiative for better education came from Santa Isabel, where the level of instruction given by the Melanesian Mission had dropped from that of the missionary Welchman's time in the 1900s. The people asked for a government school where English and commercial and technical subjects would be taught. As they became more and more involved in trading they keenly felt their inability "to read and write intelligently";[64] well aware of the old government-mission rivalry, the headmen Notare and Bako petitioned the high commissioner for a school in 1931. The district officer was sympathetic, as was the Melanesian Mission priest, Richard Fallowes. Their neighbors and coreligionists on Nggela, led by the chiefs Selwyn Aloa and Patrick Kike, presented the high commissioner with a similar request. The Nggela people were willing to pay for the education for up to four years in Fiji of two boys who, on their return, would advise the chiefs. The Nggela approach met with tepid encouragement from High Commissioner Fletcher, who pointed out that at least seven years of education in Fiji were necessary. The project foundered when Aloa became mentally disturbed and lost interest.[65]

The government was equally unhelpful with the Isabel petition, despite renewed pleas by the people. Certainly, Ashley had acknowledged the need for the government to participate in education as early as 1930, just as Woodford had in 1896, and planned to obtain aid from the Colonial Development Fund. But a man who believed that "the Solomon Islands natives generally are of a low mentality and have the minds and understanding of children"[66] was unlikely to make their education a top priority. In 1931 he had proposed a scheme whereby the government would give a modest subsidy to mission schools that were prepared to teach government-specified subjects. Although the missions were lukewarm to the proposal for fear of losing their autonomy, such was Ashley's enthusiasm that he let the matter drift for seven years.[67]

This inertia left the people of both Santa Isabel and Nggela disappointed, but, with a fair degree of prosperity, they too bided their time. In 1937 their situation changed. The trochus shell market weakened as did that for copra and ivory nuts. The overall export earnings of the Solomons declined by £192,840 from £480,741 in 1928–1929 to £287,901 in 1937–1938, while the cost of imports fell by £62,250 from £295,141 to £232,891. Not only was more than 80 percent of the export earnings being spent on imports, but also the prices of imported goods, including iron and steel implements, had increased, thus decreasing the purchasing power of the Solomon Islanders. With few money-earning exports, the cash flow within the islands declined, affecting the people's ability to buy both imported goods and locally produced items. By 1940 what trading went on in the western and central Solomons was mainly back on a barter basis.[68]

For people who had enjoyed a comparatively high standard of living, this second and overwhelming wave of the Depression initially seemed incomprehensible. As they had in the first phase of the Depression, they attempted to find a solution. The Santa Isabel people, who had grown fat on trading up to 1937, were the most discontented since they had lost the most. Onto this stage in October 1938 came Richard Fallowes, not as a missionary, but as a private individual visiting his friends.

The central Solomons and the "Chair and Rule" movement

Fallowes, conscientious and idealistic perhaps to a fault, had pushed himself beyond his strength when he worked as a priest on Isabel between 1929 and 1934. At that time, although on good terms with the district officers, Fowler and Filose, he had put himself at odds with

Tulagi by his tacit opposition to the excommunicated headman, Walter Notare. A strong if unpopular personality, Notare had been appointed as government headman in 1920 at a time when the government was trying to assert its power vis-à-vis the Melanesian Mission. The mission had long had its own system of church government, which, in the absence of any civil authority, quite naturally ruled on some secular matters, since the sacred and secular dichotomy of Europeans was an alien concept to most Melanesians. Fallowes, although never entering into conflict with Notare, revived and strengthened church administration by installing a system of church wardens *(vunagi kiloau)* in each village. As it was, there was very little disharmony between the government's headman system and the mission's system, but successors to Filose on Isabel were alert to any possible threat to government authority. Filose had been removed in 1932 when it was discovered that he had instructed his police to inflict beatings on offenders against the law on Santa Isabel and earlier on Malaita. Although there is little doubt that Filose exceeded his powers, the people sent a petition to the resident commissioner requesting that Filose be allowed to remain. Since Fallowes translated the document, Acting Resident Commissioner J. C. Barley believed that he was behind it and another petition sent by the white residents of Isabel.[69]

Fallowes was in a difficult position. He himself had administered canings to members of his church as a punishment instead of excommunication for certain offenses, particularly adultery, which neither they nor Filose wanted brought before the court. Fallowes did this openly, keeping a careful record of such punishments in his pastoral work diary.[70] But the Filose case and petitions had stirred up a hornet's nest in both Tulagi and Santa Isabel, with the result that the government put Fallowes under surveillance. Some old enemies, including Notare and George Bogesi, NMP, who Fallowes claimed could not be trusted with female patients, were not unwilling to help the government's case. Under much physical and mental strain, Fallowes left the Solomons for leave in Australia early in 1933. On his return in June, he was served with a summons as he left the steamer at Tulagi. Of the fourteen charges of common assault, he was convicted of three and fined £1 10s. Fallowes wanted to take the case further since he claimed all the punishments were inflicted with the consent of the persons involved. Bishop Baddeley talked him out of this. Fallowes returned to his pastoral duties on Isabel until recurring "nervous strain" forced him to holiday at Maravovo, Guadalcanal. Finally, in 1935, he left the islands for England where he received psychiatric attention after an attack of depression aboard ship.[71]

When Fallowes returned to Isabel in 1938 he had many discussions with the people, which resulted in three big meetings, organized mainly by Lonsdale Gada, the *soga* 'paramount chief' of Isabel and a descendant of Monilaws Soga, the unifier of the Isabel clans in the 1890s. The meetings, held at Mbughotu, Savo, and Nggela, were attended by Solomon Islander priests, chiefs, policemen, government and church leaders, teachers, and any others, including pagans, who wished to come. Among the participants were people from Malaita, the Russells, Guadalcanal, and San Cristobal, including George Gitadi, a Mbughotu chief and priest who worked on San Cristobal.

Because Fallowes thought that the traditional form of debate in Melanesian discussions resembled that of the English parliament, he suggested that a Speaker be elected to conduct the business. This was enthusiastically supported. After Fallowes outlined the business of the meeting as he stood beside the vacant chair, a Speaker was elected. Fallowes then retired and spoke only when requested to by the Speaker. Although Fallowes had no knowledge of the *vaukolu* at the turn of the century (see p. 92), many people, especially on Nggela, recalled a time when the people ran their own local affairs and received apparent support from Woodford. Out of these meetings came a number of grievances against, and petitions to, the government. The main petition, to be given to the high commissioner during his visit, was from the Nggela people led by John Palmer Pidoke, a chief of the Hongokama clan, government headman, and successor to the enfeebled Selwyn Aloa. The petition asked that the government provide, first, a technical school to teach "carpentry, boat-building, engineering, wireless, type-writing, and timber-cutting"; second, dispensaries in every district, with a Native Medical Practitioner in charge; third, a government hostel in Tulagi for the people; fourth, the repeal of the rule restricting the sale of cartridges to Islanders; fifth, the alteration of the regulation allowing married men to "sign back" on plantations for a second term; sixth, that the Solomons not be handed over to Australia or any other power; seventh, that Malaitans be given special financial assistance, namely a raise in plantation and boat crew wages; and, eighth, that the Sydney price of shell and copra be posted publicly. The petition carried an apologia tracing the history of the Church's evangelical relationship with the Solomons and the people's expectations that after "50 years" of church contact they were to get "equality with the whites in the matter of wages and prices," but that, after "78 years" this had not come to pass. It went on to defend Fallowes against the opposition of the bishop. A set of questions was also attached to the petition relating to adultery, marriage, the right to appeal in a court of law, propitiatory compensation, the customary payments of funeral attendants, and, significantly, a request for an increased wage from about 10 shillings to £12 a month.[72]

Fallowes had helped to formulate the main requests, but much of the rest was written by Pidoke. Fallowes later stated that he was "in some measure responsible for the attempt to create something of a permanent native Assembly to which representatives from the various islands could be summoned."[73]

The Nggela meeting, the third, took place on 12 June 1939. The first that High Commissioner Sir Harry Luke and Secretary to the High Commission Vaskess heard of the proposals of this Chair and Rule movement, as it came to be called, was when a group of headmen assembled to welcome them at San Cristobal on 13 June, during their voyage from Fiji to Tulagi. The headmen put forward requests for schools, hospitals, higher wages, and help with copra prices. Luke and Vaskess learned that these demands had originated from Pidoke of Nggela and had been brought to San Cristobal by the headman of Wanione Bay.[74] The following day they faced a similar group at Aola, Guadalcanal. Here the Chair and Rule movement focused the resentment that the people of the north-east had long held toward the activities of a gold-mining company that had found payable gold in 1937. In April 1939, Jimmie Bue Taburia, a headman, had registered a futile protest, reflecting the general discontent with the lack of government action on development and his people's unanimity with the ideas of political change circulating on Isabel and Nggela. He had struggled with a foreign language to tell the government,

> about 3½ years ago they have been digging the gold; but we don't know that it helps other people or our own island in the work of Priests or Deacons or teachers or Plantations or Government or Hospitals or any other different works.
> We all agree together of the thoughts of other people in the islands.[75]

Luke took no more notice of the Aola petitioners than Ashley had of the headman. The people said they favored a "native parliament," but were told by Luke that people like Pidoke could not possibly "understand the needs of the natives or what can be done for them as does the government."[76]

Luke became disturbed by the scale and extent of the spread of such opinions. When he arrived at Tulagi he received the Nggela people's petition, sent by Fallowes. Luke saw the priest as the instigator of these "absurd ideas." An Anglican, Luke was supported by the conservative Bishop Baddeley, who found this "turbulent priest" an embarrassment. In Luke's view, Fallowes was a threat to the political stability of the protectorate, "a free-lance Constitution maker [whom] no Government in a native territory could tolerate."[77] For his part, at a meeting with Luke and Vaskess on 17 June, Fallowes insisted that his role had been merely that of adviser and friend. But after being told of Fallowes' activities on Isabel, where District Officer Brownlees had considered him "a person whose presence is dangerous to peace and good order," Luke finally took out a deportation order against him.[78] Fallowes left the Solomons on 29 July 1939, but a month before he left, people from the Shortlands to San Cristobal knew of the Chair and Rule movement.[79] The district officer at the Shortlands noted "it appears that wages are to be raised to a fantastic figure and that all sorts of other good things are just around the corner."[80] The government swung into action. By the close of the year district officers throughout most of the Solomons were convinced that their many lectures to the people had stifled this "rumour of an Utopia."[81]

THE PEOPLE of both the western and the central Solomons experienced similar economic problems during the Depression. In general they adapted their life-style and their economic and political activities to cope with changing times. Although by the early 1930s the local economy was highly monetized, it still retained great flexibility because when produce prices fell drastically, exchanges between Solomon Islanders soon returned to barter. Using the structure of the mission, their lingua franca, and literacy, the people of the Gizo district organized themselves to make the first nonviolent mass protest to the government over the oppressive rate of taxation. They were largely successful, assisted as they always were by the indefatigable Goldie. Beyond the Gizo district and the rest of the western Solomons, as commercial opportunities for Solomon Islanders increased so did their awareness of their own inadequacies and the lack of government support, deficiencies all the more galling as their sources of cash subsequently shrank. The petition of the Chair and Rule movement clearly revealed what was worrying these people: they wanted practical education equal to or better than that offered by the Methodists, better medical facilities, a little assistance with marketing, and higher wages for laborers, as well as recognition of cultural values. These were simply reformist measures within the existing economic and political system. Most, including a "native assembly," could have been implemented without undue disruption of the status quo, especially in the light of policy directives emanating from the Colonial Office. Yet the government, almost as a reflex action, ridiculed and suppressed the movement, slamming the door on the possibility of cooperation with its subjects. Fallowes was no Goldie and Baddeley sided with the government. The social gospel fell victim to the Establishment and the Solomon Islanders remained without any real return for the revenue they helped to produce.

A significant feature of the protests of both the New Georgia people and the followers of the Chair and Rule movement was that the lines of communication between groups, peoples, and even islands were church based. For the first time in Solomons history, people from different groups were uniting in their own communities to bring their common concerns before the government. Despite limited successes at the time, an important precedent was established.

Since these movements were church based, the government labeled its rivals the missionaries as the instigators of the discontent. Although because of their culture the articulate white missionaries were more visible to the colonial government, they were merely the vehicles of the Solomon Islanders. The people were expressing how they felt toward a government that failed to acknowledge their identity above the level of taxpayer and laborer. Had the government listened to them, rather than concentrating attention on the missionaries, it would have discovered that the ideas behind the Gizo "revolt," the Chair and Rule movement, and other "rumours" of the time persisted in the minds of Solomon Islanders.

CHAPTER 12

More rumors:
The eastern Solomons
(c. 1930–1942)

Let it be understood that the Malaita-man has a justifiable
grievance against the Administration, a grievance which,
long simmering in the mind of an untutored, inarticulate
aboriginal, in time assumes the proportion of a serious injustice; and that mental condition has been responsible for any
"boil-over" of pent-up feelings in the past. In the Solomons
generally, and on the island of Malaita particularly, district
officers and police are primarily tax-collectors. In effect,
taxes are extorted at the point of a bayonet . . . . Government, whose paramount aim is to display a financial "profit"
in the business of administration, takes, but gives nothing—
except to Civil Servants.

Pacific Islands Monthly, November 1935

The heathen religion, springing as it does from man's impo-
tence in the face of the unknown, has as its principal function
the validation of hopes for the future . . . .

H. Ian Hogbin, *Experiments in Civilization*

RESENTMENT OF TAXATION was stronger in the eastern Solomons than
elsewhere, simply because these islands were poorer than their neighbors. In the view of their people, they received nothing from the government in return for their taxes; the tax drove many of their people to
the hated plantations. This fundamental grievance was magnified during the Depression, especially after the 50 percent wage cut of 1934 and
the near cessation of trading in primary produce in the few productive
areas, like San Cristobal. In addition to the economic decline, the bush
people of central and south Malaita were feeling the full effects of pacification in the wake of the Bell killings. Everywhere, government edicts

confronted traditional values. A spiritual revelation promised a solution to all these difficulties, and a new cult took hold. Just as with the Chair and Rule movement, the government attempted to suppress the new cult. But unlike Fallowes, the people of the Kwaio bush, who were the originators, could not be deported and the prophecies and promises of the ancestor soon underwent the mutations necessary for their survival among a colonized population.

Albeit with the difficulty born of colonial reluctance, the government read the signs. Its officers realized that the devaluation of local cultures by imposed regulations and the weakening of traditional leadership by the wage-labor and taxation systems could lead to open unrest—which any government feared. The government began introducing local courts and councils—concessions that would provide for legitimate expression of parochial concerns, make administration easier, and imply no abdication of ultimate power.

A just tax: The path not taken

Opposition to the tax by Solomon Islanders was constant. It had been a universal theme through the twenties and thirties, expressing itself most dramatically in the Bell killings on Malaita in 1927 and in the "revolt" in the Gizo district in 1934. What Malaitans and others resented, particularly in the eastern Solomons, was the apparent unwillingness of the government to provide a good administration that respected them, so giving a just return for a tax that, even on a reduced scale, represented a substantial outlay to them.

Malaitans knew that the tie between leaders and followers was reciprocity; they knew that no one got anything for nothing, that development had to be paid for. When in 1912 the north Malaitans had petitioned Woodford for higher wages on plantations, they also proposed a scheme involving a tax or a "collection," as they called it. They wanted all Malaitans in paid employment, including those still living overseas, to pay 5 percent of their income every six months into a fund entrusted to the resident commissioner and the "bishops." The funds would then be available to buy tools and equipment to clear Malaita for cultivation. The Malaitans involved wanted the taxes they paid to be spent on the means to develop their own island.[1] Perhaps the best measure of Woodford's regard for this petition was that it never got beyond his desk to Suva, but remained among his personal papers. The returned laborers' ambitious, embryonic plan for Malaita, even if feasible under the conditions of 1912, would have drained desperately needed labor away from the development of European-owned plantations, just as a higher wage scale would have hindered European enterprise in the Solomons.

Malaita and commerce during the Depression

For all the bush people of Malaita, the beach payment and plantation wages were their only cash income and virtually their sole means of paying their tax. High in the bush there were few coconuts to eat, let alone to use for copra. Most of the copra produced by Malaitan growers came from the northern coast and Small Malaita. When the price of copra fell in the early 1930s the people not only ceased making it, but those in the north also hesitated about planting new areas because they believed further production might put them into a higher tax bracket.[2] As prices improved in 1935–1936 production increased, but most of the money earned was naturally concentrated in the hands of the growers at Maluu, Fo'ondo, and, when they were able to have their produce collected, Small Malaita (Figure 10). On the coast, what little trochus shell there was went to a few people, mainly in Small Malaita, but by the mid-thirties, the reefs were almost depleted. Malaita's production was relatively insignificant. For example, 22 tons of locally produced copra were exported from the island in 1932 by a population of over 40,000, compared to 500 tons exported from Santa Isabel by only 4000. Malaita's total exports of trochus for the year 1934 were valued at £528, whereas on Isabel a single trader purchased £500 worth in *three weeks* during the same year.[3]

By far the wealthiest people on Malaita were living in the Langalanga, 'Aoke, and Lau lagoon settlements. They earned wages of 3 shillings a day each as stevedores on the steamers, which employed between one and two hundred men while in Solomon seas. Traditional sources of wealth were still exploited. Using their Nggela connections, the Langalanga people purchased pigs for their own use and to sell to their pagan Kwara'ae and Kwaio mainland neighbors, who wanted the animals to sacrifice to their *akalo* 'ancestor-spirits'.[4]

By the thirties, the Langalanga people, mostly still pagan, were the sole manufacturers of shell valuables and had a wide market for their product.[5] Since they worked on the steamers, the men took their shell valuables with them to the Shortlands people, who no longer made their own valuables or *mimisi*. From there the valuables found their way across to Bougainville where they were highly prized by the people. It seems very likely that (as today) the Langalanga men got a better price for their valuables in the far west than they could have on Malaita, especially as the movement of Christianized Malaitans to the coast, which had begun during the twenties, was reducing their output of taro and pana, which they bartered for the valuables. Inflation was affecting the worth of shell valuables on Malaita, reducing their buying power to half what it had been in pre-Christian times. With cash, the

Langalanga people could compensate for receiving decreased amounts of vegetables by buying rice, flour, and biscuits at Tulagi and Makambo (Figure 14). Moreover, following pacification, some Langalanga people had been able to acquire use-rights to land on the mainland and were able to grow some of their own food.[6]

Individuals in this prosperous region had more than one means of earning money. Of all the eastern islands, it was only to these Langalanga and Lau people with guaranteed cash incomes that Burns Philp extended credit facilities for boat buying in the 1930s. Some groups used these and other vessels to make money by transporting the steamer gangs to and from Tulagi in return for 5 shillings a head from Burns Philp. Others became involved in buying and selling cutters in areas as far apart as Kia on Santa Isabel and Mbalasuna (near Mberande) on Guadalcanal.[7]

During the early thirties such ventures represented practically all of Malaitan commercial enterprise and were almost entirely confined to the northern region of the island where the cash income was highest. For over sixty years, most Malaita men had earned cash and manufactured goods by selling their labor, since even in the early days of contact there had been little on the island to interest whalers and traders. Such was the scarcity of copra and other produce even in 1936 that when Paulo of 'Aoke wanted to start trading he planned to take his launch not around Malaita, but to New Georgia. Men like Paulo were exceptions. Most Malaitans displayed little confidence in trading because, unlike their contemporaries in the western and central Solomons, they had had scant experience in selling their own produce for cash. They preferred to leave the retailing of manufactured goods to the Chinese and Europeans. Predictably, the first Malaitan store under the reduced license fee opened in the north in 1933 at Abu, near 'Aoke.[8]

As elsewhere, such attempts at store keeping met with intense Chinese competition. Although produce exports from Malaita were low, because the island supplied almost three-quarters of the protectorate's labor force, it attracted the lion's share of the wage bill. In the early thirties, six Chinese vessels were active around Malaita, each taking between £500 and £1000 annually in turnover. Competition was keen and the Chinese always seemed to be at the center of cash exchanges. As the district officer noted in 1932:

> Price-cutting, extensive credit, and other devices to gain the patronage of the native are extensively employed, and the smallest rumour of a plantation "pay-off," a Tax Collection muster, or even a Police pay-day will attract Chinese traders with almost uncanny regularity.[9]

In 1934, besides these trading vessels, there were Chinese stores at Kwai, Kwarade, Lilisiana (near 'Aoke) and Su'u. By 1937 two more had opened. In some, Malaitans were employed as storekeepers, thus gaining some commercial experience. In the same year, there was a sudden jump of Malaitan-owned stores from a handful to 27 at the time when Burns Philp adopted its equal prices buying policy at Tulagi. Despite the fact that the company purchased at the same price from everyone, it did not sell stock at wholesale prices to Solomon Islander traders, further hindering Malaitan competition with foreign traders. Although the usual problem of excessive credit-giving ruined some of these stores there were 19 of them and 8 hawkers still licensed in 1940.[10]

Beyond Malaita

Other islands in the east were in a worse position. San Cristobal produced copra and trochus, but with low prices and the high cost of freight (£2 a ton) to the capital, practically no Islander-produced copra was sold in the thirties. Along the south coast, villagers fished for trochus, which they sold to the Chinese or to the planter at Hawa (Figure 3). The island had a population of about 7500 of whom some 50 to 200 a year (3 to 8 percent of the Solomons labor force) signed on as indentured laborers. Following the decline in plantation production in 1930 it was hardly worthwhile for recruiters to visit the island. Elkington and Palmer did some recruiting there in the mid-thirties, combining it with freight carrying and managing Carpenters' plantation at Boroni. Most San Cristobal would-be laborers signed either on contract or, more commonly, as casuals on nearby plantations. Two-thirds of their beach pay went toward paying the 5-shilling tax of their male relatives. For most, the tax was a hardship and took what money they earned. Consequently, although traditional barter trading continued, very few San Cristobal people had sufficient capital to venture in commercial operations. With the notable exception of Peter Waitasu at Uki, what sporadic trade there was remained in the hands of a couple of itinerant Chinese and one or two European trader-planters.[11] By the time war came to the Solomons, the only use that the San Cristobal people could find for their copra sacks was as clothing, a mute testimony to the decay of external trade on the island.[12]

The people of San Cristobal had little to thank the government for in the 1930s. Certainly, the yaws campaign of 1929–1930 had been a success and a "native dresser" looked after the sick at a small hospital at Kirakira until 1933. The traveling medical officer, Dr. Crichlow, visited the island occasionally, but the bulk of medical work was done by the Melanesian Mission sisters at Uki and the peripatetic Father Podevigne of the Catholic Mission at Wanione Bay. Although the missionaries were using drugs supplied freely by the government since 1928 it is unlikely that the people knew this and the government was not given any credit.[13] The government closed down its station at Kirakira for a year in 1933 and again in 1936 (see Appendix 7). Although this meant no tax for the villagers—the men on the plantations paid the reduced 1935 rate of 5 shillings regardless of their island of origin—it also meant more "lawlessness." This elicited a strong reaction from the normally apolitical SSEM missionary, Norman Deck, who told the high commissioner at 'Aoke in 1937 that since there was "no administration the people should not have to pay tax."[14] He was merely stating the feelings of the people —feelings that would find their own expression a year later in the Chair and Rule movement.

Internal trade continued, but it had been affected by the advent of Christianity. By the 1930s most people were nominal adherents to either the Melanesian Mission, the Catholic Mission, the SSEM, or the newcomers, the SDA. People on Santa Ana and Santa Catalina, for instance, found difficulty in getting the volume of vegetables from the mainland that they had in former days in exchange for their pigs and canoes. With Christianization the pagan funeral rites had been abandoned. No pigs were needed for the ancestors and no canoes to hold the bones of the dead in the "custom" houses. The government had little to offer, other than to suggest that the people of Santa Ana and Santa Catalina plant more sweet potatoes.[15]

On the neighboring island of Guadalcanal, the medical position in the 1930s remained much the same as in the 1920s. Except for continuing the yaws campaign, the government maintained one small hospital at Aola, conducted by a dresser. Nucleation and consolidation of hamlets into bigger villages in the late 1920s and early 1930s, an ill-conceived policy of the government supported by the Melanesian and South Sea Evangelical missions, had had a detrimental impact on the health of the people and probably contributed to a decline in population. During the 1930s the Melanesian Mission, the Catholics, and the Adventists supplied, at their head stations and by traveling missionaries, medical care which, with their own and the government's emphasis on sanitation, counterbalanced the adverse effects of earlier nucleation, resulting in a stabilized, if not increasing, population.

In general, the people appreciated the missions' efforts on their behalf, although between 1933 and 1936 the Catholics of southwest Guadalcanal, especially around Tangarare, were so dissatisfied with the mission that they boycotted it. Triggered in part by scandals and dissension among the Marist priests themselves, the boycott's underlying cause was the people's resentment toward the mission for failing to pay the wages promised to its catechists trained at Tangarare, and for demanding more work of them for the mission than the village economy could tolerate. A few leaders of the boycott, who had been brought to court for defamation by the mission, refused in 1935 to pay the government tax—until the district officer intervened. Much of the discontent here was economic, since the tax was perceived as yet another unjust demand, particularly in the light of the reduced plantation wage.[16]

However, Guadalcanal was slightly better off economically than San Cristobal. The tax was set at 10 shillings for the coastal region north from Wanderer Bay around to Marau Sound (Figure 12). There, the people could produce a little copra, ivory nuts, and, mainly at Marau, some trochus shell. On the weather coast, from Marau Sound west to Wanderer Bay the tax was 2s. 6d., since this area and its hinterland, like most of Malaita, produced only laborers. Until prices improved briefly in 1935, the people of the northern zone produced hardly any copra. As the demand for labor fell, cost-conscious recruiters limited their visits to the dangerous weather coast. As on Malaita, the time was the least auspicious for the introduction of cheaper trading licenses. A number of people on Guadalcanal took out store and hawker licenses, but at the end of 1932 not one showed any significant profit. When incomes increased slightly in 1935 only six Guadalcanal men had store licenses, along with two Europeans and a Chinese. On Guadalcanal, as on San Cristobal, the itinerating Chinese picked up most of what little business there was.

The rare individual who succeeded as an entrepreneur did so against considerable odds. John Rich, an illiterate pagan of Purepure, south Guadalcanal, combined traditional and new ways of accumulating wealth to buy himself a launch in the late thirties. He had been too young to go to Queensland where three of his brothers had worked, but spent four years working on plantations in the Solomons. After his return he married three wives and with their help began making copra to sell to traders, following the example of the neighboring Catholic priests at Avuavu. He next worked for a Chinese trader on the *Namunini* and saw how at Makambo Burns Philp sometimes bought local produce for laborers in transit. He started paying off £100 to a European trader to buy a three-ton launch to ship pigs and produce to Makambo from his gardens worked by his wives and brothers. He also used his vessel to go shell diving off Santa Isabel for two years, employing Malaitans as crew because some of his own villagers were jealous of his success. All this was done in an attempt to acquire enough wealth to become a big man at home, but his aspirations were blasted when the Japanese destroyed his boat during the bombing of Makambo in 1942.[17]

The Santa Cruz district, except for Vanikolo, was poorly administered in the thirties. A government station had been opened in 1923 because an officer was needed to supervise customs procedures for vessels calling to collect timber from the Vanikolo Kauri Timber Company. This duty kept him tied to the island most of the time. Although the wages of laborers of the company were usually £1 a month (double the post-1934 plantation rate), illness and fear of sorcery kept a lot of non-Vanikolo men of the district away, their places taken by Malaitans.

Compared to their neighbors in the rest of the district, the Vanikolo people were fairly well off. With the clerical assistance of the district officer, they used the direct shipping link with Sydney to order "their more elaborate requirements from Australian firms."[18]

Outside Vanikolo, the people found that with traders Cowan and Sarich ceasing operations in 1931 they could deal only with Fred Jones who then had a monopoly. Until District Officer Crawfurd intervened in 1934, Jones bought trochus at 6 shillings a tin instead of the fairer price of 10 shillings. Most trading returned to a barter basis. For many, the only source of money was plantation work and this was hard to get as few recruiters were willing to make the long voyage. Because cash was short in the outlying islands the people had difficulty paying the tax of 5 shillings. For most, the only time they ever saw the district officer was when he came tax collecting.[19]

Dissatisfaction surfaced briefly when a man from Graciosa Bay (Santa Cruz) led a small group of people into the bush to live at an abandoned village site called Nandabu. There, they built houses and a kind of spirit-house in which they prayed for the "axes, guns, glass and clothes" of the white man. Although the oral tradition relating to this cult is vague, it appears that a "Melanesian policeman," probably Lance Corporal Araga, dispersed the group and put down the cult.[20]

The outlier Sikaiana, like Ontong Java, Rennell, and Bellona, was not taxed owing to the shortage of administrative staff and transportation. Because of their isolation, Rennell and Bellona had been very susceptible to introduced diseases, particularly influenza. These islands, which produced little of commercial value, were the only ones where the Native Passes Regulation of 1933 remained in force until they were declared a closed district in 1937. The people of Rennell and Bellona were still virtually in the Stone Age. Because they had proved poor plantation workers in Queensland and in the Solomons, what few things the handful of returners brought back from about 1880 to 1933 were not replaced, except by goods cajoled from the crew of the occasional government or mission vessel visiting the islands before the prohibition order.[21] Throughout most of the decade, Ontong Java and Sikaiana had resident white traders and Japanese itinerants who bought their copra, shell, and bêche-de-mer. Without the tax, all their earnings could be spent on trade and so they suffered scant material recession during the Depression.[22]

Problems and attempted solutions

Very little had disturbed the cosmos and security of the Rennell and Bellona people because these isolated islands had little of known value for the white man and thus little to contribute to the wider world economy.

The big islands were different because they had human and nonhuman saleable commodities. For these islands, when the world economy faltered, there could be no instant retreat to precontact economic conditions because the internal structure and values of their societies had already changed, along with the needs of their people.

Consequently, when the government halved the beach payment and take-home wage of plantation labor late in 1934, the eastern islands, particularly Malaita, reeled under the shock. The government's attitude to the effects of the cut on Solomon Islanders was both contradictory and callous. Ashley, on the one hand, wanted to have copra production and recruiting maintained because, depression or not, the copra industry was the backbone of the economy. Yet, to keep the industry going, he understood that the people had to have more to look forward to spending their money on than simply the tax, and had encouraged an increase in the number of licenses for indigenous and Chinese traders. The buying power of a pound held by a Solomon Islander, as Ashley knew, was less than that of the pound in the pocket of a European or a Chinese. Despite this, Ashley cut the wages because of planter pressure.[23] As in most contemporaneous plantation economies, planters and government held the convenient assumption that a laborer's wages were never meant to provide a man and his family with a "living" or "basic wage." Such wages were merely a supplement to the living his family made by subsistence agriculture. Ashley's rationale echoed this, but was incongruent with the arguments he had used to support the encouragement of native trading:

> I am personally of the opinion that the native labourer is satisfied with 10/- per month. . . . It cannot be too often stressed that wages paid to the natives in the Protectorate are nothing more or less than so much pocket money. Apart from their tax obligation, no natives of the Protectorate have any financial responsibility in respect of either themselves or their families and very few natives have any idea of the value of money.[24]

The reaction of those affected belied their supposed satisfaction with the new wage and their assumed ignorance of the value of money. Intending recruits behaved in a similar manner to their New Georgia neighbors when the price of copra first fell. They staged a spontaneous, but unorganized boycott of recruiters. This could have worked well in times of high demand for labor, but the strategy was little more than an inconvenience in an extended period of low copra prices and reduced maintenance of plantations. In less than a year, with the tax hanging over their heads, men resumed recruiting in numbers.[25]

There were other means available to Solomon Islanders of hitting back at a system that had deprived them of half their wages. Some Malaitans, when confronted by a recruiter, would accept the beach payment of £3 and agree to take 10 shillings a month pay and then, after they were shipped to Tulagi, refuse to ratify their contracts on the grounds that they had been told the wage was to be at the old rate. This was all perfectly legal within the Labour Regulation, much to the chagrin of the government and the frustration of recruiters, who not only were legally bound to return the "recruit" home, but also often lost all or part of the distributed beach payment.[26]

Like the old returners from Queensland, many Malaitans and other Solomon Islanders realized that higher wages were a possibility when labor at any particular time was indispensable, as was the case with the steamer gang and stevedores at Tulagi. They also knew something of the strike as a worker's weapon. Returners had seen and taken part in strikes in Queensland and in Samoa in 1906 and 1916.[27] The last of those returning from Samoa to come back to the Solomons via Rabaul arrived in 1933, and almost certainly included Malaitans present during the strikes.[28] However, strikes can be successful only if labor is skilled and cannot be easily replaced by others, or if all the potential laborers are willing to act as one body. The steamer gang, which had no need to strike because of its comparatively good wages, was about the only group of Solomon Island workers to fall into both categories. Specialized and highly organized, the Langalanga group was led by Lauramo, who had worked in both Queensland and Fiji, and the Lau group by Oeta (Demisi). At 3 shillings a day these men were getting near the wage of £1 a week that Malaitans had asked Woodford for in 1912. This wage example, plus news of the methods employed by the men in the Rabaul mass strike of 1929, inspired a crew on one of Carpenters' vessels that visited Rabaul to refuse to work until they got £4 a month instead of £1 5s. Carpenters easily defeated this attempt and another in 1935 because there was a pool of experienced men always looking for jobs.[29]

Malaitans, in particular, were besieged with other difficulties besides economic pressures from the outside. An unusually severe earthquake in 1931 caused pagans to believe that their *akalo* had deserted them and Christians to think the Day of Judgment had come. In the southeast Kwaio region this phenomenon reinforced a growing religious malaise. From around the time of the Bell killings, the main food staple, taro, had been affected by a blight. The people attributed this to the displeasure of the ancestral spirits whose shrines were desecrated by north Malaitans and other Solomon Islanders taking part in the punitive expedition of 1927. In the late thirties District Officer Bengough tried to encourage the people to substitute a new variety of taro, but they refused.[30]

To the south, despite the yaws campaign, their neighbors the 'Are'are were declining in numbers. Bengough attributed the decline to certain changes in customary activities. Traditionally, when an important person died of old age, a ceremony called *houraʻa* was performed. Before pacification, such ceremonies were rare because every death, except those resulting from old age, was considered to be the outcome of sorcery and resulted in either the killing of the suspected agent or the abduction of a child to replace the deceased and appease the spirit. Following government control killing was outlawed and children could only be adopted by purchase or gift. Since these avenues for propitiating the spirit of the dead relative were closed or constrained, the ʻAreʻare extended the *houraʻa* ceremony to almost all deaths. Some months after a person had died the relatives were obliged to assemble for a feast and bring shell valuables (100 to 300 strings of red valuables) for the dead person's closest relative to present in return for the services of the undertaker.

In the opinion of the district officer, the expansion of the *houraʻa* was assisting depopulation. First, it encouraged the extension of the custom of *alu* ʻsweetheartingʼ whereby young men gained prestige by having many girl friends who gave them small gifts for their attentions. These liaisons rarely resulted in sexual intercourse or marriage, but were simply a means for young men to acquire prestige. With the availability of a variety of partners and the daunting prospect in pagan society of assembling a bride-price, men delayed marriage. Consequently fertility decreased, in contrast to the Christian Kwaraʻae to the north who, with a lower bride-price, were marrying earlier and increasing their numbers. The *houraʻa* also meant that people moved around from hamlet to hamlet, neglecting their gardens and decreasing their resistance to sickness. Finally, this mobility, along with exposure and overcrowding in the hamlet where the particular *houraʻa* was held, allowed diseases such as tuberculosis, influenza, and dysentery to spread more rapidly among the people who had once had the protection of isolation. The district officer, concerned with the population decline, persuaded the people to limit the custom, but after they had briefly done so, a severe influenza epidemic swept the region. The people attributed this to the wrath of those spirits whom they had failed to honor with *houraʻa*. Naturally, the custom resumed its former level.[31]

It is likely that the increase in *houraʻa* and other ceremonials produced a greater demand for shell valuables, at a time when the years of involvement by the Langalanga men in the steamer gang meant a decrease in production and a drain of what was produced to the Shortlands and Bougainville. Attempts to raise the required amounts of shell valuables may well have created further tensions within the society of the bush peoples.[32]

In Kwaio there was a similar intensification of funerary feasts, supporting the principle that pacification brought greater mobility and time for ceremonial. But more was involved than simply economies of time and motion. The pagan Malaitans were concerned with the role of the spirits in everyday life and the neccessity to obtain their benevolence —so demonstrably lost in the taro blight in Kwaio and the many waves of illness and death in 'Are'are.[33] In the eyes of many Malaitans, particularly the bush pagans, the source of their difficulties was the new law of the government and the missions, which so often set them at odds with their *akalo* through no fault of their own.[34]

Within the Christian communities too there were divisions. Besides the obvious sectarian differences, there was conflict between the leadership of the major Christian group, the SSEM, and the government's representatives. In the early days of the mission, as with the Anglicans on Santa Isabel and Nggela, local church leaders, be they teachers or elders, gained political as well as religious authority in the Christian coastal villages, which were made up of resettled, diverse clan and regional groups. These teachers had become more influential and independent than most of their counterparts in other sects because they had little oversight from the European missionaries, who remained aloof and apart from Melanesian concerns. As the teachers were unpaid they were left largely to their own devices to raise their subsistence, and needed to be in touch with the thinking of their congregations. Fundamentalist, Bible-centered, with Pijin as the lingua franca, the SSEM creed and structure meant that the teachers increasingly became more the leaders of the indigenous church than the agents of the foreign mission. As teachers graduated from the Onepusu Bible "school," this form of leadership continued until the 1920s, when the introduction of the government headman system produced new contenders for local political power.[35]

Pacification had inexorably drawn more and more of the Malaitan hinterland under government control. The task force led by Charles King, who patrolled the bush areas for two years after the Bell killings, filled in the blanks on the administrative map. Pagan elders and the *ramo* 'warrior-leaders' chafed under the ban on killing, which meant that deaths of kin could not be properly avenged. Secret ceremonies involving the sacrifice of a pig and a curse on the supposed sorcerer could not be as spiritually effective as revenge. Elders could no longer effectively use the threat of employing a *ramo* to dispose of rebellious and disrespectful young men and wanton young women. As had happened earlier in coastal and lowland areas, when young men became Christians with the SSEM or the SDA, they paid either a smaller brideprice of shell valuables *(tafuli'ae)* or none at all, thus reducing their dependence on, and respect for, their elders.[36] The process of weakening of the elders' authority had started in the early twenties through their dependence on the young for cash for the tax, and by the mid-thirties extended throughout the island.[37] Although in 1937 the visiting high

commissioner granted some relief to the inland people by reducing the
tax to one shilling, the elders had become impoverished after years of
using cash savings or shell valuables for the tax. As the sources of their
wealth shrank, so did their power.[38]

The power of the *fa'atabu* 'clan priest' of the pagans received a further shock in the late 1920s and 1930s in the form of the yaws and hookworm campaign. Throughout the 1930s the government's Native Medical Practitioners, Bogesi, Ravai, Piko, and Wheatley, as well as the
campaign's own officer, Gordon White, and many of the missionaries,
gave thousands of injections to eradicate yaws. Between them they covered the length and breadth of Malaita. Most people, pagan and Christian, regarded the *nila* 'needle' as semimagical and, indeed, its effect
was dramatic. Sometimes, a single injection could cure a case of painful
and disfiguring yaws, which about 90 percent of the population contracted at some time in their lives. Traditional medicine could not work
as quickly, nor was it as freely given.[39]

Pacification had brought the imposition of laws that militated against
the cultural beliefs and practices of pagans and many of the fundamentalist Christians. On Malaita and elsewhere the people particularly
resented the government's stand on adultery. Traditionally, death, exile,
or in a few cases a very heavy fine was the punishment.[40] In 1930 Eyerdam, an American collecting birds in inland Malaita, noted that a generation earlier both parties in adultery would have been tortured to
death. The woman "was sometimes seized and hung from a branch by
one foot and shot full of arrows. . . . The vagina was then cut out and
smoked over a fire and used as an armband or as an article of barter
worth about 4 shillings."[41] The man was sold off to coastal people for a
canoe-launching sacrifice in which his flesh was cut from his body while
he was still living and eaten until he died. On Guadalcanal, compensation was the usual method of solacing the injured party. Because the
British regarded adultery as an aspect of private morality and were
loath to legislate on it, they did not define in the Native Administration
Regulation of 1922 just whether and how it should be punished. Yet it
soon became evident that adultery was the cause of much of the dispu-
tation brought before the district officer. To cope with this the government was forced in 1924 to introduce legislation providing for a fine of
£5 or three months' imprisonment; in 1929 the punishment was further
increased. A compromise of British reluctance and Solomon Islander
intransigence could not appease indigenous sensibilities. Guadalcanal
people thought the 1929 punishment of six months' imprisonment too
severe. The San Cristobal people were no happier since the punishment
did not differentiate between male adulterers of varying social status.[42]
But to the Malaitans, imprisonment for six months doing light work and
gorging good food, was hardly a substitute for death, as they informed

278   *Wealth of the Solomons*

the high commissioner when he visited 'Aoke in 1931. They wanted a
minimum of two years' imprisonment and confiscation of the man's
property.[43] The weak Adultery Regulation made the offense appear
more attractive and thus more likely to occur. This could and did lead to
feuding, a clan's loss of a bride's value in shell valuables, and, for the
pagans, the possibility of punishment by the *akalo*. With such tolerance
in the introduced law, the hold of the gerontocrats over the young was
further weakened, but there seemed little else in pagan society to
replace their stabilizing control.[44] It was increasingly clear that although the pagan remained "obstinate and tenacious in his beliefs and
superstitions," young men back from plantations with money in their
boxes had "lost their reverence for the authority of their elders."[45]

The spirits, America, and new hope

The pagan Malaitans, to whom the natural and supernatural were a
unity, had found no viable solution to the myriad difficulties facing
their society in either rebellion, individual passive resistance, strikes, or
pleas to the government. Since the elders of the clan were the traditional mediums for spiritual revelation and had most to lose with the
passing of the old dispensation, it is not surprising that the ancestors
chose to speak to them of a solution to the growing social dissonance.

One of the most important female ancestral spirits of the Kwaio,
La'aka, provided such a solution in about 1939.[46] There had been an
earlier revelation and subsequent cult among the Kwara'ae to the
north. Just before the turn of the century, a spirit traditionally venerated by some pagans in the Lau area, had revealed itself in the 'Aoke
region, promising help. At the time, similar acculturative processes to
those being experienced by the bush pagans in the 1920s and 1930s were
beginning to be felt, following years of the overseas labor trade and the
start of mission and government activity. The early cult waned following the death of most of its adherents in an epidemic. In the twenties, a
similar spirit came again to two men in the Kwara'ae bush, about the
same time as seaplanes from Australia were first seen in the Solomons.
The spirit asked for offerings and a shrine, promising to

> bring plenty of different moneys including English money, rifles, car-
> tridges, etc. In the morning something like a bird will bring all the money.
> You will see that all our fathers and mothers and brothers and sisters [i.e.,
> the dead ancestors] will bring all the money.

When this did not happen, the spirit then told them to "build a house
for all the things that were to come and for the dead." Nothing happened, and the mediums asked for a girl, promising that then all would
come to pass. They got the girl, but still nothing eventuated. They were
told that the spirit wanted them to go to the coast, build canoes for por-

poise hunting, make a feast, and build a wharf. After three months, when all these things had been done and still the promises had not materialized, "the people began to mock the Bulu [a false prophetic spirit] [and] became Christians."[47]

According to anthropologist Roger Keesing, that was the last of the spirit's manifestations, but in fact a cult centering on it was imported to Uru, in the heart of Kwaio, before or during 1936. Most Kwaio came to regard this as a wandering spirit, trying to mislead people into thinking it was an ancestral spirit.[48] At some time between 1936 and 1939, the revelations of the false *bulu* faded or were taken up by La'aka. In 1939, she spoke at 'Olomburi, south of Uru, in the Kwaio region. From her revelations, rumors started

> that troops and warships of a certain great and friendly power [America] would soon arrive, and killing all who did not adhere, take over the government of the Protectorate. The rumour gained wide credence since it was alleged to originate from one of the most powerful ancestral spirits in Koio [Kwaio]. This spirit was said to have demarcated a certain area in the bush and all who did not go to live in that area would be killed by the invading troops together with all officials of the government.

The district officer also noted that two houses had been built for the expected troops at Guagware and 'Airumu. This time the government could not blame the missionaries for the rumors.[49]

Such prophecies well reflect the level of discontent of the Kwaio with their government and the search for some hoped-for solution. The American element is not totally surprising in view of the lack of accurate information available to the Malaitans. Early recruits to Fiji and Samoa would probably have had direct contacts with Americans since some of the early settlers and labor recruiters from there were Americans. As early as 1908 an American ex-convict and gold prospector, Ernest Weaver of the *Wheatsheaf*, tried to persuade the powerful and widely known big-man, Irobaua, of north Malaita to kill another white, Symonds. In discussion, Weaver promised Irobaua that he would go to the United States and get a warship to drive the white men out of Malaita.[50]

A black American sailor, Dick "Amerika" Richardson, had lived on north San Cristobal from the early 1910s. Much married, he had had a Malaitan wife and was known to people on south Malaita. Illiterate and relatively impoverished, Richardson existed most of the time on the tolerance and charity of both the European and local communities. But being a physically big man and an effusive teller of tales, he probably kept the name of his birthplace alive in the minds of the Solomon Islanders about him.[51]

Another source of knowledge of America were ships that came to the Solomons from 1919 until 1935, taking copra direct to the United

States, mainly for Burns Philp.[52] A visit to Malaita and other islands by
the flamboyant American movie-makers Osa and Martin Johnson in the
mid-twenties probably added to the people's concept of America.[53] Certainly, even in the bush of Malaita in 1930 men had heard of America
and voiced favorable opinions of it—not without some purpose, since
their audience was a party of high-paying American bird-hunters, led
by Hannibal Hamlin, grandson of Abraham Lincoln's vice-president.[54]
Their fellow countryman, the enthusiastic Dr. S. M. Lambert, had
been the moving force behind the Rockefeller contribution to the successful yaws campaign. For his time, the doctor possessed a remarkably
positive view of Pacific islanders that may well have been sensed by the
hundreds of Malaitans he treated in the north in 1933.[55]

More significant, in the early 1930s an American writer, John W.
Vandercook, his wife, and a labor recruiter off the *Kokorana* crossed the
island south of Uru in Kwaio. They stayed at an inland village where,
unlike most other Europeans, they took part in long discussions with the
people about America. Perhaps this kindly spoken American, who left
that village greatly impressed with the intelligence of the people he
spoke with, had likewise left an impression of a faraway, benevolent
land.[56]

In 1935, the *Pacific Islands Monthly*, staple reading among the white
community, ran an amusing article called "Notes on the Probable
effects of turning the Solomons into American Territory" that envisaged
an idyllic American Solomon Islands. The article had been stimulated
by the suggestion of an American admiral that the Solomons could go to
America as part payment for Britain's World War I debts. Such publicity for "their" islands must have been the subject of much idle conversation among whites at Tulagi, on plantations, and at missions.[57] Since
Islanders often got hold of magazines, there is a possibility that this
elaborate joke got jumbled and absorbed by men on plantations and
ships. With the coming of war in Europe, Europeans in the Solomons
speculated, as did the voices on their wireless sets, about just when
America might intervene, thus giving America center stage in the eyes
of the Solomon Islanders.[58] Lies, rumors, distorted jokes, colorful and
kindly individuals, and overheard snippets of conversation all combined
over the years to emerge as a major theme of hope in the revelations of
La'aka.

Institutionalizing unrest:
Reconciling "custom" and introduced law

Although the government tried to squash this relatively harmless cult,
just as it had the Chair and Rule movement, it was aware of some of the
causes of the unrest. "Custom" became a difficulty for colonial adminis-

trators as soon as they started trying to control it. In 1922 Resident Commissioner Kane had considered certain areas such as Nggela and the western district sufficiently "advanced" to have some form of native courts wherein Solomon Islanders could rule on troublesome questions of custom. But he received no support from High Commissioner Rodwell, and the matter rested. Once the Native Administration Regulation came into effect (1922), questions relating to customs such as adultery, divorce, marriage, land tenure, ownership of reefs, and compensation, created problems for district officers, not the least of which was the legality of judging these matters that varied greatly from region to region. One of Ashley's first actions as resident commissioner in 1929 had been to petition Suva for permission to set up a system of native courts to cope with these questions while retaining customs that were not "repugnant to modern ideas of justice and humanity."[59] The high commissioner favored the general concept of native courts, but insisted that the unwritten native customary law had to be codified and written down before such a system of courts could function. Although he wanted a unified code he recognized that Malaita needed a special one, since so many of its people were still pagan. Experienced officers, such as J. C. Barley in 1933, raised objections to this impractical scheme of a unified code.[60] With Ashley's tacit consent, "native tribunals" were apparently allowed to evolve naturally in districts where government officers were sensible of, and sensitive to, local conditions. In 1934, Wright of Guadalcanal permitted these courts to deal with "civil law in the form of unwritten native custom." The court decisions were generally accepted by the people. Although Ashley was encouraging, as late as 1935 the high commissioner still maintained that customary law had to be codified before such courts could become universal.[61] Support for Ashley came from an unexpected source. After fieldwork on Malaita and Guadalcanal, anthropologist Ian Hogbin gave the issue wider publicity, first among readers of *Pacific Islands Monthly* in January 1934, and a few months later in the scholarly journal *Oceania*. He maintained that councils of senior men should be established in each district in the Solomons. Hogbin warned that although the worst, in humanitarian terms, of the old customs had been suppressed, if the process continued uncontrolled there might be social chaos—a condition no administrator wanted as it created more work and interfered with the economy. Hogbin saw the reestablishment of the powers of the elders and big-men as essential.

> Councils made up of four or five such men in each district could be established under the chairmanship of the present headmen. These councils could be empowered to deal with all minor offences and civil cases, and serious offences could be investigated by them first, and a recommendation made, through the Chairman to the District Officer. Codifying native

law is not advisable, as conditions are changing so rapidly, but if this system were adopted the District Officer would have to be familiar with the usual native methods of dealing with criminals.[62]

Suva demurred, but Ashley had already embarked on a campaign of fostering a deeper study by his district officers of customs and social organization within their respective districts. As early as 1930 he had instructed Barley on Malaita to discover and record the boundaries of the various clans.[63] By 1939, probably spurred on by the Chair and Rule movement, more district officers encouraged "native arbitration courts." On Santa Isabel, where they were functioning, the district officer described them as "purely a native development [that had] long received government encouragement."[64] The same year a similar council was established experimentally at west Mbeli and To'ambaita, Malaita, and in 1940 on Small Malaita. A year later councils were operating at Baelelea and Baegu. On Malaita and function of these councils was a compromise of the Suva line and Hogbin's and Ashley's ideas. They acted to codify custom, but *within* the clans of their subdistrict. By October 1941, a single court to arbitrate on customary law for the whole of Kwara'ae was functioning and discussions between the district officer and the people were well under way for the formation of councils of elders in both Kwaio and 'Are'are, as well as the limiting of the *houra'a*, reduction and stabilization of the bride payment, and the introduction of larger permanent village settlements.[65] Likewise, in the Gizo district, Miller inaugurated a similar system of courts in 1940, a move supported by the new resident commissioner, Marchant.[66]

The councils were extended into other districts before the Pacific war and were generally popular, although many procedural details were still being worked out. On Malaita, the elders and clan leaders welcomed the development because it seemed a chance to reassert their authority. On Nggela, some of the government-appointed headmen, many of whom had returned from Queensland, and the teachers of the Melanesian Mission often found themselves superseded by informally elected representatives to the court. Nonetheless, the new system seemed to have been gaining wide acceptance when the war halted its development. As it functioned, the system still allowed the right of veto to the government and in many areas seems to have reinforced the authority of the sometimes-hated headmen.[67] Where it might have led had the war not intervened is open to conjecture. As with other reforms in Britain's empire it was seen by many of the people as too little, or too late.

ALTHOUGH AS PRODUCTS of their own culture few of the British colonial officers could have been expected to take the revelations of La'aka and the Santa Cruz cults seriously, they might well have been more sympathetic to the Chair and Rule movement, which formulated its demands and grievances in terms eminently comprehensible to any British administrator. The Chair and Rule movement, like the Gizo demonstration of 1934, began in districts that generally were long-Christianized, sophisticated, and used to dealing with at least some Europeans on terms of relative equality within the institutionalized racism of colonialism. In the west, the protest weapons of boycotts, passive resistance, petitions, and the use of sympathetic Europeans like Goldie, Boch, and Fallowes, were quite in keeping with the long history of European contact and the evolution of ways of manipulating the "ship men," even within the constraint of European-held power after 1896. In the east, the old gods still spoke to men who for decades had been only the laborers—"hewers of wood and drawers of water"—controlled abroad and even at home by the plantation economy. Their culture, origin, and occupation combined with their race to mark them off, in the eyes of the whites and some of their own compatriots, as a subservient, if not servile, class. They had to rely on wage labor to earn cash, which a parsimonious government took from them in taxes in return for laws that often conflicted with their cultural values. With only sometimes a smattering of scripture schooling and little experience of commercial trading on equal terms with the aliens, they could express their frustration only in violence, or, when they were stifled, in abortive unorganized strikes, sullen hate, and a search for a new solution. To most Europeans, that was a promised but fantastic appearance of "cargo" and a benevolent America.

Yet, for all their differences, cults like that of La'aka shared common characteristics with the Chair and Rule movement. At their base, both were manifestations of dissatisfaction with the protectorate government and the economic difficulties and inequalities that had become acute during the Depression. Although the La'aka cult was a religious phenomenon, its message was essentially political, as the government's attempts at containment showed. In expression, each movement found a different metaphor to illustrate the same fundamental theme—a metaphor that was an abstraction of decades of different experiences with Europeans and their economy, which had been determined ultimately by the number and character of human and nonhuman natural resources of the islands. Despite these expressions of their feelings, the people perceived the government's response with local councils and courts to be slow and still on its own terms.

For all this obvious discontent with the British administration there was no hint of nationalism, if with that term the Solomons are perceived as a political unit. Both the Gizo protesters and the Chair and Rule followers wanted reforms within the existing structure of British rule, whereas the La'aka cultists wanted to substitute one foreign power for another. This could hardly be interpreted as a desire for independence, even on a regional or island level. Besides a complete return to the old way, which no one seemed to want entirely, the Solomon Islanders knew of few other alternatives. The war was to change that situation and ideas shared by Fallowes and his friends would be merged with the visionary utterances of the Kwaio priests and transform the result into a common, impatient cry for political change.

CHAPTER 13

World War II and aftermath
(c. 1942–1955)

But when the enemy came they all evacuated. There was no
British white walking or living openly. Almost all saving a
few had been evacuated from the island. Previous to this we
believe we would be safely protected and safeguarded by
them but since we witnessed all those happenings all the
natives hopes utterly gone, and all what we expected was the
fact of falling into the hands of the enemy to be made slaves
of them.

Ariel Sisili, Manifesto

Like other Anglo-Saxon people, they [the Americans] were
remarkably friendly and sympathetic to other people's
natives.

Margaret Mead, *New Lives for Old*

THE SUDDEN INVASION of the defenseless Solomon Islands by the Japanese
and the evacuation of most Europeans left in their wake a legacy of
doubt and, especially to eastern Solomon Islanders, distrust toward
their colonial rulers. Although the Japanese were driven back and the
majority of the Melanesians remained loyal to Britain, the distrust
deepened among eastern Solomon Islanders when they saw the British
defense authorities take away from them the largesse bestowed by generous American troops. This, and the long history of discontent with the
colonial presence, led many Solomon Islanders to question the status
quo, an inquiry that was aided by sympathetic American personnel.
Out of this questioning grew Maasina Rule, a declaration of Malaitan
identity. Similar processes occurred elsewhere in the Solomons, varying
with the particular history and circumstances of the groups of people
involved. In the west the growth of the Eto movement and the Christian Fellowship Church transformed a foreign mission into a local
church; for all its gentleness, this was no less an assertion of Solomon
Islander consciousness than the more publicized and vociferous Maasina
Rule of the east.

285

In a few short years the war wiped out much of the colonial world of previous decades. Very slowly, the government rebuilt the colonial structure, but the old European commercial interests never quite regained their former dominance. Their absence, especially in the years following the war, meant that in order to get the external economy functioning at all, the government had to become both merchant and shipper for those producers who had not fled the invasion—the Solomon Islanders. Although the British government had no particular timetable for the future of the Solomons, the Colonial Development and Welfare Act set the protectorate on the development road with funds allocated for social, economic, and educational projects. The old certainty of the British imperialist, called into question after World War I, crumbled in the 1940s as Britain's war debts mounted and the Asian colonies gained their independence. In the Solomons, Maasina Rule and other political movements forced a new breed of postwar administrator to take note of local aspirations. The new attitude was reinforced by the protectorate's accountability to the Colonial Office as the source of the development funds that constituted about half of the Solomons' total income.

War and the Solomon Islanders

The outbreak of war in Europe in September 1939 had few immediate consequences for the Solomon Islands. Rubber reached such premium prices that a few companies, including the Solomon Islands Development Company (Burns Philp), thought it worthwhile to train tappers for work on neglected rubber trees. The price of copra rose, but optimism among the European planters quickly faded as more and more hindrances to shipping and marketing appeared with the intensification of the conflict. Rumors about enemy planes shelling their villages spread quickly among Solomon Islanders, but were contradicted by government and other Europeans.[1] The Japanese bombing of Pearl Harbor in December 1941 changed everything.

Allied forces, including Australians and New Zealanders, were concentrated in Europe, and, with the American fleet weakened, the Japanese advanced rapidly into Southeast Asia and the Pacific, with Australia as the ultimate goal. By January 1942 the Japanese had captured Rabaul, the administrative capital of New Guinea. Moving east virtually unopposed, they occupied the Shortlands in March, Tulagi and north Guadalcanal in May. Trying to get to Port Moresby by sea, the Japanese naval forces were confronted by a United States and Australian task force in the Coral Sea and were driven back. A month later the Battle of Midway weakened Japan's control of the seas and gave America the margin it needed to begin the second invasion of Tulagi and

Photo 24. Marines landing supplies on Guadalcanal, November 1942. *(US Marine Corps)*

Guadalcanal (Photo 24). There, the fighting between the Japanese and the American forces reached a crescendo in November 1942, involving an estimated 80,000 men, of whom 30,000 were Japanese. Regarding it as a temporary reverse, the Japanese withdrew and established air bases at Munda and Kolombangara. But they were constantly harassed by Allied forces using information supplied by coastwatchers working behind the Japanese lines. In June 1943 a massive Allied offensive retook most of the western Solomons—Rendova, Munda, Vella Lavella, and Mono. Except for Alu and Fauro, pockets on Choiseul, and some minor mopping up, the Solomons were free of Japanese by 1944. Guadalcanal remained a major American base and staging center for the northern advance of the Allied forces during the rest of the war.[2]

For most Solomon Islanders the war had lasted less than two years, yet its impact was considerable. The most enduring but least tangible effect was the change in the relationship between Europeans and Solomon Islanders. The status of the Europeans would never be quite the same again. The war brought about a loss of face for the whites, a process that had begun in the Solomons before the Japanese appeared. Following the fall of Rabaul in January 1942, many civilian Europeans fled the Solomons on the *Malaita* and the *Kurimarau*. Burns Philp withdrew or tied up its "mosquito" fleet (small interisland vessels) in the Solomons, managing to take or direct most of the native crew back to their homes. Many planters, on the other hand, left their laborers stranded, unfed, and unpaid. Although government officers were subsequently able to organize the repatriation of most of those laborers, what trust had existed between them and the white planters was shattered. Eventual payment of back wages could not mitigate this betrayal in the hour of crisis. Hundreds of Malaitan and south Guadalcanal men would not forget it.

Other than the monitoring of Japanese activities by an Australian air force seaplane, the Europeans had made no obvious attempts to oppose the enemy's progress. A government-ordered scorched-earth policy saw the large-scale destruction of physical plant even before the enemy advanced. All the district officers could do, with the help of headmen and chiefs, was to prepare the people for the inevitable, telling them to make secret gardens and build shelters inland in the mountains, to avoid contact with the enemy and, where possible, to bring news of Japanese movements to the government.[3]

Missionaries made individual decisions to stay or leave. Except for the Reverend Mr. Silvester and Nurse Farland, the European Methodists left, as did most of the South Sea Evangelical Mission. Goldie, who had never turned his back on his flock, was stranded outside the Solomons when the Japanese came and until 1945 was prevented by the government from returning. All the Adventists left. Bishop Baddeley of the Melanesian Mission and some of his staff stayed on in hiding, as did the Catholic Bishop Aubin and all his Marist priests, brothers, and nuns, four of whom were later murdered on Guadalcanal by the Japanese.[4]

The final evacuation of about 200 Europeans assembled at Tulagi was on Burns Philp's *Morinda* on 7 February, a week before the fall of Singapore. It was an undignified affair, with the ship initially hindered from sailing because of government hesitancy and red tape. Harried by a Japanese bomber, the loading of the vessel was chaotic, with those Solomon Islanders who had not fled witnessing a panicky rabble of officials (including military personnel from Bougainville), planters, and missionaries struggling to get aboard. Only 24 Chinese had managed to get out of the Solomons by February. Of a total of some 200 scattered around the islands, approximately a quarter ended up safe in Sydney, and half of them were children. The rest of the Chinese were left behind to face an enemy noted for its hatred of their race. Missionaries and Solomon Islanders sheltered them until the coastwatchers managed to move most of them from their scattered hideouts to San Cristobal in 1942–1943.[5]

The change in the relationship between Islanders and Europeans that began with the hurried evacuation was not to be completed until the war in the islands had finished and all the troops had gone. Meanwhile, more immediate effects of the war were being felt. At first Solomon Islanders were terrified by the fighting. The scale of operations, to say nothing of the great sea battles and overhead dogfights, was bewilder-ing. For example, in north Guadalcanal from 7 to 9 August 1942, 10,000 Americans, equal in number to two-thirds of the island's popula-tion, came ashore. On Vella Lavella 4600 US troops landed on the Mbi-lua coast on 15 August 1943, with 2300 tons of supplies.[6] Besides their initial shock, the most immediate problem for the village people was health. With the invasion, almost all the medical services that had been provided by the missions and the government broke down, compound-ing the trying conditions of living in temporary bush shelters. Many men left their families to join the Solomon Islands Labour Corps (SILC) to assist the Allies, but their absence from some areas, such as south Guadalcanal, caused hardship and cases of near starvation as the work force available for making new gardens decreased. An officer touring the weather coast of Guadalcanal to recruit laborers found that by December 1943, only 25 percent of the population were "robust," 65 percent "emaciated," and 10 percent "sick or maimed."[7] On Malaita wartime disruption was exacerbated by an extremely poor sweet-potato crop during 1943. Contact with troops of both sides introduced epi-demics throughout the islands, causing many deaths, especially of chil-dren. In many areas, such as the Shortlands where the Japanese occupa-tion lasted three years, the birthrate declined or fell off completely, probably because the women became anovulous as a result of the unset-tled conditions and scarcity of food. The overall population of the Solo-mons declined, in some areas such as south Guadalcanal by as much as 14 percent.[8]

After the evacuation of Tulagi, Resident Commissioner Marchant removed himself and a skeleton staff to the bush behind 'Aoke on Malaita. All remaining civil servants were commissioned into a military administration, the BSIP Defence Force, with former district officers as captains. These captains—Clemens, Kennedy, Wilson, Forster, and Trench, assisted closely by Horton, Josselyn, and Waddell as members of the Royal Australian Navy—became the backbone of the coast-watchers, an organization spying and reporting on the enemy to the Allies and later involved in rescuing crashed Allied pilots. Some old island hands, planters and traders like Andy Andresson, Ken Hay, Car-den Seton, Snowy Rhoades, Clarry Hart, Lafe Schroeder, and Mrs. Boye on Vanikolo, along with missionaries like Charles Fox, chose to remain in the Solomons as members of the coastwatchers.

Solomon Islanders were directly involved with coastwatching. Be-cause their lives depended on it the coastwatchers lived in close contact with the people in the bush of the western and central Solomons, sus-taining morale and a semblance of government. For all their individual courage, the coastwatchers would not have survived long without the support of the Islanders. And with few exceptions, the people succored them. Former policemen like Vouza, Goratara, Chak, Deke, and Gamu, and government employees like Daniel Pule and Silas Sitai rallied to assist with scouting, fighting, and foraging while headmen and chiefs like Ngatu, Tevai, Levai Papaku, and Peter Tavoto carried information to and from their people who picked off small Japanese patrols and rescued downed Allied airmen. The Solomon Islander sons of the old traders, Harry Wickham, Geoffrey Kuper, and Bill Bennett extended the coastwatcher network. The magnificent contribution of civilian Solomon Islanders and some six hundred Defence Force members to the war effort is a matter of record. Both coastwatchers and later Allied troops relied for their lives on Solomon Islanders and vice versa. Mutual dependence bred mutual reassessment and often respect.[9]

For the first time for some of these former district officers, the Solomon Islanders of the western and central Solomons were seen as capable human beings. As Josselyn, former acting district officer of Guadalcanal, found:

> The loyalty of the islanders never faltered, even in the most trying circumstances. Their hatred of the enemy was intense when they saw how cruelly and wantonly he behaved. They revealed qualities of body and mind which had not been suspected prior to the war and carried out tasks which had previously been thought to be beyond their capacities.[10]

Solomon Islanders perceived their former masters simply as men—vulnerable, no longer omniscient, and now in need of them. Old images were revised.

The reasons for Solomon Islander support are not difficult to discover. There had been obvious dissatisfaction with aspects of colonial rule before the war in both the western and the central Solomons. The "tax strike" in Gizo and the Chair and Rule movement bore testimony to that, just as did the Nggela people's burning of the hated law books in the judicial commissioner's house at Tulagi following the European evacuation. Nonetheless, the British were the only *masta* the people knew and prewar protest had been associated with missionaries loyal to the British flag. Moreover, Japanese suzerainty was never an attractive alternative. Unlike the early days of the New Guinea campaign, there was only a very brief honeymoon period when the Japanese offered friendship and persuasion to the indigenous people. Occupation of the Solomons came at a time when the Japanese had overextended themselves and were soon desperate for food and supplies. Their behavior won little respect. They looted churches, forced food and labor at gun point, tortured people, pillaged gardens and coconuts, and did not even promise payment.[11]

Malaita, San Cristobal, Santa Cruz, and adjacent islands were not occupied by the Japanese; here, where dissatisfaction with the government was greatest, there was no opportunity to test the loyalty of the

Photo 25. Solomon Islanders with American friends. Matthew Lova of Guadalcanal soundly whipped Pfc. Wm. F. Fey at checkers. Watching, from left, Sgt. James Sepsis, Jacob Cobro of Guadalcanal, Lt. Cmdr. Paal. (Others not identified.) 29 August 1943. *(US Marine Corps)*

people to the British or for them to weigh up the relative disadvantages of the new invader against the old. However, men from these traditional sources of labor and from south Guadalcanal, another area that saw virtually no Japanese, were actively involved in the war effort as stevedores and carriers assisting the Americans.

Like the Japanese, the Americans wanted to conscript native labor, but the Islanders never knew it. The British administrators, with an eye to the preservation of village life and probable large-scale desertion should conscription be enforced, insisted on a policy of volunteerism. The Solomon Islands Labour Corps (SILC) started recruiting in mid-1943; its organizing officers were mainly returned former managers of the big plantation concerns, such as Levers' C. V. Widdy, but included some government officials. Despite the weakening of the population due to the war, the corps had 2500 members at its maximum strength.[12] Although they occasionally came into the firing line, this disadvantage was more than offset for the Solomon Islanders by the excitement of new experiences and the extra money and goods they were given by the troops. Many may have disliked the British, but all liked the Americans (Photo 25).

From the chaos of war: Maasina Rule

The material wealth and the generosity of the Americans impressed the Solomon Islanders. The Americans gave all kinds of goods to the SILC men and to the people in villages near their camps. "Joe" (US soldiers) paid well for personal services and curios. They invited the Islanders to eat with them and jovially brushed aside the embarrassment of men who had never before been invited to sit at table with white men and did not know how to use cutlery. Many Solomon Islanders experienced the open-handedness of the Americans and saw hundreds if not thousands of them, including Blacks, attend Christian worship. For the Islanders this was the first tangible demonstration that white and black men could live together as brothers in an orderly, Christian manner. Yet they saw little evidence of these qualities in their colonial masters. SILC men were paid £1 a month by the British, but thought this insignificant in terms of what the Americans freely gave. Some soldiers claimed that the American forces gave the British authorities money for the men's wages, but that the government only passed on a small portion of it. This was widely believed by Solomon Islanders. Toward the end of the war, as former SILC men returned home, their officers, who were mainly ex-planters with an eye to future labor needs, began to object to the quantity of goods the men tried to bring aboard ships to ferry back to Malaita, San Cristobal, or south Guadalcanal. Many former plantation laborers, especially the bush Malaitans, had no liking for these old *mastas* of Levers and Burns Philp, even in prewar times. Their antipathy was intensified by the knowledge that the planters had abandoned their labor in the face of the invaders. Now this same small group of white men was trying to deprive the SILC men of what was rightfully theirs in order, it was rumored, that the officers could in future sell goods in their own plantation stores.[13] As some members of the Labour Corps complained to their officers:

> We came here without anything, but we were willing to die, so why does the government want to stop us from having these things? We should get something because of the risk. Don't spoil things for us. You whitemen never go away empty-handed so why do they [British] want to do this to the section [of the Labour Corps].[14]

The Americans sympathized with the men on this, just as they had on their complaints about the prewar regime. Some held a number of discussions with the men near Honiara, urging them to tell their leaders to negotiate with the British for a better deal. The Malaitans were forced to admit that all the leaders they had were petty local chiefs or elders or simply government headmen.[15] Without greater unity, as the colonial government had so long known, they were virtually powerless.

Many Islanders wanted the new life they shared with the Americans to continue and were determined to make this a reality. Groups of north Malaitans and Nggela people, hoping to coerce the Americans by their generosity, tried to donate several hundreds of dollars to the American commanders in an unsuccessful attempt to "buy" the American presence and keep the British out. Pro-American and anti-British feeling grew, especially as it became obvious that the British were reasserting their authority. Following the Labour Corps experience and talks with Americans on Guadalcanal during 1943–1944, a group of Malaitans, including two 'Are'are men—Nori and Aliki Nono'ohimae—and later Timothy George of south Malaita conducted meetings on Malaita that were anti-British in sentiment. Their aims were to create a unity on Malaita, a brotherhood from which to derive a unified front to negotiate with the British on local matters, especially the control by Malaitans of their own island. The movement that grew up became known as Maasina (brotherhood) Rule or Marching Rule. As five of the nine leading chiefs of the movement were members of the SSEM, they used the village contacts and the basic literacy in Pijin and Bible English provided by the mission to spread their main ideas from the heartland of the movement in 'Are'are throughout the island. By late 1945 they had achieved this and were instructing followers to stay on Malaita and work for its development. They imposed a head tax of £1 on all adult males, to be used to aid the movement and for education and economic development, a demand fairly easily met initially because of the American cash in circulation on the island. They collected, codified, and wrote down the customs of each region. Locally constituted courts, using this code of customary law as a basis, ruled on various internal and parochial disputes.[16]

The protectorate government: Response, repression, and rapprochement

As the government gradually reestablished control and the Americans withdrew in 1945, the newly created local councils on Malaita provided both vehicles and covers for the movement. Most of the Maasina Rule followers saw the small councils as government creations, not something of their own.[17] Malaitans had no monopoly on this opinion; many in the western Solomons had reached similar conclusions.

Before the war was over Major Clemens, as district officer in New Georgia, tried to influence appointments to the council, and attempted to get it to introduce regulations based on what he believed local "custom" to be. But trying to introduce such regulations as legalized prostitution and a reversion to pagan marriage practices did not appeal to the staunch Christians of New Georgia.[18] This kind of ineptitude bred

resentment. The New Georgian chiefs' opinions were best expressed by
Ngatu, who told Clemens: "You want to make the Council a farce. You
want to apparently transfer certain powers and authority to us, and yet
are unwilling to trust us and relinquish such powers yourself."[19]

To mark the end of the war in August 1945, Clemens addressed an
assembly of headmen and told them that "a new age had dawned," that
from now on the white man and black man would be one; some of the
headmen simply did not believe him.[20]

In part this suspicion of the government sprang from bitter prewar
experience, but it was not reduced by Goldie's vociferous and now near-
obsessional jealousy of the government's increasing role in affairs. Away
from the absolutes of wartime, Clemens' successors, both in New Georgia and elsewhere in the west, faced the difficult task of trying to convince people that the government was now interested in having councils
and courts that genuinely reflected the wishes of the people in both
membership and practice. Despite some reluctance by headmen to take
on expanded responsibilities, by 1950 these bodies did consist of members nominated by the people. Although the president and the headmen
were still government appointees, in most cases they were also hereditary chiefs.[21]

On populous Malaita the government did not have the staff to monitor the development of local councils closely. Many government headmen were appointed by the district officers as presidents, some supporting their *mastas*, but some joining Maasina Rule. As the movement
grew, these local government councils appear to have been seen as
emphasizing the differences among Malaitan societies, whereas the
Maasina Rule ideal, a central all-Malaita council with its own chief,
would symbolize all that was common to Malaitans and the acceptance
of local differences and religious affiliation within the bonds of broth-
erly tolerance.

When headmen loyal to the government and jealous of SSEM leaders,
all of whom supported the movement, realized that Maasina Rule was
using the councils for its own ends, they made adverse reports to the
government. Some Malaitans, especially in the north, held hopes of an
American return, an idea reinforced by the sporadic appearance of US
ships and planes throughout the islands on hydrographic survey until
1949. In the north too, economic progress before the war had been most
evident, and here the loyalists to government, led by headmen like
Maekali and Kakaluae, were concentrated. Consequently the struggle
between pro- and anti–Maasina Rule groups was strongest here, and
opinions became the most extreme, with Maasina Rule followers talking
more and more of revolt. Meanwhile in the south, cooperation with the
government for the wider aims of the movement was seen as a possibil-

ity, a view shared by the government until early 1947. At a big meeting at 'Aoke in November 1946, Maasina Rule leaders set the desired minimum monthly wage for laborers at £12 a month, reasoning that with a higher wage fewer men would have to leave Malaita. At this stage the general emphasis was still on friendly relations with the government. However, conflict with the government headman resulted in the arrest of one of the leading Maasina Rule chiefs from Lau in February 1947.[22] In retaliation Maasina Rule leaders announced a general strike in the form of a labor boycott. In June, at a meeting of 7000 with the district commissioner at 'Aoke, the angry northern leaders overplayed their hand by demanding rather than requesting recognition of Maasina Rule and its rights to determine the arbitration of customary law. The tone of this meeting and the subsequent strike polarized the protagonists. From Malaita, the disaffection spread to neighboring islands, including Guadalcanal; parts of the eastern and central Solomons were humming with talk of Maasina Rule during 1946 and 1947.[23] New Georgia people attended meetings with Malaita leaders, but regarded the movement as a Malaitan one, of little relevance to them.[24] This unrest came at a crucial time, when the government was planning the rehabilitation of the copra industry for which labor was essential.[25] Seeing its power slipping away the government "got the wind up," in Goldie's words, and overreacted.[26] Reports of coercion of others by overzealous movement members, including local Melanesian Mission clergy, provided a convenient justification for the arrest of the leaders on Malaita, Guadalcanal, and San Cristobal. Using a western Solomons militia, in August 1947 the government seized these men and charged them with sedition.[27]

On Nggela and Santa Isabel many saw the continuity between Fallowes' ideas and Maasina Rule. A representative from war hero Vouza of Guadalcanal brought to Isabel a bowdlerized version of this connection, introducing heavy "cargo cult" overtones. The Isabel people, knowing the truth, became sceptical of Maasina Rule, which finally lost support in the wake of a combination of government and Melanesian Mission opposition in late 1947.[28] The trend was much the same on Guadalcanal, although the Marau district with its Roman Catholic, 'Are'are-speaking colony long remained sympathetic to the movement.[29] On Malaita and in SSEM-controlled parts of San Cristobal, the government's actions created martyrs and intensified opposition. The people fortified their coastal villages and posted guards to oversee exit and entry. An attempted government census preparatory to the reintroduction of the hated head tax met with mainly passive noncooperation. The government arrested hundreds of people for this and later nonpayment of taxes.[30] Its attitude bewildered many villagers who had seen Maasina Rule's objectives as compatible with those of the government.[31]

Among some, confusion and stress revived hope of American intervention and "cargo"—a hope sometimes fostered by local leaders who
themselves manufactured indications of secret visits by Americans. This
strong "cargo" element among the ordinary followers of the movement
seemed fantastic to many European administrators and attracted their
scorn.[32]

Eventually the government realized it was at an impasse. Its jails
were overflowing and Malaitans were still refusing to cooperate. Although its long-term aims, as exemplified in the projected consolidation
of the smaller councils into island or regional councils, were not all that
different from Maasina Rule's, the lack of genuine dialogue had blinded
both sides to this. Maasina Rule followers wanted an all-Malaita Council that would legitimately represent the feelings of all Malaitans to the
government. The government wanted to develop councils, including an
eventual island-wide council, along certain lines so that the wishes and
workings of government could be translated to and understood by the
people.[33] Both wanted to talk, neither had particularly wanted to listen,
and neither had really come to terms with the considerable barriers to
communication inherent in any cross-cultural interaction—barriers
that were exacerbated by the entire colonial context.

In the early months of 1950 there were signs that the movement was
losing some momentum on Malaita. Continued stress, illness, especially
malaria in the big coastal settlements, the obvious suffering of women
and children, the defection of some northern followers when neither the
Americans nor their cargo materialized, and the abandonment of a proposed mass assembly led by Ariel Sisili of Kwara'ae at 'Aoke in the face
of solid government opposition all combined to weaken commitment to
Maasina Rule. Perceiving this as a possible time for rapprochement, the
government, led by a new commissioner, Gregory-Smith, had discussions with the imprisoned leaders and released them after they had promised to cooperate with the government.[34]

By the early 1950s the government had regained control, if the collection of the head tax was any index. Men offered in numbers for plantation work, as their money had been spent and cash was needed for the
tax—except that now the head tax funded the island councils.[35] In the
view of the majority of the Maasina Rule followers the movement was
successful; in 1953 it achieved its major aim of running Malaita in the
form established by the Malaita Council, along with other regional
councils in the protectorate. Continued resistance was unnecessary, a
view that was reaffirmed as Malaita became the object of many government projects. To some, especially those in the Kwara'ae-Kwaio hinterland, the council was a sham, controlled still by the government; in
this isolated area small resistance cults continued to appear until strong
government action suppressed them and imprisoned their leaders.[36]

Maasina Rule: A popular political movement

To some extent Maasina Rule was an umbrella movement sheltering Christian and pagan, hard-headed big-men politicians wanting economic and political recognition of the identity of their following, local clan elders wanting a return to the old ways with the young men under their control, and dreamers who lived in hope of the millennium. Because it was sufficiently flexible to contain all these aspirations, its appeal was wide. Although for a time both the government and the private sector viewed the movement as revolutionary, it was more accurately reformist in nature and aims and still in the mold of prewar movements. Many observers may have thought that this movement did not go far enough, yet perhaps the Melanesians in Maasina Rule, not given to suicidal protests, saw fairly realistically, in terms of the inheritance of fifty years of colonial rule and of their own culture, the strength of the existing constraints. Of them it could be said:

> Men make their own history, but they do not make it just as they please; they do not make it under circumstances chosen by themselves, but under given circumstances directly encountered and inherited from the past. The tradition of all the generations of the dead weighs like a nightmare on the brain of the living. And just when they seem involved in revolutionizing themselves and things, in creating something that has never existed before, it is precisely in such periods of revolutionary crisis that they anxiously conjure up the spirits of the past to their service and borrow names, battle cries and costumes from them in order to act out the new scene of world history in this time-honoured disguise and this borrowed language.[37]

On one level, Maasina Rule was just a composite of prewar elements: The underlying discontent with the colonial order was not new, as the Chair and Rule movement had shown. A strong belief in the importance of certain cultural values had found expression in objections to government insensitivity to the question of adultery and punishment. The emphasis on brotherhood struck a familiar chord among the Christians. Through contact on plantations, pagan Malaitans too realized that they shared religious concepts and beliefs common to most of the island. And in this alien cultural environment Islanders had learned that they could live together despite their different origins. Pijin, an artefact of the trade and plantation era, assisted them in learning this, just as it did with the communication of the ideas of Maasina Rule. On a less ideological plane, the emphasis on big central villages and crop production was as much an echo of the policies of prewar administrators and missionaries as it was an emulation of the American army camps and the military farm at Ilu on Guadalcanal. Moreover, important big-men had traditionally always been able to draw large numbers of people to swell the size of their own hamlet. The various functionaries of the movement—"head chiefs," "full chiefs," and "duties"—had close parallels in the prewar local government structure of district and village headmen and village constables. Malaita was divided among nine head chiefs into nine administrative districts, almost identical to the prewar divisions of the British, with Timothy George as head chief of Small Malaita and nominal head of the movement. The SSEM leadership network was established long before the war by missionaries who, although they doubted the Melanesians' ability to govern themselves, were convinced of their spiritual maturity. In the mid-forties, its members demonstrated their rejection of headmen who, as government puppets, had formerly been their rivals to local power. The tax Maasina Rule imposed was certainly a colonial artefact, but it also had its antecedent in the petition of 1912, when north Malaitans asked that the "collection" be spent on their own island's development. Likewise, the government-introduced councils were well under way in several areas before the Japanese invasion and provided the model for Maasina Rule assemblies. In fact, one of the great ideologues of the movement, Aliki Nono'ohimae in the disturbed 'Are'are district, developed the government's concept of a local council, when in 1943 he proposed to his people a council of traditional 'Are'are chiefs—before he joined the Labour Corps and talked with the Americans.

The collection and codification of traditional "custom" in these council areas had also been commenced under the aegis of the government. The courts ruled on local matters, but handed over murder cases to the British central government just as the district officers had done before the war. "Strikes" or boycotts by plantation labor had been tried by Malaitans in the 1930s, although they were by no means well organized. Hatred of the indenture system and low-paid plantation work was a perennial theme, expressed most dramatically in the demand for higher wages, the new wage being identical to that wanted by the Chair and Rule movement. This was no coincidence. Aliki Nono'ohimae and Harisimae, friend and mentor of Nori, along with several 'Are'are policemen, had attended Chair and Rule meetings on Nggela in 1939 and listened to Fallowes' pleas for them to organize themselves into a political force. What these men heard from the Americans reinforced Chair and Rule ideas.[38] Even the "cargo cult" aspect of Maasina Rule, involving the coming of the Americans, was a prewar element of the La'aka cult. When the war temporarily fulfilled the prophecy, the continuance and spread of such beliefs were guaranteed.

What was different and threatening to the British about Maasina Rule was its size, organization, and persistence. In geographical scope, Maasina Rule penetrated further than the Chair and Rule movement, taking in at its height all of Malaita, Nggela, Santa Isabel, eastern and southern Guadalcanal, Ulawa, and San Cristobal, its spread aided by

traditional contacts and mission linkages. Its following was consequently greater. Despite significant regional variations inevitable in
such a popular movement, it endured well into the fifties because, for
the first time, a large and fluid leadership group, many of whom met
with each other both during and after the war, shared a set of common
aspirations intensified by their experiences with the Americans. On
Malaita in particular they used the existing, totally indigenous structure
of the SSEM network of teachers in the Christian villages to create a
completely new kind of unity.

The Society for the Development of Native Races—western Guadalcanal

Although Maasina Rule took the spotlight because of its very magnitude, other movements also grew in the less developed areas of the eastern Solomons. One of these arose in the Ndi-Nggai region of Guadalcanal. There, Mathew Belamatanga who had had close contact with
the Americans during the war, started the Society for the Development
of Native Races in 1947. As well as earlier training by the Roman Catholic mission, Belamatanga had received some education from the Americans in arithmetic and geography and was sent political literature from
America after the forces left Guadalcanal. His basic tenets came from
the United Nations charter—freedom from want and fear, and freedom
of religion and speech. After one year the movement extended across
most of western Guadalcanal. Its philosophy centered on economic
development, including better formal education, but, like Maasina
Rule, followed the practice of codifying customary law and holding
courts to establish local autonomy. Its main political aim was representation on the protectorate's Advisory Council, with ultimate independence a distant and rather vague goal. According to Bathgate, in order
to gain and keep his following, Mathew Belamatanga exploited the
hope of some people that the Americans would come back, but he saw
future relations between the United States and an independent Solomon
Islands in terms of an alliance, rather than US domination. As in
Maasina Rule, coercion was sometimes used by Belamatanga's followers
against those less sympathetic to the movement; and once this became
known to government officers, they had a case for suppression of the
movement. Like the Maasina Rule leaders, Belamatanga and other
leaders were tried on charges of sedition and imprisoned.[39]

The western Solomons and the Christian Fellowship Church

Predictably the western Solomons, with a different history from the
eastern islands, produced their own kind of movement against the

strongest perceived political power, the Methodist Mission. The advent of the American forces in the western Solomons showed Goldie's followers that, although the Methodist Mission had been an equal of the government before the war, its resources were insignificant in terms of the material wealth of the Americans. By the time Goldie returned to Roviana in 1945, there had been 30,000 Americans camped around the mission land. It took the Methodists years to recover from the material losses caused by war—for almost three years a frustrated Goldie did not even have a ship to visit the outer islands regularly. The mission had given the western people some knowledge of the world of Europeans, but in their eyes it had failed to prepare them for the magnitude of the experience that was thrust on them with the coming of the planes and ships of mighty armies. The mission had given them literacy and spread Roviana as the lingua franca, but had failed to teach them English, which after their war experience seemed to be the key to the great world beyond.

The leader of the new movement was Silas Eto.[40] Before the war, in the isolated and mission-neglected Kusaghe region of New Georgia, Eto had been sent by Goldie back to his own village as teacher, contrary to normal mission practice. After the war, Eto wrote to President Roosevelt to urge the Americans to take over the Solomons. Believing such an outcome was inevitable anyway, since Americans were still in evidence, Eto hoped to steal a march on other local church leaders by associating himself with the new rulers. In the fifties the British arrested Eto for sedition, just as they had arrested the Maasina Rule leaders. But unlike those men, Eto was backed by someone who knew the limits of the white man's law. An old and ailing Goldie threatened legal action and the teacher was released, thus reinforcing his growing status in the eyes of his followers.

Eto had long been dissatisfied with aspects of Methodist teaching, organization, and worship and wished to assert a Melanesian presence in church leadership. His ambition meshed with the social malaise felt by many New Georgians. Their world was rapidly changing. The war had disrupted the pattern and predictability of their former church-centered lives; the mission was preoccupied with rebuilding its schools and other institutions; the government was asserting a more positive presence than before the war, with new schemes tried and abandoned with bewildering speed; and Goldie had died in 1954 and most of the old chiefs who had been among the early converts of Methodism were all dead. The younger chiefs, who had proven their abilities to hold the mission and people together during the war, saw their religious authority threatened by a rising generation of church-educated catechists and teachers under the control of a new European chairman and clergy who were not as sensitive to the political status quo as Goldie had been. To

Eto and his followers, including many of the chiefs, he, the "Holy Mama," was the natural inheritor of the mantle of the dead Goldie. He began to establish his own breakaway church, which became known in the fifties as the Christian Fellowship Church, soon attracting hundreds of followers. Significantly, Eto's protest focused more on the real political force in the western Solomons—the monolithic authority vested in the chairman of the Methodist Mission based at favored Roviana—rather than on the apparent authority, the government. Moreover, in trying to perform many of the welfare functions of the prewar Methodist Mission, functions increasingly taken over by the government, Eto was asserting in his own way that Solomon Islanders were capable of organizing themselves in such matters. The economic element was minor, although the Kusaghe core resented the mission's tight-fisted attitude to their area in the last years of the Depression, when its range of services to the people was declining everywhere. Power and the quest for recognition and self-expression were more the impetus and goals of Eto's movement than was any economic motive.

These movements of the immediate postwar years shared a common element. They all aimed at increased autonomy from constricting, European-imposed institutions. It would be an exaggeration to claim that they were expressions of Solomon Islands–wide nationalism, but, in terms of the pre-protectorate polity, they were certainly manifestations of regionalism, a new unity and shared feeling across large areas, involving sometimes entire island groups. To a great extent, the introduced institutions provided the structures for the development of this unity; but the Solomon Islanders sought ways to bend the new structures to their own ends when such institutions oppressed them. In the eyes of Europeans, fragmentation, local loyalties, and parochialism characterized Melanesian society throughout the prewar years. Yet, by the mid-forties and the fifties groups of Solomon Islanders, many of whom had once been deadly enemies, were able to organize themselves into movements sufficiently large and cohesive to force both civil and religious authorities to take their wishes seriously for the first time. Despite the prejudices on both sides, the Solomon Islanders found the Europeans increasingly willing to listen.

"Patching up a frayed edge of Empire": 1943–1955

What Solomon Islanders did not know was that some colonial officials[41] also had plans for a very different postwar Solomons. As part of the bureaucratic machinery established by the Colonial Development and Welfare Act of 1940, the long-serving secretary to the High Commission, H. Vaskess, under Luke and then Mitchell, prepared a detailed memorandum for the Colonial Office in August 1943, outlining pro-

posed policies for reconstruction and the reorganization of the administration in the Solomons. The war provided an opportunity for the High
Commission to take stock, to consider the future of the Solomons and
the implications of events like Fallowes' Chair and Rule movement, relatively free of the presence of the "commercials"—Europeans with
vested economic interests in the islands. The war had also brought the
little-known Solomons onto the front pages of the world's newspapers.
Now "public opinion," especially in America, was a consideration in
government planning for the future of the Solomons.

The plan was critical of prewar policies, especially the concept that
the "Solomons must support themselves" and the plantation-based
economy that had resulted in a "starvation of public services" and expatriation of profits. It recommended radical changes: "native self-government" through the councils; eventual Solomon Islander representation on the Advisory Council; localization of the lower levels of the
public service within eight to ten years; vast extension of public services,
especially education and health; the establishment of cooperatives;
diversification of the agricultural base of the economy and control of it,
including plantations, by Solomon Islanders; and the assessment and
exploitation of minerals, fisheries, and forests. For greater efficiency
and improved morale, the plan recommended partial integration of the
expatriate public service with Fiji's, as a way of providing more promotion opportunities.[42] The public service had received much-needed parity of salary with other British Western Pacific territories in 1941; for
the first time the Solomons would no longer be a virtual dead-end to the
career of an officer.

For its time and place, the plan was a visionary and revolutionary
document. Its principles had a lasting influence and, in the long term,
many of its policies came to be implemented. Yet although the Colonial
Office supported the overall concept, it was cool to the idea of government resumption of plantations and distribution of them to Solomon
Islanders, mainly because evidence suggested that European planters
would soon abandon their plantations anyway—they were becoming
uneconomic in the postwar world. In 1945 a ten-year plan based generally on these policies was prepared by the High Commission, with a
notable lack of emphasis on the rehabilitation of commercial plantations. However, the British government rejected this plan, probably
because of its estimated cost of £2.25 million, preferring to give funds on
an ad hoc basis for individual projects.

A few of the early postwar administrators found it convenient to load
much of the blame for lack of progress in the protectorate onto Maasina
Rule. Although the labor shortage was exacerbated by the movement,
the reality was more complex. The war had destroyed the infrastructure
of the administration and, more significantly, the economy. Plantations,

driers, buildings, wharves, and ships were in ruins. The government, together with a returning trickle of planters and missionaries as well as many Solomon Islanders, did the best with what was at hand, buying or appropriating surplus materials left by the Americans. Postwar plant in the Solomons was an ugly amalgam of Quonset huts, Marsdon matting, galvanized iron, and barbed wire. British reconstruction followed the American grid: the concentration of US installations and roads at Honiara determined the site of the postwar capital, despite a far superior anchorage at devastated Tulagi. Unfortunately for all in the Solomons, the Americans destroyed or sank thousands of tons of useful heavy equipment and, of course, took their ships with them.[43]

Among the European planters waiting impatiently in Sydney for permission to return to the Solomons, there was certainly the will to start again, but not the means. The majority were mortgaged to the hilt, bankrupt, or in arrears with leases despite a wartime moratorium. Their plans to return, as with the big companies, hinged on whether or not the British would grant war damage compensation. After assessing damages, the British government in 1949 decided against it.[44] The small planters, except for a few of the coastwatchers and long-established families, were finished, the war completing what the Depression had begun. Even Carpenters and Burns Philp saw little future in restoring their dispersed and derelict properties, eventually selling them to the government, as Burns Philp's subsidiary, Solomon Islands Development Company, did with its assets at Tetere and Tetepare; to individuals, as with Luti to Carden Seton; or to Solomon Islanders, as with Manning Strait to the Kia villagers.[45] Levers, which had written off the book value of its plantations during the war, had a £250,000 depreciation reserve available. Encouraged by high postwar prices for copra and the seeming recovery of its estates from premature nutfall, the company decided to concentrate on its profitable holdings in the Russells as well as investigate other economic prospects, such as oil palms.[46] Levers' neighbor on the Russells, Fairymead, also returned to its estates.[47]

With their plantations and everyone else's ruined, both Burns Philp and Carpenters had nothing to encourage a return to their retail and merchant businesses, especially since they had no facilities left and practically all their indebted clients were either bankrupt, retired, or dead. Although in the late forties Burns Philp again became involved in shipping between Australia and the protectorate, its old dominance was never reestablished, in part because of its own shipping losses, but also because of the continuance of a wartime arrangement between the British Ministry of Food, the Western Pacific territories, and Australia to control the marketing and shipment of copra, and the loss of the mail subsidy in the wake of air transport and a range of other shippers.

With the copra industry at a virtual standstill and communications primitive, few other traders or retailers returned immediately to the Solomons. In order to stimulate trade and production among Solomon Islanders and to provide somewhere for them to spend their American dollars, the government extended its wartime "Trade Scheme." It established stores, stocked them with basic trade goods (partly war surplus items purchased from the American forces), and encouraged Solomon Islanders and anyone else to set up as independent storekeepers. Although the scheme prevented the entire collapse of the cash economy, it failed, particularly in the late forties, to satisfy the desire of many Solomon Islanders for a whole range of new commodities seen and sampled during the war. On Nggela, for example, entrepreneurial servicemen had supplied the people with small power launches. Once the Americans left so too did the source of fuel, batteries, spare parts, and mechanical knowledge.[48] Had it been satisfied, this immediate postwar diversification of consumer demand might have led to a great leap in Solomon Islander participation in the economy, but with only a small supply of a limited range of commodities at a few outlets, much of the momentum was either lost or transferred to involvement in political activities.

The government continued the agreement by which all copra, except Sydney-based Levers' copra, was purchased at an agreed annual price by the British Ministry of Food with a reciprocal guarantee of shipment. To collect the copra, the Solomons government set up a Copra Board, with the Trade Scheme outlets and Fairymead as agents. But not until 1947 was any copra was produced—a mere 494 tons.[49]

The slow recovery of the copra industry was offset to some extent by funds from Britain. The Colonial Development and Welfare Act (1940) and subsequent legislation at last brought annual project grants to the Solomon Islands. Had these projects been achieved immediately, they would have provided the basis for reconstruction and a modicum of social services for the Islanders. But although the total amounts allocated up to 1955 were low—about one-third of the estimated cost of the 1945 ten-year plan—the main difficulty was in spending the money. Until the mid-fifties, the plans of both the government and private concerns were bedevilled not only by poor international and internal shipping but also by lack of equipment and supplies—like steel and cement —and a shortage of trained workers. For years new government departments, such as Education and Forestry, existed practically in name only because no personnel could be found to run them. Even when staff were obtained, the turnover was rapid, and their brave new projects halted for a year or so until a new officer appeared with yet another scheme.[50] The Kia (Santa Isabel) and Hauhui (Malaita) community development schemes are examples. Set up in haste in the wake of Maasina Rule, they were abandoned by the government in the mid-fifties, with the hope that local councils would undertake similar projects. When highly specialized expertise was necessary the Solomons government had to wait its turn—not until 1952 was the Australian navy able to survey the wreck-strewn bottom of Gizo Harbour. Until then, and at considerable cost, overseas cargo to and from Gizo had to be transshipped in small craft from and to Honiara, the nearest port with facilities for overseas shipping.[51]

Although the rebuilding of the infrastructure of the economy and administration was painfully slow, two developments of significance emerged during the decade 1945–1955—the growth of local councils and the increasing participation of local producers in the economy. As Maasina Rule reinforced the High Commission's belief in the need for recognition of local and regional aspirations, the council system was extended and strengthened to provide institutionalized expression of political feeling. By 1956 all inhabited areas except isolated outlying islands like Ontong Java, Tikopia, and the Reef Islands were under some local govenment authority administering either one subdistrict, such as southeast Guadalcanal, or an entire island, such as Malaita. Although council members were still government appointees, the power of the councils had increased as they derived revenue from the head tax, the dog tax, and interest on bank deposits, as well as fines and fees from the Native Courts, which now dealt with minor civil and criminal cases, especially ones relating to local customary practice. The councils spent some of their income on administrative costs and buildings, but increasingly on rural health—by paying dressers and assisting with the new yaws campaign—and on village development. The central government took an active role by conducting training courses for headmen, members, and clerks as well as by explaining the functions of the various and frequently new government departments.[52]

In the national arena, the government's political education activities were negligible, but at this time its main aim was to contain troublesome local political movements. In typical British fashion, the administrators' conception of national political education was to start with the councils, with local self-government a far-off goal and, in the fullness of time, when the economy and society were ready, perhaps independence. The councils, troubled by problems inherent to a non–formally educated and mainly illiterate population, took central place in government thinking. Independence in the near future, even in fifty years, was not considered to be a possibility. Nonetheless, the lessons of Chair and Rule, Maasina Rule, and Belamatanga's demands were not lost on the administration. While leading political agitators were still in jail, the government in 1950 appointed the first of a succession of nominated native members to the Advisory Council. These men—women were not considered—had been or were to be important figures in the protectorate—Vouza, Paia, Talasasa, Kakaise, Ga'a, Sisili, and Sitai. Some, like Vouza, were selected to get them "on side," to neutralize their connection with movements like Maasina Rule, by showing them that governing was a complex task. Others, like Paia and Sitai, were selected because of their loyal service or leadership potential. The current president of the Malaita Council was always a member, but the rest were nominated from the remaining districts. Their contribution to debate was modest and, to the Europeans, sometimes focused on seemingly trivial issues—like what animals should be represented on the protectorate's coat of arms. The Malaitan, Salena Ga'a, objected to the turtle favored by representatives from the western Solomons, preferring the eagle with its traditional and totemic significance to most people from Malaita, Guadalcanal, and other parts of the eastern district. But that did not suit the "outer islands" of Santa Cruz and the Polynesian outliers, whose emblem became the frigate bird. Above all, of course, loomed the British heraldic lion, and no one questioned that.

Although they had no power, the presence of these Solomon Islanders on the Advisory Council was at least some acknowledgment that they had a role to play in their own government. This development, along with the transfer of the High Commission Secretariat to Honiara in 1953, meant that the government was now in a position to be more receptive to local opinion.[53]

The participation of Solomon Islanders in the economy far excelled their national political involvement. By the late 1940s Solomon Islanders were again making copra and selling it to the Trade Scheme or to itinerating Chinese traders. As well as working their own groves, some, Islanders applied for permission to work derelict European plantations in the western and central Solomons. The government, desperate to revive its economic base, encouraged such initiatives.[54] Because these two sources of copra are indistinguishable, it is difficult to say just how much copra was "native," but "plantation" copra made up about 52 percent of the total of 22,000 tons produced in 1956, when two-thirds of the 64,000 acres of prewar coconut plantations were being worked[55] (Table 9). These developments brought closer Marchant's 1940 prediction of "the natives" taking over and running the plantations. Certainly their slice of the export pie was gradually getting bigger: from 25 percent before the war, to about 48 percent in 1954, to 52.6 percent in 1956.[56] Slowly, because of the hiatus caused by the war, Solomon Islanders were reclaiming ownership of their first and most important export industry.

The diminished commercial importance of the expatriate sector was reflected in politics. The late return of the traders meant they had to compete with both the Trade Scheme and the Chinese, a number of whom were on the spot, having been left behind in the evacuation.[57]

TABLE 9
Value of exports of copra from Solomon Islands, 1947–1978 (f.o.b.)

Year	Volume (tons)	Value (£ 000)	Value (A$ 000)
1947[a]	494 [b]	—	
1948	3,899	154	
1949	8,318	495	
1950	11,238	681	
1951	14,395	959	
1952	12,566	1,012	
1953	16,488	1,332	
1954	19,022	1,623	
1955	19,988	1,683	
1956	22,542	1,621	
1957	17,316	1,214	
1958	20,437	1,481	
1959	21,043	2,197	
1960	19,460	1,563	
1961	24,276	1,519	
1962	22,400	1,411	
1963	23,092	1,669	
1964	23,431	1,762	
1965	24,536	2,221	
1966	20,344		3,027[c]
1967	24,434		3,629
1968	17,217		3,625
1969	23,463		3,471
1970	21,050		3,633
1971	26,192		3,825
1972	20,580		1,825
1973	15,188		2,813
1974	21,440		9,012
1975	27,042		4,661
1976	22,651		3,634
1977	26,490		7,988
1978	25,685		7,856

Sources: BSIP-AR 1948–1975; SI Statistics Office 1979.
Notes: [a] For 1941–42 plantation production remained at 60–70 percent, but little was exported, stocks being deliberately destroyed because of lack of shipping or later to avoid capture by Japanese.
[b] BSIP-AR for 1948 gave 494 tons exported, but SI Statistics Office 1979 gave 1,900 tons exported.
[c] The Solomons adopted Australian decimal currency in 1966, the conversion rate being one pound (£) to two dollars ($).

The traders complained about Chinese competition, but the government's attitude was that the European traders had to eliminate the Chinese from the marketplace by reducing profits, increasing the "scandalously low prices" paid for copra.[58] Nonetheless, the government was limiting the entry of Chinese other than former residents, partly because of fears of political undesirables with loyalties to Communist China, but mainly "to leave room for native storekeepers."[59] Many of the government's Trade Scheme outlets in the western Solomons had been run by Solomon Islanders immediately after the war, and practically every Solomon Islander now knew the value of the American dollar as well as the British and Australian pound.[60] Solomon Islanders were setting up as traders and hawkers in significant numbers. By 1952 more than 300 held licenses in the central and western Solomons, compared to 66 Europeans (including plantation stores) and 35 Chinese. In the same districts, Solomon Islanders held two-thirds of the copra-buying licenses, Europeans a fifth, and Chinese the rest.[61]

The planters were also no longer a major political force, following the withdrawal of the diversified companies of W. R. Carpenter's and Burns Philp, along with dozens of small concerns. One of the last of the pioneering companies, Fairymead, eventually sold out to Levers in 1957. Former coastwatcher Ken Hay and one-time SILC officer R. C. Symes bought up some of the better estates, using capital acquired from the sale of tons of wartime scrap metal salvaged from jungle and seabed. Although—along with mighty Levers—these planters had some input into policy debates, especially during the copra boom of the early fifties, theirs was now merely one among the many interests to be considered by the government. Their diminishing influence is illustrated not only by their understandable failure to realize Levers' recurring dream of cheap imported labor, but also by their inability to persuade the government that labor contracts, now by regulation set at a maximum of one year should be extended to two.

In their dealings with Solomon Islanders too the planters found their power circumscribed. As Maasina Rule demonstrated, Solomon Islanders would not willingly return to the despised indenture system. And little real effort was made to force them back into it. For one thing, labor was at a premium as never before, with reconstruction schemes in Honiara and other centers offering more attractive alternatives to plantation work. Planters had to compromise. Work schemes devised in the Depression suited employees and most employers. Some Solomon Islanders worked for a wage as before on yearly contracts, but most worked on a share basis or by contract for a fixed price for each ton produced.[62] In 1948 the indenture system's penal clause slipped almost unnoticed into history, an outcome of negotiations started a decade before between the International Labour Organization and the British

government. Its passing went unmourned by Solomon Islanders and all
but a few of the old guard planters who, like Ken Hay, were desperate
to get their plantations functioning and wanted more clout to deal with
refractory laborers.[63]

THE WAR HAD A TREMENDOUS EFFECT on the lives of all the people of the
Solomons. It demonstrated the weakness of the colonial masters, whose
inability to protect themselves, let alone their subjects, from invasion
provided the foundation for later questioning of colonial structures. The
advent of thousands of Allied troops, mainly American, gave Solomon
Islanders a much broader concept of the outside world and of alternatives they had not previously been able to consider. American questioning of Malaitans and others regarding leadership and politics in their
respective islands made them aware not only of what they had lost but
also of how they needed to change to regain their self-respect in the face
of the colonial power.

Eastern Solomon Islanders, especially Malaitans, felt a double betrayal by their colonial masters: First, as laborers they were deserted by
the planters to fend for themselves as the enemy advanced; later, after
they had rallied to serve in the Labour Corps they found themselves
stripped (often by the very same men) of the spoils of victory. They felt
that both their wages and their American gifts were unjustly appro-
priated while the government stood by and did nothing. Many now
thought it time to redefine their relationship with those who had considered themselves their masters and protectors. So Maasina Rule began,
springing to life in one of the most troubled areas of Malaita—'Are'are.

Maasina Rule achieved few of its material aims; the lack of commercial crops and trained workers precluded this far more effectively than
simple government opposition. In terms of political institutions too
Maasina Rule achieved little. The codification of custom, the jurisdiction of the local courts on such matters, and the entity of the council
would have come eventually with or without the movement, just as sim
ilar institutions became established in the western Solomons. But such
institutions only functioned well where there was a will for them to do
so. In the western Solomons most groups already had district unity
before the war. On Malaita, Maasina Rule created an ideological consensus, a real feeling and practice of brotherhood and unity. The movement restored Malaitan pride. Without the catalyst of the war there
would have been no pan-Malaitan, or indeed pan–eastern Solomons,
Maasina Rule and without that Malaita would have long remained a
fractious conglomeration of communities, suspicious of one another and
of the outside world. The Malaitans had transformed themselves from
an assortment of clans and tribes into a people. Their name now signified a social identity, not simply a geographical location. If the new

council worked it was because Malaitans, not the government, had confronted and resolved their differences.

New Georgia was different. Here articulate chiefs successfully challenged initial government interference in the representation on councils. This kind of negotiation was nothing new to them and they did it with some skill within the existing structure of government. The real struggle for identity took place in what for so long had been the most potent institution in the western Solomons, the Methodist Mission. The emergence of Eto's Christian Fellowship Church was as much a symbol of the rejection of the colonial relationship in the west as was Maasina Rule in the east.

These movements and their resultant institutions emerged from regional forces that flourished during the administrative hiatus caused by the war. Fortuitously, many of their aims broadly coincided with new policies outlined by the High Commission, although many Solomon Islanders had little knowledge or understanding of the government's plans to achieve them. Similarly, Solomon Islanders regained a major role in production because of the failure of most expatriate entrepreneurs to return after 1945. It was simply too costly under immediate postwar conditions for major commercial interests to reestablish themselves in the Solomons, where plantations had proved risky enterprises. Major firms could afford to wait ten, twenty, or even thirty years for more favorable circumstances and government backing. With good postwar prices for copra and the government acting as merchant and shipper, the way was open for Solomon Islanders to take up the slack, an outcome of necessity as much as of deliberate government policies.

CHAPTER 14

Independence:
Coming, ready or not!
(1955–1978)

Unity is indeed desirable, but mutual unity and respect can
only be grown, not imposed . . . the process of unity and
identity has been a tribe to a village, to a locality, to a whole
island, to a district. A further process of growth should bring
us a state and national unity.

　　　　Submission of the Western Council, August 1978

We appreciate the help and guidance given to us over the
years, but we feel that this is no more than we deserved, since
we became Britain's colonial subjects through no wish of
our own.

　　　　　　　　　Willie Betu, September 1977

THROUGHOUT MOST OF THEIR COLONIES, the British responded to international anticolonial feeling in the fifties and sixties by granting independence. Yet despite this trend, Britain gave only limited consideration
to constitutional development for the small and struggling Solomon
Islands until the mid-sixties when the protectorate's economy had
strengthened and self-government began to become more of a possibility. As the palmy days of the sixties gave way to the early seventies, with
the fuel crisis and the realities of membership in the European Economic Community (EEC), Britain's gentle amble toward the protectorate's internal self-government rapidly escalated into a breakneck gallop
toward independence. Both constitutional and economic policies directed at that goal were suddenly introduced. Just as suddenly, the people and politicians in the Solomons had to face many hitherto unre-
solved issues. Forms of government had to be decided; ideas about
regionalism and secession had to be dealt with; and policies on education and exploitation of resources needed to be formulated. In some
ways the politicians followed the practices of their colonial mentors
only to find that the results were not always what the people wanted. In

311

part, the wishes of the people were to hinder government plans for national economic growth, although they proclaimed some cultural values and, less propitiously, perpetuated the attitude that the government was there to be exploited.

Paternalistic policies for progress, 1955–1965

British colonial policy after the war soon became one of disengagement. Because of the war, Britain had changed from being the world's largest creditor nation to being the largest debtor nation, owing £6,000 million.[1] The Atlantic Charter of 1941, more broadly interpreted than Britain intended by major colonial states, and certainly by America, seemed a manifesto, if not a guarantee, of future independence for colonial peoples. American demands, as well as those of the Communist bloc in the United Nations during the fifties, were soon to be echoed by the newly independent Asian states in both the United Nations and the Commonwealth of Nations: Britain must grant independence to its colonies. As time went by, and Britain's aid expenditure soared, these colonies were becoming less and less economic. Moreover, the costs of suppressing the more radical elements that were bound to emerge would become so great that, recent evidence suggests, Britain actively stimulated so-called nationalist movements among the growing urban elites in the larger colonies, especially in Africa.

Although Britain in the late forties and fifties was willing to relinquish its major possessions, some minor dependencies were considered totally unviable as nation-states, mainly for economic, but occasionally for sociopolitical reasons. On the basis of information from the High Commission, the Colonial Office judged the Solomons—and all the Western Pacific territories for that matter—to be in this category.[2] In the fifties the British government considered the Solomons to be incapable of self-government, but by 1964, although the protectorate was still "backward" and in receipt of substantial budgetary aid, its people were to be given an increasing but very gradual responsibility in the national management of their own affairs.[3] This new policy was predominantly a response by Britain to international anticolonial pressure, but its feasibility arose from developments within the Solomons that were outcomes of financial aid from Britain during 1955–1964.

By 1955 the protectorate was back on its feet. Essential reconstruction had been completed and district administration restored—except, predictably, in neglected Santa Cruz—and the economy was far healthier than in the dark days of the Depression and the war. Moreover, several Commonwealth Development and Welfare (CDW) projects had been commenced for survey and research of resources—forestry, geological survey, extended entomological research, rice and cocoa research, and the special lands commission. These sometimes took years to become really functional because of shortages, but by 1955 they were beginning to provide the government with some of the information it needed for more coherent planning. Mistakes had been made in the past because of precipitous decisions—the cocoa project on Malaita being the classic example. In 1951 CDW provided £13,375 for trial cocoa plots, one on Malaita (the object of much expenditure at this time because of Maasina Rule) and one on Guadalcanal. As soon as the trees produced seeds, seedlings were distributed throughout Malaita by enthusiastic agricultural officers. Little consideration was given to such primary factors as climate and soil suitability. By 1956 the officers had persuaded people to clear land and plant some forty-two thousand trees, which were soon attacked by the boring weevil, *Pantorhytes biplagiatus*, and later by the disease "black pod." That particular strain of cocoa was doomed, a fact the government did not publicly admit until the sixties.[4]

There was a need for long-term planning now that the emergency conditions of the early postwar years were over. The process was assisted in 1955 by the first of the British government's direct "grants-in-aid" to supplement the protectorate's revenue on an annual basis. Unlike CDW grants, this money was not tagged to specific projects, allowing planning to be broader and more integrated. From 1955 total British aid and CDW grants doubled the protectorate's own revenue, the bulk of which was derived from import and export duties. Under the new system, the first (1955–1960) of many development plans commenced with a budget of £1,777,000 to broaden the economy and provide basic services. Continued surveys and research of natural resources including agriculture took 25 percent, communications 33 percent, education (mainly mission subsidies) and medical each 12 percent, and most of the remainder was allocated to works schemes. A second (1960–1964, revised 1963) and third (1963–1966) development plan followed, with emphasis in the latter on labor planning.

All of these plans looked good on paper—they had to if they were to winkle funds from the British government. Although the protectorate government managed its finances very competently throughout the postwar period, a lot of the data collected and collated for planning were often useful only to the British government for its own statistical and comparative purposes. The information was of little value in getting the Solomon Islanders really involved in the development process because data on such important matters as culture were not assembled. In essence, much of the money provided went into strengthening the protectorate government and correspondingly the benefits were felt in the capital, Honiara.[5]

Despite these flaws, by the early sixties the protectorate was on a planned and secure road to gradual economic development. As well, the government was in the process of distancing itself from the merchant functions it had assumed in the commercial vacuum during the war. The Copra Board had been operating since the late forties and after the Ministry of Food contract expired in 1957 the Board proved itself effective in grading, shipping, and marketing copra and negotiating firm contracts with overseas buyers. It bought copra at the major centers, leaving the Chinese traders to pick up most of the village copra, especially in isolated areas.[6] With the growth of cooperatives some beginnings were made by local groups to cut out intermediaries. Rural cooperatives begun in the early fifties received substantial government encouragement from 1956 on, and by 1965 had a capital investment of almost £50,000 and a turnover of £170,000.[7] To assist both local and expatriate entrepreneurs the government set up the Agricultural and Industrial Loans Board. The most potent symbol of the government's control of commerce, the British Solomons Trading Corporation, the statutory heir to the Trade Scheme, was eventually sold in 1962 to the British Solomons Trading Company, consisting of Australian and Japanese interests. Another promising development for both producers and consumers was the increasing volume of international shipping calling at the Solomons, encouraged by the government's ports building program. As well as Burns Philp and the Bank Line (which had the Copra Board contract), the Australia–West Pacific Line, the Australia–New Guinea Line, and the China Navigation Company were regular shippers by 1960 and were soon competing against two newcomers, the Nederlands-Lloyd and the Rotterdamsche-Lloyd lines.[8]

Although still rough and ready, the capital of the Solomons, Honiara, was a substantial Pacific island town by 1960, with a population of about 5000. The labor shortage of the early fifties was past, with 9000 in the work force. For the first time there was a large concentration of laborers in one place, free from the restraints of the old indenture system. Encouraged by the Labour Department, the first workers' union was formed in Honiara in 1961. There was certainly a need for a united front. The plantation system had left its imprint on labor policy. As in prewar times, wages were based on subsistence for a single man, not for a family. Married men were discouraged from bringing their families to town because of this, as well as the high cost of urban living and the failure of employers to provide married accommodation. Skilled workers received little if any extra remuneration for their abilities. Consequently the workers, as ever mainly Malaitans and south Guadalcanal men, tended to work to target, resulting in a high turnover in the work force. Despite this, in 1962 the BSI Workers Union conducted its first strike, involving both government and privately employed workers, and gained a 20 percent wage increase. The union split in 1963, forming the

BSI Port and Copra Workers Union and the BSI Building and General Workers Union. At this time the basic wage was £7 16s. a month for unskilled labor, but actual wages ranged from about £8 to £10. Real conflict developed between the government and the unions following two strikes in 1964–1965 over further wage increases. One of these, in Honiara, involved mainly government employees, but the other, in the Russells, involved workers on Levers' plantations and was labeled unlawful and ineffective by the government. Police used tear gas to break up demonstrations and threatened to forcibly repatriate workers to their home district. Rumors about the misappropriation of union funds and the resignation of a union leader also weakened support. The outcome for many workers was a loss of confidence in the unions and a return to joint consultative committees on labor matters; for employers it was an apparently "tamed" workforce.[9]

Developments such as stable, long-term government planning, increasing government disengagement from direct involvement in commerce, reliable shipping, safe ports, and an adequate labor supply on still relatively low wages gave more confidence to the private sector. Moreover, the government could now offer extensive information on the resources of the protectorate and had passed a considerable body of legislation to enable their exploitation. The government's plans now included the encouragement of plantation agriculture, as one way to ensure a leap forward in the economy. Overseas investors were drawn once again to the Solomons. Between 1962 and 1965 four timber companies started operations, including a Levers subsidiary to work Levers' former "waste lands," many of which had indeed lain waste and unused for over half a century in the western Solomons. The Commonwealth Development Corporation, in partnership with the government, began field trials of rice, soybeans, and oil palms on the Guadalcanal plains; at the same time Ken Hay's Guadalcanal Plains Limited had 800 acres under dry rice, sorghum, and soybeans as well as plans to extend into hotel accommodation in Honiara. Although international shipping was the preserve of the private sector, interisland transportation had been largely government operated until 1965–1966, when there were plans for higher charges to introduce economic rates that would be competitive for private enterprise. Air transport became an independently owned operation in 1963, when Megapode Airways (later Solair) inaugurated services between the major islands.[10]

Solomon Islanders' involvement in the economy was less spectacular than their gains in the early fifties had been. As an outcome of a CDW grant made first in 1954 and work by the Agriculture Department and the Copra Board, cheap hot-air driers ("Kukum") were developed and then made available to Solomon Islanders and provision was made for a three-grade system of copra classification by government inspectors.[11]

The price differentials inherent in this system eventually proved an incentive for Solomon Islanders to produce higher grade copra. In 1956, 76.6 percent of the copra produced by Solomon Islander growers was still third grade (smoke-dried). By 1965 this had dropped to 55.6 percent, with 27.2 percent in the first-grade (good quality, hot-air dried) category. Prospects for greater production by local groups were promising, but government support was inadequate and complaints of neglect were being voiced in some of the more isolated areas. In the early sixties, planting programs using improved seed under the aegis of the Agriculture Department had resulted in increased areas being planted, with four thousand acres under coconuts on Malaita alone. In effect, this only compensated for the senescence of old prewar groves; total copra production remained fairly stable at 24,000 tons in 1965, with Solomon Islanders maintaining their share at around 52 percent.[12] The government provided little investment capital through the Agricultural and Industrial Loans Board since, between 1955 and 1966, only 6 percent of loans went to coconut and cocoa development and most of those to expatriates.[13]

Some of the few loans that did go to Solomon Islanders went to people on the isolated weather coast of Guadalcanal, an area that received little government attention in the mid-fifties, despite its density of population and relative proximity to Honiara. Local dissatisfaction with central government and the 'Are'are-dominated Marau-Haumba Council in the Moli district found a focus during 1957–1958 in Moro of Makaruka, a man who displayed many of the behavioral characteristics of a "cargo cult" leader—visions, coma, reputed resurrection from the dead, and a plan for a new order based on local self-sufficiency and a revival of old customs. The Moro "Custom Company" had a platform and grievances similar in some respects to Fallowes' Chair and Rule movement:

> Tomorrow, the peoples of Moro's Custom Company will be looking forward. The principal aid [from] civilization is money. We are now starting with our fashion of marketing. We realise that money makes better education, better business, and better development of civilization. Without money we can do nothing. Money makes things possible.
>
> We have been waiting for many years. Since the missions came to the Solomons, we have not seen any change from our old habit of living except the changing of faith and a bit of education.
>
> The traders and the Government also came and lived in the Solomons for many years, but there has been no changed made [sic] . . . .[14]

Moro attracted a large following throughout Moli, southern Mbirao and as far west as the Koloula River valley and the Viso district. In the early sixties, the company's attempts at economic development—a communal coconut plantation, pig farming, gold mining, and the building of a boat to market produce—were not particularly successful, mainly because of lack of skilled personnel, especially at the managerial level. Until the mid-sixties, Moro and his followers remained aloof from government and council, which both began to pay more attention to the area as a consequence of Moro's growing political influence. Ironically, the non-Moro supporters and, west of Avuavu, the nominal Moro followers initially reaped much of the benefit of this new interest in the weather coast. Early in 1959 the government began a shipping service to the area that, although erratic, did generate interest in cash cropping. More significant, the government—with council cooperation—started work in 1961 on a tractor road from sheltered Marau through to Avuavu and the Kuma River to provide a regular outlet for produce. Helped by government loans, local producers in the Moli area by 1964 had 100 acres under cacao and 350 acres under coconuts.[15]

The extension of cash cropping here and elsewhere underlined the difficulties Solomon Islanders faced in defining changing concepts of land use and ownership. In an attempt to resolve these difficulties and to spur further economic development in both the local and the expatriate sectors, the government altered the land laws. Prior to 1959 the government had registered deeds of land transactions, but this did not necessarily guarantee their validity. The tracing of deeds was a long and often costly process and they were not available to the general public. Under a series of acts from 1959 to 1965, the government introduced the Torrens system, establishing a land register to record the ownership of all titles that had been investigated and proved, along with survey data on boundaries. These ordinances did not apply directly to customary or native title. However, in the belief that security of tenure would be an incentive to the smallholder entrepreneur's investment of time and money in long-term crops and projects, the government established extensive machinery for the settlement and registration of customary land, vested in either a group or an individual—but only upon request by traditional claimants.[16]

Minor constitutional developments opened the sixties. In 1960 an Executive and a Legislative Council replaced the Advisory Council. The Legislative Council consisted of three ex officio members, eight official members and ten nominated unofficial members, six of whom were Solomon Islanders. The Executive, with a smaller membership, had a similar composition, all drawn from the Legislative Council. In both bodies the official members dominated proceedings and nominated members had no powers. More significant from the point of view of exercise of adult suffrage, local government councils at last became elective in 1963. They had extended responsibilities in primary education, rural health services, village hygiene, communications, and market supervision. Two years later electoral colleges of local government councillors elected seven members of the Legislative Council, and an eighth member for Honiara was elected by direct ballot. These elections saw the emergence of the first, if ephemeral, political party—the Democratic Party headed by Mariano Kelesi with a moderate platform of eventual self-government for the Solomons within the Commonwealth —and the election of the first (and so far only) woman member, Lili Ogatini.[17]

By 1965 the protectorate government could look back with some satisfaction over the preceding years at "the steady rate of progress in development" in the Solomons and anticipate eventual internal self-government on a secure economic base.[18] A major project had just begun in conjunction with WHO to eradicate malaria, a scourge that retarded development as much as lack of specialized skills among the population. In education, the government's policies, it was hoped, would eventually provide some people with those skills. Working in liaison with the missions, the government aimed to devise an integrated education system. It was a nice plan on paper: Of an intake into a four-year junior primary school, half would pass on to senior primary, and of these half again would be selected for secondary school, so that the most able would perhaps go to tertiary and other training institutions, such as the newly opened Teachers' College. But by 1965 there was hardening resistance from Solomon Islanders and the missions to the social costs and the inherent philosophy of such a scheme.[19] One of the first tasks of the elected Solomon Islander members of the Legislative Council was to voice this criticism to the government. This was but one of the many storms that would trouble the years leading to self-government.

Rapid constitutional and political change, 1965–1978

The storms that disturbed this steady development were not only metaphorical. One cyclone after another hit the Solomons in the mid-sixties. In 1966 Cyclone Angela devastated north and west Malaita, and the south and east of Guadalcanal, including the plains, leaving many homeless, without gardens and cash crops. Early in 1967 another cyclone severely damaged the central Solomons, and later that year Cyclone Annie ripped through much of the New Georgia group, Choiseul, north Malaita, and Santa Isabel, as well as destroying half of Ontong Java's coconut palms. Late in 1968 Cyclone Becky caused considerable losses on Malaita and in the eastern Solomons. Copra production, which had been 24,500 tons in 1965, fell to 20,500 in 1968 as a result of cyclone damage coupled with low world prices. The timber industry, promising its first real profit on vast government investment in the preceding decade, again recorded a loss in 1966–1967, mainly because of the cyclones.[20]

The aftermath of the cyclones emphasized more than simply the vulnerability of the Solomons' agricultural economy to natural catastrophe. Each disaster saw the government take relief action to help stricken communities. In precontact times, and even in the colonial years before the war, communities had had to rely on their own resources and ties with neighbors for recovery. But now the ample breasts of the colonial government fed the hungry and comforted the homeless, giving the government a new dimension. From early colonial times, the government had always been to Solomon Islanders a foreign, imposed institution exercising apparently arbitrary power. In the post-war period it was still seen as this, but increasingly benevolent, ready with aid whenever a need was articulated. Sometimes action might be delayed, but eventually, it seemed, most needs were satisfied. For example, from 1965 on, members of the Legislative Council kept up a barrage of complaints about the problems faced by local producers in getting the maximum price for high grade copra because of the Chinese traders' practice of buying all local copra at third-grade prices, a policy justified in the traders' eyes because of the small lots involved and the loading and shipping difficulties on many dangerous coasts. The official government members explained that to set up more buying points with requisite grading agents would be an expensive operation and, if financed by the Copra Board, would reduce overall returns to all producers. Yet by 1973, the British government allocated A$75,000 for this under a special Development Aid Project.[21] Of course, many members of the Legislative Council, by then with an elected majority of Solomon Islanders, realized what was happening. One of the Malaitan members, David Kausimae, summed up the process:

> In a way . . . we are suffering from a father figure type of government in the past and we still want things done for us . . . we are not fools and we know that in the long term our natural resources must pay for the social services we want. We all know that we cannot keep expecting handouts or gifts of aid.[22]

Politicians in Honiara had the impossible task of trying to satisfy their vociferous constituents' rising aspirations while dealing with financial reality. As long as there was still a colonial government they took the only political option—the continued milking of Britain.

The British were not unaware of what was going on since they had largely underwritten the policy. In their view, the sooner self-government was a reality, the sooner more responsibility for administrative management would grow. In the late sixties, although each year saw a new constitutional development in the Legislative Council, the pattern

of government and debate remained very much "us" versus "them"—
Solomon Island elected members versus official members and their public service backing—a pattern that served only to reinforce the idea of
the government as a colonial artefact answerable to and exploitable by
Solomon Islanders, but not an institution in which they were both participants and accountable.[23]

Consequently, in 1970 the government accelerated the localization of
the public service. In the same year, the British introduced a new constitution, drawing on experiments in other small colonies as models. A
committee system came into existence and a new parliament, called the
Governing Council. Basically, there were five committees responsible
for given departments (such as Commerce and Industry) and each
elected member had to be a member of one of those committees, which
included official members and public servants. Financial Secretary
T. Russell, later chief secretary to the High Commission, provided questionable ideological justification for this new system, claiming that it
was more "Melanesian," an opinion shared by Peter Kenilorea, a leading public servant. But the real reasons were more pragmatic. It was
hoped that the Solomon Islanders, now an elected majority, would
work with the official members and the bureaucracy as part of a team,
rather than as an opposition, and at the same time gain greater experience with policy formulation.[24]

Government by committee found little favor with the new house. It
was too cumbersome, too slow, and it robbed aspirants to political leadership of a stage on which to star. Solomon Mamaloni, a member from
Makira, was a consistent critic, and at the end of 1971 he led the elected
members of the council in rejecting it and opting for a return to what
was to be, in the absence of strong parties, a distinctly Melanesian variant of the Westminster system with ministerial responsibility. The
change was endorsed by a special select committee the following year.[25]

The committee system had been an expendable and expensive experiment, but the time for such luxuries was fast drawing to a close. Even as
late as 1970, few members, let alone colonial officials, spoke publicly of
independence. Solomon Islander politicians were wary of such talk,
since the existing constitutional changes were little understood by ordinary villagers—a consequence of decisions made from the top and of the
lack of effective protectorate-wide news media.

Within Honiara there was intense criticism of the colonial government, which throughout the sixties consisted more and more of overseas
public servants transferred from newly independent African states. The
time-serving "Africa Corps," as they were labeled, seemed content to
while away their leisure hours within the narrow social world of the
Guadalcanal Club or the Mendaña Hotel. Few showed any willingness
to learn about the rural people and their needs and most had little sensi-

tivity to the aspirations of Solomon Islanders within the government bureaucracy. Solomon Islanders who were open in their resentment of such attitudes were considered "Communists," as were nongovernment observers and researchers who dared offer constructive advice.

Some criticism of the colonial power was published in the cyclostyled *Kakamora Reporter*, edited by Henry Raraka and Ella Bugotu from 1970 to 1975. Usually in the English language, but sometimes in Pijin, it aired the views of the emerging Western-educated elite, some of whom were still studying overseas, but its circulation and support remained largely Honiara based throughout its brief existence. Most village people at this time perceived the status quo as generally satisfactory. British postwar policies had answered almost all the limited demands of movements like Chair and Rule and Maasina Rule, so why change things? Internally then, there was no momentum for independence except among a handful of tertiary graduates and university students and most of these were whisked into the public service after their studies. Russell and his advisers in 1970 passed off talk of independence as premature while the protectorate was still getting budgetary aid and warned that any timetable for independence would only scare off potential overseas investors. In Britain, the possibility of a kind of free association status for the Solomons was seriously but only briefly considered. Experiments with small territories in the Caribbean in the late sixties had shown Britain that it was a troublesome arrangement. Officially, at least, self-government for the Solomons was the immediate goal, but in reality the British government envisaged independence as the inevitable outcome and the shorter the twilight period before independence of diminished power yet all responsibility for the colonial authority, the better.[26]

By 1974 Britain had clearly abandoned its gradualist, evolutionary approach. Independence was to come—and soon. Slow decolonization, the British knew, was a thankless task. But the real impetus to Britain's disengagement lay in its own economic and social troubles, the fuel crisis, and the practicalities of membership in the European Economic Community, coupled with the probable reaction of Western-educated, urban-based Solomon Islanders to the coming independence of Australia's Papua New Guinea.[27] Without any general clamor for independence in the Solomons and with the near exhaustion of the worldwide anticolonial movement of the postwar decades, Britain was very much the instigator of independence for the Solomons. The British saw the process as one of their gaining independence from the Pacific rather than of territories like the Solomons winning independence from them. The Solomons, a bare decade before considered only a possible candidate for eventual self-government, were now to be prepared for independence as quickly as the appropriate legal and constitutional niceties would allow.[28]

Part of the niceties required a Solomon Islander leader or group of leaders who would create and sustain some momentum for independence. In 1974 the Governing Council was reorganized as the Legislative Assembly with a ministerial system, and Solomon Mamaloni as its first chief minister. Educated at tertiary level in New Zealand and considered somewhat radical in his criticisms of the British, Mamaloni was perceived by many of those same officials as the man of the moment— he seemed to be the only politician likely to command a majority. The officials' need for an independence leader meshed with Mamaloni's ambition to be that leader; in the period before independence in a small place like the Solomons, where personalities can loom large, this one man was to have considerable influence on developments.

In January 1975 Mamaloni represented the Solomons in discussions in Honiara with Joan Lestor, the British minister responsible for dependent territories. From this and further talks in London emerged a timetable for constitutional development, with self-government scheduled for late 1975 and independence twelve to eighteen months later. January 1976 saw limited internal self-government, with the deputy governor retaining the right to sit in Cabinet and Council.

British retention of powers like this, as well as their continuing control of the public service and the police, meant that Solomon Islander politicians, ministers especially, were often hamstrung in the exercise of their own power since they were also accountable to their constituents who were oblivious of the nice divisions of authority at this transition stage. This situation produced increasing frustration and, as the British were aware, reduced the likelihood that government ministers would try to postpone independence. During this twilight period any chief minister was particularly vulnerable because he had to deal with his ministers' dissatisfaction. To complicate matters, party loyalty in the tradition of Westminster was all but nonexistent in Solomon politics, where parliamentarians kept their options as open as possible, so that no chief minister could count on the continuing support of even his ministers, let alone the party back bench.

This political fact and its implications were not fully recognized by the British, used as they were to African precedents. In their usual fashion, they insisted on a preindependence election in mid-1976, the aim being to have a clear public mandate that would legitimize the independence government. But this practice had been useful in states where independence was the platform of popular movements and their stable political parties. The 1976 election resulted in Peter Kenilorea, an independent, being selected as chief minister (on the seventh ballot by members), a result neither the British nor Mamaloni had anticipated. The fluidity of support was such that Kenilorea was soon in the trying position of being head of a minority government—hardly an ideal circumstance for a leader who was expected to speak on behalf of an emerging nation.

Kenilorea, Mamaloni, and a sometime–Mamaloni supporter and former union leader, Bart Ulufa'alu, to say nothing of a half-dozen other politicians, all had hopes of leading their country at independence. Although Kenilorea had no party to back him, as a former public servant he had support from this quarter that his leading rivals in opposition, Mamaloni, Ulufa'alu, and Francis Talasasa Aqorau (president of the Western Council), lacked. The power struggles came to a head in November 1976 when the government barely managed to get the Budget through the House following a motion of no confidence. In a cabinet of "independent" ministers and a divided Opposition, alliances continued unstable. This instability, coupled with members' inexperience of the ministerial system, as well as the odd political scandal, hindered finalization of negotiations on the constitution for independence.

Typical of the uncertainties of the time were the events surrounding the sudden death of western member Aqorau in January 1977. Honiara was already nervous on the "law and order" issue following three unsolved murders on Guadalcanal. The capital buzzed with speculation, recalling Mamaloni's recent criticisms of the police for their failure to find the killers. Soon rumor had it that Aqorau too had been murdered by poisoning. Mamaloni, having twice failed to recapture the chief ministership, announced his resignation from the House and planned to concentrate on his business interests back on Makira. Further rumors suggested a "Malaita Mafia" was responsible for Aqorau's death and was out to dispose of other leading non-Malaitan politicians and public servants. The intent behind such rumors was not lost on Malaitans like Kenilorea and Opposition leader Ulufa'alu. Mamaloni, now perceived as a possible victim of the "Mafia," left the House for the time being with new support not only from his own electorate and Guadalcanal members, but also from Aqorau's westerners who, almost two years before, had been at odds with him as chief minister because of their embarrassing demands for statehood.[29]

As well as trying to survive this internal political turmoil, Kenilorea had to negotiate major constitutional issues with Britain. One of the problems was the fate of nonindigenous peoples, including the Gilbertese who had been resettled from overcrowded Micronesian atolls between 1955 and 1971. Agreement as to where they could settle and their rights to land, quite naturally for the times, had been between the protectorate government and local Solomon Islander communities and their leaders in the west, rather than any indigenous national forum. For the British, the future of such people was a lively issue since they, in their role as colonial power, were being censured by the High Court in London in 1977 for their dealings with another group of resettled dependent Pacific Islanders, the Banabans. The British did not want any displaced non–Solomon Islanders having postindependence claims on them as British citizens and they wanted to have the Gilbertese confirmed in the land rights given them in 1955. Initially, this was a government-to-government issue, but some politicians saw it as a possibly powerful weapon to use against Britain to obtain a more favorable financial settlement for the Solomons at independence. They stirred up public opinion. The Gilbertese question quickly became a focus for popular resentment against apparent colonial high-handedness in resettling the Gilbertese in the Solomons in the first place. Another popular issue was the future of alienated land, but because the Kenilorea government, like its predecessors, recognized the complexity of any proposed redistribution, it did not dare make a publicly unequivocal stand, preferring to shelve the problem until a later date. This sort of pressure on Solomon Islander politicians threatened negotiations because it placed them in a double bind: They had to appear sensitive to their electorate, yet bear in mind the wider national and constitutional concerns.

In May 1977, with these issues hanging over him but still the leader of a minority government, Kenilorea headed a small delegation of parliamentarians to London to negotiate the financial settlement for independence with British Minister of Overseas Development Judith Hart. The British agreed to provide £ stg. 18 million for development purposes by way of a loan, £ stg. 5 million for a Production Resources Development Fund as a grant, and £ stg. 3 million for a budgetary deficit as and when agreed. Aid in the form of technical assistance and various consultants would continue.

Some members of the Kenilorea delegation were unhappy with aspects of the agreement. At home, parliamentarians criticized the lack of consultation. Consequently, the Solomons parliament refused to allow the agreement before the House and negotiations were deadlocked. Britain attempted to retrieve the situation by sending a constitutional expert to the Solomons for further talks. Although this was unsuccessful, a shift in the factions within the parliament lessened resistance to Kenilorea.

After Aqorau's death and Mamaloni's resignation, Ulufa'alu was the clear leader of the Opposition group, but he lost some support when a new party was formed in mid-1977. Soon after, Kenilorea's plan to involve the entire House in another round of London talks drew cries of extravagance from the public. Sensing political capital to be gained, Ulufa'alu refused to attend, but in the process lost support from Opposition members who wanted to visit London. Just at this time too, Ulufa'alu, as former head of the Solomon Islands General Workers Union, conveniently came under suspicion of misappropriation of union funds which, although disproved, lessened his credibility.

With the return of the large Kenilorea party from London in September 1977, effective parliamentary opposition to constitutional change was silenced. On the citizenship issue the Solomons government conceded that nonindigenous people who had "belonger" status (for example, long-term residence, through having been born in the Solomons or married to a Solomon Islander) could apply within a set period for citizenship, which they would automatically receive. This partly solved the question of the Gilbertese, but their right to land was left to the decision of the Solomons parliament. Britain had successfully rid itself of responsibility for these British subjects, but in doing so bequeathed yet another problem to the future independent government.

Britain made some concessions: a slight increase in the overall financial settlement, and—more important from the Solomons point of view—the conversion of £ stg. 18 million for development aid from loan to grant. Under these conditions independence would proceed mid-1978.[30] These negotiations were extremely successful if the satisfaction of both parties was any index. The British, who had wanted the Solomons "independent, by hook or by crook," felt they had got off lightly since the Solomons party had been in a position to push for an even costlier settlement; and the Solomon Islanders returned home in triumph claiming a victory in gaining the grant.[31]

Developments at the local level: Devolution and its cost

Obviously, the rate of constitutional change was rapid and very much at the center. Central government was the natural focus for the colonial power, which wanted to deal with only one forum of Solomons opinion. But the concentration on constitutional development and its trappings, very much a part of "the rituals of decolonisation" and a key feature of the seventies, tended to steal the limelight from important political developments at the local level.[32]

In 1972 the Governing Council had set up a select committee to examine the role of local government within a new constitution leading to self-government and to gauge the feelings of villagers on such matters. Plans were set in motion to consolidate a number of councils too small to be viable and to decentralize decision making, so that the local council became "the principal agency for progress within its area" as well as a partner of the central administration "for the promotion of national government."[33] The fact that the five separate councils of the western Solomons had amalgamated voluntarily in 1972 augured well for the plan. Originally "devolution" was intended to streamline local government by giving officials in a particular area control over the functions of administration (for example, health, works, education), so giving local people a feeling of participation.

Villagers believed that Honiara received most of the money spent on the development of an infrastructure. And they were right, for in the late sixties the annual budget allocation to Honiara was about two-thirds of all capital expenditure on public utilities, building, and communications at a time when only about 5 percent of the population lived in Honiara. The planners of devolution hoped that more decision making and spending at the local level would lessen rural resentment.

By 1976, most of the reforms were being implemented. Twenty-one local councils were reduced to eight, exclusive of an urban one for Honiara. Although councillors were elected, the bodies that established grassroots priorities and mobilized local resources, including the basic council "rate" (replacing the "tax") in any one council ward, were the area committees. Local practice determined committee membership— in one ward heads of families might meet, in another the local chiefs or big-men—but the elected councillor from that ward was always a member. To the councils themselves, the central administration supplied and paid technical staff for both field services and clerical support. In order to supplement the local revenue, most of which came from the "rate," the central administration gave annual grants constituting at least two-thirds of the council finance, in the form of a service or running costs grant and General Development Aid for new capital projects such as road building. Staff transfers from central government to councils began in 1975.

The concept of devolution, especially in the unsettled preindependence period, was attractive to many. On paper, it seemed to the British a neat way of satisfying local aspirations with the least conflict. To the politicians in Honiara, it would take off some of the pressure imposed by their rural constituents. These people, especially in the less economically productive regions, had long felt that the central government should do more for them. The new arrangement held out the promise of improvement, a promise central politicians would only reinforce.

The inauguration of local councils and courts in the late thirties and early forties had created an expectation among local leaders that their importance would be recognized and their influence extended. Maasina Rule had further raised their hopes, but the central colonial government always seemed to have the final word. Now, with devolution as a policy, presidents and councillors (some themselves chiefs and big-men, or certainly dependent on such men for their positions) seized the opportunity to assert their own power vis-à-vis the politicians and government in Honiara. What had begun as an administrative reform had been transformed into a political exercise, more by the efforts of Solomon Islander local and national politicians than those of any back-room British planners in Honiara.

Many of the changes were pushed through precipitously. Councils had not been prepared for the complexities of the task and suffered because they insisted that the district commissioners, the old heads of the district administrations and the most potent symbol of central government, be phased out in favor of council clerks. The commissioners became transitional government agents, supposedly liaison officers smoothing the way for eventual full local government control of each district administration. The council clerks, paid by the central government, found themselves in a cleft stick, pulled by loyalties to their employer and to their council. Everywhere the standard of services fell and overall costs rose and remained at a level far above estimates.[34]

The western Solomons "breakaway"

Devolution was not proving the panacea it had seemed. Virtually on the eve of independence, years of dissatisfaction with central government culminated in the western Solomons in the declaration of a "breakaway" movement. Initially in 1975, the westerners wanted a bigger financial allocation from Mamaloni's central government, claiming they were highly productive and supplying a disproportionate amount of government revenue. It might have seemed that way, but the bulk of earnings came from Levers and the timber companies. In fact, where they had once been leaders in smallholder production of copra, westerners were now lagging behind other districts in the quality of their product. Moreover, they already had superior services, though some admittedly were mission operated and financed.

It seems that few westerners were aware of these basic economic facts and that those who were, were not above the standard postwar political tactic of screaming loudly until the government offered some solace. To add to their unrest, the fear grew that with the new political alignment of 1977, the removal of the British lion would see the western turtle overshadowed by the eastern eagle, that Malaitan interests would dominate the central government and that government would in turn dominate the west. These fears were magnified by Mamaloni's resignation from politics in the wake of Aqorau's death and the Malaita "Mafia" scare.

"Breakaway" was the first real challenge that the now fully self-governing Solomon Islands had to face. Its basic origins are not hard to find. Even before the war, westerners had resented the drift of land-hungry Malaitans into their islands by migration and marriage. They considered Malaitan plantation laborers wild men and troublemakers, only useful when there was hard work to be done. Some westerners still recalled the depredation of the Malaitan militia in the wake of the Binskin murders and feared that Malaitans retained memories of the more recent involvement of westerners in raids against followers of

Maasina Rule. Even that great claim to Malaitan fame, Maasina Rule, was regarded by many westerners as having been little more than rabble-rousing to blackmail the government into all kinds of unmerited concessions and grants. Now, a Malaitan, Peter Kenilorea, was leading the country from Malaitan-dominated Honiara, and Malaita, with many of its sixty thousand people yet backward and pagan, was still attracting an undue amount of government spending. The magnification of the Gilbertese issue gave the westerners another grievance, as they had taken the burden of Gilbertese resettlement. To make things worse, in 1977, amendments to the land laws made the central government landlord of all formerly expatriate-held freehold as well as leasehold and resulted in 12 percent of all land in the west being transferred to central government ownership.

All this only confirmed the westerners' strong sense of identity and apartness. Their blackness, their Roviana lingua franca, their Christian religious affiliations, their beautiful and influential women, and their pride in being smallholder producers rather than migrant laborers marked them off as a distinct group from their brown neighbors. Their confidence in themselves was reinforced by the model of the thriving indigenous Christian Fellowship Church and their successful creation of a single Western Council in 1972, an ideal that had been conceived by some of their representatives in the mid-fifties but ignored by the administration at the time. In fact, the new council at Gizo became one of the few loci of leadership for "breakaway."[35]

The tactics of "breakaway" had been inspired in part by neighboring copper-rich Bougainville, whose leaders had threatened amalgamation with the western Solomons in the early seventies and, later, possible secession to extract concessions from the central Papua New Guinea government. Unlike Bougainville, the west had no mine and its leadership group was dispersed and poorly coordinated, ranging from Western Council members like Jerry Buare, parliamentarians like Francis Billy Hilly, and public servants, to leading members of the Christian Fellowship Church. One group, led by an opportunistic former parliamentarian and would-be leader of the west, actually asked the central government to fund a western delegation to visit Australia for legal advice on constitutional matters. The central government declined, but the Christian Fellowship Church supplied the finance. Armed with a new constitution for the west, the group then sought outside advice on running costs, only to discover that the western Solomons would be financially better off under the old dispensation. Another group asked the protectorate governor, Sir Colin Allan, to be its first governor. He declined. It was time to reconsider.

In an effort to settle some of the west's grievances, the Kenilorea government gave the Western Council a slightly increased grant based on

Photo 26. Peter Kenilorea and friends, Independence Day 1978, Honiara. *(Solomon Islands Information Office)*

new and, to the Council, more satisfactory criteria. Some government land was transferred to the council and westerners were placed in important parliamentary and public service positions. But Kenilorea remained adamant on the issue of state government, just as the Western Council refused to back down on its demands. Negotiations ended in stalemate, with independence just around the corner.

The council's worst fears seemed confirmed by the unfortunate and ill-advised publication in the government-owned newspaper of "Ode to the Westwind," which denigrated the west and its people and revealed a Malaitan perspective, just a bare month before independence. Rumor had it—later found to be untrue—that a Kenilorea assistant was the author. After considerable vacillation, a public government apology followed and $9000 was paid to the Western Council in compensation for hurt sensibilities. On 7 July 1978, independence was celebrated in every district except the west (Photo 26). Yet the central government had managed to defuse the situation to such a degree that a year later the west too joined in the festivities marking the first anniversary of independence—paid for by funds from the central government.[36]

For all its farcical elements, "breakaway" was a reflection of the wide spectrum of uncertainty about independence at both village and district level throughout the Solomons. Solomon Islanders, with their highly developed political sense, were suspicious of their own government, or at least of their own politicians. The old colonial government had been capricious and generally ignorant of its subjects, but it had been basically impartial. This explains why devolution had appealed; it seemed to be a way of limiting the powers of the emerging national government. That government still retains two trump cards that could be used to assist poorer districts in the face of resistence by their richer neighbors: in most areas it heavily subsidizes the councils; and it secures at least one third of its revenue in aid from overseas. It could use this for its own purposes, such as the rapid exploitation of certain resources like minerals and forestry—measures that in the past always met with such steadfast opposition at the grass roots that the colonial administration of the sixties and seventies dared not force the issue.

The economy: Limitations, frustrations, and old values

With internal self-government in view in the early sixties, the colonial administration had concentrated on achieving a greater diversity of exports along with increased overall production. Although generally successful if measured by a 7 percent annual growth rate of the gross domestic product between 1973 and 1977, the thrust for diversification was mainly through encouragment of large-scale and usually foreign-controlled agriculture, mining, timber extraction, and fisheries. Rural development, to the administrator a far slower and more costly process, was patchy and generally unimpressive.

The Solomons cash economy was still mainly based on agriculture. In the sixties the country's dominant money-spinner, especially for the smallholder, remained copra—with all its vulnerability to world price fluctuations. However, by 1977–1978 copra made up only a quarter of the Solomons' export earnings. Palm oil, from the concentrated plantations on the Guadalcanal Plains, added another 16 percent to the export statistics, but being an oil was subject to the same market pressures as copra. Timber products and fish, making up almost a quarter each of total exports, provided diversity and put the Solomons in a secure position compared to many other Pacific island states.[37]

Overall annual copra production remained around 25,000 tons, a mere 3000–5000 tons more than prewar, from a population of 195,000, double that of the 1930s. At best, production by smallholders was about 60 percent of the total output, but the volume of their first-grade copra had increased to more than 60 percent, while more than 90 percent of plantation copra was in that category. One bright spot for all growers in the late 1960s was the success of protracted entomological research on control of premature nutfall and *Brontispa* in coconuts. The government also assisted growers by providing high-yielding seed stock and continued the joint efforts of the Department of Agriculture and Levers to develop improved hybrid coconuts.[38]

The government hoped to encourage the potential of still large reserves of arable land through its land development policies. In the early seventies it began buying up alienated land, usually planted with senescent palms, for subdivision and development, as well as supplying loans to groups for similar community undertakings. Unrealistically high prices demanded by expatriate owners slowed the process until the new land legislation of 1977 converted all nonindigenously held freehold and leasehold to 75-year government leases. As a development clause forces owners to rehabilitate derelict plantations or develop virgin land, those expatriates who had hoped to make great profit on their run-down holdings began selling out. But this project, as well as the schemes registering customary land in the name of groups or individuals to "free" it for commercial development, has been hindered by demarcation disputes as well as questions as to which local people should have the right to work the land. This problem is a very real one. Although there is no shortage of land in the Solomons, prime land with ready access to sea or road transport is not abundant relative to the population. There are simply more people in the Solomons than there have been for more than three generations, an outcome of improved postwar medical facilities and the success of the WHO-funded malaria control campaign of the late sixties and seventies. A startling 3.4 percent annual growth of population and the upsurge of coastward migration after the war have brought many "incomers" to already populated areas where they have few rights to even subsistence usufruct. Their rights to use the land for commercial purposes, of course, become a far more contentious issue and one that has sometimes been inflamed, rather than reconciled, by the conscientious probings of land settlement officers. Yet with cases of coastal owners cold-bloodedly sitting back and waiting until incomers develop the land before making assertions about ownership, the situation will only deteriorate.[39] The colonial government skirted the settlement of a land policy congruent with the kind of economic development it had encouraged and its immediate successor did no better. The problem remains.

The government's continuing support of large-scale commercial agriculture has also been demonstrated by its interest in the "agricultural opportunity areas"—forty-three widely dispersed areas with above average potential—assessed by the land resources survey of Hansell and Wall in 1976. Many of these areas are suited to large-scale agriculture and, providing shipping services can be improved to serve them, they might well fulfill their economic potential.

The government's interest in commercial agriculture in the 1970s might have seemed unfashionable for the time and imprudent in the light of the prewar experience with plantations. But conditions had changed somewhat. First, by the mid-seventies there was an expanding potential supply of labor, with almost 50 percent of the population under fifteen years of age. Second, many Solomon Islanders want wage-labor if they can get it for periods that suit them.[40] As ever, these people are predominantly from isolated or less-productive areas, but others also seek short-term employment if they want cash quickly and cannot wait until, say, their cocoa is harvested and sold. Third, in terms of national expenditure, large-scale agriculture is less costly than trying to push smallholder development on people not convinced of the need for it. As well, plantations can provide trial runs for new crops, rather than smallholders—who have more to lose, as in the cocoa fiasco on Malaita. Fourth, with either government or council ownership, partnership, or shareholding, there is not the same expatriation of profits as in the colo-nial plantation economy. Fifth, a diversity of crops like rice, cacao, palm oil, and coconuts gives some insurance against a fall in world prices for a single product. Finally, if (and it is a big "if") the govern-ment can get land in the agricultural opportunity areas for resettlement of people from crowded or nonproductive areas, it is certain that the returns to Solomon Islanders will be far greater than under the old plan-tation system. This will take careful planning, lest the new settlers reap the benefits of government interest at the cost of the neighboring origi-nal ownership group, as has been the case with similar schemes in Papua New Guinea.[41] And as always, agricultural development takes place in an unpredictable environment where cyclones and insect pests can inflict as much damage as can world price fluctuations and in-creases in costs of the long voyage to world markets.

The land provided another major product—timber. Unlike copra production, much timber was logged by privately owned overseas com-panies, the leading one being Levers Pacific Timbers. The projected spin-offs in local employment, road building, and local milling had not yet been realized in the mid-seventies.

Disputes over timber rights during the sixties and seventies high-lighted the tenacity of the attachment Solomon Islanders have for their land. Tradition aside, such attachment is understandable since the land directly gives a living to nine out of ten Solomon Islanders. One major dispute has centered on Kolombangara. Of the land granted to Levers as part of their huge "waste land" parcel at the turn of the century, the company only ever developed 2500 acres of the 120,000 allowed by them by readjustments of the Phillips Commission. Under pressure from the high commissioner in the mid-seventies, Levers gave 100,000 acres of it to the government in return for timber-cutting rights there for Levers Pacific Timbers, the retention of 20,000 acres of the best cultivable land for agricultural purposes as perpetual estate (with a 30-year development clause), and government assistance in persuading people on neighboring customary land to allow Levers to log there too. Levers really sacrificed very little. By the sixties they had at last accepted the fact that a cheap foreign labor supply was a pipe dream. Even with their sponsored resettlement of families from crowded Tikopia as a resident labor force in the Russells, they calculated that it would be a long time before they would get skilled Solomon Islands labor in the numbers they wanted and certainly not at rates comparable to prewar wages. And the low copra prices of the 1960s were no incentive. The Kolombangara land would have had to remain undeveloped anyway; by getting rid of it they saved themselves lease fees on land that seemed good only for timber. Nonetheless, the administration considered it had pulled off a coup, as did some of Levers' officials. The colonial administrators looked on the deal as providing an asset for the future Solomon Islands government. Solomon Islanders, especially on Kolombangara, viewed it from a different perspective. To them, the government merely replaced Levers as the owner and the government's reafforestation plans clearly demonstrated its intention to keep the land. On this issue and by the 1977 law, the independent government continued the policy, now owning almost 8 percent of all Solomons land. But the majority of the people see this as merely a continuation of colonial alienation policy, and they still want the land returned to the traditional claimants.[42]

The people have a similar attitude toward mining. Extensive surveys by the government in the fifties and by private companies such as Conzinc Riotinto of Australia (CRA), Utah Mining, and Mitsui Mining and Smelting in the sixties and early seventies revealed the presence of a range of minerals including copper, nickel, bauxite, and phosphate, but in currently uneconomic quantities. Bauxite reserves on Rennell and Vaghena are substantial, but the Japanese firm involved on Rennell eventually withdrew because of a decline in prices coupled with the costs of various concessions demanded by the government. Although the Rennellese with their bauxite and the Bellonese with their phosphate remain divided on whether or not mining is what they wanted, if the projects had gone ahead conflict with the government seemed inevitable on several fronts. The Polynesian Rennell and Bellona people were suspicious of a central government increasingly controlled by Melanesians. Along with other Polynesian minorities in the Solomons, many considered the people of the "black islands" to be little better than barbarians.[43] The exploratory work on these islands and elsewhere gave both Polynesians and Melanesians an awareness of other, broader issues. The people were not so much opposed to mining as to the allotment of royalties. Following British practice the government claimed all royalties. Consistent pressure by members from possible mining areas wrought minor concessions—in 1970 the Mining Amendment Act gave 5 percent of royalties to landholders and the rest to central government, although the landholders wanted 100 percent. Interestingly, the original amendment proposed that the 5 percent should go to the local council, but this was rejected, an indication of the continuing primacy of family and village loyalties.[44] For the present, these issues remain merely dormant, until mining becomes economic, but like the land problem they will not go away.

The colonial government's concentration on these large projects was to the detriment of rural development in that it failed to find a second staple village crop in the twenty years prior to independence. As early as the forties the government had encouraged village rice projects and they were extended in the fifties. Although the people responded well, at the same time as self-government became an option the government abandoned the projects in favor of a quicker and more cost-efficient return from concentrated plantings on the Guadalcanal Plains by overseas companies. As with rice, the cocoa project's initial collapse made villagers cautious about planting any improved varieties. Experts talked of "conservatism" among villagers, but with competitive demands on labor and land, for most people it was simply a case of once bitten, twice shy. Similar experiments and failures, by and large due to erratic or superficial follow-up by agriculture extension services, as with chillies on the weather coast of Guadalcanal for example, have left many villagers disillusioned with government plans for rural agricultural development. On the positive side, when copra prices dramatically fell in 1975 Malaitans, especially, saw the value of having another major cash crop. The renewed interest they showed in the improved cacao stock resulted in a doubling of smallholder production in 1977–1978, contributing about a quarter of the country's total export of cocoa.[45]

Sometimes the government launched into major projects without fully assessing the likely consequences, a weakness in the development plans. The cattle project is a case in point. Throughout the fifties and sixties rural interest in cattle raising was expressed. It could certainly substitute for imports and, in the view of some expatriates, raise Islander self-confidence because the cattle that planters had so long grazed under their coconut palms were very much white men's business. Many Solomon Islanders wanted only small herds, or one or two cows, which they could manage without the expense of clearing and fencing large pasture areas; but the Agriculture Department urged big farms because they were more efficient—that is, easier for its field officers to inspect. By the seventies the project had grown out of all proportion. The aim was now export, and export standards and infrastructure forced operations to be centered, along with so many other industries, around Honiara. Although exports remain insignificant, Australia for instance being able to do it all cheaper and better, the reorientation to the domestic market continues to labor under a legacy of centralization and unnecessarily high standards. At independence much of the cattle project was funded by Australian aid and neither donor nor recipient wanted to admit publicly that the project was in trouble.[46] Had the same investment been put into pig raising, the home and perhaps the export market would have guaranteed success for rural areas. In the seventies that the government could not meet the demand for improved pig stocks was evidence of the people's high interest. Solomon Islanders are already expert pig raisers and, as prewar practice has shown, can contract and expand herds as the price of copra rises and falls. Moreover, a live pig can be carried in a canoe, a cow never. The argument that pigs are traditional wealth and only killed for ceremonial occasions may well hold a lot of truth, but with prosperity occasions for ceremony and celebrations are not hard to find.

Minor crops like cocoa, chillies, and turmeric along with the old staple, copra, provide a little cash for most coastal Solomon Islanders outside paid employment.[47] But marketing difficulties in many areas have reduced income from them. The collecting and marketing of produce have never been easy, but in the period immediately preceding independence shipping to more isolated districts fell off because of the decreased Chinese involvement in trading. As is often the case, decolonization meant a totting up of old scores to be settled. Only the very powerful planters were left, and with Levers cooperating closely with the government on coconut research, Tikopian resettlement, and timber exploitation, it was unlikely an independent government would single them out. New overseas companies, some with the government as shareholders, displayed little of the arrogance of the old colonials, leaving the Chinese as the primary focus for the opprobrium of a few young nationalists and fellow travelers. Unfortuntely, many of the 580 Chinese lacked British passports. There was talk in Honiara circles of driving them out of the country at independence and the occasional opportunistic politician used this as a lever to obtain unlimited credit in Chinese stores. This fear campaign may well have been part of a wider Solomons strategy, as was the threatened expulsion of the resettled Gilbertese, as independence neared. Whatever the intention, about a third of the Chinese, using their links with relatives in Australia, Canada, and the United States, took the hint and left permanently despite subsequent constitutional protection. This left empty trade stores in Honiara's Chinatown, but more significantly it left villagers in places like Choiseul and parts of Makira without any external trade link. Whether the burgeoning cooperative movement or other Solomon Islander entrepreneurial combines will take up the slack remains to be seen, but local investment in coastal shipping has been mainly in the more prosperous and accessible areas.[48]

Beyond the land lies the largest resource of the Solomons, its territorial waters. Except for inshore fishing, it is a resource untapped by Islanders and therefore one that both the colonial and independent governments could offer for exploitation with relative impunity. In 1971 David Kausimae, as chairman of the Natural Resources Committee of the Governing Council, signed an agreement with the Japanese company Taiyo for a survey of the fishing potential of the Solomons. Although heavily criticized by other members, Kausimae defended his stand on the grounds that the venture could provide revenue for a future independent Solomons. After the success of the survey and renegotiation of inshore limits, a joint agreement between Taiyo and the government was finalized in 1972, opening the way for the first major commercial fishery since the whaling era. The government held 25 percent equity (plus an option for a further 24 percent) and some five hundred Solomon Islanders were trained and employed in the industry, based at Tulagi and later Noro, involving the catching, freezing, and canning of tuna-like fish.[49] On the one hand the new industry provided import substitution, but on the other, Solomon Islanders are buying fish from their waters in tins rather than catching their own because bait fishing by Taiyo has reduced the numbers of fish caught by villagers. In balance, the government had made the best of a difficult situation, although future generations may condemn them for selling the fishery to foreigners, just as they condemn their own ancestors for selling land to planters. As it was, both before and after the Taiyo agreement, foreign fishing boats were poaching in Solomons seas. No government then or in the foreseeable future would have the air and sea forces to detect, let alone capture, poachers in the vast waters of the Solomon Islands. At least with the agreement $8 million and more is made annually in export earnings, with some return to government and people.[50]

The people—change and continuity

As their past has demonstrated, the Solomon Islanders are willing to try new ideas and ways—if they can see a probability of benefit and if they can experiment while sacrificing little of their existing security. In economic matters this characteristic has been labeled risk minimization, but it also applies to Solomon Islanders' general attitude to life.[51]

Christianity has been one new way that Solomon Islanders have adopted as their own. By 1970, 90 percent were affiliated with one or other of the Christian denominations, with the remaining 10 percent following "traditional religious customs," mainly in inland Malaita and Guadalcanal.[52] After the establishment and consolidation of the protectorate, Christianity helped Solomon Islanders to reduce some of the risks apparent in the changing circumstances of the islands. For some, the initial conversion was a way of dealing with the arbitrary power of the government; for many, it was a way to discover the basis of this power and the wealth of the Europeans; and for others, it was simply conformity with a growing trend, experimenting with a new movement to see if it had anything real to offer. Christ's assurance, "I came that they may have life and have it abundantly" was appealing for its practical fulfillment in the schools and medical aid provided by the missions.[53] Many missionaries like Goldie and Fallowes demonstrated their concern for not only the spiritual but also the material needs of Solomon Islanders. Just as some prewar missionaries had anticipated the colonial government in their appreciation of the Solomon Islanders' political abilities, in the sixties the missions were assisting with the creation of local churches before talk of constitutional independence for the group was in the wind. Starting with the South Sea Evangelical Mission, which became the South Sea Evangelical Church in 1966, church organization and leadership became Solomon Islands and Islander based. The Methodists followed in 1968, as a part of the United Church of Papua New Guinea and the Solomons; the Adventists localized the important positions of district presidents in 1970. The Melanesian Mission, which first ordained Solomon Islander clergy in the late nineteenth century, by this time claimed a third of the islands' Christians. Early in 1975 it became the Church of Melanesia and at the end of the year installed its first Melanesian archbishop, Norman Palmer, a grandson of Norman Wheatley and half-brother of the recruiter Ernie Palmer. The Roman Catholics were slower to localize because of a shortage of local ordained clergy, partly a result of the extensive education required for their priests and partly of the alien ideal of priestly celibacy in a society where marriage is universally valued. In 1975, however, the Daughters of Mary Immaculate, a religious order for Solomon Islander women, elected its own superior and became largely autonomous.[54]

Despite the growth of Christianity and its independent churches, Solomon Islanders continue with many of their old beliefs. A Christian villager will have no qualms about making gardens around a rock that was a shark-deity shrine in the old days. And the same man will say prayers to spirits for the successful growth of the yams he is planting. Likewise, in villages where there are church services morning and evening, sorcery or the "evil eye" is still feared, magical potions (for success, say, in love) still sought from elderly experts, and unusual occurrences in nature still read as portents. All this may seem incongruous to European outsiders, but would be less so if they knew more of the history of their own ancestors' syncretism in their conversion to Christianity. To most Solomon Islanders, Christianity is a valued system that has provided answers to many of their problems, but since some practices of the old religion still seem effective, why dispense with yet another way of minimizing the many risks of the world—seen or unseen?

In the village economy, Solomon Islanders demonstrate a similar approach. They invest their time, energy, and resources in a variety of economic activities rather than one. The most obvious and long-established sources of cash income are wage labor and cash cropping. With wage labor, the Solomon Islanders of today are in a better position than their pre–World War II counterparts. Certainly they still have various payments to meet—the council rate, school fees for children—but they are no longer bound by penal sanctions to work for a set period for a particular employer. Besides casual paid work for neighbors and kin, they can opt to work in a town or on another island for as long as necessary and when it is most convenient to absent themselves from family and village. There is less disruption of village life than under the old contract system. On wages a worker earns about $400 a year. In marginal areas, wage labor as an alternative source of cash takes considerable pressure off villagers to concentrate their resources on cash cropping where returns might often be far less in terms of both input and upheaval in village routine. On Guadalcanal for example, wage earners in villages on the western north coast connected by road to Honiara's market and port facilities, contributed only 13 percent to the mean annual income of about $80 a head, whereas on the isolated central south coast they contributed about 70 percent to an income of about $19 a head.[55] The sporadic involvement of villagers in the wage sector has other benefits. It helps keep them informed about developments in the towns and other districts as well as providing reliable contacts for forwarding store goods and produce between village and town.[56]

As before the war, cash crops vary from one area to another in importance as a source of income. Malaita, which produced about 30 tons of smallholder copra annually in the early thirties, was by 1978 producing some 2700 tons, 16 percent of the Solomons total. The Western District (excluding Isabel) contribution was 39 percent, whereas Makira-Ulawa's was only 10 percent. Cocoa, on the other hand, was a major cash crop for Malaita, which produced 57 percent of the Solomons smallholder total, compared to the west's 8.7 percent; Guadalcanal was a significant second-place producer of both crops.[57] Although the underlying production pattern for copra is similar to the prewar period, the dichotomy between western and eastern regions is not as stark and, in fact, is reversed for cocoa. District figures can mask significant detail. Areas like north Choiseul, for instance, contributed relatively little in smallholder production to the western total.

Even where cash cropping is a significant source of income, people usually have plantings of more than one crop, say coconuts with cocoa. In addition, a particular household might have interests in the cooperative, a small trade store, and will almost certainly earn some cash from the sale of livestock—pigs, chickens, or the occasional cow. Some cash comes from the invisible "other sources" of government statistics—the sale of local artefacts (wooden bowls, "pudding" mortars, axe handles, oars, canoes, string bags), odd lots of shell and bêche-de-mer, bush foodstuffs (flying foxes, yams, pigeons), betel nut, lime, fish, tobacco, eggs, and so on. Diversification is the cornerstone of the village cash economy and provides maximum flexibility when any one source fails or market prices fall. Most villagers have one main source of income and one to four subsidiary ones. In Mbughotu (Isabel) for example, Herlihy found that 21 percent of area income came from export cash crops, about 17 percent from livestock, about 9 percent from business, 40 percent from regular wages, and 13 percent from "other sources." There is, of course, considerable variation in the contribution to each category with location, but the underlying pattern of diversification remains.[58]

In many Solomon Island societies, villagers, through kinship and inheritance, possess interests in widely dispersed lands. Often they reside away from their home village for a time, to cultivate their cash-crop and subsistence lands and to strengthen ties with relatives in other areas. Again, they spread their energies, but at the same time reduce possible losses should a garden fail or a house be destroyed.[59] These practices relating to the cash economy were well established by the 1930s and probably reflect far more ancient experience of a social and physical environment that threw people into emergency situations on a frequent, if intermittent, schedule. To the economic and agricultural planners of the modern Solomon Islands government, such practices, in the narrow view, are inefficient simply because they limit productivity in terms of any specific item. To the villagers, particularly in marginal areas where cash cropping is comparatively new or marketing uncertain, they provide a guarantee of survival in a wider world, which they rightly recognize is largely beyond their control. More recently, such practices have also been to them protection from the succession of high-risk, "development" fads and fashions that emanate from those same salaried and secure central planners. Adherence to this behavior is their way of slowing change to suit themselves, rather than being swept along in its wake uncontrollably.[60]

In the poor, more isolated areas, the people, as in the past, perceive wage labor as the most reliable source of income.[61] Their need for a cash income has increased as an inevitable concomitant of the development and decolonization process. The massive exposure of Solomon Islanders to Western technology and products during the war years was eventually followed by major aid projects, a dramatic growth in numbers of expatriate public servants and their families, and the rapid development of Honiara and district centers, as well as greater access by Solomon Islanders to modern media and schooling. All these combined to produce, by example as well as precept, a huge leap in the people's aspirations and wants, far beyond the limited demands of the prewar era.

Quite simply, many Solomon Islanders, especially the young who are the most numerous segment of the population, want more than life on the land can presently offer them, as is evident in their attitudes to education.

The conflict over the three-tiered primary-secondary scheme (see p. 318) was largely resolved by the government's retreat from insistence on mission participation in 1967 and a concentration on teacher training. Subsequently, as part of devolution in 1975 primary education increasingly became the responsibility of local education boards. But as well as producing candidates for the next educational step, the primary schools also produced dropouts who were ill fitted for ordinary village life and lacked sufficient formal education to work elsewhere. It is probably no coincidence that on Santa Isabel, whose leaders had pressed for government aid in education in the 1930s, the council took the initiative in 1969 and set up its own Rural Training Centre at Kamaosi (southern Mbughotu) to train primary school leavers for a year in skills relevant to village life. The idea had enormous grass roots support and seemed so promising that other regions adopted it. But all of these rural training centers faltered for much the same reasons—lack of trained staff; funds, time, and enthusiasm wasted on delays in building and delivery of supplies; and the shift of the overall goal from education for village life to education for paid employment within the island or region. Nonetheless, the concept appealed to the central government and became policy as a result of the 1973 White Paper on education, produced by a committee chaired by Francis Bugotu. The paper stipulated that this new middle level in the education system should only be established and funded by the central government if the catchment area would allow the purchase of land for the graduates to farm. The project involved the establishment of a "New Secondary" school in each major rural district with plans for twenty-two eventually. These were not to be just practical vocational schools, but schools with a two-year curriculum attuned to local needs and aimed at educating young men and women in village craft and culture as well as some basic business knowledge, health principles, and village cash cropping. By providing education at and for the local level it was hoped by legislators and educationists alike to reaffirm the importance of traditional values, as well as to avoid a crop of primary dropouts discontented with village life. However, just before independence members of the Legislative Assembly put forward plans to incorporate the New Secondaries into the existing national secondary school system with an academic curriculum of three years. This change was forced by their constituents. Expatriate educationists argued that the New Secondaries were never given a chance. The central government, fearful of the touchy land question, had lacked the courage to push the requirement that land be reserved for the graduates. Moreover, the schools had been poorly organized and were set up in great haste.[62] Whatever the reasons, the local people saw as well as any visitor that the schools were "a shambles," reconfirming their fears that their children were being fobbed off with a second-rate education by a selfish government, even though that education was cloaked in the garb of reaffirming traditional culture and local values.[63]

The quest by villagers for education for their children reflects their concern for advancement and participation in both the cash economy and the wider Solomons society. But it would be a misconception to see this as a spurning of the societal values of the village and local community. Today, as traditionally, the possession of wealth is both a prerequisite for and concomitant of prestige and leadership. Solomon Islanders see Western education as the key to the most versatile form of wealth—cash. Although the means are transformed, the end is the same.

Sophisticated national parliamentarians, for example, also want their children to receive a Western education, but will often set one child aside for *kastom*, for education by the family and clan in things of traditional value, things that are important in the micro politics of the village. Although a person's ability to acquire, mobilize, and channel wealth, especially cash, is the basis of modern big-manship, the means to acquire this wealth involve knowledge of matters like customary land tenure, genealogy, local history, and ecology. Educating a child in these matters bestows the chance to become a future big-man, and at the same time, acknowledges and reconfirms the significance of current big-men or chiefs who still continue to be important in village and local politics. Although frequently unable to participate directly in the national arena because of lack of English and formal education, such leaders do influence national politics by giving support or withholding it from parliamentary candidates, as some have found to their sorrow.

Other aspects of village society continue to be important in the eyes of Solomon Islanders. Urban-based parents frequently return to their home village, often leaving their children there with relatives, not simply for convenience or for blatant political reasons, but to learn village ways, the language, and to keep warm their claims to membership in that community. And with good reason. A Solomon Islander who has relatives is never alone against the world. In Honiara, where the supports and sanctions of village society are absent, marriages often falter. Wife-beating fueled by alcohol is an increasing problem. Women and children, if they can find the fare home, still have the village as a refuge. Where claims are acknowledged by clan and village, no Solomon Islander would be denied garden land and the means to subsistence. The village still represents life and livelihood. Solomon Islanders who sustain these kinds of village links can be seen as keeping their options open, getting the best of both worlds, or as providing yet another example of risk minimization.

The urban population of Honiara, the only real town in the Solomons, numbered almost 15,000 in 1976.[64] This population is fluid. Although professional and skilled Solomon Islanders employed by the administration and business periodically absent themselves from the town to revive village relationships, by far the most mobile and numerous section of the population is the nonskilled and semiskilled labor force. These men and increasing numbers of women come to town to work for a few months or years on an intermittent basis before returning to their villages. Many like the experience and all want the wages, but few commit themselves entirely to the town and town living. There is no permanent urban proletariat, although a small urban-based class is beginning to emerge among the higher-paid Western-educated public servants and employees of major business firms. These people have not renounced their village affiliations, but most perceive the "subsistence affluence" of village life as being relatively deprived without a constant inflow of cash to satisfy the range of new material and social needs associated with their town life-style. Their commitment to the new state is not simply ideological, but also economic. The state feeds its workers, it is their new *kumara* garden. Although they may not yet be engaged in activities that permit them to accumulate capital, they are its brokers since they make and implement decisions as to where and how government revenues—of which one third is the result of the productivity of other countries—will be spent.

When the central government talks of national interests, the bulk of the population tends to see this group, in the main those who live, work, and play in Honiara, as the main beneficiaries. The reasons for this lie partly in the transference of the old distrust of the colonial government to its heir and partly in even older traditions of local autonomy. But they also lie in the perceived disparity in living standards and opportunities between town and village. The government's attempts to narrow the gap or, in the words of the National Development Plan 1975–1979, ". . . to improve the distribution of available wealth, to avoid the growth of privileged and powerful minorities, and to ensure a fair sharing of opportunity and welfare among all the people of the Solomon Islands . . ."[65] have thus far led to economic policies which, while they may result in a higher rate of growth in national income, are incompatible with such national goals. Growth, or even maintenance, of national income means continuing reliance on other countries for aid as well as reliance on big projects such as timber extraction, fisheries, or agribusiness, like the rice-growing project on Guadalcanal—all of which are controlled by foreign companies or are joint ventures of the same with the government. Either way, rural development tends to become an agglomeration of piecemeal projects or to be relegated to second place in any planning. Yet, while the rapidly growing population continues to expect and demand of the government a greater share of health and education services—to say nothing of individual desires for material possessions like radios, watches, and outboard motors—these economic policies and their inherent contradictions are unlikely to be resolved without major social or political upheaval. The resolution of these issues and the tensions between macro and micro politics are certain to be dominant themes in the history of the independent Solomon Islands.

DURING THE PERIOD FROM 1955 until independence, Britain largely dictated the timetable of economic and political change in the Solomons, laying the foundations of the modern state. The pace was slow at first, but it quickened when the British government reached the inescapable conclusion that the Solomons must either become independent or become the junior partner in some kind of special relationship. The latter would only keep the British embroiled in Pacific affairs when their national interests were no longer involved there, even indirectly. By the early seventies, independence was by far the better option for Britain.

Economic policy concentrated less on the immediate postwar goal of restoring Solomon Islanders to their old role of self-employed primary producers and the retention of marketing functions and profitability within the Solomons. From the sixties on, the British increased aid funds to build the infrastructure necessary for more rapid national development, once again turning to plantation agriculture, albeit diversified, as a major money spinner. However, in relation to these projects as much as rural development, central planners learned that social factors, like the Solomon Islanders' attachment to their lands, presented obstacles to increasing the gross domestic product.

Political and constitutional development was also set on the "fast-forward" switch. National elections, a House of Assembly, variations of the Westminster system, political parties, a chief minister, and all the paraphernalia of the decolonization process came in rapid succession. Yet Solomon Islander parliamentarians delayed Britain's nice timetable for independence in the final stages. Their political style of risk minimization resulted in constant shifts in party and leadership allegiances along with a predictable exploitation of the vulnerability of colonial administrators during this transition period. In the districts, provincial governments were established hastily in a bid to recognize regional differences, just when fears of impending independence had made them a potent force. Neither acknowledgment of regional interests, nor many of the policies of a Solomon Islander–elected House at self-government, were sufficient to quieten such fears. Nor did they lessen the demands for financial grants from the central government, whose representatives not long before had been the leading voices calling for the same from the colonial authorities. With independence, the time of real nation building had only just begun.

Epilogue

FROM THIS STUDY of the Solomon Islanders and their relationships with their environment, one another, and the outside world has emerged the dominance of the plantation economy. Buttressed by the colonial government, this economy affected Solomons societies throughout most of the colonial period, creating both challenges and choices.

Solomon Islanders avidly sought the prized metal and other manufactured goods of the early European visitors. What had once been a want became a need and inevitably a dependency. In their quest for the new goods Solomon Islanders could perceive no loss of control in dealing with the traders and no abdication of local autonomy in offering for contract work on overseas plantations. But to the European entrepreneurs, the early coconut-oil and copra trading, together with migrant labor, were merely first steps toward the logical conclusion that overheads would fall and profits rise if they themselves were to control the sources and means of production with the help of a compliant, inexpensive government. That conclusion may have been logical until the close of the second decade of the twentieth century, but other, unaccountable variables could and did influence profitability. In the Solomon Islands, an unexpected shortage of labor soon became the prime hindrance. And this on a backdrop of a range of variable if not uncontrollable factors such as climate, insect and fungal parasites, and distance from markets —enduring facts of life on most tropical islands, but often underestimated by investing Europeans. Beyond the islands, the leveling off of demand for vegetable oil, along with its overproduction, combined with the Great Depression in the 1930s to produce stagnation of the cash economy in the Solomons. World War II knocked the tottering economy completely off its feet. Yet the plantation-based economy had been so dominant that even during postwar reconstruction it remained central to government planning; at independence, it retained a signifi-

344

cant place although some superficial features such as forms of ownership and types of crops had altered by then.

Throughout, the plantation economy impinged on Solomon Islanders' lives. For some, its influence was indirect; in much of the western
and some of the central Solomons, where productivity was high relative
to population, Solomon Islanders retained their roles as small-scale producers of copra. Yet the structures and strictures of government, along
with the marketing and shipping network controlled by Europeans, had
all been premised on the plantation economy, and these Islanders inevitably felt its influence. In the eastern Solomons, the source of most plantation labor, men were employed directly at some time in their lives in
working on or around plantations. Until recently this involvement,
whether indirect or direct, was for Solomon Islanders at the lowest level
—simply as small producers or laborers, with no control of the plantation economy's infrastructure, organization, or policies. Nonetheless,
that economy and its bedfellow, the colonial government, created
unique challenges to the small-scale and disparate societies of the
islands. In a remarkably short time those societies replied, developing
ways of forging new identities and of asserting them. Many grasped and
exploited the potential of the new life offered by Christianity. Others
consolidated a less homogeneous mixture of ancient cultural values, an
inchoate, plantation-formed island awareness, and Western concepts of
political representation. In the 1930s, after years of gradually extending
its control into village life, the protectorate government found itself
confronted not by little bands of axe-wielding "savages," but by large
groups of people assembling peacefully to express their grievances either
directly or through petitions. Except for the successful "tax strike" with
its limited goals in the western Solomons, the government ignored such
pleas. The Pacific War proved a catalyst for both unrest and its expression, culminating in movements like Maasina Rule.

But Maasina Rule and similar movements were limited. They were
island or region based and lacked any pan-Solomons support. Fundamental elements—such as a literate, Western-educated leadership
group who could talk the same language and play the same game as
their masters—would have had to have been present to make them
more than temporary, localized threats to the government and the plantation economy. Given time and an intransigent colonial power this
might have happened, but it is no more the historian's brief to dwell on
past possibilities than it is the humanitarian's wish that oppression
might have been greater. Just as the anti-British and anticolonial feelings manifest in such movements reached their highest since the days of
pacification, many of the basic reasons for discontent either vanished or
weakened as the British found themselves in a world where colonialism
had become a dirty word. Although still operating very much within its

own political idiom, the protectorate government, as an instrument of British control, was as willing to change its policies as groups of Solomon Islanders were to demand such changes. To a large extent, the years from the mid-fifties until independence were a period of denouement, when the details of that changed will and concomitant relationships were worked out.

Although in the immediate postwar decade there was a strong grassroots antipathy toward British authority in many districts, it was largely countered by the economic, social, and regional political development that resulted from the new governmental policies. In the late sixties and early seventies only a very small group, mainly a handful of the first university and other tertiary graduates, began to be conscious of what they saw as the moral injustice of colonialism. Before they could even develop a coherent ideological expression of their intellectual discontent, the Solomons were on the short constitutional journey to independence. Britain had again upstaged its critics.

The Solomons were catapulted into independence without any semblance of a great national struggle or even a shared patriotic ideology that might have bound their people together. Some would see this as a weakness in the new state. However, the force most likely to hold the Solomons together as a political entity is the reality of its economic and international position. The wealth of the Solomons is limited. In 1978 when the islands became independent they joined the long line of Pacific mendicant states. Although not as dependent as some on outside aid, over a third of the Solomons' income is from overseas—a proportion that is unlikely to decrease before the year 2000. As the western "breakaway" demonstrated, any politically secessionist island or group would have to face this fact, together with the desire of major donor states like Britain, Australia, New Zealand, and Japan for stability in Melanesia. And as the Japanese invasion in 1943 and, more recently, Indonesian control of Irian Jaya have illustrated, colonialism is not simply a nineteenth-century European prerogative. Old allegiances can alter too. In 1984, the government's justified detention of an American tuna-fishing boat for illegal operations in its territorial waters met with a United States ban on Solomons' exports, thereby stripping Solomon Islanders of any illusions they might have had about contemporary international political realities. Today, as nations rather than as islands inhabited by various peoples, the postcolonial Solomons and their Pacific Island neighbors remain vulnerable to forces beyond their beaches, including the consequences of the nuclear wargames of the great powers. Although regional tensions originating in island-based resource disparities and frustrated aspirations are likely to characterize the domestic politics of the Solomons, a united front on national and external issues, whether or not actively backed by concerned foreign states, will continue to be presented internationally. As Solomon Islands leaders know, to do otherwise, could well invite the beginning of a new and vastly more destructive colonial age.

The significance of a nation, like that of an individual, is not to be measured merely in terms of material wealth and the brute force of arms. That the many and varied small societies of the Solomons responded with intelligence and creativity to the challenges of contact with the outside world and a mighty colonial power augurs well for the new nation. As their history shows, the diversity of the Solomons, far from being a drawback, provides a rich, sustaining culture for the seeds of new visions—visions that will not only guide their own people, but may one day influence those in the wider world whose exploring ancestors less than two centuries ago forever ended the islands' isolation.

APPENDIXES

APPENDIX 1
Whaling contacts and sightings, c. 1800–1890

Year	Ship[1]	Flag[2]	Type of encounter,[3] by island or group[4]					
			Shs	Chl	NGw	NGe	SIl	RIs
1799	*Resource*	USA						
1803	*Patterson*	USA	C	C	C	S		
1806	*Eliza*	USA						
1822	*Roscoe*	USA						
c. 1824	?							
c. 1825	?							
1827	*Clay*	USA						
1828	Alfred	ANZ						
1828	*John Bull*[5]	ANZ					C	
1828/29	*Alfred*	ANZ						
	Cadmus	ANZ						
1828	Hibernia	USA					C	
1828	Zephyr	ANZ					S	
	John Bull	ANZ						
1829	*Australian*	ANZ						
1829	Elizabeth Collins							
	?							
	Lynx	ANZ						
c. 1830	Wolf							
1830/31	*Australian*	ANZ					S	
1830/31	New Zealand	ANZ					S	
1830/31	Woodlark	ANZ						
1830/31	Elizabeth	ANZ					S	
	Devernon	ANZ						
	Old Ham	ANZ						
	Caroline	Br/ANZ			S			
	Proteus	ANZ						
	Albion	ANZ						
1830/31	Dolt	ANZ						
1831/32	Hashmy							
1832	Lady Rowena							
1832	*Primrose*						S	
1832	*Vigilant*	Br	S		S			
	Albion	ANZ	S					
	Ashing				S			
	Pocklington	ANZ			S			
	?				S			
	Lord Rodney	ANZ						
	Proteus	ANZ						
1835	Anastasia							
1835	Lord Rodney	ANZ						
1835/36	?	ANZ		S?		S	C	
c. 1836	Cornwallis							
1836	Marshall Bennett		C?	C?				
1837	Fabius[6]	USA						
1837	*Addison*	USA				S	S	
1838	Achilles							
1839	*William Hamilton*	USA	C		C		C	
	Caernarvon	Br			C			
	Gem		S					
1840	Elizabeth	ANZ?						
1841	*Fortune*	USA	S					
c. 1842	Offley	Br	D					
1842	*Gipsy*	Br	C		S			
	Proteus	ANZ						
	Sarah and Elizabeth							
	Caroline	ANZ			S			

350

Nga	Gul	Maa	SCl	SCz	R&B	OJa	Sia	Tia	Source
S	S	S	S						*Resource*
									Patterson
							S?		*Eliza*
		S							*Roscoe*
								C	Dillon 1829
								C	Dillon 1829
		C					S		*Clay*
		D							*SGSGTL* 11 Dec. 1852
		D							*SGSGTL* 11 Dec. 1852
	S	C		D			C	C	*SGSGTL* 11 Dec. 1852, *Alfred*
		S							Cattlin 1828
		D		D					T. W. Smith 1844 (unreliable)
		S							Cattlin 1828
		D							Cattlin 1828
		S	S		C				Cattlin 1829–1831
		S							Cattlin 1829–1831
			S						Cattlin 1829–1831
				S					*SG* 13 Feb. 1830
								C	*SGNSWA* 22 Jan. 1839
		S		S					Cattlin 1829–1831
		C?							Cattlin 1829–1831
		S?	S?						Foster 1975
		C							Cattlin 1829–1831
		S							Cattlin 1829–1831
		S							Cattlin 1829–1831
		C	C?	S	C?				Cattlin 1829–1831
				S					Cattlin 1829–1831
				S?					Cattlin 1829–1831
				S?					Cattlin 1829–1831
		C							*SH* 16 July 1832; *AJMR* June 1832, 103
								C	*SH* 16 Jan. 1832
	C	S	C						*Primrose* (PMB 12)
	S				S				Swain 1835
									Swain 1835
									Swain 1835
									Swain 1835
									Swain 1835
S					S				Swain 1835
S					S				Swain 1835
				C					*AJMR* Dec. 1835, 236
			C						*SGSGTL* 11 Dec. 1852
			C						Cattlin 1835–1836
							C		Cattlin 1835–1836
									NM 9 (1840)
						D			*RRAACP* 1950: *Salem Gazette*, 16 June 1837
		S							*Addison*
								D	*SGNSWA* 22 Jan. 1839
		C	C		C				*William Hamilton* (PMB 376, 819)
		C					C		*William Hamilton* (PMB 376, 819, 898)
									William Hamilton (PMB 376)
		C							*SGSGTL* 11 Dec. 1852
									Fortune
									SMH 5 Jan. 1843; *Gipsy*
									Gipsy
		S							*SMH* 16 March 1842
		S							*SMH* 16 March 1842
									Gipsy

(continued)

Year	Ship[1]	Flag[2]	Shs	Chl	NGw	NGe	SIl	RIs
			Type of encounter,[3] by island or group[4]					
1842/43	Clarice	USA	S					S
1843	Tuscaloosa	USA						
1845	WOODLARK	ANZ	C					
1845	Levant	USA					S	
1846	BROUGHAM	Br			S	S		
	NELSON	ANZ	D					
	Eliza Ann	USA						
	AUSTRALIAN	ANZ						
1846	Navigator	USA						
1847	Christopher Mitchell	USA						
1848	FAME	ANZ						
1848	Atlantic	USA						
	NELSON	ANZ						
	BOYD	ANZ						
1849	Olympia	USA			S		S	
	Alfred	USA					C	
	Elizabeth	USA						
	BROTHERS	USA						
	Planter	USA						
1850	Herald	USA	C					
1851	JANE	ANZ						
	STAR	ANZ	C					
	Fellowes	USA						
	EARLE HARDWICKE							
1854	Gay Head	USA	S				S	
	WOODLARK	ANZ						
	BELLE							
c. 1855	Young Hector	USA						
	POST BOY	ANZ?			C			
1855	Peruvian	USA		S			S	
1855	Martha	USA						
	Lion	USA	S					
1856	Woodlark	USA						
	Belle	USA						
	POST BOY		C					
	Alfred Gibbs	USA						
	Young Hector	USA						
	Peruvian	USA		S				
1856/57	Zone	USA						
1857	Young Hector	USA						
	WOODLARK	ANZ						
1857	GANGES	ANZ						
	KATE	ANZ						
	CAERNARVON	ANZ						
	ELIZA	ANZ						
c. 1858	James Arnold	USA	C	S	C			
1858	JOSEPH BUTLER				S			
	JANE		C		S			
1859	Belle	USA						
	Hope	USA						
	Two Brothers	USA	S	C	S	S		
1860	Two Brothers	USA						
1860	INDEPENDENCE	ANZ						
	ONYX	ANZ						
	MAURY							
	HIAWATHA	USA						
	SEABIRD				S			
	Superior	USA	D		C			
	HENRIETTA						D	C
	Eugenia		S					

Nga	Gul	Maa	SCl	SCz	R&B	OJa	Sia	Tia	Source
	S	S	S						*Clarice*
				S					*Tuscaloosa*
									SGSGTL 22 Nov. 1845
		S					C		*Levant*
									NM 16 (1847)
									SGSGTL 7 March 1846
		S							*Eliza Ann*
				S?					*Eliza Ann*
				S					*Navigator*
		C					C		*Christopher Mitchell;*
									SGSGTL 23 Oct. 1847
	S								*Atlantic*
	C						C		*Atlantic*
	S								*Atlantic*
	S								*Atlantic*
	S						S		*Olympia* (PMB 273–274)
	C		C						*Alfred*
			C						*Elizabeth*
	S								*Alfred*
					C				Paddock 1893
				S					*Herald* 1847–1854
		C							*SGSGTL* 3 Jan. 1852
									SGSGTL 13 March 1852
				S[7]					*Fellowes*
				S[7]					*Fellowes*
	C?	S	C						*Gay Head*
	S		C						*SMH* 16 Oct. 1854
	S								*SMH* 16 Oct. 1854
						C?			*Young Hector*
									SMH 21 Aug. 1855
									Peruvian
		S							*Martha*
		C	C	C					*Lion*
	S		2C	2C					*Woodlark;*
									SGSGTL 19 Oct. 1857
			C				C		*Belle*
									SMH 8 Jan. 1856
		S	C				C		*Alfred Gibbs*
		S		S				S	*Young Hector*
									Peruvian
				S					*Zone*
		S							*Young Hector*
		S?							*SGSGTL* 19 Oct. 1857
		C							*Young Hector*
		C							*SGSGTL* 10 Oct. 1857
		C							*SGSGTL* 19 Oct. 1857
		C							*SGSGTL* 19 Oct. 1857
									James Arnold
									James Arnold
									James Arnold
				S					*Belle*
							C		*Hope; SMH* 21 Dec. 1860
C?	C	C					C		*Two Brothers*
	C	C		S					*Two Brothers*
		C							Bradford 1861
		C							Bradford 1861
		C							*Two Brothers*
		C		S					*Two Brothers*
									Superior
									Superior
									RRAACP 1950
									Eugenia

(continued)

Year	Ship[1]	Flag[2]	Type of encounter,[3] by island or group[4]					
			Shs	Chl	NGw	NGe	SII	RIs
1861	*Eugenia*		S		S	S		
1861	MISSION							
	Jirah Perry	USA						
	Sun	USA	S		S	S		
	Mohawk	USA						
	Cambria	USA						
1861	CLEMATIS[8]							
	DRAPER							
1863	*Massachusetts*	USA				S		
	Sunbeam	USA						
	Parachute	USA	S		C	S		
	Ontario	USA						
1864	*Ontario*	USA		S				
c. 1865	*Aurora*	USA					S	
1867	*Stephanie*	USA						
1868	*Stephanie*	USA						
	ARTHUR PICKERING							
	RAINBOW							
1869	*Stephanie*	USA						
1870	*Helen Snow*	ANZ						
1873	VICTORIA	ANZ						
	Marengo	USA						
	Adeline Gibbs	USA	C					
1874	BENJAMIN CUMMINGS	USA						
	Matilda Sears	USA						
1875	*California*	USA						
c. 1875	*Arnolda*	USA						
c. 1880	*Velocity*	ANZ						
	ONWARDS	ANZ						
1884	*Swallow*	USA						
1887	*John and Winthrop*	USA						

NOTES: 1. Ship names in *italics* indicate information from log, journal, memoirs, etc., of crew members; names in SMALL CAPITALS indicate mention in other ships' logs, newspapers, etc.
2. Vessel originated in America (USA), Britain (Br), or Australian or New Zealand colonies (ANZ).
3. C, communication; S, sighting; D, disturbance, conflict, or fight between crew and Islanders.
4. Shs, Shortlands; Chl, Choiseul; NGw, west New Georgia Islands; NGe, east New Georgia Islands; SII, Santa Isabel; RIs, Russell Islands; Nga, Nggela; Gul, Guadalcanal; Maa, Malaita; SCl, San Cristobal, Santa Ana, etc.; SCz, Santa Cruz; R&B, Rennell and Bellona; OJa, Ontong Java; Sia, Sikaiana; Tia, Tikopia.

		Type of encounter,[3] by island or group[4]							
Nga	Gul	Maa	SCl	SCz	R&B	OJa	Sia	Tia	Source
			C						*Eugenia*
			C						*Eugenia*
				S					*Jirah Perry*
									Sun
	S	S	C			S			*Mohawk*
			C				C		*Cambria*
			C						*RRAACP* 1950
			C						*Mohawk*
						S			*Massachusetts* (PMB 349)
						C			*Sunbeam*
									Parachute
			C	C		S	C	S	*Ontario*
							C		*Ontario*
C	S	S	S				C	C	*Aurora*
							C		*Stephanie* (PMB 221)
							C		*Stephanie* (PMB 221)
			C?						*SMH* 27 Oct. 1868
							C		*Stephanie* (PMB 221)
			S				S	S	*Stephanie* (PMB 221)
							S		*Helen Snow*
			C?						*UK-RNAS* 13: Rendle to Stirling, 14 Sept. 1873
							C		*Marengo*
									Adeline Gibbs
			C						*UK-RNAS* 13: Williams to Governor of NSW, 4 Jan. 1875
			C		S				*Matilda Sears*
				S					*California*
		C	C						*Arnolda*
C			C						J. W. Robinson 1904
			C						J. W. Robinson 1904
						C			*Swallow*
						C			*John and Winthrop*

5. The master of the *John Bull* appears to have investigated this attack with the hope of somehow finding Matthews, the man kidnapped from the *Alfred* (*AJMR* 1828, 757).

6. The source states that this ship was taken at Hawl's or Howe's Group. No coordinates are given, nor any other indication of location. There is a Lord Howe Island in the Santa Cruz group and another in Tonga. The neighboring atolls to Ontong Java (Lord Howe's Group)—the Mortlocks and the Nukumanu Islands—were often confused with Lord Howe's Group by early navigators.

7. Sighted Mitre Island.

8. *Clematis* was wrecked on Indispensable Reef and the crew went to San Cristobal in boats.

APPENDIX 2

Castaways, deserters, and runaway convicts in the Solomon Islands, c. 1820–1870

Date	Location	Person(s)	Remarks	Sources
c. 1820s	North Malaita	14 Englishmen and 6 Lascars	Extremely unlikely as the source is unreliable	T. W. Smith 1844
c. 1820s	Maana'oba, North Malaita	"Doorey"	Was this Matthews?	Marwick 1935; *AJMR* June 1832, 103
1826	Tikopia	5 Englishmen, including T. Reader and James Coutts	Two men claimed to be deserters from *Harriet*. Three claimed to be castaways from a wrecked whaler. Evidence suggests they were escaped convicts from Tasmania	Dillon 1829, 117–119
c. 1830	Mahia, San Cristobal	3 white men	Two died and one boarded a passing ship for Sydney	Verguet 1885, 193–232; Woodford Papers: Account of . . . Marist Mission . . .
1839	Simbo	1 white man	Left a ship at Sikaiana and the *Caernarvon* of London took him to Simbo	*William Hamilton*; *Caernarvon*
1844	Simbo	James Dornin, George Macleod, Warren Minerley, James Jones	Found there by Andrew Cheyne	Shineberg 1971b, 313
1851	Makira Harbour, San Cristobal	7 men from *Jane*	Deserters	*SGSGTL*, 3 Jan. 1852

Date	Location	Name/People	Description	Reference
1854	Southwest Guadalcanal	Denis Griffiths (Dani)	Griffiths was a convict aboard HMS *Herald* which came to Wanderer Bay to investigate Benjamin Boyd's death. Griffiths ran away and lived for many years with the Ghari people	Denham 1855
1854	San Cristobal	1 white man		*Gay Head*
1857	Makira Harbour	11 crewmen from *Kate* and *Caernarvon*	Deserters	*SGSGTL* 19 Oct. 1857
1858	Sikaiana	John Davis	Left on island against his will by the notorious Captain Ross, sandalwooder	Scherzer 1861:2, 603–609
1858	Makira Harbour	2 crewmen from *Independence*	Deserters	Bradford 1861
1860	Makira Harbour	F. J. Bradford	Signed off from *Hiawatha*	Bradford 1861
1862	Makira Harbour	1 white man		*Eugenia*
1862	San Cristobal	Henry Dady, Nicholas King	Discharged at Makira Harbour from *Eugenia*	*Eugenia*
1865	Hada, San Cristobal	1 American black and 1 white man	Shipwrecked on Indispensable Reef, probably off the *Clematis*	Rietman 1868, 183–184
c. 1868	Sulufou, Malaita	John Renton and companions	Companions either died of natural causes or were killed before Renton was rescued	Marwick 1935
1873	San Cristobal	W. Perry		See Appendix 5 and *NM* 40 (1871), 125
1874	San Cristobal	John Murray, J. J. Coleman, W. Wenquist, R. Jackson	Deserters from the *Matilda Sears* at Makira Harbour. One drowned	*Matilda Sears*

APPENDIX 3

Items of trade, where mentioned, of whaling ships and other non-trading vessels, 1798–1860

Year	Ship	Place	Received	Given	Sources
1798	Ann and Hope	Sth San Cristobal	Coconuts, spears, shells, tapa	Knives, trinkets, biscuits	Ann and Hope
1802	Canada	NE Guadalcanal	Two-three spears	Not mentioned (N/M)	Canada
1803	Buffalo	Simbo	Coconuts, breadfruit, tortoiseshell ornaments, mother-of-pearl, spears, and arrows	Old iron knives, nails. *Stolen:* two bayonets, buckle with belt, glass	Kent Family Papers
1803	Patterson	Simbo	Coconuts, plantains, trinkets	Iron hoop, knives, nails, bottles. *Stolen:* a cap	Patterson
1813*	Hunter	Tikopia	Yams, fruit	Fish hooks, cloth	Dillon 1829
1827	Clay	Santa Ana	Coconuts, armlets, necklaces	Iron	Clay
1828	John Bull	Isabel	N/M	Iron hoop	Cattlin 1828
1828	John Bull	Nth Malaita	Cooked taro (poisoned?)	N/M	Cattlin 1828
1828	John Bull	Sikaiana	Coconuts, taro, fruit, two "turtles"	N/M	Cattlin 1828
1828	Alfred	Nth Malaita	Coconuts and "apples," two "old coconuts"	Iron hoop	Cattlin 1829
1828	Alfred	Santa Cruz	Coconuts	N/M	Cattlin 1829
1828	Alfred	Tikopia	Yams and fowls	N/M	Cattlin 1829
1830	Alfred	Rennell	"Took" wood at Rennell		Cattlin 1829
1832	Primrose	New Georgia or Simbo	Coconuts and tortoiseshell	N/M	Tregurtha Autobiography

Year	Primrose	Tinakula	Coconuts, nuts, yams, weapons, shells	Iron hoop, gimlets, nails, mirror, coloured beads, and necklaces	Tregurtha Autobiography
1833					
1835	(Cattlin)	Isabel? or	Taro, bananas	N/M	Cattlin 1836
1835	(Cattlin)	Choiseul?	Fruit	N/M	Cattlin 1836
1835	(Cattlin)	Isabel?	Taro, fruit	N/M	Cattlin 1836
1835	(Cattlin)	Isabel	Breadfruit, taro, coconuts, wood, water, pig	N/M	Cattlin 1836
1836	(Cattlin)	Ulawa	Coconuts	N/M	Cattlin 1836
1839	William Hamilton	Sth San Cristobal	Yams, plantains	Iron hoops	William Hamilton (PMB 376, 819)
1839	William Hamilton	Malaita	Coconuts, yams	Iron hoop	William Hamilton (PMB 376, 819)
1839	William Hamilton	Shortlands	Tortoiseshell	N/M	William Hamilton (PMB 376, 819)
1839	William Hamilton	Mono	Tortoiseshell, taro	Iron hoop, hatchets	William Hamilton (PMB 376, 819)
1842	Gipsy	Mono	Wood, taro, a few shells	N/M	Gipsy
1845	Levant	Sikaiana	Pigs, fowls	N/M	Levant
1847	Christopher Mitchell	Sikaiana	Coconuts	N/M	Christopher Mitchell
1847	Christopher Mitchell	Ulawa	N/M	Iron hoop	Christopher Mitchell

(continued)

APPENDIX 3: *Items of trade, where mentioned, of whaling ships and other non-trading vessels, 1798–1860 (cont.)*

Year	Ship	Place	Received	Given	Sources
1847	Christopher Mitchell	San Cristobal	Yams, fruit, water	N/M	Christopher Mitchell
1848	Atlantic	Sikaiana	Coconuts	N/M	Atlantic
1848	Atlantic	Gower Island	50 coconuts	N/M	Atlantic
1849	Alfred	Santa Cruz	Bows, arrows, coconuts	Fish hooks, beads	Alfred
1849	Alfred	Malaita	Green coconuts	N/M	Alfred
1849	Alfred	NW Isabel	Tortoiseshell, nuts	Iron hoop, 1–2 hatchets	Alfred
1849	Alfred	Shortlands	Tortoiseshell	N/M	Alfred
1850	Havannah	Vanikolo	N/M	Fish hooks, cap, shirt	Vigors 1850
1850	Havannah	Santa Catalina	Coconuts, bananas, clubs, wooden bowl	Knives, hooks, calico	Vigors 1850
1850	Havannah	Sth San Cristobal	Spears, bowls, clubs, fruits, tortoiseshell, bracelets	Fish hooks, bottles	Vigors 1850
1850	Havannah	Ulawa	3 waist belts	3 tomahawks	Vigors 1850
1851	Wanderer	Sikaiana	Pigs	Knives, tomahawks, tobacco, calico	Webster 1863, 60
1851	Wanderer	Sth San Cristobal	Yams	Tomahawks, files, beads, knives	Webster 1863, 67, 73
1852	Herald	Sth San Cristobal	Yams, taro, coconuts, nuts, pigs, birds, spears, clubs, ornaments, shell, tortoiseshell	Nails, knives, beads, axes, tomahawks, iron hoop, glass bottles	MacGillivray Dec. 1852
1852	Herald	Sth Guadalcanal	Vegetables	Axes, "etc."	MacGillivray Dec. 1852
1854	Gay Head	Nth San Cristobal	Yams	N/M	Gay Head

1855	*Lion*	Santa Cruz	Yams, "etc."	N/M	*Lion*
1855	*Lion*	Nth San Cristobal	Yams	N/M	*Lion*
1856	*Young Hector*	Gower Island	Took 500 coconuts (probably stolen)	N/M	*Young Hector*
1856	*Alfred Gibbs*	Sikaiana	13 hogs and 3 boat-loads of coconuts	N/M	*Alfred Gibbs*
1856	*Alfred Gibbs*	Sth San Cristobal	Water, wood, yams	N/M	*Alfred Gibbs*
1856	*Belle*	Sth San Cristobal	Water, wood	N/M	*Belle* 1852
1858	*James Arnold*	Mono	"Trading"	N/M	*James Arnold*
1858	*James Arnold*	Simbo	Pigs, coconuts	Tobacco, pipes	*James Arnold*
1859	*Hope*	Sikaiana	10 hogs, 26 barrels of coconuts	N/M	*Hope*
1859	*Hope*	Santa Cruz	10 barrels yams	N/M	*Hope*
1859	*Two Brothers*	Sikaiana	Coconuts, pigs	N/M	*Two Brothers*
1859	*Two Brothers*	Florida?	Yams	N/M	*Two Brothers*
1859	*Two Brothers*	Fauro or Choiseul	Tortoiseshell	Hatchets	*Two Brothers*
1859	*Two Brothers*	Sth San Cristobal	Wood, water	N/M	*Two Brothers*
1860	*Two Brothers*	Sth Guadalcanal	Yams	N/M	*Two Brothers*
1860	*Superior*	Simbo	Coconuts, yams, hogs, eggs	N/M	*Superior*
1860	*Superior*	Mono	Water, taro, tortoiseshell	N/M	*Superior*
1860	*Superior*	Mono	Water, wood, vegetables	N/M	*Superior*

* When Dillon came to Tikopia and Vanikolo in 1827 searching for La Pérouse's wrecked ships, he gave many presents in exchange for relics of the expedition. This did not constitute normal trade and so has been omitted.

APPENDIX 4
Exports and shipping from Solomon Islands to port of Sydney, c. 1854–1896

Year	Month	Ship	Tonnage	Captain	Agent
1854	Aug.	*Oberon*	47	Truscott	
	Dec.	*Oberon*		Truscott	
	Dec.	*Post Boy*	96	Blake	
	TOTAL				
1855	April	*Jenny Lucie*	98	Blair	
	July	*Oberon**		Devlin	R. T. Ford
	Aug.	*Post Boy*		Blake	R. T. Ford
	TOTALS				
1856	Feb.	*Post Boy*		Moffatt	R. T. Ford
	July	*Oberon**		Devlin	
	Dec.	*Oberon*		Devlin	R. T. Ford
	TOTALS				
1857	Aug.	*Scotia*	70	Barrack	Korff
	Aug.	*Oberon**		Devlin	R. T. Ford
	Dec.	*Scotia*		Blake	Korff
	TOTALS				
1858	Feb.	*Oberon**		Devlin	
	April	*Henrietta*	104	Larrack	"a cruise"
	TOTALS				
1859	Jan.	*Alice Brown*		Brown	
	July	*Oberon**		Slater	
	Aug.	*Jenny Lucie*		Pugh	captain
	Dec.	*Post Boy*		Gilroy	
	TOTALS				
1860	Mar.	*Oberon*		Slater	R. T. Ford
	Dec.	*Hope*			
	TOTALS				
1861	Jan.	*Rebecca*	68	J. Devlin	
	Jan.	*Ariel**	69	J. Slater	
	TOTALS				
1862	June	*William*	62	E. Rodd	
	July	*Rebecca*	68	J. Devlin	J. Cuthbert
	Nov.	*Rebecca*	68	E. Rodd	
	TOTALS				
1863	July	*William*	62	T. Dawson	
	TOTALS				
1864	Mar.	*William**	62	T. Dawson	
	Oct.	*Chance**	68	J. McGregor	
	TOTALS				
1865	Jan.	*William*	62	Dawson	
	June	*Chance*	68	McGregor	J. A. Buttery
	TOTALS				

Coconut oil (T/B)**	Coconuts (No.)	Copra (Tons)	Bêche-de-Mer (Tons)	Pearl-shell (Tons)	Tortoise-shell (Lbs.)	Ivory nuts (Tons)	Other
					1480		
					1456		Sperm oil 70 barrels oil
					2936		
2.0T					100		
					1300		
					800		Sperm oil
2.0T					2200		
					350		Sperm oil
				0.5	1520		
				1.0	1700		
				1.5	3570		
	2,000			1.0	400		
				1.0	1713		
					600		
	2,000			2.0	2713		
				6.0	1600		
				6.0	1600		
				2.5	448		
				4.0	1680		
				0.5	100		
				?	?		Whale oil
				7.0	2228		
				3.0	1850		
40B							Whale oil
40B				3.0	1850		
	2,000				1200		
No cargo listed							
	2,000				1200		
			0.5	5.0	1500		
				10.0	1700		
				5.0	700		
			0.5	20.0	3900		
				8.0	1700		
				8.0	1700		
				8.0	1953		
				8.0	1700		
				16.0	3653		
			7.0	8.0	1000		
			0.5	2.0	1500		
			7.5	10.0	2500		

(continued)

Year	Month	Ship	Ton-nage	Captain	Agent
1866	Feb.	*Chance*	68	McGregor	J. A. Buttery
	Oct.	*Dart**	153	J. Lloyd	J. A. Buttery
	Nov.	*Chance**	68	McGregor	J. A. Buttery
	TOTALS				
1867	June	*Chance*	68	McGregor	J. A. Buttery
	TOTALS				
1868	Jan.	*Chance*	68	McGregor	J. A. Buttery
	Oct.	*Chance*	68	McGregor	J. A. Buttery
	TOTALS				
1869		*No ships listed*			
1870	Mar.	*Rose & Thistle*		McFarlane	
	Aug.	*Captain Cook*		N. Brodie	O'Dowd
	Oct.	*Aurora*	240	Dawson	H. Burnes
	Dec.	*Rose & Thistle*		McFarlane	
	TOTALS				
1871	April	*Captain Cook*	55	A. M. Ferguson	O'Dowd
	May	*Lavinia*	57	N. Brodie	
	Oct.	*Aurora*	240	Bennett	
	Nov.	*Lavinia*	57	N. Brodie	
	TOTALS				
1872	Jan.	*Traveller*	116	McFarlane	
	July	*Star of the Sea*	59	Ormiston	
	July	*Lavinia*	62	Brodie	Biffen & Clark
	Aug.	*Prince of Wales*	25	Saintz	
	Nov.	*Prince of Wales*	25	Saintz	
	Nov.	*Traveller*	116	McFarlane	
	Dec.	*Star of the Sea*	59	Ormiston	O'Dowd
	Dec.	*Wainui**	87	Gray?(Gay?)	captain
	TOTALS				
1873	Feb.	*Lavinia*	57	Brodie	Biffen & Clark
	Dec.	*Traveller*	116	H. Kennett	Bird & Co.
	Dec.	*Maid of Erin**	72	J. Cairnes	
	TOTALS				
1874	April	*Kate Kearney*		A. M. Ferguson	O'Dowd
	Oct.	*Lucy*		H. Nicholas	J. Campbell
	TOTALS				
1875	Jan.	*Kate Kearney*		Ferguson	O'Dowd
	Dec.	*Margaret Chessel*		Lawrence	
	Dec.	*Margaret Chessel*		Ferguson	
	TOTALS				
1876	Jan.	*Sydney*	192	T. Woodhouse	Cowlishaw
	July	*Sydney*	192	T. Woodhouse	Cowlishaw
	Nov.	*Martha Ellen*	124		J. Biffen
	TOTALS				

Coconut oil (T/B)**	Coconuts (No.)	Copra (Tons)	Bêche-de-Mer (Tons)	Pearl-shell (Tons)	Tortoise-shell (Lbs.)	Ivory nuts (Tons)	Other
			1.0		1900		
			10.0		300		
			2.0		1800		
			13.0		4000		
1.0T			0.5		1700		
1.0T			0.5		1700		
4.0B					1904		
3.0T			0.5		1700		
3.0T/4.0B			0.5		3604		
2.0T		1			1100		
5.5T			1.5		1200		
		50	7.0				Sulphur
7.0T		2	2.0		1200		
14.5T		53	10.5		3500		
22.0B		20			7 pks		
2.0T	1,000	18		0.1	1260		0.5 ton rattan, 15 tons sulphur
No cargo listed							
3.0T	600	18	8.0	5.0	630		15 tons sulphur
5.0T/22.0B	1,600	56	8.0	5.1	1890		
4.0T	12,000		12	1.0	1100		1 ton rattan
5.0T		40	3		1000		20 tons sulphur
3.5T	5,000	25	10				
No cargo listed							
1.5T					1 box		3.5 tons rattan
		3	25		500		
5.0T		40	5	'some'	550		Sulphur
				0.2			
19.0T	17,000	108	55	1.2	>3150		
1.5T	1,000	36	3		800		4 cwt rattan
		20	18		800		
				.25	45		
1.5T	1,000	56	21	.25	1645		
17.0T		4	9	.5	1700		
			16		1030		
17.0T		4	25	.5	2730		
No cargo listed							
			12	5.0	700		
1.0T		7	1	0.1	600		
1.0T		7	13	5.1	1300		
4.0T		15	0.5	0.5	11 cases		6 tons sulphur
2.0T		80			600		
		60	2.0	7.0	600		3 tons rattan
6.0T		155	2.5	7.5	>1200		

(continued)

APPENDIX 4: *Exports and shipping from Solomon Islands to port of Sydney, c. 1854–1896 (cont.)*

Year	Month	Ship	Ton-nage	Captain	Agent
1877	Feb.	*Sydney*	192	T. Woodhouse	Cowlishaw
	May	*Ripple*	59	Ferguson	Cowlishaw
	June	*Ariel*	133	Brodie	
	Sept.	*Zephyr*	57	W. Schwartz	Montifiore
	Nov.	*Emu*	131	R. Davis	Cowlishaw
	Nov.	*Iserbrook*	208	J. Fraser	Bell
	Dec.	*Douglas*	93	F. S. Beaver	
	TOTALS				
1878	Jan.	*Zephyr*	57	Schwartz	Montifore
	Mar.	*Melrose*	287	Kenny	Cowlishaw
	May	*Ariel*	133	Brodie	J. Bros
	June	*Melrose*	284	Kenny	Cowlishaw
	June	*Zephyr*	57	Schwartz	Montifiore
	Aug.	*Loelia*		Foreman?	Rabone, Feez & Co.
	Aug.	*Princess Louise*	90	Craig	
	Sept.	*Venture*	168	Wolsch	Biffen
	Sept.	*Gazelle*	324	Davis	Cowlishaw
	Oct.	*Sir I. Newton*	121	Cable	Biffen
	Oct.	*Zephyr*	57	Schwartz	Montifiore
	Nov.	*Lalia*	57	Boer?	Rabone, Feez & Co.
	Dec.	*Gazelle*	327	Runcie	Cowlishaw
	TOTALS				
1879	Jan.	*Ariel*	120	Brodie	Biffen
	Jan.	*Princess Louise*	100	Craig	Bond
	Jan.	*Pacific*	100	Davis	Biffen
	Feb.	*Zephyr*	120	Schwartz	Montifiore
	Mar.	*Venture**	169	Verney	Biffen
	Mar.	*Loelia**	50	Boer	
	April	*Gazelle*	324	Runcie	Cowlishaw
	May	*Ripple*	58	Ferguson	Cowlishaw
	June	*Pacific*	69	Davis	captain
	June	*Zephyr*	57	Schwartz	Montifiore
	July	*Black Hawk**	44	Chipperton	captain
	July	*Avoca*	268	Runcie	Cowlishaw
	Aug.	*Ariel*	130	Brodie	captain
	Aug.	*Minnie Low**	75	McDougall	captain
	Aug.	*Lalia**	40	Magness	Mason Bros.
	Sept.	*Princess Louise*	90	Craig	C. B. Bond
	Oct.	*Avoca*	160	Runcie	Cowlishaw
	Nov.	*Daphne*	51	Callaghan	Rabone, Feez & Co.
	Dec.	*Zephyr*	57	Schwartz	captain
	Dec.	*Venture*	167	Wolsch	Young & Lark
	TOTALS				
1880	Jan.	*Avoca*		Runcie	Cowlishaw
	Jan.	*Ariel*	134	Brodie	captain
	Feb.	*Queen*		McGregor	captain
	Feb.	*Loelia*	50	Magnus	captain
	Mar.	*Vibilia*		Davis	J. Williams
	Mar.	*Gazelle*		McIntosh	Cowlishaw
	April	*Emu*		T. Woodhouse	Cowlishaw
	May	*Princess Louise*	90	Craig	C. B. Bond
	May	*Daphne*		Fitzhardinge	Rabone, Feez & Co.

Coconut oil (T/B)**	Coconuts (No.)	Copra (Tons)	Bêche-de-Mer (Tons)	Pearl-shell (Tons)	Tortoise-shell (Lbs.)	Ivory nuts (Tons)	Other
		70	60.0		900		
No cargo listed							
		100	5.0	1.5	600		
		50	2.0	2.0			
		130	2.0	3.0			
			12.0				
	6,000	29					
	6,000	379	81.0	6.5	1500		
		53	4.0				
		176	20.0	16.5	5 cases	5	
		50	2.0	2	400		
	5,230	129	14.0	4	4 cases	7	
		50	5.0	1			
		'some'					
		50					
		35	7.0	0.5			
		80	16.0			90	
	10,000	60	7.0	1.75	2 cases		
		40	5.0	0.1		5	
No cargo listed							
		80	7.5	3.5	401	180	
	15,230	>803	87.5	29.35	>801	287	
	1,000	80	5.0	1.5	200	20	
	6,000	60	10.0			4	
		1				74	
		40	2.0			15	
		20				20	
		11	3.5	0.2	180	22	
		86	2.0	8.0	2 pkts	116	
		30			56	3	
			10.0			21	
		30	9.0	0.45	60	12	
		1		0.4		30	
		100	2.9	1.5		111	
		74		0.3	40	24	
		30		2 sacks	700		
		10	9.0	1.5	300	9	
		70	1.0	2.0		10	
		160	4.0	3.0	750	117	
		40	0.5	0.5			
		45	2.0	0.5	60	5	
		106	6.0	4 cases	2 cases	6	
	7,000	994	66.9	>19.9	>2346	619	
	"a quantity"	100	1.0	1.0	3 pkts	45	
	5,000	78	1 pkt	1 pkt	1 pkt	14	
		33	0.13	10 cases		8	
		8	15.0	3.0	336	3	
	2,800	47	1.35	0.3	1 case	9	
		100	6.0			45	5 tons sulphur
		100	1.5	5 casks		8	
		40	5 bags	2 cases		10	
		10	0.5	0.25	161	2	

367

(continued)

APPENDIX 4: *Exports and shipping from Solomon Islands to port of Sydney, c. 1854–1896 (cont.)*

Year	Month	Ship	Tonnage	Captain	Agent
	June	*Avoca*		Cable	Cowlishaw
	June	*Zephyr*	57	Schwartz	Montifiore
	Aug.	*Queen*		R. Haddock	
	Sept.	*Venture*		Wolsch	Young & Lark
	Sept.	*Mavis*		Rosen	J. Williams
	Oct.	*Gazelle*	350	Woodhouse	Cowlishaw
	Nov.	*Ariel*		Brodie	captain
	Dec.	*Princess Louise*	90	Craig	C. B. Bond
	Dec.	*Restless**		Flech	
	Dec.	*Leslie*		Schwartz	Montifiore
	TOTALS				
1881	Jan.	*Lotus*	38	Bowers	Kelly, Williams & Woodhouse
	Jan.	*Mavis*	80	Rosen	K, W & W
	Jan.	*Queen*	71	Kemp	captain
	Feb.	*Venture*	160	Wolsch	Young & Lark
	Feb.	*Victor**	58	McIntosh	captain
	Feb.	*Avoca*	258	Cable	K, W & W
	Mar.	*Leslie*	108	Robinson	Montifiore
	July	*Mavis*	80	Rosen	J. Williams
	July	*Avoca*	258	Cable	J. Williams?
	Aug.	*Leslie*	108	Robinson	Montifiore
	Aug.	*Victor*	58	Chew?	captain
	Oct.	*Queen*	71	Kemp	
	Nov.	*Venture*	160	Wolsch	Young & Lark
	Nov.	*Lizzie Davis**	84	Lessing	
	Nov.	*Ariel*	134	Brodie	captain
	Nov.	*Dancing Wave*	67	Lennon	Scott, Henderson & Co.
	Dec.	*Avoca*	274	Cable	K, W & W
	TOTALS				
1882	June	*Venture*	160	Wolsch	Young & Lark
	June	*Black Hawk*	44	Hays?	
	Aug.	*Princess Louise*	90	Craig	C. B. Bond
	Oct.	*Avoca*	228	Cable	J. Williams
	Nov.	*Venture*	167	Wolsch	Young & Lark
	Nov.	*Dancing Wave*	67	Leman	Scott, Henderson
	Nov.	*Ariel*		Brodie	captain
	TOTALS				
1883	Feb.	*Ripple*	58	T. Woodhouse	J. Williams
	Mar.	*John Hunt*	61	Martin	Rev. Kelunaek
	May	*Princess Louise*	90	Craig	C. B. Bond
	May	*Venture*	170	Wolsch	Young & Lark
	Sept.	*John S. Laine*	82	Brodie	Kelly & Williams
	Sept.	*Venture*	170	Wolsch	Young & Lark
	Dec.	*Avoca*	258	Cable	Kelly & Williams
	Dec.	*Upolu*	112	Southgate	
	TOTALS				
1884	Jan.	*Renard*	81	P. F. Hurley	K, W & W
	Feb.	*John S. Laine*	82	Brodie	captain
	Feb.	*Venture*	167	Wolsch	Young & Lark

Coconut oil (T/B)**	Coconuts (No.)	Copra (Tons)	Bêche-de-Mer (Tons)	Pearl-shell (Tons)	Tortoise-shell (Lbs.)	Ivory nuts (Tons)	Other
		111	4.0		117	15	362 lb old copper
		52	7.0	2.1	40		
		50		6 cases	1 pkt	8 bags	
		95	4.0	2 cases	3 cases		
		45	1.0	15.0			
		200	5.0	3.0	1 pkt		
		85	2.0	14.0	250		12 tons snail shell
	2,000	80	1 pkt	0.5		1	
No cargo listed							
No cargo listed							
	>9,800	1234	>48.48	39.15	>904	>160	
		18	3.0	2.0	30		
		45	0.5	0.4	25		
		56		0.5	112		
		65	3.5	0.15	100		
		20	10.0	1.0	100		
		135	1.5	0.9	255		
		20	3 bags				
		70		4.0	1 case		
		150	1.0		1 case		
			60 bags	4 bags	20		1 ton snail shell
	1,500	35	1.5	0.5	1 box		
		50		1.25			
		120	6.0	0.5	112		
			4 bags	1.0	"a quantity"		
		42	9.0	5.0	230		20 tons green snail
			20.0	10.0			
		188	4.5	1.5	560		1 bag shark fins
	1,500	1014	>60.5	28.7	>1544		
		"full cargo of copra"					
No cargo listed							
No cargo listed except "islands produce"							
		198		2.5	4 cases		
		120	3.5	5 cases	1 case		
		5	4.0	14.5	40		
		45	20.0	26.0			
		>368	27.5	>43.0	>40		
		25				10	
	In ballast						
		70					
		140	23 pkts	6 cases	30		2 boxes sundries, 1 case rings
		80	1.0	1.0			
		50			336		
		270	2.0	0.5	3 boxes		
		40	2.0	0.4	140		
		675	>5.0	>1.9	>506	10	
		45	4.0	2.0			Sundries
		75		0.45	336		
		"full cargo of copra"					

369

(continued)

Year	Month	Ship	Ton-nage	Captain	Agent
	May	*Avoca*	259	Cable	J. Williams
	June	*Princess Louise**	90	Craig	C. B. Bond
	Aug.	*John S. Laine*	82	Brodie	J. Bros
	Aug.	*Venture*	167	Wolsch	Young & Lark
	Sept.	*Renard*	80	Hurley	captain
	Oct.	*Avoca*	258	Cable	J. Williams
	TOTALS				
1885	Jan.	*Fairlie*	175	E. Hawkins	G. J. Waterhouse
	Jan.	*Princess Louise*	90	Craig	C. B. Bond
	Jan.	*Albert*	42	E. Ancell	G. J. Waterhouse
	Feb.	*John S. Laine*	83	Brodie	captain
	Feb.	*Renard*	81	Knowles	J. Williams
	Feb.	*Lizzie**	191	Cable	J. Williams
	Mar.	*Venture*	175	T. Davies	Young & Lark
	June	*Ripple*		Woodhouse?	K, W&W ?
	June	*Fairlie*	177	J. Hawkins	G. J. Waterhouse
	Aug.	*Lizzie**	223	Cable	
	Sept.	*Fairlie*	177	Hawkins	G. J. Waterhouse
	Sept.	*Venture*		Wolsch	
	Dec.	*Princess Louise*		Craig	C. B. Bond
	Dec.	*Fairlie*	177	J. E. Hawkins	G. J. Waterhouse
	Dec.	*John S. Laine*	82	Brodie	
	TOTALS				
1886	May	*Fairlie*	177	J. E. Hawkins	G. J. Waterhouse
	Sept.	*Renard*	81	Brodie	Brodie & Clarke
	Sept.	*Fairlie*	177	Hawkins	G. J. Waterhouse
	Oct.	*Princess Louise*	96	Craig	C. Bond
	Nov.	*Lizzie*	220	Cable	J. Williams
	Dec.	*Fairlie*	177	Hawkins	G. J. Waterhouse
	TOTALS				
1887	Jan.	*Renard*	81	Rose	Brodie & Clarke
	Mar.	*Belle Brandon*	65	Ingham	G. J. Waterhouse
	April	*Eudora**	69	Ericksen	Bremner (American)
	May	*Lizzie*	223	Cable	J. Williams
	June	*Renard*	81	W. Rosen	Brodie & Clarke
	Aug.	*Fairlie*	186	Hawkins	A. H. Waterhouse & Co.
	Aug.	*Hally Bally*	113	Wolsch	J. Williams
	Aug.	*Mary Ogilvie*	68	Garth	A. H. Waterhouse
	Oct.	*Lizzie*	220	Cable	J. Williams
	Oct.	*Renard*	81	Rosen	Brodie & Clarke
	TOTALS				
1888	Jan.	*Lizzie*	223	Cable	J. Williams
	Jan.	*Loch Lee*	248	J. Bower	G. J. Waterhouse
	Feb.	*Renard*	81	Rosen	Brodie & Clarke
	June	*Lizzie*	223	Cable	J. Williams
	June	*Thistle*	139	Brodie	Brodie & Clarke
	June	*Spunkie*	132	Wolsch	A. H. Waterhouse
	Oct.	*Lizzie*	223	Cable	J. Williams
	Oct.	*Thistle*	139	Brodie	Brodie & Clarke
	Oct.	*Marshall S*	179	Wolsch	G. J. Waterhouse
	TOTALS				

Coconut oil (T/B)**	Coconuts (No.)	Copra (Tons)	Bêche-de-Mer (Tons)	Pearl-shell (Tons)	Tortoise-shell (Lbs.)	Ivory nuts (Tons)	Other
		170	2.0		300		
		50		1.0	"a quantity"		Sundries
		75		5 cases			Sundries
		130	1.0	0.5	2 cases		
		60	1.0	3.0	70		
		180	1.0	1.0			
		>785	9.0	>7.95	706		
		135	0.35	0.25	100		8 pks curios
		75					
		25		9.5			0.5 ton blackhead shell
		70					
		25		3.0			
		170	1.5	1.0	250		
		100	2.0	0.5			
		40		0.25	1 case	8.0	
		166	1.35	0.9	400		
		97					
		175	4.0	3.0	300		
		36	1.0		100		
5 pks	3,000	75	2.0	1.0			
		155	2.0	2.0	200		
No record in Sydney Morning Herald							
5 pks	3,000	1344	14.2	21.4	>1350	8.0	
		176	1.0	1.0	650		
		56	0.4	0.15	168	12.0	
		170	1.0	1.0	150		
		30		0.1			
		175				35.0	
		130	0.5	0.5	200	2.5	
		737	2.9	2.75	1168	49.5	
		30				30.0	
		30	1.0		"a quantity"	6.0	
		15				35.0	
		100			1 case	120.0	
		40			1 case	25.0	
		165			1 case	16.0	
		76		4 bags	403	23.0	
		67			250	7.0	
		129.27		0.17		68.09	
		50		2 packs	130	15	
		702.27	1.0	>0.17	>783	345.09	
		80			2 cases	80.0	
		159			700	47.0	
		135			1 pack	25.0	
		80	13 packs		13 packs	"quantity"	
		100			224	"large quantity"	
		113		2.5	2 cases	21.0	
		172	2.15	3.65	500	14.0	
		145		1.9	1 case	20.0	Curios
		175					
		1159	>2.15	8.05	>1424	>207.0	

(continued)

Year	Month	Ship	Ton-nage	Captain	Agent
1889	Jan.	*Renard*	81	Rosen	Brodie & Clarke
	May	*Maroon*	362	Cable	J. Williams
	June	*Thistle*	139	Brodie	Brodie & Clarke
	Sept.	*Edith May**	212	F. E. Stewart	G. J. Waterhouse
	Oct.	*Maroon*	369	Cuttle	J. Williams
	Dec.	*Thistle*	139	Brodie	Brodie & Clarke
	TOTALS				
1890	Jan.	*Enterprise*	81	Craig	
	Jan.	*Edith May**	213	F. E. Stewart	John Taylor & Sons
	Feb.	*Marshall S*	179	Cable	J. Williams
	Feb.	*Renard*	81	Rosen	Brodie & Clarke
	Mar.	*Buster**	305	Wolsch	J. Williams
	Mar.	*Forest King**	158	Le Blanque	J. Williams
	May	*Oamaru*	156	T. Richards	G. J. Waterhouse
	July	*Marshall S*		Cable	J. Williams
	Aug.	*Sandfly*	76	Kirkpatrick	J. Bros
	Aug.	*Thistle*		?	Brodie & Clarke
	Sept.	*Marshall S*		Cable	J. Williams
	Nov.	*Hally Bayley*		Rosen	?
	Dec.	*Flying Scud*		Wolsch	?
	TOTALS				
1891	Jan.	*Marshall S*	179	Cable	J. Williams
	Jan.	*Thistle*	139	Hawkins	Brodie & Clarke
	Jan.	*Sandfly**	76	Kirkpatrick	G. J. Waterhouse
	July	*Thistle*	139	Hawkins	Brodie & Clarke
	July	*Marshall S*	179	Wolsch	G. J. Waterhouse
	Aug.	*Sandfly*	76	Kirkpatrick	Bros & Smith
	Sept.	*Pet**	268	S. J. Read	J. Vos
	Nov.	*Marshall S*	179	Wolsch	G. J. Waterhouse
	Dec.	*Elangowan**	33	Clynne	
	Dec.	*Thistle*	139	Hawkins	Brodie & Clarke
	TOTALS				
1892	Jan.	*Vailele*	159	Woodhouse	J. Williams
	Jan.	*Hally Bayley*	113	Rosen	Kelly & Williams
	Jan.	*Sandfly*	76	Kirkpatrick	Bros & Smith
	Jan.	*Senta**	76	Bohermann	
	Mar.	*Renard*	91	Brodie	Brodie & Clarke
	Mar.	*Saucy Lass*	41	F. Wickham	G. J. Waterhouse
	Mar.	*Borough Belle*	20	J. Williams	G. J. Waterhouse
	May	*Hally Bayley*	113	Rosen	Kelly & Williams
	June	*Thistle*	139	Hawkins	Bros & Smith
	Aug.	*Borough Belle*	210	Williams	G. J. Waterhouse
	Sept.	*Vailele*	158	Cable	J. Williams
	Sept.	*Escort*	130	Rosen	J. Williams
	Sept.	*Thistle*	139	Hawkins	Bros & Smith
	Oct.	*Renard*	91	Brodie	Bros & Smith
	Nov.	*Clara Jackson*	32	S. Buchart	J. H. Buchart
	Nov.	*Borough Belle*	210	Williams	G. J. Waterhouse
	Dec.	*Thistle*	139	Hawkins	Bros & Smith
	Dec.	*Escort*	130	Rosen	T. G. Kelly
	TOTALS				

Coconut oil (T/B)**	Coconuts (No.)	Copra (Tons)	Bêche-de-Mer (Tons)	Pearl-shell (Tons)	Tortoise-shell (Lbs.)	Ivory nuts (Tons)	Other
	50				2 packs	10.0	
	286	3.0		1.3		75.0	
	134			0.25	130	20.0	
	121					17.0	
	190	1.0		2 packs	1 case	166.0	8000 snail shells
	140	2 bags		0.5	208	27.0	
	921	>4.0		>2.05	>338	315.0	
	60			3 packs	1 pack		
	21			0.07	472	22.0	
	148	0.5		0.5	248	55.0	
	40	1 bag		2 bags	1 case	15.0	
	147	0.5		0.4	1 case	153.0	Sundries
	40					120.0	
	125	5.0		0.13	448	30.0	
	160					30 sacks	
	60						
	98			0.05	45	60.0	
	150	2.0		0.5	100	13.0	
	80			0.35	336	20.0	
	157	3 sacks		4 bags	3 cases		Curios
	1286	>8.0		>2.0	>1649	>488.0	
	136	1.0		0.15	100	60.0	
	125	0.05		0.13	65	30.0	
	30	3 packs		0.1	100		
	115	1 bag		2 bags	2 bags	30.0	
	168					18.0	
	65	2 bags		2 bags	35	6.0	
No cargo, crew ill							
	180	3.0		0.4	1 case	10.0	
No cargo							
	155			0.25	100		
	974	>4.05		>1.03	>400	154.0	
	156	0.05		0.01			
	100	1.0		0.05			4 tons snail shell
	70						
In ballast							
	56	"quantity"					
	17			2.0	300		
	151					40.0	
	30						
	150						
	171	34 bags		4 bags	9 packs		
	60	7.0				30.0	
	120					15.0	
	150	2.0		0.5	1 case		
	60	32 bags		17 packs +0.26	6 packs +224	14.0	
		3.0			20		
	174			9 bags	370	13.0	
	135	5.0		0.5	300	14.0	
	50				1 case		
	1650	>18.05		>3.26	>1214	126.0	

(continued)

Year	Month	Ship	Ton-nage	Captain	Agent
1893	Feb.	*Renard*	81	Brodie	J. Williams
	Mar.	*Isabel**	69	Wolsch	W. S. Preddy
	April	*Escort*	130	Rosen	Kelly & Williams
	June	*Saucy Lass*	41	T. Sheridan	Bros & Smith
	June	*Thistle**	139	Hawkins	Bros & Smith
	July	*Borough Belle*	210	J. Williams	G. J. Waterhouse
	Aug.	*Renard*	81	Brodie	Bros & Smith
	Sept.	*Thistle*	139	Hawkins	Bros & Smith
	Nov.	*Borough Belle*	210	Hawkins?	G. J. Waterhouse
	Nov.	*Meg Merrilees**	143	Kirkpatrick	Bros & Smith
	Dec.	*Thistle*		Kirkpatrick?	Bros & Smith
	TOTALS				
1894	Mar.	*Thistle*	139	McGregor	Bros & Smith
	June	*Lark*	197	Rosen	J. Williams
	June	*Hesketh†*	640	W. Robinson	Burns Philp
	June	*Thistle*	139	Hawkins	Bros & Smith
	June	*Kurrara*†*	386	McGeorge	G. J. Waterhouse
	Sept.	*Lark*	197	Rosen	J. Williams
	Sept.	*Thistle*	139	Hawkins	Bros & Smith
	Sept.	*Flinders*†*	948	J. Williams	Burns Philp
	Oct.	*Kurrara*†*	386	McGeorge	G. J. Waterhouse
	Dec.	*Kurrara†*	386	McGeorge	Burns Philp
	TOTALS				
1895	Jan.	*Saucy Lass*		Kunson	Bros & Smith
	Jan.	*Kurrara†*		McGeorge	Burns Philp
	Jan.	*Lark**	197	Rosen	J. Williams
	Mar.	*Chittoor†*	217	S. Keating	G. J. Waterhouse
	April	*Meg Merrilies**	143	Rendora?	
	May	*Kelloe†*	501	H. Johnson	Burns Philp
	May	*Lark*	197	Hawkins	Bros & Smith
	June	*Kelloe†*	501	Johnson	Burns Philp
	July	*Chittoor†*	217	S. Keating	G. J. Waterhouse
	Aug.	*Kurrara*†*	386	McGeorge	Burns Philp
	Sept.	*Lark*	197	Hawkins	John Smith
	Sept.	*Kurrara*†*	386	McGeorge	Burns Philp
	Nov.	*Chittoor*†*	217	Keating	G. J. Waterhouse
	Dec.	*Lark†*	197	Hawkins	John Smith
	Dec.	*Kelloe*†*		Johnson	Burns Philp
	TOTALS				

Sources: Register of Arrivals of Vessels, Port of Sydney, Maritime Services Board 1841–1843, 1851–1853, 1854–1886, 1890–1893, SP 729, Commonwealth Archives (NSW Branch), Sydney; Register of Arrivals, Port of Sydney, Maritime Services Board, 1867–1882, 4/7738, New South Wales State Archives, Sydney; *Sydney Morning Herald,* Shipping column, 1854–1895. (After the government was established in 1896, totals of exports were included in the annual reports.)

Notes: Only ships which gave their last port of call as Solomon Islands have been included here. Ship tonnages are as given in the original sources, with no attempt to resolve discrepancies. In converting the original data for copra, bêche-de-mer, pearlshell, and

Coconut oil (T/B)**	Coconuts (No.)	Copra (Tons)	Bêche-de-Mer (Tons)	Pearl-shell (Tons)	Tortoise-shell (Lbs.)	Ivory nuts (Tons)	Other
	52			0.2		20.0	
	15					7.0	
	105	2.5			1 case	26.0	
	30	2.0					
	75			0.05	1 parcel	80.0	
	178					12.0	
	40				1 bag	86.0	3 tons shell
	130			4.0	2 packs	25.0	
	187.15	0.25		0.2			
	12		6 bags			60.0	
	138	0.65			448	15.0	
	962.15	5.4		4.45	>448	331.0	
	140				100.0	11.0	
	75		0.09		53.5	17.0	
	+1248 bags		+5 bags				
	260		7 bags		40.0	21.0	
	80		6 bags	53 cases +9 bags	5 cases		
	190					30.0	
	160					10.0	
	125						
	120					15.0	
	223			50 cases +8 bags		26.0	
	243		4 bags	6 bags	379.0	31.0	
	1616		>0.09	—	>572.5	161.0	
	20				60.0	6.0	
	110				370.0	65.0	
	120		2 bags	2 boxes +26 bags			
	116		3 packs	1 case		116.0	
No cargo listed							
	73		1 bag		264.0	266.0	
	91					21.0	
	100			2.1	256.0	39.0	
	95	2.0		22 cases		116.0	
	96.05	1.41		1.6	348.5	147.15	
	120	0.5		1.5		37.0	
	58.85			0.13		106.25	
	90	6.0			1 pack	92.0	
	130			3.0		21.5	
	41	1.1				28.0	
	1260.9	>11.01		>8.33	>1298.5	1060.9	

ivory nuts from tons, hundredweights, quarters, and pounds to tons and decimal fractions, some rounding has occurred; to minimize distortion, totals have been converted to the nearest decimal place, rather than re-added. Because the weight of "1 case" or "1 bag" is unknown, such items are indicated in the totals only by the inclusion of a "greater than" symbol.

*Visited other islands in addition to Solomon Islands
**T = tons; B = barrels
†Steamer

APPENDIX 5

Location of resident traders and non-Melanesian staff, c. 1860–1900

Year	Place	Person	Employer or buyer of produce	Remarks	Sources
Santa Cruz Islands					
1898	Nendö	A. E. C. Forrest	Burns Philp	In debt to Burns Philp and others. Left islands for Torres group c. 1900	WPHC 233/98: Woodford to O'Brien, 18 June 1898; WPHC 336/98: Woodford to O'Brien, 30 Oct. 1901 and encls.
1898	Carlisle Bay	A white man	A. E. C. Forrest		WPHC 336/98: Woodford to O'Brien, 30 Oct. 1901 and encls.
1898	Reef Islands	A white man	A. E. C. Forrest		Ibid.
1899	Banks Islands (Vanuatu)	Frank Whitford		Involved in illegal recruiting on the Reef Islands	WPHC 241/99: Woodford to Whitford, 9 Mar. 1900
San Cristobal and Adjacent Islands					
c. 1868–1870	Uki (?)	J. Stephens			UK-RNAS 16: Bruce to Wilson, 4 June 1881
1871	Makira Harbour	W. Perry	Independent	Died 1874	UK-RNAS 14: Effects of W. Perry, 2 Mar. 1875 and encls.; Edwin Redlich, Notes . . . *Journal of Royal Geographical Society* 44 (1874): 31
1876	Makira Harbour	J. Stephens	A. M. Ferguson (?)	Station closed 1877	*Daphne* 12 May 1876; *Dauntless* 14 Apr. 1877
1876	Uki	A "Manila man"	A. M. Ferguson (?)		Penny Diary, 14 Aug. 1876
1877	Uki	W. Aitkins	McArthur & Co.	New Zealand traders, who left after less than a year's stay	UK-RNAS 14: Wright to Capt. of *Beagle*, 6 Oct. 1877

Date	Location	Name	Employer/Company	Remarks	Reference
1877	Uki (?)	R. Cundall	McArthur & Co.		Ibid.
1877	Uki (?)	J. Howland	McArthur & Co.		Ibid.
1877	Uki (?)	F. Kripper	McArthur & Co.		Ibid.
1877	Hada (?)	G. Atkinson	MacArthur & Co.		Ibid.
1877	Ubuna	F. Howard	McArthur & Co.		Ibid.
1877	Santa Ana & east San Cristobal	J. C. Macdonald	Houng Lee	Lee, a Levuka merchant	WPHC 4/78: Leefe Report on New Hebrides and Sol. Is., 10 Mar. 1878; *Marion Renny* 5 Nov. 1877
1878	Uki	A white man (H. Wright?)	Ferguson	Ferguson's partners were Cowlishaw Bros.	WPHC 15/79: Houghton to HC, 9 June 1878
1878	Uki	H. J. Townsend	Swartz	Killed by local people after a few days' residence	WPHC 15/79: Houghton to HC, 9 June 1878
1878	Uki (?)	H. Wright / J. Stephens			Ibid.
1879	Hada/Wango	J. Martin	Brodie (?)	Left Hada and went to Wango	UK-RNAS 14: Capt. [Brodie] of *Ariel* to Capt. of HM ship, 27 Apr. 1879, encl.
1880	Uki	F. Howard	J. Stephens	Stephens away in Australia or New Zealand	*SMH*, 2 Jan. 1880
1880	Makira Harbour and ?	Stanley Bateman and 2 brothers		One at Makira Harbour	*SMH*, 11 Oct. 1880; WPHC 139/80: Wilson to Gordon, 23 Sept. 1880 and encls.; Hernsheim Diary, 23 Jan. 1880
late 1880	Uki	J. Stephens			UK-RNAS 15: Bruce to Wilson, 4 June 1881
1881	Uki	J. Stephens	Kelly, Williams & Woodhouse		Ibid.

(continued)

Year	Place	Person	Employer or buyer of produce	Remarks	Sources
1881	Santa Ana	J. C. Macdonald W. Macdonald Sproul	Independent	J. C. Macdonald's wife, Melinda, with him Sproul was a partner of the Macdonalds	Ibid.; Ferguson 28–30 Sept. 1881
1882	Santa Ana	J. C. Macdonald W. Macdonald Sproul	Independent		WPHC 121/82: Capt. of *Diamond* to Gordon, 3 Sept. 1882
		Heuglan	J. C. Macdonald		
1884	Santa Ana	5 white men incl. 2 Macdonalds			*Ethel*, 14 Mar. 1884 (QSA)
1885	Santa Ana	A. Gunderson		J. C. Macdonald and family left Santa Ana about December 1885	*Albatross*, 27 Mar. 1885 (FNA)
1885	Hada	E. Griffiths A white man	Baker, Crossen & Co. of Fiji	Baker bought land for station for Crossen at Hada	Blyth 29 Aug.–2 Sept., 31 Oct. 1885
1886	Santa Ana	F. Nyberg	G. J. Waterhouse	Nyberg was renting Macdonald's land	Woodford Diary, 11 May 1886; Blyth 15 Feb.–3 Mar. 1886
1886	Uki	J. Stephens W. & T. Dabelle	G. J. Waterhouse G. J. Waterhouse	Selling goods to Waterhouse	Woodford Diary, 14 May 1886
1887	Uki	F. Howard			Elton 1888
early 1889	Hada	W. & T. Dabelle	G. J. Waterhouse	W. Dabelle left for Roviana	WPHC 191/89: Meredith to Cmdr. *Royalist*, 18 May 1889; WPHC 125/90: Comins to Thurston, 10 Apr. 1890
1889	Anuta	T. Dabelle	G. J. Waterhouse	T. Dabelle murdered at Anuta	WPHC 191/89: Meredith to Cmdr. *Royalist*, 18 May 1889

1889	Santa Ana	F. Nyberg		Off to Sydney for visit	*SMH*, 21 June 1889
1890	Uki	J. Stephens A Frenchman	G. J. Waterhouse J. Stephens	An escaped convict?	Woodford Papers: Corresp. Respecting Outrages, Grenfell to CC, 21 Aug. 1890, encl., Case 31.
1890	Uki	F. Howard	T. Woodhouse	Managing for J. Stephens whose agent was G. J. Waterhouse	WPHC 230/90: Comins to HC, 26 July 1890, encl.
1891	Santa Ana	Arthur Lette		In charge of Nyberg's stations	WPHC 102/92: Corresp. Davis to CC, 12 July 1891
1891	Uki	Williams		Howard murdered, Williams in charge	
1892	Santa Ana	F. Nyberg		Killed after shooting a Santa Ana man	
1894	Santa Ana	C. Olsen			WPHC 293/95: Goodrich to CC, 28 May 1894, Corresp. 1894
1894–1895	Uki	Devine Robert Burkett	T. Woodhouse	Apparently agent for Waterhouse; J. Stephens died c. 1893	WPHC 402/96: Burkett to HC, 8 Oct. 1896; WPHC 293/95: Goodrich to CC, 28 May 1894, Corresp. 1894; Welchman 2 Oct. 1893
1895	Santa Ana	C. Olsen			WPHC 141/96: English and Foreign Traders in SI, Dec. 1895, App. 4, Corresp. 1895
1896	Uki	T. Woodhouse		Woodhouse, formerly of Kelly, Williams & Woodhouse	WPHC 199/96: Woodford to Thurston, 6 June 1896
1896	Uki	John Fleming	T. Woodhouse		Ibid.
1896	Uki	A Frenchman			Ibid.
1896	near Makira Harbour	Sullivan		(Confusion with Sheridan?)	Ibid.

(continued)

Year	Place	Person	Employer or buyer of produce	Remarks	Sources
1896	Santa Ana	C. Olsen			Ibid.
1896		2 Rotumans			WPHC 477/96: AR 1896
1896	Uki	T. Woodhouse			Ibid.
1896		J. Druce	T. Woodhouse	Mixed-race Fijian	Ibid.
1896		J. Fleming	T. Woodhouse		WPHC 416/96: Woodford to HC, 25 Nov. 1896
1896	Waimamura	H. Wright		According to documents, Wright's station was at Bauro, but map of location places it in the Waimamura area. Murdered by Maiwasiwasi bush people	Ibid.
1896	Makira Harbour	Thomas Sheridan	Sheridan	Cook	WPHC 477/96: AR 1896
		Thomas Campbell	Sheridan	Mate	
		William Price			
Nggela and Savo					
1869	Savo	Laurence	Henderson & MacFarlane	New Zealand traders	Woodford Papers: Notes on History of SI
1876	Vaturua, Nggela	Lewis			Penny Diary, 5 Aug. 1876
July 1877	Savo	Miller			Penny Diary, 3 July 1877
1877	Savo	C. Edwards	McArthur	New Zealand traders	UK-RNAS 14: Wright to Capt. *Beagle*, 6 Oct. 1877, and encls.
1877	Savo	Nielsen			Ibid.
1878	Savo	?	Ferguson	Ferguson's partners were Cowlishaw Bros.	WPHC 4/78: Leefe Report on New Hebrides and SI, 10 Mar.

Year	Place	Trader	Owner	Notes	Source
1878–1879	Savo	Cartwright	Ferguson (?)		UK-RNAS 14: Houghton to Wilson, 16 May 1879
1878–1879	Savo	Martin	Brodie (?)	Martin went to Wango, San Cristobal, in 1879	Ibid.
1878–1879	Savo	J. Morrow	Brodie		WPHC 54/79: Cmdr. *Wolverine* to Gorrie, 9 June 1879; UK-RNAS 14: Houghton to Wilson, 16 May 1879
1880	Savo	Cartwright	Brodie	Cartwright trading also for Callaghan	Mair 28 Sept. 1889; WPHC 160/80: Brodie to Capt. *Sandfly*, 13 Oct. 1880, encl.; Hernsheim Diary, 23 Jan. 1880
1882	Savo	L. Nixon	Wolsch		UK-RNAS 16: Dale to Erskine, 3 Sept. 1882, Corresp. 1882
1883	Savo	Bealeman			*SMH*, 30 May 1883
1886–1887	Savo	"Jack" Cooper	Wolsch (?)	Also resided part-time at Marau, Guadalcanal	Woodford Papers: Letter to Thurston, Nov. 1886; Woodford Diary, 25 Mar. 1887
1888	Vatilau, Nggela	J. Emmanuel	Kelly, Williams & Woodhouse		Woodford Diary, 16 Nov. 1888
1888	Nggela	A. Thrower	Kelly, Williams & Woodhouse		WPHC 102/92: Davis Memo, 16 Oct. 1891, Corresp. 1891
1890	Honggo, Nggela	Charles Horsman			Woodford Papers: Castle to CC, 19 Sept. 1890, Corresp. 1890
1891	Honggo, Nggela	Charles Horsman			WPHC 102/92: Davis to CC, 12 July 1891, Corresp. 1891
1891	Chavutu, Nggela	L. Nielsen			Ibid.
1891	Chavutu, Nggela	Wilson			Ibid.
1894	Naghotono, Nggela	J. Emmanuel			WPHC 345/94: ? to Thurston, 14 Dec. 1894

(continued)

APPENDIX 5: *Location of resident traders and non-Melanesian staff, c. 1860–1900 (cont.)*

Year	Place	Person	Employer or buyer of produce	Remarks	Sources
1895	Savo	John Newman Thomas Young			WPHC 141/96: Case 69, Corresp. 1895
1896	Bangai, Nggela	G. Creswell		Died 1896	WPHC 280/96: Woodford to Thurston, 26 June 1896
1896	Savo	John Newman			Ibid.; WPHC 477/96: AR 1896
1896	Savo	J. Emmanuel			WPHC 477/96: AR 1896
1896	Chavutu	L. Nielsen			Ibid.
1896	Chavutu	J. Anderson	Nielsen		Ibid.
1896	Chavutu	F. Ericsen		Mate	Ibid.
1896	Chavutu	J. Wilson			Ibid.
1896	Olevugha, Nggela	A. Ellingson			WPHC 477/96: AR 1896
1900	Chavutu	L. Nielsen			UK-CRSI: Langdale to Denson, 30 May 1900
1900	Savo	J. Newman			Ibid.
Santa Isabel					
1877	Cockatoo Is.	N. P. Sorenson (& others?)	McArthur	Diving station	UK-RNAS 14: Wright to Capt. *Beagle*, 6 Oct. 1877 and encls.; Penny Diary, 27 May 1877
1878	Thousand Ships Bay	A white man			WPHC 4/78: Leefe Report on New Hebrides and SI, 10 Mar. 1878
1879	?	A white man			UK-RNAS 14: Wilson to CC, 3 June 1879
1880	?	Harrison	Ferguson (?)		Hernsheim Diary, 23 Jan. 1880
1882	Cockatoo Is.	Schwartz		Also trading at Russells where he was murdered	UK-RNAS 16: Dale to Erskine, 8 Sept. 1882

Russell Islands

1900	Russell Is.	Butchart Griffiths			UK-CRSI: Langdale to Denson, 30 May 1900

Guadalcanal

c. 1876	Marau?	J. Morrow	A. M. Ferguson	Cowlishaw Bros. (Ferguson's partners)	UK-RNAS 14: Houghton to Wilson, 16 May 1879 and encls.
Aug. 1877	Island off Rere	Robinson	Henderson & MacFarlane	Island was possibly Rua Sura	*Marion Renny*, 12 Aug. 1877
June 1877	Ruavatu	Robinson			Penny Diary, 8 June 1877
July 1877	Tadhimboko	L. Nixon			Penny Diary, 3 July 1877
1877	Tadhimboko	H. Jury	McArthur	New Zealand traders	UK-RNAS 14: Wright to Capt. *Beagle*, 6 Oct. 1877
1877	Marau	Braidwood plus 1 or 2 whites	Ferguson		*Dauntless*, 19 Apr. 1877 (FNA)
1878	Visale	Robert Provis / W. D. Cartwright		Provis murdered at Ngalimbiu River in November	WPHC 4/78: Leefe Report on New Hebrides and SI, 10 Mar. 1878; UK-RNAS 14: Houghton to Wilson, 16 May 1879
1878	Marau	C. Halgate	Ferguson	Murdered 1879	UK-RNAS 14: Houghton to Wilson, 16 May 1879
1879	Tadhimboko	L. Nixon	Ferguson		*SMH*, 9 Apr. 1879
1880	?	L. Nixon	Ferguson		*SMH*, 2 Jan. 1880
1881	Marau	Sidey		"Collecting trade"	WPHC 20/81: Maxwell to Wilson, 31 Jan. 1881, encl.
1882	No white traders residing on Guadalcanal				
1885	Gera (Mbara Is.)	L. Nielsen / J. C. Mcdonald			*Albatross*, 25 Apr. 1885 (FNA)
1886	Gera	L. Nielsen	Kelly, Williams & Woodhouse	Also sold to Waterhouse	Woodford Papers: Diary, 30 May 1886, and Woodford to Thurston, Nov. 1886

(continued)

APPENDIX 5: *Location of resident traders and non-Melanesian staff, c. 1860–1900 (cont.)*

Year	Place	Person	Employer or buyer of produce	Remarks	Sources
1886	Aola	Harrison	Waterhouse	Owned a cutter	Woodford Papers: Woodford to Thurston, Nov. 1886
1887	Gera	L. Nielsen			Woodford Papers: Diary, 1 Apr. 1887
1888	Marau	"Jack" Cooper	Kelly, Williams & Woodhouse		Woodford Papers: Diary, 30 Nov. 1888
1889	Marau	"Jack" Cooper	Kelly, Williams & Woodhouse	Killed in attack by Malaitans on Savo	Woodford Papers: *Whitgift Magazine* 8 (4) (June 1890), and Case 33, Corresp. 1889
1889	Marau	"Charlie" (Charles Ladden)		Killed in attack by Malaitans on Savo	*Daily Telegraph*, 7 Aug. 1889; Woodford Papers: Case 33, Corresp. 1889
1890	Marau	Theodore Svensen S. B. Nerdrum		Both died of illness	WPHC 69/93: Case 56, Corresp. 1892
1891	Gera (Mbara)	Alfred Thrower	Woodhouse		WPHC 102/92: Thrower to Davis [Oct. 1891], Corresp. 1891
1892	Marau	Oscar Svensen J. G. B. Nerdrum		O. Svensen, "Kapitan Marau," one of the partners of the Marau Company	WPHC 102/92: Davis to CC, 29 Aug. 1891; WPHC 69/93: Case 56, Corresp. 1892
1894	Aola	H. Atkinson		Said to have been trading at Malaita	Welchman Diary, 17 Jan. 1894
1895	Aola	W. Fraser			WPHC, 141/96: English and Foreign Traders in SI, Dec. 1895, Corresp. 1895
1895	Neal Is. (Vulelua)	W. & G. Grace			Ibid.
1896	Marau	O. Svensen			WPHC 477/96: AR 1896
1896	Marau	J. G. B. Nerdrum		Partner in Marau Co.	Ibid.
1896	Marau	C. Trachet	Marau Co.		Ibid.

Date	Place	Name	Buyer	Note	Reference
1896	Marau	J. Bengai	Marau Co.		Ibid.
1896	Marau	Thompson	Marau Co.		Ibid.
1896	Aola	J. Porret	Marau Co.		Ibid.
1896	Aola	W. Fraser			Ibid.
1896	Gera (Mbara)	W. Pope			Ibid.
1896	Gera (Mbara)	W. Pitt			Ibid.
1896	Gera (Mbara)	A. Thrower			Ibid.
1896	Gera (Mbara)	J. Weldon			Ibid.
1896	Gera (Mbara)	W. T. Issott		Mate of ship	Ibid.
1896	Gera (Mbara)	Thompson		Cook	Ibid.
1896	Gera (Mbara)	A. Kunell		Seaman	Ibid.
1896	Neal Is. (Vulelua)	C. H. E. Butchert			Ibid.
1896	Neal Is. (Vulelua)	G. L. Griffiths			Ibid.
1896	Neal Is. (Vulelua)	H. Niemayer	Griffiths		Ibid.
1899	Aola	A. J. Rabut		Partner of O. Svensen, one-time partner of A. E. C. Forrest	WPHC 48/99: Woodford to HC, 18 Feb. 1900 and encls.; Welchman Diary, 23 Mar. 1899
1900	Aola	W. Pitt	best buyer		UK-CRSI: Langdale to Denson, 30 May 1900
1900	Aola	O. Svensen	Justus Scharff		Ibid.
1900	Gera	W. Pope	Justus Scharff	Shipped through Burns Philp to Justus Scharff	Ibid.

East New Georgia Islands (New Georgia, Rendova, Vonavona, Kolombangara, Tetepare, Vangunu, Nggatokae)

Date	Place	Name	Buyer	Note	Reference
c. 1859	Roviana	2 white men		Left to collect produce for *Oberon*	*Empire*, 26 Dec. 1859
c. 1869–1870	Roviana	Jack Brookfield		Living under protection of Gorei and Bitia	Woodford Papers: Notes on History . . . .

(*continued*)

APPENDIX 5: *Location of resident traders and non-Melanesian staff, c. 1860–1900 (cont.)*

Year	Place	Person	Employer or buyer of produce	Remarks	Sources
1877	Roviana	Jack Brookfield	Ferguson	Cowlishaw Bros.	*SMH*, 4 Nov. 1877; WHPC 4/78: Leefe Report . . ., 10 Mar. 1878
1880	Marovo	James Martin	Brodie		WPHC 160/80: Wilson to Gordon, 19 Dec. 1880 and encls.
1880	Marovo	T. Evans	Brodie		Ibid.
1880	Roviana?	J. Jones			UK-RNAS 15: Statement of John Jones of Rubiana [c. Aug. 1880]
1880	Roviana	F. Wickham (?)	Ferguson		*SMH*, 2 June 1880
1881	Roviana	A white man			WPHC 158/81: Romilly to HC, 6 Aug. 1881
1881	Nusa Zonga (?) Roviana	Nelson			WPHC 192/81: Dawson to Wilson, 11 Nov. 1881, encl.
1883	Marovo (?)	F. Thomassen		Died there of fever	*SMH*, 4 Sept. 1883
1886	Nusa Zonga	W. Harland	Kelly, Williams & Woodhouse	Woodhouse resided at Nusa Zonga when not captaining *Ripple. Ripple* had a white crew of six. The schooner *Freak* of Kelly, Williams & Woodhouse had a white crew of two	WPHC 160/86: Brook to Tryon, 18 May 1886; Woodford Papers: Woodford to Thurston, Nov. 1886
1886	Roviana	F. Wickham	Waterhouse	Owned cutter *Rubiana*	Woodford Papers: Diary, 24–25 Sept. 1886, and Woodford to Thurston, Nov. 1886
1886	Roviana	A white man	F. Wickham		Ibid.
1886	Roviana	P. E. Pratt	Kelly, Williams & Woodhouse	Owned cutter *Martha*	Ibid.

1886	Roviana	A white man	P. E. Pratt		Woodford Papers: Woodford to Thurston, Nov. 1886
1886	Lilihina (?) Marovo	George Cresswell	Kelly, Williams & Woodhouse		Ibid.; Woodford Papers: Diary, 11 Oct. 1886
1887	Nusa Zonga	A white man	Kelly, Williams & Woodhouse		Woodford Papers: Diary, 27 Feb. 1887
1887	Lilihina	G. Cresswell			Ibid., 19 Mar. 1887
1887	Hombuhombu	P. E. Pratt			Ibid., 6 Mar. 1887
1890	Nusa Zonga	Woodhouse			Woodford Papers: Grenfell to CC, 23 July 1890, Corresp. 1890
1890	Marovo	Eric Ellingson	Woodhouse		Ibid., Castle to CC, 10 Sept. 1890, Corresp. 1890
1891	Nusa Zonga	C. Atkinson	Woodhouse	Killed September 1895	WPHC 102/92: Davis to CC, 29 Aug. 1891, Corresp. 1891
1891	Nusa Zonga	T. H. Easson			WPHC 344/94: Easson to Thurston, 13 Dec. 1894
1891	Lilihina	A. Griffiths			WPHC 102/92: Bain to CC, 4 Dec. 1891, Corresp. 1891
1892	Nusa Zonga	N. Wheatley			WPHC 69/93: Bremer to Kelham, 29 Sept. 1892, Corresp.
1892	Nusa Zonga	T. H. Easson			WPHC 344/94: Easson to Thurston, 13 Dec. 1894
1892	Hombupecka	F. Wickham			WPHC 69/93: Bremer to Kelham, 29 Sept. 1892, Corresp.
1893	Nusa Zonga	Kelly			WPHC 350/94: Gibson to Bowden-Smith, 13 July 1893
1893	Nusa Zonga	T. H. Easson			WPHC 344/94: Easson to Thurston, 13 Dec. 1894

(continued)

Year	Place	Person	Employer or buyer of produce	Remarks	Sources
1894	Lilihina	Donald Guy	G. Atkinson/Woodhouse	Murdered	WPHC 293/95: Goodrich to CC, 28 May 1894, Corresp. 1894
1894	Roviana	A. Griffiths			Somerville, 1897, 396
early 1896	Hombuhombu	T. H. Easson	F. Wickham	Wickham in England	WPHC 283/96: Woodford to HC, 12 July 1896; Welchman Diary, 4 Mar. 1896
1896	Roviana area	F. Wickham			WPHC 477/96: AR 1896
1896	Roviana area	N. Wheatley			Ibid.
1896	Roviana area	W. Keith		Seaman	Ibid.
1896	Roviana area	James Gibbins			Ibid.
1896	Vonavona	2 white men			Ibid.
1900	Roviana	F. Wickham N. Wheatley	Burns Philp		UK-CRSI: Langdale to Denson, 30 May 1900

West New Georgia (Vella Lavella, Simbo, Ranongga, Gizo)

Year	Place	Person	Employer or buyer of produce	Remarks	Sources
1869–1870	Gizo	N. Brodie			Woodford Papers: Notes on History . . .
1869–1870	Gizo	2 white men			Ibid.
1873	Gizo	2 white men	N. Brodie		UK-RNAS 13: Rendle to Stirling, 14 Sept. 1873
1896	Simbo/Narovo	J. P. Pratt		Ship's mate	WPHC 477/96: AR 1896
1896	Simbo/Narovo	P. Surville			Ibid.
1896	Simbo/Narovo	P. E. Pratt			Ibid.
1896	Simbo/Narovo	D. Langreen		Seaman	Ibid.
1896	Simbo/Narovo	C. Grinot		Cook	Ibid.
1898	Narovo	J. P. Pratt			WPHC 344/98: Woodford to HC, 14 Oct. 1898

Year	Place	Name	Employer	Notes	Source
1900	Narovo	L. Keith		Ship's mate	Ibid.
1900	Narovo	P. E. Pratt			Welchman Diary, 13 June 1900
Choiseul					
1897	Warisi	Wagenbret	N. Tindal		CO 225/54: Tindal to Imperial Magistrate, 9 June 1897 and encls.
1897	?	At Cham	N. Tindal	At Cham, a Chinese, died shortly after his arrival	Ibid.
1898	Tambatamba	William Peter Leonard	W. Macdonald(?)	Driven out by head-hunters from New Georgia group	CO 225/56: Castell to Foreign Office, 3 Nov. 1898 and encls.
Shortland Islands					
late 1885	Siniasoro, Fauro	J. C. Macdonald			Woodford Papers: Diary, 30 June 1886
1886	Fauro	J. C. and W. Macdonald			Ibid.
1893	Siniasoro	J. C. Macdonald		Sold some produce to German trading ships	Ribbe 1903, 56–75
1895	Faisi	N. Tindal			Chewings 1900, 22; Festetics von Tolna 1903, 374
1896	Fauro	Atkinson			WPHC 287/96: Woodford to Thurston, 18 July 1896; WPHC 91/00: Woodford, General Information . . .
Ontong Java					
1889	Ontong Java	Otto Asche		Left ship *Thistle*	*SMH*, 21 June 1889
1899	Ontong Java	?	E. Forsyth & Co.	E. Forsyth or "Queen Emma"	WPHC 32/99: Woodford to HC, 18 Nov. 1899
1900	Ontong Java	Schwartz	Forsyth	Bismarck Archipelago	WPHC 91/00: Woodford to HC, 29 Aug. 1900, Information on Lord Howe Group
1900	Ontong Java	Monrod	Mouton	Bismarck Archipelago	Ibid.

APPENDIX 6

Violent conflicts between Solomon Islanders and Europeans engaged in trading, c. 1860–1896

Date	Place	Vessel/person	Killed*		Supposed motives and remarks	Sources
			SI	E		
1859	Rendova	*Pearl*		8	Also killed, Chinese cook and two Erromanga men	*Empire*, 26 Dec. 1859
1860	Roviana, New Georgia	*Rebecca*	1	2	Crew attacked while loading water on ship. Solomon Islander crewman killed	*SMH*, 2 Jan. 1861
1862	Cape Marsh, Russells	*William*'s party		2	Shore party including 11 Lifu Islanders collecting bêche-de-mer massacred. Station plundered	*SMH*, 7 June 1862
1863	?	*William*		1	G. Fowlis seized by natives when trying to trade	*SMH*, 12 July 1863
1867	Banietta, Rendova	*Marion Renny*		12		*SMH*, 20 Jan. 1868; UK-RNAS 14: Ponsonby to Delaney, 13 Sept. 1869 and encls.
1873	Nggela	*Lavinia*	2	6	Porakasi and Dukwa instigated attack	*SMH*, 15 Jan. 1875; UK-RNAS 13: Stirling to Cmdr. *Sandfly*, 1 Sept. 1873
1874	East Choiseul	*Kate Kearney*	1		Killed by war party from Vella Lavella, seeking head for chief's death	*SMH*, 27 Apr. 1874
Oct. 1874	Ontong Java	*James Burnie*	15	8	Solomon Island Melanesians burned bêche-de-mer drying shed, blamed Ontong Javanese. Ontong Javanese retaliated. No record of Ontong Javanese being killed in affray	UK-RNAS 13: Williams to Gov. NSW, 4 Jan. 1875 and encls.

Date	Place	Ship/Person	No.	Description	Source
1875	Gizo	*Kate Kearney*	8	Attacked while landing a native "chief" who had been aboard ship	*SMH*, 5 July 1876
1877	Cockatoo Is., Santa Isabel	*Mary Anderson's* station	1	N. P. Sorenson ill-treating natives	UK-RNAS 14: Wright to Capt. *Beagle*, 6 Oct. 1877, encl.
Nov. 1878	Ngalimbiu River, Guadalcanal	Robert Provis and Visa e men	3	Said to have been killed because of enmity between Visale and Ngalimbiu people. Capt. Schwartz burned village in retaliation	UK-RNAS 14: Houghton to Wilson, 16 May 1879 and encls.
May 1879	Uki	Townsend	1		WPHC 15/79: Townsend to HC, 27 Jan. 1879, and encls.
1879	"Ferguson" Is., Marau Sound, Guadalcanal	Charles Halgate	1	Washari and Alick killed Halgate because of Capt. Ferguson's punishment of Washari for "stealing" pearlshell	UK-RNAS 14: Houghton to Wilson, 16 May 1879 and encls.
1879	Marau Sound	Jimmy Morrow and Wilson, a Savo man	1	Vessel, *Sylph*, plundered and stolen. Man-of-war destroyed canoes and village as punishment. People of Paro and Maraunia implicated	Ibid.; WPHC 54/79: Cmdr. *Wolverine* to Gorrie, 9 June 1879 and encls.
1879	Marau Sound	J. Macdonald's boat crew	3	Boat seized	UK-RNAS 14: Houghton to Wilson, 16 May 1879 and encls.; UK-RNAS 15: Accounts of white men, 30 Sept. 1879
1879	Kolombangara	McIntosh and Jaffney of *Esperanza*	2	Kolombangara people wanted plunder. Two crewmen were from Tanna, Vanuatu. Another source says eight Islanders and three whites were killed	UK-RNAS 15: Statement of John Jones of Roviana, c. Aug. 1880 and encls.; *Mackay Mercury*, 1 Sept. 1880
1880	Tambatamba, Choiseul	*Zephyr*	2	"Chief" Koka of Kangipassa implicated. Man-of-war punished village	WPHC 20/81: Maxwell to Wilson, 31 Jan. 1881 and encls.

(*continued*)

APPENDIX 6: *Violent conflicts between Solomon Islanders and Europeans engaged in trading, c. 1860–1896 (cont.)*

Date	Place	Vessel/person	Killed* SI	Killed* E	Supposed motives and remarks	Sources
1880	Northwest Guadalcanal	People at Yaro			Capt. Haddock of *Queen* quarreled with the villagers re price of copra. He struck one man in the mouth knocking teeth out, hit another with the butt of his pistol, and failed to return 3 of his boat crew to their homes, landing them instead among their enemies	Mair, 30 Sept. 1880
Aug. 1880	Ubuna, San Cristobal	"Ourna" (Aurua)	1		Local trader, "Ourna," accidentally shot by mate of *Venture*	WPHC 139/80: Bateman to Wilson, 13 Sept. 1880, encl.; WPHC 150/80: Nixon to Bowen, 3 Sept. 1880, encl.
1881	Russell Islands	Schwartz of *Leslie*		1	Quarrel over trade. Schwartz had given advance to "Cookey" and Harry, but they sold to *Mavis*. Capt. Wolsch said to have burned down village of suspects as punishment	WPHC 70/81: Wilson to Gordon, 22 Mar. 1881 and encls.; WPHC 167/81: Wilson to Gordon, 16 Aug. 1881, and encls.; WPHC 192/81: Wilson to Gordon, 28 Nov. 1881 and encls.
1881	Mundimundi, Vella Lavella	*Atlantic*	1		Head money offered by a Roviana chief. Man-of-war destroyed village and canoes	WPHC 192/81: Wilson to Gordon, 28 Nov. 1881 and encls.
May 1885	Near Banietta, Rendova	*Elibank Castle*	3	2	J. Howie and K. Johns among those killed. "Chief" Noah and Poogey behind attack because Poogey wanted heads and plunder	WPHC 43/86: Tryon to Thurston, 8 Jan. 1886

Date	Location	Vessel/Person	No.	Description	Reference
1886	Gisu, Fauro	T. Woodhouse		Boat stolen at Roviana by Shortland Islanders. Woodhouse attacked village of Gisu to get vessel back	Woodford Papers: Diary, 24 Aug. 1886
Oct. 1886	Near Ruavatu, Guadalcanal	Louisa		Vessel looted after running on reef	Ibid., 18 Oct. 1886
1886	Hada, San Cristobal	A boy		Shot by E. Griffiths, trader, but recovered. The "chief" protected the trader	WPHC 79/86: Acting Agent General to Sec. to HC, 18 May 1886 and encls.
1886	Bauro area, San Cristobal	Acams of Lucy Acams	1	Murdered while drunk by bushmen who wanted a head following the death of a big-man	WPHC 106/86: Tryon to Thurston, 17 June 1886 and encls.
1887	Hughli, Rendova	Spec alias Progress	2	G. Queen and M. Madson ex Fiji murdered by Gassa, Rangi, Miyana, Tomu, and Zahey for plunder. Man-of-war punished village	Woodford Papers: Diary, 16 Sept. 1887
1888	Roviana, New Georgia	Malaita men	2	Employed by P. E. Pratt. Killed by Banietta or Simbo people	WPHC 102/92: Case 32A, Corresp. 1891
1889	Marovo, New Georgia	Malaita men	2	Working for T. Woodhouse, were murdered while collecting copra off beach	Woodford Papers: Case 35, Corresp. 1889; WPHC 96/91: Case 35, Corresp. 1890; WPHC 102/92: Case 35, Corresp. 1891; WPHC 69/93: Case 35, Corresp. 1892
Sept. 1889	Lokokongo, Rendova	Enterprise	4	Lars (?) Nielsen and boat crew attacked while getting copra off beach	WPHC 96/91: Case 34, Corresp. 1890
Mar. 1889	Anuta Is., San Cristobal	T. Dabelle	1	Killed to avenge the death of a man on plantations in Fiji. Man-of-war shelled villages. Supposed "murderer" hanged by Royal Navy	Woodford Papers: Case 31, Corresp. 1889; WPHC 96/91: Case 31, Corresp. 1890; WPHC 102/92: Case 31, Corresp. 1891; WPHC 69/93: Case 31, Corresp. 1892

(continued)

APPENDIX 6: *Violent conflicts between Solomon Islanders and Europeans engaged in trading, c. 1860–1896 (cont.)*

Date	Place	Vessel/person	Killed* SI	Killed* E	Supposed motives and remarks	Sources
June 1889	Roviana, New Georgia	W. Dabelle	2	1	Brother of T. Dabelle	Woodford Papers: Case 31, Corresp. 1889; WPHC 96/91: Case 32, Corresp. 1891; WPHC 102/92: Case 32; WPHC 69/93: Case 32
1889	Waisisi, Malaita	"Jack" Cooper, Charles Ladden and 12 crew of *Savo*	12	2	Shell "money" said to have been offered for deaths. Man-of-war shelled village	Woodford Papers: Case 33, Corresp. 1889; WPHC 69/91: Case 33; WPHC 102/92: Case 33; WPHC 69/93: Case 33
1890	Sirumbai, Vella Lavella	"Chief" Rosen	1		Killed by P. E. Pratt in argument involving Ontong Javanese boy and Maghratulo	WPHC 96/91: Case 42, Corresp. 1890; WPHC 102/92: Case 42, Corresp. 1891
1891	Makira Harbour, San Cristobal	Sam Craig of *Sandfly*		1	Killed by Tamahine (Taiemi) to avenge death of laborers in Fiji. Taiemi executed by Davis of HMS *Royalist*	WPHC 102/92: Case 46, Corresp. 1891
Jan. 1891	Uki	Fred Howard		1	Killed by Malaitans for guns and blood "money" paid by Uki people	WPHC 102/92: Case 49, Corresp. 1891; WPHC 69/93: Case 49, Corresp. 1892; WPHC 293/95: Case 49; WPHC 141/96: Case 49
1891	Roviana, New Georgia	A man	1		Employed by P. E. Pratt; killed during Pratt's absence	*SMH*, 2 Sept. 1891

Date	Place	Victim(s)	No.	Circumstances	Source
May 1891	Roviana, New Georgia	2 Savo crew of *Marshall S*	2	Killed by Buko at Dulavi after being enticed to leave ship. For this and killing of W. Dabelle, HMS *Royalist* destroyed villages of Roviana and Munda. Buko was also flogged	WPHC 102/92: Case 52, Corresp. 1891; WPHC 69/93: Case 52, Corresp. 1892
Mar. 1891	Ndovele, Vella Lavella	4 crewmen of *Freak*	4	Tono wanted heads for canoe launching. Tono also in debt to Atkinson. Atkinson, Woodhouse, and crew were fired on a month later. Although one boy was wounded they got back 2 skulls and burned Tono's people's homes. HMS *Royalist* destroyed canoes	WPHC 102/92: Case 53, Corresp. 1891
Nov. 1891	Danae Bay, Marau	Olsen of *Myrtle*		Attacked while bathing in river. Escaped	WPHC 102/92: Davis to CC, 4 Nov. 1891
1892	Santa Ana	F. Nyberg	1?	Killed following the shooting of a Santa Ana man during a drunken quarrel	WPHC 69/93: Kelham to Keating, 18 Apr. 1892
1893	Ubuna	*Elna* crewman	1	Man murdered in retaliation for rifling of graves and stealing of *mbakia* (armrings)	WPHC 141/96: Case 66, Corresp. 1895; WPHC 89/95: Bridges to Thurston, 1 Mar. 1895 and encl.
May 1894	Lilihina, Marovo	D. Guy	4	People of Soy wanted heads to launch canoes. Villages burned	WPHC 293/95: Case 61: Corresp. 1894
Oct. 1894	Santa Ana	1 man	1	Joseph Emmanuel of *Elna* killed man for wanting to go ashore	WPHC 141/96: Case 66, Corresp. 1895
c. 1894	Kolombangara and Vonavona	8 Malaita men	8	Employed by P. E. Pratt. Stole boat and goods from J. P. Pratt and ran away. Killed by people of Kolombangara and Vonavona	WPHC 293/95: Case 65, Corresp. 1895; WPHC 141/96: Case 65, Corresp. 1894

(continued)

APPENDIX 6: *Violent conflicts between Solomon Islanders and Europeans engaged in trading, c. 1860–1896 (cont.)*

Date	Place	Vessel/person	Killed* SI	Killed* E	Supposed motives and remarks	Sources
early c. 1895	Bulani, Roviana	Daniel Kerr John Smith of *Amelia*		2	Oro, Bekala, and Soka at Bulani behind killings. Motivated by need for heads for canoe launching	WPHC 283/96: Woodford to HC, 12 July 1896
July 1895	Roviana	The mate of *Wana Wana*			Malaitan, Oha, attempted to kill mate because the European had earlier slapped him. Punished by man-of-war	WPHC 141/96: Case 71, Corresp. 1895
Aug. 1895	Nggatokae, New Georgia Islands	C. Atkinson F. Floyd 1 Malaitan	1	2	Atkinson and Floyd killed by Malaitan crew, partly in retaliation for a blow by Atkinson that had killed a Malaitan crewman	WPHC 141/96: Case 69, Corresp. 1895
c. 1895	Choiseul	German trader?			Said to have been killed by local people. No details	WPHC 283/96: Woodford to HC, 12 July 1896
1896	Uki	E. Hamilton Wright		1	Murdered by Maiwasiwasi people from Bauro bush	WPHC 416/96: Woodford to Thurston, 21 Sept. 1896 and encls.
Nov. 1896	Hughli, Rendova	J. Gibbons		1	Attacked in cabin. Rengi behind killing. Village and canoes destroyed by man-of-war and Resident Commissioner Woodford	WPHC 36/97: Woodford to Collet, 25 Jan. 1897 and encls.

NOTE: Whalers, labor recruiters, missionaries, and crew of vessels drifting from outside the Solomons are excluded.
* SI, Solomon Islanders; E, Europeans

APPENDIX 7

*Resident commissioners and district officers before World War II,
by districts*

Resident commissioners, Solomon Islands

1896–1915	C. M. Woodford
1915–1917	F. J. Barnett (Acting)
1917–1921	C. R. M. Workman
1921–1929	R. R. Kane
1929–1939	F. N. Ashley
1940–1943	W. S. Marchant

District Officers, Shortland Island (District)
Compiled from Western Pacific Archives by Patrick Macdonald

1906 N. S. Heffernan, 24 October 1906 to 24 November 1909. (Appointed as District Magistrate)

1910 N. S. Heffernan, 14 April 1910 to 21 March 1911. (This appointment lacks absolute certitude, since the Civil List merely records "Resumed duty," though it is presumed that it was in the same post.)

1911 N. S. Heffernan, 29 May to 12 November 1911 (also as above)
W. R. Bell, 13 November 1911 to 30 July 1912

1915 Dr. N. Crichlow, Medical Officer, 7 December 1915 to 14 November 1916 (conjoint). (It is not possible to confirm the date on which he relinquished the post, but, as he was still Medical Officer, Shortland, in April 1917, and did not take leave between the two above dates, it may be presumed that he filled the post until relieved by his successor.)

1916 C. E. J. Wilson, 15 November 1916 to 21 January 1917

1919 S. G. C. Knibbs, Commissioner of Lands and Crown Surveyor, 4 April to 26 July 1919
C. F. Swift, Third Clerk and Boarding Officer, Treasury and Customs Department, 5 August 1919 to 18 March 1920

1920 H. D. Curry, 29 October 1920 to ? (Despite a thorough search it has not been possible to say on what date he gave up this post, but it must have been before 9 August 1921, when another officer succeeded him.)
ADO Nicholson, October 1920

1921 A. Middenway, 9 August 1921 to 9 December 1923

1923 Dr. N. Crichlow, Medical Officer, 10 December 1923 to 2 January 1925

1925 R. F. Thomson, Chief Inspector of Labourers, 2 January 1925 to 19 February 1927

1927 W. H. C. C. Miller, 20 February 1927 to 9 January 1930

1930 B. E. Crawfurd, 9 January to 2 November 1930

1931 W. H. C. C. Miller, 3 November 1931 to 25 March 1933. (Assigned the district of Shortland Islands.)

1933   Dr. N. Crichlow, Medical Officer, 26 March to 26 June 1933 (conjoint)
        L. W. S. Wright, 26 March 1933 to 27 January 1934
1934   F. L. Barlett, 28 January to 1 September 1934
        W. H. C. C. Miller, 1 September 1934 to 26 September 1935
1936   R. J. Keegan, 6 October 1936 to 29 March 1937
1937   C. N. F. Bengough, 19 October 1937 to 11 August 1938
1938   R. J. Keegan, 11 August 1938 to 1 April 1940
1940   D. C. C. Trench, 1 April to 6 May 1940
1941   W. H. C. C. Miller, 7 May 1941 to 24 September 1941
        A. N. A. Waddell, 25 September to ? (The date on which he relin-
        quished this post is uncertain; he was granted, like others, leave of
        absence for naval service on 2 August 1942.)

District Officers, Gizo

1904   T. W. Edge-Partington, District Magistrate, December 1904 to August
        1905
1906   T. W. Edge-Partington, District Magistrate, January 1906 to 12 May
        1908
1908   T. W. Edge-Partington, District Magistrate, 20 July 1908 to 31 May
        1909
1909   R. B. Hill, 20 July 1909 to 7 February 1911. (He and his successors were
        all designated District Officers.)
1911   R. B. Hill, 17 April 1911 to 31 October 1912
1912   J. C. Barley, 1 November 1912 to 15 April 1913
1915   J. C. Barley, 12 February to 25 March 1915
        H. D. Curry, 25 May to 23 June 1915
        Dr. N. Crichlow, Medical Officer, 23 July to 6 December 1915 (conjoint)
        H. D. Curry, 6 December 1915 to 30 November 1917
1919   C. C. Francis, 13 October 1919 to 5 October 1922
1922   W. V. J. Blake, Sub-Inspector of Constabulary, 6 October to 22 Novem-
        ber 1922
        C. C. Francis, 23 November 1922 to 19 October 1923
1923   A. Middenway, 10 December 1923 to 7 January 1925
1925   Dr. N. Crichlow, Medical Officer, 8 January to 6 July 1925 (conjoint)
        J. C. Barley, 1 July 1925 to 26 January 1928
1928   A. Middenway, 26 January to 9 October 1928
        R. A. Crompton, Cadet (attached to District Officer, Gizo), 28 July to 8
        October 1928
        R. A. Crompton, 9 October 1928 to 18 March 1929
1929   A. Middenway, 18 March 1929 to 6 January 1932
        W. Fowler, Cadet (attached to District Officer, Gizo), 23 December
        1929 to 23 February 1930
1930   A. D. C. Stephens, 29 June to 28 September 1930
        A. J. F. White, Cadet (attached to District Officer, Gizo), 21 September
        to 7 November 1930
        B. E. Crawfurd, Cadet (attached to District Officer, Gizo), 5 November
        1930 to 9 August 1931

1932 C. E. J. Wilson, 6 January to 21 August 1932
      A. Middenway, 22 August 1932 to 1 September 1934
1934 C. N. F. Bengough, Cadet (assigned for duty to the Gizo District), 2 January to 5 February 1934
      C. E. J. Wilson, 1 September 1934 to 31 July 1937
1937 R. J. Keegan, 31 July 1937 to 1 March 1938
1938 C. E. J. Wilson, 1 March to 7 November 1938
      D. C. Horton, 7 November to 30 November 1938
      W. H. C. C. Miller, 14 December 1938 to 9 December 1940
1940 J. K. Brownlees, 9 December 1940 to 29 January 1941
1941 A. N. A. Waddell, 29 January to 17 June 1941
      J. K. Brownlees, 18 June to 30 September 1941
      W. H. C. C. Miller, 30 September 1941 to ? (The date of his relinquishment of this post cannot be traced, but his successor took over on 1 July 1942—see below.)
1942 D. G. Kennedy, 1 July 1942 to ? (The date on which he relinquished this post cannot be traced, but he proceeded on overseas leave on 13 September 1942, and may well have been in the post until just before then.)

District Officer, Marovo Lagoon

1913 J. C. Barley, 22 October 1913 to 27 January 1915. (It would be helpful if the latter date could be further verified.)

District Officers, Santa Isabel

1917 N. S. Heffernan, 10 October 1917 to ? (The date of relinquishment of this post is uncertain, but was probably August 1918—see note regarding District Officer, Cape Marsh.)
1924 N. S. Heffernan, 17 July 1924 to 27 July 1925. (There can be no absolute certitude about these dates. The Civil List merely records "Resumed duty" and, as he was serving previously in Isabel, it is possible, or probable, that he resumed duty there.)
1925 S. G. Masterman, Inspector of Laborers, 27 July to 26 September 1925
      A. Middenway, 27 September 1925 to 2 September 1926
1926 E. D. D. Davis, Sub-Inspector of Constabulary, 3 September to 26 November 1926
      A. H. Studd, 27 November 1926 to 3 April 1927
1927 R. B. Hill, 4 April 1927 to 4 January 1929
1929 P. C. Hubbard, 5 January to 30 January 1929
1930 W. Fowler, 24 February 1930 to 5 June 1932
1932 F. B. Filose, 6 June 1932 to ? (The precise date upon which he relinquished control of the district cannot be traced, but his successor took over on 19 January 1933.)
1933 S. G. Masterman, Inspector of Laborers, 19 January to 16 February 1933
      W. H. C. C. Miller, 34 April to 13 October 1933. (He was assigned the District of Isabel *and* the Russell Islands.)
      W. Fowler, 19 October 1933 to 15 May 1935

1935 J. K. Brownlees, 16 May 1935 to 27 December 1936
1937 D. C. Horton, 7 September 1937 to 1 March 1938
1938 J. K. Brownlees, 8 March 1938 to 14 April 1940
1940 L. W. S. Wright, 16 April 1940 to 10 April 1941. (Assigned the District of Isabel.)
1941 D. G. Kennedy, 11 October 1941 to ? (It is not possible to trace the date when he relinquished this post. He was, however, assigned the District of Gizo on 1 July 1942.)

District Officer, Cape Marsh
(*Note:* Cape Marsh is the colloquial name for the Russell Islands)

1917 N. S. Heffernan, 10 October 1917 to ? (There is no date ascertainable as to when he relinquished this post, but the Gazette records that he went on overseas leave on 10 August 1918, so he could not have been there longer than that. He is also shown in the Civil List for 1925 as District Officer, Isabel, for the same period.)

District Officers, Savo, Florida, Tulagi and Nggela

1923 E. N. Turner, Officer in charge of Constabulary, 31 March 1923 to 10 September 1924. (Appointed Acting District Officer "for Savo and Florida comprised in the District of Tulagi"; conjoint.)
1928 E. N. Turner, Officer in charge of Constabulary, 2 June to 23 November 1928. (Appointed on the same basis as in 1923.)
      G. E. D. Sandars, Sub-Inspector of Constabulary, 24 November 1928 to 27 August 1929. (Appointed Acting District Officer "for the District of Tulagi.")
1934 E. N. Turner, Officer in command of Constabulary and Superintendent of the Prison, 28 July 1934 to 14 May 1935. (Appointed Acting District Officer, Nggela; conjoint.)
1935 G. E. D. Sandars, Sub-Inspector of Constabulary, 14 May to 13 October 1935. (Appointed Acting District Officer, Nggela; conjoint.)
1940 P. Colley, Clerk, Resident Commissioner's Office, 10 March to 25 July 1940. (Appointed District Officer, Nggela.)
      D. G. Kennedy, 27 July 1940 to 6 October 1941 (conjoint)
1942 G. E. D. Sandars, Secretary to Government, 8 December 1942 to 12 June 1943. (Assigned to District of Nggela; conjoint.)

District Officers, Guadalcanal

1914 C. C. Francis, Passed Cadet; provisionally appointed District Officer, Aola, 9 November 1914
1915 C. E. J. Wilson, Boarding Officer and Clerk, Acting District Officer, 18 January to 14 May 1915
      C. G. Norris, Cadet, Acting District Officer, 15 May 1915 to 9 September 1919
1919 H. W. P. Newall, Acting District Officer, 9 September 1919 to 31 March 1920. (There is some doubt as to whether Newall did in fact act as Dis-

trict Officer. Originally, the Resident Commissioner proposed that C. C. Francis assume these duties from 13 October 1919 to March 1920.)

1920 R. B. Hill, District Officer, 1 April to 4 November 1920

1921 R. B. Hill, District Officer, 18 April 1920 to 14 July 1923

1923 C. E. J. Wilson, Accountant and First Clerk, Treasury and Customs Department; Acting District Officer, 2 July to 9 December. (Ralph Brodhurst Hill resumed duty 21 December 1923 and served as Acting Resident Commissioner until 6 October 1924, apparently at Tulagi.)

1924 R. B. Hill, District Officer, 6 October 1924 to 6 September 1925

1925 F. B. Filose, Clerk to the Resident Commissioner; Acting District Officer, 3 September 1925 to 5 August 1926

1926 C. E. J. Wilson, District Officer, 6 August 1926 to 12 October 1927

1927 R. A. Crompton, Cadet; attached to District Officer, 24 May to 6 October 1927
Arthur Middenway, District Officer, 13 October 1927 to 29 January 1928

1928 C. E. J. Wilson, District Officer, 23 January to 23 November 1928
L. W. S. Wright, Assistant District Officer, 24 November 1928 to 30 April 1930

1930 C. E. J. Wilson, District Officer, 1 May 1930 to 19 May 1931
A. D. C. Stephens, Cadet; attached to District Officer, 29 September 1930 to 29 June 1931

1931 L. W. S. Wright, District Officer, 20 May to 18 November 1931
C. E. J. Wilson, 18 November 1931 to 5 January 1932

1932 L. W. S. Wright, 6 January to 21 September 1932
C. E. J. Wilson, 22 September 1932 to 5 February 1934

1934 L. W. S. Wright, 6 February 1934 to 12 September 1935

1935 C. N. F. Bengough, District Officer, 13 September 1935 to 2 March 1936

1936 L. W. S. Wright, District Officer, 3 March 1936 to 28 February 1938

1938 T. P. Kneen, 1 March 1938 until after the outbreak of World War II

District Officers, Malaita

1909 T. W. Edge-Partington, District Magistrate, 1 September 1909 to 22 February 1912

1913 T. W. Edge-Partington, District Magistrate, 26 February 1913 to 26 January 1915 (on which latter date he resigned)

1915 F. M. Campbell, Officer in command of Native Police, 21 January to 31 March 1915 (conjoint)
R. B. Hill, 10 May to 7 August 1915
F. M. Campbell, Officer in command of Native Police, 7 August to 22 October 1915 (conjoint)
W. R. Bell, Inspector of Laborers, 22 October 1915 to 25 January 1916

1916 W. R. Bell, Inspector of Laborers, 29 May 1916 to February 1917. (The precise date cannot be traced.)

1917 W. R. Bell, Inspector of Laborers, May 1917 to 4 March 1921. (The date of appointment cannot be traced; he was appointed a District Officer on 21 May 1919.)

1921   W. R. Bell, 21 June 1921 to 17 July 1924
1923   A. H. Studd, 7 September 1923 to 16 July 1924 (Assistant District Officer)
1924   A. H. Studd, 17 July 1924 to 1 April 1925
1925   W. R. Bell, 2 April 1925 to 4 October 1927. (On the latter date he met his death on Malaita.)
      K. C. Lillies, 20 November 1925 to 18 March 1927 (Cadet attached to District Officer, Malaita)
1927   K. C. Lillies, 14 April to 4 October 1927 (Cadet until he met his death on Malaita)
      *S. G. Masterman, Inspector of Laborers, 7 October to 30 November 1927
      *R. A. Crompton, 7 October 1927 to 12 February 1928
      *A. W. Dickes, Survey Office Clerk, 20 September to 16 December 1927
      *C. E. J. Wilson, 13 October 1927 to 22 January 1928
      (The last four officers were seconded for special service on Malaita.)
1928   F. B. Filose, 9 January 1928 to 8 May 1929
      R. A. Crompton, 7 February to 12 February 1928 (Acting Assistant District Officer, Malaita)
      R. H. Garvey, 11 August to 18 October 1928 (Acting Assistant District Officer, Malaita)
      P. C. Hubbard, 18 October 1928 to 4 January 1929 (Acting Assistant District Officer, Malaita)
1929   C. E. J. Wilson, 8 May 1929 to 29 January 1930 (assigned the District of Malaita)
1930   J. C. Barley, 29 January 1930 to 5 January 1932
      L. W. S. Wright, 1 October to 8 November 1930 (Assistant District Officer, Malaita)
      A. J. F. White, 8 November 1930 to 5 January 1932 (attached to the District Officer, Malaita)
      R. H. Garvey, 3 December 1930 to 19 April 1931 (assigned the District of South Malaita)
1932   A. J. F. White, 5 January 1932 to 19 May 1933
1933   W. Fowler, 11 May 1933 to 2 June 1934 (Assistant District Officer, Malaita)
      J. C. Barley, 19 May to 23 November 1933
      G. E. D. Sandars, Sub-Inspector of Constabulary, 23 November 1933 to 6 May 1935
1934   C. N. F. Bengough, 10 February 1934 to 4 May 1935 (assigned for duty to the District of Malaita)
1935   C. N. F. Bengough, 6 May to 20 May 1935
      W. Fowler, 20 May 1935 to 4 March 1936. (The latter date cannot be precisely verified but it is the day before he proceeded on overseas leave. He was assigned the District of Malaita.)
      J. K. Brownlees, 30 December 1935 to 26 January 1937 (Assistant District Officer, Malaita)
1936   C. N. F. Bengough, 5 March to 1 October 1936
      G. E. D. Sandars, 2 October 1936 to 26 September 1938
1937   A. N. A. Waddell, 4 September 1937 to 11 May 1938 (assigned for duty to Malaita)

1938 C. N. F. Bengough, 26 September 1938 to 7 August 1939
      W. F. M. Clemens, 29 October 1938 to 1 August 1940 (assigned for duty
      to Malaita)
1940 J. K. Brownlees, 3 August to 5 December 1940 (assigned to the District
      of Malaita)
      M. J. Forster, 5 August to 24 November 1940 (assigned for duty to
      Malaita)
      M. J. Forster, 25 November to 4 December 1940
      C. N. F. Bengough, 5 December 1940 to 3 May 1943
1941 D. C. C. Trench, 7 May to 6 September 1941 (assigned for duty to
      Malaita)

District Officers, Eastern Solomon Islands

1917 F. M. Campbell, Officer in charge of Armed Constabulary, 9 November
      1917 to 21 June 1919. (Campbell was DO Eastern Solomons with Newell
      under him, but the later transferred c. November 1919 to Guadalcanal.)
1919 E. N. Turner, Officer in command of Constabulary; Acting District
      Officer, 1 September to 2 November 1919
      J. C. Barley, 13 October 1919 to 11 September 1921. (He was appointed
      to act as Resident Commissioner on the latter date, and, as there is no
      other item gazetted in the interim, it is assumed that he was District
      Officer in the Eastern Solomon Islands until then.)
1922 J. C. Barley, 18 February 1922 to 2 April 1923. (The Civil List shows
      "Resumed duties of substantive post" which may simply mean "District
      Officer" or "District Officer, Eastern Solomons." The latter seems more
      likely as it fits in with the date of assumption of duty by his successor.)
1923 C. E. J. Wilson, 2 April to 1 July 1923
      Dr. N. Crichlow, Medical Officer, 1 August to 9 December 1923 (con-
      joint)
1925 A. H. Studd, 28 April to 11 October 1925
      Dr. N. Crichlow, Medical Officer, 11 October 1925 to 29 April 1926
      (conjoint)
1926 E. D. D. Davis, Sub-Inspector of Constabulary, 30 November 1926 to
      19 March 1927
1927 K. C. Lillies, 20 March to 12 April 1927
      A. H. Studd, 12 April to 4 October 1927
      F. B. Filose, 5 October 1927 to 8 January 1928
1930 R. F. Thomson, Chief Inspector of Laborers, 14 May 1930 to 19 April
      1931
1931 R. H. Garvey, 20 April to 29 June 1931. (He was "assigned the district of
      the Eastern Solomon Islands." He was then "assigned the district of Santa
      Cruz on 1 August 1931.")
      A. D. C. Stephens, 30 June 1931. (He was appointed "Acting District
      Officer, Eastern Solomon Islands." There are no later items in the Civil
      List for 1933, and his name does not appear in that for 1934; it is
      believed he resigned.)
1932 F. M. Campbell, as Acting District Officer
1933 W. Fowler, 6 July to 15 October 1933. (The latter date is not precise but
      he was appointed as Acting District Officer, Isabel, on 19 October 1933.)

1934   J. K. Brownlees, 12 September 1934 to 11 May 1935. (The latter date is
       not precise but he was appointed as Acting District Officer, Isabel, on 16
       May 1935.)

1938   A. N. A. Waddell, 12 May 1938 to 4 August 1940. (The latter date is not
       precise but he went on leave overseas on 7 August 1940.)

1940   W. F. M. Clemens, 5 August 1940 to 28 February 1942. (The latter date
       is not precise but he was appointed District Officer, Guadalcanal, on 1
       March 1942.)

1941   M. J. Forster, 1 November 1941 to ? (No date is given for his relinquish-
       ment of this appointment; his next gazetted appointment is as District
       Officer, Nggela, on 13 June 1943 and, as the next gazetted appointment
       was 27 May 1943, it may reasonably be assumed that his appointment in
       San Cristobal lasted until May 1943.)

District Officers, Santa Cruz

1923   C. E. J. Wilson, 10 December 1923 to 5 December 1924

1925   N. S. Heffernan, 28 July 1925 to 17 September 1926

1926   A. Middenway, 18 September 1926 to 7 October 1927
       A. H. Studd, 8 October 1927 to 4 October 1928

1928   R. H. Garvey, 21 October 1928 to 7 October 1929

1929   Dr. N. Crichlow, Medical Officer, 17 October to 4 November 1929 (con-
       joint)
       F. B. Filose, 29 November 1929 to 2 July 1931

1931   R. H. Garvey, 1 August 1931 to July 1932. (The precise date is not ascer-
       tainable, but he became Assistant Secretary of the Western Pacific High
       Commission on 10 August 1932. He was not appointed "District Officer,
       Santa Cruz" as were his predecessors but was "assigned the district of
       Santa Cruz.")

1932   B. E. Crawfurd, 10 October 1932 to 25 September 1935

1935   W. H. C. C. Miller, 27 September 1935 to 27 March 1937 (assigned the
       District of Santa Cruz)

1937   Dr. N. Crichlow, Medical Officer, 27 March to 29 November 1937 (con-
       joint)
       W. H. C. C. Miller, 30 November 1937 to 17 November 1938 (assigned
       the District of Santa Cruz)

1938   C. E. J. Wilson, 18 November 1938 to 17 August 1940 (assigned the Dis-
       trict of Santa Cruz)

1940   Dr. N. Crichlow, Medical Officer, 17 August to 9 December 1940 (con-
       joint)
       C. E. J. Wilson, to 10 December 1943. (No precise date of his relin-
       quishment of the post is ascertainable but he proceeded on overseas
       leave on 9 December 1943.)

District Officer, Lord Howe Islands

1915   J. C. Barley, 27 July 1915 to 27 March 1916

APPENDIX 8

Petitions to Resident Commissioner, 1912

First petition

Octo. 16th 1912

the Government residence Commissioner Tulagi

Dear sir we maent if the boy. whatever money he is earning he can spente it or saved it. for his Father and mother or any of his relation and Banking it. through thee and us is here. in the Island. and sir. this is great mistake on untreatment is. the boy obey enough and do their work with anxious mine and may be few solow hand there amonges the crowde or staveness for food may be fell upon them all. of course we know the living soul must filled his stamuch with usefull Food befor they can hurry on the hard duing or hard works. as soon as the master for boy come along in evening or morning and see the work carrie on not so well. and he start Barcking at the boss boy. immediately arose the rough nature wosce the boy with loyer cane in his hand without fault from the boys. for therefore no daily the boy stold boat. or connoo and skoot Back again to their home land malayta through the untreater. just as they declare their agony to the Judge. it maent if He can wipe away their tears. I do believe thou wilte thou can smoote the mather between us and Farmer. Prosper. of course we under the British Flages now. much be Equal food and wage. for we are join in one is given from above to all mankind on earth is Jesus and lord. so we layout the boy were they weekly work on Boardship or any different Popurse on the land for 18 mont it they have no enough money to deliver it. on the colliction Book. but if he Passe to or 18 monht. must be toul for him and we leaveht him unts thy hand must bonde in Prison. we layout every boy. imploy their name must be writen in the Book of (it maent not in Prison but fraid them) the collection every 6 or 18 monht. above their money. and sir while thou Prove this. we.ll start rear up our navye trooper. then we ll let thee know again of [?] is the Facte if the messege is fulfile there is not enough plantation to imploy the whole Islanders mane and woman and chidren here in the island. would be Queen land and Fiji will be specting nough room for them all. for we are waiting and looking for somthing better well appeare from thee in the island sir. after all

we are your.

faithfull

and truely servent sir.

Ben. Bowra Footaboory and
P. A., J. K., J. G., H. R.,
H. U.

Fair English version

16 October 1912

To the Resident Commissioner, Tulagi

A boy should be able to spend or save what he earns. He can spend it on his parents or relations or he can bank it. We all live in these islands. But there is mistreatment.

A boy does what he is told and tries his best. A few might be slow, some perhaps because of hunger. Of course, we all realize a person must be well fed before he can work hard. Anytime the master comes along to check on the work he starts yelling at the boss boy. He gets very angry and hits the boy with a *loia* cane for no reason at all. As a result of this mistreatment a boy might be forced to steal a boat or a canoe to get back to his homeland, Malaita.

If they could tell of their sufferings to a judge they could get redress. I think you can clear up the trouble between our people and the planters.

Of course, we are now under the British flag so we should get equal wages and treatment equal to the whites. We are all one in the law and in the eyes of Jesus, our Lord.

We say that if a boy works at a weekly rate aboard ship or on land for eighteen months his employer should set aside enough money to the collection. If a boy works more than eighteen months [and has not paid] then that is his own fault and he should be imprisoned. Every employer's name must be written in a book so that they will know that if they break the law there is a record. The laborer's contribution to the collection must be recorded every six or eighteen months.*

While you are considering this we will start a militia [or navy], then we will talk about this again. If there is not enough work on plantations here for every man, woman, and child then there would be scope for them to work in Queensland or Fiji. We are waiting and seeking an improvement in life in these islands.

Ben. Bowra Footaboory and P. A.,
J. K., J. G., H. R., and H. U.

Alternative: All employers' names must be recorded and the money they owe [to their employees], every six to eighteen months.

Second petition

Octo. 17th 1912

The Government residance commissioner Tulagi

Dear sir Mr. C. Woodford.

we are trifling this article sir that we know thou can handled this collaction for us throughout whole the Islander district. wherever the Farmer taker employ the boys. and the collaction is the Boy from 15 year of age £1.0. each every 6 monht and the boy from 12 up to 14 year of age £0.10. each every 6 monht also the boy must be get their Piyment every 6 monht. but as soon as the boys Payment is due and the Boys master just renounced every boy before he can Keepeht it back this money of every boys wage. and the commissioner we layout £0.1.0 out of each £1.0 and the £0.0.6d. out of each £0.10.0 this is thine own commissioner. and the money were is collacting the master of the boy must handled to thee. and thou to us. as this collaction is carrie on from Generation to Generation. this is what we call the mission collaction for to helping thee and the bishops for the Poorer and the nakedness we are Dear sir. again I try to Bring up our nation unto the civilisation states. also we can train them about the good work. sir. do Passe this message to whole the Farmer Prosper through-out whole the Islander district. and also sir kindly Passe it to the Fiji. Goverer and Australian government to Published for those who are still remaine in Fiji and Australia must sign their name for the collaction every 6 monht. but their money were they earning Every year they can do what they like with. they can spente it or Bankeht it by thee and us. now am going to tell thee about the great Exisitance between us and the Farmer Prosper is. First of all the Good treat-ment and the wage. it is the facte that nearly whole the boy have been out and return from Australian Queensland and Fiji and they sould remember the treat-ment there. is lot different from here. so the treatment here is bring them down to the ignorntment druction. and the untreatment is sir. first of all wanting Bread and meal and tea and sugar and rice and Potato all kind of food every meal. and the next of it. the wage seeker and riasing a wage. the boys From 15 year of age up to the full age. muchly get 35 shilling a week and tuker. for those who are will known and anxiously and the overhim. it maent. those train them already. and the £. 25s. a week for some. and the boy from 12 to 14 year of age £.20.s. a week. and the boy must find their own cook and the cloht for usesing at work and the cook must get 10 schilling a week from each Boy out of 35 schilling and 25s. and 5s. out of the £ 1.0 each boy this is the cooks wage. and the cook must find his own mane servent for to clean up the boys dwelling and helping for the clean cook. supposes in the maenthim do thou can opente up Australian queensland again sooner for thine own children here in the Island. can out once more to the australia as soon as thou Provid this messeage. throughout whole the solomon Island district and newhabrigedis I do believe thou at will. but the labour trip captain must get the boy Free from the Island without Present to the Father and mother only. Plentifull of food on boardship to reach the Place were they Go to. and sign their name above their wage. so when the maneger of the Plantation must look after their boy with charity and gentleness as much as thyself. sir. as soon as thou fullfile the message. we can Exercised the mission boy some work wherever the mission is. but the same wage also and while we started our scrup claring then we can ordered what we want from thee. nothing but usesing tool and storstock but we cannot starte our Possession untill thou receive the collaction. sir.

the harbour.   and.   the member.

Quarra Harbour . . . . .Benjamin Bowra Footaboory
Marlu mission . . . . . . .Peter. ambuover.
urrasie . . . . .Jackson. Kefeety and Bro.
Feu mission . . . . .Jack. Gwoefoon.
Aoke . . . . .Harry. Rumsalla.
lunga lunga . . . . .Harry. Umfirra.
this member must be Found in every Parht on

Fair English version

17 October 1912

To the Resident Commissioner, Mr C. Woodford, Tulagi

We are writing to tell you about the collection throughout the islands. When a planter employs a boy of fifteen years of age he must take from him £1/-/- every six months. A boy of twelve to fourteen years should have 10/- held by the planter. The boys should be paid every six months. The master can hold back this part of the boy's due wage. We want to suggest that 1/- from each £1 or 6d from 10/- be taken by you for yourself. The rest of this retained money should also be handed to you and then passed on to us. This collection is to continue from generation to generation. We will call this the mission collection to help you [the government] and the bishops and our own poverty.

I want, sir, to bring our nation into a state of civilization. We want our young to be educated to do good work.

Pass this message on to the planters throughout these islands and also to the governments of Fiji and Australia so that islanders remaining behind there will know. They too must sign on to give money to the collection every six months. They can do what they like with the rest of their money—they can spend it, bank it or send it to you or to us to look after.

Now I am going to tell you about conditions of employment on plantations. Firstly, concerning treatment of labourers and their wage: It is a fact that practically all the men have worked in Queensland or Fiji and they are aware that the treatment there is a lot different from here. Here, they are treated as if they are ignorant. What they want [on the plantations] is bread, meat, tea, sugar, and potatoes at every meal. Next, they want an increase in wages. Boys from fifteen years of age up to adulthood must be paid 35/- a week and food, providing they are already trained and proficient at their jobs. If they are 'new chums' they should be paid 25/- a week. Boys from twelve to fourteen should get 20/- a week, but the boys must be allowed to choose their own cook and clothing for wearing at work. The cook should be paid 10/- a week by the men who earn 35/- and 25/- a week and 5/- by those paid £1 a week. This is to be the cook's wage, but he must find his own assistant to clean up the mens' houses and to help with the cooking.

In the meantime do all you can to open up Queensland again for recruiting for your people [Solomon Islanders] so they can once again go to Australia. If this can be done the word will soon spread throughout the Solomons and the New Hebrides [Vanuatu]. However, the captains of the labor ships should give the beach pay only to the parents of the boy. On ship the recruits must get plenty of food while they are on their way to the plantation. The planter must look after the boy with charity and gentleness, just like he would treat you [or, just like you would treat him].

As soon as you carry out these things, sir, the mission boys can set to work in those places where the missions are, but at the same wage rate.

Sir, we can then use our collection funds held by you to buy tools and hardware so we can clear the bush, but we cannot begin until you make the collection.

The harbor	and	the member
Quarra Harbour		Benjamin Bowra Footaboory
Maluu mission		Peter Ambuover
Urasi		Jackson Kefeety and brother
Fiu mission		Jack Gwoefoon
'Aoke		Harry Rumsalla
Langalanga		Harry Umfirra

These members live at the above address

ABBREVIATIONS

AC	Advisory Council
AC-AR	Annual Report of Armed Constabulary
ADC	Acting District Commissioner
ADO	Acting District Officer
AJMR	*Asiatic Journal and Monthly Register*
ANA	Australian National Archives
ANU	Australian National University
AR	Annual Report
BP	Burns Philp
BPA	Burns Philp Archives
BSI	British Solomon Islands
BSIP	British Solomon Islands Protectorate
BSIP-AR	Annual Report of BSIP
BSIP-CS	BSIP Confidential Series
CAO	Commonwealth Archives Office
CC	Commander-in-Chief
CDW	Commonwealth Development and Welfare
CJEP	Correspondence of James Edge-Partington
CO	Colonial Office (United Kingdom)
COR	Companies Office Records
CP	Commons Papers
CRS	Commonwealth Records Series
CRSI	Correspondence relating to the Solomon Islands
CS	Confidential source
DC	District Commissioner
DO	District Officer
FNA	Fiji National Archives
FP	Fallowes papers
FRCP	Fairley Rigby company papers
FT	*Fiji Times*

411

GC	Goldie Correspondence
GCD	Governing Council Debates
GCO	German Colonial Office records
GEIC	Gilbert and Ellice Islands Colony
GNA	German National Archives
GOV	Government
Ham P	Hamilton Papers
HC	High Commissioner
HP	Hocart Papers
HMSO	Her Majesty's Stationery Office
IC	Inwards Correspondence
IP	Island Properties
IPI	Island Properties Inspection file
IR	Inspection Reports
K	Kindar file
KR	King's Regulation
LAD	Legislative Assembly Debates
LB	Lever Brothers file
LC	Lands Commission
LCD	Legislative Council Debates
LCR	Lands Commission Report
LD	Labour Department
LPP	Lever's Pacific Plantations
LTR	Land Titles Records
MAR	Manager's Annual Report
MD	Medical Department
MDHD	Ministry of Defence Hydrographic Department
MMP	Methodist Mission Papers
MP	Metcalfe Papers
NID	Naval Intelligence Division
NLA	National Library of Australia
NM	*Nautical Magazine*
NMP	Native Medical Practitioner
NSWSA	New South Wales State Archives
P	Papers
PI	Pacific Islands
PIM	*Pacific Islands Monthly*
PMB	Pacific Manuscript Bureau Microfilm
PMUA	Pacific Material on Unilever Archives
PP	Parliamentary Papers
QSA	Queensland State Archives
QR	Queen's Regulation
Reg	Regulation
RNAS	Royal Navy, Australian Station

RRAACP	Research in Records of American Activities in the Central Pacific
SCL	*Southern Cross Log*
Sec	Secretary
SecS	Secretary of State
SG	*Sydney Gazette*
SGNSWA	*Sydney Gazette and New South Wales Advertiser*
SGSGTL	*Shipping Gazette and Sydney General Trade List*
SH	*Sydney Herald*
ShI	Shortland Island miscellaneous file
ShIPC	Shortland Island Plantation Company
SI	Solomon Islands
SIDC	Solomon Islands Development Company
SILC	Solomon Islands Labour Corps
SIM-1	Solomon Islands Miscellaneous File no. 1
SIM-2	Solomon Islands Miscellaneous File no. 2
SM	*Sydney Mail*
SMH	*Sydney Morning Herald*
SMO	Senior Medical Officer
SS	South Seas
SSEM	South Sea Evangelical Mission
Syn	Syndicate
TL	Tetiri Lands file [Tetere]
UA	Unilever Archives
UK	United Kingdom
UPNG	University of Papua New Guinea
WPA	Western Pacific Archives
WPHC	Western Pacific High Commission
WRCP	W. R. Carpenter and Company Papers

NOTES

Chapter 1: The Solomon Islands in 1800

Chatterton in *Pacific Islands Monthly*, July 1982, 53–54.

1. Amherst and Thompson 1901, 1:17, 88–89, 107–108.
2. Grover 1958, 25–26, 148; Brookfield with Hart 1971, 84, 124n.
3. Brookfield with Hart 1971, 97–111; Ross 1973, 73–77.
4. Hansell and Wall 1976, 1:106, 117–118.
5. Brookfield with Hart 1971, 226–229; Zoleveke 1979, 1–4.
6. Brookfield with Hart 1971, 86; Ross 1973, 75.
7. Wall and Hansell 1974b, 5.30; Scheffler 1965, 3; Ross 1973, 34.
8. Wall and Hansell 1974b, Figure 5.6.
9. Brookfield with Hart 1971, 5–6; Gabites 1960; Wall and Hansell 1974b, 5.19–5.20; Hansell and Wall 1976, 36, 41, Map 6. See also Ross 1973, 30–32.
10. Miller 1980, 461–462; Ross 1973, 73.
11. Ross 1973, 48–50; Scheffler 1965, 7–8.
12. Bellwood 1978, 119–122, 244; Roger Green 1976, 55–87; Tryon 1979, 35–36.
13. Tryon 1979, 35–36.
14. Bellwood 1978, 244–255.
15. Wheeler 1943, history; WPHC 3845/32: Trench to Sec. of Govt. 4 Jan. 1941 encl.
16. Bennett 1974, 74–77.
17. Ivens 1927, 26.
18. Bennett 1974, 21–25, 42–46; Hopkins 1928, 40; Miller 1980, 455–456.
19. Bennett 1974; Miller 1980, 456–457.
20. Chapman 1970, 60–73; Scheffler 1965, 25–26.
21. WPHC BSIP F 46/35: Kuper to DO 2 Oct. 1933 encl.
22. Bennett 1974, 121–126; Wright 1974, 3.78, 3.82. See, for other Pacific peoples in pre-European times, Snow 1974, 11; Pietrusewsky 1976, 8; Houghton 1980, 95–97.
23. Barrau 1958, 25, 33; Ross 1973, 80; Scheffler 1965,11; Hogbin 1964, 41; Ivens 1927, 355.
24. Tedder 1976, 41–48.
25. Barrau 1958, 41, 48; Burman 1981, 257.
26. Brookfield with Hart 1971, 85; Barrau 1958, 46–47, 53, 54–60; Ivens 1927, 36; Woodford 1890a, 201.

416   *Notes to chapter 1*

27. Barrau 1958, 75–76; Witt 1974, 6.5–6.7, 6.24, 6.26–6.29; Ross 1973, 83.
28. Chapman 1970, 67–73; Burman 1981, 257; Ivens 1927, 356, 370; Barrau 1958, 46.
29. Barrau 1958, 65–68.
30. Ivens 1927, 158.
31. Woodford 1889, 477; Somerville 1897, 374; WPHC 292/96: Woodford to Thurston 26 June 1896; Belshaw 1950, 173–174.
32. Dalton 1967, 255–281.
33. WPHC 292/96: Woodford to Thurston 26 June 1896; Nerdrum, 1901–1902, 22–58.
34. Hogbin 1964, 47–50; Ivens 1927, 40–41, 153.
35. Tedder 1975, 15–16.
36. Bogesi 1948, 213–214; Fox 1924, 10–17, 33–38, 64–67, 71–75; HP, Roviana—Relation of the sexes and marriage; Birth, children; Hogbin 1938, 398–400; Hogbin 1939, 25–60; Scheffler 1965, 110–178; Wheeler 1943.
37. Ivens 1927; Hogbin 1964, 84–85; Ross 1973, 118–125; Burman 1981.
38. Bennett 1979a, 265.
39. HP; Bennett 1974, 20; Allan 1957, 103; Hogbin 1964, 19–21.
40. Ivens 1927, 43.
41. WPHC BSIP 42/3: Grass "Native monies, Guadalcanal" 17 May 1945 encl. Old Tour Reports Central District; Laracy 1983, 53–80.
42. The sketch of the big-man is a composite from the research of early observers, as well as anthropologists, geographers, and historians working since the thirties in the Solomon Islands and southern Bougainville, and various recorded oral sources. HP, Chieftainship, Eddystone (c. 1908); Monneron 1914, 258; Elton 1888; Somerville 1897; Codrington 1891, 49–60; Wheeler 1943. Fox 1924; Ivens 1930; Thurnwald 1934, 119–141; Thurnwald 1936, 347–357; Hogbin 1934; Hogbin 1939, 61–121; Hogbin 1964, 62–71; Oliver 1955; Keesing 1967, 1968, 1978; Scheffler 1965, 144, 180ff., 196; Ross 1973, 11, 53, 55, 188–202, 224–247; Bathgate 1975, 178–180; Prendeville 1975; WPHC 274/32: Wright "Guadalcanal," Census Report 1931, encl.
43. Miller 1978a, 3.
44. Guppy 1887, 4, 6, 21, 23; Capell 1943, 27; Ivens 1930, 84–92; Ivens 1927.
45. Fox 1924, 305–306; Bennett 1974, 26–32, 40–42; Monneron 1914, 258.
46. Fox 1975, 21, 24.
47. Throughout this section I have relied heavily on Lawrence and Meggitt's excellent introduction to *Gods Ghosts and Men in Melanesia* (1965). The overall pattern they described appears to apply to most Solomons societies.
48. Codrington 1891, 124, 151–152; Tuza 1975, 17–20; Prendeville 1975, 20; Fox 1962, 62.
49. Prendeville 1975, 20–21; Hogbin 1964, 72–79.
50. Codrington 1891, 125–127, 253–254, 258; WPHC 274/32: Wright "Guadalcanal," Census Report 1931, encl.; Hogbin 1964, 83; Ivens 1927, 179–180.
51. Ivens 1927, 181, 199–207.
52. Codrington 1891, 128–149, 208–209, 221; Ivens 1927, 179, 187–188, 243, 250, 464–465, 467. Ross 1973, 55, 189–190; Wheeler 1943, 629.
53. Codrington 1891, 95, 132–133, 138–139; Fox 1962, 59–60; Burman 1981, 259–260; Prendeville 1975, 24–28.
54. Prendeville 1975, 21–23, 28–31; Codrington 1891, 118–120, 194–209; Hogbin 1964, 55–59.
55. Hogbin 1964, 89–90.

56. Prendeville 1975, 23; Codrington 1891, 253–265.
57. For a typical mental map of known territory, see Ross 1973, 112.
58. Jack-Hinton 1969, 3–32.
59. Amherst and Thompson 1901.
60. Shineberg 1971a.
61. Allen and Green 1972.
62. Jack-Hinton 1969, 227–307.

Chapter 2: The ship men

Luana 1969, 15.
De Orosco, quoted in Jack-Hinton 1969, 80.
1. SCL 14 May 1898, 3; SCL 15 Sept. 1898, 7–9; Vigors 1850, 201–204; Ivens 1927, 49–50; Bogesi 1948, 354–355; Bennett 1974, 50–51.
2. Jack-Hinton 1969, 79–83; Wallis 1965, 160–164; Bougainville 1772, 320; Monneron 1914, 256–257.
3. Hocart Papers. See also Dillon 1829, 133; *Ann and Hope* 1798; *Nile* Mar. 1802; *Minorca* Mar. 1802; *Canada* Mar. 1802.
4. Phillip 1789, 196.
5. Jack-Hinton 1969, 315; Dillon 1829, 162.
6. Marwick 1935, 30.
7. Ibid., 36.
8. See for example, Dillon 1829, 133.
9. Wallis 1965, 160–164; Bougainville 1772, 320; Monneron 1914, 231–232, 252–263.
10. The choking effects of the East India Company's monopoly on Australian colonial shipping before 1820 are discussed in Bach 1976, 46–49.
11. Jack-Hinton 1969, 296–324.
12. Hocart Papers, Notes on Whiteman.
13. *Patterson* 15 Dec. 1803.
14. cf. Miller 1978b, 292.
15. Shineberg 1971b, 305; Deposition of George Bowen quoted in Dillon 1829, ixvi–ixix; *New Bedford Daily Gazette* 4 June 1836, in AACP.
16. Shineberg 1971a; Cheyne 1852; Cheyne 1855; Cheyne [?] in *Nautical Magazine* 18 (1849): 27–28. Captain R. L. Hunter of the *Marshall Bennett* made a vague reference to the cutting out of "one or two vessels" in New Georgia. Perhaps he too gained his information from the Simbo people (*Nautical Magazine* 9 [1840]: 467).
17. Cattlin 1828.
18. Bradford 1861.
19. *SH* 20 Dec. 1832.
20. Guppy 1887, 43.
21. Whalemen c. 1840–1870 (PMB 402).
22. Bradford 1861.
23. MacGillivray 14 Dec. 1852.
24. Informants, 1976. See also Hogbin 1964, 19–20.
25. Hocart Papers, Notes on Whiteman.
26. Cattlin 1836.
27. MacGillivray 1852.
28. Cattlin 1828, Feb.
29. Jack-Hinton 1969, 345.
30. In this same area, a vessel was said to have been wrecked and all but two

of its twenty-man crew eaten. This appears in a rather sensational account of whaling adventure and should be treated with some caution. See Smith 1844, 203–206.

31. Cattlin 4 Mar. 1828.
32. *Atlantic* Nov. 1848; *Alfred* 1849; *William Hamilton* 15 Oct. 1839 (PMB 376); *Liverpool* 1865.
33. *Gipsy* 12 Mar. 1842.
34. *SMH* 5 Jan. 1843; *RRAACP* 1950, *The Bay State Democrat*, 23 Dec. 1842.
35. *Superior* May–Sept. 1860; *Two Brothers* 1858–1863.
36. See Appendix 1; *SGSGTL* 14 Mar. 1846.
37. *SMH* 21 Jan. 1861; *The Empire* (Sydney), 26 Dec. 1859.
38. *Superior* May–Sept. 1860.
39. In the oral account *all* those who did not fight were spared. Wheeler 1943; Guppy 1887, 22.
40. Bradford 1861. For a similar incident see *Woodlark* 19 July 1856.
41. Bennett 1979a, 33–34.
42. The term 'world economy' is borrowed from Immanuel Wallerstein. It does not necessarily imply that an economy is world-wide, but rather that, in common parlance, it is a 'world' of its own: that is, it is a social system largely self-contained economically (Wallerstein 1974, 347–348).
43. Czarkowska Starzecka and Cranstone 1974, 18–19, 34, 36.
44. Webster c. 1863, 77, 81, 88, 89.
45. Salisbury 1962, 110, 220; see also Godelier 1969, 5–37; Belshaw 1954, 60; Sarfert and Damm 1929, 30–40.
46. Salisbury 1962, 110.
47. Woodford 1888, 372; Barrau 1958, 9.
48. Salisbury 1962, 109.
49. Hocart Papers, Trade and Money; Somerville 1897; Piko 1976, 101–103.
50. Ivens 1930, 273.
51. Salisbury 1970, 10.
52. Jackson 1972; Tippett 1967, 147–159. Guppy in the 1880s appears to have been the first European to make this observation (Guppy 1887, 17).
53. Shineberg 1971b, 303–304. For a perceptive examination of the trade-raid linkages in the New Georgia islands, see McKinnon 1972.
54. Ivens 1930, 186; Bogesi 1948, 210.
55. Miller 1978b, 292–294.
56. Fox 1924, 305–306.
57. McKinnon 1972, 64.
58. Wheeler 1943, 630.
59. Wheeler 1943.
60. Wheeler 1943, history.
61. Chiefs of a later era on Mono made very sure any transactions with outsiders remained in their hands. (See Guppy 1887, 73.)
62. *SMH* 21 Jan. 1861.
63. Wheeler 1943.
64. WPHC F46/35: Kuper to DO 2 Oct. 1933 encl.
65. Davenport 1975, 76.
66. *SH* 16 July 1832.
67. Firth 1959, 34.
68. Codrington 1891, 12n; Bradford 1861.
69. Somerville 1897, 394.

70. Leber 1914.
71. *Ontario* 19 Dec. 1863.
72. Scherzer 1861, 613.
73. Sarfert and Damm 1929, 47.
74. *SG* 16 Feb. 1837; Firth 1959, 36; Verguet 1885, 193–232; Woodford Papers, Account of the First Attempt of the Marist Mission to form an Establishment in the Protectorate.
75. Cattlin 1829; *SGNSWA* 22 Jan. 1839; *SG* 22 July 1830.
76. *SGSGTL* 11 Dec. 1852.
77. *Eugenia* July–Aug. 1862; Rietmann 1868, 195.
78. *Stephania* 15 Aug. 1868.
79. *Two Brothers* Sept. 1861; Woodford Papers, Some Account of Sikaiana.
80. *Ontario* Dec. 1863–Feb. 1864.
81. Carroll 1975, 299.
82. Dumont d'Urville 1843, 62.
83. Cheyne 1855, 67.
84. For examples, see *James Arnold* 8 Nov. 1858; *SCL* 14 May 1898, 4.
85. WPHC 1512/30: Notes on history of Sikaiana encl.
86. Brenchley 1873, 265–270, 273.
87. Ivens 1927, 50; Fox 1924, 339. In western San Cristobal, the word *haka*, used in the twentieth century for ship, was before 1850 *waka (uaka)*. This shift may have been due to whalers' influence (see Verguet 1885, 230).
88. Dumont d'Urville 1843, 53.
89. Ivens 1927, 392–395.
90. Laracy 1976, 17–18, cf. Bogesi 1948, 355.
91. Laracy 1976, 18–22.
92. Bradford 1861.
93. Hocart Papers; Woodford Papers; Kerry Prendeville, pers. com. 1976–1977; Marwick 1935, 37.
94. Scherzer 1861, 602–603.
95. Cheyne 1855, 67.
96. *James Arnold* 7 Nov. 1858; *SCL* 14 May 1898, 4.
97. Rietmann 1868, 187, 193; Brenchley 1873, 268; Liverpool 1865.
98. *SGSGTL* 19 Oct. 1857.
99. Scherzer 1861, 616.
100. *Gipsy* 7 Feb. 1842.
101. Ross 1973, 16.
102. *SGNSWA* 22 Jan. 1839; Scherzer 1861, 603.

Chapter 3: The traders and their masters

Judith Wright, 1971, 12.
Ross 1973, 57.
1. NSWSA List of vessels arrived, Arrivals for 19 Jan. 1848, 18 Jan. 1849. *SMH* shipping arrivals for 22 Dec. 1851, 22 Oct. 1853, 16 Oct. 1854, 4 Dec. 1854.
2. Bach 1976, 76.
3. Ibid.; Derry and Williams 1960, 517–521, 689.
4. *The Empire* (Sydney), 26 Dec. 1859; *SMH* arrivals for 7 Feb. 1858, 29 July 1859, 30 Mar. 1860.
5. Shineberg 1967, 1–15.
6. Wilson 1954, 6–8, 31. As a result of the shortage of tallow following the

Crimean War, English soap manufacturers experimented with vegetable fats. Coconut oil, when used in combination with other fats, made a superior soap to that made from tallow. Soap-making left glycerine as a by-product. When this substance is treated with a strong mixture of sulphuric acid and nitric acid, nitroglycerine is produced (Wilson 1954, 10–11; Derry and Williams 1960, 547).

7. Leubuscher 1951, 57–58; Lewthwaite 1962, 142; Tetens 1958, 51, 69. See also Maude with Leeson 1968, 281.

8. *SMH* shipping columns, 1877.

9. Corris 1973. See also Cromar 1935.

10. Mair 1880.

11. Bolton 1963, Chaps. 4, 7, 9; Blainey 1963, 86–87. See, for examples, *SMH*, arrivals for 9 June 1875, 5 Jan. 1876; UKRNAS 1857–1896: Coffin to Hopkins 25 Oct. 1877, and encls., vol. 14; Haddock 22 June–28 Dec. 1877; *SMH* shipping column, 12 Feb. 1880; *SMH* shipping departures for 15 Mar. 1881.

12. *SMH* shipping arrivals for 11 Feb., 11 Mar., 24 Apr., 21 Aug. 1880, and 13 Nov. 1882. Ivory nuts were exported and used in the manufacture of buttons.

13. Bennett 1979a, 59.

14. *SMH* shipping columns, 1860–1895; WPHC 163/02: BSIP-AR 1901.

15. UKRNAS 1875–1896: Effects of W. Perry 2 Mar. 1875, and encls., vol. 13; *SMH* shipping arrivals for 8 Feb. 1873; *SMH* 21 Apr. 1875, 16 May 1877, 2 Jan. 1880; Woodford n.d. Notes upon History of SI; *FT* 30 June 1877; see also Appendixes 5 and 6.

16. *SMH* shipping columns, 22 Apr. 1875; 24 Apr., 27 Nov. 1880; *FT* 30 June 1877; UKRNAS, vol. 15: List of traders in SI, 30 Sept. 1879. The Sydney merchants and commission agents, Biffen and Clark, T. Bros, Rabone, Feez and Company, A. Buttery, Montifiore, and Young and Lark, each had two or three ships they backed in the Solomon trade. Mason Bros., C. B. Bond, Bird and Company, Campbell and Company, and Bell also sponsored occasional vessels in the 1870s and 1880s (see Appendix 4).

17. Ribbe 1903, 259–260; WPHC 160/80: Wilson to Gordon 19 Dec. 1880, and encls.; WPHC 193/81: Wilson to Gordon 28 Nov. 1881, and encls.

18. WPHC 193/81: Wilson to Gordon 28 Nov. 1881, and encls.

19. Ribbe 1903, 260; WPHC 193/81: Wilson to Gordon 28 Nov. 1881, and encls.

20. Biskup 1974, 69n.; Chewings 1900, 25; Ribbe 1903, 233–254; Ribbe 1894, 134; Coote 1883, 146; Woodford Papers, Diary 23 Oct. 1886.

21. WPHC 477/96: BSIP-AR 1896.

22. Ibid.

23. UKCRSI 1903: Langdale to Denson c. March 1900.

24. Ibid.

25. Woodford Papers, Diary, 25 May, 9 July 1887.

26. WPHC 1267/15: Barnett to HC 6 Apr. 1915, and encls.; BSI-AR, 1914–1918; WPHC 2471/14: Barnett to HC 16 Sept. 1914; WPHC 2259/15: Law to Sweet Escott 7 July 1915.

27. WPHC 477/96: BSIP-AR 1896.

28. WPHC 477/96: BSIP-AR 1896.

29. Woodford Papers, Notes taken on board *Pylades*, 1896; WPHC 199/96: Woodford to Thurston 6 June 1896.

30. WPHC 297/97: Woodford to Collet 3 May 1897; WPHC 305/97: Woodford to Berkeley 21 June 1897.

31. Bennett 1981, 170–177.

32. WPHC 203/02: List of deceased estates. See also, Bennett 1979a, 67.

33. WPHC 141/96: Case 69 1895; Woodford Papers, Notes taken on board *Pylades*, 1896; WPHC 199/96: Woodford to Thurston 6 June 1896.

34. WPHC 187/06: Woodford to HC 28 June 1906.

35. WPHC 160/80: Wilson to Gordon 19 Dec. 1880, and encls.; WPHC 203/85: Otto Asche, c. 1885; Woodford Papers, Diary 22 Mar. 1887.

36. WPHC 191/89: Keating to Captain of man-of-war 21 May 1889, encl.

37. WPHC 230/90: Comins to HC 26 July 1890, and Comins to HC 10 Apr. 1890; WPHC 96/91: Case 31 1890.

38. Woodford Papers, Diary 27 Aug. 1886.

39. Penny, 21 July 1878; Hernsheim, 23 Jan. 1880; *SMH* shipping arrivals for 24 Sept. 1878, 31 Jan., 15 June 1879, 1, 27 Mar. 1880; WPHC 193/81: Memo of Agreement between Cowlishaw Brothers and John Stephens 12 Mar. 1880, Copy of receipts 1880, encls.; Biskup 1974, 21–22; Firth 1973, 13–14. In later years the British traders displayed the same proprietorial attitude when the German naturalist Carl Ribbe visited the Solomons in 1893. They suspected him of being "a spy of the New Guinea Kompagnie" (Ribbe 1903, 302–303).

40. Brown 1908a, 371; Woodford Papers, Notes on History of SI; UKRNAS, vol. 13: Ponsonby to Delaney 13 Sept. 1869, and encls.; *SMH* shipping arrivals for 19 Jan. 1868, 25 Apr. 1874; *SM* 25 Sept. 1880.

41. *SM* 25 Sept. 1880; Brown 1908a, 516; WPHC 313/94: Griffiths to Sec. HC 24 Oct. 1894; Guppy 1887, 21; WPHC 141/80: Wilson to Gordon 8 Oct. 1880, and encls.; Festetics von Tolna 1903, 376.

42. *SM* 25 Sept. 1880; Brown 1908a, 357–359, 363, 371–372; *SMH* shipping columns, 11 Mar. and 8 Apr. 1880.

43. *SMH* shipping columns, 5 Nov. 1877; *FT,* 1 Dec. 1877; UKRNAS, vol. 15: Account of white men and natives killed . . . 30 Sept. 1879; *SMH* shipping columns, 11 Mar., 8 Apr., 27 Nov. 1880; UKRNAS, vol. 15: Ferguson to Wilson, 1 Aug. 1880; Bennett 1974, 74–76.

44. WPHC 141/80: Wilson to Gordon 8 Oct. 1880, and encls.; *SM* 25 Sept. 1880.

45. For other examples see Bennett 1979a, 72–74.

46. Phillip Palmer 1976; *SM* 25 Sept. 1880.

47. Thurston, 14 Oct. 1804.

48. *FT* 31 Mar., 27 June, 21 July 1877, 17 Apr. 1878; WPHC 4/78: Leefe to HC 10 Mar. 1878; Haddock 5 Nov. 1877; Ferguson 28, 29 Sept. 1881; Ferguson 31 July 1882; Reilly 15 June, 28 Aug. 1882; WPHC 1225/13: Woodford to HC 2 June 1913.

49. UKRNAS, vol. 14: Wright to Capt. HMS *Beagle* 6 Oct. 1877, and encls.; WPHC 193/81: Stephens to Cowlishaw Bros. 31 Jan. 1881 encl.; WPHC 461/96: Meredith to Collet 11 Oct. 1896, and encls.; Metcalfe 1902–1964: Notes on Harry Wickham; Cromar 1935, 133–134; WPHC 477/96: BSIP-AR 1896, List of merchant vessels . . .

50. Mauler and Kesslitz 1899, 37. Welchman 17 May 1896; Hagen 1893, 338, 371, 378.

51. WPHC 15/79: de Houghton to O'Brien 9 June 1878, and encls.

52. Woodford Papers, Diary, 16 Sept. 1887; WPHC 250/87: Fairfax to Mitchell 9 Sept. 1887, and encls.

53. Phillip Palmer, 1976.
54. Rannie 1912, 27.
55. *The Whitgift Magazine* 8 (4), June 1890, among Woodford Papers.
56. Welchman 5 June 1900; Festetics von Tolna 1903, 316.
57. WPHC 141/96: Rason to CC 29 Oct. 1895, Case 65, 1895.
58. Dorothy Gardner, 1976; WPHC 223/00: Woodford to O'Brien 14 Oct. 1900; see also Thurston 14 Oct. 1894.
59. Elton 1888, 91.
60. *FT* 30 June 1877.
61. Ibid.; Ribbe 1903, 76.
62. Ribbe 1903, 76, 259–260.
63. In 1879, ships in Solomons waters employed 200 hands of whom 124 were Europeans exclusive of about 20 on shore stations. (UKRNAS vol. 15: List of merchant vessels . . . 30 Sept. 1879 and Report of HMS *Wolverine*, 29 Oct. 1879 [?].)
64. For white missionary strength in the Solomons from 1860 to 1895, see Hilliard 1978, 79–189.
65. WPHC 141/96: Statement of Olsen encl. Case 72, 1895.
66. GDRNA 1893; Ribbe 1903, 145; John Henry Macdonald 1976. *Tanutanu* is a title which means 'of a chiefly clan.'
67. WPHC 102/92: Case 32A, 1869.
68. WPHC 43/86: Nelson to Thurston 8 Jan. 1886, and encls.; Woodford Papers, Diary, 4 Oct. 1888; see also WPHC 160/86; WPHC 7/87.
69. WPHC 19/11: Log of *Narovo*.
70. WPHC 285/96: Woodford to HC 12 July 1896.
71. Boutilier 1975, 31.
72. Penny 11 Aug. 1876.
73. Penny 5 June 1878.
74. WPHC 102/92: Case 50, 1891; WPHC 342/98: Woodford to O'Brien 14 Sept. 1898; Welchman 1892–1906.
75. WPHC 134/99: Woodford to O'Brien 15 May 1899, and encls.; Bennett 1974, 39, 91–95; Laracy 1976, 40–42.
76. *Australian Methodist Mission Review*, Apr. 1901, 8; Metcalfe 1902–1964: The Gumi Family.
77. Hilliard 1966, 245, 263–266, 273, 296, 416–417; MMP: Goldie to Danks, 23 Oct. 1912; Burnett 1911, 95–99; Leslie Gill, 1975.
78. UKRNAS, vol. 17: Davis to Scott 18 Oct. 1891.
79. See, for examples, UKRNAS, vols. 14–17: Cases relating to SI, 1870 to 1892; WPHC 293/95: 1894; WPHC 141/96: 1895; Carter n.d. Notes on Oral History of New Georgia Islands.
80. WPHC 121/81: Bruce to Wilson 4 June 1881; Wilson to Gordon 2 July 1881 encls.
81. UKRNAS, vol. 15: Ferguson to Wilson 1 Aug. 1880, and Statement of John Jones n.d.; WPHC 192/81: Dawson to Wilson 11 Nov. 1881 encl.; UKRNAS, vol. 16: Dale to Erskine 3 Sept. 1882.
82. Ribbe 1903, 56–57, 67–70; GDRNA 1893 (30 Mar.) encl. RKA 2982; Festetics von Tolna 1903, 374–376.
83. Cromar 1935, 203, 255–256, 278; Woodford Papers, Notes on history of SI; Hilliard 1966, 95–96, 110–112.
84. *FT* 30 June 1877; Nicholls 19 Apr. 1877; UKRNAS, vol. 14: Wright to Captain of HMS *Beagle* 6 Oct. 1877, and encls.

85. Ribbe 1903, 76–77.
86. Ibid., 79–83.
87. Somerville 1897, 389–390.
88. Woodford Papers, Diary 27 Aug. 1886. See also Hocart 1931, 315.
89. Ribbe 1903, 76; Guppy 1887, 67; Geoffrey Kuper, John H. Macdonald, 1976.
90. Ferguson 28 Sept. 1881; Guppy 1887, 15, 91, 160, 163; *SMH* 12 Nov. 1881.
91. WPHC 150/80: Nixon to Bower 3 Sept. 1880 encl. Aurua was the brother of Oubasiaro, an important "chiefess" of Ubuna. He became "chief" after her death (Teresa Rora'ei, 1976).
92. Woodford Papers, Diary 23 Aug. 1886; Festetics von Tolna 1903, 317.
93. *SCL* Sept. 1895, 5.
94. Woodford Papers, Diary 10 Sept. 1886.
95. For example of similar reaction, see Woodford Papers, Diary 18 Oct. 1886; *SMH* 6 Dec. 1886.
96. Woodford Papers, Case 32 1889, encl.; see also Sarfert and Damm 1929, 183, 310; WPHC 96/91: Cases 32 and 42 1890.
97. Guppy 1887, 18–20, 162.
98. As late as the 1950s, 40 percent infant mortality was common in New Ireland. (Scragg 1954, 47.)
99. Bennett 1979a, 91.
100. Chesterman 1960, 19–25.
101. Gunther quoted in Ryan 1969, 34.
102. Ribbe 1903, 233.
103. Woodford Papers, Diary 12 June 1886. See also Woodford Papers, Case 6, 1889, and Diary 1 Apr. 1887.
104. Woodford Papers, Diary 11 May 1886; Bernatzik 1935, 48–49; WPHC 69/93: Keating to Kelham 18 Apr. 1892.
105. Ribbe 1903, 27–28.
106. Welchman 27 Aug. 1892; WPHC 83/98: Woodford to O'Brien 25 Jan. 1898, and encls.; WPHC 2327/30: Death notice of Wheatley, 13 May 1930; Hocart var. genealogies 36, 82, 88, 132; Ribbe 1903, 80; Festetics von Tolna 1903, 375. Most of Melinda and John's children—John A. C., Minnie, Edith, Clara, and Linda—were later to be linked with prominent Solomon Island families and trader-planter circles (Dorothy Gardner, John Henry Macdonald, grandchildren of Melinda, 1975–1976; see also Reilly 31 July 1882; MMP: Rooney to Goldie, 3 Aug. 1910).
107. Penny 16 May 1880; *SMH* shipping arrivals for 23 Oct., 1 Nov. 1879, 11 Nov. 1886, 17 May, 8 Sept. 1889; Woodford Papers, Diary, 23 Oct. 1886; Dorothy Gardner, 1975.
108. Hyam 1976, 135–137.
109. Coote 1883, 126.
110. Ribbe 1903, 81.
111. Hocart 1931, 306; Penny 29 May 1879; WPHC 506/97: Ivens to Woodford 4 Sept. 1897.
112. Ribbe 1903, 145; John Henry Macdonald, 1976.
113. Hocart var. genealogies 36, 82, 88, 132; WPHC 259/32: Marriage registration of Henry Wickham 16 Oct. 1931. See also WPHC 345/94: ? to Thurston 14 Dec. 1894.
114. Ribbe 1903, 145; John Henry Macdonald, 1976.

115. Festetics von Tolna 1903, 317–318; Somerville 1897, 386; WPHC 308/94: Pratt to HC 18 Oct. 1894; WPHC 293/95: Thurston to CC 15 Dec. 1894. Somerville 1897, 363, 386; Hocart var. genealogies 36, 43, 82, 88, 132.
116. Cromar 1935, 256–257.
117. Ribbe 1903, 81, 272.
118. Ribbe 1903, 81.
119. WPHC 143/97: Woodford to Thurston 27 Mar. 1897; WPHC 144/97: Woodford to Collet, 27 Mar. 1897.
120. WPHC 83/98: Woodford to O'Brien 25 Jan 1898, and encls.
121. Festetics von Tolna 1903, 316–317, 375; WPHC 313/94: Griffiths to Sec. HC 24 Oct. 1894 and annotations; UKRNAS, vol. 15: de Houghton to Wilson 10 Sept. 1880; Brown 1908a, 371.
122. WPHC 151/02: Woodford to HC 5 Aug. 1902; Woodford Papers, Notes . . . 1896; WPHC 187/06: Woodford to HC 28 June 1906; WPHC 141/96: Rason to CC 29 Oct. 1895, Case 65 1895.
123. Ribbe 1903, 79.
124. Ribbe 1903, 27.
125. Ribbe 1903, 81–82.
126. Biskup 1974, 126–127.
127. Williamson 1914, 19; Boutilier 1975, 37.
128. WPHC 764/31: Probate, will of Norman Wheatley.
129. Festetics von Tolna 1903, 317–319.
130. Willy Paia pers. com., 1977; WPHC 141/96: Rason to CC, 29 Oct. 1895, Case 65 1895; Welchman 23 Mar. 1899; WPHC 74/01: Woodford to HC 7 Apr. 1901.
131. MMP: Goldie to Pratt 27 Sept. 1918.

Chapter 4: The attractions of trade

Raymond Firth 1936, 36.
Sarawia 1973, 8.
1. WPHC 158/81: Romilly to HC 6 Aug. 1881; Woodford Papers, Diary 12 June 1886.
2. UKRNAS, vol. 14: Brodie to Capt. of H.M.'s ship 27 Apr. 1879; Penny 3 Oct. 1879; 23 July, 13 Sept. 1880; 12, 25 Jan. 1881; WPHC 139/80: Bateman to Wilson 13 Sept. 1880; WPHC 70/81: Wilson to Gordon 22 Mar. 1881, and encls.; WPHC 158/81: Romilly to HC 6 Aug. 1881; WPHC 192/81: Dawson to Wilson 11 Nov. 1881 encl.; Hernsheim 22 Jan. 1880.
3. WPHC 477/96: BSIP-AR 1896.
4. Nerdrum 1901–1902, 22–58.
5. WPHC 19/81: Wilson to Gordon 24 Feb. 1881, and encl.
6. WPHC 76/98: Woodford to O'Brien 22 Dec. 1897, and encl.; WPHC 70/81: Wilson to Gordon 22 Mar. 1881, and encls.
7. GDRNA: Wirtersheim an den Chef der Admiralität, 25 Okt. 1886; Woodford Papers, Diary 24 June, 18 July, 1 Sept 1886.
8. Guppy 1887, 21; Ribbe 1894, 134–135.
9. Parkinson 1887, 85; Biskup 1974, 69; Coote 1883, 146.
10. The man-day concept used in Table 2 was taken from Ian Frazer's field observations on north Malaita in 1970. There, about 18–19 man-days were taken to make a ton of copra (about 6000–6500 nuts). However, McKinnon's figure for production in New Georgia at the same period is much higher. He calculated that 50 man-days would be required. This shows the degree of varia-

tion possible, depending on such factors as speed of working, actual weight of each coconut, time spent in getting coconuts to and from a drying shed, spoilage, and so on (Frazer 1973, 76–77; McKinnon 1972, 85).

11. Guppy 1887, 18.

12. Woodford Papers, Diary 1 Sept. 1886; *SM* 20 Sept. 1880.

13. See, for examples, Wheeler 1943, 599, 868; *SCL* May 1896.

14. *SMH* shipping columns 1850–1880; *SGSGTL* 1850–1860.

15. Penny 2 Aug. 1877.

16. For early Choiseul recruiting see Metcalfe 1902–1964, Notes on Lauru; Bennett 1974, 51.

17. Corris 1973, 31–36. Corris stated that there is no evidence of recruits having gone to Queensland from New Georgia. There must have been a few because the New Georgians complained to the captain of HMS *Beagle* of the non-return of some of their friends who went on board the *Woodlark* to Queensland in about 1871 (UKRNAS vol. 13: Proceedings of HMS *Beagle* 6 Sept. 1875; see also Corris 1973, 26; Price with Baker 1976, 114–116; Bevan 12 June 1882).

18. Woodford Papers, Diary 24 June 1886, 21 Apr. 1887; Guppy 1887, 76; see also GDRNA: Wirtersheim an den Chef der Admiralität, 25 Okt. 1886.

19. Ribbe 1903, 292, 302; Somerville 1897, 375.

20. Guppy 1887, 76, 120.

21. On Nggela in 1877, tomahawks were the hardware most desired by the people. Fifteen years later, not only were a labor recruiter's standard trade goods refused, but also cash was demanded in return for birds and shells (Melvin 1977, 91). In the fertile Gazelle Peninsula of New Britain the transition took only about ten years (Epstein 1968, 35).

22. WPHC 141/96: Rason to Commander 21 Dec. 1895.

23. Woodford Papers, Diary 25 May, 9 July 1887.

24. WPHC 461/96: Hamilton to Lamb 15 Dec. 1895 encl.; Boaz Bebeni.

25. *The Empire* 26 Dec. 1859. See also Shineberg 1967, 156–157.

26. WPHC 292/96: Woodford to Thurston 26 June 1896; WPHC 477/96: BSIP-AR 1896.

27. Penny 27, 29 May 1877; Woodford Papers, Diary 11 May 1886.

28. Ribbe 1903, 260.

29. Ribbe 1903, 292–293.

30. Hocart Papers, Trade and Money.

31. Guppy 1887, 132; Ribbe 1903, 260, 294; WPHC 447/96: BSIP-AR 1896.

32. Woodford Papers, Diary 25 May, 9 July 1887; Penny 7, 10 Sept. 1877, 7 June 1879; Hirst n.d.

33. LPP n.d.*a*; *SCL* 15 Oct. 1898.

34. Brook 1940, 191. See also UKRNAS, vol. 15: Bruce to Wilson 4 June 1881; Ribbe 1903, 294; Wheeler 1943, 893; Woodford 1888, 359.

35. WPHC 477/96: BSIP-AR, 1896; Hirst n.d.; Belshaw 1950, 172.

36. Salisbury 1962, 112–122.

37. Bennett 1979a, 118.

38. WPHC F46/30: Kuper to DO 2 Oct. 1933 encl.

39. Elton 1888, 93; Guppy 1887, 35, 41.

40. Woodford 1888, 365–369.

41. Corris 1973, 150; UKRNAS, vol. 16: Correspondence respecting outrages . . . 1882; for Gorai's trading in recruits, see Guppy 1887, 27.

42. Woodford 1888, 359; Ribbe 1894, 134.

43. Corris 1970.

44. Corris 1973, 32–38, 60–67; Melvin 1977, 21–27. For further information on the overseas labor trade, see Saunders 1975; Scarr 1968, 15–17. See also Cooper 1979, 39.

45. Corris 1973, 39–40; see Table 2 for basis of calculation.

46. This process might have been even more intensive had it not been for natural restrictions on the availability of suitable garden land and the introduction of diseases, such as dysentery and pulmonary sickness, from ships (see, for example, Bennett 1974, 21–73).

47. Penny 26 Sept. 1879; UKRNAS, vol. 15: Bruce to Wilson 4 June 1881; WPHC 158/81: Romilly to HC 6 Aug. 1881; Guppy 1887, 6, 28, 50; Woodford papers, Diary 23 Oct. 1886, 3–4 Oct. 1888; WPHC 96/91: Case 40 1890; WPHC 102/92: Cases 49 and 51 1891; Ribbe 1903, 40, 46; WPHC 154/95: Gov. of Queensland to Thurston 2 May 1895; WPHC 88/95: O'Brien to Gov. of Queensland 14 Jan. 1895, encl.; WPHC 461/96: Meredith to Collett 14 Oct. 1896 encl.; WPHC 378/97: Woodford to Thurston 7 Aug. 1897; see also Bennett 1974, 58–61.

48. McKinnon 1972, 95–101; WPHC 192/81: Dawson to Wilson 6 Oct. 1881, 11 Nov. 1881, encls.; BSI-LTR: Claim 21, 16 May 1923, Proceedings of Lands Commission; see also MMP: Goldie to Brown 1 Feb. 1911 Book 118; WPHC 248/11: Indenture between Tulo and John Macdonald and Jesse Davis 15 Feb. 1885 encl. This prominence was a two-edged sword as Maghratulo was held responsible for any attacks against Europeans. See WPHC 102/92: Case 32 1891; WPHC 69/93: Kelham to CC 25 July 1892 and Case 32 1892.

49. WPHC 19/11: Log of *Narovo* 14 Apr. 1894.

50. McKinnon 1972, 100.

51. Tippett 1967, 139–142; Hocart Papers, Chieftainship; WPHC 4/78: Leefe to HC 10 Mar. 1878; WPHC 160/86: Tryon to Thurston 27 July 1886; WPHC 250/87: Fairfax to Mitchell 9 Sept. 1887; Woodford Papers, Diary 2 Oct. 1888.

52. Woodford 1888, 360–361.

53. Woodford Papers, Diary 25 Sept. 2, 3, 5 Oct. 1888; Hocart 1931, 301.

54. WPHC 268/89: Hand to Scott 6 Nov. 1889.

55. Woodford 1890a, 150–152.

56. Brooke to Tryon 18 May 1886, Correspondence respecting outrages . . . , 1886, copy in Woodford Papers; WPHC 102/92: Davis to CC 4 Nov. 1891, Correspondence . . . , 1891.

57. WPHC 69/93: Bremer to Kelham 29 Sept. 1892; WPHC 350/94: Gibson to CC 10 Aug. 1893 encl.; WPHC 293/95: Goodrich to CC 22 Sept. 1894; Thurston to CC, 15 Dec. 1894; WPHC 283/96: Woodford to HC 12 July 1896; WPHC 36/97: Woodford to Collet 25 Jan. 1897; WPHC 296/97: Woodford to Berkeley 30 Apr. 1897; WPHC 300/97: Woodford to Berkeley 8 June 1897.

58. Brown 1908a, 517.

59. WPHC 308/94: Pratt to Thurston 18 Oct. 1894.

60. Hocart Papers, Chieftainship.

61. Hardy and Elkington 1907, 99–100. Elkington may have been repeating with small variations the account Somerville had written in 1896. See Somerville 1897, 399.

62. WPHC 300/97: Woodford to Berkeley 9 June 1897; WPHC 285/98: Woodford to O'Brien 3 Oct. 1899, extracts from Mahaffy's Report of Proceedings, May 1900, encls.

63. Woodford Papers, Diary 25 Sept. 1888; *SCL* 15 Oct. 1898, 15 Oct. 1900; Edge-Partington 1907, 22–23; Brown 1908a, 515–517, 520–521.

64. Hilliard 1966, 75–76, 95–96, 110–112; Jackson 1975; White 1979.
65. Corris 1970.
66. Bennett 1979a, 126–128.
67. Guppy 1887, 15.
68. Ivens 1927, 48.
69. Ibid., 94; Elton 1888, 91; Chewings 1900, 23.
70. Woodford Papers, Diary 15 May 1886; WPHC 134/99: Woodford to O'Brien 15 May 1899.
71. Coote 1883, 146.
72. *FT* 30 June 1877; Martin Manganimate, 1972.
73. Rannie 1912, 34; Woodford 1890a, 139; WPHC 2099/21: Barley to Acting HC 19 Nov. 1921.
74. Festetics von Tolna 1903, 309.
75. Rannie 1912, 34; see also Specht 1975.
76. *Christopher Mitchell*, Sept. 1847; Scherzer 1861, 619; [Cheyne] 1867; Shineberg 1971b, 303, 312–314; *SMH* 7 June 1862; Woodford Papers, Notes on Ontong Java; Sarfert and Damm 1929, 307; UKRNAS, vol. 13: Proceedings of HMS *Beagle* . . . , Case of *James Burnie* 6 Sept. 1875.
77. Somerville 1897, 369; Brown 1908a, 8–9.
78. Somerville 1897, 375, 378–389.
79. Coote 1883, 99; WPHC 233/98: Woodford to O'Brien 18 June 1898; *SMH* shipping columns, 1880–1900.
80. Woodford Papers, Diary 21 June 1886.
81. WPHC 292/96: Woodford to Thurston 26 June 1896.
82. When Guppy was at Mono on the HMS *Lark*, Mule Kopa wanted the leading stoker, Mr. Isabell, to stay on because of "his readiness to employ his mechanical skill for their various wants." In return, Mule Kopa promised to make Isabell a "chief" and give him a number of wives. This was probably one of the reasons the people wanted traders to reside with them (Guppy 1887, 24–25).
83. Rannie 1912, 31; Woodford Papers, Diary 1 Sept. 1886; Ferguson 17 Sept. 1881.
84. In the last year of the century the steamer brought, on one trip alone, 17 whaleboats ordered by traders for local people (WPHC 133/99: BSIP-AR, 1899 encl.; see also Ribbe 1903, 289).
85. Guppy 1887, 149.
86. Guppy 1887, 65–66, 158; Woodford Papers, Diary 19 Aug. 1887; Welchman 15 Nov. 1897.
87. Nerdrum 1901–1902.
88. Ferguson 9 June, 11 Aug. 1883; Hamilton 1852–1937; Rannie 1912, 32.
89. Zöller 1891, 349 (translation).
90. WPHC 173/94: Pelldrum to Thurston 3 July 1894, and encl.; Festetics von Tolna 1903, 378; Somerville 1897, 367; Zöller 1891, 341–349; Rannie 1912, 31; *SCL*, 15 Feb. 1901.
91. WPHC 477/96: BSIP-AR 1896; Hilliard 1966, 46. Penny of the Melanesian Mission was one of the exceptions. He saw the main benefit of the white trader to the community as being a source of clothing (Hilliard 1978, 101–102).
92. Somerville 1897, 363; Vera Clift, 1975.
93. Coppet 1977, 35.
94. Fox 1924, 339.
95. Scherzer 1861, 614; Guppy 1887, 130–131; Somerville 1897, 362.
96. Rannie 1912, 46.

97. Zöller 1891, 341–349.
98. Festetics von Tolna 1903, 303; WPHC 343/98: Woodford to HC 3 Oct. 1898 encl.
99. Penny 14 June 1878; Elton 1888, 96; Welchman Mar.–Aug. 1898.
100. Guppy 1887, 169, 173.
101. WPHC 84/98: Woodford to O'Brien 30 Apr. 1898; see also Ribbe 1903, 18.
102. Ribbe 1903, 67–68, 70, 274.
103. *SMH* shipping columns 1860–1900.
104. Penny 3 Sept. 1878, 29 May 1879; BSI-LTR Conveyance of Tavanipopo (Crawford Island), 30 Apr. 1890, 5/66, 222-001-1.
105. Somerville 1897, 381.
106. Ibid.
107. WPHC 477/96: BSIP-AR 1896.
108. WPHC 286/96: Woodford to Thurston 18 July 1896, and encl.
109. Luvusia Willy, 1973; WPHC 416/96: Woodford to Thurston 21 Sept. 1896.
110. WPHC 416/96: Woodford to Thurston 21 Sept. 1896; Luvusia Willy; Biskup 1974, 118; WPHC 91/99: Woodford to O'Brien, 29 Aug. 1900, and encls.; Sarfert and Damm 1929, 310–311.
111. WPHC 345/94: ? to Thurston 14 Dec. 1893; Lands Commission Report, in BSI-LTR Native Claim 34, 21 Apr. 1925.
112. WPHC 477/96: BSIP-AR 1896.

Chapter 5: The colonial government and pacification

Australian Parliamentary Papers 1919, 10.
WPHC 72/1899: Woodford, 8 June 1899 encl.
1. Morrell 1960, 332–349; Scarr 1967, 252–256, 260–263.
2. Morrell 1960, 344.
3. Scarr 1967, 259; WPHC 477/96: BSIP-AR 1896 encl.; WPHC 297/97: QR: The Solomons (Revenue) Regulation 1897 encl. For a discussion of the legal status of protectorates, see Wolfers 1971; Newbury 1973. For legal issues in land purchases in protectorates, see Bayne 1979.
4. WPHC 477/96: BSIP-AR 1896; WPHC 240/00: Woodford to HC 11 May 1901 encl.
5. WPHC 350/94: Gibson to Bowden-Smith 13 July 1893 encl.
6. WPHC 286/98: BSIP-AR 1898; WPHC 133/1899: BSIP-AR 1899; WPHC 239/00: BSIP-AR 1900.
7. WPHC 8/98: Woodford to O'Brien 17 Apr. 1898; WPHC 285/98: Woodford to O'Brien 11 Sept. 1899, and encls.; UKCO 225/55 COR: Mahaffy to Woodford 1 Aug. 1898, and encls.; O'Brien to CO 11 Oct. 1898; Jackson 1978, 125–139, cf. McKinnon 1975, 305, and Zelenietz 1979, 4–107.
8. WPHC 508/17: Woodford to O'Brien 25 Sept. 1897.
9. MMP: Teki to Danks 16 Aug. 1908.
10. MMP: Goldie to Danks 14 Jan. 1909.
11. Burnett 1911, 102–129; WPHC 98/08: Woodford to HC 13 Apr. 1908. WPHC 261/08: Woodford to im Thurn 22 Aug. 1908; WPHC 422/08: Woodford to im Thurn 22 Aug. 1908; Metcalfe Papers, Pitu, How the Marovo chief . . .
12. WPHC 261/08: Woodford to Major 11 Jan. 1909.
13. WPHC 28/85: Tryon to Thurston 5 Jan. 1886; WPHC 106/86: Tryon to

Thurston 16 June 1886; Woodford Papers, Case 8, Correspondence Respecting Outrages . . . , 1886; WPHC 41/02: Woodford to O'Brien 28 Dec. 1901, and encls.; MMP: Nicholson to Danks 4 Oct. 1909, Nicholson to Danks 7 Dec. 1909, Nicholson to Danks 27 Jan. 1910, Goldie to Danks 7 Feb. 1910, Nicholson to Danks 1 Mar. 1910, Goldie to Danks and encl. 11 Mar. 1910, Nicholson to Danks 10 Apr. 1910, Goldie to Danks 29 May 1910, Nicholson to Danks 13 June 1910; Burnett 1911, 145–157; WPHC 1121/1909: Woodford to HC 23 Sept. 1909, and encls.; Boutilier 1975, 34.

  14. Luxton 1955, 96.

  15. Laracy 1976, 79; Hilliard 1974.

  16. Woodford 1890a, 185; WPHC 213/00: Woodford to O'Brien 21 Sept. 1900 encl.; Hilliard 1966, 74, 114–115.

  17. WPHC 782/09: Barnett to Major 23 June 1909.

  18. WPHC 830/08: Mahaffy Report on SI, 21 Dec. 1908.

  19. WPHC 98/08: Woodford to HC 13 Apr. 1908; WPHC 442/08: Woodford to HC 22 Aug. 1908; WPHC 260/08: Woodford to HC 22 Aug. 1908; UKCO 225/96: Edge-Partington to Barnett, 15 July 1911 encl.; CO 225/102: Carver to CO 13 Oct. 1911; CO 225/98: Carver to King-Hall 11 Nov. 1911, encl.; CO 225/90: Woodford to CO 28 Nov. 1911; CO 225/90: Carver to King-Hall 23 Dec. 1911 encl.; CO 225/103: Edge-Partington to Woodford 6 Dec. 1911.

  20. Bertreux 1905, 369; Chatelet 1905, 370–375; Raucaz 1928, 110–112, 116.

  21. WPHC 62/14: Edge-Partington to Barnett 26 Sept. 1914 (Mala); BSIP-AR 1918–1919, 1920; Bennett 1974, 80, 82–84, 97, 231.

  22. WPHC 1707/32: AR Guadalcanal, 1931; Bennett 1974, 152–154.

  23. Bennett 1974, 231.

  24. Report of DO Eastern district 1918, quoted at length in Green 1976, 42–43; WPHC F46/35: Kuper to DO 2 Oct. 1933 encl.; Laracy 1976, 46–47, 67; WPHC 426/21: Kane to HC 25 Apr. 1921 and encls.

  25. WPHC 306/19: AC-AR 1918. For other examples of action against customary practice, see WPHC 146/78: Woodford to O'Brien 1 Mar. 1898, and encls.; WPHC 285/99: Woodford to O'Brien 3 Oct. 1899 and encls.

  26. Woodford Papers, Diary 15 Oct. 1886, 6–8 Oct. 1888; Somerville 1897, 399; WPHC 293/1895: Balfour to CC 22 Oct. 1894; WPHC 283/1896: Woodford to HC 12 July 1896; WPHC 296/1897: Woodford to HC 30 Apr. 1897; WPHC 300/1897: Woodford to HC 8 June 1897; WPHC 8/1898: Woodford to HC 17 Apr. 1898; WPHC 91/98: Woodford to HC 29 May 1900 encl. "Kolombangara"; Chewings 1900, 20; Ribbe 1903, 254.

  27. WPHC 3051/1923: Francis to RC 20 Feb. 1923; Hilliard 1966, 252.

  28. Goldie 1914, 568, 573.

  29. WPHC 192/81: Dawson to Wilson 11 Nov. 1881.

  30. Hilliard 1966, 249, 250; Carter n.d., Notes on Oral History; Tippett 1967, 139–142; Edge-Partington 1907.

  31. Hocart Papers, Chieftainship.

  32. Cromar 1935, 280–282; Bennett 1974, 20.

  33. BSIP-AR 1912–1913; Laracy 1976, 52–53.

  34. For examples, see MMP: Goldie to Danks 11 Mar. 1910; see also WPHC 1121/09.

  35. See, for example, Collinson 1926, 126–127, 178–179; Burnett 1911, 120–122.

  36. Hocart Papers, Roviana . . . , 6–7.

  37. WPHC 830/08: Mahaffy Report on SI, 21 Dec. 1908; Rivers 1922, 98 ff; Burnett 1911, 84–85; Fox 1975, 47.

38. WPHC 281/11: Woodford to im Thurn 13 Feb. 1908; WPHC 63/13: Vernon's, Notes on the SIP, 7 Dec. 1912 encl.; see also WPHC 2471/14: Barnett to HC 16 Sept. 1914.

39. Hocart Papers, Chieftainship; Allan 1957, 95–97.

40. WPHC 261/08: Woodford to im Thurn 22 Aug. 1908 and encl.; Metcalfe Papers, Pitu, How the Marovo chief . . . ; LTR: 143-002-02, Application for first registration 16/64, Parcel Description Lot 4 and Remainder of Lot 1, LR 250 Sege.

41. Metcalfe Papers, How the Marovo chief . . . ; LTR: 121-003-1, Application 149/68, LR 189, Humbupecka, Roviana; LTR: 120-003-1, Application no. 275/70, LR, Kolohite Islands.

42. Hilliard 1966, 114–115; WPHC 213/1900: Woodford to im Thurn 21 Sept. 1900, and encls.; LTR: 190-005-1, 96/68 LR Lovoro no. 2 West Guadalcanal.

43. Woodford 1890a, 183–184; Rudd 1877, 12 May; Rannie 1912, 190–191; UKMDHD 1887–1888, Sec. H 363/1889, Guadalcanal north coast, B2073 Shelf PV; WPHC 91/90: Woodford to O'Brien 17 Mar. 1901.

44. Ferguson 1882, 12 June.

45. Andrews 1876, 21 July; Rudd 1877, 12 May; Haddock 1877, 15, 17 Aug.; Mair 1880, 21–30 Sept., 12 Oct.; Reilly 1882, 29–30 July, 3, 7, 10 Aug.; Cromar 1935, 278–279.

46. LTR: 190-001-7, Application no. 5/63 and 10/04; Bathgate 1975, 58.

47. Corris 1973, 126–134.

48. *SCL* 8 Jan., 13 Aug. 1910.

49. Bathgate 1975, 59–60; Woodford 1909, 20.

50. WPHC 274/32: Guadalcanal Census Report 1931 encl.

51. Bathgate 1975, 60. For examples elsewhere, see Tutty n.d.; WPHC 2195/40: AR Nggela 1940 encl.

52. *SCL* 2 Oct. 1916.

53. *SCL* 16 Feb. 1912, 1 June 1916.

54. Where there were disputes regarding this land it was usually over actual boundaries rather than the validity of the transfer. (See for example LTR: 237-004-1, 18/68 and 19/69, LR 287, Ma'alu.)

55. Hilliard 1966, 138, 158; see LTR: land titles 237-003-0 to 253-001-1, San Cristobal, and 190-001-1 to 193-001-3, Guadalcanal.

56. WPHC 106/02: Woodford to HC 7 May 1902. The records relating to this intended sale are either nonexistent or among the then unregistered land titles which, because of local considerations, I was not permitted to examine in 1976 in Honiara. Atkinson had ownership of this island in 1931 when he died (LTR: 020-002-2, application for first registration, no. 9/1/73, Lot 2 of LR 9 Ballalae).

57. WPHC 477/96: BSIP-AR 1896 encl.; BPA: Lucas Reports on SI Plantation Properties Oct. 1910; *Prospectus of Mamara Plantations Limited* c. 1905.

58. WPHC 107/03: Woodford to Jackson 15 May 1905.

59. Burnett 1911, 136–137.

60. WPHC 69/10: Edge-Partington to Woodford 1 Nov. 1910 (Mala).

61. Ivens 1930, 198. As late as 1916, around Rohinari alone, the Marist Catholic priest knew of sixty to seventy murders or killings and guessed there were many more in the hinterland, of which he knew nothing (WPHC 2/16: Bell to Barnett 17 Jan. 1916 [Mala]).

62. Corris 1973, 112–125.

63. WPHC 1779/16: Murray to Minister for External Affairs 29 Apr. 1916;

WPHC BSIP Series CF 81/7: Noel 29 Dec. 1943 encl.; see also Report of the Labour Commission in WPHC 827/30: BSIP 1929.
 64. WPHC 1716/12: RC to HC 3 Aug. 1912; WPHC 73 (?)/19: Bell to ARC 7 Apr. 1919 (Mala); WPHC 2048/20: Bell to RC 14 Oct. 1920 encl.
 65. Ross 1973, 55–56; Hogbin 1939, 91–99, 109, 157, 185.
 66. Hilliard 1966, 370–371, 380–381; Hilliard 1978; Laracy 1976, 72, 180–181; WPHC 164/07: Barnett Report on visit to Western SI July 1907 encl.
 67. Scheffler 1965, 20–25; Luxton 1955, 69–91; Hilliard 1966.

Chapter 6: The colonial government and land alienation

Woodford Papers, Hand to Commander-in-Chief, Correspondence respecting outrages . . . , 1890.
Lever, May 1912, quoted in Smith and Pape 1912, vii.
 1. WPHC 199/96: Woodford to Thurston 6 June 1896; WPHC 281/96: Woodford to Thurston 4 July 1896; Woodford Papers, Diary 4 Oct. 1886; WPHC 102/92: Case 49 Correspondence respecting outrages . . . , 1891.
 2. *SMH* 9 June 1894.
 3. *SMH* 9 June, 22 Aug., 4 Dec. 1894, 16 Jan., 17 June, 26, 30 Sept., 14 Nov. 1895.
 4. *SMH* 9 June 1894.
 5. *SMH* 16 Jan., 7 Feb., 4, 11 Mar., 20 Apr., 16 June, 1 Aug. 1896. See Appendix 4; WPHC 238/05: BSIP-AR 1904–1905.
 6. WPHC 281/96: Woodford to Thurston 4 July 1896.
 7. WPHC 477/96: BSIP-AR 1896.
 8. Hookey 1971, 230.
 9. Ibid.; Wallerstein 1976, 43; Scarr 1967, 265.
 10. Hookey 1971, 234, 236–237.
 11. Wilson 1954, 105–106.
 12. Wilson 1954, 160; Jolly 1976, 96.
 13. Lever Bros., Lever to Cooper Bros. 26 Feb. 1902.
 14. BPA: Memo to MD re letter from Lever Bros.; MD, BP, to Chairman, Levers 6 May 1903; Campbell to Burns 26 Sept. 1902; Tillotson to BP, 20 Oct. 1902; BP to Campbell 2 Dec. 1902, and encls., LB.
 15. Wilson 1954, 160–163; Hookey 1971, 237; Jolly 1976, 75.
 16. See letter Aug. 1904 quoted in Fieldhouse 1978, 460–461; Lever Bros., Lever to Meek 19 Oct. 1916.
 17. Edge-Partington Correspondence, Giblin to Stanmore 20 Mar. 1905.
 18. Secretary of State, 13 Aug. 1906, quoted in Scarr 1967, 266.
 19. Hookey 1971, 237.
 20. BPA: Gordon to MD 28 Aug. 1907 IPI; Lucas to MD 15 May 1901, and encls.; Memo for MD; Offer of Svensen's SI Business 31 Aug. 1903, SIM-1; LTR: 181-000-3, no. 210/71, Parcel Description L.P. 75 Guvutu.
 21. WPHC 233/00: Woodford to O'Brien 19 Feb. 1901; LTR: Application for first Registration no. 67/65, L.R. 158, Lofung.
 22. BPA: Lucas (?), Memo to the Board of BP, 25 Feb. 1904, and encls., ShI.
 23. Lever Bros., Lever to Greenleigh 18 Sept. 1903; Wilson 1954, 160, 163.
 24. BPA: Forsyth, Report on New Guinea and SI Trade, 12 Sept. 1906; Firth 1982, 88.
 25. BPA: Forsyth, Report on New Guinea . . . ; Memo to Gerald Gordon . . . ; 12 July 1907; Gordon to BP 25 July 1907, IPI.

26. Allan 1957; Scheffler 1965, 34, 48–52, 120–139; Ross 1973, 159–169; Lasaqa 1972, 98–101.

27. WPHC 91/98: Woodford to O'Brien 29 May 1900, and encls.

28. Woodford 1890a, 139, 145; WPHC 12/98: Woodford to O'Brien 9 Nov. 1898.

29. WPHC 240/98: KR, no. 1 of 1904 encl.

30. Hamilton Papers, Log of *Jessie Kelly* 1883.

31. Hamilton Papers, Report on a Voyage . . . 1899–1900; WPHC 113/00: Woodford to Jackson 21 Mar. 1904, and encls.

32. WPHC 109/00: Woodford to O'Brien 24 June 1900, and encls.

33. WPHC 113/00: Woodford to Jackson 21 Mar. 1904.

34. Hamilton Papers, Log of *Canomie* 6 Sept. 1905; WPHC 113/00: Hamilton to Woodford 28 Mar. 1902, Woodford to Jackson 31 Oct. 1902.

35. WPHC 113/00: Woodford to O'Brien 14 May 1900.

36. WPHC 113/00: Woodford to Jackson 21 Mar. 1904.

37. Hamilton Papers, Log of *Canomie* 28, 29 June, 29 July, 21–26 Aug., 7, 13 Sept. 1905; WPHC 282/05: BSIP-AR, 1904–1905; BPA: Villiers Brown to Philp 15 June 1907 IP.

38. BPA: Appendix, Summary of SI Clients, in Burns Memo to George Gordon 12 July 1907 IPI.

39. BPA: Burns Memo to Gerald Gordon 12 July 1907, and encls., IPI; LTR: 051-001-1 Application no. 7/63.

40. WPHC 73/08: BP to Woodford June 1909.

41. WPHC 830/08: Mahaffy to HC Report on SIP, 21 Dec. 1908 encl.

42. BPA: Burns Memo to Gerald Gordon 12 July 1907 IPI.

43. BPA: Lucas to MD 25 Nov. 1907 encl., Lucas Report on SI.

44. BPA: Lucas to MD 28 July 1908; Burns Memo . . . , 12 July 1907 IPI; Lucas to Woodford 21 Oct. 1912 File 3a.

45. BPA: Lucas to Forsyth 3 Nov. 1908.

46. BPA: Lucas to Woodford 14 Oct. 1913, TL. See also BPA: Woodford to Burns 16 July 1907 File 3a.

47. BPA: Woodford to Burns 16 Jan. 1914, TL; Forsyth to Burns 18 Dec. 1914; WPHC 1233/16: Burnett to Eyre Hutson 14 Apr. 1916.

48. WPHC 61/13: Vernon, Report on BSIP, 7 Dec. 1912; BPA: TL, passim; Resumé of BP's case for the information and guidance of Lord Inchcape, n.d.

49. BPA: Jose to Lucas 18 Feb. 1915, and encl.; Lucas to Burns 20 Feb. 1915. Noted for his pro-Australia sentiments as London *Times* correspondent in Australia until 1915, A. W. Jose became an intelligence officer with the Royal Australian Navy. Much of the intelligence he and Prime Minister William Morris Hughes received on western Pacific matters came from Walter Henry Lucas, BP's island manager. (James Gibbney, Australian Dictionary of Biography project, ANU.)

50. [Jose] 1915.

51. Woodford Papers, Lucas to Woodford 14 Jan. 1911.

52. WPHC 2933/15: Bonar Law to HC 9 Oct. 1915; WPHC 620/17: Barnett to HC 12 Feb. 1917.

53. WPHC 63/13: Vernon, Report on BSIP, 7 Dec. 1912.

54. Jackson 1968, 226, 247.

55. Biskup 1974, fn 27.

56. WPHC 70/06: Giblin to Chairman, SI Syn. 21 July 1905 encl.

57. See for example *Truth* (London) 1 June 1910; *Sun* (Sydney) 3 Aug. 1911.

58. Smith and Pape 1912, v–viii.

59. NSWSA COR: No. 3148, Ullberg's Plantations Ltd. (Union Plantation and Trading Co.) 3/5789; No. 4388, Hamilton Plantation Choiseul Bay Co. Ltd. 3/5838. WPHC 782/09: Barnett to Major, 23 June 1909 and encls.; QSA COR: Fairley, Rigby & Co. Ltd., 30/1912; Hivo Plantations Ltd., 139/1912; Lavoro Plantations Pty. Ltd., 40/1910; Mamara Plantations Ltd. 106/1911; SI Rubber Plantation Ltd., 28/1919. WPHC BSIP CF 33/6, Vol. I: Svensen to HC 1 Aug. 1940 encl.

60. Committee on the Rubber Industry in Ceylon 1947, 6; Vickery and Vickery 1979, 29; BPA: Lucas, Report on SI Plantation Props 1 Oct. 1907, 6–7; Smith and Pape 1912, 88.

61. Woodford 1909. The capitation tax of £5 annually on all European residents except missionaries, was abolished in 1907–1908. By 1907 a customs tariff on a wide range of goods compensated for the tax (BSIP *Handbook* 1911).

62. WPHC 70/06: Giblin to Chairman, SI Syn. 21 July 1905 encl.; WPHC 830/08: Mahaffy Report . . . , 21 Dec. 1908; WPHC 74/01: Woodford to HC 7 Apr. 1901.

63. See LTR, passim.

64. Land sold from 1896 on came under Queen's Regulation No. 4 of 1896, by which one-tenth of freehold land bought for agricultural purposes had to be cultivated within five years (Copy of Reg. in WPHC 240/98).

65. *SCL* 16 Feb. 1912, 283–284.

66. LTR: 063-001-1 Application no. 83/66, Lot 2 of LR 1, Mundi Mundi, Vella Lavella; 063-003-1 Application no. 3/1/72, Lot 3, LR 1 [Mundi Mundi].

67. BPA: Lucas to MD 15 May 1901, SIM-1; BPA: Memo to the Board of BP 25 Feb. 1904, Correspondence re Shortland Island Estate 1905–1906, SHI; LTR: 273-002-1 Application no. 133/66 under Part III of LTO (Cap 93), Santa Ana; 073-002-2 Application no. 133/66, LR 89, Santa Ana; 192-004-12, no. 198/70 Lots 20 and 27 LR 83/R; 181-001-3, 181-001-4 and 181-001-5, no. 210/71, Parcel Descriptions LR 75 Gavutu, LR 76 Gaomi and LR 93 Tanamboga.

68. LTR: LR 81 Logar; BPA: Casley to MD 6 Nov. 1913 SIM-2.

69. LTR: 120-006-1 Application no. 37/1/73, Parcel Description LR 64 Barakai Island, Roviana Lagoon; BPA: K.

70. LTR: 192-011-1, no. 112, 65 LR 166, Berande; BPA: Lucas to Forsyth 13 Oct. 1915; Lucas, Report on the SI Plantation Props, 1 Oct. 1910.

71. Young c. 1926, 127–129; WPHC 2015/13: Woodford to Sweet Escott 21 Aug. 1913, and encls.; LTR: 177-003-1, nos. 226-229/70, Lots 4, 5, 6 and 7 LR 50, Yandina, Banika.

72. LTR: 191-049-1, no. 102/67 LR 40 Doma.

73. WPHC 1708/12: Woodford to Major 26 July 1912; LTR: 123-003-1, Application no. 55/71, LR Buka Buki (Bukibuki); 123-003-2, Application no. 56/71 LR 25, Veuru or Araro Island; 120-005-1, Application no. 81/67, LR 625, Kenelo plantations, part of LR 58, Kenelo and part of LR 59 Banyatta.

74. BPA: Burns Memo . . . , 12 July 1907 IPI.

75. BPA: Lucas, Report on SI 25 Nov. 1907.

76. BPA: Caseley to MD 6 Nov. 1913, SIM-2.

77. BPA: Lucas, Report . . . 25 Nov. 1907; LTR: 141-001-1 Application no. 8/65, Parcel Description Remainder of Lot 1, LR 173, Tetepare; BPA: Lucas to Wheatley, 18 Nov. 1907, encl. in Lucas, Report . . . 25 Nov. 1907. Wheatley was also involved in other land negotiations for BP on Rendova (BPA: Lucas to Burns 28 Dec. 1909 File 3a).

78. WPHC 111/08: Woodford to HC 21 Feb. 1908 and HC's annotations on minute paper.

79. Bennett 1979a, 179; BPA: Lucas to Gordon 27 Aug. 1907 encl. Gordon, Report, 19 Aug. 1907, IPI; Lucas, Report . . . 25 Nov. 1907; Corris 1973, 140–141.

80. WPHC 49/10: Edge-Partington to Woodford 4 July 1910; WPHC 74/10: Edge-Partington to Woodford 1 Dec. 1910.

81. Wall and Hansell 1974a, 48–49; Sandars 1928–1943, Autobiography; WPHC 74/10: Edge-Partington to Woodford, 1 Dec. 1910; WPHC 14/11: Edge-Partington to Woodford 27 Feb. 1911; WPHC 46/11: Edge-Partington to Woodford 13 June 1911; WPHC 44/11: Edge-Partington to Woodford 13 June 1911; WPHC 6/1912: Edge-Partington to Woodford 1 Feb. 1912; WPHC 14/17: Bell to ARC 26 Aug. 1917; WPHC 27/17: Bell to AHC 11 Nov. 1917; WPHC 35/19: Bell to AHC 28 Aug. 1919; WPHC 2/20: Bell to RC 5 Jan. 1920; WPHC 30/20: Bell to RC 19 June 1920; WPHC 46/20: Bell to RC 24 Oct. 1920; Simion Funasi'a; Lizba Luda Bata; Salimauri; Seti Mato'ofeli; Jo Ariana; Jo Gonai'ilae 1976. For an account of the initial Malayta Co. negotiations see Brook 1940, 143–147, 201.

82. Ivens 1930, 84–85, 269.

83. WPHC 834/11: Woodford to Clark 26 Apr. 1911; see also WPHC 61/05: Woodford to im Thurn 8 Apr. 1910 encl.

84. WPHC 107/03: Woodford to Jackson 15 May 1905.

85. WPHC 111/10: Woodford to im Thurn 26 Dec. 1909.

86. Scarr 1967, 292–294; WPHC 830/08: Mahaffy Report . . . , 21 Dec. 1908. As late as 1931, this view was still current, partly as a result of the 1931 census which placed the population at 93,000 instead of the estimated 150,000 (WPHC 83/32: Hewitt to Sydney Office 7 Sept. 1931 encl.).

87. WPHC 134/99: Woodford to im Thurn 27 Oct. 1906 encl.

88. WPHC 134/99: im Thurn to Woodford 15 Dec. 1906 encl.

89. Scarr 1967, 282–285.

90. WPHC 977/09: Extracts from a letter from Woodford to im Thurn 14 Feb. 1910, and encls.

91. WPHC 830/08: Mahaffy Report . . . 21 Dec. 1908; WPHC 63/13: Vernon . . . 7 Dec. 1912.

92. WPHC 799/13: Lists of lands leased on behalf of natives and by government 1913.

93. The terms of government leaseholds stated that the lessee had to pay for the first five years 3 pence per acre per annum, for the second five years 6 pence per acre per annum, for the next ten, 3 shillings per acre per annum. From the thirty-first year until the ninety-ninth the rental was 5 percent of the unimproved capital value, to be reappraised every ten years. An improvement clause required that one-tenth of the area leased had to be cultivated within the first ten years (WPHC 240/98: KR, no. 11 of 1912 encl.; WPHC 1734/13: BSIP-AR 1912–13).

94. See BSIP-AR 1898–1919, passim. Scarr 1967, 297.

95. WPHC 1734/13: BSIP-AR 1912–13.

96. Even in the early 1970s the total area under coconuts (all types of holdings) came to only 2.18 percent of the land area of the Solomons (Hansell and Wall 1976, 125–126).

97. WPHC 1734/13: BSIP-AR 1912–13.

98. Roberts 1964, 169–170; Robinson 1965, 6–7, 22; Scarr 1967, 290–297; see also Heussler 1963, 5, 15.

Chapter 7: The colonial government and labor

WPHC 827/30: Report of Labour Commission 1929.

1. WPHC 83/32: Raucaz 1928, and encls.; WPHC 1734/13: BSIP-AR 1912–1913, encl.
2. Grant, May 1900 in UK-CRSI 1903; Jolly 1976, 103–104.
3. BPA: Walter Lucas, Reports on SI Plantation Properties, 1 Oct. 1910.
4. WPHC 774/09: Woodford to im Thurn 26 Dec. 1909; HC to GG 7 Nov. 1909; GG to HC 8 Nov. 1909, and encls. (formerly at WPHC 111/10).
5. WPHC 784/10: Woodford to HC 8 Apr. 1910 encl.; WPHC 779/09: 27 June 1911 encl.
6. WPHC 1505/13: Stubbs to USecS 23 Oct. 1911, and encls. For a study of Indian migration to Fiji, see Gillion 1962.
7. WPHC 63/13: Vernon, Notes on SI Protectorate, 7 Dec. 1912, encl.; WPHC 1154/13: RC to HC 16 May 1913, and encls.; WPHC 1784/14: Woodford to HC 26 June 1914, and encls.
8. WPHC 1154/13: RC to HC 16 May 1913, and encls. WPHC 1149/17: Hamilton to HC 3 Apr. 1917; WPHC 445/18: Monckton to RC [1918] encl. BPA: [Bateson?], Notes on the General History of BP's Pacific Plantations; Lucas to Black 19 Oct. 1915; [Lucas?] Resumé of negotiations . . . 24 Mar. 1916. Bassett 1969, 15, 38. Rowley 1958, 55–56, 118, 151.
9. WPHC 1994/23: Fulton to RC 1 Aug. 1923, and encls.; WPHC 3073/23: Rodwell to Devonshire 31 Oct. 1923, and encls.; WPHC 1956/24: Leverhulme to SecS 30 Apr. 1924; Davis to Lever 19 June 1924. UA: Notes with regard to labour . . . 17 Jan. 1924; Memos regarding labour . . . 29, 30 Jan. 1924.
10. Roberts 1964, 172.
11. Moorhouse 1929.
12. WPHC 1956/24: Davis to Lever 19 June 1924, encl.; WPHC 1184/25: Deputation to HC 29 Sept. 1925, encl.
13. WPHC 1912/20: Workmen to Sec. of Planters' Association 24 June 1920, encl.
14. QSA Premier's Dept.: SI (Labour) Reg. 1897 encl., Papers relating to labour trade, Pre 85.
15. WPHC 830/08: Woodford to im Thurn 13 Feb. 1908.
16. WPHC 830/08: Mahaffy to HC 21 Dec. 1908, and encls. Re Hermes in Shortlands, WPHC 131/05; WPHC 156a/05.
17. Choranga; Moi'ea Pepechi; Jack Kwalau.
18. Alike Tae; Irlan Pope; Alveti Tongorova, Samuel Bau; Jorji Feleni'i. For other violent incidents involving overseers and labor: Simion Funasi'a; Alike Ghandokiki; Hari Roro; John Rich; Herman Lambuvia; James Piro.
19. WPHC 2738/15: Barnett to HC 31 Aug. 1915, and encls. See also WPHC 3086/16. WPHC 1437/18: *Sydney Truth* 12 May 1917, and other encls.; WPHC 2735/15: Barnett to HC 30 Aug. 1915, and encls.
20. WPHC 258/16: Norris to Barnett 15 Dec. 1915.
21. Moi'ea Pepechi, translated from Pijin; see for example WPHC 74/06, 517/09, 1779/14, 268/20. In the 1920s the administration of justice improved with most alleged murderers being brought to trial (see, for example WPHC 2989/22).
22. WPHC 206/09: Meek to RC 30 Mar. 1909, and encls.
23. WPHC 66/11: Edge-Partington to Woodford 7 July 1911, Malaita Series (Mala); WPHC 97/11: Edge-Partington to Woodford 6 Dec. 1911, (Mala); WPHC 22/12: Walsh to Woodford 24 Apr. 1911 (Mala); WPHC 55/12: Walsh to

Woodford 5 Sept. 1912 (Mala); WPHC 63/12: Walsh to Woodford 30 Sept. 1912; WPHC 64/13: Edge-Partington to Woodford 16 June 1913 (Mala); WPHC 73/13: Campbell to RC 29 Jan. 1914 (Mala); WPHC 38/15: Bell to Barnett 17 Nov. 1915 (Mala); WPHC 4/16: Bell to Barnett 11 June 1916 (Mala); WPHC 29/17: Bell to Barnett 20 Nov. 1917 (Mala); WPHC 489/17: Barnett to HC 27 Jan. 1917, and encls.

24. FRCP: Mumford to Fairleys 21 May 1914.
25. WPHC 830/08: Mahaffy to HC 21 Dec. 1908, and encls.; WPHC 801/14: LD-AR 1913, encl. Bell 1936, 39.
26. FRCP: Wardle to Mulock 7 Mar. 1913.
27. McLaren 1923, 219–220.
28. WPHC 830/08: Mahaffy to HC 21 Dec. 1908.
29. WPHC 1605/12: King's Reg. III, 1910 as amended in KR VIII, 1912 encl.
30. WPHC 281/11: Woodford to im Thurn 13 Feb. 1908, encl.; WPHC 1605/ 12: King's Reg. VIII, 1912, encl. Following the Anglo-German agreement in 1899, Santa Isabel, the Shortlands, and Choiseul ceased to be German territories and became British. Germany, however, retained the right to recruit labor from the British Solomons for Samoa until World War I. The numbers of Islanders recruited are not yet known, but were probably not great (WPHC 1154/13: Woodford to HC 10 May 1913 encl.).
31. WPHC 830/08: Woodford to im Thurn 13 Feb. 1908 encl.; WPHC 63/13: Vernon, Notes on SIP, 7 Dec. 1912 encl.; WPHC 937/13: Bell to SecS 10 Apr. 1913, and encls.; WPHC 1995/13: Bell to HC 28 Aug. 1913, and encls.; WPHC 801/14: LD-AR, 1913 encl.; WPHC 698/15: LD-AR 1914, encl.
32. WPHC 698/15: LD-AR 1914, encl.
33. WPHC 876/16: LD-AR 1915 encl.; WPHC 701/17: LD-AR, 1917 encl.; WPHC 2316/14: Barnett to HC 28 Aug. 1914; WPHC 2811/14: Barnett to Bell 26 Oct. 1914; WPHC 3033/14: Bell to Barnett 11 Nov. 1914; WPHC 1987/15: Bonar Law to Sweet-Escott, 9 June 1915, encl.
34. WPHC 876/16: LD-AR 1915 encl.; WPHC 701/17: LD-AR 1917 encl.
35. WPHC 2747/15: Bell, Statement 28 Aug. 1915.
36. WPHC 2738/15: Barnett to Eyre Hutson 31 Aug. 1915, and encls.; WPHC 258/16: Barnett to Norris 15 Dec. 1915, and encls.; WPHC 661/16: Bonar Law to HC, 11 Jan. 1916; WPHC 2307/16: RC to HC, 6 Aug. 1916.
37. WPHC 2464/14: Barnett to HC 10 Sept. 1914, and encls.; WPHC 2811/ 14: Barnett to Inspector of Labour 26 Oct. 1914, encl.; WPHC 2316/14: Barnett to HC 28 Aug. 1914; WPHC 1912/20: Workman to HC and encls. 8 July 1920; WPHC 2902/20: Workman to HC 19 Oct. 1920, and encls.; also WPHC 1187/17: Heffernan to Barnett, 24 Mar. 1917, and encls.
38. WPHC 2299/13: Bell to RC 15 Oct. 1913.
39. WPHC 806/21: Symington to ARC 12 Jan. 1921 encl.
40. WPHC 806/21: Hill to HC 10 Jan. 1921, and encls.
41. WPHC BSIP Series F34/1, Nos. 1 to 6: Requests for extension . . . and encls.
42. Peter Plowman, 1975; Norden 1926, 72–73; WPHC 850/24: Fell to ARC 24 Apr. 1924, and encls. See also WPHC 1284/18: LD-AR, 1917, encl.
43. WPHC 1554/23: LD-AR 1922 encl.
44. WPHC 20/09: Edge-Partington to Woodford 18 Dec. 1909 (Mala); WPHC 7/10: 24 Jan. 1910 (Mala); Irlan Pope; Hari Roro; WPHC 13/10: Edge-Partington to Woodford, 4 Mar. 1910.
45. Leslie Gill, 1976.

46. Corris 1973, 49–51; see also QSA Premier's Dept.: Brenan to Under Chief Sec. 3 Oct. 1901, Pre 88. (Reference kindly provided by P. M. Mercer.)
47. *Bulletin*, 9 June 1894.
48. Melvin 1977, 51–52, 56–57, 60.
49. *Cairns Morning Post*, 25 Feb. 1897; *Mackay Mercury*, 4 June 1906. (References supplied by P. M. Mercer.)
50. Mercer, pers. com.
51. WPHC 286/96: Woodford to Thurston 18 July 1896, and encls.; Corris 1973, 44; Grant 1900 in UK-CRSI 1903.
52. WPHC 801/14: LD-AR 1913, encl.; WPHC 698/15: LD-AR 1914 encl.; WPHC 875/16: LD-AR 1915 encl.; see also WPHC 63/13: Vernon, Notes 7 Dec. 1912 encl.
53. QSA Premier's Dept.: Minutes of Meeting, McDermott, Forsythe and Svensen, 10 May 1905 Pre 89.
54. Woodford 1909.
55. CO 225/80: Ambuover to HM the King 2 May 1907.
56. See also WPHC 292/96: Woodford to Thurston 26 June 1896.
57. WPHC 1779/16: Murray to Minister for External Affairs 29 Apr. 1916 encl.; WPHC 824/21: *The Planters Gazette*, vol. 1, December 1920 encl. Some of this increase in 1914 can be attributed to wartime inflation (WPHC 2818/14: Barnett to HC 2 Nov. 1914).
58. WPHC 25/22: Minutes AC 10 Nov. 1921 encl.; WPHC 185/23: Minutes AC 8 Dec. 1922 encl.
59. WPHC 1714/22: Thomson, Comments on Allardyce's Report 11 July 1922, and encls.; WPHC 1912/20: Workman to HC 8 July 1920, and encls.; WPHC 2902/20: 19 Oct. 1920, and encls.
60. The tax was scaled so that in very poor areas it ranged from 5 to 10 shillings per head (WPHC 2408/19: King's Reg. No. 10 of 1920); WPHC 2929a/20: Rodwell to Workman 3 Oct. 1920 and encl.; WPHC 2667/22: Bell to RC 8 Aug. 1922, and encls.; WPHC 2902/20: Workman to HC 19 Oct. 1920, and encls.
61. WPHC 1137/23: Symington to RC 21 Feb. 1923 encl.; WPHC 850/24: Fell to ARC 24 Apr. 1924, and encls.; WPHC 661/23: Fell to RC 16 Nov. 1922 encl.; WPHC 2667/22: Bell to RC 8 Aug. 1922. Brook 1940, 164; Mamara Plantations c. 1905, 23–24.
62. Justus Malalifu; Dickinson 1927, 147; WPHC 1779/16: Murray to Minister for External Affairs, 29 Apr. 1916 encl.
63. WPHC 1912/20: McKerlie to RC 1 Mar. 1020 encl.
64. WPHC 827/30: Report of the Labour Commission in BSIP 1929.
65. Herr and Rood 1978, 175–177; Dickinson 1927, 156–157; WPHC 1912/20: Knibbs to HC 8 July 1920, and McKerlie to RC 1 Mar. 1920, encls. Justus Malalifu; Alike Tae.
66. WPHC 2902/20: Workman to HC 19 Oct. 1920, and encls.; WPHC 1912/20: Workman to HC 8 July 1920, and encls.; WPHC 2399/21: Kane to AHC 5 Aug. 1921; WPHC 850/24: Fell to ARC 24 Apr. 1924, encl.; WPHC 2667/22: Bell to RC 8 Aug. 1922, encl.; WPHC 827/30: Report of Labour Commission, 1929; WPHC 25/22: Meeting of AC 1921, encl.; Justus Malalifu; Jo Ariana; Kika. See also Tommy Elkington, 8 Mar. 1968.
67. WPHC 1197/25: LD-AR 1924 encl. Some Islanders attributed this wage increase to the influence of William Bell (Mageli Leban).
68. WPHC 3343/26: Barley to GS 23 Aug. 1926 encl.; Jotam Finou.
69. Jotam Finou.
70. Of the total number of laborers, 6152, employed in 1923, about 63 per-

cent or 3855 would have been Malaitans. Since 1504 were recruited in 1923, most at the new rate, the total income to Malaitan labor for 1923 would have been around £32,152 (WPHC 350/23: LD-AR 1921 encl.; WPHC 1554/23: LD-AR 1922 encl.; WPHC 1121/24: LD-AR 1923 encl.; WPHC 1117/24: Barley to RC 26 May 1924 encl.; WPHC 3343/26: Bell to RC 9 Aug. 1926 encl.).

71. Salimauri; Dickie Panna; Choranga; Elison Kavaro.

72. WPHC 1184/25: Deputation to HC . . . 29 Sept. 1925.

73. WPHC 490/28: Minutes of AC 5–8 Dec. 1927.

74. WPHC 2907/31: RC to HC 29 Apr. 1934, encl.; WPHC 827/30: Report of the Labour Commission 1929; WPHC 1184/25: Clift, Deputation to HC . . . 29 Sept. 1925.

75. LD-AR 1913–1940, in WPHC files 801/14, 698/15, 875/16, 701/17, 1284/18, 535/20, 350/23, 1554/23, 1121/24, 1197/25, 1170/26, 1510/27, 1835/28, 1426/29, 809/30, 755/31, 1228/32, 506/33, 920/34, 1612/35, 1598/36, 2744/36, 1638/38, 2469/40, 2399/41; WPHC 284/32: Census of BSIP for 1931, 23 Dec. 1931.

76. WPHC BSIP Series 16: Hobgin, Secret Memo, Oct. 1943, and encls.

77. See, for example, Brook 1940, 164.

78. See WPHC 1760/30; WPHC 236/30; WPHC BSIP Series F34/4; WPHC 3726/31: Tour Notes, Dec. 1929, encls.; Roberts 1964, 180–181.

79. WPHC 1184/25: Clift, Deputation to HC . . . 29 Sept. 1925.

Chapter 8: The plantation

Welchman in *SCL*, 6 Mar. 1906.

Hewitt in WPHC 3698/36: Meeting of AC 1931 encl.

1. ANA Canberra: Chief Sec. to Lt. Gov. 29 Nov. 1901, encl. Prime Minister's Department, papers relating to External Affairs CAO CRS A1108, vol. 57; Hogbin 1939, 48; Geoffrey Kuper, 1976.

2. Kika; Salimauri; Jonathen Kuka; Urumbangereni Rubano; John Christian. Of course, in labor trade days, the aim of many recruits was to get guns and ammunition to contribute to their group's effectiveness in warfare (see, for example, ANA Canberra: Labour Trade, Prime Minister's Department, collected papers relating to External Affairs CAO CRS A1108, vol. 57; Bennett 1974, 48–72; Corris 1973, 37–38, 111–113).

3. Bennett 1973, 52–54; Hogbin 1964, 23–25; Codrington 1891, 94–100; Ivens 1927, 130–142.

4. Bennett 1973, 52–53; Hogbin 1964, 44–48, 130, 166; Hilliard 1978, 264–265. Within the Melanesian Mission there were differences of opinion. A. Hopkins disliked plantation life while Charles Fox thought it beneficial to the men (Hopkins 1928, 224; Charles Fox, pers. com. 1976; *PIM* 24 Jan. 1936, 41–42).

5. Recruits from c. 1870–1911 numbered on average about 800 each year from the Solomons with almost a third going to Fiji. Price with Baker 1976; Bennett 1974, 211–217; Corris 1973, 149–150; see Table 6.

6. Moi'ea Pepechi; James Piro; Irlan Pope; Joseph Odofia.

7. Timmy Lotufana; Abraham Te'fa'adi; Pita Mafane.

8. Seti's mother of Vatumanivo; WPHC 1634/38: AR Santa Isabel 1937 encl.; Jotam Finou; WPHC BSIP F34/11/7: ADO to Manager, Levers 27 Jan. 1937 encl.; Hogbin 1939, 211; Sandars Papers, Autobiography.

9. Elkington 1965.

10. WPHC 3423/27: Barley to Sec. Gov. 13 Sept. 1927 encl. WPHC 1422/29: AR Gizo district 1929; WPHC 827/30: Report of Labour Commission 1929;

Svensen n.d.; Hirst, 1975 interview and TS; Peter Plowman; Tommy Elkington, 1968; Knibbs 1929, 73; Mytinger 1942, 108–110; Brook 1940, 193; Bell 1936, 7–36; Romasio Ngura; Aliesio Tavoruka; Sove Kimbo; see also WPHC 3842/33: Barley to HC 12 Dec. 1932 encl.

11. John Rich; Mageli Leban; Vichi Chio; Chamali Hesikia; Chapasere; Choranga; Alike Ghandokiki; Reo Dick; Heman Lambuvia; Urumbangereni Rubano. Jack Mainagwa; Peter Plowman; Tommy Elkington, 1968; WPHC 827/30: Report of Labour Commission, 1929; WPHC 3842/32: Filose to RC 5 Dec. 1932 encl.

12. WPHC F34/3/1: Letter, translation 19 July 1934 encl.

13. Knibbs 1929, 69–71; Stanley Maurione.

14. WPHC 1073/34: Report on burning of copra driers in BSIP, 1935. See also *PIM*, 24 Aug. 1934; Mytinger 1942, 131–132, 136–138.

15. Justus Malalifu. See also WPHC 2925/26; WPHC 1896/40.

16. WPHC 1734/13: BSIP-AR 1912 encl. See also WPHC 92/18.

17. Jack Mainagwa.

18. FRCP: Rigby to Fairley 16 May 1913; WPHC 1090/33: Middenway, Labour troubles 1932 encl. WPHC 1284/18: LD-AR 1917 encl.; WPHC 1510/27: LD-AR, 1926 encl.; WPHC 1426/29: LD-AR 1929 encl.; WPHC 67/10: Edge-Partington to Woodford 1 Nov. 1910, (Mala); Hopkins Autobiography, 152–153.

19. WPHC 3343/26: Kane to HC 23 Sept. 1926 encl.

20. WPHC 2608/20: Pinching to RC 17 Sept. 1920, and encls.

21. WPHC 1035/22: Thompson to RC 7 Apr. 1922 encl.

22. Peter Plowman, 1975; see also WPHC 350/23: LD-AR 1921.

23. Timmy Lotufana; Jotam Finou; James Piro; Choranga; Charles Fox Ha'amouri; Peter Plowman. In New Georgia the laborers sometimes took their complaints to the Reverend John Goldie, who then told the district officer (Joseph Odofia).

24. Sandars 1928–1943; Peter Eiatarogari; Stanley Maurione.

25. Peter Plowman, 1975; Jack Mainagwa. See also WPHC 1585/35 and Simone Maa'eobi.

26. WPHC 1236/16: MD-AR 1915 encl.; WPHC 452/18: Workman to HC 17 Jan. 1918 and encls.; WPHC 2593/31: Lotze to RC 18 Sept. 1937 and encls.; Informants.

27. Chapasere; Mbumbukimbo; Heman Lambuvia; Chamali Hesikia; James Piro; Alike Tae; Jones Bulangi; Vichi Chio; Reo Dick; Mageli Leban; John Rich; Alveti Tongorova; Kaspa Arabae'awa; Nelson Anuanulabu; Thomas Ta'ae'ke'kerei; Gilbert Suniaru; Robinson Wakii'a; Morris Ohairangi; Daniel Tougageita; Abraham Te'fa'adi; Pita Mafane; Anifanaia; Thomas; Jo Ariana; Jack Mainagwa; Romasio Ngura; Timmy Lotufana; Lamofanageni (of Waileni); Kika; Hirst Memoirs; WPHC 827/30: RLC 1929. For an account of a killing of a Guadalcanal man (Frank) by a Malaitan (Olini) at Yandina see Chamali Hesikia.

28. Jo Tiakapu; Jack Kwalau; Romasio Ngura; Kaspa Arabae'awa, Alveti Tongorova; Dickie Panna; Aliesio Tavoruka.

29. Moi'ea Pepechi; John Tologhomba.

30. Mageli Leban. See also Debora Atoubora.

31. Jones Bulangi; Dickie Panna; Reo Dick; Alike Ghandokiki; Debora Atoubora; Jo Ariana; WPHC 827/30: Report of Labour Commission 1929; Bell 1936, 27.

32. Tommy Elkington, 1976; WPHC 2831/28.

33. Tommy Elkington; see also WPHC 1284/18: LD-AR 1917.

34. WPHC 2831/28: HC to Amery 10 Oct. 1928, and encls. In the Santa Cruz group the Reef Islanders, so long impervious to the Christian message, still practiced institutionalized prostitution. The high commissioner instructed that this must cease in order to bring the Solomons into line with the convention (Hilliard 1978, 184–186; WPHC 1187/26: HC to RC 29 June 1926 encl.). Up to the World War II, on Santa Ana, the "abode of frail sisterhood," prostitutes (urao) were a normal part of most feasts with European visitors sometimes assisting with transportation. The government turned a blind eye to this, but not so Norman Deck, the SSEM leader (Herr and Rood 1978, 145; Tommy Elkington, 1976).

35. John Bana; Thomas; Tommy Elkington 1976; Bell 1936, 27, 49–51. Some of the Shortland Islands chiefs offered young women, usually adoptees or descendants of captives, as prostitutes to various Europeans in the thirties. It is likely that laborers who could pay were similarly encouraged (Seton n.d.; J. H. Macdonald). When male strangers annoyed village women, it was usually after they had ceased employment on a plantation and managed to insinuate themselves into a nearby village (WPHC 2100/26: Younger to RC 12 Mar. 1926, and encls.).

36. Leslie Gill, 1977.

37. WPHC 1284/18: LD-AR 1918 encl.; WPHC BSIP Series F34/4 Part II: Keegan to Sec. Gov. 14 Aug. 1939 encl.; Peter Plowman.

38. Some informants must remain confidential. Jack Campbell, 1976; Irlan Pope; Leslie Gill, 1977; Hogbin 1939, 47, 163, 164; Struben 1961, 69; Norden 1926, 118; Tommy Elkington, 1976; WPHC BSIP F34/4, Part II: Keegan to Sec. Gov. 14 Aug. 1939; see also WPHC 3156/38; 3159/38; 1752/39.

39. Beni Kai; John Tologhomba; Reo Dick; Matthew Mairotaha.

40. Joseph Odofia; Choranga; Alike Ghandokiki; WPHC 2352/25: Eyre Hutson to Sec. State 26 Oct. 1925 encl.; WPHC 1770/26: Gizo district, quarterly report 31 Mar. 1926 encl.; WPHC 2894/27: AR Gizo district 1926 encl.; WPHC 1443/28: Report of Constabulary, 1927 encl.

41. WPHC BSIP F34/11/7: Manager Levers to RC 20 Apr. 1938, and encls. For a description of piro and vele, see Bennett 1974, 10–12.

42. Jo Ariana; Jack Mainagwa; Joseph Afe'ou and elders of Igwa village.

43. Jotam Finou; also Stanley Maurione.

44. WPHC 801/14: LD-AR 1913, encl.; WPHC 698/15: LD-AR 1914; WPHC 875/16: LD-AR 1915; WPHC 701/17: LD-AR 1916; WPHC 1284/18: LD-AR 1917; WPHC 539/20: LD-AR 1919; WPHC 350/23: LD-AR 1921; WPHC 1554/23: LD-AR 1922; WPHC 1121/24: LD-AR 1923; Crichlow 1921. See also WPHC 2279/24.

45. WPHC 2329/25: Kidson to HC 14 Apr. 1926, and encls.; WPHC 1453/28: MD-AR 1927 encl. See also James 1956, 54, 65; WPHC 535/20: LD-AR 1919.

46. WPHC 2867/33: Hetherington to RC 8 Aug. 1933, and encls. WPHC 2122/36: SMO to Hetherington 9 Mar. 1940, and encls.; Vichi Chio; Charles Fox Ha'amouri; Stanley Maurione.

47. WPHC 698/15: LD-AR 1914 encl.; WPHC 1050/19: Bates to HC 14 Apr. 1919 encl.; WPHC 2491/20: Bates to RC 16 July 1920 encl.; WPHC 2491/20: LD-AR 1929 encl.; WPHC 809/30: LD-AR 1929 encl.

48. WPHC 1581/12: Woodford to Major 17 July 1912 encl.; WPHC 1890/12: Woodford to HC 9 Sept. 1912; WPHC 1143/13: Woodford to HC 10 May 1913,

and encls.; WPHC 3251/17: Barnett to HC 16 Feb. 1917, and encls.; WPHC 1121/24: LD-AR 1923 encl.

49. Phillips 1940, 53; WPHC 1554/23: LD-AR 1922 encl.; WPHC 1170/26: LD-AR 1925 encl.; WPHC 1426/29: LD-AR 1929 encl.; *PIM*, Aug. 1934, 17; *PIM*, Sept. 1946, 16. Usually, carbon tetrachloride or tetrachlorethylene was used for hookworm and neoarsphenamine injections for yaws (Lambert 1941, 142, 149, 244; BSIP-AR 1931; see also WPHC 1103/31: Wilson to Sec. Gov. 23 Jan. 1931). WPHC 639/29: Kidson to HC 8 Feb. 1929, and encls.; WPHC 827/30: Report of Labour Commission 1929; all male informants; WPHC 2907/31: Inquiry into the death of Franki Sorro Dec. 1930 encl.

50. WPHC BSIP F34/4, Part II: Keegan to Sec. Gov. 14 Aug. 1939; Timmy Lotufana; Mageli Leban; Jack Campbell; Samuel Ramohuni; Thomas Taʻaeʻke-ʻkerei; Timothy Tarorua; Kaspa Arabaeʻawa, Hari Taisubaurona; Daniel Tawariʻi; Rubin Siro; Morris Ohairangi; Leonard Haʻanimaraha; Stanley Maurione. See also John Bana; Alpons Mule Mangila, John Baptista Mauroi.

51. Leslie Gill, 1977. Tommy Elkington; John Kevisi; Sunauni.

52. WPHC 1064/33: Barley, Memo (n.d., c. Mar. 1933) encl.

53. M. Hirst; Leslie Gill; see also Hogbin 1939, 164.

54. WPHC 1284/18: LD-AR 1917.

55. All male informants; Vera Clift; Seton n.d.; *PIM*, 23 July 1935, 58; *PIM*, 24 Oct. 1935, 64; Timmy Lotufana.

56. No matter if priest, planter, or trader was involved, suicide, flight, deportation, or a ban on re-entry to the protectorate put an end to the activities of reputed European male homosexuals in the Solomons before the war. Only one European, F. E. Gilbert, was brought to trial in 1917, on his own insistence, and was sentenced to seven years' imprisonment in Suva (Tommy Elkington; Vera Clift; see, for example, WPHC files 336/98, 77/00, 12/02, 10/04, 121/08, 515/12, 2540/17, 2831/17, 1663/19; WPHC 2148/33: Barley to HC 10 Nov. 1933 encl.).

57. Tommy Elkington; Vera Clift; Timoti Fiʻfounia; Timmy Lotufana; Bese Ghaura; Boaz Bebeni. Except for one case in 1908 involving Edge-Partington and a "notorious female native of Simbo," resident commissioners ignored sexual relationships between officers and local women. J. C. Barley, for instance, was well-known for his involvements with Island women by whom he fathered several children (WPHC 836/08: Woodford to im Thurn 22 Dec. 1908, and encls.; Sandars 1928–1943). Justus Malalifu.

58. Bell 1936, 26–44. (See also WPHC 1426/29: LD-AR 1928 for native desertions at Lunga during the time Bell was overseer there.) Norden 1926, 30; Bese Ghaura; Tommy Elkington.

59. WPHC 2400/23: FT, 22 May 1923, encl.; WPHC 248/32: Barley to HC 10 Apr. 1933, and encls.; WPHC 4065/33: Minute by legal adviser 1933, and encls.; WPHC 226/34: Minutes of Trial 29 Nov. 1933, and encls. WPHC 1124/34: Report by legal adviser 25 Apr. 1934, and encls.; *PIM*, 21 Mar. 1935, 3–4; WPHC 4028/33: Meetings of AC Oct. 1933 encl.; WPHC 2722/34: Meeting of AC Oct. 1934, encls. Unlike the White Women's Protection Ordinance of 1926 in Papua, the new law in the Solomons covered offenses against Solomon Islands as well as European women (Inglis 1974, 71–88; King's Reg. No. 7 of 1934; see also WPHC 2722/34: Correction, Meeting of AC Oct. 1934).

60. Phillips 1940, 50–51.

61. John Bana.

62. WPHC 24779/19: Rodwell to SS 29 Oct. 1920, encls.; Timothy Ianitaro.

63. Mytinger 1942, 194, 211–212, 230; Tommy Elkington; Phillips 1940, 22, 50–51, 54; Hogbin 1939, 164; LPP n.d. *b*.

64. Smith 1967, 230.

65. Averages calculated from statistics in LD-AR 1913–1940; see WPHC files 801/14, 698/15, 875/16, 701/17, 1284/18, 535/20, 350/23, 1554/23, 1221/24, 1197/25, 1170/26, 1510/27, 1835/28, 1426/29, 809/30, 755/31, 1228/32, 506/33, 920/34, 1612/35, 1598/36, 2744/36, 1638/38, 2469/40, 2399/41. Malaita, Guadalcanal, and San Cristobal, by the 1931 census, had a combined population of 61,812 out of the Solomons total of 93,415 (WPHC 274/32: Census of SI 1931 encl.); see also Hogbin 1939, 222; Sandars 1928–1943.

66. Bennett 1974; Sayes 1976.

67. Tommy Elkington, 1976.

68. Erastus Eda'kwa'ou.

69. Jo Ariana; Seti Mato'feli; Salimauri; Simion Funasi'a; Jo Gonai'ilae; Sisto Alui; Brown Foufou. For place of birth and religion of informants see interviews, *passim*; Dickinson 1927, 179–202; Hogbin 1939, 173.

70. Robinson Wakii'a; Nelson Anuanuiabu; Louisa Hutairongo; Elders of Igwa village; Jack Kwalau; Phillips 1940, 58, 235.

71. See, for examples, Michael Mai'lee'a; Sosimo Sikulu; Erastus Eda-'kwa'ou.

72. The "steamer gang" came across the Indispensable Strait from Langalanga or Lau lagoon in their cutters, sailing through the Mboli Pass on Nggela to Makambo, where they would load the steamer. The steamer worked slowly westwards to Faisi, deposited the gang at the Shortland Islands Plantation Company's headquarters at Lofung, then crossed the border to do the New Guinea run. After calling at Rabaul it returned to Faisi, collected the men and, again visiting various plantations, made its way to Tulagi, where it left the men to return to Malaita while it sailed for Australia. At various times Faisi was the terminus for the steamer (James Petersen, 1975; G. Seton, 1976. For a description of a typical round trip on a Burns Philp steamer, see Cameron 1923, 267–311).

73. James Petersen, 1975; BPA: Report of Inspector, Makambo Branch, 31 Aug. 1922, Inspection Reports. The wage rate in the 1910s was 2 shillings a day. Burns Philp attempted to avoid paying this by using plantation recruits in transit to unload and load the steamer. The labor inspector, Bell, stopped the practice in 1913 (WPHC 1995/13: Bell to HC 28 Aug. 1913 encl.).

74. For labor trade activities, see Corris 1973, 32, 61, 64–66, 112–113. Besides the good wages, one of the early attractions of steamer employment was the possibility of getting smuggled arms and ammunition. Levers' *Kulumbangara*, not being registered in Australia, took its gang to Australia where some obtained firearms in 1913 (WPHC 17/13: Woodford to Edge-Partington, 17 Apr. 1913; WPHC 62/14: Edge-Partington to ARC 26 Sept. 1914; WPHC 2313/13: Woodford to HC 10 Nov. 1913).

75. Sandars 1928–1943.

76. Jack Mainagwa; Timoti Fi'founia; Joseph Odofia; Sisto Alui; K. G. Seton.

77. WPHC 1121/24: LD-AR 1923.

78. Ibid.; Informants; Sandars 1928–1943. See also Ross 1973, 55–56.

79. Vandercook 1937, 356–357.

80. See Chapter 9; BSIP Meeting AC Oct. 1953, 1954; Hirst, 1975 interview and TS; Boaz Bebeni.

81. WPHC F34/15: ADO to Sec. Gov. 8 Nov. 1938, encl.; Informants.
82. Hogbin 1964, 49.
83. Thomas; Beni Kai; Joseph Odofia; Samuel Ramohuni; Nelson Anuanuiabu; Bese Ghaura; Daisi Sauha'abu; Matthew Mairotaha; Thomas Ta'ae'ke'kerei; Kaspa Arabae'awa; John Bana. See also Hogbin 1964, 5–6.
84. Bennett 1979*b*; Keesing 1977.

Chapter 9: Producers and consumers

Meek, 1916 in Australian Parliamentary Papers 1919, 67.
Gann and Duignan 1969, 22.
  1. WPHC 2763/22: Bell to RC 9 Aug. 1922; WPHC 2352/25: HC to SecS 26
Oct. 1925; WPHC 1679/22: Kane to HC 10 May 1922; WPHC 1770/26: Gizo
district, quarterly report 31 Mar. 1926; WPHC 1422/29: AR Gizo district,
1928; WPHC 1290/30: AR Gizo district, 1929; WPHC 3051/23: Francis to RC
26 Feb. 1923; WPHC 2932/26: Filose to HC 10 Jan. 1926; WPHC 3349/26:
Kane to HC 27 Sept. 1926; Bennett 1974; Hendren 1976, 150, 157–159; Luvusia Willy, 1972.
  2. Metcalfe Diaries 9 May 1922, 9 Apr. 1923, 26 July, 30 Aug. 1925, (PMB
75); WPHC 1290/30: AR Gizo district, 1929; GC: Goldie to Sinclair, 6 Apr.
1932; PMB #925; Bennett 1974; Report of DO Eastern district, 1918 quoted in
Green 1976, 42–43; WPHC 2763/22: Bell to RC 9 Aug. 1922.
  3. Allan 1957, 42–43.
  4. GC: Goldie to Sinclair, 6 Apr. 1932; LTR: LCR Native Claims, 30–37, re
lands claimed by LPP, Item 16, 18/1.
  5. WPHC 1328/21: General Sec. to Rodwell 2 May 1921 and encls.; GC:
Goldie to Sinclair 7 Mar., 3 June 1922, 1 Mar., 6 May 1923; LTR: LCR Native
Claim 29, respecting land at Bagga Island claimed by Joseph Binskin, Item 14,
18/1; Allan 1957, 43.
  6. Captain G. G. Alexander began the commission in 1919, but his judg-
ments were heavily criticized (WPHC 532/20: Workman to Capt. Alexander 24
Jan. 1920; WPHC 779/29: Alexander to RC 26 Mar. 1920, and encls.; WPHC
904/20: Alexander to RC 9 Apr. 1920, and encls.; WPHC 1059/20: Alexander to
RC 19 Apr. 1920, and encls.; WPHC 1208/20: Alexander to RC 11 May 1920,
and encls.; WPHC 1999/20: LC, Summary of works done to 22 Sept. 1920, and
encls.; Allan 1957, 43. For a description of his work, see Alexander 1927, 252–
277; Allan 1957, 45–47.
  7. GC: Goldie to Sinclair 7 Mar., 3 June 1922, 1 Mar., 6 May 1923. See, for
example, LTR: LCR Native Claims nos. 30–37. The conflict between the
Methodists and the Seventh Day Adventists paralleled traditional divisions
between various "tribal" groups who were using the new law and religion, as is
often still the case today, to resolve old differences about marginal lands (LTR:
LCR Native Claim no. 25, Items 10, 18).
  8. GC: Goldie to Sinclair 1 Mar. 1923; Allan 1957, 36–50. For the question of
the validity of Crown title over waste lands, see Bennett 1979a, 214.
  9. WPHC 1716/12: Walsh to Woodford 14 June 1912; WPHC 2667/22: Bell
to RC 8 Aug. 1922; Herr and Rood 1978, 169, 172–173. See also and compare
Corris 1973, 141; Ivens 1930, 85–86, 269.
  10. WPHC 2600/23: Wilson to RC 20 Sept. 1923; Thomas.
  11. Corris 1973, 146; WPHC 3022/30: Hug to ADO 10 Mar. 1930; Bese
Ghaura.

12. WPHC 1233/16: Barnett to Eyre Hutson 14 Apr. 1916; WPHC 128/99: Woodford to Mayor 20 June 1904, and encls.; see also LTR: 192-009-1, no. 159/66, Tenavatu.

13. WPHC 1736/13: BSIP-AR 1912 encl.; Hilliard 1978, 101–102.

14. MMP: Goldie to Danks 22 Dec. 1909 and 28 Sept. 1910, Shackell to Danks 7 Nov. 1910; GC: Goldie to Sinclair 7 May, 7 Aug., 6 Oct. 1928; Metcalfe diaries 1 Sept. 1924, 10 Apr., 27 May, 1, 12 July 1925, 3 Sept. 1927, 2 Aug., 21 Nov. 1928, 20 Nov. 1929, (PMB 75).

15. WPHC 1184/25: Goldie's comments, Deputation to the HC of Representatives of Residents, 29 Sept. 1925; WPHC 1422/29: Gizo district report 1929; GC: Goldie to Sinclair 3 Dec. 1930, Goldie to RC 29 Dec. 1931.

16. Metcalfe Diary, 26 June 1921 (PMB 75).

17. Tutty n.d.

18. Hilliard 1978, 226; *SCL* 16 (185) 20 Oct. 1910, 18 (215) 2 June 1913, 12 (2) Apr. 1917.

19. WPHC 1184/25: Chaperlin's comments, Deputation to HC . . . , 29 Sept. 1925; Laracy 1976, 93–95, 97.

20. FRCP: Rigby to Fairleys 7 Feb. 1913.

21. WPHC 2015/13: Woodford to Sweet-Escott 21 Aug. 1913; Hilliard 1966, 375–379.

22. WPHC 267/22: Bell to RC 8 Aug. 1922, and encls.; WPHC 287/27: Bell to HC 11 June 1927; WPHC 888/27: Wilson to RC, 2 Apr. 1927, and encls. See Chapter 7, p. 162 and n. 60.

23. WPHC 2929a/20: Rodwell to Workman 3 Oct. 1920, and encls.

24. WPHC 2205/19: Workman to HC 21 Oct. 1919 encl.

25. UK-NID 1944, 188–192; GEIC-AR 1924–1926; 1927–1928; West 1968, 185–186.

26. WPHC 638/23: AC-AR 1922; WPHC 1117/24: Bell to RC 26 May 1924; WPHC 659/23: Bell to RC 29 Jan. 1923; Hopkins 1928, 224.

27. WPHC 2600/23: Wilson to RC 20 Sept. 1923.

28. WPHC 1707/32: Wright to RC n.d. 1931 encl.

29. Hogbin 1939, 168, fn.; Keesing and Corris 1980.

30. WPHC 937/25: Heffernan to RC 18 Mar. 1925; WPHC 2352/25: Kane to HC 12 Apr. 1926; WPHC 1184/25: Goldie, Deputation to HC . . . 25 Sept. 1925.

31. WPHC 1644/28: Hill to RC 24 Nov. 1928.

32. Bennett 1979a, 222, fn. See also BSIP-AR 1931.

33. GC: Goldie to Sinclair 4 July 1922. This was raised to £1 early in 1921, but was lowered to 12s. 6d. following a fall in copra prices (WPHC 122/21: McKerlie to HC 23 Feb. 1921; WPHC 3306/21: Manager of BP [SS] to HC 28 Nov. 1921; WPHC 185/23: Minutes of AC 8 Dec. 1922); WPHC 2205/19: Greene, Memo on Tax encl. Woodford to HC 28 July 1919; WPHC 122/21: King's Regs., no. 7 and no. 12 of 1911, McKerlie to HC 23 Feb. 1921, and encls.; WPHC 1855/17: Précis of correspondence, The Sale of Copra . . . ; WPHC 1562/17: Barley to HC 21 May 1917.

34. Minutes of Committee appointed to deal with the allocation of freight space in connection with the shipment of copra from Sydney, 14 June 1916, 9 Feb. 1917, copy in BPA; FRCP: Mumford to Fairleys 25 Sept., 2 Oct. 1918.

35. WPHC 2818/14: Barnett to HC 2 Nov. 1914; WPHC 241/18: Pugh to RC 7 Nov. 1917; FRCP: Mumford to Fairleys 26 Feb. 1917, 10 Jan., (?) Feb., 11 May 1918, 1 Jan. 1919.

36. WPHC 638/23: AC-AR 1922; WPHC 1679/22: Kane to HC 10 May 1922,

and encls.; see also WPHC 3251/17; BPA: BP (SS) IR Faisi, 2 Oct. 1922; WPHC 1290/30: AR Guadalcanal, Santa Isabel, Shortlands, Gizo district, Malaita, 1929 encls.; WPHC 1422/29: AR Nggela and Savo, 1929.

37. FRCP: Mumford to Fairleys Jan., 3 Oct. 1918, Apr. 1919.

38. WPHC 1184/25: Deputation to HC, 29 Sept. 1925.

39. WPHC 622/22: Kane to HC 9 May 1922, and encls.; WPHC 1647/23: Kane to HC 11 June 1923, and encls.; WPHC 3010/24: Fell to SecS (?) 20 Dec. 1924, and encls.; WPHC 2659/22: Kane to HC 16 Aug. 1922. This was further extended in BP's case to 1926 and again to 1931 (WPHC 1647/23; WPHC 2760/25: Amery to Hutson 3 Nov. 1925 encl.).

40. WPHC 3101/24: Fell to SecS (?) 20 Dec. 1924; WPHC 83/24: Thomas to HC 16 May 1924.

41. WPHC 2760/25: Amery to HC 3 Nov. 1925; WPHC 947/26: Amery to HC 13 Feb. 1926, and encls.; WPHC 1770/26: Gizo district quarterly report, 31 Mar. 1921; see also Hilliard 1978, 237.

42. WPHC 947/26: Amery to HC 13 Feb. 1926, and encls.

43. Tobacco, for the years 1920–1930, usually ranked as one of the most valuable imports into the Solomons, second only to rice. In 1922–1923, for example, the total revenue of the protectorate was £56,741. Of this copra export duty contributed £11,893, tobacco import duty £11,750 and native taxation (exclusive of dog tax, licenses for native hawkers, etc.), £7,516. With Solomon Islander production of copra at 25 percent of the whole at the time, Solomon Islanders paid indirectly £2,973 5s. 0d. in copra tax. In all then, the Solomon Islander contribution in direct and indirect taxation was £22,239 5s. 0d. or almost 40 percent of the government's revenue for 1922–1923. (*BSIP Blue Book for 1922–1923*; WPHC 2099/21.)

44. WPHC 2099/21: Barley to AHC 19 Nov. 1921; WPHC 1097/29: Davis, Auditor's Report 25 Mar. 1929 encl.; BPA: papers on SI; WRCP: papers on SI.

45. See LPP n.d.*b*, entries for 20 Aug., 12 Nov. 1923, 3 May, 7 June, 22 July, 1 Aug. 1924; FRCP: Mumford to Fairleys 26 Feb. 1917; WPHC 26/20: Knibbs to RC 14 July 1920, and encls.; WPHC 1561/23: Cost of living table; WPHC 1650/24: Knibbs, Cost of living 1920–1924, and encls.; BSIP-AR 1920–1930: Value of Main Exports and Imports to BSIP.

46. Corris 1973, 34; WPHC 32/14: RC to HC 11 Dec. 1914; WPHC 350/23: LD-AR 1921; WPHC 1554/23: LD-AR 1922; WPHC 1121/24: LD-AR 1923; WPHC 1197/25: LD-AR 1924; WPHC 827/30: Report of the Labour Commission in BSIP 1929, 99–100; UK-NID 1944, 138, 140; GEIC-AR, 1924–1926; WPHC 2352/25: HC to Kane 8 Sept. 1926 encl.

47. WPHC 4028/33: Meeting of AC Oct. 1933 encl. WPHC 2288/16: Barnett to HC 31 July 1916 encl.

48. WPA: Native Contracts Reg., Queen's Reg. no. 2 of 1896 encl. HC to SS 26 June 1896, in bound volume of despatches from HC to SecS, 1896–1897; FNA: Native Dealings Ordinance 1891, Ordinance no. XVIII of 1895, Rotuma Native Dealings Ordinance no. XIX of 1895, in bound volume of ordinances; WPHC 297/97: Woodford to Collet 3 May 1897; WPHC 305/97: Woodford to Berkeley 21 June 1897; WPHC 219/08: Woodford to Meek, and encls. 20 May 1908.

49. WPHC 1813/16: RC to HC 21 June 1916.

50. WPHC 2288/16: Barnett to HC 31 July 1916 encl.

51. WPHC 282/05: BSIP-AR 1905; WPHC 1734/13: BSIP-AR 1913.

52. WPHC 128/18: Holloson and Vider to HC 7 Sept. 1912; WPHC 2099/21: Barley to AHC 19 Nov. 1921; WPHC 1184/25: Kane to HC 3 Mar. 1926 encl.;

WPHC 2830/28: Moorhouse to HC 22 Sept. 1928; Leslie Gill, 1975; Herr and Rood 1978.

53. See, for example of European attitudes to Solomon Islanders, WPHC 4028/33: Meeting AC Oct. 1933 encl.

54. BPA: Gordon Report on Faisi estate 27 Aug. 1907, Lucas to Gordon 27 Aug. 1907, encl. IPI.

55. BPA: Report of Inspector 9 Nov. 1920, Gizo Branch, BP (SS) IR; Hopkins 1928, 247.

56. BPA: Managing Director to Gordon 25 July 1907, Gordon to Managing Director 28 Aug. 1907, IPI.

57. BPA: Gordon to Managing Director 28 Aug. 1907, Managing Director to Gordon 25 July 1907, IPI; Lucas Report on the SI 25 Nov. 1907.

58. BPA: Gordon to Managing Director 31 Aug. 1907.

59. BPA: Mitchell to Haycock 24 Apr. 1925, Makambo Branch, MAR.

60. WPHC 1991/13: Bell to RC 9 Sept. 1913 encl.; WPHC 1810/14: Harcourt to Sweet-Escott 10 June 1914; WPHC 3033/14; Bell to RC 11 Nov. 1914; BPA: Barnett to Burns 24 Nov. 1914 SIM-1; Lucas to Burns 5 June 1913; Shipping, SI Service, 1915; BP, General History, Pacific Personnel; Woodford 1909; Luvusia Willy.

61. WPHC 2402/28: Kwong Ying Cheon to HC 18 June 1928 encl.; WPHC 2047/18: Workman to HC 9 Aug. 1918; WPHC 702/17: List of Government lands on lease, 1917 encl. See also LTR: 181-003-6, no. 214/69 (181-003-10), Parcel Lot 101; 181-003-7, no. 330-70, Parcel Lot 102; 181-003-10, no. 214-69, Tulagi, LR 198 and LR 634 Remainder; Phillips 1940, 22.

62. WPHC 2905/20: Petition of British Residents, 1920, encl.

63. WPHC 281/11: Woodford to im Thurn 13 Feb. 1908 encl.; WPHC 1587/12: Woodford to Major 18 July 1912; WPHC 2047/18: Workman to HC 8 Aug. 1918; WPHC 2905/20: Workman to HC 25 Oct. 1920, and encls.; see also WPHC 2613/27: RC to HC 3 Oct. 1927; WPHC 1184/25: Kane to HC 6 May 1925, and encls.

64. WPHC 1538/16: Barnett to HC 11 May 1916, and encls.; BPA: Burns to Pope 9 Nov. 1920, Gizo Branch; BPA: Report of Inspector, 31 Aug. 1922, Burns to Kirkham, 24 Oct. 1922, 27 Apr. 1926, Makambo Branch BP (SS) IR; BPA: Report of Manager, 31 Jan. 1925, Makambo Branch, MAR; Moi'ea Pepechi; Jotam Finou; Anifanaia; Jorji Feleni'i; Timmy Lotufana; Joseph Odofia; Gilbert Suniaru; Boaz Bebeni; Hugo Kereruku; John Erei; Morris Ohairangi; Peter Eiatarogari; Tommy Elkington, 1976.

65. WRCP: Scrymgour to Carpenter 19 Feb., 4 May, and 29 July 1926; BPA: Report of Inspector, 31 Aug. 1922 Makambo Branch, BP (SS) IR.

66. WPHC 2905/20: Workman to HC 25 Oct. 1920.

67. WPHC 59/30: Barley to HC 13 Jan. 1931; WPHC 1184/25: Kane to HC 6 May 1925; WPHC 2564/26: Kane to HC 19 July 1926, and encls.; BPA: Report of Manager 13 Jan. 1928 Gizo Branch, MAR. Some of the European opposition to Akun's license stemmed from the belief that he was "dummying" for the German firm of Hernsheim. Akun had tried to obtain a mortgage over Risby's trading station at Savo. W. R. Carpenter feared the advent of the German firm because it would "flood the trade with cheap German goods" (WRCP: Scrymgour to Carpenter 7 Apr. 1927).

68. WPHC 1993/27: Bell to RC 12 June 1927; WPHC 243/24: Hill to HC 22 Dec. 1923, and encls.; WPHC 265/25: Kane to HC 9 Jan. 1925; WPHC 1197/25: Kane to HC 6 May 1925, and encls.; WPHC 3343/26: Kane to HC 23 Sept. 1926, and encls.

69. Akun did not take up the license for a store in the Shortlands, probably because of competition from trader-planters like Atkinson and Scott as well as BP's store at Faisi. Settlements were scattered and adequately served by shipborne Europeans and Chinese (BPA: Report of Inspector 2 Oct. 1922, Faisi Branch, IR; BPA: Report of Manager 14 Jan. 1928, Faisi Branch, MAR).

70. WPHC 3022/30: Hug to ADO 10 Mar. 1930; Thomas of Fulo; WPHC 294/27: Minutes of AC 9–13 Dec. 1926 encl.

71. WPHC 1184/25: Kane to HC 3 Mar. 1926 encl.

72. WPHC 2613/27: RC to HC 3 Oct. 1927 encl.

73. WRCP: Carpenter to Scrymgour 19 Aug. 1929.

74. BPA: Report of Inspector 27 Apr. 1926, Makambo Branch, IR.

75. WPHC 35/15: MD-AR 7 Dec. 1914; WPHC 730/28: Kane to HC 16 July 1928 encl. The first census in 1931 established the population at about 93,000 (Groenewegen 1972, 1–2).

76. CO 856/1: *BSIP Blue Book*, 1922 encl.; *BSIP Handbook . . . 1923*, 29; WPHC 3033/14: Bell to HC 11 Nov. 1914.

77. WPHC 1236/16: MD-AR 28 Feb. 1916.

78. WPHC 730/28: Kane to HC 16 July 1928 encl.; WPHC 2886/27: Crichlow to SMO 15 Aug. 1927; WPHC 287/27: Bell to HC 11 June 1927.

79. WPHC 185/23: Minutes of AC 8 Dec. 1922; BSIP Minutes of AC Oct. 1953 (1954); WPHC 1160/30: Ashley to HC 25 June 1930 encl.

80. WPHC 1160/30: Ashley to HC 25 June 1930 encl.; for details of the yaws and hookworm campaign, see Lambert 1942.

81. WPHC 2768/22: KR, no. 17 of 1922 encl.

82. In 1923 there were twenty-eight European government personnel, including the RC and two female nurses. Officers' salaries ranged from £250 to £500 per year (WPHC 1309/23: Kane to HC, Annual Confidential Reports, 1922–1923; *BSIP Handbook . . . 1923*, 63).

83. WPHC 2558/26: List of appointments for the year 1926–1927, under KR no. 17 of 1922; BSIP-AR 1927.

84. WPHC 2912/21: Kane to AHC 6 Oct. 1921, and encls.; WPHC 1448/22: Kane to HC 6 May 1922; Hilliard 1978, 237; WPHC 2290/22: Rodwell to RC 24 Aug. 1922, and encls.; WPHC 2768/22: KR no. 17 of 1922.

85. WPHC 849/24: Hill to RC 22 Feb. 1924.

86. WPHC 1160/30: Ashley to HC 25 June 1930; Moorhouse 1929; see also WPHC files 1039/28, 1795/28, 1802/28, 2288/28, 3623/28. For an account of the Bell incident see Keesing and Corris 1980.

87. WPHC 2831/28: HC to Amery 10 Oct. 1928.

88. WPHC 2558/26: List of Appointments for 1926–1927; WPHC 849/24: Kane to HC 22 Feb. 1924; Report on Guadalcanal district, 1929; WPHC 1290/30: Report on Gizo district, encls.; Moorhouse, 1927.

89. Moorhouse, 1927; BSIP-AR, 1920–1929.

90. UKPP, Colonial Development Bill, 1, 1929–1930.

91. WPHC 1103/31: Report on Guadalcanal district, 1930; WPHC 3698/36 (?): Meeting of AC Nov. 1934.

92. Hilliard 1978, 155, 180, 252n; Laracy 1976, 62.

93. GC: Goldie to Sinclair 7 May 1928.

94. Norden 1926, 42; Leslie Gill, 1975; BPA: Reports of Inspector 1920–1930, IR.

95. Bennett 1979a, 376–378; see also Norden 1926, 81.

96. WPHC 2894/27: AR Gizo district 1926; WPHC 1422/29: AR Gizo district 1928.

97. Goldie Correspondence.
98. Laracy 1976, 53–54; Hilliard 1978, 87–95.
99. Laracy 1976, 42, 48–49, 77–78; Hilliard 1978, 177–178, 180–181.
100. Woodford Papers, Footaboory and others to RC, 16 Oct. 1912 (see Appendix 8).
.101. Woodford Papers, Footaboory to RC, 17 Oct. 1912 (see Appendix 8).
102. WPHC 1690/22: Kane to HC 22 May 1922.

Chapter 10: Weathering the storm

Australian Parliamentary Papers 1919, 43.
Ashley in BSIP Meeting of AC 11 Nov. 1931 encl. WPHC 3698/[32].

1. Young 1968, 34–78, 321, 347–352, 450–455; Page 1975; Firth 1973; Australian Parliamentary Papers 1919.
2. Australian Parliamentary Papers 1919, 31–32, 73; Lever 1935; Lewis 1970, 232–234, 258, 300. Compare with *Vegetable Oils and Oilseeds* (1938): 67 (an annual publication of HMSO, London), which assessed the Solomons as higher contributor to world copra production. However, these figures do not include all producers, nor are they broken down according to copra grade.
3. WPHC 2535/26: Hedstrom to Sec. of WPHC, 31 Aug. 1926; WPHC 2674/26: Payne to SecS for Colonies 20 Aug. 1926.
4. QSA: Fairley Rigby and Co. Ltd., 30/1912 COR; NSWSA: Ullberg's Plantation Ltd. (Union Plantation and Trading Co.) COR 3/5789; see also NSWSA: Hamilton Choiseul Bay Co. Ltd., COR 3/5838.
5. Lewis 1952, 1.
6. CAO: Report on Pacific Islands Shipping Facilities 1926–27 Territories Branch Corresp. File, Multi-number series, Classes relating to External Territories, PI Mail Services 1927–30, CR 5 A518, item B112/2; WPHC 827/30: Report of Labour Commission 1929. Between 1923 and 1925 Levers planted 1002.5 acres at Linggatu, Russell Islands (Allied Forces . . . no. 47, Russell Islands 9 Feb. 1943, Map 7).
7. WPHC 1850/34: Ashley to HC 14 (?) May 1934; WPHC 1540/34: AR Gizo District 1933. The upper limit of £9 was the cost calculated when interest on capital was included along with direct production costs. (WPHC 2098/29: Seymour to SecS 30 Sept. 1929.)
8. WPHC 1850/34: Ashley to HC 14 (?) May 1934. The Solomon Islands Planters and Settlers Association estimated costs accordingly: Wages £24, Hospital £5, Recruiting fees £12, Rations & clothing £32 7s., Cost of passage to plantation £2, Ratification of contract 1s. 6d., Repatriation £3 10s., Tax, 1 year 7s. 6d. (WPHC 2637/30: Timms to RC 14 July 1930).
9. WPHC 2467/36: Meeting of AC Oct. 1936; Gill, letter in *Papuan Courier* 23 Oct. 1923 (reference kindly provided by D. C. Lewis); KR 15 of 1921, Section 43; see also WPHC 2902/20: RC to HC 19 Oct. 1920.
10. WPHC 3496/30: Knibbs, Cancelled Crown and Native Leases 13 Feb. 1932; WPHC 1081/31: Ashley to HC 10 Mar. 1931, and encls.
11. WPHC 1228/32: Ashley to HC 16 Mar. 1932; WPHC 72/33: Barley to HC 14 Dec. 1932; WPHC 755/31: Ashley to HC 16 Feb. 1931 encl.; WPHC 1214/31: AR Gizo district 1931; WPHC 1522/32: AR Gizo district 1932; WPHC 1589/35: AR Gizo district 1934.
12. In the 1920s a community or family settlement scheme had been considered as a possible solution to the perennial labor shortage. Under this scheme time-expired laborers and their families were allocated an uncultivated portion

of a plantation estate in return for a fixed number of days' paid labor a week for the planter. Clift and Clift Ltd. tried the scheme in 1925, but it was not a success. With its abundance of land the Solomon Islands Protectorate was never a suitable place to develop a *metayage* system, although the idea was revived periodically, even as late as 1939. (WPHC 1184/25: Deputation to HC of Representatives of Residents 29 Sept. 1925; WPHC 827/30: Report of the Labour Commission 1929; WPHC 1752/33: Replacement of Recruiting n.d. encl.; WPHC BSIP 21/11: Seton to DO 28 Dec. 1939 encl.

13. WPHC 1290/30: AR Gizo district 1929; WPHC 1228/32: Ashley to HC 16 Mar. 1932; WPHC 2381/32: Ashley to HC 14 June 1932; WPHC 2222/31: Quarterly Report Gizo district 30 June 1931; see also WPHC 1522/33: AR Guadalcanal 1932; WPHC 3267/34: Notes of a discussion between Middenway and the Sec. of the WPHC 23–24 Oct. 1934.

14. WPHC 1359/34: District Diary Eastern Solomons Nov. 1933; WPHC 1540/34: AR Gizo district 1933.

15. WPHC 293/25: Acting Chairman to Sec. HC 22 Jan. 1925 encl.; WPHC 1589/35: AR Gizo district 1934; BPA: SIDC Minute Book.

16. WPHC 1589/35: AR Malaita 1934.

17. WPHC 1589/35: AR Gizo district 1934.

18. WPHC 1589/35: AR Shortlands district 1934; WPHC 1589/35: AR Eastern District 1934.

19. WPHC 1920/30: AR Shortlands district 1929; WRCP: Scrymgour to Carpenter 19 July 1930; WPHC 1771/32: DO to SecS to Government 8 Dec. 1931, and encls.

20. WPHC 3269/30: Meeting of AC Oct. 1930; WPHC 3698/[36]: Meeting . . . Nov. 1931; WPHC 4028/33: Meeting . . . Oct. 1933.

21. WPHC 2722/34: Meeting of AC Oct. 1933 encl.; BSIP-AR 1931.

22. WPHC 3461/33: Minutes of Proceedings 8 Mar. 1934.

23. WPHC 2722/34: Meeting of AC Oct. 1934.

24. WPHC 3296/30: Meeting of AC Oct. 1930 encl.; WPHC 2722/34: Meeting . . . Nov. 1931 encl.

25. WPHC 2722/34: Meeting of AC Oct. 1934 encl.

26. WPHC 3496/30: Knibbs to Sec. of Gov. 13 Feb. 1932 encl.

27. WPHC 1081/31: Ashley to HC 14 Feb. 1935 encl.

28. WPHC 1081/31: Macdonald to Fletcher 22 Aug. 1935, and encls.

29. Collinson 1926, 78, 216–217; WPHC 3296/30: Meeting of AC Oct. 1930 encl.; WPHC 3698/[36]: Meeting of AC Nov. 1931 encl.; WPHC 4028/33: Meeting . . . Oct. 1933 encl. Norman Wheatley, for example, owed Carpenter's over £6,000 in 1924. He was forced to sell them land at Marovo Lagoon, Roviana, Rendova and northwest Santa Isabel to clear the debt (LTR: 100-002-1, LR 36, Hamarai).

30. W. R. Carpenter's bought out lands held by Morris Hedstrom, a major merchant company in Fiji (LTR: 181-003-1A [4–16], No. 214/69 and Part III, LR 298 and LR 634, Tulagi, Lots 27–29; 192-009-1, No. 159/66, Tenavatu); *PIM*, 24 Aug. 1934, 23; *PIM*, 21 Sept. 1934, 60.

31. LTR: 079-007-4, LR 213, Emu Harbour, Ranongga; 098-001-1, LR 28, Nusa Sivi Island; 098-006-2 (Title deduction under LTO Part III); 100-002-1, LR 36, Hamarai Plantation, Roviana; 120-003-1, LR, Kolohite Island; 120-006-1, LR 64, Bara Kai; 121-001-1, Lots 1 & 2 and the remainder of Lot 5, LR 57, LR 476, LR 477; 122-001-5, LR 270, Tombe, Viru Harbour; 141-002-2 to 141-002-59, LR 313, Hazoari and Ruvirai; 143-006-1, LR 37, Nggatirana (Gatera), New Georgia; 237-001-1, LR 218, Boroni, San Cristobal; 237-004-1,

LR 287, Ma'ahi; 252-001-4, LR 409, Ngona Ngona; 252-009-1 (Title deduction under LTO part III); 070-001-1, LR 38, Wohinarah or Gill Island; 671-002-1 and 071-003-1, LR 23 (1), Papatura Island and Suavanau, north Santa Isabel; 072-001-1 LR Papatura, Hite and Sasakatura Island; 089-001-3, LR 211, Ghehe and James Island, Estrella Bay; 089-001-4, LR 309/1 Kesero Cove, Estrella Bay; 089-001-5, Lot 1, of LR 272/1, Sikali, Lot 2 of LR 272/1, Legha-hana Island and Lot 3 of LR 272/1, Bane Island, San Cristobal; 089-002-4, LR 232, Sakalina, Estrella Bay; 089-002-5, LR 33, Kahinge, Santa Isabel, 108-002-2, LR 277, Holokama (Guguha); 108-003-1, LR 396, Fera Island, Maringe Lagoon; 190-003-1, LR 275, Tenamba, Guadalcanal; 190-004-1, LR 244, Taievo; 191-005-1, LR 282, Tanakomba and LR 207, Ruanu'u.

32. Tommy Elkington, 1976; James Petersen, 1975.

33. Phillips 1940, 55; Tommy Elkington, 1976; BPA: Reports of Inspector 1 Dec. 1933, 26 Apr. 1937, 7 June 1939, Makambo Branch, IR.

34. WPHC 1214/32: AR Gizo district 1931; see also WPHC 1850/34: Ashley to HC 26 Nov. 1934, and encls., re-filed under WPHC BSIP Series F33/6/1.

35. Vanikolo, where there were no commercial plantations, was a special case and at least one trader prospered there. The island had regular links with Australia and New Zealand because kauri timber was exported from Vanikolo by the Vanikolo Timber Company (WPHC 1290/30: AR Santa Cruz, 1929 encl.; WPHC 1214/32: AR . . . 1931; WPHC 1522/33: AR . . . 1932; WPHC 1359/34: AR . . . 1933; WPHC 1052/36: AR . . . 1935; WPHC 1881/37: AR . . . 1936; WPHC 1634/38: AR . . . 1937.

36. WPHC 222/31: Quarterly report Gizo district 30 June 1931; Leslie Gill, 1975. Both Green and Gill always dealt with Islanders on a strictly cash basis (Leslie Gill).

37. WPHC 954/34: RC's notes 19 Mar. 1934.

38. *PIM*, 19 Dec. 1934, 38–39; *PIM*, 24 Jan. 1935, 47–48; *PIM*, 24 Jan. 1936, 34; *PIM*, 22 Jan. 1937, 72.

39. WPHC 59/31: ARC to HC 13 Jan. 1933, and encls.; WPHC 954/34: HC to RC 4 July 1934 encl. The new high commissioner, Sir Murchison Fletcher, formerly in service in Hong Kong, was pro-Chinese (Laracy 1974, 33–34).

40. WPHC 1522/33: AR Gizo district 1932; WPHC 1540/34: AR . . . 1933; WPHC 1589/35: AR . . . 1934; WPHC 1589/34: AR Santa Isabel, 1934; BSIP-AR 1931 and 1933; WPHC BSIP F33/6/1: Ashley, Report on the Position of the Copra Industry in the SI 14 (?) May 1934 encl.; see, for effects of Depression on Europeans, Sandars 1928–1943, and *PIM*, 21 Sept. 1934, 31.

41. An attempt has been made to calculate Levers' Solomons profits from 1911 to 1942, but the basic statistics are lacking (Fieldhouse 1978, 468, 492). BPA: SIDC Minute Book; *PIM:* 18 Dec. 1931, 21; 19 Oct. 1932, 43; 24 Apr. 1933, 24; 22 Aug. 1933, 20; 22 Jan. 1934, 28; 22 June 1934, 34; 21 Sept. 1934, 60; 22 Aug. 1935, 4; 24 Oct. 1935, 11; 19 Aug. 1936, 74; 23 Apr. 1937, 75; 25 Aug. 1937, 73; 22 Apr. 1938, 82; 14 Oct. 1939, 26; 14 Sept. 1940, 42.

42. BPA: SIDC Minute Books 1925–1956.

43. WPHC 1758/30: Ashley to HC 19 May 1930, and encls.; WPHC 827/30: Report of the Labour Commission 1929.

44. WPHC 1522/33: AR Santa Isabel and Russell Islands 1932. When wages were halved in 1934, the "bonus" was likewise reduced to 1½d. for every additional 28 lb. (WPHC 1587/35: AR Santa Isabel, 1934). By 1940 this rate was down to three farthings (¾d.) for 28 lb. (WPHC 2399/41: LD-AR 1940 encl.).

45. See, for example, Seton n.d.

46. Vera Clift, 1975; see also WRCP: Scrymgour to Carpenter 14 Jan. 1927.
47. BPA: SIDC Minute Books 1925–1956.
48. Seton n.d.; WPHC 3461/33: Clift to HC 6 Nov. 1933 encl.; WPHC 3698/36: Meeting of AC Nov. 1931, encl. Compare with Bathgate 1975, 75.
49. Levers n.d. *a.*
50. Lever Bros.: Meek to Leverhulme 19 Mar. 1923, and Leverhulme to Meek 18 Sept. 1923; WPHC 2034/34: Kidson to HC 23 July 1924.
51. WPHC 1605/37: Hewitt to HC 10 May 1937 encl.; WPHC 3296/30: Meeting of AC Oct. 1930 encl.; WPHC 3215/38: Meeting of AC Nov. 1938 encl. In 1928 Levers formed a new company, Levers Pacific Plantations Proprietary Limited, registered in Sydney to replace Levers Pacific Plantations (1902, British registry), and included a new subsidiary with holdings in Papua, the Commonwealth Copra Company Proprietary Limited. The audited assets of the new company were valued at £712,423 (Levers n.d. *a;* LTR: 121-004-0, LR 65, LR 66, LR 67, LR 68).
52. Fieldhouse 1978, 472.
53. GC: Goldie to Scrivin 23 July 1934; *PIM,* 25 Jan. 1933, 6; *PIM,* 20 Feb. 1934, 3; *PIM,* 21 Feb. 1935, 43; Brookfield 1972, 78.
54. WPHC 1188/32: The History of Nutfall from 1911 to Oct. 1935, 15 Sept. 1936, encl.; WPHC 1103/31: AR Guadalcanal 1930; WPHC 3698/[36]: Meeting of AC Nov. 1931; WPHC 1052/36: AR Santa Isabel 1935 encl.; Stapley 1971; Leach 1948.
55. WPHC 1734/13: BSIP-AR 1913 encl.; WPHC 3726/31: RC, Report of a Tour 30 Dec. 1929; GC: Goldie to Scrivin 15 Oct. 1934.
56. WPHC BSIP F33/6/1 (formerly 1880/34): Ashley to HC 26 Nov. 1934, and encls.; BSIP-AR 1934.
57. M. Hirst, 1975; *PIM,* 22 Nov. 1934, 48; WPHC 3726/31: RC, Report of a Tour 30 Dec. 1929.
58. WPHC 4028/33: Meeting of AC Oct. 1933 encl.; WPHC BSIP F33/6/1: Ashley to HC 26 Nov. 1934, and encls.; see also WPHC BSIP F1/1: Meeting of AC Nov. 1941.
59. WPHC 665/31: HC to Sec. of S. Nov. 1931, and encls.; BPA: Report of Inspector 1 Dec. 1933 Makambo Branch; BPA: 22 Apr. 1932, 14 Dec. 1933, Gizo Branch IR; *PIM,* 21 Feb. 1935, 27; see also Phillips 1940, 60.
60. Vera Clift, 1975; WPHC 3602/32: Mitchell to MacKenzie 18 Nov. 1932, and encls.; WPHC 3490/33: Burns to HC 16 Oct. 1933, and encls.; BSIP-AR 1932; WPHC 3461/33: Meek, Turnbull, and Wood to HC 20 Feb. 1934, and encls.
61. BPA: Report of Inspector Makambo Branch 26 Apr. 1937, 7 June 1939; Gizo Branch 30 Apr. 1937, 7 July 1939, IR; Report of Manager, Gizo Branch 13 Jan. 1928, 16 Feb. 1933, 15 Feb. 1934, 28 Jan. 1936, 22 Jan. 1939; Makambo Branch 11 Jan. 1930, 6 Feb. 1934, 31 Jan. 1936, 12 Feb. 1937, 10 Feb. 1938, 31 Jan. 1939, 3 Feb. 1940; Faisi Branch 10 Feb. 1935, MR.
62. WPHC 1052/36: AR Gizo district 1935; BPA: Report of Manager, Gizo Branch 15 Feb. 1937, MR.
63. WPHC 1851/37: AR Gizo district 1936.
64. John Bana; WPHC 1634/38: AR Shortland district 1937; WPHC 2199/40: AR . . . 1939; WPHC 1779/39: AR Santa Isabel 1938; WPHC 1634/38: AR Malaita district 1937, encl.
65. WPHC BSIP F33/6/1: Ashley, Report on the Copra Industry in the SI, 14 (?) May 1934.

66. Ibid.

67. WPHC 1277/35: Meeting of AC May 1935; WPHC 2467/36: Meeting . . . Oct. 1936.

68. BSIP-AR, 1934–1937; WPHC 3116/37: Ormsby-Gore to HC 15 Mar. 1937 encl.; WPHC 1277/35: Meeting of AC May 1935 encl.; WPHC 3116/37: Ashley to HC 12 July 1938 encl.

69. WPHC 1634/38: AR Gizo district; WPHC 397/38: Meeting of AC Apr. 1938 encl.

70. WPHC 3526/26: RC to HC 7 Mar. 1940; WPHC 2199/40: AR Gizo district 1940; WPHC BSIP CF 33/6, vol. 1: SecS to Gov. of Fiji 1 June 1940, 13 July 1940, encls.

71. WPHC 2578/37: Meeting of AC Oct. 1937, encl.; WPHC 3154/38: RC to HC 13 Sept. 1941, and encls.

72. WPHC 2578/37: Meeting of AC Oct. 1937 encl.; see also WPHC BSIP CF 33/6, vol. 1: RC to HC 14 Sept. 1940, encl.

73. These were W. Francis, F. M. Campbell, C. Younger, Mrs. Edith Gaskell, J. Oien (estate), Mrs. Clara Scott, H. Markham, F. Hickie, M. Harper, H. Kuper, A. Musgrave, Mrs. E. Cruickshank, C. R. M. Gorringe, R. C. Laycock, H. R. Sim, Ruravai Syndicate (L. Gill), H. Corry, M. Monckton, H. Beck, W. Atkinson, L. Austen, J. Svensen, A. Cant, J. H. Macdonald, M. Olsen, G. Clift (estate), and J. Klaucke (WPHC 3154/38: List of leases with rentals remitted 1941 encl.).

74. In 1941, there were approximately 63,103 acres under Crown leases, including mission properties and over 11,000 acres of Levers in the Russell Islands. Excluding the missions' and Levers' holdings there were about 49,000 acres leased to planters and traders. Traders' holdings were relatively insignificant, amounting to less than 100 acres (WPHC 3386/27: List of lands Mar. 1927 encl. Quarterly returns of leases: WPHC 1436/28: 1928, WPHC 1122/29: 1929, WPHC 3308/30: 1930, WPHC 1491/33: 1933, WPHC 1358/34: 1934, WPHC F48/4: 1936, 1937–1941, and encls.; WPHC 3496/30: Ashley to HC 15 Apr. 1932, and encls.; WPHC 3496/30: Knibbs to Sec. of Gov., 13 Feb. 1932 encl.; WPHC 3154/38: List of Native and Crown leases on which rentals were remitted 13 Sept. 1941 encl.; WPHC 1894/33: Ashley to HC 19 May 1933).

75. WPHC 3154/38: Marchant to HC 13 Sept. 1941, and encls.

76. WPHC 3116/37: Reports of Mamara Plantations Ltd. and SI Rubber Plantations, 31 July 1939 encls.; WPHC BSIP Series CR 33/6, vol. 1: Svensen to HC 1 Aug. 1940 encl.

77. WPHC 2467/36: Meeting of AC Oct. 1936 encl.

78. WPHC 1486/41: AR Shortlands district 1940 encl.; K. G. Seton, 1978; BPA: War Damage Claims; LTR: 190-004-1 to 190-005-2; WPHC 2399/41: LD-AR 1940 encl.

79. WPHC 1634/38: AR Shortlands district 1937 encl.; WPHC 1779/39: AR . . . 1938; WPHC 1486/41; AR . . . 1940 encl.; WPHC 2199/40: AR Gizo district 1940 encl.; WPHC 2399/41: LD-AR 1940 encl.; WPHC BSIP series CF 33/6, vol. 1: Marchant to Luke 5 Aug. 1940 encl.; BPA: Minutes of the SIDC; K. G. Seton, 1975.

80. WPHC BSIP 2/5/1(?): Trench to Sec. of Gov. 6 Sept. 1940.

81. WPHC BSIP CF 82/3: Vaskess 1943 encl.

82. WPHC 1015/35: Allan to Ashley 6 Aug. 1935, and encls.

83. WRCP: Carpenter to Scrymgour 19 Aug. 1929.

84. WPHC 3698/[36]: Meeting of AC Nov. 1931 encl.

85. WPHC 1015/35: Allan to Ashley 6 Aug. 1935, and encls.
86. Had the revenue of the protectorate fallen off proportionately to the poverty of the small planter, perhaps the government, through sheer desperation, might have been pushed to more radical remedies. As it was, from 1935 on, the Solomons obtained thousands of pounds in windfall revenue from selling postage stamps to philatelists. In 1937–1938, the protectorate earned £10,760 or one-eighth of its income from stamp sales (WPHC 397/38: Meeting of AC Apr. 1938).
87. WPHC 1160/30: Ashley to HC 25 June 1930 encl.
88. WPHC 1605/37: Ashley to HC 12 Aug. 1937 encl.
89. Ibid.
90. WPHC 1605/37: Richards to Sec. of S. 18 May 1937 encl.
91. WPHC 1605/37: Ormsby-Gore to HC 3 Dec. 1937.
92. WPHC 1605/37: Hewitt to Sec. to HC 12 Feb. 1940, and encls.; see also Phillips 1940, 63–66.
93. WPHC BSIP CF 33/6, vol. 1: Marchant to HC 30 Mar. 1940.
94. WPHC BSIP Series CF 33/6, vol. 2: Information re copra, [Dec. 1940] encl.
95. Roberts 1964, 182–189.
96. UKPP: Statement of Policy on Colonial Development and Welfare, *Commons Papers* 10, 1939–1940.
97. Groves 1940, 1–2; *PIM*, Jan. 1941, 14, 40–41.

Chapter 11: A rumor of utopia

WPHC 2811/39: Pidoke, June 1939, encl.
1. WPHC 1214/32: AR Gizo district 1931 encl.; WPHC 1522/33: AR Gizo district 1932 encl.; WPHC 1540/34: AR Gizo district, 1933 encl.; WPHC 1103/31: AR Guadalcanal district 1930, encl.; WPHC 1522/33: AR Guadalcanal district 1932, encl.; WPHC 1522/33: AR Nggela and Savo district 1932 encl.; WPHC BSIP Series F46/40: Bartlett to RC 2 Aug. 1934, encl.
2. WPHC 2222/31: Quarterly report, Gizo district 30 June 1931.
3. *PIM*, 15 Mar. 1932, 25.
4. WPHC 1540/34: AR Gizo district 1933 encl.
5. WPHC 1589/35: AR Shortlands 1934 encl.; WPHC 1522/33: AR Guadalcanal 1932; WPHC 1214/32: AR Nggela and Savo 1931 encl.
6. Willy Paia pers. com., 1979; GC: Goldie to Sinclair 20 Nov. 1930, Goldie to Scrivin 29 Nov. 1938, Goldie to Scrivin 21 June 1939.
7. WPHC 1522/33: AR Gizo district 1932, encl.
8. BPA: Report of Inspector Gizo Branch 22 Apr. 1932 IR; WPHC 1522/33: AR Gizo district 1932 encl.; Metcalfe Diary, 9 Apr. 1933 (PMB 76); WPHC 2722/34: Minutes of the AC Oct. 1934 encl.; *PIM*, 25 Jan. 1932, 29; GC: Goldie to Sinclair 23 Aug. 1932.
9. WPHC 1540/34: AR Gizo district 1933 encl.
10. WPHC 1214/32: AR Gizo district 1931, encl.; WPHC 1522/33: AR . . . 1932 encl.; WPHC 1540/34: AR . . . 1933 encl.; WPHC 1522/33: AR Guadalcanal 1932 encl.; WPHC 1522/33: AR Nggela and Savo 1932 encl.; WPHC 1522/33: AR Santa Isabel district 1932 encl.; WPHC 1540/34: AR . . . 1933 encl.; WPHC 1589/35: AR Shortlands 1934 encl.; BPA: Report of Manager Makambo Branch 31 Jan. 1936 MR.
11. WPHC 1542/34: AR Gizo district 1933 encl.

12. WPHC 643/35; Bankruptcy of Sydney Marks encl.; WPHC 1052/36: AR Gizo district 1935 encl.; WPHC 1522/33: AR Gizo district 1932 encl.

13. WPHC 1851/37: AR Gizo district 1936 encl.

14. WPHC 1589/35: AR Gizo district 1934 encl.; WPHC 1052/36: AR . . . encl.; WPHC 1851/37: AR . . . 1936 encl.

15. WPHC 1540/34: AR Gizo district 1933 encl.; WPHC 1589/35: AR . . . 1934 encl.; WPHC 1587/35: Quarterly Report Gizo district Dec. 1936 encl.

16. BSIP-AR 1928.

17. WPHC 1540/34: AR Gizo district 1933 encl.; BSIP-AR 1933; WPHC 274/32: Census of the SI 1931.

18. WPHC 1540/34: AR Gizo district 1933 encl.; Metcalfe Diary 20 Nov. 1929.

19. WPHC 3808/33: Goldie to Vaskess 22 June 1935 encl.

20. Hilliard 1974, 110–111.

21. GC: Vella Lavella Circuit Report 1934.

22. WPHC 1290/30: AR Gizo district 1929 encl.; WPHC 2593/31: Ability of Natives to pay tax 1937 encl.; WPHC 2397/31: Ashley to HC 13 July 1931; WPHC 1540/34: AR Gizo district 1933 encl.

23. WPHC 1876/33: Native Passes Reg. Nov. 1933 encl.; WPHC 3808/33: Goldie to RC 20 Sept. 1933 encl.

24. WPHC 2593/31: Ability of Natives to pay tax 1937 encl.

25. WPHC 1359/34: AR Gizo district 1933 encl.

26. WPHC 1589/35: AR Gizo district 1934, encl.; GC: Goldie to Scrivin 22 Nov. 1934, Goldie to Scrivin 1 Aug. 1945; WPHC 3808/33: Goldie to Vaskess 22 June 1935, and encls. See also Metcalfe Papers: extracts from *Missionary Review* 1902–1918.

27. WPHC 1589/35: AR Gizo district 1934, encl.; *PIM*, 21 Feb. 1935, 25; Willy Paia, 1979; GC: Goldie to Scrivin 22 Nov. 1935. Ashley in 1931 was prepared to take a harder line on tax than his predecessor and revoked Kane's district-wide exemptions. There is evidence to show that Ashley, following a survey of the economy in 1932, recommended general tax reduction in certain areas. The high commissioner, Murchison Fletcher, stated that, instead, the district officers should be given discretionary authority to defer, reduce, or remit tax. The onus was shifted from the government to the Solomon Islander to prove a case for reduction or exemption. This was not made clear to all the people in every district. In the Gizo district Middenway exercised his "discretionary powers" in 1933 in two cases only, allowing a reduction from £1 to 15 shillings "on account of sickness" (WPHC 3698/32: Meeting of AC, Nov. 1931 encl.; WPHC 2593/31: Ability of Natives to pay tax 1937 encl.; WPHC 1540/34: AR Gizo district 1933 encl.).

28. WPHC 1587/35: District Diary Gizo, Dec. 1934 encl.; WPHC 1589/35: AR Gizo district 1934 encl.; WPHC 1052/36: AR . . . 1935 encl.; WPHC 3808/33: Goldie to Vaskess 22 June 1935; WPHC 2593/31: Ashley to HC 1 Dec. 1934 encl.; GC: Goldie to Scrivin 19 Feb. 1935; *PIM*, 21 Feb. 1935, 25, and 17 Apr. 1935, iii.

29. WPHC 1851/37: AR Gizo district 1936 encl.

30. WPHC 1779/39: AR Gizo district 1938 encl.

31. WPHC 1540/34: AR Gizo district 1933 encl.; WPHC 1634/38: AR . . . 1937 encl.; WPHC 2195/40: AR . . . 1939, encl.; WPHC 1486/41(?): AR . . . 1941 encl.

32. Groves 1940, 12. Cf. Harwood 1978, 242.

33. Mikelo Ebinuwi; John Bana; Silverio Ilaha; Luka; Katherine Mangila;

Alpons Mule Mangila; John Henry Macdonald; Bernard Pilow; Joseph Nikolas; Teresia Tapasi; Timothy Sikori; Andrew Kimisi; John Marehasi; Jeremiah Makila; Paul Kaputuku; Nathaniel Misu; John Baptista Mauroi; Joseph Normani; Jacob Piopio; John Bitiai; Maekel Meibo Tanutanu; Joseph Maike; Chief of Koliae; Bariri; notes of discussion with Remesio Eresi, 1976; WPHC 2351/17: Barnett to (?), 16 Feb. 1917 encl.; WPHC 1522/33: AR Shortlands Islands district 1932 encl.; WPHC 1540/34: AR . . . 1933 encl.; WPHC 1589/35: AR . . . 1934 encl.; WPHC 1634/38: AR . . . 1933 encl.; WPHC 1779/39: AR . . . 1938 encl.; WPHC 2195/40: AR . . . 1939 encl.; WPHC 1486/41: AR . . . 1940 encl.; K. G. Seton, pers. com., 1976 and 1978.

34. BPA: Campbell to Manager, BP, 8 Jan. 1930 encl. ShIPC Corres.

35. WPHC 274/32: Census of SI 1931; WPHC 426/21: Heffernan to ARC 14 Feb. 1921; WPHC 927/25: Heffernan to RC 18 Mar. 1925; R. Fallowes, pers. com., 1978.

36. Fallowes Diary 15 Jan. 1932.

37. WPHC 927/25: Heffernan to RC 18 Mar. 1925; WPHC 1589/35: AR Gizo district 1934 encl.

38. WPHC 2892/31: Ashley to HC 12 Aug. 1931, and encls.; WPHC 99/33: Trading by Natives in the BSIP, 25 May 1937 encl.

39. WPHC 1214/32: AR Gizo district 1931 encl.

40. WPHC 3698/32: Meeting of AC Nov. 1931 encl.; WPHC 1277/35: . . . May 1935 encl.

41. WPHC 1851/37: AR Santa Isabel district 1936 encl.

42. WPHC 1052/36: AR Santa Isabel district 1935 encl.

43. KR no. 6 of 1916 provided, among other things, that "a hawker's licence shall not entitle a licensee to sell goods in or upon any premises or building but only from a cart or boat or from a pack or basket carried by him" (WPHC 4028/33: Meeting of AC Oct. 1933 encl.).

44. WPHC 1052/36: AR Santa Isabel district 1935 encl.

45. WPHC 2214/32: AR Santa Isabel district 1931 encl.; WPHC 1522/33: AR . . . 1932 encl.; WPHC 1540/34: AR . . . 1933 encl.; WPHC 1589/35: AR . . . 1934 encl.; WPHC 1851/37: AR . . . 1935 encl.; WPHC 615/30: DO to RC 8 May 1935 encl.

46. WPHC 1290/30: AR Nggela and Savo district 1929 encl.; WPHC 1214/32: AR . . . 1931 encl.; WPHC 1522/33: AR . . . 1932 encl.; WPHC 1540/34: AR . . . 1933 encl.; WPHC 1589/35: AR . . . 1934 encl.; WPHC 1052/36: AR . . . 1935 encl.; WPHC 1851/37: AR . . . 1936 encl.; WPHC 3698/32: Meeting of the AC Nov. 1932 encl.

47. WPHC 1589/35: AR Shortlands district 1935 encl.; WPHC 1634/38: AR . . . 1937 encl.; BPA: Report of Inspector Gizo Branch, 7 July 1939, IR.

48. Leslie Gill, 1975.

49. McKinnon 1972, 138–140; Hilliard 1966, 263–266, 312–340; Harwood 1971, 32, 37–38; LTR: 063-001-1 application for first registration no. 83/66, Lot 2 of LR I, Mundi Mundi; 063-003-1, Application for first registration, no. 3/1/72, Parcel Description Lot 3, LR I; Metcalfe Diary 6 Aug. 1920; GC: Goldie to Sinclair 22 Aug. 1923, 16 Nov. 1923, 6 Apr. 1932; GC: Goldie to Scrivin 20 Nov. 1933.

50. GC: Goldie, Roviana Circuit Report for 1937.

51. WPHC 1540/34: AR Gizo district 1933 encl.; WPHC 2195/40: AR . . . 1939 encl.

52. Metcalfe Diary 7 Oct. 1936; WPHC 1522/33: AR Gizo district 1932, encl.; WPHC 1540/34: AR . . . 1933 encl.; WPHC 1540/34: AR Santa Isabel

district 1933 encl.; WPHC 1589/35: AR . . . encl.

53. WPHC 1277/35: Meeting of the AC May 1935 encl.; *PIM*, 18 Dec. 1931, 29.

54. BPA: Report of Inspector, Gizo Branch 7 July 1939 IR; Report of Manager 22 Jan. 1939 MR.

55. Fallowes Diary 15 June 1931; WPHC 1540/34: AR Santa Isabel district 1933 encl.; WPHC 1779/39: AR . . . 1938 encl.

56. WPHC 1214/32: AR Santa Isabel 1931 encl.; WPHC 1522/33: AR . . . 1932 encl.; WPHC 1540/34: AR . . . 1933 encl.; WPHC 1589/35: AR . . . 1934 encl.; WPHC 1522/33: AR Gizo district 1931 encl.; WPHC 1540/34: AR . . . 1933 Gizo district encl. According to Hilliard, bride-payment had been abolished in the days of the missionary Henry Welchman. It seems likely that the custom revived in the mid-thirties, when there was no foreign missionary on Isabel and when trade was flourishing (Hilliard 1978, 263–264).

57. Metcalfe Diary, 29 Jan. 1924.

58. Luke 1945, 180; Metcalfe Diaries, 8 Apr. 1927, 16 July 1936; GC: Goldie to Sinclair 28 Sept. 1923; BSIP-AR 1931; WPHC 1540/34: AR Gizo district 1933 encl.; WPHC 1539/35: AR . . . 1934 encl.; WPHC 1052/36: AR . . . 1935 encl.; WPHC 1851/37: AR . . . 1936 encl. In some societies the deliberate destruction or burying of valuables by a big-man was a sign of very high status and a challenge to that of other big-men (Hogbin 1964, 70–71).

59. WPHC 1540/34: AR Gizo district 1933 encl.; WPHC 1540/34: AR Santa Isabel district 1933 encl.; WPHC 1589/35: AR . . . 1934 encl. In New Georgia as elsewhere there were probably various degrees of ownership depending on how the inner reef was used. Commercial exploitation seems to have produced more definite and stronger claims (Allan 1957, 150–155).

60. WPHC 292/96: Woodford to Thurston 26 June 1896.

61. Vandercook 1937, 337; Hilliard 1966; Hogbin 1939, 179–181; Laracy 1976, 99–107; GC: Goldie to Scrivin, 30 May 1939; WPHC 1214/32: AR Santa Isabel 1931, encl.; WPHC 2195/40: AR Shortlands district 1939 encl. See also WPHC 1707/32: Wright, Native Administration Guadalcanal 1931 encl.

62. Hilliard 1966, 334–336, 339–340, 442–443, 458; WPHC 2894/27: AR Gizo district 1926 encl.; WPHC 855/30: RC to HC 18 Mar. 1930; WPHC 1832/28: AR Guadalcanal 1927 encl.; GC: Goldie to Scrivin 30 May 1939; WPHC 614/33: Selection of Medical students for training 31 May 1937 encl.; WPHC 3297/38: List of NMP to 31 Dec. 1948 and encls.

63. Hilliard 1978, 280; Hilliard 1966, 374, 377, 385–387, 400–401; Laracy 1976, 74–76, 83–84, 88; Hogbin 1939, 179–181.

64. WPHC 1290/30: AR Santa Isabel district 1929 encl.

65. Hilliard 1978, 280; WPHC 1214/32: AR Santa Isabel district 1932 encl.; WPHC 3058/31: Report of Sir Murchison Fletcher on Tour 1931; WPHC 2588/31: Notes of discussion at Tunabuli, Isabel 18 July 1931; Fallowes Diary 30 July, 31 Aug., 17 Nov. 1932; WPHC 423/32: Fletcher to RC 16 Feb. 1932, and encls. In Isabel, and after some delays, the people themselves started to build a school on mission land at Mara-na-tabu, but Fallowes could not teach there himself as his round of pastoral duties took him all over the island and the mission had no other personnel available (Fallowes Diary).

66. WPHC 2892/31: Fowler to HC 22 Oct. 1931, HC to RC 2 Aug. 1932 encls.; WPHC 1160/30: Ashley to HC 25 June 1930; WPHC 292/96: Woodford to Thurston 26 June 1896; Hilliard 1978, 262–263.

67. WPHC 1387/37: Ashley to HC 11 Mar. 1937 encl.

68. BSIP-AR 1929, 1938; WPHC 426/21: Heffernan to ARC 14 Feb. 1921 and encls.; WPHC 2195/40: AR Santa Isabel district 1940 encl.; WPHC 1634/ 38: AR Gizo district 1937 encl.; WPHC 2195/40: AR Gizo district 1940 encl.

69. WPHC 426/21: Statement by R. Hill 28 Apr. 1921, and encls.; see also WPHC 1679/22; Fallowes Diary; Fallowes to his sister, 22 July 1934; Fallowes pers. com. 1978; WPHC 1064/33: Barley to HC 11 Mar. 1933, and encls.; WPHC 849/24: Kane to HC 22 Feb. 1924; WPHC 1214/32: AR Santa Isabel district 1931 encl.; WPHC 1589/35: AR . . . 1933 encl. For another study of Fallowes' activities see Hilliard 1974, 19–74, 93–116; Hilliard 1978, 281–285.

70. Because of a legal technicality on Santa Isabel involving changes in the traditional form of marriage under Melanesian Mission influence, there were in fact no lawful marriages from about the turn of the century to 1938, and thus in theory there could be no adultery to bring before the court. Some district officers preferred to leave rulings on these matters to the church. However, when Fowler returned to Isabel in 1933 he tried such cases, although he had no right to do so under the existing law. (See Hilliard 1978, 263–264; WPHC 1540/34: AR Santa Isabel 1933 encl.; Fallowes Diary; Fallowes to his sister 22 July 1934.)

71. Fallowes, pers. com. 1978; Notare's son, Hedley Vekasi, was Ashley's personal servant and doubtless an informant on Isabel matters (Tommy Elkington, pers. com. 1977); *PIM*, 23 Mar. 1933, 26, and 22 Aug. 1935, 10; WPHC 1214/32: AR Santa Isabel district 1931 encl.; WPHC 1540/34: AR . . . 1933 encl.; WPHC 1589/35: AR . . . 1934 encl.; WPHC 1605/33: Ashley to HC 28 June 1933 and encls. Fallowes' opinion of Bogesi was shared, in relation to the Shortlands' women, by the Catholic priest, Fr. Boch (WPHC 3055/34: DO to SMO 25 Oct. 1934 encl. See also GC: Goldie to Scrivin 15 Mar. 1944).

72. WPHC 2811/39: Petition to HC June 1939 encls.

73. WPHC 2811/39: Fallowes to HC 15 June 1939 encl.; Fallowes, pers. com. 1978. See also Keesing 1980, 103–104.

74. WPHC BSIP Series CF 33/6, vol. 1: Notes of a discussion at meeting of HC with headmen at Kirakira 13 June 1939 encl.

75. WPHC 2839/39: Taburia to government 29 Apr. 1939.

76. WPHC 2811/39: Notes of a meeting with headmen at Aola 14 June 1939. Cf. Luke 1945, 84–92.

77. WPHC BSIP Series CF 33/6, vol. 1: Notes of an interview of Rev. R. Fallowes with His Excellency, 17 June 1939.

78. WPHC 2811/39: Brownlees, Sworn Statement 20 June 1939 encl.

79. WPHC 2811/39: Fallowes to HC 21 Aug. 1939 encls.; Fallowes, pers. com. 1978; *PIM*, 15 Aug. 1939, 1; Willy Paia pers. com. 1979.

80. WPHC BSIP F21/5, Part 1: DO to RC 30 June 1939 encl.

81. WPHC 2195/40: AR Eastern district 1939 encl.; WPHC 1779/39: AR Isabel district 1939 encl.; WPHC 2195/40: AR Nggela and Savo 1939 encl.

Chapter 12: More rumors: the eastern solomons

PIM, 20 Nov. 1935, 10.
Hogbin 1939, 266.

1. Woodford Papers, Petitions to Woodford, Oct. 1912. See Appendix 8 for originals and my fair English version.

2. WPHC 1290/30: AR Malaita District 1929 encl. This belief was not without logic, for wherever coconuts were abundant in the Solomons the district

officers refused to accept that the people might have difficulty paying the tax
(WPHC 1634/38: AR Malaita District 1937 encl.).

3. WPHC 1290/30: AR Malaita District 1929 encl.; WPHC 1214/32: AR
. . . 1931 encl.; WPHC 1522/33: AR . . . 1932 encl.; WPHC 1589/35: AR
. . . 1934 encl.; WPHC 827/30: Report of Labour Commission 1929; WPHC
1522/33: AR Santa Isabel District 1932 encl.; WPHC 1589/35: AR . . . 1934
encl.

4. WPHC 1290/30: AR Malaita District 1929 encl.; WPHC 1522/33: AR
. . . 1932 encl.; WPHC 1052/36: AR . . . 1935 encl.; WPHC 1851/37: AR
. . . 1936 encl.; WPHC 1637/38: AR . . . 1937 encl.; WPHC 2667/22: Bell to
RC 8 Aug. 1922 encl.; WPHC 3343/26: Barley to Gov. Sec. 23 Aug. 1926 encl.;
WPHC 827/30: Report of the Labour Commission 1929; WPHC 2267/34: Sandars to Sec. of Gov. 12 June 1934 encl.; WPHC 1522/33: AR Nggela and Savo
district 1932 encl.; WPHC 292/96: Woodford to Thurston 26 June 1896; see also
WPHC 2195/40: AR Nggela and Savo district 1939 encl.

5. The retention of the old religion on Langalanga had its advantages. Since
polygamy was permitted, a man with a number of wives could have more shell
valuables produced as the women carried out most of the operations involved in
their manufacture. As the Langalanga people obtained land on the mainland,
the bulk of the gardening was done by the men when they were not working on
the steamers; this more economic division of labor permitted the women to be
more profitably employed making shell valuables (Cooper 1971, 267, 270–271;
WPHC 827/30: Statement of Lauramo, Report of Labour Commission 1929
encl.). The shell valuable industry in the Haununu-Waihora area of south San
Cristobal appears to have ceased in the late 1920s or early 1930s due to the
acceptance of Christianity (Dickinson 1927, 59; Belshaw 1950, 179).

6. WPHC 274/32: Native Industries Malaita District encl.; WPHC 1522/33:
AR Malaita District 1932 encl.; WPHC 1052/36: AR . . . 1935 encl.

7. BPA: Report of Inspector, Makambo Branch, 1 Dec. 1933, 26 Apr. 1937
(see also 30 Apr. 1930 IR); WPHC 1052/36: AR Malaita District 1935 encl.;
WPHC 1587/35: District Diary Malaita Nov. 1936 encl.; WPHC 1634/38: AR
Malaita District, 1937 encl.; WPHC 1587/35: District Diary Santa Isabel Nov.
1936 encl.; *PIM*, 22 Nov. 1934, 28; Struben 1961, 68–69; WPHC 827/30: Statements of Lauramo and Oeta, Report of the Labour Commission 1929.

8. WPHC 1540/34: AR Malaita District 1933 encl.; WPHC 1052/36: AR
. . . 1935 encl.; WPHC 1587/35: Malaita Diary, Dec. 1936 encl.

9. WPHC 1522/33: AR Malaita District 1932 encl.

10. WPHC 1589/35: AR Malaita District 1934 encl.; WPHC 1634/38: AR
. . . 1937 encl.; WPHC 2095/40: AR . . . 1940 encl.

11. WPHC 1290/30: AR Eastern District 1929 encl.; WPHC 1214/32: AR
. . . 1931 encl.; WPHC 1522/33: AR . . . 1932 encl.; WPHC 1589/35: AR
. . . 1934 encl.; WPHC 1775/39: AR . . . 1938 encl.; WPHC 1359/34: Eastern
District Diary Nov. 1934 encl.

12. Boaz Bebeni; Charles Fox Ha'amouri.

13. Hilliard 1978, 369; Hilliard 1966, 201; WPHC 3296/30: Meeting of AC
Oct. 1930 encl.; WPHC 3698/33: Meeting of AC Nov. 1931 encl.; WPHC 2722/
34: Meeting of AC Oct. 1934 encl.; George Hurunani; Timothy Ianitaro;
Tommy Elkington, 1976; WPHC 1290/30: AR Eastern District 1929 encl.;
WPHC 1214/31: AR . . . 1931 encl.; WPHC 1522/33: AR . . . 1932 encl.;
WPHC 3296/30: Meeting of AC Oct. 1930 encl.

14. WPHC 1404/37: Interview of His Excellency with Norman Deck 14 July
1937.

15. Hilliard 1966; Laracy 1976; WPHC 2195/40: AR Eastern District 1939 encl. For bone canoes, see Mead 1973.

16. Bennett 1974, 121–155; Hilliard 1966, 201.

17. WPHC 1103/31: AR Guadalcanal District 1931 encl.; WPHC 1522/33: AR . . . 1932 encl.; WPHC 1052/36: AR . . . 1935 encl.; John Rich.

18. WPHC 1522/33: AR, Santa Cruz district 1932 encl.

19. BSIP-AR 1923; WPHC 229/25: Kane to HC; WPHC 2531/29: Santa Cruz, DO's log Mar. 1929 encl.; WPHC 1290/30: AR Santa Cruz district 1929 encl.; WPHC 1214/32: AR . . . 1931 encl.; WPHC 1359/34: AR . . . 1933 encl.; WPHC 1589/35: AR . . . 1934 encl.; WPHC 1052/36: AR . . . 1935 encl.; WPHC 1851/37: AR . . . 1936 encl.

20. Yen 1976, 205, 212.

21. Wawn 1893, 236–238, 243, 288; WPHC 955/34: Lambert "Health Survey 1933," encl.; WPHC 2722/34: Minutes of AC Oct. 1934 encl.; Deck 1945; WPHC 1121/24: LD-AR 1923 encl.

22. WPHC 887/37: Ashley to HC 19 Feb. 1937 and encl.; WPHC 1707/32: Reports on Ontong Java and Sikaiana 1932 encl.

23. WPHC 2397/31: Ashley to HC 13 July 1931 encl.

24. WPHC 2307/34: Ashley to HC 28 Oct. 1936 encl. See also WPHC 1538/ 16: Barnett to HC 11 May 1916.

25. BPA: Report of Manager, Makambo Branch, 18 Feb. 1935 MR; WPHC 1587/35: District Diary, Santa Cruz, Oct. 1935 encl.; WPHC 1587/35: District Diary Malaita, Dec. 1934 encl.; WPHC 1052/36: AR Malaita 1935 encl.; WPHC 1585/35: District Diary, Santa Cruz Oct. 1936 encl.; WPHC 1052/36: AR Guadalcanal, 1935; WPHC 1779/39: AR . . . 1938; see also WPHC 2593/ 31. Malaitans had not forgotten this wage cut as late as 1960 (see "From Sinerango," 1960, in File L21/1 vol. 1, Labour Historical, Labour Dept., Honiara).

26. WPHC 2307/34: Ashley to HC 21 June 1935 encl.; *PIM*, 23 July 1935, 63.

27. QSA: Staines to Brenan, Brenan to Staines, 24 July 1906 and Staines to Brenan, 27 July 1906 encl. 3647/1906, inward letter, M167(a), Chief Sec.'s Dept.; QSA: Senior Constable to Police Inspector Brisbane 26 June 1890, M 11, POL/JI Police Dept., Commissioner's Office: Misc. Corres. and Reports (references kindly provided by P. M. Mercer); see also Harris 1968; WPHC 289/08: Trood to im Thurn 13 Oct. 1908, and encls.

28. *PIM*, 24 Oct. 1933, 40; O'Connor 1968, 13, 22.

29. Vandercook 1937, 356; WPHC 827/30: Statements of Lauramo and Oeta, Report of Labour Commission 1929 encl.; WRCP: Manager to R. B. Carpenter 22 May 1929, see also Manager to W. R. Carpenter 4 May 1929; *PIM*, 21 Feb. 1935, 22. For a study of the Rabaul strike, see Gammage 1975.

30. WPHC 1214/32: AR Malaita District 1931 encl.; WPHC 1589/35: AR . . . encl.; WPHC 1779/39: AR . . . 1939 encl.; WPHC 1849/28: Eyre Hutson to SecS 5 July 1928 encl.

31. WPHC 1290/30: AR Malaita District 1929 encl.; WPHC 1638/38: AR . . . encl.; WPHC 879/37: Nutrition Survey . . . encl.; WPHC 3653/34: Report on the Depopulation of 'Are'are 8 Oct. 1934, and encls. See also Phillips 1940, 233.

32. Certainly, in the days of the first conversions by Deck and his Queensland-return teachers in the Siesie region (west Kwaio), the indigenous teachers of their own accord acted as a body to put a ban on customary feasting because it was making the people too poor (Erastus Eda'kwa'ou). WPHC 1779/39: AR Malaita 1938 encl.

33. WPHC 1952/36: AR Malaita district 1935 encl. See also Eyerdam Journal 1 Mar. 1930.

34. WPHC 1634/38: AR Malaita 1937 encl.; Eyerdam 1930, 25 Jan. to 18 Apr.

35. Hilliard 1966, 365–371, 402–403, 407; Hilliard 1969.

36. For the expansion of Christianity on Malaita, see Hilliard 1966; Laracy 1976.

37. Hogbin 1939, 47–48, 166–168, 213–214, 222–225.

38. WPHC 1814/28: King Patrol Report 1928; WPHC 1849/28: Eyre Hutson to SecS 5 July 1928, and encls.; WPHC 3198/28: King Patrol Report 25 Sept. 1928; WPHC 1021/29: KPR 28 Jan. 1929; WPHC 1411/29: KPR 30 Mar. 1929; WPHC 2528/29: KPR 12 Aug. 1929; WPHC 2729/29: Ashley to HC 16 Sept. 1929, and encls.; Hogbin 1934; WPHC 1634/38: AR Malaita district 1937 encl.; WPHC 1779/30: AR . . . 1938 encl.; WPHC 1779/39: AR . . . 1939 encl.

39. WPHC 1422/29: DO's log Malaita Sept. 1928 encls.; WPHC 1290/30: AR Malaita District 1929 encl.; WPHC 1214/31: AR . . . 1930 encl.; WPHC 1522/33: AR . . . 1932 encl.; WPHC 1540/34: AR . . . 1933 encl.; WPHC 1589/35: AR . . . 1934 encl.; WPHC 1052/36: AR . . . 1935 encl.; WPHC 1851/37: AR . . . 1936 encl.; WPHC 1634/38: AR . . . 1937 encl.; WPHC 1779/39: AR . . . 1938 encl.; WPHC 1779/39: AR . . . 1939 encl.; WPHC 25/28: Crichlow to SMO, 3 Mar. 1928 encl.; Lambert 1942, 299–302, 346–347, 350, 352–355. See also Eyerdam 1930, 8 Mar., 26 Mar. It could be argued that the yaws campaign was paid for by the tax. Even at 1 to 5 shillings a year from the adult men, the cost was lower than payments for traditional medicine and treatment was given to every man, woman, and child on the island.

40. Hogbin 1939, 97, 115, 119.

41. Eyerdam 1930, 26 Feb.; see also Dickinson 1927, 184–190.

42. Hogbin 1934, 258; Cochrane 1969, 281–288.

43. WPHC 190/23: Hill to HC 5 Mar. 1924 encl.; WPHC 1448/22: Kane to HC 6 May 1922; WPHC 2290/22: Rodwell to RC, and encls.; WPHC 2768/22: KR no. 17 of 1922 encl.; WPHC 2829/29: Ashley to HC 16 Sept. 1929 encl.; WPHC 3202/29: HC to SecS 6 Jan. 1931; WPHC 2211/31: Notes of a Meeting of Native Chiefs and Headmen with HC June 1931 encl.; see also Hogbin 1939, 155–156.

44. See, for examples, WPHC 3824/35: sentence for adultery on Tuita, 17 Oct. 1935, encl.; WPHC 2008/36: sentence . . . Lao encl.; WPHC 3764/37: sentence . . . Sarah Sano encl.; WPHC 1626/38: sentence . . . Waruhanua 20 Feb. 1938 encl.; WPHC 1627/38: sentence . . . Hauto 10 Mar. 1938 encl.; WPHC 246/39: sentence . . . Maesikisia 22 Nov. 1938 encl.; WPHC 4434/39: sentence . . . Fafefea encl.; WPHC 186/40: sentence . . . Kakite'e Dec. 1937 encl.; WPHC 1587/35: Malaita Diary July 1936 encl.; see also Hogbin 1939, 223–236.

45. WPHC 1851/37: AR Malaita 1936 encl.

46. Keesing 1978.

47. Allan 1974.

48. Keesing 1978; WPHC 1587/35: Malaita Diary Nov. 1936 encl.; WPHC 1587/35: AR Malaita 1936 encl.; WPHC 1851/37: AR Malaita 1936 encl.; Keesing 1980, 107.

49. WPHC 1779/39: AR Malaita District 1939 encl.

50. Young 1968; Gilson 1970, 276–280, 293–321; WPHC 540/08: Order of Prohibition against Ernest Weaver 25 Sept. 1908, and encls.; Sandars 1928–1943. See also Herr and Rood 1978, 167–168.

51. FRCP; WPHC 3509/36: Brownlees to Sec. of Gov. 10 Sept. 1936 encl.; Muspratt 1931, 91–100; Dickinson 1927, 129–130, 135, 137–139; Sandars 1928–1943; George Hurunani; Norden 1926, 91–92.

52. WPHC 857/19: Bates to HC 10 Mar. 1919; WPHC 2622/19: Greenwood to RC 27 Nov. 1919; BSIP-AR 1929–1935.

53. Johnson 1945; Johnson 1940; Norden 1926, 96.

54. Eyerdam 1933; Lambert 1942, 306; Eyerdam 1930, 15 Feb. At the same time, they told Eyerdam that they also liked Queensland, where so many had been years before as labor recruits. Cf. Keesing 1980.

55. Lambert 1942.

56. Vandercook 1937, 359–367.

57. *PIM*, 17 Apr. 1935, 5.

58. See, for example, *PIM*, 20 Oct. 1935, 64; *PIM*, 15 July 1939, 1. Re wireless, see *PIM*, 21 Dec. 1937, 15.

59. WPHC 2729/29: Ashley to HC 16 Sept. 1929 encl.

60. WPHC 4053/33: Barley to HC 19 Nov. 1932, and encls.; WPHC 2290/22: Rodwell to RC 24 Aug. 1922 encl.; WPHC 1448/22: Kane to HC 6 May 1922, and encls.

61. WPHC 3845/32: Native Administration in the BSIP, 31 May 1937, and encls.

62. Hogbin 1934, 264.

63. WPHC 3296/30: Meeting of AC Oct. 1930 encl.; for AR of Districts, see WPHC files 1290/30, 1214/32, 1522/33, 1540/34, 1589/33, 1052/36, 1851/37, 1634/38.

64. WPHC 1779/39: AR Santa Isabel 1939 encl. See also WPHC 2195/40: AR Santa Isabel 1941 encl., and WPHC 1589/35: AR 1934, encl.

65. WPHC 1779/39: AR Malaita District 1939 encl.; WPHC 3901/32: AR . . . 1940 encl.; WPHC BSIP Series F21/5, Part 2: Malaita Diary Oct. 1941 encl.

66. WPHC 3901/32: AR Gizo district 1940 encl. Kennedy claimed the courts were the brainchild of Marchant who became RC in 1939. This new rule, under which the Nggela courts were set up by Kennedy, became known as Marchant's Rule—hence, so Kennedy says, the term Maasina Rulu, or Marching Rule, of the postwar period. While Marchant undoubtedly furthered the establishment of the councils it was Ashley who gave the initial, if tacit, encouragement (Kennedy n.d.).

67. WPHC 3901/32: AR Eastern District 1940 encl.; WPHC 2195/40: AR Shortlands district 1941 encl.; WPHC 1779/39: AR Malaita 1939 encl.; WPHC 3901/32: AR Nggela and Savo 1940 encl.; Kennedy n.d.

Chapter 13: World War II and aftermath

NOTE: I have relied extensively on secondary sources in both this and the next chapter because under the Thirty Year Rule I was not granted access to post–World War II government records. Some sources and informants are confidential. CS (Confidential Source) indicates where they have been cited.

Ariel Sisili, quoted in Laracy 1983, 169.

Mead 1956, 168.

1. WPHC BSIP 17/6: ADO to Sec. to Gov. 1 Oct. 1939 Guadalcanal Quarterly Report no. 44/39; *PIM*, July 1955, 35; *PIM*, July 1971, 53–55.

2. For the history of the war in the Solomon Islands see J. Miller 1949; Rentz 1952; Zimmerman 1949; Feldt 1967; UKCO 1946; Horton 1970.

462   *Notes to chapter 13*

3. Hay, in BSIP Minutes of AC 16 and 19 Oct. 1953 (published 1954); *PIM*, June 1955, 23; Horton 1970, 10–19; Fieldhouse 1978, 481; Bennett 1974, 157; Moi'ea Pepechi; Vichi Chio; Kikiti; Reo Dick; Salimauri.

4. Horton 1970, 21; Laracy 1976, 111–117.

5. Horton 1970, 14–18, 191, 201, 222, 229; Ashby 1978, 94–95; *PIM*, July 1971, 53–55; WPHC BSIP F 33/4/2: Johnson to HC 19 Feb. 1942, and encls.; GC: Goldie to Scrivin 29 May 1942.

6. Horton 1970, 80–81; McKinnon 1972, 153; CS.

7. Bennett 1974, 159–160.

8. Shortland Islands informants; Groenewegen 1972, 10; Bennett 1974, 161.

9. Horton 1970.

10. Ibid., 225–226.

11. Ibid., 58–59; Belshaw 1954, 73.

12. Bennett 1974, 159n; UKCO 1946, 34.

13. Boaz Bebeni; John Erei; Morris Ohairangi; Charles Fox Ha'amouri; Habit Aharohei'a; Hari Taisubaurona; John Mark Dauhenia; Daniel Tawari'i; Timothy Ianitaro; Moi'ea Pepechi; Vichi Chio; Sove Kimbo; Jones Bulangi; Kikiti; Chapasere; Reo Dick; Aliesio Tavoruka; Justus Malalifu; Elia Maikoto; Sedrak Ufamari; Fo'afuna; Jo Gonai'ilae; Joseph Afe'ou; Dick Sawalo; Joseph Odofia; John Siteageni; Elders of Maravari; Francis Nisbule; Dicko Vaevo. See also Simone Maa'eobi (Keesing interview) 1979.

14. Boaz Bebeni (my translation from Pijin).

15. I am indebted to Hugh Laracy for his generosity in giving me a copy of his 1979 manuscript, "Maasina Rule: Resistance to Colonialism in the Solomon Islands" in 1981, now available as *Pacific Protest . . .* (see Laracy 1983). For earlier studies see Worsley 1957; Allan 1950; Tippett 1967, 217 ff; Laracy 1971; Keesing 1978.

16. Laracy 1983, 85–88, 89, 109, 138.

17. Ibid., pp. 85–87, 95–96; Belshaw 1954, 113.

18. GC: Goldie to Scrivin 14 Jan. 1946.

19. Ngatu, quoted in ibid.

20. McKinnon 1972, 157.

21. GC: Goldie to Scrivin 19 June, 30 Dec. 1947, 20 Mar. 1948, 10 Aug. 1949; BSIP-AR 1948, 29; CS.

22. Laracy 1983, 27–29, 91, 92–93, 114–116, 136–138; BSIP-AR 1948, 26–28.

23. Laracy 1983, 26; BSIP-AR 1948.

24. Allan, paper read to seminar at Research School of Pacific Studies, ANU, Canberra, July 1978. The Savo people also displayed little interest (Allan 1982b, 227).

25. BSIP-AR 1948.

26. GC: Goldie to Scrivin 22 Sept. 1947.

27. Laracy 1983, 28. The government called for recruits in New Georgia to serve against the rebels. Goldie Sakiri, chief of Roviana, was afraid that if they did a feud between the New Georgians and Malaitans would result. He suggested that if any fighting was to be done they should arm the European officials who had so much time on their hands (GC: Goldie to Scrivin 22 Sept. 1947).

28. Laracy 1983, 23; Allan 1950, 60.

29. Bennett 1974, 162–164.

30. BSIP-AR 1948; Laracy 1983, 21.

31. Jo Gonai'ilae.

32. See for example the tone of Allan 1951.
33. For typical government statement of policy see BSIP-AR 1948, 28–29. See also WPHC BSIP CF 81/7: Noel, Notes on Future Economic Development of BSIP, 29 Dec. 1943 encl.
34. Laracy 1983, 50, 109–110, 163–171; *PIM*, July 1982, 17–18; BSIP Minutes of AC 4, 6 Sept. 1951.
35. BSIP Minutes of AC, 5, 8, 9 May 1952; BSIP-AR 1953–54, 51.
36. Laracy 1983, 30–31, 192–193.
37. Marx 1978, 9–10.
38. Laracy 1983, 85; Keesing 1980, 103–104.
39. Bathgate 1975, 102–108.
40. For the growth of Eto's church I have drawn extensively on Harwood 1971 and on Tuza 1975.
41. The phrase "patching up a frayed edge of Empire" is borrowed from Goldie in GC: Goldie to Scrivin, 24 Jan. 1948, and was said to be the description an early post-war administrator gave to his role in the Solomons (Leslie Gill).
42. Vaskess 1943, 2.
43. WPHC BSIP CF 82/3: CO to Mitchell 28 Jan. 1944, and encls.; Morgan 1980 vol. 1, 239; Herlihy 1981, 198–199; *PIM*, Oct. 1946, 38–39; *PIM*, July 1955, 47.
44. BSIP-AR 1948, 1953–54; BSIP Minutes of AC Oct. 1945, Sept. 1951, May 1952, Oct. 1953, Feb. 1954; WPHC BSIP CF 80/38/2: Noel to Rushworth 11 Mar. 1948, and encls.; WPHC BSIP 2/37: Hodgress to HC Nov. 1943, and encls.; WPHC BSIP CF 33/6, vol. 10: SecS to HC, 8 July 1946, Files Relating to Copra Marketing and Trade Schemes; BPA: files G30–G34, Relating to War Damage Claims; GC: Goldie to Scrivin 29 Nov. 1945, 29 Sept. 1949, 14 Mar. 1950; *PIM*, May 1943, 40.
45. Tommy Elkington 1976; BPA: Minutes of Directors' Meetings, SIDC Nov. 1947–Mar. 1955.
46. Fieldhouse 1978, 477.
47. BSIP-AR 1948, 1953–54.
48. WPHC BSIP CF 33/6, vol. 10: AHC (?) 24 July 1947 encl.; BPA: Seton to Sec. SIDC 18 Oct. 1947 File G31; GC: Goldie to Scrivin 25 Jan., 20 Dec. 1948; BSIP-AR 1948; *PIM*, Sept. 1946, 10; *PIM*, Aug. 1946, 11; *PIM*, June 1955, 23; *PIM*, July 1955, 161–164; Belshaw 1954, 65, 89.
49. BSIP-AR 1948. See also WPHC BSIP CF 33/6: throughout vols. 1–14, 1940, 51, files relating to Copra Marketing and Food Schemes; *PIM*, July 1955, 35.
50. BSIP-AR 1948, 1953–54; Herlihy 1981, 199; BSIP Minutes of AC, Sept. 1951, May 1952, Feb. 1954; GC: Goldie to Scrivin 28 May 1948; *PIM*, Sept. 1954, 21; *PIM*, Dec. 1954, 26–28.
51. BSIP Minutes of AC, Sept. 1951, May 1952, Apr. 1956; *PIM*, Sept. 1954, 21; *PIM*, Dec. 1954, 26–28.
52. BSIP-AR 1953–54, 1955–56.
53. Morgan 1980, 1: 239; BSIP Minutes of AC, Sept.-Oct. 1948, Sept. 1951, May 1952, Oct. 1953, Feb., Oct. 1954, Oct. 1955, Apr. 1956; BSIP-AR 1953–54, 1955–56. For the continuing importance of the relationship implied by these emblems, see Allan 1982a, 223 and *PIM*, Oct. 1975, 23.
54. Bennett 1974, 166–167; Davidson to Barnes 6 Oct. 1954, Unnumbered BSIP-DO file; BPA: Minutes of Directors' Meeting, SIDC 21 Nov. 1947; BSIP-AR 1953–54.
55. BSIP-AR 1953–54.

56. Ibid., and 1955–56; BSIP Minutes of AC, Oct. 1955.

57. *PIM*, Sept. 1946, 10; *PIM*, Oct. 1946, 59–60; *PIM*, Dec. 1946, 26; BSIP Minutes of AC, Sept. 1951, May 1952.

58. WPHC BSIP CF 48/2 (2225/39): Brief to HC of Chinese petition, 9(?) Sept. 1950.

59. WPHC BSIP CF 48/2 (2225/39): Notes by ASec to Gov. 25(?) Sept. 1950.

60. WPHC BSIP CF 48/2 (2225/39): Notes on Chinese Immigration policy 28 Jan. 1953; Extract from Minutes of Gov. House Meeting 30 Jan. 1953; WPHC BSIP CF 48/2 (2225/39): Chief Sec. to Chau Chu 6 Mar. 1953, encls.; *PIM*, Aug. 1946, 11.

61. BSIP Minutes of AC, May 1952.

62. Fieldhouse 1978, 478, 481–483; BPA: Seton to Barnes 6 Sept. 1954, and Sale of Manning Straits file; BSIP-AR 1953–54, 1955–56; Records of LTR; BSIP Minutes of AC, May 1952, Oct. 1953.

63. BSIP Minutes of AC, Oct. 1953, Feb. 1954.

Chapter 14: Independence: Coming, ready or not!

NOTE: I have relied extensively on secondary sources in this and the previous chapter because under the Thirty Year Rule I was not granted access to post–World War II government records. CS (Confidential Source) indicates where confidential sources and informants have been cited.

SI Western Council Submission 1978, 1.

Willie Betu in UKPP: Report of the SI Constitutional Conferences, Sept. 1977.

1. Morgan 1980, 5: 89.

2. Morgan 1980, 5: 1–25, 32–39, 61–62; Robinson 1980, 50–72.

3. Morgan 1980, 5: 202, 210, 223–224.

4. BSIP-AR 1953–54, 1955–56, 1957–58, 1966, 1967.

5. BSIP-AR 1955–56, 1957–58, 1961–62, 1963–64; Herlihy 1981, 201–205.

6. BSIP-AR 1955–56, 1957–58.

7. BSIP-AR 1955–56, 1963–64, 1965.

8. BSIP-AR 1955–56, 1961–62; *PIM*, Oct. 1960, 53–55. Capital to establish the Loans Board came mainly from Japanese reparations payments (BSIP-AR 1957–58 and CS).

9. BSIP-AR 1961–62, 1963–64, 1965, 1966; *PIM*, May 1965, 15; *PIM*, July 1965, 13; *PIM*, July 1979, 49; CS; Sykes 1958; Fieldhouse 1978, 483.

10. BSIP-AR 1961–62, 1963–64, 1965, 1966; *PIM*, Sept. 1960, 65.

11. BSIP-AR 1953–54, 1955–56.

12. BSIP-AR 1961–62, 1963–64, 1965.

13. Bellam 1969, 13 and fn.25.

14. Quoted in Davenport and Çoker 1967, 138.

15. Bennett 1973, 1–7.

16. BSIP-AR 1961–62, 1963–64, 1965; Ruthven 1979, 246; Hughes 1979, 232.

17. BSIP-AR 1961–62, 1963–64, 1965; Geoffrey Beti, *Kakamora Reporter* May 1971, 8; Campbell 1977, 230; Paia 1975, 83; BSIP-LCD June–Dec. 1965; *PIM*, July 1965, 15.

18. BSIP-AR 1965.

19. BSIP-LCD Nov.–Dec. 1967; see also Palmer n.d.; Laracy 1976, 156.

20. BSIP-AR 1965, 1966, 1967, 1968.

21. BSIP-LCD June 1965; BSI-GCD Mar.–Apr. 1973.

22. BSI-GCD Mar.–Apr. 1973.

23. Russell 1970, 229–230. See also Clark 1980, 136; Morgan 1980, vol. 5, 296.

24. BSIP-AR 1970, 1971; Clark 1980, 136–137; Russell 1970, 236–237; Kenilorea 1973, 25; Paia 1975, 84–89.

25. BSI-GCD Nov. 1971, Nov. 1973; *PIM*, Aug. 1971, 51–53.

26. Clark 1980, 138; Saunana 1973; Murray Chapman pers. com.; Herlihy 1981, 209; Russell 1970, 231–232; BSI-GCD Nov. 1970; see also *PIM*, Sept. 1971, 21–22; *PIM*, Nov. 1977, 13; Nazareth, 1971; Barrie Macdonald pers. com. 1983; CS.

27. BSIP-AR 1975; Walker 1981; Morgan 1980, vol. 5, 295–296; Clark 1980, 139.

28. Clark 1980, 138–139.

29. Potterton 1979, 27–29; Herlihy 1980, 5–13; Saemala 1979; *PIM*, Oct. 1975, 23, 27; *PIM*, Dec. 1975, 9; *PIM*, Aug. 1976, 19; *PIM*, Mar. 1977, 19; *News Drum*, 12 Mar., 10 Dec. 1976; *Melanesian Nius*, 19 Jan. 1977; (for Mamaloni's relationship to *Melanesian Nius*, see *PIM*, June 1977, 27). Ulufaʻalu, formerly student leader at the University of Papua New Guinea and graduate in economics, unlike most other graduates, was not given any position in the public service. A radical, branded by some colonial officials as a Communist, he joined the union movement. The Solomon Islands General Workers Union was formed in 1975 and he was its president until his election to the Honiara seat in 1976 (*PIM*, Oct. 1977, 38).

30. Herlihy 1980; *PIM*, July 1977, 13; *PIM*, Nov. 1977, 12; CS; cf. Potterton 1979, 28–29; Saemala 1979, 7–9.

31. Solomon Islands Bill, *House of Lords Debates*, 23 May 1978 and quoted in Potterton 1979, 28–29; Herlihy 1980, 12–13; Saemala 1979, 8–9.

32. Herlihy 1982 revised ed.; CS.

33. Campbell 1977, 230–239.

34. Bellam 1969, 113; *PIM*, Sept. 1975, 19–22; Herlihy 1980, 19; CS.

35. SI Western Council Submission 1978; SI-LAD 1977; *PIM*, June 1978, 18; Bobai 1979; BSIP Minutes of AC Sept. 1951, Oct. 1954, Apr. 1956; CS.

36. SI Western Council Submission 1978; *News Drum*, 17 Feb., 7, 14, 28 Apr., 9 June, 28 July, 20 Aug., 8 Sept., 20 Oct. 1978, 20 Aug. 1979, 1 Feb. 1980; Larmour 1979, 249; Hastings 1976; *PIM*, July 1978, 10–11; *PIM*, Sept. 1978, 10; *PIM*, Oct. 1978, 55; CS.

37. *PIM*, June 1977, 8; *PIM*, May 1979, 73–75; SI Statistics Office 1978, 12.

38. SI Statistics Office 1978, 28; BSIP-AR 1969, 1975.

39. BSIP-AR 1970–1975; Wright 1974, 377–393; Hughes 1979; Herlihy 1981, 125; Joan M. Herlihy, pers. com. 1983.

40. Hansell and Wall 1976, 135–138; Ward and Proctor 1980, 410–411.

41. Dick and McKillop 1976, 34–35.

42. BSIP-AR 1970–1975; see also *PIM*, May 1979, 74; *PIM*, Nov. 1977, 12; Fieldhouse 1978, 482–483, 484–491; also Larson 1966; Riogano 1979, 85–89; Ruthven 1979, 247–249.

43. BSIP-AR 1966–1975; *PIM*, July 1971, 51; *PIM*, Aug. 1977, 66; *PIM*, Sept. 1977, 60; *PIM*, Sept. 1978, 42; Monberg 1976, 25, 37; Feinberg 1982, 8–9, 12.

44. BSI-GCD July 1970, Mar.–Apr. 1973.

45. Allan 1980, 111. BSIP-AR 1953–54, 1975; SI Statistics Office 1979, 67–

73; *PIM*, June 1977, 8; *PIM*, July 1978, 15–16; Witt 1974, 6.42–6.81.

46. Lea 1972, 258; Rev. Fr. Brunz, Sept. 1976; BSIP-AR 1973–1975; *PIM*, Sept. 1971, 97–98; *PIM*, May 1979, 75; *PIM*, Aug. 1979, 5; *PIM*, Oct. 1979, 52; Herlihy 1981, 326–328.

47. Witt 1974, 6.42–6.81; Herlihy 1981, 317–322; *PIM*, May 1979, 75.

48. *PIM*, Dec. 1971, 43; *PIM*, Oct. 1975, 25; *PIM*, Sept. 1977, 8; *PIM*, July 1978, 17; *PIM*, Dec. 1978, 74–75; *PIM*, May 1979, 75; Tommy Elkington; Bart Ulufa'alu; Rolph Novak, 1976; see also Ward and Proctor 1980, 412–413.

49. BSIP-AR 1972; *PIM*, Sept. 1971, 21–22; *PIM*, Oct. 1971, 57–58; *PIM*, Sept. 1978, 41–42.

50. *PIM*, Sept. 1971, 21–22; *PIM*, Sept. 1978, 41–42; *PIM*, May 1979, 73–74; see also Sipolo 1981, 5–6.

51. Brookfield with Hart 1971, 262.

52. BSIP-AR 1973.

53. John 10:10.

54. BSIP-AR 1966–1975.

55. Herlihy 1981, 310–312, 314.

56. Ibid., 288–290.

57. SI Statistics Office 1978, 60–61, 67, 71.

58. Herlihy 1981, 313; McKinnon 1973, 44; Lasaqa 1972, 269; Brookfield with Hart 1971, 364–370.

59. Herlihy 1981, 111–112.

60. Joan M. Herlihy, pers. com., 1983.

61. Herlihy 1981, 310–312.

62. Laracy 1976, 156; BSIP-AR 1975; Herlihy 1981, 338–348; *PIM*, July 1978, 21–23.

63. CS.

64. SI Statistics Office 1978, 8.

65. BSI 1975, vol. 2, 1.

BIBLIOGRAPHY

NOTES: Whalers' logs and journals are listed by the name of the ship. The original manuscripts relating to the whaling vessels are located in the United States. All of those listed were read on microfilms of the Pacific Manuscripts Bureau, Australian National University, Canberra. They are available at the National Library of Australia, Canberra; the state libraries of Victoria, South Australia, Tasmania, and Western Australia; the Mitchell Library, Sydney; the National Library of New Zealand, Wellington; and Hamilton Library, University of Hawaii, Honolulu.

The records of the Western Pacific High Commission were consulted at the Western Pacific Archives, Suva. They have since been transferred to the Foreign and Commonwealth Office, London. Records for the years from about 1876 to 1925 have been microfilmed and are available in the National Library of Australia, Canberra.

Adams, Emma H.
    c. 1890 *Two Cannibal Archipelagoes.* Oakland, CA: Pacific Press Publishing.

Addison
    [1834– Log in Nicholson Whaling Collection, Providence, RI. PMB 571.
    1837]

Adeline Gibbs
    [1870– Log in Old Dartmouth Whaling Museum, New Bedford, MA. PMB
    1875] 277.

Alexander, Gilchrist
    1927   *From the Middle Temple to the South Seas.* London: John Murray.

Alfred
    [1845– Whaling log. Kendall Whaling Museum, Sharon, MA. PMB 801.
    1849]

Alfred Gibbs
    [1854– Whaling log. Nicholson Whaling Collection, Providence, RI. PMB
    1858] 572.

Allan, Colin Hamilton
    1950   The Marching Rule Movement in the British Solomon Islands Protectorate. Dip. Anthropology thesis, Cambridge University.

1951   Marching Rule, a Nativistic Cult of the British Solomon Islands. *Corona* 3 (3): 93–100.

1957   *Customary Land Tenure in the British Solomon Islands Protectorate.* Report of the Special Lands Commission. Honiara: Western Pacific High Commission.

1974   Some Marching Rule Stories. *Journal of Pacific History* 9:182–186.

1980   An Early Marching Rule letter by Nori of Waisisi, 'Are'are, Malaita. Manuscript 15. *Journal of Pacific History* 15:110–112.

1982*a* Further Marching Rule Documents: Manuscript 16—Anaefolo of Uru and the Federal Council Decision 1951. *Journal of Pacific History* 17:222–225.

1982*b* The Special Lands Commissioner's Note on the Nggela people and Marching Rule 1954. Manuscript 17. *Journal of Pacific History* 17:225–227.

Allen, Jim, and Roger C. Green
1972   Mendaña 1595 and the Fate of the Lost "Almiranta": An Archaeological Investigation. *Journal of Pacific History* 7:73–91.

Allied Forces, Southwest Pacific Area, Allied Geographical Section
1942– *Terrain Study no. 11, Guadalcanal; no. 39, Ysabel; no. 41, Short-*
1943   *land Islands; no. 47, Russell Islands; no. 48, Choiseul; no. 54, New Georgia.* N.p.

Alpha
[1860– Whaling log. Whaling Museum, Nantucket, MA. PMB 372.
1865]

Amherst, Lord, and Basil Thomson, eds.
1901   *The Discovery of the Solomon Islands by Alvaro de Mendaña in 1568.* 2 vols. London: Hakluyt Society.

Andrews, T.
1876   Journal aboard *Jessie Henderson*, 5 June to 4 October. Government agent's journal no. 3. FNA, Immigration Dept.

Angas, George F.
1866   *Polynesia: A popular description of the physical features, inhabitants, natural history and productions of the islands of the Pacific* . . . London: Society for Promoting Christian Knowledge.

Ann and Hope
[1798– Whaling log. John Carter Brown Library, Providence, RI. PMB 540;
1799]   Rhode Island Historical Society, Providence, RI. PMB 769.

Arctic
[1871– Whaling log. Nicholson Whaling Collection, Providence, RI. PMB
1872]   791.

Arnolda
[1872– Whaling log. Old Dartmouth Whaling Museum, New Bedford, MA.
1876]   PMB 721.

Ashby, Ted
1978   *Blackie: A story of the old-time bushmen.* Wellington: Reed.

[AJMR] *Asiatic Journal and Monthly Register for British India and its Dependencies*
1821–
1835

Atlantic
[1846– Whaling log. Whaling Museum, Nantucket, MA. PMB 396.
1849]

Aurora
[1865– Whaling log. New Bedford Free Public Library, New Bedford, MA.
1871] PMB 310, 311.

Australian National Archives
Canberra office
var.　Papers relating to External Affairs, CAO CRS A1108, vol. 57.

Sydney office
[1841– List of vessels arrived, Port of Sydney, 1841–1843, 1851–1853,
1893] 1854–1886, 1890–1893. Maritime Services Board, SP729.

Australian Parliamentary Papers
c. 1919 *British and Australian Trade in the South Pacific*, vol. 5, 1917–1919.
Report of Interstate Commission. Melbourne: Commonwealth of
Australia.

Bach, John
1976　*A Maritime History of Australia*. Melbourne: Nelson.

Barrau, Jacques
1958　*Subsistence Agriculture in Melanesia*. Bulletin 219. Honolulu:
Bishop Museum Press.

Bassett, Marnie
1969　*Letters from New Guinea, 1921*. Melbourne: Hawthorn.

Bathgate, Murray Alexander
1975　Bihu Matena Golo: A Study of the Ndi-Nggai of West Guadalcanal
and their involvement in the Solomon Islands cash economy. PhD
dissertation, Victoria University of Wellington.

Bayne, Peter
1979　Opinion: The validity of the Crown title to land at Kolombangara
Island, Solomon Islands. La Trobe University.

Beckford, George L.
1972　*Persistent Poverty: Underdevelopment in Plantation Economies of
the Third World*. New York: Oxford University Press.

Bell, H. M. [Rikard]
1936　*Man No Good, An Autobiography of the South Seas*. London: Hurst
& Blackett.

Bell, W. R.
[1908– Journal aboard *Clansman*. Government agent's journal no. 65, 25
1909] October 1908 to 17 February 1909. FNA, Immigration Department.
[1910] Journal aboard *Clansman*. Government agent's journal no. 66, 14
February to 3 August 1910. FNA, Immigration Department.

Bellam, M. E. P.
1969　"Walkabout Long Chinatown": Aspects of Urban and Regional
Development in the British Solomon Islands. In *Papers presented at
a Seminar on Urbanisation and Resettlement in the South Pacific*,
convened by J. R. McCreary, pp. 1–16. Wellington: Victoria University.

Belle
[1852] Whaling log. E. J. Bliss, Edgartown, MA. PMB 680.

Belle
[1857–   Whaling log. New Bedford Free Public Library, New Bedford, MA.
1862]   PMB 311.

Bellwood, Peter
1978   *Man's Conquest of the Pacific: The Prehistory of Southeast Asia and Oceania.* Auckland: Collins.

Belshaw, C. S.
1950   Changes in Heirloom Jewellery in the Central Solomons. *Oceania* 20 (3): 169–184.
1954   *Changing Melanesia: Social Economics of Culture Contact.* Melbourne: Oxford University Press.

Bennett, Judith A.
1973   Weather Coast History 1955 to 1972. Paper, University of Hawaii.
1974   Cross-Cultural Influences on Village Relocation on the Weather Coast of Guadalcanal, Solomon Islands, c. 1870–1953. MA thesis, University of Hawaii.
1979a   Wealth of the Solomons: A History of Trade, Plantations and Society in the Solomon Islands, 1800–1942. PhD dissertation, Australian National University.
1979b   Some English-based Pidgins in the Southwestern Pacific: Solomon Islands Pidgin. In *New Guinea and Neighbouring Areas: A Socio-Linguistic Laboratory*, edited by Stephen A. Wurm, pp. 64–72. The Hague: Mouton.
1981a   Oscar Svensen: A Solomons trader among "the few." *Journal of Pacific History* 16:170–189.
1981b   Personal work histories of Solomon Islands plantation labourers: Methodology and uses. *Pacific Studies* 5:34–56.

Bernatzik, Hugo Adolf
1935   *Südsee: Travels in the South Seas.* London: Constable.

Bertreux, R. P.
1905   Lettre, 4 Décembre 1904. *Annales des Missions de l'Océanie* 11 (3): 368–370.

Best, Lloyd
1968   Outlines of a Model of Pure Plantation Economy. *Social and Economic Studies* 17 (September): 283–326.

Bevan, F. P.
[1882]   Journal aboard *Surprise*. Government agent's journal no. 37, 9 December 1881 to 19 July 1882; 27 July [1882?] to ? Medical journals kept on two successive voyages; last pages of second journal missing. FNA, Immigration Department.
[1883–   Journal aboard *Winifred*. Government agent's journal no. 51, 10
1884]   October 1883 to 13 January 1884. FNA, Immigration Department.

Biskup, Peter, ed.
1974   *The New Guinea Memoirs of Jean Baptiste Octave Mouton.* Pacific History Series no. 7. Canberra: Australian National University Press/ Honolulu: University Press of Hawaii.

Blainey, Geoffrey
1963   *The Rush That Never Ended: A History of Australian Mining.* Melbourne: Melbourne University Press.

Blyth, J.
[1885] Journal aboard *Glencairn*. Government agent's journal no. 56, 1 August to 8 December 1885. FNA, Immigration Department.

Bobai, Tebano
1979 Gilbertese Settlement. In Larmour 1979:131–141.

Bogesi, George
1948 Santa Isabel, Solomon Islands. *Oceania* 18 (3): 208–232; (4): 327–357.

Bolton, G. C.
1963 *A Thousand Miles Away: A History of North Queensland to 1920*. Brisbane: Jacaranda.

Bougainville, Louis de
1772 *A Voyage Round the World*. Ridgewood, NJ: Gregg Press (1967 Reprint).

Boutilier, J. A.
1975 The New Georgia Days of Norman Wheatley. *Journal of the Solomons Islands Museum Association* 3:29–41.

Bradford
1861 Letter to British Consul, 7 Sept. 1861. In British Consulate Papers, Set 24, Item 8.

Brenchley, Julius L.
1873 *Jottings during the Cruise of HMS Curaçoa among the South Sea Islands in 1865*. London: Longmans, Green.

[BSI] British Solomon Islands [*see also* BSIP, Solomon Islands]
1912– *Annual Report on the British Solomon Islands for the year[s]*. . . .
1958 London: HMSO [Title varies.]
1961– *Report for the year[s]*. . . . Honiara: BSIP/London: HMSO.
1975
1970– *Governing Council Debates*. Honiara: Government Printing Office.
1974
1975 *National Development Plan 1975–1979*. 3 vols. Honiara: Office of Chief Minister.

[BSIP] British Solomon Islands Protectorate [*see also* BSI, Solomon Islands]
1911 *Handbook . . . with returns up to 31 March 1911*. Tulagi: n p
1923 *Handbook . . . with returns up to December 1921 [and] through 1922*. New ed. Suva: n.p.
1923– *Blue Book for the year* . . . [1923–24 to 1937–38]. Suva: WPHC.
1938
1930– *Minutes of Advisory council, 1930–1953*. Suva: WPHC. (Minutes
1954 before 1930 located in WPHC Archives.)
1934 *Agricultural Gazette*. Tulagi. Quarterly.

Brook, James A.
1940 *Jim of the Seven Seas: A true story of Personal Adventure*. London: Heath Cranton.

Brookfield, H. C.
1972 *Colonialism, Development and Independence: The Case of the Melanesian Islands in the South Pacific*. Cambridge: University Press.

Brookfield, H. C., with Doreen Hart
1971 *Melanesia: A Geographical Interpretation of an Island World.* London: Methuen.

Brown, George
1908a *George Brown, D.D., Pioneer-Missionary and Explorer: An Autobiography.* London: Hodder and Stoughton.
1908b Notes of a Voyage to Isabel Island, Solomons Group, and Le ua Niua (Ontong Java or Lord Howe), and Tasman Groups. In *Report of the Eleventh Meeting of the Australasian Association for the Advancement of Science, . . . held at Adelaide, 1907,* 11:528–538.

Burman, Rickie
1981 Time and Socioeconomic change on Simbo, Solomon Islands. *Man* 16:251–267.

Burnett, Frank
1911 *Through Polynesia and Papua: Wanderings with a Camera in Southern Seas.* London: G. Bell.

[BPA] Burns, Philp & Company Limited
[1898– Letters and papers relating to Solomon Islands, 1898–1956. In
1956] Burns, Philp & Company Limited offices, Bridge St., Sydney.

California
[1872– Whaling log. Nicholson Whaling Collection, Providence, RI. PMB
1876] 578.

Cambria
[1858– Whaling log. Old Dartmouth Historical Society, New Bedford, MA.
1862] PMB 914.

Cameron, Charlotte
1923 *Two Years in Southern Seas.* London: T. Fisher Unwin.

Campbell, Michael J.
1977 Devolution in the Solomon Islands: A Study of Major Reforms. *Journal of Administration Overseas* 16 (4): 228–239.

Canada
1802 Logbook. In India Office Library, London; on microfilm, Department of Pacific and Southeast Asian History, ANU.

Capell, A.
1943 Notes on the islands of Choiseul and New Georgia, Solomon Islands. *Oceania* 14:20–29.

Carpenter, W. R. and Company Limited (Tulagi)
[1925– Letters and papers, 1925–1931. In writer's care.
1931]

Carroll, Vern, ed.
1975 *Pacific Atoll Populations.* ASAO Monograph no. 3. Honolulu: University Press of Hawaii.

Carter, George G.
n.d. Papers in possession of Rev. G. G. Carter, Auckland. PMB 716.

Cattlin, E.
[1828] Journal of *John Bull,* 1828.
[1829] Journal of *Alfred,* 1828–1829.
[1833] Journal of *Australian,* 1829–1831, *Primrose* 1831–1833.

[1836]   Journal of unnamed vessel, 1835–1836.
         All journals in MS 1800, Mitchell Library, Sydney.

Chapman, Murray
1970   Population movement in a tribal society: The case of Duidui and
         Pichahila, British Solomon Islands. PhD dissertation, University of
         Washington.

Chapman, Murray, and Peter Pirie, eds.
1974   *Tasi Mauri: A Report on Population and Resources of the
         Guadalcanal Weather Coast.* Honolulu: University of Hawaii and
         East West Center.

Chatelet, P.
1905   Lettre, 15 Janvier 1905. *Annales des Missions de l'Océanie* 11 (3):
         370–377.

Chesterman, Clement C.
1960   *Tropical Dispensary Handbook.* London: Lutterworth.

Chewings, Hannah
1900   *Among Tropical Islands: Notes and Observations during a visit of
         S.S. Moresby to New Guinea, New Britain and the Solomon Islands
         in 1899.* London: J. L. Bonython.

Cheyne, Andrew
1852   *A Description of Islands in the Western Pacific Ocean . . .* London:
         Potter.
1855   *Sailing Directions from New South Wales to China and Japan . . .*
         London: Potter.

[Cheyne, Andrew]
1867   Sikyana or Stewart's Island and the Sea Slug. *Nautical Magazine,*
         609–613.

Christopher Mitchell
[1845–   Whaling log. Whaling Museum, Nantucket, MA. PMB 389.
1848]

Clarice
[1841–   Whaling log. New Bedford Free Public Library, New Bedford, MA.
1845]   PMB 319.

Clark, A. Trevor
1980   Decolonisation: Three Fields of View. *Journal of Commonwealth
         and Comparative Politics* 18:127–144.

Clark, Jeffrey T., and John Terrell
1978   Archaeology in Oceania. *Annual Review of Anthropology* 7:293–
         319.

Clay
[1827–   Whaling log. Peabody Museum, Salem, MA. PMB 216.
1829]

Coates, A.
[1884–   Journal aboard *Sea Breeze.* Government agent's journal no. 54, 3
1885]   October 1884 to 30 January 1885. FNA, Immigration Department.

Cochrane, D. G.
1969   Conflict Between Law and Sexual Mores on San Cristobal. *Oceania*
         39 (4): 281–289.

Codrington, R. H.
1891   *The Melanesians: Studies in their Anthropology and Folk-lore.*
        Oxford: Clarendon Press.
Coghlan, T. A.
1918   *Labour and Industry in Australia . . . 1788–1901.* Vol. 4. London:
        Oxford University Press/New York: H. Milford.
Collinson, Clifford W.
1926   *Life and Laughter 'Midst the Cannibals.* London: Hurst & Blackett.
Committee on the Rubber Industry in Ceylon
1947   Report . . . on the Rubber Industry in Ceylon. Colombo: Govern-
        ment Printer.
Cooper, Matthew
1971   Economic Context of Shell Money Production in Malaita. *Oceania*
        41 (4): 266–276.
1979   On the Beginning of Colonialism in Melanesia. In *The Pacification
        of Melanesia*, edited by Margaret Rodman and Matthew Cooper, pp.
        25–41. ASAO Monograph no. 7. Ann Arbor: University of Michigan
        Press.
Coote, Walter
1883   *The Western Pacific.* London: Sampson Low, Marston, Searle, and
        Rivington. (New York: Praeger, 1969.)
Coppet, Daniel de
1977   First Exchange, Double Illusion. *Journal of the Cultural Association
        of the Solomon Islands* 5:23–39.
Corris, Peter
1968   "Blackbirding" in New Guinea Waters, 1883–84: An episode in the
        Queensland Labour Trade. *Journal of Pacific History* 3:85–105.
1970   Kwaisulia of Ada Gege: A strongman in the Solomon Islands. In
        Pacific Islands Portraits, edited by J. W. Davidson and Deryck
        Scarr, pp. 253–265. Canberra: Australian National University Press.
1973   *Passage, Port and Plantation: A History of Solomon Islands Labour
        Migration, 1870–1914.* Melbourne: Melbourne University Press.
Crichlow, Nathaniel
1921   *A Brief Guide for the Layman on the Recognition, Treatment and
        Prevention of the Common Diseases of the Solomon Islands.* Olea,
        Guadalcanal: Melanesian Mission.
Cromar, John
1935   *Jock of the Islands: Early days in the South Seas . . .* London: Faber
        & Faber.
Czarkowska Starzecka, Dorota, and B. A. L. Cranstone
1974   *The Solomon Islanders.* London: British Museum.
Dalton, George
1967   Primitive Money. In *Tribal and Peasant Economies: Readings in Eco-
        nomic Anthropology*, edited by George Dalton, pp. 254–281. Gar-
        den City, NY: Natural History Press.
Davenport, William
1962   Red-feather Money. *Scientific American* 206 (3): 94–104.
1964   Notes on Santa Cruz Voyaging. *Journal of the Polynesian Society* 73
        (2): 134–142.

1975 The population of the Outer Reef Islands, British Solomon Islands Protectorate. In *Pacific Atoll Populations*, edited by Vern Carroll, pp. 64–116. Honolulu: University Press of Hawaii.

Davenport, William, and Gülbün Çoker
1967 The Moro Movement of Guadalcanal, British Solomons Protectorate. *Journal of the Polynesian Society* 76 (2): 123–175.

Day, J.
[1881] Journal aboard *Sea Breeze*. Government agent's journal no. 30, 8 April to 19 July 1881. FNA, Immigration Department.

Deck, Northcote
1945 *South from Guadalcanal: The Romance of Rennell Island*. Toronto: Evangelical Publishers.

Denham, H. M.
1855 Report of Proceedings of HMS *Herald*, November 1854 to January 1855. Mitchell Library, Sydney.

Derry, T. K., and Trevor I. Williams
1960 *A Short History of Technology from the earliest times to A.D. 1900.* Oxford: Clarendon Press.

Dick, Gordon, and Bob McKillop
1976 A brief history of agricultural extension and education in Papua New Guinea. Extension Bulletin no. 10. Port Moresby: Department of Primary Industry.

Dickinson, Joseph H. C.
1927 *A Trader in the Savage Solomons*. London: Witherby.

Dillon, Peter
1829 *Narrative of La Pérouse's Expedition*. Vol. 2. London: Hurst, Chance.

Dumont d'Urville, M. J.
1843 *Voyage au Pole Sud et dans l'Océanie sur les corvettes l'Astrolabe et La Zélée . . . pendant les années 1837 . . . 1840. . . . Vol. 5, Histoire du Voyage . . .* Paris: Gide.

Edge-Partington, James
var. Correspondence relating to the Solomon Islands. In Alexander Turnbull Library, Wellington, New Zealand; on microfilm, Department of Pacific and Southeast Asian History, ANU.

Edge-Partington, T. W.
1907 Ingava, Chief of Rubiana, Solomon Islands: died 1906. *Man* 7:22–23.

Eliza
[1805– 1806] Whaling log. Peabody Museum, Salem, MA. PMB 217, 222.

Eliza Ann
[1845– 1848] Whaling log. Essex Institute, Salem, MA. PMB 211, 212.

Elizabeth
[1847– 1851] Whaling log. Peabody Museum, Salem, MA. PMB 217; Kendall Whaling Museum, Sharon, MA. PMB 808.

Elkington, Tommy
  1965   Typescript of interview with official of Department of Labour,
          Honiara.
Elton, F.
  1888   Notes on natives of the Solomon Islands. *Journal of the [Royal]
          Anthropological Institute* 17:90–99.
Epstein, T. Scarlett
  1968   *Capitalism, Primitive and Modern: Some Aspects of Tolai Economic
          Growth.* Manchester: Manchester University Press.
Eugenia
  [1859– Whaling log. Falmouth Historical Society, Falmouth, MA. PMB
  1864]   785.
Eyerdam, Walter J.
  1930   Journal, 1930. Papers of the Whitney South Sea Expedition, Ameri-
          can Museum of Natural History; photocopy of excerpts in possession
          of Professor Roger Keesing, ANU.
  1933   Among the Mountain Bushmen of Malaita. *Natural History* 33:430–
          438.
[FRCP] Fairley, Rigby and Company Limited
  1912–   Correspondence and papers. In University of Melbourne Archives.
  1920
Fallowes, R. P.
  1929–   Letters, diary, and papers. In NLA, Canberra.
  1934
Fay, C. R.
  1940   The Movement towards Free Trade 1820–1853. In *Cambridge His-
          tory of the British Empire*, edited by J. Holland Rose et al. Vol. 2,
          The Growth of the New Empire, pp. 388–414. Cambridge: Univer-
          sity Press.
Feldt, Eric A.
  1967   *The Coast Watchers.* Sydney: Angus and Robertson.
Feinberg, Richard
  1982   Structural Dimensions of Sociopolitical Change on Anuta, S.I.
          Pacific Studies 5 (2): 1–19.
Fellowes
  [1850– Log in Nicholson Whaling Collection, Providence, RI. PMB 861.
  1853]
Ferguson, R. J. C.
  [1881] Journal aboard *Jessie Kelly.* Government agent's journal no. 32, 9
          July to 13 November 1881; portion from 22 October to 13 November
          missing. FNA, Immigration Department.
  [1882] Journal aboard *Jessie Kelly.* Government agent's journal no. 38, 1
          April to 20 August 1882. FNA, Immigration Department.
Festetics von Tolna, Count Rudolf [Rudolphe Festetics de Tolna]
  1903   *Chez les Cannibales.* Paris: Plon-Nourrit.
Fieldhouse, David K.
  1978   *Unilever Overseas: The Anatomy of a Multinational, 1895–1965.*
          London: Croom Helm/Stanford: Hoover Institution Press.

Fiji Gazette and Central Polynesian
1871–1874
Fiji Times
1875–   Daily. Suva.
1885
Firth, Raymond
1936   *We, the Tikopia: A sociological study of kinship in Primitive Polyne-sia.* London: George Allen & Unwin.
1959   *Social Change in Tikopia: Re-study of a Polynesian community after a generation.* London: George Allen & Unwin.

Firth, Stewart
1973   German Firms in the Western Pacific Islands, 1857–1914. *Journal of Pacific History* 8:10–28.
1982   *New Guinea under the Germans.* Melbourne: Melbourne University Press.

Fletcher, J. J.
[1883]   Journal aboard *Hally Bayley.* Government agent's journal no. 45, 11 April to 9 August 1883. FNA, Immigration Department.
[1884]   Journal aboard *Winifred.* Government agent's journal no. 53, 21 July to 12 November 1884. FNA, Immigration Department.

Fortune
[1840–   Whaling log. Old Dartmouth Whaling Museum, New Bedford, MA.
1844]   PMB 862.
Foster, Honore
1975   A Sydney Whaler 1829–32: The Reminiscences of James Heberley. *Journal of Pacific History* 10 (1–2): 90–104.

Fowler, Wilfred
1959   *This Island's Mine.* London: Constable.

Fox, Charles E.
1924   *The Threshold of the Pacific: an Account of the Social Organization Magic and Religion of the People of San Cristoval in the Solomon Islands.* London: Kegan Paul, Trench, Trubner.
1962   *Kakamora.* London: Hodder and Stoughton.
1975   *The Story of the Solomons.* Rev. ed. Sydney: Pacific Publications.

Fraser, John A.
1954   *Gold Dish and Kava Bowl.* London: Dent.

Frazer, Ian L.
1973   North Malaita Report: A Study of Socio-Economic Change in North-West Malaita. Victoria University of Wellington, Department of Geography.

Gabites, J. F.
1960   A Survey of Tropical Cyclones in the South Pacific. *New Zealand Meteorological Service Technical Information Circular* no. 107. Wellington: Government Printer.

Gammage, Bill
1975   The Rabaul Strike, 1929. *Journal of Pacific History* 10 (3–4): 3–29.

Gann, L. H., and Peter Duignan, eds.
1969   *Colonialism in Africa, 1870–1960.* Vol. 1, *The History and Politics of Colonialism, 1870–1914.* Cambridge: University Press.

478 Bibliography

478   *Bibliography*

Garanger, José
1966   Recherches archéologiques aux Nouvelles-Hébrides. *L'Homme* 6 (1): 59–81.
1972   *Archéologie des Nouvelles Hébrides.* Publication de la Société des Océanistes, no. 30. Musée de l'Homme. Paris: Office de la Recherche Scientifique et Technique Outre-Mer.

Gay Head
[1852– Whaling log. New Bedford Free Public Library, New Bedford, MA.
1856] PMB 327.

General Scott
[1855– Whaling log. New Bedford Free Public Library, New Bedford, MA.
1859] PMB 327, 328.

[GDRNA] German Democratic Republic National Archives
1886   Wirtersheim an Chef der Admiralität, 25 Oktober 1886, Berichtüberdie Reise SM Kr *Adler.*
1893   Fischer an Ober-Kommando der Marine, 8 Februar 1893. RKA 2982, Records of the German Colonial Office.
       (Copies kindly provided by Dr. Stewart Firth.)

[GEIC] Gilbert and Ellice Islands Colony
1926– *Report for [year]. Colonial Reports—Annual.* 1924–1928. London:
1929   HMSO.

Gillion, K. L.
1962   *Fiji's Indian Migrants: A History to the End of Indenture in 1920.* Melbourne: Oxford University Press.

Gilson, R. P.
1970   *Samoa 1830 to 1900: The Politics of a Multi-cultural Community.* Melbourne: Oxford University Press.

Gipsy
[1839– Log of, 1839–1843. TS 198, Department of Pacific and Southeast
1843] Asian History, ANU.

Godelier, M.
1969   La "monnaie de sel" des Baruya de Nouvelle-Guinée. *L'Homme* 9 (2): 5–37.

Goldie, John F.
1914   The Solomon Islands. In *A Century in the Pacific,* edited by James Colwell, pp. 559–585. Sydney: Beale.
var.   Correspondence, Joint Board for Overseas Mission, Wellington Street, Auckland. PMB 925.

Golson, Jack
1968   Archaeological Prospects for Melanesia. In *Prehistoric Culture in Oceania: A Symposium,* edited by I. Yawata and Y. H. Sinoto, pp. 3–14. Eleventh Pacific Science Congress, Tokyo, 1966. Honolulu: Bishop Museum Press.
1972   Both sides of the Wallace Line: New Guinea, Australia, Island Melanesia and Asian Prehistory. In *Early Chinese Art and its Possible Influence in the Pacific Basin: A Symposium . . .* Vol. 3, *Oceania and the Americas,* edited by Noel Barnard, pp. 533–595. New York: Intercultural Arts Press.

Goodenough, V. H., ed.
1876   *Journal of Commodore Goodenough . . . 1873–1875.* London: Henry S. King.

Green, Kaye C.
1976   The History of Post-Spanish European Contact in the Eastern District Before 1939. In Green and Cresswell 1976:31–46.

Green, Roger C.
1976   New Sites with Lapita Pottery and their implications for an Understanding of the Settlement of the Western Pacific. In Colloque 22, *La Préhistoire Océanienne*, edited by José Garanger, pp. 55–87. Ninth congress of Union International des Sciences Préhistoriques et Protohistoriques, Nice. Paris: Centre National de la Recherche Scientifique.

Green, Roger C., and M. M. Cresswell, eds.
1976   *Southeast Solomon Islands Cultural History: A Preliminary Survey.* Wellington: Royal Society of New Zealand.

Groenewegen, K.
[1972]   *Report on the Census of the Population, 1970.* Honiara: WPHC, BSIP.

Grover, John C.
1958   *The Solomon Islands: Geological Exploration and Research, 1953–1956.* The Geological Survey of the B.S.I., Memoir no. 2. London: WPHC.

Groves, W. C.
1940   Report on a Survey of Education in the British Solomon Islands Protectorate. Mimeograph in Barr-Smith Library, Adelaide.

Guppy, Henry B.
1887   *The Solomon Islands and their Natives.* London: Swan Sonnenschein, Lowrey.

Hackman, Brian D.
1968   *A Guide to the Spelling and Pronunciation of Place Names in the British Solomon Islands Protectorate.* BSIP Lands and Surveys Department. Honiara: Government Printing Office.

Haddock, R
[1877]   Journal aboard *Marion Rennie*. Government agent's journal no. 4, 24 June to 28 December 1877. FNA, Immigration Department.

Hagen, A.
1893   Voyage aux Nouvelles-Hébrides et aux Iles Salomon. *Le Tour du Monde* 22 (3 Juin): 338–384.

Hamilton, William
[1852–   Papers of Captain William Hamilton, 1852–1937. In Oxley Memo-
1937]   rial Library, Brisbane. PMB 15.

Hansell, John R. F., and John R. D. Wall
1976   *Land Resources of the Solomon Islands.* Vol. 1: *Introduction and Recommendations.* Land Resource Study 18. Surbiton, Surrey: Land Resources Division, Ministry of Overseas Development.

Hardy, Norman H., and E. Way Elkington
1907   *The Savage South Seas.* London: A. & C. Black.

Harris, Joe
  1968   The Struggle Against Pacific Island Labour, 1868–1902. *Labour History* 15 (November): 40–48.

Harwood, Frances Hine
  1971   The Christian Fellowship Church: A Revitalization Movement in Melanesia. PhD dissertation, University of Chicago.
  1978   Intercultural Communication in the Western Solomons: The Methodist Mission and the Emergence of the Christian Fellowship Church. In *Mission, Church, and Sect in Oceania*, edited by James A. Boutilier, Daniel T. Hughes, and Sharon W. Tiffany, pp. 231–250. ASAO Monograph no. 6. Ann Arbor: University of Michigan Press/ Lanham, MD: University Press of America.

Hastings, Peter
  1976   Bougainville and the Solomons: An Inevitable Union? *New Guinea and Australia, the Pacific and South-east Asia* 10 (3): 33–41.

Helen Snow
  [1867–   Whaling log. New Bedford Free Public Library, New Bedford, MA.
  1871]   PMB 332.

Hendren, Gilbert H.
  1976   Recent Settlement Pattern Changes on Ulawa, Southeast Solomon Islands. In Green and Cresswell 1976:149–159.

Herald
  [1804–   Log in Essex Institute, Salem, MA. PMB 201.
  1805]

Herald
  [1847–   Log in Nicholson Whaling Collection, Providence, RI. PMB 867.
  1854]

Herlihy, Joan M.
  1980   Decolonization Politics in Solomon Islands: The Model That Never Was. Seminar paper, Canberra, Australian National University. Published in *Melanesia Beyond Diversity* (vol. 2), edited by R. J. May and Hank Nelson, pp. 571–600 (Canberra: ANU Research School of Pacific Studies, 1982).
  1981   "Always we are Last": A Study of Planning, Development and Disadvantage in Melanesia. PhD dissertation, ANU.
  1982   Rituals, Rhetoric and Reality: Decolonization and Associated Phenomena. Seminar paper, ANU.

Hermant, Paul, and R. W. Cilento
  1929   *Report of the Mission Entrusted with a Survey on Health Conditions in the Pacific Islands.* Geneva: League of Nations.

Hernsheim, Eduard
  [1880–   Diary, 7 January 1880 to 17 June 1881. Manuscript in English in pos-
  1881]   session of Dr. Peter Sack, Department of Law, ANU.

Herr, Richard A., and E. A. Rood, eds.
  1978   *A Solomons Sojourn: J. E. Philp's Log of the "Makira," 1912–1913.* Hobart: Tasmanian Historical Research Association.

Heussler, Robert
  1963   *Yesterday's Rulers: The Making of the British Colonial Service.* London: Oxford University Press/Syracuse: Syracuse University Press.

Hilliard, David L.
1966   Protestant Missions in the Solomon Islands, 1849–1942. PhD dissertation, ANU.
1969   The South Sea Evangelical Mission in the Solomon Islands: The Foundation Years. *Journal of Pacific History* 4:41–64.
1974   Colonialism and Christianity: The Melanesian Mission in the Solomon Islands. *Journal of Pacific History* 9:93–116.
1978   *God's Gentlemen: A History of the Melanesian Mission, 1849–1942.* Brisbane: University of Queensland Press.

Hirst, M.
n.d.   Memoirs. Typescript in Burns Philip Archives, Sydney.

Hocart, Arthur M.
1931   Warfare in Eddystone of the Solomon Islands. *Journal of The Royal Anthropological Institute of Great Britain and Ireland* 61:301–324.
var.   Papers. In Alexander Turnbull Library, Wellington; on microfilm, Department of Pacific and Southeast Asian History, ANU.

Hogbin, H. Ian
1934   Culture Change in the Solomon Islands: Report of Field Work in Guadalcanal and Malaita. *Oceania* 4 (3): 233–267.
1938   Social Organization of Guadalcanal and Florida, Solomon Islands. *Oceania* 8 (4): 398–402.
1939   *Experiments in Civilization: The Effects of European Culture on a Native Community of the Solomon Islands.* London: George Routledge and Sons; reprinted 1969 by Routledge and Kegan Paul.
1964   *A Guadalcanal Society: The Kaoka Speakers.* New York: Holt Rinehart and Winston.

Hookey, J. F.
1971   The establishment of a plantation economy in the British Solomon Islands Protectorate. In *The History of Melanesia: Second Waigani Seminar,* pp. 229–238. Canberra: Research School of Pacific Studies, Australian National University and University of Papua New Guinea.

Hope
[1863]   Whaling log. Peabody Museum, Salem, MA. PMB 222; Old Dartmouth Whaling Museum, New Bedford, MA. PMB 279.

Hopkins, Arthur I.
[1928]   Autobiography: Melanesian Mission 1900–1925. At diocesan office of Church of Melanesia, Honiara. PMB 557.
1928   *In the Isles of King Solomon.* London: Seeley, Service.

Horton, D. C.
1965   *The Happy Isles: A Diary of the Solomons.* London: Heinemann.
1970   *Fire Over the Islands: The Coast Watchers of the Solomons.* Sydney: Reed.

Houghton, Philip
1980   *The First New Zealanders.* Auckland: Hodder and Stoughton.

Hughes, Tony
1979   Evaluating Land Settlement. In Larmour 1979:232–238.

Hunter, J.
1793   *An Historical Journal of the Transactions at Port Jackson and North Island.* London: Stockdale.

Hyam, Ronald
1976   *Britain's Imperial Century, 1815-1914.* London: Batsford.
Ianthe
[1844–   Whaling log. Essex Institute, Salem, MA. PMB 210.
1845]
Imperial Economic Committee
1938   *Vegetable Oils and Oilseeds.* London: HMSO.
Inglis, Amirah
1974   *Not a White Woman Safe: Sexual Anxiety and Politics in Port Moresby, 1920-1934.* Canberra: ANU Press.
Innes, James Ross
1938   *Report of Leprosy Survey of the British Solomon Islands Protectorate.* Suva: WPHC.
Irwin, G. J.
1972   An Archaeological Survey in the Shortland Islands, BSIP. MA thesis, University of Auckland.
Ivens, Walter G.
1927   *Melanesians of the South-east Solomon Islands.* London: Kegan Paul, Trench, Trubner.
1930   *The Island Builders of the Pacific* . . . London: Seeley, Service.
Jack-Hinton, Colin
1969   *The Search for the Islands of Solomon, 1567-1838.* Oxford: Clarendon Press.
Jackson, James C.
1968   *Planters and Speculators.* Kuala Lumpur: University of Malaya.
Jackson, K. B.
1972   Head-hunting and Santa Isabel, Solomon Islands, 1568-1901. BA Hons thesis, ANU.
1975   Head-hunting in the Christianization of Bugotu 1861-1900. *Journal of Pacific History* 10 (1): 65–78.
1978   Tie Hokara, Tie Vaka: Black Man, White Man, a Study of the New Georgia Group to 1925. PhD dissertation, ANU.
James, Clifford S.
1956   *Diseases Commonly met with in Melanesia and Polynesia: Their Diagnosis, Prevention and Treatment.* Auckland: Institute Printing and Publishing Society.
James Arnold
[1857–   Whaling log. Old Dartmouth Whaling Museum, New Bedford, MA.
1859]   PMB 260.
Jirah Perry
[1860–   Whaling log. Nicholas Whaling Collection, Providence, RI. PMB
1864]   884.
John and Winthrop
[1885–   Whaling log. Kendall Whaling Museum, Sharon, MA. PMB 811.
1858]
Johnson, Osa H. L.
c. 1940 *I Married Adventure.* London: Hutchinson.
1945   *Bride in the Solomons.* London: Harrap.

Jolly, W. P.
  1976   *Lord Leverhulme, a Biography.* London: Constable.
[Jose, Arthur W.]
  1915   *British Mismanagement in the Pacific.* Sydney: Websdale, Shoo-
          smith. (Pamphlet.)

Keesing, Roger M.
  1967   Christians and Pagans in Kwaio, Malaita. *Journal of the Polynesian
          Society* 76:82–100.
  1968   Chiefs in a Chiefless Society: The Ideology of Modern Kwaio Poli-
          tics. *Oceania* 38:276–280.
  1977   *Kwaio Religion.* Honiara: Cultural Association of the Solomon
          Islands.
  1978   Politico-Religious Movements and Anticolonialism on Malaita:
          Maasina Rule in Historical Perspective. *Oceania* 48 (4): 241–261 and
          49 (1): 46–73.
  1980   Antecedents of Maasina Rule: Some Further Notes. *Journal of
          Pacific History* 15:102–107.

Keesing, Roger M., and Peter Corris
  1980   *Lightning Meets the West Wind: The Malaita Massacre.* Melbourne:
          Oxford University Press.

Kenilorea, Peter
  1973   Political Development. In *Priorities in Melanesian Development:
          Sixth Waigani Seminar,* edited by Ronald J. May, pp. 23–26. Can-
          berra: ANU Research School of Pacific Studies and UPNG.

Kennedy, D. C.
  n.d.   Marching Rule in the British Solomon Islands Protectorate. Copy of
          manuscript in Department of Pacific and Southeast Asian History,
          ANU.
Kent Family Papers
  1803   Mrs. William Kent's Journal, 13 May–13 October 1803. Vol. 4.
          A3968, Mitchell Library, Sydney.

Knibbs, S. G. C.
  1929   *The Savage Solomons as They Were and Are: A Record of a Head-
          hunting People Gradually Emerging from a Life of Savage Cruelty
          and Bloody Customs, with a Description of their Manners and Ways
          and of the Beauties and Potentialities of the Islands.* London: Seeley,
          Service.

Lambert, S. M.
  1928   Medical Conditions in the South Pacific. *Medical Journal of Austra-
          lia,* (September): 364–375.
  1942   *A Doctor in Paradise.* Melbourne: Jaboor/London: Dent. (Published
          in USA under title *A Yankee Doctor in Paradise,* Boston: Little,
          Brown, 1941.)
Laracy, Hugh M.
  1971   Marching Rule and the Missions. *Journal of Pacific History* 6:96–
          114.
  1974   Unwelcome Guests: The Solomons' Chinese. *New Guinea and Aus-
          tralia, the Pacific and South-east Asia* 8 (4): 27–37.

1976   *Marists and Melanesians: A History of Catholic Missions in the Solo-mon Islands.* Canberra: ANU Press/Honolulu: University Press of Hawaii.

Laracy, Hugh M., ed.
1983   *Pacific Protest: The Maasina Rule Movement, Solomon Islands, 1944–1952.* Suva: Institute of Pacific Studies, University of the South Pacific.

Larmour, Peter, ed.
1979   *Land in Solomon Islands.* Suva: University of the South Pacific Insti-tute of Pacific Studies and Ministry of Agriculture and Lands, Solo-mon Islands.

Larson, Eric H.
1966   *Nukufero: a Tikopian Colony in the Russell Islands.* Eugene: Univer-sity of Oregon Department of Anthropology.

Lasaqa, I. Q.
1972   *Melanesians' Choice: Tadhimboko Participation in the Solomon Islands Cash Economy.* New Guinea Research Unit Bulletin no. 46. Canberra: ANU.

Lawrence, P., and M. J. Meggitt, eds.
1965   *Gods Ghosts and Men in Melanesia: Some Religions of Australian New Guinea and the New Hebrides.* Melbourne: Oxford University Press.

Lea, David A. M.
1972   Indigenous Horticulture in Melanesia. In Ward 1972, 252–279.

Leach, R.
1948   Report on Amplypelta Nutfall of Coconuts in Palms in the Solomon Islands, Lever's Pacific Plantation. National Library of the Solomon Islands.

Leber, A.
c. 1914   Vorlaufiger Bericht der Medizinische-Demographische Deutsch-Neuguinea-Expedition des Reichskolonialamtes: Salomons-Inseln. Australian National Archives, Melbourne.

Leubuscher, Charlotte
1951   *The Processing of Colonial Raw Materials: A Study in Location.* London: HMSO.

Levant
[1844–   Whaling log. Peter Foulger Museum, Nantucket, MA. PMB 782.
1845]

Lever Brothers
var.   Pacific Material in Unilever Archives. TT 3734, 112A, Sunlight Works, England; on microfilm Department of Pacific and Southeast Asian History, ANU.

Lever, R. J.
c. 1935   The Present Economic Position of the Coconut Industry. *BSIP Agri-cultural Gazette* 3 (2): 10–11.

[LPP] Lever's Pacific Plantations Limited
n.d. *a*   Brief History of Lever's Plantations in the Pacific. Typescript. Copy in Department of Pacific and Southeast Asian History, ANU.
n.d. *b*   Ufa Estates Record. MS in Alderman Library, University of Virginia,

Charlottesville, VA. Microfilm MS 424, Alexander Turnbull Library, Wellington.

Lewis, W. Arthur
1952   World Production, Prices and Trade, 1870–1960. *Manchester School of Economics and Social Studies* 20 (2): 105–138.
1970   *Tropical Development, 1880–1913*. London: Allen and Unwin.

Lewthwaite, G. R.
1962   Land, Life and Agriculture to Mid-Century. In *Western Samoa: Land, Life and Agriculture in Tropical Polynesia*, edited by J. W. Fox and K. B. Cumberland, pp. 130–176. Christchurch: Whitcombe & Tombs.

Lion
[1854– Whaling log. Nicholson Whaling Collection, Providence, RI. PMB
1856]   875.

Liverpool, C. C. S. Foljambe
1865   Letter from the *Curaçoa;* on microfilm C18295, NLA, Canberra.

Luana, Casper, [pseud.]
1969   Buka! A Retrospect. *New Guinea and Australia, the Pacific and South-east Asia* 4 (1): 15–20.

Luke, Sir Harry
1945   *From a South Seas Diary, 1938–1942*. London: Nicholson & Watson.

Luxton, Clarence T. J.
1955   *Isles of Solomon: A tale of Missionary Adventure*. Auckland: Methodist and Foreign Mission Society of New Zealand.

MacGillivray, John
[1852– Private Journal aboard HMS *Herald* to the South Pacific. Admiralty
1855]   Library, London; on microfilm, NLA, Canberra.

McKinnon, John M.
1972   Bilua Changes: Culture Contact and its Consequences, a Study of the Bilua of Vella Lavella in the British Solomon Islands. PhD dissertation, Victoria University of Wellington.
1973   Bilua Report: Preliminary results of research into rural economic development . . . Vella Lavella . . . B.S.I.P. Victoria University of Wellington, Department of Geography.
1975   Tomahawks, turtles and traders: A reconstruction in the circular causation of warfare in the New Georgia group. *Oceania* 45 (4): 290–307.

McLaren, Jack
1923   *My Odyssey*. London: Jonathan Cape.

McNeill, William H.
1977   *Plagues and Peoples*. Oxford: Blackwell.

MacQuarrie, Hector
1946   *Vouza and the Solomon Islands*. Sydney: Angus and Robertson.

Mair, H. A.
[1880]   Journal aboard *Flirt*. Government agent's journal no. 27, 24 August to 26 December 1880. FNA, Immigration Department.

Mamara Plantations
c. 1905 Prospectus. Sydney: Mamara Plantations.

Marengo
[1871– Whaling log. Essex Institute, Salem, MA. PMB 214.
1875]

Martha
[1854– Whaling log. New Bedford Free Public Library, New Bedford, MA.
1858] PMB 347.

Marwick, J. G., comp.
1935   *The Adventures of John Renton.* Kirkwall: Kirkwall Press.

Marx, Karl
1978   *The Eighteenth Brumaire of Louis Bonaparte.* Peking: Foreign Language Press.

Matilda Sears
[1873– Whaling log. Nicholson Whaling Collection, Providence, RI. PMB
1877] 879.

Maude, H. E., with Ida Leeson
1968   The Coconut Oil Trade of the Gilbert Islands. In *Of Islands and Men: Studies in Pacific History,* edited by H. E. Maude, pp. 233–283. Melbourne: Oxford University Press.

Mauler, J. von, and Wilhelm Kesslitz
1899   The Scientific Mission of SM *Albatros,* 1895–1898. In *Report from the 'K.K.' Geographical Society in Vienna,* vol. 1, edited by A. B. E. von Böhmerscheim, translated by V. C. Wasem. Vienna: Lechner. Mimeograph in writer's possession.

Mead, Margaret
1956   *New Lives for Old: Cultural Transformation—Manus, 1928–1953.* London: Victor Gollancz/New York: Morrow.

Mead, Sidney
1973   *Material Culture and Art in the Star Harbour Region, Eastern Solomon Islands.* Toronto: Royal Ontario Museum.

Melvin, J. D.
1977   *The Cruise of the Helena: A Labour-recruiting Voyage to the Solomon Islands.* Edited by Peter Corris. Melbourne: Hawthorn.

Metcalfe, John R.
[1902– Miscellaneous Papers on the Solomon Islands, 1902–1964. Depart-
1964] ment of Pacific and Southeast Asian History, ANU (to be deposited at Mitchell Library, Sydney). PMB 413.
[1911– Diaries, 1 Jan. 1911 to 30 Nov. 1969. Department of Pacific and
1969] Southeast Asian History, ANU (to be deposited at Mitchell Library, Sydney). PMB 74–79.

[MMP] Methodist Mission
var.   Papers. Mitchell Library, Sydney.

Miller, Daniel
1978a The Development of Solomon Island Politics to Independence. *Journal of the Cultural Association of the Solomon Islands* 6:1–17.
1978b An Organizational Approach to Exchange Media: An Example from the Western Solomons. *Mankind* 11 (3): 288–295.
1980   Settlement and Diversity in the Solomon Islands. *Man* 15 (3): 451–466.

Miller, J.
1949   *The War in the Pacific, Guadalcanal: the First Offensive.* Washington: Department of the Army.

Minorca
1802   Logbook. In India Office Library, London; on microfilm, Department of Pacific and Southeast Asian History, ANU.

Mohawk
[1859– Whaling log. Whaling Museum, Nantucket, MA. PMB 390.
1863]

Monberg, Torben
1976   *Mobile in the Trade Wind: the Reactions of People on Bellona Island towards a Mining Project.* Copenhagen: National Museum of Denmark.

Monneron, P.
1914   Extracts from the Journal of a Voyage . . . on . . . *Saint Jean Baptiste.* . . . In *Historical Records of New Zealand*, vol. 2, edited by Robert McNab, pp. 231–295. Wellington: Government Printer.

Moorhouse, H. C.
1929   *BSIP, Report of Commissioner Appointed . . . to inquire into the circumstances in which murderous attacks took place in 1927 on Government Officials on Guadalcanal and Malaita.* London: HMSO for GBCO.

Moresby, John
1876   *Discoveries and Surveys in New Guinea and the D'Entrecasteaux Islands.* London: Murray.

Morgan, D. J.
1980   *The Official History of Colonial Development*, vol. 1: *The Origins of British Aid Policy, 1924–1945;* vol. 5: *Guidance Towards Self-Government in British Colonies, 1941–1971.* Atlantic Highlands, NJ: Humanities Press.

Morrell, Benjamin
1832   *A Narrative of four voyages to the South Sea, north and south Pacific Ocean, Chinese Sea, Ethiopic and Southern Atlantic Ocean, Indian and Antarctic Ocean . . . 1822–31 . . .* New York: J. & J. Harper. (Upper Saddle River, NJ: Gregg Press, 1070.)

Morrell, William P.
1960   *Britain in the Pacific Islands.* Oxford: Clarendon Press.

Moynagh, Michael
1978   Brown or White? A History of the Fiji Sugar Industry, 1873–1973. PhD dissertation, ANU.

Muhlhauser, George H. P.
1924   *The Cruise of the "Amaryllis."* London: John Lane, The Bodley Head.

Muspratt, Eric
1931   *My South Sea Island.* London: Hopkinson.

Mytinger, Caroline
1942   *Head-hunting in the Solomon Islands around the Coral Sea.* New York: Macmillan.

[NM] *Nautical Magazine and Naval Chronicle*
1832– London. Monthly.
1860
Navigator
[1845– Whaling log. Essex Institute, Salem, MA. PMB 211.
1847]
Nazareth, G. P.
1971   Free Association and the Decolonization of Micro-Territories. Paper,
        ANU.

Nerdrum, J. G. B.
1901–   Indtryk og oplevelser under et 7 aars ophold paa Salomon-oerne,
1902   *Norske Geog. Selskabs Aarbog* 13:22–58. (*Norwegian Geographical
        Society Yearbook;* translated by P. Stenbo, Auckland; copy in
        writer's possession.)

Newbury, Colin
1973   Treaty, Grant, Usage and Sufferance: The Origins of British Colonial
        Protectorates. In *W. P. Morrell: A Tribute,* edited by G. A. Wood
        and P. S. O'Connor, pp. 69–84. Dunedin: University of Otago Press.
New South Wales Customs House Statistics, 1882, 1883
1883,   Sydney: NSW Government Printer.
1884
New South Wales State Archives
var.   Companies Office Records
var.   List of vessels arrived, Port of Sydney. Colonial Secretary, COD 92.

Nicholls, F.
[1880] Journal aboard *Dauntless.* Government agent's journal no. 19, 4
        April to 6 July 1880. FNA, Immigration Department.
Nile
1802   Logbook. In India Office Library, London; on microfilm, Depart-
        ment of Pacific and Southeast Asian History, ANU.
Norden, Hermann
1926   *Byways of the Tropic Seas: Wanderings Among the Solomons and in
        the Malay Archipelago.* London: Witherley.
Norman
[1855– Whaling log. Whaling Institute, Nantucket, MA. PMB 380, 381.
1860]
O'Connor, P. S.
1968   The Problem of Indentured Labour in Samoa Under the Military
        Administration. *Political Science* 20 (2): 10–27.
O'Ferrall, W. C.
1908   *Santa Cruz and the Reef Islands.* London: Melanesian Mission.
Oliver, Douglas L.
1955   *A Solomon Island Society: Kinship and Leadership among the Siuai
        of Bougainville.* Cambridge, MA: Harvard University Press.
Ontario
[1863– Whaling log. Nicholson Whaling Collection, Providence, RI. PMB
1866]   886.
Otway, Franc
[1895– Journal aboard *Sydney Belle.* Government agent's journal no. 63, 7

1896] September 1895 to 24 February 1896; entries for 31 January to 5 February missing. FNA, Immigration Department.

[1899] Journal aboard *Rotuma*. Government agent's journal no. 64, 27 April to 1 November 1899. FNA, Immigration Department.

Pacific Islands Company, the Pacific Phosphate Company, and Levers Pacific Plantations Ltd.

 var. Papers. Unilever House, London; on microfilm, Department of Pacific and Southeast Asian History, ANU.

Pacific Islands Monthly
 1930– Sydney.
 1978

Paddock, William C.
 1893 *Life on the Ocean or Thirty-five years at Sea*. Cambridge: Riverside Press.

Page, K. R.
 1975 Western Economic Impact on Indigenous Life in Fiji and Tonga, 1868–1875. BA Hons thesis, Macquarie University, Sydney.

Paia, Warren
 1975 Aspects of Constitutional Development in the Solomon Islands. *Journal of Pacific History* 10 (1–2): 81–89.

Palmer, B. S.
 n.d. The Interaction of Churches and State in the British Solomon Islands Protectorate or in the Designated Schools Scheme, 1964–67. Paper, n.p.

Parachute
 [1859– Whaling log. Old Dartmouth Whaling Museum, New Bedford, MA.
 1864] PMB 271.

Parkinson, Richard H. R.
 1887 *Im Bismark-Archipel*. Leipzig: F. A. Brockhaus.

Patterson
 [1803– Whaling log. Rhode Island Historical Society, Providence, RI. PMB
 1804] 770.

Penny, Alfred
 1876– Diaries. MS B807–17, Mitchell Library, Sydney.
 1886

Peruvian
 [1852– Whaling log. Whaling Museum, Nantucket, MA. PMB 382.
 1856]

Phillip, Arthur
 1789 *The voyage of Governor Phillip to Botany Bay* . . . Compiled by John Stockdale. London: Stockdale.

Phillips, J. S.
 1940 *Coconut Quest: The Story of a Search in the Solomon Islands and the East Indies*. London: Jarrolds.

Pietrusewsky, Michael
 1976 *Prehistoric Human Skeletal Remains from Papua New Guinea and the Marquesas*. Honolulu: Social Science and Linguistics Institute, University of Hawaii.

Potterton, Philip
    1979   The Solomon Islands Today. *Current Affairs Bulletin* 56 (6): 24–31.

Prendeville, Kerry F.
    1975   Socio-Religious Change Among the Gari Speaking People of Guadal-
            canal Island, British Solomon Islands. Seminar paper, Department
            of Anthropology and Sociology, University of Papua New Guinea.

Price, Charles A., with Elizabeth Baker
    1976   Origins of Pacific Island Labourers in Queensland, 1863–1904: A
            Research Note. *Journal of Pacific History* 11 (1–2): 106–121.

Purdy, John
    1816   *The Oriental Navigator or Directions for Sailing to, from, and upon
            the Coasts of the East Indies, China, Australia, ...* London:
            Laurie.

Rannie, Douglas
    1912   *My Adventures among South Sea Cannibals: An Account of the
            Experiences and Adventures of a Government Official among the
            Natives of Oceania.* London: Seeley, Service.

Raucaz, Louis M.
    1928   *In the Savage South Solomons: The Story of a Mission.* Lyon: Society
            for the Propagation of the Faith.

Rebman, C.
    [1879– Journal aboard *Dauntless.* Government agent's journal no. 18, 16
    1880]   November 1879 to 19 February 1880. FNA, Immigration Depart-
            ment.

Reilly, E.
    [1882] Journal aboard *Oamaru.* Government agent's journal no. 39, 1 July
            to 6 December 1882. FNA, Immigration Department.
    [1883] Journal aboard *Mavis.* Government agent's journal no. 46, 11 April
            to 19 August 1883. FNA, Immigration Department.

Rentz, John N.
    1952   *Marines in the Central Solomons.* Washington, DC: U.S. Marine
            Corps.

[*RRAACP*] *Research in Records of American Activities in the Central Pacific,
1790–1870. Data collected on the activities of New England seamen and
whalers in the Central Pacific Ocean.*
    c. 1950 Central Pacific Islands Project, Boston. (Mostly excerpts from Amer-
            ican newspapers and periodicals.) Microfilm, Department of Pacific
            History, ANU. (Published under title *American Activities in the Cen-
            tral Pacific 1790–1870*, 8 vols., edited by R. Gerard Ward. Ridge-
            wood, NJ: Gregg Press, 1966–1967.)

Resource
    [1799– Whaling log. San Francisco Maritime Museum, San Francisco. PMB
    1800]   790.

Ribbe, Carl
    1894   Reise nach Bougainville (Salomonen). *Globus* (August): 133–136.
    1903   *Zwei jahre unter den Kannibalen der Salomo-Inseln.* Dresden:
            Beyer.

Rietmann, O.
    1868   *Wanderungen in Australien und Polynesien.* St. Gallen: Scheitlin & Zollikofer.

Riogano, Josiah
    1979   Kolombangara. In Larmour 1979:85–89.

Rivers, William H. R., ed.
    1922   *Essays on the Depopulation of Melanesia.* Cambridge: University Press.

Roberts, Benjamin C.
    1964   *Labour in the Tropical Territories of the Commonwealth.* London: School of Economics and Political Science/Durham, NC: Duke University Press.

Robinson, J. W.
    1904   Whaling Reminiscences. Crowther Collection, Public Library of Tasmania, Hobart.

Robinson, Kenneth
    1965   *The Dilemmas of Trusteeship: Aspects of Colonial Policy Between the Wars.* Oxford: Oxford University Press.

Robinson, Ronald
    1980   Andrew Cohen and the Transfer of Power in Tropical Africa, 1940–1951. In *Decolonisation and After: The British and French Experience*, edited by W. H. Morris-Jones and Georges Fischer, pp. 50–72. London: Frank Cass.

Roscoe
    [1821– Whaling log. Peabody Museum, Salem, MA. PMB 270.
    1824]

Ross, Harold M.
    1973   *Baegu: Social and Ecological Organization in Malaita, Solomon Islands.* Illinois Studies in Anthropology no. 8. Urbana: University of Illinois Press.

Rowley, Charles D.
    1958   *The Australians in German New Guinea, 1914–1921.* Melbourne: Melbourne University Press.

Royalist, HMS
    1891   Log of. PRO/2001, ADM 53/15479, British Admiralty Records, London; on microfilm, NLA, Canberra.

Rudd, C.
    1877   Journal aboard *Dauntless.* Government agent's journal no. 6, 10 January to 23 June. FNA, Immigration Department.

Russell, T.
    1948   The Culture of Marovo, British Solomon Islands. *Journal of the Polynesian Society* 57:306–329.
    1970   The 1970 Constitution for the British Solomon Islands. In *The Politics of Melanesia: Fourth Waigani Seminar*, edited by Marion W. Ward, pp. 225–238. Canberra: ANU, Research School of Pacific Studies.

Ruthven, David
    1979   Land Legislation from the Protectorate to Independence. In Larmour 1979:239–248.

Ryan, Peter
1969   *The Hot Land*. Melbourne: Melbourne University Press.

Saemala, Francis J.
1979   *Our Independent Solomon Islands*. Honiara: Institute of Pacific Studies, University of the South Pacific.

Salisbury, Richard F.
1962   *From Stone to Steel: Economic Consequences of a Technological Change in New Guinea*. Melbourne: Melbourne University Press.
1970   *Vunamami: Economic Transformation in a Traditional Society*. Melbourne: Melbourne University Press/Berkeley: University of California Press.

Sandars, E.
1928–   Papers, 1928–1943. In care of Mrs. Joan Laws, Laura, NSW. PMB
1943   553.

Sarawia, George
1973   *They Came to My Island: The Beginnings of the Mission in the Banks Islands*. Honiara: Provincial Press, reprint edition. (Originally published at Taroaniara by Diocese of Melanesia Press, 1968.)

Sarfert, Ernst, and Hans Damm
1929   *Ergebnisse der Südsee Expedition 1908–1910*, 2, B, edited by G. Thilenius. Vol. 12: *Luangiua und Nukumanu*. Hamburg: Friederichsen, De Gruyter.

Saunana, John S.
1973   The Politics of Subservience. In *Priorities in Melanesian Development: Sixth Waigani Seminar*, edited by Ronald J. May, pp. 429–436. Canberra: ANU Research School of Pacific Studies and UPNG.

Saunders, Kay
1975   Uncertain Bondage: An Analysis of Indentured Labour in Queensland to 1907 with particular reference to Melanesian servants. PhD dissertation, University of Queensland.

Sayes, Shelley A.
1976   The Ethnohistory of Arosi, San Cristobal. MA thesis, University of Auckland.

Scarr, Deryck
1967   *Fragments of Empire: A History of the Western Pacific High Commission 1877–1914*. Canberra: ANU Press. (Honolulu: University of Hawaii Press, 1968.)

Scheffler, Harold W.
1965   *Choiseul Island Social Structure*. Berkeley: University of California Press.

Scherzer, Karl ritter von
1861   *Narrative of the Circumnavigation . . . by the Austrian Frigate "Novara" . . . in the Years 1857, 1858 & 1859*. London: Saunders, Otley.

Scott, Christopher, and Georges Sabagh
1970   The Historical Calendar as a Method of Estimating Age: The Experience of the Moroccan Multi-Purpose Sample Survey of 1961–63. *Population Studies, A Journal of Demography* 24:93–109.

Scragg, Roy F. R.
1954　*Depopulation in New Ireland: A Study of Demography and Fertility.* Port Moresby: Administration of Papua New Guinea.

Selwyn, Bishop George A.
1872　Papers. Letters re cruise of *Rosario,* 1872. Auckland Institute and Museum; microfilm, NLA, Canberra.

Seton, K. G. (Georgina)
n.d.　Frigate Bird. Manuscript of a novel in possession of K. G. Seton, Brisbane; copy in Department of Pacific and Southeast Asian History, ANU.

Shineberg, Dorothy
1967　*They Came for Sandalwood.* Melbourne: Melbourne University Press.
1971*a*　Guns and Men in Melanesia. *Journal of Pacific History* 6:61–82.

Shineberg, Dorothy, ed.
1971*b*　*The Trading Voyages of Andrew Cheyne, 1841–1844.* Pacific History Series, no. 3. Canberra: ANU Press.

Shipping Gazette and Sydney General Trade List
1844–　Sydney.
1860

Shutler, Mary Elizabeth, and Richard Shutler, Jr.
1965　*A Preliminary Report of Archaeological Explorations in the Southern New Hebrides, 1963–1964.* Honolulu: Bishop Museum.
1967　Origins of the Melanesians. *Archaeology and Physical Anthropology in Oceania* 2:91–99.

Simons, Linda, and Hugh Young
1978　*Pijin Blong Yumi: A Guide to Solomon Islands Pijin.* Honiara: Solomon Islands Christian Association.

Sipolo, Jully
1981　*Civilized Girl: Poems.* Suva: South Pacific Creative Arts Society.

Smith, Harold Hamel, and Fred A. G. Pape
1912　*Coconuts: The Consols of the East.* London: Tropical Life.

Smith, R. T.
1967　Social Stratification, Cultural Pluralism and Integration in West Indian Societies. In *Caribbean Integration,* edited by S. Lewis and T. G. Mathews, Puerto Rico: University of Puerto Rico, Institute of Caribbean Studies.

Smith, T. W.
1844　*A Narrative of the Life, Travels and Sufferings of Thomas W. Smith.* New Bedford, MA: Wm. C. Hill.

Snow, Charles
1974　*Early Hawaiians: An Initial Study of Skeletal Remains from Mokapu, Oahu.* Lexington: University Press of Kentucky.

[SI] Solomon Islands [*See also* BSI, BSIP.]
　Legislative Assembly
　1975–　*Legislative Assembly Debates.* Honiara: Government Printing
　1978　Office.

Ministry of Agriculture and Lands
var.   Lands sales records and titles. Lands Titles Office, Lands Division. National Archives, Honiara.
Statistics Office
1978   *Statistical Bulletin 1978.* Statistics Office no. 14/78. Honiara: Statistics Office.
1979   *Statistical Year Book 1979.* Honiara: Ministry of Finance.
Western Council
1978   Submission of Western Council, August 1977, to Special Committee on Provincial Government. Background Paper no. 28. Mimeo.

Somerville, Boyle T.
1897   Ethnographical Notes in New Georgia, Solomon Islands. *Journal of the [Royal] Anthropological Institute* 26:357–412.

[SCL] *Southern Cross Log*
1896–   Auckland: Melanesian Mission. Irregular.
1904,
1913–
1919
1904–   Sydney: Melanesian Mission.
1913

Specht, Jim
1975   Smoking Pipes and Cultural Change on Buka Island, Papua New Guinea. *Journal of the Polynesian Society* 84 (3): 356–364.

Speiser, Felix
1913   *Two Years with the Natives in the Western Pacific.* London: Mills and Boon.

Stapley, J. H.
c. 1971   Field Studies on the Ant Complex in Relation to Premature Nutfall of Coconuts in the Solomon Islands. Honiara: BSIP Department of Agriculture.

Stephania
[1864–   Whaling log. Peabody Museum, Salem, MA. PMB 221.
1868]

Struben, Roy
1961   *Coral and Colour of Gold.* London: Faber & Faber.

Sun
[1860–   Whaling log. Nicholson Whaling Collection, Providence, RI. PMB
1862]   894.

Sunbeam
[1871–   Whaling log. New Bedford Free Public Library, New Bedford, MA.
1876]   PMB 364.

Superior
[1857–   Whaling log. Kendall Whaling Museum, Sharon, MA. PMB 818.
1860]

Svensen, J.
n.d.   Early Pioneering of the Solomon Islands. Manuscript in Department of Pacific and Southeast Asian History, ANU.

Swain, Samuel
1835   Log of *Vigilant.* MS 4796, NLA.

Swallow
[1833–   Whaling log. New Bedford Free Public Library, New Bedford, MA.
1887]   PMB 542.

Sydney Gazette
1837–   Sydney.
1840

Sydney General Trade List
1828–
1842

Sydney Herald
1832–   Sydney.
1835

Sydney Mail
1880   Sydney.

[*SMH*] *Sydney Morning Herald*
1842–   Sydney.
1900

Sykes, H. O. E.
1958   Report on a Short Survey of the Labour Position in the British Solomon Islands Protectorate. Honiara: BSIP.

Tedder, Margaret M.
1975   Nataghera Custom Houses Reopening 1973. *Journal of the Solomon
Islands Museum Association* 3:10–23.
1976   Old Kusaghe. *Journal of the Cultural Association of the Solomon
Islands* 4:41–95.

Tetens, Alfred
1958   *Among the Savages of the South Seas: Memoirs of Micronesia, 1862–
1868.* Translated by Florence M. Spoehr. Stanford, CA: Stanford
University Press.

Thurnwald, Richard C.
1934   Pigs and Currency in Buin. *Oceania* 5 (2): 119–141.
1936   The Price of the White Man's Peace. *Pacific Affairs* 9 (3): 347–357.

Thurston, W. B.
1894   Diary. NLA, Canberra.

Tippett, A. R.
1967   *Solomon Islands Christianity: A Study in Growth and Obstruction.*
London: Lutterworth.

Tregurtha, Edward
   Autobiography. In the care of Dr. Norman Wettenhall, Toorak, Victoria. PMB 12. (Published by Blubber Press, Hobart, c. 1980.)

Tryon, D. T.
1979   Remarks on the Language Situation in the Solomon Islands. In *New
Guinea and Neighboring Areas: A Sociolinguistic Laboratory*, edited
by Stephen A. Wurm, pp. 33–51. The Hague/New York: Mouton.

Tuscaloosa
[1840–   Whaling log. Old Dartmouth Whaling Museum, New Bedford, MA.
1844]   PMB 289.

Tutty, R. H.
n.d.   History of the Dovele Mission. MS 1206, NLA, Canberra.

Tuza, Esau Togasabo
1975   The Emergence of the Christian Fellowship Church: A Historical
        View of Silas Eto, Founder of the Christian Fellowship Church. MA
        thesis, University of Papua New Guinea.

Two Brothers
[1858–   Whaling log. Old Dartmouth Whaling Museum, New Bedford, MA.
1863]   PMB 284, 285.

Unidentified vessel
[1835–   Whaling log. Houghton Library, Cambridge, MA. PMB 737.
1836]

United Kingdom
  British Consulate (Sydney)
    1857–   British Consulate Papers, vol. 5: Letters, 1857–1866. Mitchell
    1866   Library, Sydney.

  Colonial Office (CO)
    1946   *Among those Present: The official story of the Pacific Islands at
            war.* Central Office of Information. London: HMSO.
    var.   Colonial and Foreign Office correspondence. CO 225, PRO, Lon-
            don. Microfilm, NLA.

  Correspondence Relating to the Solomon Islands (CRSI)
    1903   London: HMSO. Available in Alexander Turnbull Library, Wel-
            lington, and on microfilm 182, Department of Pacific and South-
            east Asian History, ANU.

  Ministry of Defence, Hydrographic Department (MDHD)
    1887–   Map of Guadalcanal Island. London: Ministry of Defence.
    1888

  Naval Intelligence Division (NID)
    1944   *Pacific Islands*, vol. 3: *Western Pacific.* Geographical Handbook
            Series. London: HMSO.

  Parliamentary Papers (PP)
    1929–   Bills to House of Commons.
    1940

  Royal Navy, Australian Station (RNAS)
    1857–   Records of Commander-in-chief, vols. 13–19. New Zealand Na-
    1896   tional Archives, Wellington. Microfilm, NLA.

Vandercook, John W.
1937   *Dark Islands.* New York: Harper and Brothers.

Vansina, Jan
1965   *Oral Tradition: A Study in Historical Methodology.* Translated by
        H. M. Wright. Chicago: Aldine.

Vaskess, H.
1943   *Post War Policy, Reconstruction and Reorganization of Administra-
        tion.* Suva: WPHC.

Verguet, L.
1885   Arossi ou San-Christoval et ses Habitants. *Revue d'Ethnographie*
        4:194–232.

Vickery, Margaret L., and Brian Vickery
1979   *Plant Products of Tropical Africa.* London: Macmillan.

Vigors, Philip D.
  1850   Journal aboard HMS *Havannah*. Typescript in Auckland Institute and Museum Library; on microfilm G2261, NLA, Canberra.

Walker, David
  1981   The British Decline. *Current Affairs Bulletin* 57 (11—April): 15-24.

Wall, J. R. D., and J. R. F. Hansell
  1974*a*   *Land Resources of the British Solomon Islands Protectorate*, vol. 3: *Malaita and Ulawa*. Surbiton, Surrey: Ministry of Overseas Development.
  1974*b*   Natural Environment. In Chapman and Pirie, eds., pp. 5.1-5.54.

Wallerstein, Immanuel
  1974   *The Modern World System: Capitalist Agriculture and the Origins of the European World-economy in the Sixteenth Century*. New York: Academic Press.
  1976   The Three Stages of African Involvement in the World Economy. In *The Political Economy of Contemporary Africa*, edited by Peter Gutkind and I. Wallerstein, pp. 30-57. Beverly Hills: Sage Publications.

Wallis, Helen, ed.
  1965   *Carteret's Voyage Round the World 1766-1769*. London: Cambridge University Press for Hakluyt Society.

Ward, R. Gerard
  1972   *Man in the Pacific Islands: Essays on Geographical Change in the Pacific Islands*. Oxford: Clarendon Press.

Ward, R. Gerard, and Andrew Proctor, eds.
  1980   *South Pacific Agriculture Choices and Constraints: South Pacific Agricultural Survey 1979*. Canberra: ANU Press

Ward, Russel
  1977   *A Nation for a Continent: The History of Australia, 1901-1975*. Melbourne: Heinemann/New York: Harper & Row.

Wawn, William T.
  1893   *The South Sea Islanders and the Queensland Labour Trade . . . 1875 to 1891*. London: Swan Sonnenschein.

Webster, John
  c. 1803 *The Last Cruise of the "Wanderer."* Sydney: Cunninghame.

Welchman, Henry
  1892–   Diaries, 1892-1906. Melanesian Mission English Committee Office,
  1906   Watford, Hertfordshire; on microfilm at NLA, Canberra.

West, Francis J.
  1968   *Hubert Murray: The Australian Pro-Consul*. Melbourne: Oxford University Press.

Whalemen
  c. 1840– Shipping Papers, c. 1840-1870. New Bedford Free Public Library,
  1870   New Bedford, MA. PMB 402-408.

[WPHC] Western Pacific High Commission
  1876–   Inwards Correspondence, General. PRO, London.
  1945
  1910–   Mala Series c. PRO, London.
  1935

c. 1940–BSIP Series c. PRO, London.
1950

Wheeler, G. C.
c. 1943   Mono Alu notes. MS 184245, School of Oriental and African Studies,
London. (Pagination inconsistent.) Microfilm, NLA, Canberra, and
Mitchell Library, Sydney.

White, Geoffrey M.
1977   Symbols of Solidarity in the Christianization of Santa Isabel, Solomon Islands. Manuscript, University of California.
1979   War, Peace, and Piety in Santa Isabel, Solomon Islands. In *The Pacification of Melanesia*, edited by Margaret Rodman and Matthew
Cooper, pp. 109–139. ASAO Monograph no. 7. Ann Arbor: University of Michigan Press.

William Hamilton
[1838–   Logs in New Bedford Free Public Library, New Bedford, MA. PMB
1842]   376, 377; Kendall Whaling Museum, Sharon, MA. PMB 819;
Nicholson Whaling Collection, Providence, RI. PMB 898.

Williamson, Robert W.
1911   Solomon Islands Notes. *Man* 11:65–68.
1914   *The Ways of the South Sea Savage*. Philadelphia: Lippincott.

Wilson, Charles
1954   *The History of Unilever: A Study in Economic Growth and Social
Change*. Vol. 1. London: Cassell.

Witt, Eric
1974   Agriculture and Economic Resources. In Chapman and Pirie, eds.,
pp. 6.1–6.180.

Wolfers, Edward
1971   The Significance of Protectorate Status. *Institute of Current World
Affairs*, Publication no. EPW-29, BSIP-11, (5 February).

Woodford, C. M.
1888   Exploration of the Solomon Islands. *Proceedings of the Royal Geographical Society and Monthly Record of Geography* n.s. 10:351–
376.
1889   Life in the Solomon Islands. *Popular Science Monthly* (August):
476–487.
1890a   *A Naturalist Among the Head-hunters*. London: Philip and Son.
1890b   Further Explorations in the Solomon Islands. *Proceedings of the
Royal Geographical Society and Monthly Record of Geography* n.s.
12:393–418.
1909   *Protectorate of British Solomon Islands: Statistics to 31 March 1909*.
Sydney: WPHC.
n.d.   Papers. Department of Pacific and Southeast Asian History, ANU.

Woodlark
[1856–   Whaling log. Alexander Turnbull Library, Wellington. PMB 196.
1857]

Worsley, Peter
1957   *The Trumpet Shall Sound: A Study of "Cargo" Cults in Melanesia*.
London: MacGibbon & Kee.

WRCP—See Carpenter.

Wright, Judith
1971   "The Idler." In *Collected Poems*. Sydney: Angus and Robertson.

Wright, Paul
1974   Population: The Project Census. In Chapman and Pirie, eds., pp. 3.1–3.139.

Yen, Douglas E.
1976   Inland Settlement on Santa Cruz Island (Nendö). In Green and Cresswell 1976:203–224.

Young, Florence S. H.
c. 1926 *Pearls from the Pacific*. London: Marshall Brothers.

Young, John M. R.
1968   Frontier Society in Fiji, 1858–1873. PhD dissertation, University of Adelaide.

Young Hector
[1853– Log in Kendall Whaling Museum, Sharon, MA. PMB 819.
1857]

Zelenietz, Martin
1979   The End of Headhunting in New Georgia. In *The Pacification of Melanesia*, edited by Margaret Rodman and Matthew Cooper, pp. 91–108. ASAO Monograph no. 7. Ann Arbor: University of Michigan Press.

Zimmerman, John L.
1949   *The Guadalcanal Campaign*. Washington, DC: U.S. Marine Corps.

Zoleveke, Gideon
1979   Traditional Ownership and Land Policy. In Larmour 1979:1–9.

Zöller, Hugo
1891   *Deutsch Newguinea und meine Ersteigung des Finisterre-Gebirges*. Stuttgart: Deutsche Verlagsgesellschaft.

Zone
[1855– Logs in Athenaeum Library, Nantucket, MA. PMB 227; Whaling
1858]   Museum, PMB 391, 397; Kendall Whaling Museum, Sharon, MA. PMB 831.

INFORMANTS

NOTE: Typescripts of interviews with informants will, in time, be lodged in the Solomon Islands National Library.

Solomon Islands Informants, 1976

Guadalcanal coast villages

Marisiliano Chuke and John Tologhomba of Taupanda; Dickie Panna and Elison Kavaro of Ghiliatu; Moiʻea Pepechi, Setiʻs Mother (f), and Luvusia Willy of Vatumanivo; John Rich of Purepure; Samuel Bau and Sove Kimbo of Nduindui; Alveti Tongorova of Kolina; Jones Bulangi of Kolochachara; Alike Tae, Keolesi (f), and Kikiti of Kolokiki; Kelemu (f) of Vatukulau; Hari Roro and Maria Teresia Manasa (f) of Inadoa; Chapasere of Ulusughu; Mbumbukimbo and Reo Dick of Mandakacho; Kapini of Alidauva; Alike Ghandokiki of Raurembo; Irlan Pope of Sughu (Talise); Dominico Alebua of Haimatua; Aliesio Tavoruka of Longgu; Martin Manganimate of Sughu, Wanderer Bay.

Guadalcanal bush villages

Choranga and Kenghau (f) of Marao; James Piro of Valeboghobogho; Heman Lambuvia of Kologhasi; Vichi Chio of Sughulonga; Chamali Hesikia of Valevuru; Mageli Leban of Koloniu; Urumbangereni Rubana of Sumbanariki; Simon of Ghaivogha; Deobe Leone of Chaunamarao.

Malaita villages (coast or bush)

Salimauri, Lamofanageni, and Lowasi Lobosi (f) of Waileni; Seti Matoʻfeli, Sedrak Ufamari, and Thomas of Fulo; Jo Gonaiʻilae, Beni Kai, and Jo Tiakapu of Kwaiʻgilu; Bart Ulufaʻalu; Jonathen Kuka; Anifanaia.

Malaita coast villages

Abraham Teʻfaʻadi and Elia Maikoto of Loulana; Jo Ariana of Kwaʻa; Lizba Luda Bata (f) and Erastus Edaʻkwaʻou of Kwoifala; Simion Funasiʻa, Michael Maiʻleeʻa, and Foʻafuna of Bona; Obedi Alike Moisimae of Baunani; Elders of Igwa, Martin Suafunua, and Joseph Afeʻou of Igwa; Sisto Alui and Brown Foufou of Kwareʻekwa; Dick Sawalo of Bulu; Jotam Finou and Jorji Feleniʻi of Gonahili; Timoti Fiʻfounia, Justus Malalifu, and Timmy Lotufana of Maoa;

501

502   *Informants*

Joseph Odofia of Mari Mari; Sisto Faaramoa, Romasio Ngura, John Siteageni, and Pita Mafane of Ngalingela; Sosimo Sikulu and Margaret Fokonala (f) of Buma; Jack Mainagwa of Isisi.

Malaita bush villages

Kika and Sali Toasi of Elingamanu; Jack Kwalau and Lamafanageni of Sinaba.
Simone Maaʻeobi of Kwaio, Malaita: taped interview by Roger Keesing, September 1979.

San Cristobal coast villages

John Christian, Hari Taisubaurona, Rex Taki, George Hurunani, John Mark Dauhenia, James Huʻongisimai, May Kaharisi (f), and Leonard Haʻanimaraha of Tawatana; Samuel Ramohuni, Robert Raurua, and Moses Maimurinihoasi of Haʻaghaura; Hugo Kereruku, Matthew Mairotaha, and Louisa Hutairongo (f) of Marunuʻu; Margaret Sauwereiʻa (f) of Hausongo; Thomas Taʻaeʻkeʻkerei, Robinson Wakiiʻa, Debora Atoubora (f), and Teresa Roraʻei (f) of Ubuna; Timothy Tarorua of Tawaniʻau; Rubin Apwahi, Kaspa Arabaeʻawa, Habit Aharoheiʻa, Nelson Anuanuiabu, Frederick Taʻaru, Andrew Abenihaʻa, and Gilbert Suniaru of Heuru; Daniel Tawariʻi of Aboro; Bese Ghaura (f) of Robo; Jones Dingianimai and Timothy Ianitaro of Hada; Victor Buaniramo and John Erei of Asmanioha; Hilda Waritaiʻi (f) of Takiri; Rubin Siro and Daniel Tougageita of Tadahadi; Morris Ohairangi of Niu Niu; Peter Eiatarogari and Stanley Maurione of Aringana; Daisi Sauhaʻabu (f), Alis Rahageni (f), and Charles Fox Haʻamouri of Maniora; Sunauni of Macedonia; Jack Campbell of Kirakira; Geoffrey Kuper of Ghupuna.

San Cristobal bush villages

Boaz Bebeni of Herenia; Junia Wawenihaʻa (f) of Ruarua.

Shortland Islands—all coastal villages

Mikelo Ebinuwi, John Bana, and Remesio Eresi of Nuhu; Silverio Ilaha, Luka, Katherine Mangila (f), and Alpons Mule Mangila of Maleae; John Henry MacDonald of Munia; Bernard Pilow of Toumua; Joseph Nikolas and Teresia Tapasi (f) of Samanago; Timothy Sikori, Andrew Kimisi, John Marehasi, Jeremiah Makila, and Paul Kaputuku of Falamae; Nathaniel Misu of Kariki; John Baptista Mauroi, Jacob Piopio, and Joseph Normani of Pirumeri; John Bitiai of Alliang (interviewed at Nila); Maekel Meibo Tanutanu of Sanae; Joseph Maike of Hari Hari; chief of Koliai; Bariri of Nila.

New Georgia Islands—all coastal villages

Elders of Maravari and Gideon Tolopitu of Maravari; Francis Nisbule and Dicko Vaevo of Bunaporo, Vonunu; David Voulos of Samaboro; Rubin Elobule of Uzamba; Billy Binskin of Mbava; Edwin Kombe of Buliana; Kitchener Wheatley and Willy Paia of Munda; John Kevisi of New Lambete.

European Informants

Colin H. Allan, paper read, but not circulated at Research School of Pacific Studies, ANU, Canberra, July 1978
Reverend Father Brunz, of Wanione Catholic Mission (Interview, 1976)
Vera Clift of Toowoomba, Queensland (Interview, 1975)

Tommy Elkington,* of Tulagi (Interview, 1976; correspondence, and type-script)
The Reverend Richard Fallowes (Correspondence, 1978–1979)
The Reverend Charles E. Fox,* of New Zealand (Correspondence, 1977)
Dorothy Gardner,* of Sydney (Interviews, 1975, 1977, and correspondence)
Leslie Gill,* of Melbourne (Interviews, 1975, 1977)
M. Hirst of Sydney (Interviews, 1975, and typescript)
Rolph Novak of Choiseul (Interview, 1976)
Phillip Palmer of Gizo (Interview, 1976)
James Petersen (Interview and correspondence, 1975–1977)
Peter Plowman,* of Apia (Interview, 1975)
K. G. ("Georgina") Seton of Brisbane (Interview, 1976, and correspondence)

* deceased

GENERAL INDEX

Page numbers for photographs are in boldface type

Acts, Parliamentary: Colonial Development Act (1929), 212, 236, 239; Colonial Development and Welfare Act (1940), 286, 301, 304; India Emigration Act (1922), 152; Mining Amendment Act (1970), 334; Native Administration Regulation (1922), 277, 281; Native Contracts' Regulation no. 2 (1896), 203; Navigation, 24; relating to land holding, 119, 135, 328, 331; Solomons (Labour Amendment) Regulations (1912), 159; Waste Land Regulations, 125, 131–133, 138, 148, 149, 195

Adultery, 182–183, 261, 277–278, 281

Advisory Council, 162, 165, 299, 302, 305–306, 317

"Africa Corps," 320

Agricultural and Industrial Loans Board, 314, 316

Agriculture, 2–4, 10–11, 131, 302, 332. See also Crops

Agriculture Department, 315, 316, 331, 334

Aho (laborer), 154

Air services, 315

'Airumu, 279

Akun, Alois, 208, 213, 446n67, 447n69

Alcohol, 69, 99–100, 208, 341. See also Distilling

Alisifiona, Jonah, 163

Allan, Sir Colin, 328

Allardyce, K. J., 160

Allen (overseer at Baunani plantation), 154

Almond, canarium, 2, 8, 10

Aloa, Selwyn, 258, 259, 261

Alu Island: 7, 249, 287; people of, 32, 37, 203

Ambuover (or Ambuofa), Peter, 161

Americans: during war, 285, 286–287, **287**, 289, 291, **291**, 292–293, 300; hoped-for return of, 294, 296, 298, 299; property of, 285, 292, 303. See also United States of America

Ameriga (Mrs. Frank Wickham), 70

Amplypelta cocophaga China, 227–228, 238

Ancestors: 12, 15, 17–18, 122, 267; and *houra'a*, 275; *La'aka*, 278, 279, 280; and land rights, 4, 130; shrines of, 122, 146; skulls of, 35, 85; spirits of, 17–18, 175, 274, 276, 278–279

Anderson, Pastor, 245, 247

Andressen, Albert M. ("Andy"), 180, 289

Anglicans, 262, 276. See also Melanesian Mission

Anuta: island, 2; village, 55

'Aoke: 2, 112, 270, 278, 295, 296; people of, 267

Aola: Chair and Rule movement at, 262; Chinese store at 208–209; government station at, 111–112, 270; land alienation at, 143; trade, traders at, 71, 82, 159

Aqorau, Francis Talasasa, 306, 323, 324, 327

Araga, Lance Corporal, 272

'Are'are: 276, 282, 298; and Maasina Rule, 293, 298, 309; people from, 8, 97, 185, 274–276

Arimauri (laborer), 154

Arosi: 14, 178, 185; people of, 97

Artifacts, 11, 12, 27, 35, 38, 46, 94, 95, 96, 267, 339. See also Valuables

Aruliho, 229

Arundel, John Thomas, 127, 128

Ashley, Resident Commissioner: 223, 247, 262; and Chinese immigration, 237–238;

332, 451n51; and Depression, 226–228; economic problems of, 221; and government, 335; hot-air driers of, 228–229; and hybrid coconut, 331; and labor, 237–238, 315, 333; lands of 233–235, 332–333; plantations of, 212, 221–222, 233–235, 303; and World War II, 303. *See also* Colonial Office (U.K.)
Levers Pacific Timbers (1963), 315, 327, 332–333
Levuka, 58
Lewis (Captain), 39
Lewis (trader), 380
Liapari, 88, 100
Life expectancy, 9
Lifu Islanders, 390
Likin (Solomon Island woman), 154
Lilihina, 64
Lilisiana, 268
Lillies, K. C., 211, 402, 403
Lingi Lingi clan, 88
Lloyd, J., 364
Lobi (of Simbo), 27
Local government councils, 293–296, 305, 317–318, 325–327. *See also* Western Council
Logha, 143, 145
Lord Howe Group. *See* Ontong Java
Lova, Matthew, 291
Lucas, Walter Henry: 144, 151, **156**, **184**, 205, 432n49; and labor, 151, 171; and land, 133–137
Luke, Sir Harry, 262–263, 301
Lungga, 143

Maasina Rule: 286, 293, 298, 302, 308, 309, 326, 345; and "Chair and Rule" movement, 293, 298; and government, 293, 294–299, 304, 305–306, 313, 321, 328; leaders arrested, 295–296; on Malaita, 285, 294–296, 297–299, 304, 309, 313, 328; opposition to, 293, 295; SSEM involvement in, 293, 294, 295. *See also* Kwaio
McAlpine (at Tetepare), 154
McArthur and Company, 58, 65, 322, 376, 377, 380, 383
Macdonald, J. H., 452n73
Macdonald, John A., 60, 67, 423n106
Macdonald, Mrs. John A. *See* Tanutanu Galaga
Macdonald, John Champion: 58, 60, 67, 69, 88, 129, 377, 378, 383, 389, 391, 423n106; family of, 64, 80, 129
Macdonald, Melinda (Mrs. John C. Macdonald), 69, 378, 423n106
Macdonald, Patrick, 397
Macdonald, William, 58, 64, 69, 70, 75, 378, 389

Macdonald, Mrs. William (first). *See* Male, Alice
Macdonald, Mrs. William (second). *See* Marota
McDougall (Captain), 366
McFarlane (Captain), 364
McGeorge (Captain), 374
MacGillivray, John, 29
McGregor, J. (Captain), 362, 364
McGregor (Captain of *Queen*), 366
McGregor (Captain of *Thistle*), 374
McIntosh (Captain), 366, 368
McIntosh (of *Esperanza*), 391
McIntyre (Captain), 154
Mackenzie, C. C., 109
MacKinnon, D., 231, 235
McLaren, Jack, 157
Macleod, George, 356
McMahon, L. C., 181
Madson, M., 393
Maekali, 294
Maghratulo (of Vella Lavella), 68, 88, 100, 394, 426n48
Magness (Captain), 366
Magnus (Captain), 366
Magusaiai, 80
Mahaffy (Woodford's assistant), 107, 157
Mai (of Santa Ana), 69
Mainagwa, Jack, 170, 175
Maiwasiwasi people, 380, 396. *See also* Wright, E. Hamilton
Makambo, 158, 206, **206**, 207, 213, 224, 268, 271. *See also* Burns Philp; Tulagi
Makira. *See* San Cristobal
Makira Harbour: 28, 34, 40; trade at, 27, 42, 43, 50, 56, 83–84, 94; whalers at, 27, 29, 31, 32, 39, 41
Malaita: 1, 2, 5, 8, 24, 27, 92, 161, 212, 214, 281, 306; Bell killings on, 211; bush people of, 43, 121, 267 (*see also* 'Are'are; Kwaio); castaways at, 23; "Chair and Rule" movement at, 261, 298; closed societies at, 120–121; cocoa production at, 313, 334, 338; coconuts and copra at, 195, 316, 338, 457n2; cyclone damage on, 318; and Depression, 267–269; descent on, 12; government spending at, 313, 328; head taxes at, 164, 198, 211, 215, 458n2; health on, 274–275, 277; laborers from, 122, 162, 168, 173, 185, 187–188, 189, 191, 268, 273–274, 437n70; land dealings at, 145, 146, 214; languages of, 6, 8; leadership on, 15–16, 92, 111, 122–123, 213, 215, 256–257, 276–277, 278, 283, 294–295; local councils of, 282, 294, 305; Maasina Rule on, 293–299, 309; and Pacific War, 290–291; people of, 108, 173, 185, 187, 194, 266, 309, 323, 327, 328, 462n27; police beat-

INDEX OF SHIPS

ABOUT THE AUTHOR

Judith A. Bennett is an Australian and was educated at All Hallows' School, Brisbane, and the University of Queensland. She is currently lecturer in history and warden of St. Margaret's College, University of Otago, Dunedin, New Zealand. Prior to that she taught at Massey University, Palmerston North, New Zealand, and she also taught for several years in Papua New Guinea. She received her M.A. from the University of Hawaii, and Ph.D. from the Australian National University. She also holds a Dip.Ed. in Developing Countries from the University of Papua New Guinea.

Dr. Bennett first went to the Solomon Islands in 1972 as a member of an interdisciplinary research team seeking to identify population pressure on south Guadalcanal. She returned to the Solomons in 1976 to conduct the oral and supplementary documentary research on which her doctoral dissertation and this book are based.

Production Notes

This book was designed by Roger Eggers.
Composition and paging were done on the
Quadex Composing System and typesetting
on the Compugraphic 8400 by the design and
production staff of University of Hawaii
Press.

The text typeface is Compugraphic Caledonia
and the display typeface is Compugraphic
Palatino.

Offset presswork and binding were done by
Vail-Ballou Press, Inc. Text paper is Glatfelter
Offset Vellum, basis 45.

Tokyo
JAPAN
CHINA
Wake
Northern
Marianas
Marshall Islands
Guam
Majuro
Kwajalein
Manila
Pohnpei
Truk
Kosrae
Yap
PHILIPPINES
Palau
Caroline Islands
Gilbert Islands
International Dateline
Sunday
Saturday
K I R I
equator
Nauru
Banaba
Bougainville
New Ireland
Solomon
Islands
Tuvalu
IRIAN JAYA
PAPUA NEW GUINEA
New Britain
Santa Cruz Is
Guadalcanal
SOLOMON ISLANDS
Wallis
Futun
Fiji
Vanuatu
Vanua Levu
Viti Levu
Coral Sea
Loyalty Is
New Caledonia
AUSTRALIA
Northern Territory
Queensland
Brisbane
Norfolk
Western Australia
South Australia
New South Wales
Sydney
Auckland
New Zealand
Victoria
Tasman Sea
Tasmania
175°E
160°E
145°E
130°E
115°E